COMPLETE COURSE

20th Century® Typewriting

NINTH EDITION

By

D. D. LESSENBERRY
Professor of Education, Emeritus
University of Pittsburgh

T. JAMES CRAWFORD
School of Business
Indiana University

LAWRENCE W. ERICKSON
Graduate Business Education
School of Education
University of California, Los Angeles

With the assistance of

Lee R. Beaumont
School of Business
Indiana University of Pennsylvania

Jerry W. Robinson
Senior Editor
South-Western Publishing Company

Library of Congress
Catalog Card Number: 67-19455

T30 14 15 16 H 2 1 0 *Printed in the U.S.A.*

SOUTH-WESTERN PUBLISHING COMPANY

Cincinnati Chicago Burlingame, Calif. New Rochelle, N.Y. Dallas

Contents (First Year)

PART 1 Learning to Typewrite

PART 2 Building Typewriting Competence

Contents (Second Year)

PART 3 Preparing for Business

PART 4 Applied Office Typewriting

Preface

TO THE STUDENT

You will have three partners to help you learn to type: your teacher, a typewriter, and this Ninth Edition of *20th Century Typewriting, Complete Course.*

Your teacher will guide, stimulate, and challenge your daily practice; the typewriter will do exactly what you direct your fingers to have it do; and this textbook provides all the structured practice materials needed for maximum growth in typing skill.

Learning to type can be as exciting as it is demanding, but it is mostly a do-it-yourself activity. What your partners can do to help you achieve your best typing skill is limited, but what you can do in cooperation with them knows no bounds.

Some special features of this book of particular interest to you are:

1. Line identification and marginal notations to increase your understanding of what and how to type.
2. Built-in cues for improved practice.
3. Easy-to-read "telegraphed" directions.
4. Alternate drives for speed and accuracy in the same lesson.
5. Tryout drills on new learnings before application in problems.
6. Communication aids: guides for typing numbers, dividing words, punctuating, and other points of technical English, taught in drill and realistic "use" situations.
7. Alertness training (corrections to be made as you type) to lead to a thinking typist, not a mere copyist.
8. A look-it-up-yourself Reference Guide section of 16 pages (pages i-xvi) to avoid the necessity of asking for needless repetition of explanations and directions.

You can learn to type if you want to learn and will work to learn. Expect and exact much of yourself. Emphasize correct techniques, efficient problem-solving procedures, and good work habits. Your teacher will give you cues for improved practice; follow these carefully. When you reach one skill goal, practice vigorously, hopefully, and confidently to reach the next goal. To the extent that you desire excellence and will work for excellence, you will achieve it.

TO THE TEACHER

Many features in this textbook have been proved through research, tryout results, and teacher preferences and practices to improve student performance in learning to type. Some of these features, in addition to those listed in Column 1, are:

1. Increased page size (a half inch wider *and* longer) to give maximum readability.
2. A 3-1 plan for presenting the letter keyboard: three lessons for teaching, followed by one lesson for integrating new learning.
3. Figure-symbol mastery through teaching just one figure key in a lesson and its shifted symbol in the next lesson.
4. Easy-to-difficult copy progression, paragraphs triple controlled for syllable intensity (SI), average word length (AWL), and percent of high-frequency words (HFW).
5. Preapplication manipulative drills to develop readiness and to improve performance in problem-production typing.
6. Longer "dwell" on one type of problem before moving to the next, with fewer different applications in a lesson.
7. Simplified letter-placement table which will lead more quickly to judgment placement of letters.
8. Emphasis on learning transfer: straight copy to script, rough draft, statistical copy, letters, manuscripts, tables, and the like.

In teaching this book, identify, explain, and repeatedly demonstrate the techniques that are to be initiated and refined. These techniques, with speed and control of individual motions, are the underlying cause of both speed and accuracy. Appraise the pattern of practice more than the results of practice (the typed line or page).

Involve each student in determining the purpose of practice and in selecting the materials of practice. The greater the involvement, the more intelligently he will practice to achieve excellence in his daily work. Give cues for improved practice and fewer specific directions for ways to practice. This is teaching at its best, for it places on the student a fair share of responsibility for success in achieving his highest typing potential.

ABOUT THIS BOOK

This Ninth Edition has 300 carefully structured lessons, each planned for 50 minutes of goal-directed practice. The lessons are grouped into 4 parts of 75 lessons each. Part 1 provides the foundation for all subsequent typewriting learning (whether personal or vocational). Part 2 improves basic skills, broadens personal applications, and provides intensive practice on basic typing operations. Part 3 develops production typewriting competence. Part 4 provides vocational work-experience activities.

A wide variety of carefully designed and tested learning materials and practice procedures has been included to develop overall typewriting competence. These include:

1. Individualized-goal practice, using progressive-difficulty sentences and paragraphs.
2. Specially designed skill-building drills on selected skill elements.
3. Simple-to-complex sequence of problems, moving smoothly from model to semiarranged, and to unarranged copy.
4. Time-pressure activities that motivate the student to succeed and that reinforce his learning by providing knowledge of results.
5. Three-phase problem-production cycle: (1) learning the nature of the problem; (2) short-interval and sustained skill building; and (3) measurement of developed knowledge and skill.

Although specific practice procedures and time schedules are suggested for each of the lessons as aids to the teacher, the materials are easily adaptable to the special needs of the individual class or school.

ACKNOWLEDGMENTS

Appreciation is expressed to the teachers, students, and business workers who have contributed helpful criticisms, ideas, and materials. Very special appreciation is expressed to the 5,400 teachers who participated in the survey of practices and preferences in teaching typewriting. This book has been written to help achieve the goal of excellence all teachers seek for their students.

DDL / TJC / LWE

Learning to Typewrite

SOME THINGS YOU WILL LEARN

YOU WILL LEARN to type by touch—without looking at the keyboard—as you type words, sentences, and paragraphs.

YOU WILL LEARN to type numbers and certain special symbols that are important for your own use and for business typing.

YOU WILL LEARN to type with acceptable speed and with good control, and to put your basic skill to work in typing notes, letters, postal cards, themes, manuscripts, simple tables, and other papers. You will learn to proofread your own typing and will develop skill in finding and correcting errors in your typed copy. This is effective training in alertness.

YOU WILL LEARN to compose at the typewriter—a wonderful substitute for the laborious process of writing in longhand. You will learn all this—and more—in this first course in typewriting.

Unit 1 | Lessons 1-12

Learning the Letter Keys

LESSON 1

1A: Get Ready to Type

1. ARRANGE YOUR WORK AREA

a. Clear the desk or table of unneeded books and papers.
b. Place this book to the right of the typewriter on a bookholder, or put something under the top to raise it to better reading position.
c. Have the front of the typewriter even with the edge of the desk.

2. KNOW YOUR TYPEWRITER

Study the following diagram carefully.

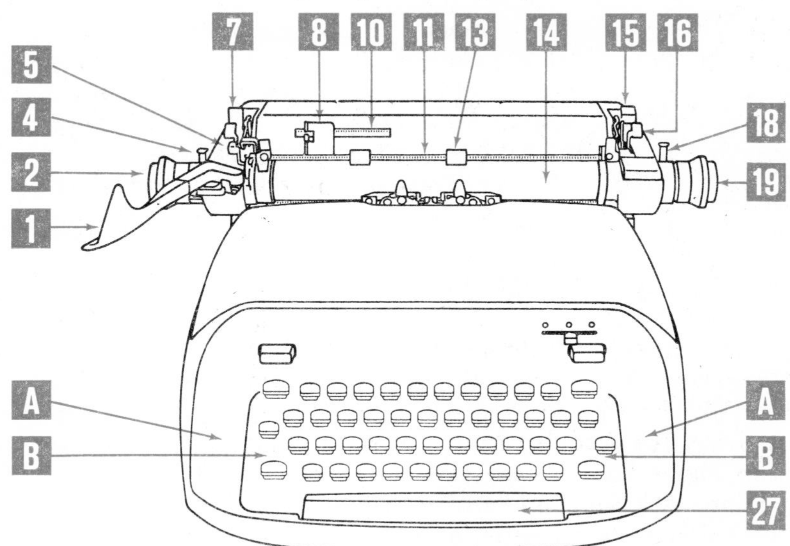

The numbers in boldface type are those assigned to the machine parts shown above and in the illustrations on Reference Guide pages i and ii.

1 Return Lever and Line Spacer
2 Platen (Cylinder) Knob, Left
4 Carriage Release, Left
5 Line-Space Regulator
7 Margin Set, Left
8 Paper Guide
10 Paper Table
11 Paper Bail and Bail Scale
13 Paper-Bail Roll
14 Platen (Cylinder)
15 Margin Set, Right
16 Paper-Release Lever
18 Carriage Release, Right
19 Platen (Cylinder) Knob, Right
A Typewriter Frame
B Keyboard
27 Space Bar

Job 3: Interoffice Memorandum *(1" side margins)*

Words

TO:	All Retired Employees	DATE:	*(Current)*	5 / 7
FROM:	Eliot Duval, Manager	SUBJECT:	Group Health Insurance	13 / 16

(¶ 1) Arrangements have been made with the 24
Hospital Care Foundation to provide Blue Cross 33
and Blue Shield coverage for our retired em- 42
ployees on a group basis. All retired employees 51
who become members of this group will be 60
entitled to the same group benefits now avail- 69
able to our active employees. The group rates 78
for both Blue Cross and Blue Shield are outlined 88
below: 89

	Single Contract	Family Contract	Words
			92 / 99
Blue Cross	$2.75	$6.95	103
Blue Shield	.60	1.90	108

(¶ 2) Please let me know soon if you want to join 117
this group insurance plan. If you elect to be- 126
come a member of this group, deductions cover- 135
ing the premium will be made from your pension 145
checks. 146

Job 4: Invoice *(Type the following invoice on the appropriate form)*

Words

		Date	*(Current)*	3
Sold To	Tridea Engineering, Inc.	Our No.	JM–1936	10
	22 North Grand Avenue	Cust. Order No.	L–10385	16
	Long Beach, California 90806	Shipped Via	REA Express	24
Terms	2/10, n/30			26

Quantity	Description	Unit Price	Amount	Words
20 cases	10W–30 quart cans Modern Motor Oil	13.95 case	279.00	39
12 sets	FH 291 Bushing Driver Sets	5.98 set	71.76	49
3 M	3/8-inch Coupling—Copper to Copper	20.00 M	60.00	60
1 doz.	50-foot Steel Tapes	40.00 doz.	40.00	69
50 rolls	KC 91, 1-inch Clear Repair Tape	.50 roll	25.00	81
1 M	1/2-inch, Galvanized Reducing Elbows	100.00 M	100.00	94
			575.76	95

Job 5: Night Letter

Words

Charge message to: Institute of Life Insurance 6
New York, New York, April 22, 19—— William 14
C. Mills 169 Strawberry Drive Encino, Califor- 23
nia Arriving Los Angeles April 23, 6:30 p.m., 32
American Flight 508. Please save April 24 for 42
our meeting. Ask Simi and Farris to join us. Will 52
need school reports on experiences with Adult 61
Money Management Guide. Bob Gibson *(Your* 69
initials for reference) Address not to be transmitted: 70
380 Park Avenue 72

Job 6: Letter on Half Sheet
(5½" x 8½"—short side up)

Block, open; ½" margins; date on Line 10
Address on 4th line below date *Envelope*

Words

(Current date) | Mr. Robert Debussy | 356 Oak 8
Grove Park | Pasadena, Calif. 91103 | Dear Mr. 17
Debussy | (¶ 1) This is the year for your Great 25
Escape! Go where Silver Caravans of the Con- 34
quistadores sought the sea. Go where coaches of 44
Cortez carried vacation-seekers long ago. Go 53
where Emperor Maximilian and Empress Carlotta 62
held Court. Go to the playground of the 70
world—FAMOUS ACAPULCO. (¶ 2) Acapulco— 77
the world's most "in" spot—is just a few hours 87
away. Join Hollywood celebrities and the jet set 97
on Western's Fiesta Flights to Acapulco—non- 106
stop from Los Angeles. (¶ 3) The fare is so low, 115
you can't say no. Only $184 round trip from 124
Los Angeles. Convenient deferred payment 132
privileges are available to you. Make your plans 142
now. Call 776–2311 and ask for Dave Holt, our 152
Acapulco Tour Manager. Sincerely yours 160
WESTERN AIRLINES Reservations Manager TJ 168
Smith | xx (138) 170/183

3. INSERT PAPER

a. Adjust the paper guide **8** as directed on Reference Guide page iii, at the back of the book.

b. Place a full-size sheet of paper on the desk to the left of the typewriter, turned so the long side of the paper is close to you.

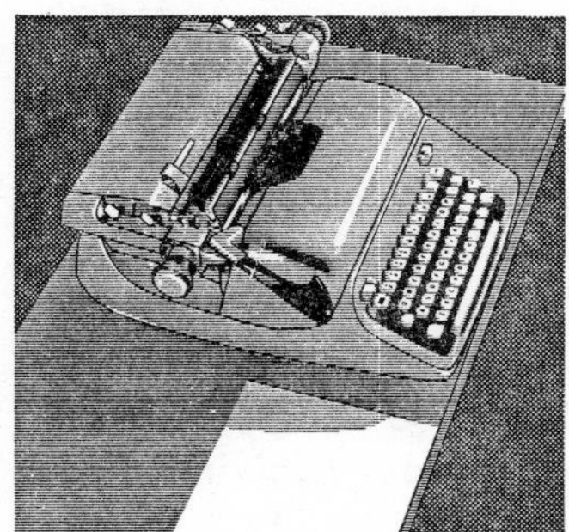

c. Pull the paper bail **11** forward—toward you—with your right hand.

d. Grasp the paper with your left hand, the thumb under the sheet, as shown in the following diagram.

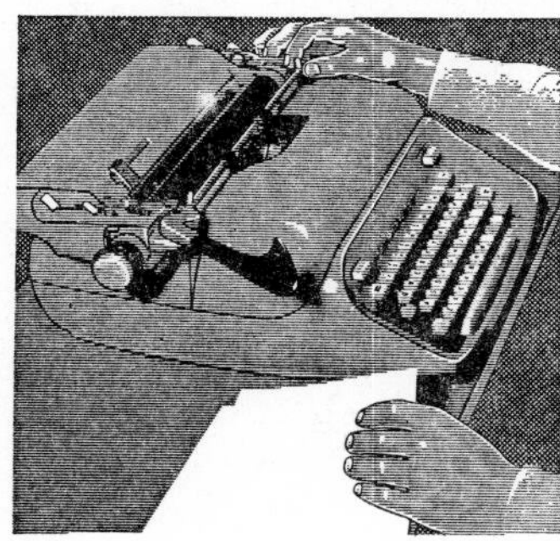

e. Bring the paper to the platen **14** and drop it between the platen and the paper table **10**, against the paper guide **8**; *at the same time*, bring the right hand to the right cylinder knob **19** and twirl the knob with a quick movement of the fingers and the thumb. Push the paper bail down to hold the paper against the platen.

4. SET LINE-SPACE REGULATOR 5

a. On "1" for single spacing the lines you are to type in this lesson and the following ones of this unit.

And when so directed—

b. On "2" for double spacing.
c. On "3" for triple spacing.

The first two lines shown below are single-spaced (*SS*); the next line is a double space (*DS*) below the second line; and the last line is a triple space (*TS*) below that.

```
1 This is single spacing.
2 This is single spacing.    SS
3 (one blank line)           DS
4 This is double spacing.
5
6 (two blank lines)          TS
7 This is triple spacing.
```

5. SET MARGIN STOPS

First study the diagrams shown below to determine whether your typewriter has hand-set or key-set margin stops.

Then, move the left margin stop **7** to the left of the center of the paper 25 spaces. Move the right stop **15** to the end of the scale. *You will type the copy line for line and do not need the right margin stop to indicate the end of the line.*

HAND-SET MARGIN STOPS

KEY-SET MARGIN STOPS

6. TAKE CORRECT TYPING POSITION

a. Body erect; sit back in the chair.

b. Feet on the floor, one just ahead of the other.

c. Fingers curved and upright over the second row of keys.

d. Wrists low and relaxed.

e. Elbows near the body; forearms parallel to the slant of the keyboard.

f. Eyes on the copy.

Words
$1, it will mean that ten children in your com- 162
munity can receive this test. Certainly the health 172
of our children––and the assurance of an adult 182
life free of tuberculosis––is worth this small in- 191
vestment. (¶ 3) Won't you please make your 199
contribution TODAY. Just use the enclosed enve- 208
lope. Your thoughtfulness and concern now can 218
insure a healthier, happier tomorrow for all our 228
children. Sincerely yours, James L. Drissen, 237
M.D. | Campaign Director | Enc. (206) 242/255

Job 2: Manuscript Report

Leftbound manuscript style	*Use judgment in*
2" top margin, first page; DS	*arranging tables*
5-space ¶ indention	*SS data of columns*

Words
THE FEDERAL BUDGET 4

The Federal budget is a financial plan encom- 13
passing the program of action proposed by the 22
President to meet the nation's needs at home 31
and abroad. It is prepared every year by the 40
Bureau of the Budget under the direction of the 50
President from information submitted by all Fed- 59
eral Government agencies. The budget contains 68
estimates of the amount the Federal Govern- 77
ment will spend and the revenues it will collect. 87
It includes funds for the President's new legisla- 97
tive proposals as well as his recommendations 106
for existing activities. 111

The 1966 Budget 117

In the fiscal year 1966, Federal cash ex- 125
penditures were $137.6 billion and cash receipts 135
totaled $134.4 billion. The $3.2 billion deficit 145
was financed by borrowing, resulting in increas- 154
ing the public debt. About two thirds of the 163
public debt was incurred in wartime––primarily 173
in World War II. Although the debt has risen 182
since then, it has continued to decline in rela- 191
tion to the size of the economy. As a percent 201
of Gross National Product, the public debt has 210
declined sharply from a peak of 133 percent in 219
1947 to about 45 percent today. 226

Sources of Revenue 233

Cash receipts come mainly from income 241
taxes––$85.5 billion or over 60 percent of the 250
total in fiscal year 1966. Employment or payroll 260
taxes totaled $20.0 billion in that same year. 270
Sources of revenue, or where the Government 278
dollar comes from, are shown in the table that 288
follows: 290

Words
THE GOVERNMENT DOLLAR 294
(Where It Comes From) 299

Source	Amount	Words
Individual Income Taxes	$0.40	310
Corporation Income Taxes	.22	316
Employment Taxes	.15	320
Excise Taxes	.10	324
Borrowing	.02	326
Other	.11	329
TOTAL	$1.00	334

(Header line "Source Amount": 304)

Government Expenditures 344

The Government's tax and other revenues 352
are used for providing a wide range of public 361
services to meet the needs of our growing popu- 370
lation and increasingly urban society. The fol- 379
lowing table gives a breakdown of how the 388
Government dollar (total cash expenditures) was 397
spent in 1966: 401

(Use same stops as for previous table)

THE GOVERNMENT DOLLAR 405
(How It Was Spent) 409

Expenditure	Amount	Words
National Defense	$0.42	421
Health, Labor, and Welfare	.24	427
Space Research and Technology	.04	434
Veterans Funds	.04	438
Fixed Interest Charges	.07	443
Agriculture	.03	446
International Affairs	.03	452
Education	.02	454
Other	.11	457
TOTAL	$1.00	462

(Header line "Expenditure Amount": 416)

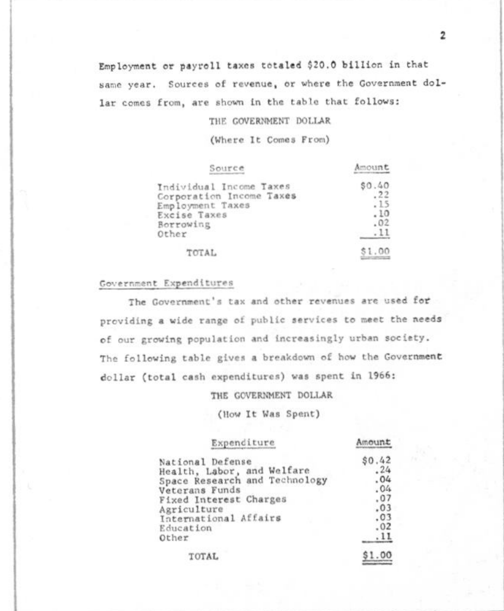

2

Employment or payroll taxes totaled $20.0 billion in that same year. Sources of revenue, or where the Government dollar comes from, are shown in the table that follows:

THE GOVERNMENT DOLLAR
(Where It Comes From)

Source	Amount
Individual Income Taxes	$0.40
Corporation Income Taxes	.22
Employment Taxes	.15
Excise Taxes	.10
Borrowing	.02
Other	.11
TOTAL	$1.00

Government Expenditures

The Government's tax and other revenues are used for providing a wide range of public services to meet the needs of our growing population and increasingly urban society. The following table gives a breakdown of how the Government dollar (total cash expenditures) was spent in 1966:

THE GOVERNMENT DOLLAR
(How It Was Spent)

Expenditure	Amount
National Defense	$0.42
Health, Labor, and Welfare	.24
Space Research and Technology	.04
Veterans Funds	.04
Fixed Interest Charges	.07
Agriculture	.03
International Affairs	.03
Education	.02
Other	.11
TOTAL	$1.00

PAGE 2 OF MANUSCRIPT REPORT

1B: Finger Position

Look at the keyboard shown at the right and locate **asdf** (home keys for the left hand) and **jkl;** (home keys for the right hand).

Look at your typewriter keyboard and locate the home keys. Place the fingers of your left hand on **asdf** and the fingers of your right hand on **jkl;**. Keep your fingers curved and upright.

Remove your hands from the keyboard; then place your curved fingers in home position again, holding them *lightly* on the keys. *Repeat two or three times.*

1C: Key Stroking and Spacing

If you are using an electric typewriter, turn the ON-OFF switch to ON position.

Type **f** with the *left first finger*; then type **j** with the *right first finger*. Strike each key with a down motion and with the finger pulled slightly toward the palm of the hand, as illustrated at the right.

To space after typing a letter or between groups of letters, operate the space bar **27** with a quick *down-and-in* motion of the *right thumb*.

SEQUENCE OF KEY STROKING

1—(*Illustration at left*) Each key should be struck with a firm, sharp stroke and released quickly. Keep most of the stroking action in the fingers; hold the hands and arms quiet.

2—(*Illustration at right*) The finger is snapped *slightly* toward the palm of the hand as the key is released. The finger does not follow the key all the way down. Striking and releasing a key should be thought of as one motion with the release motion started almost at the same instant as the downward motion of the finger.

Type **f j** (with a space after each letter) five times:

```
f j f j f j f j f j
```

On the same line on which you typed **f j** a few times, type the home keys **asdf jkl;** twice, with a space between the grouped letters. The completed line should look like this:

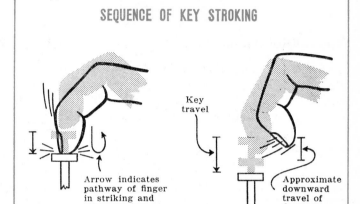

```
f j f j f j f j f j asdf jkl; asdf jkl;
```

Study 1D, below; then make the return.

1D: Carriage (or Element Carrier) Return

To space the paper forward and return to the beginning of the line, use Lever **1** on a manual typewriter or Key **1** on an electric typewriter. Locate this machine part on your typewriter; then make the return as directed below and as illustrated at the right.

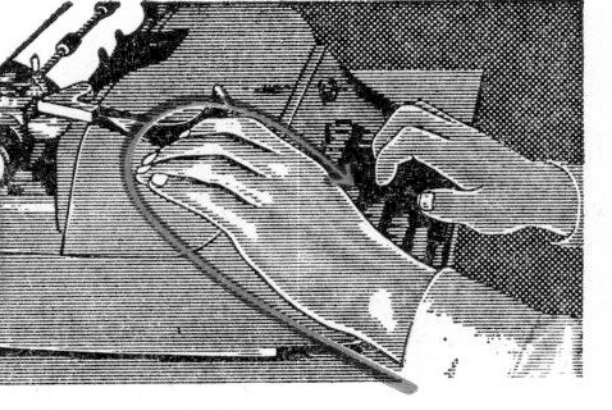

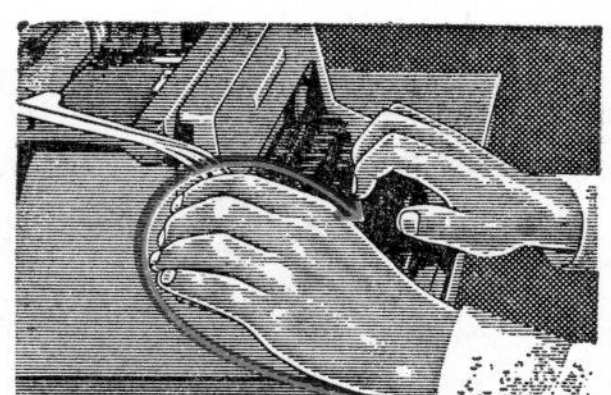

Manual (Nonelectric). Move the left hand, fingers bracing one another, to the carriage return lever and move the lever inward to take up the slack; then return the carriage with a quick wrist and hand motion. Drop the hand to typing position without letting it follow the carriage across.

Electric and Selectric. Reach the little finger of the right hand to the return key, flick the key lightly, release it quickly, and return the finger to its typing position.

On the Selectric the return key returns the *element carrier* (not the carriage) to the left margin.

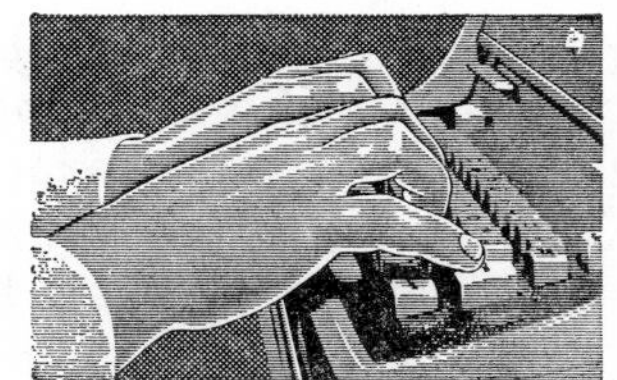

LESSONS 299-300

299–300A: Conditioning Practice (5) *each line three times*

Alphabet	Kag was thrilled by the exquisite, unchained harmony of Peruvian jazz.	*Finger action; hands quiet*
Figure-symbol	Please shift VOA to #13–690 jacks on the DC Control Panel #78–245–398.	
Outside reaches	A zebra slipped on the wet terrazzo of the pavilion as I left the zoo.	
Fluency	While it may be nice to be important, it is more important to be nice.	
	| 1 | 2 | 3 | 4 | 5 | 6 | 7 | 8 | 9 | 10 | 11 | 12 | 13 | 14 |	

299–300B: Skill Comparison (5) *one 1′ writing on each sentence of 299–300A above*

299–300C: Measuring Applied Typewriting Skill (40)

Type the following jobs for 30 minutes in each lesson. Begin with Job 1 below and type as many jobs as you can. Prepare a carbon copy of each job. Erase and correct errors. On the second day, start the timed writing where you left off in the previous timing (re-insert materials for any partially completed job). If you complete all jobs, start over. At the end of Lesson 300, determine *n-pram*: Total acceptable words typed ÷ 60.

Job 1: Business Letters

Modified block, 5-space ¶ indentions
Mixed punctuation *Address envelopes*

Words

Letter 1. (*Current date*) | Western Aircraft Cor- 7
poration | 2608 Colorado Blvd. | Santa Monica, 16
Calif. 90405 | Attention Dr. Allen R. Campbell, 25
Medical Director | Gentlemen: (¶ 1) Mr. Virgil 33
Frohling has recently undergone his semiannual 42
physical examination under my direction. It is 52
my opinion that he is physically sound to per- 61
form the duties of test pilot as required by your 71
Company. (¶ 2) A copy of the medical report 79
is being prepared. It will be sent to you as soon 89
as possible. (¶ 3) Mr. Frohling is about fifteen 98
pounds overweight. I have suggested to him 107
that he watch his diet carefully. I have, there- 116
fore, recommended that he visit my office again 126
in three months so that I may check this condi- 135
tion. Sincerely yours, James L. Drissen, M.D. 145/160
(104)

Letter 2. June 12, 19–– | Mr. David E. Meyers | 7
5746 Hiawatha Drive | Glendale, Calif. 91208 | 16
Dear Mr. Meyers: (¶ 1) In your recent letter you 24
inquired about the filing of insurance claims to 34
cover your medical examination of May 10. Miss 44
Hunter, my office secretary, reports that those 53
papers were processed and sent to the Occi- 62
dental Insurance Company on May 29. (¶ 2) 69
The amount of the claim was $40. This claim 79
consisted of charges for a chest x-ray and lab- 87
oratory blood tests. The $5 charge for a small- 96
pox vaccination was not filed with the insurance 106
company. It is considered preventive care which 116
is not applicable under the terms of your insur- 125
ance contract. (¶ 3) If you have any further 133
questions, do not hesitate to call my office. 143
Please ask for Miss Hunter. If she cannot answer 153
your questions satisfactorily, I shall be glad to do 163
so. Sincerely yours, James L. Drissen, M.D. 173/185
(146)

Letter 3. (*Current date*) | Mr. James Van Dyck | 7
3657 Terra Bella Avenue | Van Nuys, Calif. 15
91402 | Dear Mr. Van Dyck: (¶ 1) At our last 23
volunteer meeting, I was told by our campaign 32
chairman that we have a good chance of reach- 41
ing our goal this year if we hear from our past 50
friends and supporters. However, we cannot be 60
sure everyone will remember us and we are 68
faced with a crucial problem, one that only you 78
can help solve. (¶ 2) Our Christmas Seal Cam- 86
paign closes soon, and we find that we are short 95
of funds needed to maintain one of our most 104
important community health services––tuberculin 114
testing programs in the schools. The tuberculin 124
test determines if a child has been exposed to 133
tuberculosis and should have a chest x-ray and 142
treatment. If you are able to make a gift of just 153

1E: Stroking Technique Practice

Curve your fingers and place them *lightly* on the home keys. **Strike** each key with a *quick, snap stroke*; then **release** the key quickly and type the next key.

Type the typewritten lines below: Single-space (*SS*) the two typings of a line of copy; double-space (*DS*) between two-line groups by operating the return lever or key twice.

1 f | j f ff f ff j jj j jj f ff j jj fj fj fj ff jj fj fj
2 f ff f ff j jj j jj f ff j jj fj fj fj ff jj fj fj
DS (operate the return twice)

Return without spacing after final letter in line

3 d | k d dd d dd k kk k kk d dd k kk dk dk dk dd kk dk dk
4 d dd d dd k kk k kk d dd k kk dk dk dk dd kk dk dk
DS (double-space)

Keep right thumb close to space bar

5 s | l s ss s ss l ll l ll s ss l ll sl sl sl ss ll sl sl
6 s ss s ss l ll l ll s ss l ll sl sl sl ss ll sl sl
DS

7 a | ; a aa a aa ; ;; ; ;; a aa ; ;; a; a; a; aa ;; a; a;
8 a aa a aa ; ;; ; ;; a aa ; ;; a; a; a; aa ;; a; a;
DS

Space with down-and-in motion

9 Home keys fd fds fdsa jk jkl jkl; fd fds fdsa jk jkl jkl; fj
10 fd fds fdsa jk jkl jkl; fd fds fdsa jk jkl jkl; fj
DS

11 Home keys as ask ask ad lad lad all fall all fall ask a lad;
12 as ask ask ad lad lad all fall all fall ask a lad;

TS (triple-space)

1F: Continuity Practice *type the lines as shown*

Continuity Cue	Type one stroke after the other without pausing between them. Keep the carriage moving at a steady, even pace.

ad lad fad sad lad as ask ask lad fad all fall all
ad lad fad sad lad as ask ask lad fad all fall all
DS

Return quickly

Space once after ;

ask dad; dad asks all lads; lads ask dad all fall;
ask dad; dad asks all lads; lads ask dad all fall;
DS

all fall; all fall ads; ask a lad; dad asks a lad;
all fall; all fall ads; ask a lad; dad asks a lad;

Space quickly; use a down-and-in motion

1G: Remove the Paper and Center the Carriage

To remove the paper, raise or pull forward the paper bail **11** with your right hand; operate the paper-release lever **16** with your right hand.

Remove the paper with your left hand. Leave the release lever in forward position to release the pressure on the platen after final daily use.

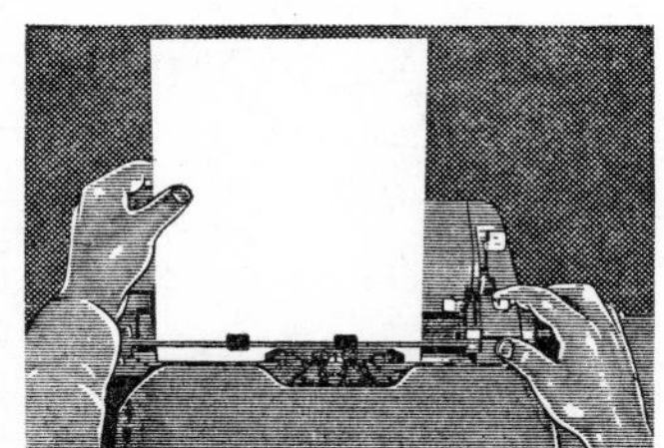

To center the carriage, depress the right carriage release **18** and hold the platen knob firmly. Move the carriage so it is approximately centered.

298B: Statistical Rough-Draft Measurement (45)

three 10′ writings; circle errors; determine nwam *(2 best)*

All letters are used.

	10′ GWAM	
 By mid 1967 the population *of the United States* was around the 200 million mark.	2	38
In the 10-year ~~period~~ *interval*--1955 to 1965--our population ~~increased~~ *multiplied* by	3	39
more than 30 million. By the year 2000, the population of the	4	40
United States probably will be ~~some~~ *nearly* 340 million--about a 150%	6	42
acceleration ~~over~~ *from* 1967. In 1980, young adults *(16 to 24 years of age)* will account for	7	43
well over 40% of the aggregate population. *At that time,* supersonic planes	9	45
will be flying over 1,800 miles per hour; by the year 2000,	10	46
hypersonic planes *flying 5,000 m.p.h. or faster* will be in use.	11	47
 In 1954, population experts projected a world population of	12	49
3.6 billion by 1980. *We have just reached that point.* These experts now are estimating a world	14	51
population of 4.3 billion by 1980 *and about 7.5 billion by 2000.* The population growth rate	16	52
is ~~greater~~ *higher* in underdeveloped ~~countries~~ *regions* than it is in developed	17	54
~~countries~~ *regions*. There is a similar disparity, except in reverse, in	19	55
terms of ~~GNP/C.~~ *gross national product per capita.* For instance, in 1965 the GNP/C of the	20	57
United States was $3,800; in India, it was $80.	24	60
 ~~Great~~ *Amazing* technological ~~advances are forthcoming~~ *progress is being made*. Take as one	25	61
area the magical laser beam. Even though it has been said that	27	63
present-day lasers are ~~exceedingly~~ *very* primitive, ~~hardly~~ *not much* better than	28	64
airplanes were in 1910, annual laser sales *are* now ~~exceed~~ *more than* $125 million.	29	65
Such sales will ~~exceed~~ *be more than* $674.3 million by 1980. Today the laser	31	67
has many uses--in medicine, in research, and in industry. Tomorrow	32	68
a laser eraser may be available for a typist. It has already been	33	69
~~demonstrated~~ *shown* that the black ink of ~~the~~ *an* incorrectly typed letter *can*	35	71
instantly *be* vaporized under the laser beam, leaving no telltale	36	72
eraser smudges.	36	72

It is estimated that by 1995 the GNP/C of the United States will have increased to $15,360, while in India it will rise to only $130.

10′ GWAM | 1 | 2 |

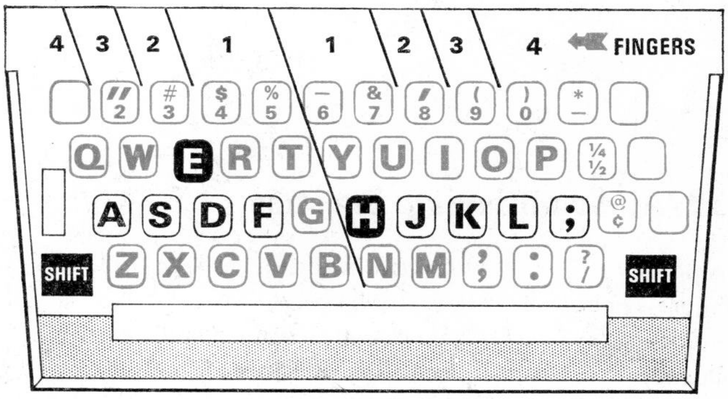

LESSON 2

2A: Get Ready to Type

1. **Desk:** Clear it of unneeded books and papers.
2. **Book:** Place it to the right of the typewriter with the top raised slightly.
3. **Typewriter Frame:** Have front frame even with edge of desk.
4. **Paper Guide 8:** Adjust it as directed for your machine.
5. **Paper Bail 11:** Adjust it as directed for your machine.
6. **Paper:** Place at left of typewriter, long side toward you. Insert as directed on page 2.
7. **Paper Release 16:** Be sure it is engaged.
8. **Line-Space Regulator 5:** Set on "1" for single spacing.
9. **Margin Stops:** Set left stop **7** to left of center of paper 25 spaces; move right stop **15** to end of scale.

TYPING POSITION

Take correct typing position: sit erect; feet on floor; wrists low and relaxed; fingers curved. When typing, keep eyes on the copy.

2B: Conditioning Practice *type the lines as shown*

RECALL: To double-space when the line-space regulator is set for single spacing, operate the return lever or key *twice* as you make the return. Do this after the second typing of the line.

STROKING TECHNIQUE: Snap the finger slightly toward the palm of the hand as you release the key. Do not let the finger follow the key all the way down. Strike and release the key in one motion.

Fingers curved

```
ff jj fj fj dd kk dk dk ss ll sl sl aa ;; a; a; fj
ff jj fj fj dd kk dk dk ss ll sl sl aa ;; a; a; fj
```

Use a quick, snap stroke

DS (double-space)

Start new line without a pause

```
fj dk sl a; fd fds fdsa jk jkl jkl; fdsa jkl; asdf
fj dk sl a; fd fds fdsa jk jkl jkl; fdsa jkl; asdf
```

Space quickly with a down-and-in motion

DS

```
ad lad fad lad sad lad as ask as all all fall af;j
ad lad fad lad sad lad as ask as all all fall af;j
```

TS (triple-space)

2C: New Key Location – h, e, and Left Shift Key

1. Find the new key on the keyboard chart above.
2. Locate the new key on the typewriter keyboard.
3. Study the reach illustration for the new key.
4. Type the reach technique drill.

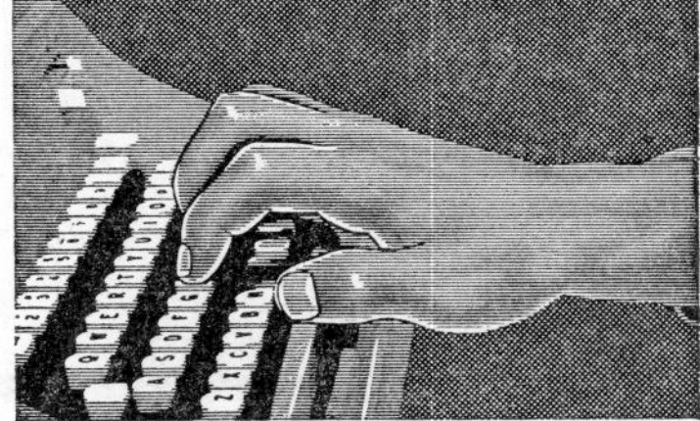

REACH TECHNIQUE FOR H

Reach the *right first finger* to the left to type **h** without moving the other fingers from their home keys.

```
hh hj hj hh jhj hj hh jhj
hj has had hj has had has
```

DS

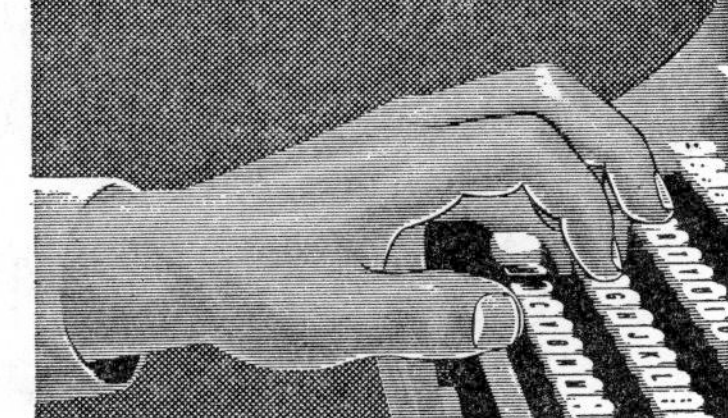

REACH TECHNIQUE FOR E

Reach the *left second finger* to **e**, lifting the first finger slightly to free the controlling finger.

```
ee dd ed ee ded ed ee ded
ed led led ed led fed led
```

DS

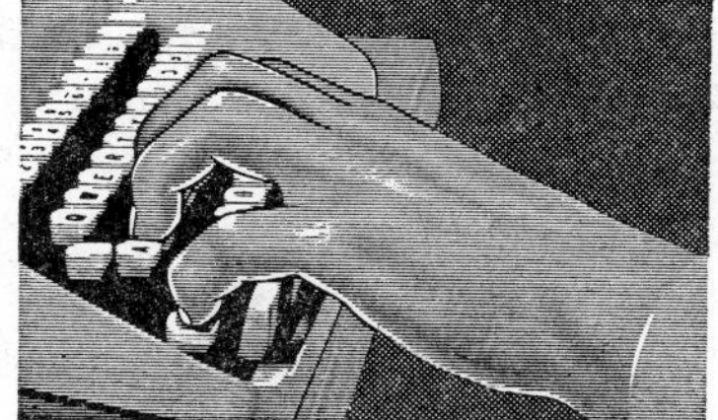

CONTROL OF LEFT SHIFT KEY

Hold the left shift key **28** down with the *left little finger* until the capital letter has been typed. Release quickly.

```
Ha Hal Hall Ha Hale Hakes
Hal Hakes led; Jake fled;
```

TS

LESSON 297

297A: Conditioning Practice (5) *each line three times*

Alphabet	The commander quizzed J. G. Kaplyn about the use of five new sextants.	*Use quick, snap strokes*
Figure-symbol	I-T-E is 51¢ vs. 39¢, N&E is 84¢ vs. 67¢, and PQ&G is $2.70 vs. $1.65.	
Adjacent key	Aza Wert's opinions were not received with great favor by politicians.	
Fluency	If nothing is demanded which you cannot do, you do not do all you can.	
	| 1 | 2 | 3 | 4 | 5 | 6 | 7 | 8 | 9 | 10 | 11 | 12 | 13 | 14 |	

297B: Composition (45)

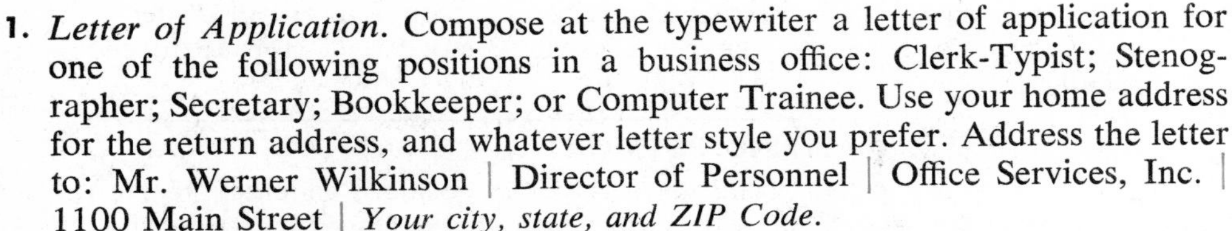

1. *Letter of Application.* Compose at the typewriter a letter of application for one of the following positions in a business office: Clerk-Typist; Stenographer; Secretary; Bookkeeper; or Computer Trainee. Use your home address for the return address, and whatever letter style you prefer. Address the letter to: Mr. Werner Wilkinson | Director of Personnel | Office Services, Inc. | 1100 Main Street | *Your city, state, and ZIP Code.*

Tell Mr. Wilkinson (1) how you learned of the position (school placement office); (2) when you will be graduated from high school (assume next June); the names of some specific courses that you have taken which you think will strengthen your application, and any specific skills you have, plus any work experience; (3) that you are enclosing a personal data sheet. Give any other information you think appropriate.

After you have composed the letter, make any needed pencil corrections, and retype the letter in good form.

1327 Valley Heart Drive
Burbank, California 91506
Current date

Mr. Robert J. Thomas
Director of Personnel
National Computers, Inc.
4567 Washington Boulevard
Los Angeles, California 90023

Dear Mr. Thomas:

Your announcement of openings for the position of "Computer Programmer Trainee" was given to me by my school adviser, Mr. Charles Wheelock. Programming is an area of interest to me, and I should like to apply for the position.

I shall be graduated from Burbank High School in June. My field of study has been business management. This program includes courses in general business, business law, economics, typewriting, bookkeeping, office practice, and introduction to data processing. In addition, I have completed the regular required high school courses. I can type 60 words a minute on straight-copy materials, and I have learned appropriate production skills. I have been active in school organizations. Last year I was president of the Junior Achievement Club. This year I am student body treasurer.

The enclosed personal data sheet will give you additional information. I believe my high school grade average, my work experience, and my participation in school activities are an indication that I can succeed in the position for which I am applying. May I come for an interview at a time that is convenient for you? In case you wish to call me, my telephone number is 224-6539.

Sincerely,

John L. Beck

Enclosure

LETTER OF APPLICATION

2. *Personal Data Sheet.* Compose at the typewriter a data sheet to enclose with your letter of application. Arrange the material on the data sheet in good form. Include information under each of these principal categories:

(1) *Personal Information:* Age; Place of Birth; Height and Weight; etc.

(2) *Education:* Name of High School; Major Field; perhaps something about your scholastic attainment.

(3) *School Activities:* List any appropriate school activities in which you may have participated, or any honors you may have received.

(4) *Work Experience:* List any work experience you have had.

(5) *References:* Give three references other than relatives (teachers, previous employers, etc.).

After you have composed the data sheet, make any needed pencil corrections, and retype the data sheet in good form. Address an envelope for your letter of application and personal data sheet.

PERSONAL DATA SHEET

John L. Beck
1327 Valley Heart Drive
Burbank, California 91506
Telephone: 224-6539

Personal Information

Age:	18
Place of Birth:	Logan, Utah
Height and Weight:	6'1", 175 pounds
Health:	Excellent

Education

High School:	Burbank High School
Degree:	High school diploma, pending graduation
Major:	Business management--Academic
Grade Average:	B+ (Upper 15% of graduating class)

School Activities

Member of varsity baseball team for three years. Regular shortstop during junior and senior years.

President of Junior Achievement Club during junior year. Formed the Allied Products Company, which manufactured and sold tie racks.

Student body treasurer during senior year. Prepared purchase requisitions and kept records of receipts and disbursements of student body funds.

Work Experience

Newspaper route for one year. Delivered 120 papers a day. Made collections monthly.

Clerk-Typist in an insurance office for two summers. Typed insurance forms and letters, sorted company mail, and did other general clerical work.

References (by permission)

Mr. Charles Wheelock, Boys' Adviser; Burbank High School; 525 N. Glenoaks Boulevard; Burbank, California 91502

Mr. Lloyd Bartholome, Business Instructor; Burbank High School; 525 N. Glenoaks Boulevard; Burbank, California 91502

Mr. Edward Nelson, Office Manager; Western States Insurance Company; 2613 W. Olive Avenue; Burbank, California 91506

PERSONAL DATA SHEET

LESSON 298

298A: Conditioning Practice (5) *each line three times*

Alphabet	Judge Namy will be quite perplexed to realize the five checks are bad.	*Type with continuity*
Figure-symbol	Stock reports show W & S $3.45 vs. $2.78, and M & G $16.90 vs. $16.75.	
Shift key	Mrs. T. James O'Malley gave a report on life in San Juan, Puerto Rico.	
Fluency	No invention can ever take the place of honesty, sincerity, and faith.	
	| 1 | 2 | 3 | 4 | 5 | 6 | 7 | 8 | 9 | 10 | 11 | 12 | 13 | 14 |	

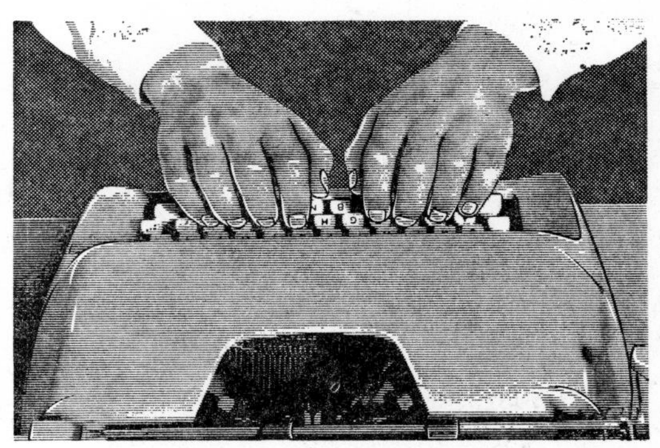

2D: Stroking Technique Practice

RECALL: Operate the return lever or key three times (triple-space) to leave two blank line spaces between lesson parts.

TYPE: The lines as shown below. (Do not type the numbers or identifications at the beginning of the lines.)

STROKING CUE	Snap the finger slightly toward the palm of the hand as you release the key. Do not let the finger follow the key all the way down. Strike and release the key with one continuous motion.

1 **h** hj hh hj ha hal half half hj ha hal half hall hall — *Return without spacing after final stroke*
2 hj hh hj ha hal half half hj ha hal half hall hall
DS (double-space)

3 **e** ed ee ed led fled fed led fled led sled fled sleds
4 ed ee ed led fled fed led fled led sled fled sleds
DS

5 *Caps* Ha Hal Hall Hale Ja Jake La Ladd Lee Leed Hal Hale — *Space quickly with a down-and-in motion*
6 Ha Hal Hall Hale Ja Jake La Ladd Lee Leed Hal Hale

7 *Reinforcement practice* f j h j e d h e d k h j s l a ; e d h j h e h e he
8 f j h j e d h e d k h j s l a ; e d h j h e h e he

9 *Continuity practice* Hal Hall held a lash; Lee has a sled; he has fled;
10 Hal Hall held a lash; Lee has a sled; he has fled; — *TS (triple-space)*

2E: Continuity Practice *type the lines as shown*

STROKING CUE	Keep typing action in fingers. Hold hands and arms quiet—almost motionless. Type a key—lightly and quickly—then type the next key. Keep typing at a steady pace.

1 *Space quickly between words* he she he she shed led sled fled he held self half — *Return quickly*
2 he she he she shed led sled fled he held self half
DS

3 fell sell jell sell shell feel feel heel keel dell
4 fell sell jell sell shell feel feel heel keel dell

5 Les Lee sells jade; Jeff Hess has had a fall sale;
6 Les Lee sells jade; Jeff Hess has had a fall sale;

7 Hal Hale has a desk; he had a desk shelf all fall;
8 Hal Hale has a desk; he had a desk shelf all fall;

2F: Remove the Paper and Center the Carriage (*See page 4.*)

DO: Lift the paper bail or pull it forward. Operate the paper release and remove the paper. Leave the paper release in forward position.

DO: Depress the carriage release and move the carriage to the approximate center of the typewriter. Do this at the close of each practice period.

Taking an Employment Test

LESSON 296

296A: Conditioning Practice (5) *each line three times*

Alphabet	Amazing as it is, we have liked Quebec for all the months except July.	*Fingers close to keys*
Figure-symbol	Was the Multiplex Recorder #45–638 (Serial AMA 2790) listed at $1,395?	
Long words	Computer programming requires a knowledge of compressible flow theory.	
Fluency	Excellence of the highest order is the truest measure of your success.	
	| 1 | 2 | 3 | 4 | 5 | 6 | 7 | 8 | 9 | 10 | 11 | 12 | 13 | 14 |	

296B: Straight-Copy Measurement (45) *three 10′ writings; circle errors; determine* nwam *(2 best)*

All letters are used.

	GWAM 1′	GWAM 10′	
The ability to plan and organize work which can be completed in	13	1	37
an efficient manner will be expected of you in an office. All duties	27	3	39
must be performed with a minimum of waste time and motion. Studies	40	4	40
conclude that many office tasks are done inefficiently simply because	54	5	41
the work was not properly planned and organized.	64	6	42
Cooperation is a word which refers to an attitude that is valued	13	8	44
in office work. If you cooperate with fellow workers, you are destined	27	9	45
to make numerous friends; and your day will be a pleasant and worthy	41	11	46
adventure. Be sure to recognize the importance of teamwork, and realize	56	12	48
that the highest goal in working with others is to cooperate.	68	13	49
Our personality is one of life's greatest assets; but, personality	13	15	51
cannot be wrapped in a container labeled "the acceptable thing." There	28	16	52
is only one acceptable thing for any person to do, and that is the right	42	17	53
thing. The ethical or right thing often goes beyond the acceptable	56	19	55
thing and, in terms of a valid or a genuine achievement, it indicates	70	20	56
much more.	72	20	56
Competition with your own record often leads to superior work habits.	14	22	58
A pattern of superior work habits is yet another way to spell success	28	23	59
in office work. You are aware of the huge cost of paper work in most	42	25	60
business offices. If all office employees learn to operate with effi-	56	26	62
ciency and if they establish a goal of speed and accuracy, these tremen-	70	27	63
dous costs can be diminished.	76	28	64
Respectability may indicate a kind of plan, a scheme, or a pattern	13	29	65
of behavior to some. Genuine respectability has a greater implication.	28	31	67
It implies honesty of thought, word, and deed. It begins with being so	42	32	68
honest with yourself that you cannot be dishonest with others. Such complete	58	34	69
honesty may lead to some understanding; but be of good faith, for in	72	35	71
the long run it leads to esteem and honor.	80	36	72

1′ GWAM | 1 | 2 | 3 | 4 | 5 | 6 | 7 | 8 | 9 | 10 | 11 | 12 | 13 | 14 |

10′ GWAM | 1 | 2 |

LESSON 3

3A: Get Ready to Type

1. Clear the desk.
2. Place book to right of typewriter.
3. Align machine with edge of desk.
4. Review machine parts diagram (page 1).
5. Adjust paper guide and paper bail.
6. Insert the paper and readjust the paper bail.
7. Set machine for single spacing ("1").
8. Move left margin stop 25 spaces to left of center; right stop to end of scale.

3B: Conditioning Practice *type each line twice*

Type the first line twice with single spacing; then double-space and type the other lines in the same way. (Note the illustration given at the right.)

TECHNIQUE CUE	Begin to type at a slow, even pace. Strike and release the key quickly. Move from one letter to the next without pausing between strokes. Keep typing.

```
fdsa jkl; fdsa jkl; eded hjhj eded hjhj he she she
fdsa jkl; fdsa jkl; eded hjhj eded hjhj he she she

ed hj he she shelf held head heal held shelf shall
ed hj he she shelf held head heal held shelf shall

Hal led all; Les fled; Lee fell; Jake held a sale;
Hal led all; Les fled; Lee fell; Jake held a sale;
```

```
fdsa jkl; fdsa jkl; eded hjhj eded hjhj he she she        Space quickly

ed hj he she shelf held head heal held shelf shall

Hal led all; Les fled; Lee fell; Jake held a sale;        TS (triple-space)
```

Space once after **;**

3C: Know Your Typewriter

LEARN: The large letters and figures in the illustrations below are in *pica* type; the small, in *elite* type. Look at your typed lines. Does your typewriter have pica type or elite type?

```
1234567890      Pica type has 10 spaces to the horizontal inch.
123456789012    Elite type has 12 spaces to the horizontal inch.
```

LEARN:

Typing paper is usually 8½ inches wide. It has 85 pica or 102 elite spaces (8½ × 10 = 85; 8½ × 12 = 102). The center of the paper is at 42½ for pica type and at 51 for elite type; but you will *use 42 for pica and 50 for elite center.*

By changing the placement of the paper guide, you can insert the paper so that 50 will be the center point for pica as well as for elite type, if you are so directed.

DO:

Remove the paper from the machine. Place the top left and right edges together. Make a slight crease at the exact center at the top. Reinsert the paper with the center at 42 for pica or at 50 for elite (or whatever center you are directed to use).

Move the paper guide against the left edge of the paper. Check to see that it is in this position at the beginning of each practice period.

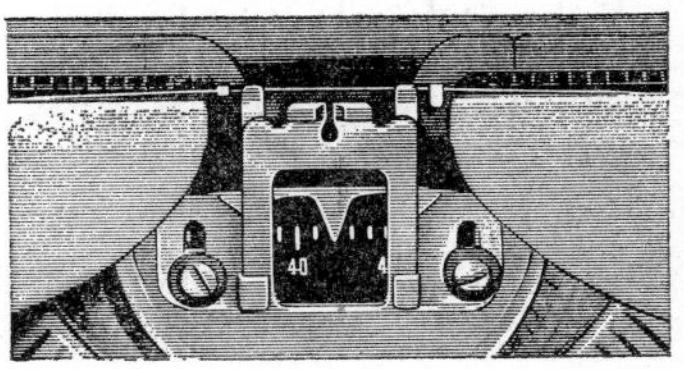

Job 8: Two-Page Medical Letter

TYPE the letter using current year for the date. In the first paragraph use date two years ago, and in the second paragraph use date one year ago.

1 cc; modified block	*Block heading, page 2*
Mixed punctuation	*Correct errors*

January 3, 19—– | State Department of Rehabilitation | Division of Disability Determination | Room 5040, 1111 Jackson Street | Oakland, California 94607 | Gentlemen: | *(Note to typist: Center RE [regarding] lines in subject-line position.)*

RE: Henry, Thomas
File 032–92–34

(¶ 1) The patient is a 64-year-old white male, who underwent resection of an aortic valve for aortic stenosis, aortic insufficiency, as well as resection of an ascending aortic aneurysm on April 6, 19—–. A Starr–Edwards prosthetic valve and a Teflon tube aortic graft were used as replacement. Postoperatively, the patient did well. He, however, was readmitted to the CENTER on May 7, 19—–, because of hemorrhage resulting from his anticoagulation. This was corrected, but it was noted that he had sustained a large hematoma in the area of his upper right thigh. Following discharge from the hospital, the patient was left with residual pain, numbness, and weakness in the right lower extremity. He was seen by the Orthopedic Clinic. Varying grades of exercises were prescribed, all of which provided slow improvement in the numbness and weakness of the right leg. (¶ 2) The patient has continued to be followed by the Surgical Clinic, the Orthopedic Clinic, and the cardiologists. He was at the CENTER in November, 19—–, where he was described as having some numbness along the inner aspects of the right leg, but his strength in his right foot was better. He was able at that time to do only light work. On November 30, 19—–, he was seen in the Cardiology Clinic at his home in Bakersfield, California, and was described as having had an episode of tachycardia with shortness of breath and dizziness. He was seen in a local emergency room, but no medication was affected. A summary of recent laboratory data shows an EKG revealing left ventricular hypertrophy, and a chest x-ray showing left ventricular hypertrophy and pulmonary vascular congestion. (¶ 3) Physical examination reveals that his lungs are clear and that he continues to have a Grade V pansytolic murmur over the left precordium, as well as a Grade IV diastolic murmur. Clinically, however, he appears to be relatively stable. He will be followed closely by his private physician in Bakersfield. He is scheduled for follow-up visits at the above-mentioned clinics at regular intervals. His present medications include only Digitalis leaf. (¶ 4) It is my opinion that this patient is unable to do any physical labor. Clinically, he would be classified as totally disabled, since he is, at present, qualified to do only physical labor of an unskilled kind. I shall be glad to furnish any other information you may need. | Sincerely yours, | Kurt Templeman, M.D. | Chief Resident | Department of Medicine | KT:xx (481)

Job 9: Typing Master Copy for Photo Reproduction

TYPE a master copy. Be sure type is clean. Use uniform stroking. All errors must be neatly corrected.

Top margin: 1½″	*DS copy*
Side margins: 1″	*TS before side headings*

INTENSIVE CARE UNIT | at | SAINT JOHN'S HOSPITAL

FOR THE PATIENT . . .

Embodying a new concept of personalized "around-the-clock" care for acutely ill or post-operative patients with possible complications, the INTENSIVE CARE UNIT (I.C.U.) at Saint John's Hospital provides the patient with CONSTANT audio and visual observation and highly skilled nursing care at a cost considerably lower than previously possible.

Located on the third floor in the main section of the hospital, I.C.U. is composed of a suite of air-conditioned rooms especially equipped and staffed to meet all emergencies. In this section, removed from the regular activities of the hospital, I.C.U. patients receive the full benefit of the medical team and specialized equipment throughout the day and night. A family room has been provided adjacent to I.C.U., permitting the family to remain near the patient.

FOR THE DOCTOR . . .

The INTENSIVE CARE UNIT, staffed by skilled nursing personnel and the latest in medical instrumentation, assures the physician or surgeon that his or her patient is receiving CONSTANT audio and visual observation and care as needed.

The suite also serves as a recovery room for emergency surgical cases during those times and hours when the recovery room is not available. Admissions and dismissals of patients to and from the unit are always ordered by the doctor. A fully stocked section of medications is maintained in I.C.U. and is readily available at all times as another reassurance to both patient and physician.

3D: New Key Location – i, t, and . *(period)*

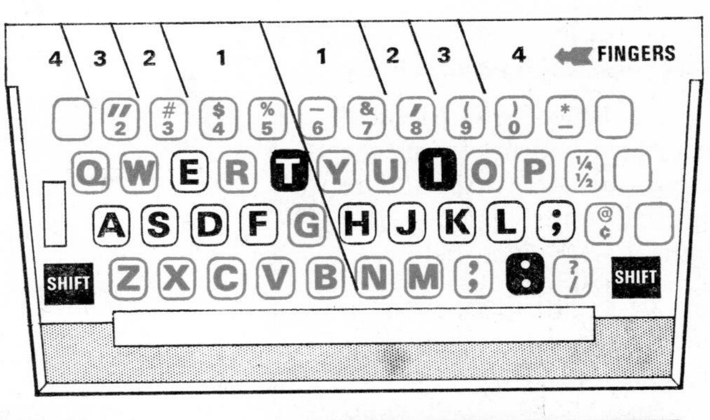

DO: 1. Find new key on keyboard chart.
2. Locate new key on typewriter keyboard.
3. Study reach illustration.
4. Type reach technique drill.

REACH TECHNIQUE FOR i

Reach the *right second finger* to **i**; lift the right first finger slightly for improved stroking control.

```
ii ik ik ii kik ik ii kik
if ik is his kid aid laid
```
DS

REACH TECHNIQUE FOR T

Reach the *left first finger* to **t** without arching the wrist or moving the hand forward.

```
tt tf tf tt ftf tf tt ftf
tf the flat the left that
```
DS

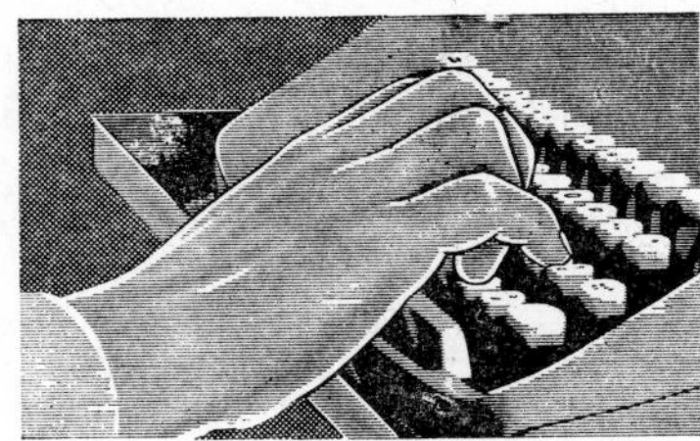

REACH TECHNIQUE FOR .

Extend the *right third finger* down to type **.** (period) without moving the hand downward.

```
l.l .l .. .l .. .l .. l.l
adj. del. stk. def. hdkf.
```
TS

3E: Stroking Technique Practice *type a line twice; DS; then type the next line twice*

SPACING RULE	Space twice after a period at the end of a sentence, except when it is the last stroke in a line; then return without spacing.

1 i — ik if is kid lid aid kid laid said fill kill skill — *Strike space bar quickly*

2 t — tf the theft flat that left take felt these health

3 . — It fits. It is a hit. Kit said that I had skill.

4 *Reinforcement* — i f if i t it i s is h i s his it fit is this .l.l

5 *Space once after* **;** — Jeff still has that file; let Keith Leeds take it. — *TS (triple-space)*

3F: Continuity Practice *type a line twice; DS; then type the next line twice*

1 if it is did kit fit sit hit lit aid laid his this — *Return without spacing after final stroke in line*

2 *Depress shift key firmly* — I shall take this hat. It is a hat that fits Kit.

3 Let Kit aid Jake Leff. He said he likes his life. — *Space quickly*

4 Keith said that Kit Hiss has his file at the lake.

AT THE END OF THE PERIOD	Remove the paper. Leave paper release in forward position. Center the carriage. Pick up all waste paper. Push the chair to the desk as you leave the room.

Job 6: Medical Insurance Form

Type a Blue Cross Medical Insurance Form from the partial illustration at the right (Items 1-12) and Items 13-19 given below.

Blue Cross of Southern California BOX 27747 LOS FELIZ STATION LOS ANGELES, CALIFORNIA 90027	PHYSICIAN'S REPORT and Outpatient Report for Non-contracting Hospitals REFER TO BLUE CROSS PHYSICIAN'S MANUAL FOR INSTRUCTIONS		
1 PATIENT'S NAME (LAST, FIRST, MIDDLE INITIAL) Sabina, Rosemary E.	4 DATE OF BIRTH MONTH DAY YEAR 9 14 1922	5 CERTIFICATE NUMBER 573-12-3713	6 GROUP NUMBER 16212A
2 STREET ADDRESS (PLEASE CHECK ADDRESS) 4399 Laurel Canyon	7 SUBSCRIBER'S NAME David Sabina	8 REL. TO SUBSCRIBER Wife	9 UNION LOCAL #
3 CITY AND STATE No. Hollywood, Calif.	10 PT'S OCCUPATION Housewife	11 COMPANY EMPLOYING SUBSCRIBER California Products, Inc.	
12 IF REFERRED CASE ENTER PHYSICIAN'S NAME AND ADDRESS			

13 X CONTINUED CASE
14 X NO *15* (*Blank*)
16 CBC 11/14/-- $6.00
PBI " 6.00
17 Subtotal left lobectomy of thyroid gland 11/17/-- $350.00 *18* (*Blank*) *19* Aaron Bond, M.D. | 2200 Santa Monica Blvd. Santa Monica, Calif. 90405

Job 7: Report of Operation

Type heading lines as shown in illustration →
SS the lines of the PROCEDURE
2 cc's; correct errors

038-95-96

SABINA, Rosemary E.
GENERAL SURGERY 4 East

Aaron Bond, M.D.

CENTER FOR THE HEALTH SCIENCES

REPORT OF OPERATION

DATE OF OPERATION: 11/17/--
NAME OF DICTATOR: Paul Orlando, M.D.

PREOPERATIVE DIAGNOSIS: Benign nodule, left lobe of thyroid
POSTOPERATIVE DIAGNOSIS: Same
OPERATION: Subtotal left lobectomy of thyroid gland
SURGEON: Aaron Bond, M.D. ASSISTANTS: Paul Orlando, M.D.
Steven Josephs, M.D.

PROCEDURE: Under satisfactory general anesthetic the skin of the

PROCEDURE: Under satisfactory general anesthetic the skin of the neck was prepared and draped in the usual manner. A 3-inch transverse incision, skinline, was made in the lower portion of the anterior surface of the neck, approximately two fingerbreadths above the jugular notch. Sharp dissection was carried out through the area to the level of the platysmal muscle, and to the cervical fascia. Midline dissection was carried out separating the two external hyoid muscles. These were both deflected laterally and the sternothyroid muscles were then dissected free. The thyroid gland was then identified. The right lobe of the thyroid was examined and found to be normal. Dissection along the left lobe of the thyroid was then carried out, and the thyroid nodule identified. The superior parathyroid gland was identified. Roughly one half of the left lobe of the thyroid included the left thyroid nodule, which was then dissected free from the remaining tissue. Bleeders were ligated with 4-0 silk sutures. The mass on each side of the trachea inferior to the thyroid gland was then dissected, freed, and found to be the large cervical extension of the thymus gland on each side. A portion of the thymus gland on the left was removed and submitted for frozen section. Pathologically the specimen was found to be a normal thymus gland. Frozen section report on the thyroid nodule confirmed the diagnosis of benign thyroid nodule. The area was then reexamined and careful hemostasis undertaken, with both Bovie and 4-0 silk ligatures. With 4-0 silk sutures, the cervical fascia was then approximated using interrupted sutures. Subcutaneous tissues and platysma were then reapproximated with 4-0 silk interrupted sutures and skin was closed using 4-0 silk mattress sutures. A thyroid-type dressing was then applied. The patient tolerated the procedure well and left the operating room in good condition.

TS

PAUL ORLANDO, M.D.

PO: (*Your initials*)
DICT: 12/19/--
TRANS: 12/27/--

LESSON 4

4A: Get Ready to Type (3)*

1. Clear the desk.
2. Place book to right of typewriter.
3. Align machine with edge of desk.
4. Adjust paper guide, paper bail, and paper release.
5. Insert the paper.
6. Set line-space regulator on "1" for single spacing.
7. Move left margin stop 25 spaces to left of center; right stop to end of scale.

4B: Know Your Typewriter – Ribbon Control (5)

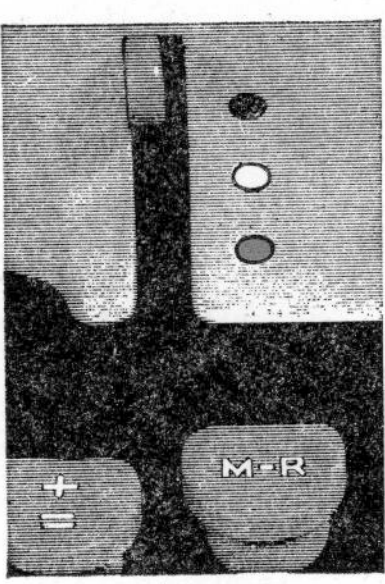

The ribbon control **22** can be set to type on the upper or lower part of the ribbon if there are three adjustments on your typewriter for this control. If there are four adjustments, the typing will be on the upper, middle, or lower part of the ribbon. Set the ribbon control to type on the upper part of the ribbon. Make this a part of your daily Get Ready to Type.

REMEMBER:

1. A full-length line on paper 8½ inches wide has 85 pica or 102 elite spaces. (See illustration on page 7.)
2. There are 10 pica or 12 elite spaces to a horizontal inch; therefore, use 42 for pica or 50 for elite center unless directed to use another center point.

4C: Conditioning Practice (7) *type a line twice; DS; then type the next line twice*

SPACING RULE	Space once after a period used at the end of an abbreviation; twice after . at the end of a sentence.

Begin slowly fd jk sa l; ed hj tf ik tf ik .l La. Lt. Ill. Hts. *Space quickly*

Use quick snap stroke is his it fit is his this list Ike Kidd Jill Heiss

I had the lease. I let Kit take it; she filed it. *TS (triple-space)*

4D: Reinforcement Practice (15) *type a line twice; DS; then type the next line*

REMEDIAL CUE	If a capital letter is typed above (not on) the line, depress and hold down the shift key firmly until the letter has been typed.

1 e | h eded else deal see seed hjhj he she he held he she *Return quickly*

2 t | i tftf the these late last set ikik it fit this list

3 i | e lie die tie tied side this files field these still

4 *Space twice after . and* I like this. I like this set. Jeff has the list.

5 *once after ;* Lee is at Lake Heid; he has the last sheets I did.

*A time schedule for the parts of this lesson and the following ones is given as a guide for your minimum practice. The number of minutes is shown as a figure within a circle: (3) If the schedule permits, retype selected lines from the various drills of the lesson.

Job 3: Patient Identification Cards

USE: 6″ x 4″ cards. TYPE: Two Patient Identification Card forms as illustrated; use judgment in arranging the form; save cards for Job 4.

PATIENT IDENTIFICATION CARD

Patient's Name and Address:

1 ______________________ Date: ________

2 ______________________ File No.: ________

3 ______________________ Age: ________

Name of Spouse or Parent: Height: ________

4 ______________________ Weight: ________

Employer's Name and Address: Telephone: ________

5 ______________________ Insurance: ________

6 ______________________ ________

7 ______________________

PATIENT IDENTIFICATION CARD

Job 4: Completing Patient Identification Cards

Complete cards prepared in Job 3 by typing the information given below on the appropriate blank lines.

(1) Patient's Name and Address: **Cowan, John Joseph** | **1099 Oleander Drive** | **Los Angeles, Calif. 90042** | Name of Spouse or Parent: **Helen Cowan (Wife)** | Employer's Name and Address: **(Patient retired)** | Date: **4/3/--** | File No.: **057–8153A** | Age: **69** | Height: **5′ 11″** | Weight: **189** | Telephone: **987–6543** | Insurance: **Medicare**

(2) Patient's Name and Address: **Sabina, Rosemary E.** | **4399 Laurel Canyon** | **No. Hollywood, Calif. 91604** | Name of Spouse or Parent: **David Sabina (Husband)** | Employer's Name and Address: **California Products, Inc.** | **308 Catalina Avenue, So.** | **Torrance, Calif. 90503** | Date: **11/14/--** | File No.: **038–95–96** | Age: **45** | Height: **5′ 3½″** | Weight: **123** | Telephone: **783–8418** | Insurance: **Blue Cross of California**

Job 5: Medicare Insurance Form

TYPE a Medicare Insurance Form, completing appropriate blanks, from the material shown below. Part II of the form is partially illustrated below.

Upper Left Corner: **CALIFORNIA PHYSICIANS' SERVICE** | **P. O. Box 7968, Rincon Annex** | **San Francisco, California 94119** Name of Beneficiary: **COWAN, John Joseph** Claim Number: **057–8153A** (Use **X** in box for Male) **Medi-Cal No. 023|90|69|1–M**
Item 1: **CATARACT, O.D.**
Item 2: (**X** in **NO** box)
Item 3: **NO** Item 4: **YES**
Item 5: (Leave **SIGNATURE** line blank); Date: **4/10/--**
Item 6: (Supply information from appropriate Patient Identification Card, Job 4.) Telephone: (Get from Patient Identification Card)
Items 7–13: (Type from illustration at right.)

PART II—REPORT OF SERVICES—TO BE COMPLETED BY PHYSICIAN— This Part, Including Physician's Signature, Need Not Be Completed If Paid, Itemized Bills Are Submitted.

7. A. DATE OF EACH SERVICE	B. PLACE OF SERVICE[1]	RVS PROC. NO.[1]	C. FULLY DESCRIBE SURGICAL OR MEDICAL PROCEDURES AND OTHER SERVICES OR SUPPLIES FURNISHED FOR EACH DATE GIVEN	D. NATURE OF ILLNESS OR INJURY REQUIRING SERVICES OR SUPPLIES (Diagnosis)	E. CHARGES	Leave Blank
3/23	IH	5611	Extraction, intra-capsular, cataract, O.D.	Senile cataract, O.D.	$ 560.00	
			Surgeon: G. O. Dayton, M.D. Anesthesia: Local			
3/23	IH	8922	PATHOLOGY: Gross examination of surgical specimen		2.00	

8. NAME AND ADDRESS OF PHYSICIAN OR SUPPLIER (Number and street, City, State, ZIP Code)
G. O. Dayton, M.D.
11455 Sunset Blvd.
Los Angeles, Calif. 90049

TELEPHONE NUMBER: 654-3789
CODE NO.:
STATE LIC. NO.[1,2]: XY039

9. Total Charges: $ 562.00
10. Amount Paid: $ 0
11. Any Unpaid Balance Due: $ 562.00

12. ASSIGNMENT OF PATIENT'S BILL (See reverse) [X] I ACCEPT ASSIGNMENT [ ] I DO NOT ACCEPT ASSIGNMENT

13. SIGNATURE OF PHYSICIAN OR SUPPLIER (A physician's signature certifies that physician's services were personally rendered by him or under his personal direction) [X] MD [ ] DO [ ] DDS OR DMD | DATE SIGNED: 4/12/--

PART II OF MEDICARE INSURANCE FORM

4E: Sentence Guided Writings (20)

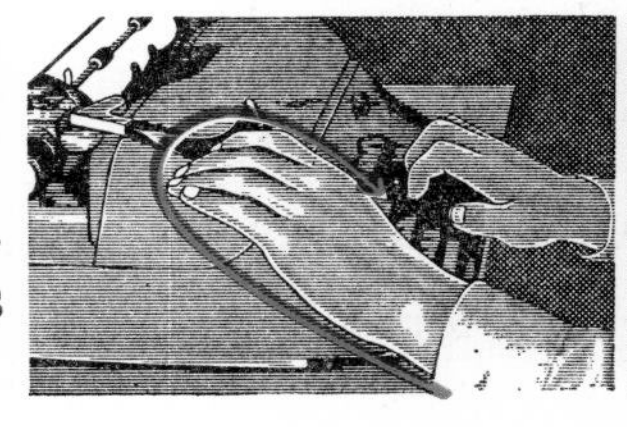

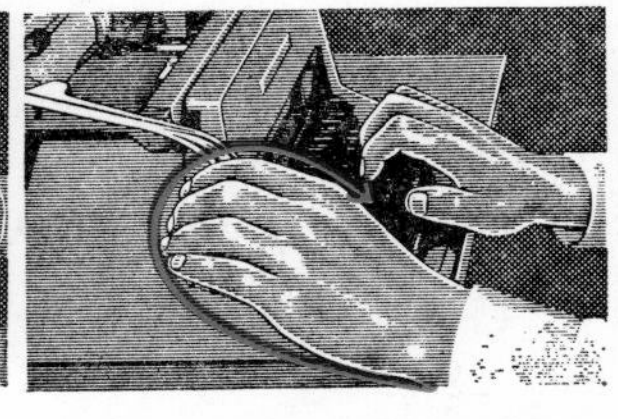

1. **Type** each sentence twice untimed; then double-space.
   a. First, type at an easy pace and with even, continuous stroking.
   b. Then, speed up the stroking. Avoid pausing between strokes and between words—just keep on typing.

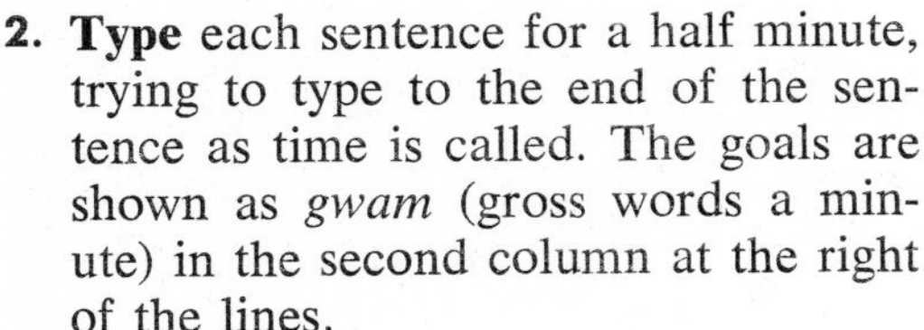

2. **Type** each sentence for a half minute, trying to type to the end of the sentence as time is called. The goals are shown as *gwam* (gross words a minute) in the second column at the right of the lines.

3. **Type** each sentence for 1 minute without the call of the line ending. Type until time is called.

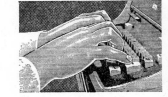

RETURN CUE	Make the return without looking up from the copy.

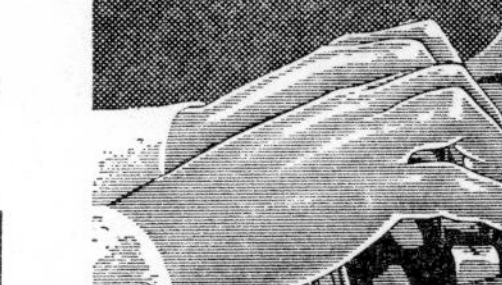

All letters that have been taught and only one-syllable words are used in the sentences.

		Words in Line*	GWAM 30" Guide
1	I had a jade sale at the lake.	6	12
2	Jeff said Jake had failed the test.	7	14
3	Kit asked Keith if he had the last list.	8	16
4	Hal asked Lee if he had filed the state list.	9	18
5	It is this desk file that Les Leith had Kate take.	10	20
	. . . . 1 . . . . 2 . . . . 3 . . . . 4 . . . . 5 . . . . 6 . . . . 7 . . . . 8 . . . . 9 10		

***HOW TYPEWRITTEN WORDS ARE COUNTED:**

Five strokes are counted as one standard typewritten word. The figures in the first column at the right of the foregoing sentences show the number of 5-stroke words in each of the lines. The scale beneath the copy shows the word-by-word count (5 strokes at a time) for each of the lines.

TO DETERMINE TOTAL WORDS TYPED:

1. List the figure at the end of each complete line typed during a writing. **2.** Note from the scale the figure directly below the point at which you stopped typing. **3.** Add these figures to determine the total gross words typed. (Gross words are the same as *gwam* for a 1-minute writing.)

4F: Bonus (Extra-Credit) Typing *type a line twice; DS; then type the next line*

SPACE-BAR CONTROL	Strike the space bar in the center with a quick down-and-in motion of the right thumb. Make spacing a short, quick stroke in rhythm with the typing.

1 as see seed fee feed ill kill hill test date state

2 Kit had the file. Jake has it. He did this list.

3 I failed the last test. Lee said that he is safe.

4 Les asked Keith if he has set the state test date.

. . . . 1 . . . . 2 . . . . 3 . . . . 4 . . . . 5 . . . . 6 . . . . 7 . . . . 8 . . . . 9 10

Lessons 292, 293, and 294

Use the following plan for Lessons 292, 293, and 294:

Conditioning Practice (5′): Type 291A, page 417.

Sustained Skill Building (15′): Type a timed writing on 291C, page 418, using the following plan:

Lesson 292: 10′ writing; circle errors; determine *gwam*.

Lesson 293: 10′ writing; correct errors as you type; proofread; add ½′ to 10 for each uncorrected error; use this total time to compute corrected-words-a-minute rate (*cwam*).

Lesson 294: 10′ writing; circle errors; determine *nwam*.

Applied Typing (30′): Type the Jobs on pages 419–422. Use an eraser, when necessary, and your best correction techniques for acceptable work.

Lesson 295

Use the following plan for Lesson 295:

Conditioning Practice (5′): Type 291A, page 417.

Accuracy Emphasis (25′): Type a 1′ writing on each sentence of 291B, page 417. **Goal:** Accuracy.

Applied Typing (20′): Continue with the Jobs you have been typing. At the end of the lesson, assemble all jobs you have completed, arrange them in job number order, evaluate each job as *acceptable* or *unacceptable*, and submit them to your teacher.

Applied Typing: Lessons 292 – 295

Job 1: Abstract of a Medical Research Report

Leftbound manuscript style	*4 carbon copies; DS*
10-space ¶ indentions	*Correct errors*

ABSTRACT OF SOME REPRESENTATIVE FINDINGS CONCERNING THE ECOLOGY OF THIRD-GRADE SCHOOL CHILDREN (¶ 1) In ecology, interest is centered upon the mutual relations between the individual and his environment. It is presumed that, since the human organism functions as a whole, a substantial change in any one aspect of either its internal or external environment may bring about alterations both in general well-being and in specific types of functions. (¶ 2) The report presents a limited number of representative findings that arose from a study of 336 third-grade boys and of 336 third-grade girls. The data were obtained upon nearly eighty different variables pertaining to such diversified dimensions as anthropometric and physical characteristics, maturity factors, respiratory function, physiological measures indicative of nutrition (such as blood sugar, total cholesterol, and hemoglobin), cardiac factors such as the P-R, Q-R-S, and Q-T intervals in the electrocardiogram records, heart rate at various stages of temporal proximity to exercise, intellectual status, achievement on standardized tests, perceptual function, personal and social adjustment, social acceptance, and certain sociological measures such as parental occupation and number of siblings. (¶ 3) From the findings presented in the report, it is apparent that a substantial degree of interdependence exists between various aspects of organic function and different types of observable activities in the human organism. Interrelationships are apparent between certain pairs of such diversified variables as achievement in arithmetic, respiratory function, maturity level, physiological indices of blood sugar, total cholesterol, and hemoglobin, measures of cardiac function, and social adjustment. The data secured lend support to the hypotheses of the existence of a degree of relationship between selected pairs of variables. *(Medical research report upon which this abstract is based furnished by courtesy of Milton Tobias, M.D.)*

Job 2: Composing an Office Memo

TYPE a brief office memo (on plain paper using your name in the FROM line) addressed to the three persons listed at the right, telling them that you are enclosing for their reference the ABSTRACT OF SOME REPRESENTATIVE FINDINGS CONCERNING THE ECOLOGY OF THIRD-GRADE SCHOOL CHILDREN (prepared as Job 1). Make needed pencil corrections in your composition; then type the memo in proper form with three carbon copies.

William Ross, M.D., Medical Research
H. L. Edwards, Research Contracts Division
Brian R. McCarthy, Reports Analyst

LESSON 5

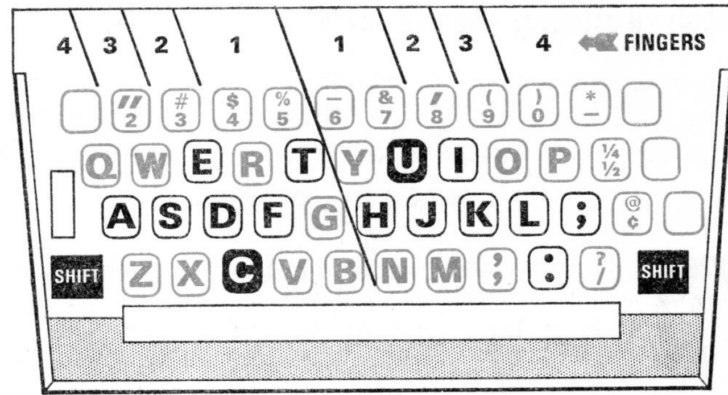

5A: Get Ready to Type (3)

1. Insert full sheet.
2. Set machine for single spacing ("1").
3. Set left margin stop 25 spaces to left of center of paper; move right stop to end of scale.

5B: Know Your Typewriter (5)

LEARN: When one key is struck before the preceding one is released, the keys collide and may stick together, or "jam." (*On the Selectric typewriter, jamming is mechanically impossible.*)

To correct this technique fault, align fingers directly over the home keys and improve timing of key strokes.

IF KEYS JAM: **1.** Use the special jammed-key release, if your typewriter has this special key.

2. Depress the shift key; this sometimes works.

3. If keys are still tangled, gently flick with your finger the stuck key nearest you; or push keys slightly toward the platen and untangle them.

5C: Conditioning Practice (7) *type a line twice; DS; then type the next line*

TECHNIQUE CUE	Sit erect, feet on floor. Fingers curved. Space quickly with down-and-in motion of the right thumb. Eyes on copy as you type.

Space once after . ending abbreviation, twice after . at end of sentence

Return without spacing after .

```
ik tf fit ed hj the a; sl last l. Lt. La. La. Ill.

I like Hal.  He failed a test.  Kate had the list.

I shall see if Lee has the state file at the lake.
....1....2....3....4....5....6....7....8....9....10
```

5D: New Key Location – u, c, and Right Shift Key (10)

DO: Find new key on chart, above. | Locate new key on keyboard. | Study reach diagram. | Type the drill.

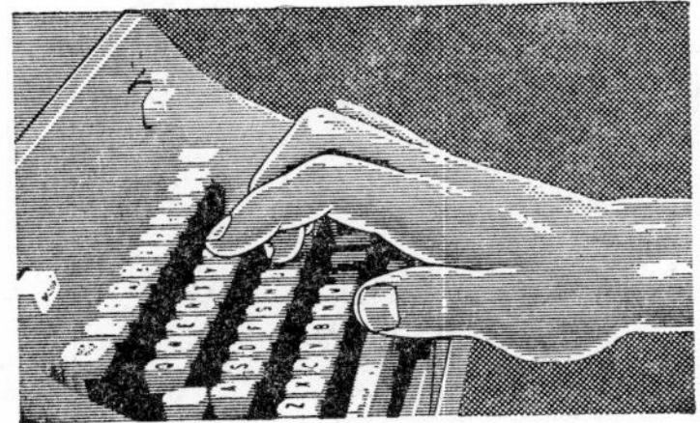

REACH TECHNIQUE FOR U

Reach the *right first finger* to **u** without moving the other fingers from their home keys.

```
uu uj uj uu juj uj uu juj

uj us just dust husk just DS
```

REACH TECHNIQUE FOR C

Reach down to **c** with the *left second finger* without twisting the elbow in or out or moving the hand down.

```
cc cd cd cc dcd cd cc dcd

cd clad sick deck cd each DS
```

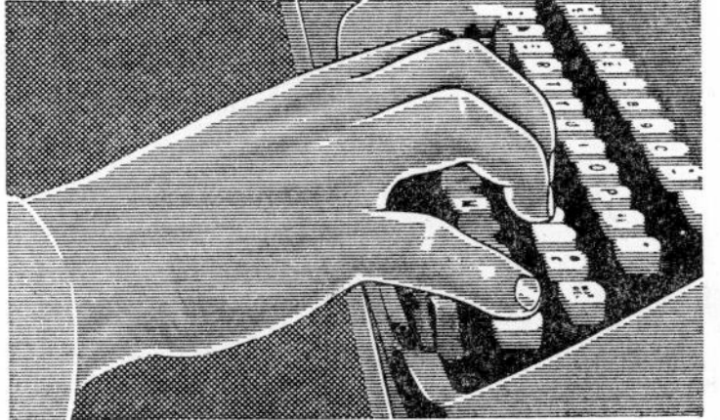

CONTROL OF RIGHT SHIFT KEY

Hold the right shift key **26** down with the *right little finger* until the capital letter has been typed.

```
Al El Alf Sal File Stiles

Alf led Sue.  El is sick. TS
```

291C: Building Speed and Control (30)

1. **Speed.** Select a *speed goal* 4 to 8 *wam* above your average speed rate; type three 1′ guided writings on each ¶ at this goal rate.

2. **Control.** Type two 1′ *control* guided writings on each ¶. Select a *control rate* about 8 *wam* below your average speed rate on Step 1.

All letters are used.

HA		10′ GWAM	
1.6 HA 5.8 70	Because of the numerous one- or two-doctor medical offices, a	1	37
	top medical secretary must be trained in three basic job fields––those	3	38
	of receptionist, bookkeeper, and stenographer. In a small clinic a	4	40
	girl may be called upon to perform all of these duties. In a big office	5	41
	a different girl is responsible for each task.	6	42
1.6 HA 5.8 70	A medical receptionist has to be neat in appearance and dress.	8	44
	Her manner must not antagonize the patient. She should be able to	9	45
	put patients at ease but not let them control the situation. She must	10	46
	be polite, friendly, considerate, and alert. She must have the ability	12	48
	to execute oral and written directions that are given by a doctor.	13	49
1.6 HA 5.8 70	A capable bookkeeper must be skilled in the use of the double-entry	15	51
	theory of keeping books. It includes daily recording of income and	16	52
	expenses as well as orderly posting to ledgers. Charges and credits to	17	53
	each account have to be kept current. It is her duty to submit insurance	19	55
	claims and orders for patients. The records are audited at regular	20	56
	intervals.	20	56
1.6 HA 5.8 70	A doctor may refuse to hire a stenographer who does not have the	22	58
	ability to type, spell, and take dictation. She has to acquire such	23	59
	skill prior to applying for a job. Some of her many duties are: take	25	61
	dictation, submit letters and reports in an acceptable style, keep records	26	62
	neatly filed in proper sequence, have appropriate supplies available,	27	63
	and assist in any office task.	28	64
1.6 HA 5.8 70	Duties of individual office employees may vary according to the	29	65
	desires of a doctor. This is why it is vital that staff members know	31	67
	specific areas of work assigned to each girl. Girls are expected to	32	68
	aid each other. There must be a feeling of rapport among the respective	34	70
	workers. Then, the office will function in an efficient style, and the	35	71
	doctor can spend his time administering to patients.	36	72

10′ GWAM | 1 | 2 |

5E: Stroking Technique Practice (15) *each line twice; DS between pairs; then type from dictation*

REACH CUE	Reach up to **u** without moving the hand forward and down to **c** without twisting the elbow out.

SPACING RULE	Space once after **.** used at the end of an abbreviation; twice after **.** used to punctuate a sentence.

1	u	uj u juj due sue jut us uj u use used hut hue just	*Quick, snap stroke*
2	c	cd c dcd cash deck each teach chief checks checked	
3	*Right shift*	St. Ala. Del. Fla. Tues. Fed. Sat. Dec. Chas. Cat.	*Eyes on copy*
4	*Reinforcement*	u s us h e he i t it c u t cut c u e cue a c t act	
5	*Sentence typing*	Al called. Sue has the facts. Ed cashed a check.	

5F: Continuity Practice (10) *each line twice; DS between pairs*

1	u | c	us just such clue chute cluck latch clutch checked	*Reach—don't "leap" to the key*
2	u | c	cue cut such duck luck tuck stuck cede cult caused	
3	*Double letters*	fuss cuff dull cull full cuss less tell sell still	
4	*Caps and .*	Cal cashed a check. Sue checked the cash Cal has.	
5	*Sentence typing*	Dick said that Chuck let Sue Duff use these files.	

. . . . 1 . . . . 2 . . . . 3 . . . . 4 . . . . 5 . . . . 6 . . . . 7 . . . . 8 . . . . 9 10

5G: Bonus (Extra-Credit) Typing *type a line twice; DS; type the next line*

All letters taught are used in the lines.

1	us use thus cd clad such just haul duck deck chute	*Hold hands quiet; type with fingers*
2	case cast cede hill kill hull fact seat face faced	
3	Cliff has filed the deed. Sue had shut this case.	
4	The cause is just; thus the cause shall shield us.	
5	Dick said it is a fact that Chuck failed the test.	

. . . . 1 . . . . 2 . . . . 3 . . . . 4 . . . . 5 . . . . 6 . . . . 7 . . . . 8 . . . . 9 10

END-OF-PERIOD ACTIVITY: Remove the Paper; Center the Carriage

REMEMBER: Pull the paper-release lever forward (toward you) and remove the paper with the left hand. Leave the release lever in forward position to release the tension on the platen after final daily use. Center the carriage. Pick up all paper. Push the chair to the desk as you leave.

Unit 52 | Lessons 291-295

A Day in a Medical Office

LESSON 291

291A: Conditioning Practice (5) *each line three times*

Alphabet	Even Jerome Quixote was puzzled by the incorrect spelling of Siskiyou.	*Type with fluency*
Figure-symbol	The code on the telegram was CINCY #3405, MRC*, 8/13/67, LAX 291, NLT.	
One-hand	The opinions he expressed during the address were greatly exaggerated.	
Fluency	Our primary task is not to surpass others; it is to surpass ourselves.	
	| 1 | 2 | 3 | 4 | 5 | 6 | 7 | 8 | 9 | 10 | 11 | 12 | 13 | 14 |	

291B: Common-Error Correction Drill (15) *each line twice, without error; more as time permits*

Adjacent Key and Long Reaches

In my opinion, few errors of a covert type were made by the policeman.
The new colonel quickly assumed responsibility in all troop companies.
A number of economic reports predict a bright outlook for the economy.
| 1 | 2 | 3 | 4 | 5 | 6 | 7 | 8 | 9 | 10 | 11 | 12 | 13 | 14 |

Error: Adjacent key
Cause: Hands out of position
Cure: Quiet hands; finger action

Double Letters

Full summers for swimming, tennis, and football seem too good to miss.
Teen-agers ate Swiss cheese and apples on a grassy hill in the valley.
A book of well-written essays on freedom was appreciated by the class.
| 1 | 2 | 3 | 4 | 5 | 6 | 7 | 8 | 9 | 10 | 11 | 12 | 13 | 14 |

Error: Omitted or faint letter
Cause: Weak or uneven stroking
Cure: Uniform stroking

Outside Fingers

Paul saw a plump polo pony near the old wax owl in that ancient plaza.
Zaza quickly saw and pointed out a loophole in the antique quota laws.
An old wagon lost an axle as it was pulled from a cold swamp by Sally.
| 1 | 2 | 3 | 4 | 5 | 6 | 7 | 8 | 9 | 10 | 11 | 12 | 13 | 14 |

ie, ei

A thief stole a pie from my neighbor during the weird but quiet storm.
I tried to seize the foreign piece before it was weighed by the chief.
Neither he nor I will receive a science degree because of our beliefs.
| 1 | 2 | 3 | 4 | 5 | 6 | 7 | 8 | 9 | 10 | 11 | 12 | 13 | 14 |

Error: Opposite hand
Cause: Weak reading impulse
Cure: Concentrate on copy

Short Words; y, n, m, k, p Endings

If he is to do the work for us, she may not be able to work with them.
Many men and women may share my interest in this work of pop artisans.
If Leon does not return soon, Jim may go to the swamp to look for him.
| 1 | 2 | 3 | 4 | 5 | 6 | 7 | 8 | 9 | 10 | 11 | 12 | 13 | 14 |

Error: Spacing
Cause: Hand out of position
Cure: Correct keyboard position; thumb close to space bar

Long, Difficult Words

A living language is a changing, diversified, and creative phenomenon.
Double negatives are grammatically improper but semantically harmless.
Technically, hypersonic speed may revolutionize aeronautical concepts.
| 1 | 2 | 3 | 4 | 5 | 6 | 7 | 8 | 9 | 10 | 11 | 12 | 13 | 14 |

Error: Reading
Cause: Failure to adjust typing level
Cure: Decrease speed; eyes on copy; concentrate

LESSON 6

6A: Get Ready to Type ③

1. Check paper guide and paper bail.
2. Insert full sheet.
3. Set machine for single spacing.
4. Set left margin stop 25 spaces to left of center; right stop at end of scale.

6B: Recall ⑤

1. Typing position (page 2).
2. Stroking keys and space bar (pages 3 and 4).
3. Pica and elite spaces (page 7).
4. Center point for pica or elite type (pages 7 and 9).
5. Spaces after **.** at end of sentence (page 8); after **.** used to punctuate an abbreviation (page 9).
6. How to determine total words typed (page 10).
7. What to do when keys "jam" (page 11).

6C: Conditioning Practice ⑦ *each line twice; DS between pairs*

CONTINUITY CUE	Begin to type at a slow, even pace. Increase stroking rate gradually.

```
uj uj ed ed used cd cd ik cite cede such lack fact

jut cut hut act hit ace kick luck deck fast clutch

Cal Duff said the cause that failed is still just.
....1....2....3....4....5....6....7....8....9....10
```

6D: New Key Location – r, o, and z ⑩

DO: Find key on chart. | Locate key on keyboard. | Study reach diagram. | Type the drill.

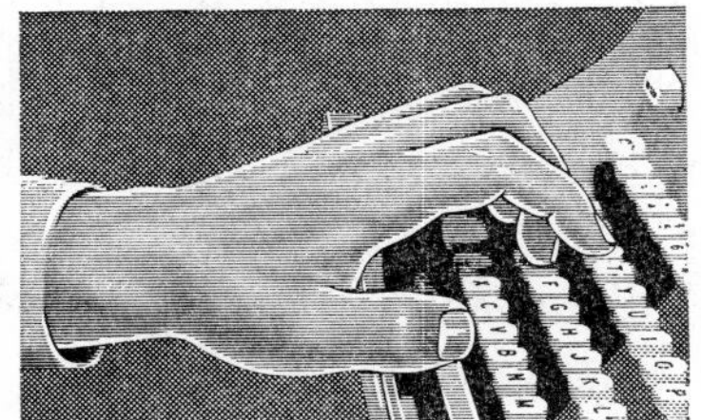

REACH TECHNIQUE FOR R

Reach the *left first finger* to **r** without moving the other fingers from their home keys.

```
rr rf rf rr frf rf rr frf

rf fir fur fur surf drill   DS
```

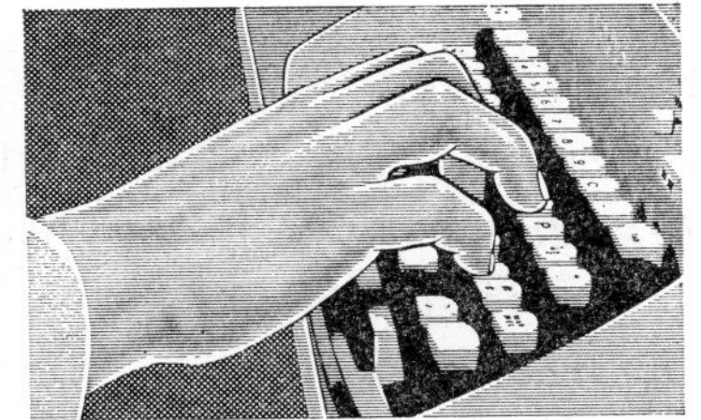

REACH TECHNIQUE FOR O

Reach the *right third finger* up to type **o** without moving the hand forward or the elbow outward.

```
oo ol ol oo lol ol oo lol

ol of so sold old cold of   DS
```

REACH TECHNIQUE FOR Z

Reach the *left little finger* down to type **z** without moving the hand and without moving the elbow in or out.

```
zz za za zz aza za zz aza

za haze zeal za size zeal   TS
```

receipt and acceptance of this revised page 8 by signing and returning the original copy of this letter to us. Sincerely yours | Allen J. Mason | Specifications Department | Enclosure | *(TS)* THE UNDERSIGNED ACKNOWLEDGES RECEIPT OF REVISED PAGE 8, PROCESS SPECIFICATION RA0112–003: *(TS)* Date ______________

By ________________________________
Supplier

```
Enclosure

THE UNDERSIGNED ACKNOWLEDGES RECEIPT OF REVISED PAGE 8,
PROCESS SPECIFICATION RA0112-003:

Date_________________ By_____________________________
                                  Supplier
```

LETTER WITH SPECIAL CLOSING PARTS

Job 5: Specifications Sheet *(Left margin 1½"; other margins approx. 1")*

Process Specification RA0112–003 Page 8

TS

<u>3.10 Curing the Coating</u>:

DS

3.10.1 <u>Air Drying</u>: After application of the solid film dry lubricant, the coated parts must be baked to eliminate the alcohol carrier and to cure the coating. The parts shall be air dried for 15 to 30 minutes after coating and prior to baking.

3.10.2 <u>Support While Curing</u>: The parts shall be placed on wire mesh trays or otherwise suitably supported in the baking oven so as to avoid damaging the coating.

3.10.3 <u>Curing Cycle</u>: The baking cycle for the approved coating for PC shop application shall be in accordance with Table II.

DS

4.0 <u>QUALITY ASSURANCE</u>:

4.1 <u>Qualification Requirements</u>: Quality Control shall conduct all the tests on every outside processing source and each individual (PC only) to demonstrate their proficiency in applying each type coating for which they are to be approved. The qualification tests are described in Paragraph 4.3 and 4.4 and are as follows: Film Appearance, Film Thickness Determination, Film Adhesion, and Wear Life Performance. Failure to pass any one of these tests shall be cause for disqualification until it is demonstrated that all the requirements can be met.

4.1.1 <u>Test Specimens</u>: The test specimens for all tests are described in Paragraphs 4.1.1.1 and 4.1.1.2. Pretreat and apply dry film lubricant to test parts per the requirements of this specification.

4.1.1.1 <u>Type I and II (Qualification Test and Inspection Tests</u>): The test specimens shall consist of an NAS 1008 (A–286) steel bolt about two inches in length and a PACIFIC RD114–8003–008 (A–286) steel locking nut. The coating shall be applied to the threads and the shank of the bolt for testing. Only locking nuts which have been cleaned and are free of all lubricant coatings, platings, and other type finishes shall be used in the tests.

4.1.1.2 <u>Type II (Qualification Tests Only</u>): In addition to those required in Paragraph 4.1.1.1, the test specimens for this coating shall consist of a chrome plated 4340 steel shaft and a 52100 steel bushing. The coating shall be applied only to the cylindrical portion of the shaft and to the inner circumference of the bushing.

6E: Stroking Technique Practice (15) *each line twice; DS between pairs; then type from dictation*

TECHNIQUE CUE	Make low, quick reach-strokes; keep the hands and arms almost motionless.

1 r rf rid fir jar fur hard read hair care frail drill

2 o ol so sold to told do does cold hold too took cook

3 z za haze size zest za zeal haze fizz adz daze seize

4 *Reinforcement* tf ol to rf ik rid or for cd uj cut za ol zoo zeal

5 *Sentence typing* Zoe asked to see the zoo. Joe took Liz for a ride.

6F: Continuity Practice (10) *each line twice*

CONTINUITY CUE	Keep your eyes on the copy as you type. Read each word letter by letter just now. Do not pause between strokes, words, or lines. Keep on.

1 *Space quickly* or for our four sour hours course door food school *Sit erect*

2 size raze haze their there chose oil are air route

3 Roz has a school course that lasts for four hours.

4 The size of their razed house is the size of ours. *Wrists low*

5 Kirk Ford took the lot. Jack Rolf rode the horse.

. . . . 1 . . . . 2 . . . . 3 . . . . 4 . . . . 5 . . . . 6 . . . . 7 . . . . 8 . . . . 9 10

6G: Bonus (Extra-Credit) Typing *each line twice*

TECHNIQUE REMINDER	Hold the shift key down firmly until the capital letter has been typed. Do not space at the end of the line; return quickly and start the new line.

1 or for ford hard hark doze zoo door floor oz. doz. *Hands and arms quiet*

2 Joe said he sold our oil; I heard the deal is off.

3 Dr. Fitz should see that Liz rides for four hours.

4 Ruth said she should sell their old house to Lars.

5 The hour is too short for Zoe to do all the drill.

. . . . 1 . . . . 2 . . . . 3 . . . . 4 . . . . 5 . . . . 6 . . . . 7 . . . . 8 . . . . 9 10

YOUR WORK STATION

Keep your work station free of unneeded books and papers. At the end of each period, pick up all waste paper; center the typewriter carriage; and push the chair to the desk as you leave the room.

(Job 2 continued)

methods of data preparation are growing in importance. For example, a special type font has been developed which can be read by an optical scanner attached to the computer. This development permits both humans and the computer to utilize the data without the intermediate step of keypunching. Such things as record length, placement on the page, format and precision of figures, and the set of characters used must be strictly controlled within the restrictions imposed by the operating system and the program. (¶ 7) After the object program has been compiled and the data have been prepared, they are loaded into the computer and the program is "executed." The result is usually a printed report, which is distributed to the user or users. These reports can be anything––paychecks, organization charts, mathematical tables, accounting records, orbit calculations. The list is as long as the list of human problems. Normally someone thinks, "I wish I had a report that would tell me such-and-such. Maybe I could write a computer program that would give it to me." So, the need for the print-out in most cases antedates the need for the program, and "what to do with the print-out" is self-evident.

Job 3: Two-page Technical Letter

Modified block	*1 carbon copy*
Mixed punctuation	*Block enumerations; envelope*

(Current date) Dr. Eric Rostvold | Pacific Corporation | 6200 Blucher Avenue | Van Nuys, Calif. 91401 | Dear Dr. Rostvold: (¶ 1) When I tried to make a computer run of our water isentropes for you shortly after the Detonation Symposium, I was unable to find the data deck I had used. The other day I found the deck, so I am sending you the output from a run. The output was generated from our equation of state of water as follows:

1. A program (not this one) computed a point on the Hugoniot curve for our equation by solving simultaneously $E - E_o = \frac{1}{2}(p + p_o)(V_o - V)$ and $p = P(E,V)$, where $E_o = O$, p_o and V_o are 1 atmosphere 20°C, and p was pre-selected. The program then integrated $(aE/aV)_s = -p$ to get the isentrope from (p,V,E) down to zero pressure.
2. We then found graphically the p,V point where this isentrope cut the 1 atmos line below 100°C (for isentropes from about 55 kb or less on the Hugoniot) or the saturation line (from 100°C to the neighborhood of the critical point) or the 1000 bar line (for the highest Hugoniot pressures), and the temperature at this p,V point was noted (from the 1 atmos data).
3. The p,V,E,T base point above was given to the present program which then integrated $(aE/aV)_s = -p$ and $(aT/aV)_s = -T(ap/aE)_v$ back up the isentrope to the Hugoniot point (actually to the Hugoniot pressure; however, the values of V and E agreed with the original Hugoniot values to within 1 or 2 in the fifth place). Note that at the base point we used the E which, when put in our equation with V, gave the correct p. It is hence more or less different from the true E at that p,V from water data based on E = 0 at 20° C, 1 atmos.

(¶ 2) The heading "ISOTHERMS" in the output refers to points linearly interpolated at 10° intervals between the isentrope points you see in the print-out. This was simplest and seemed adequate although we could, of course, have calculated these points more accurately during the integration. (¶ 3) I can send you some other isentropes if you wish; specifically, those cutting the Hugoniot at 250, 500, 750 bars, 1, 2, . . ., 65 kb, and some whose base points cluster around 100, 175, and 250°C. If you need any other data, I'll be happy to try to get such data for you. (¶ 4) I assume you have our equation of state and information on its derivation. In any case, this information is contained in the Detonation Symposium materials. If you find a good equation of state of water in the low, medium, or high pressure region, let me know. Sincerely yours, Philip Gardner Enc.

Job 4: Specifications Letter

Block style	*Start date on Line 14; 1 cc*
Open punctuation	*Space closing parts as directed*

(Current date) Fortner Engineering and Manufacturing, Inc. | 918 Thompson Avenue | Glendale, California 91201 | Attention Mr. W. L. Fortner, Jr., President | Gentlemen | (¶ 1) Enclosed is the latest revision of Process Specification RA0112–003 (page 8 only), issued by Pacific Corporation. Our records indicate that you already have this document on file. Do not destroy the copy you now have on file; merely replace the superseded page with the revised page. (¶ 2) You are directed to perform work under existing purchase orders of this corporation in accordance with the applicable revised document, beginning at the earliest possible date. In the event that price or delivery schedule, or fit, form, or function of supplies is affected, please notify our buyer immediately and do not apply process specifications until advised in writing by our buyer. (¶ 3) Please acknowledge

LESSON 7

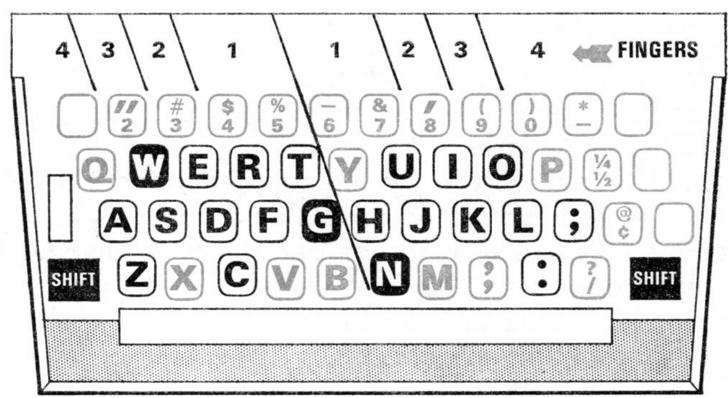

7A: Get Ready to Type (3)

Full sheet | Single spacing
Left margin stop 25 spaces to left of center;
right stop at end of scale

7B: Conditioning Practice (7) *each line twice; DS between pairs*

Begin slowly

```
hj ed he uj cd such ik rf fir ol tf told za .l oz.
so sold cold cord size zeal haze fizz seize stroke
Fritz does like to ride.  He rode for three hours.
....1....2....3....4....5....6....7....8....9....10
```

Return quickly

7C: Know Your Typewriter – Backspacing (5)

LEARN: To fill in an omitted letter or to position the carriage, depress the backspace key **30.** Locate the key on the keyboard.

TYPE: The groups of letters as given in the first line below; then backspace and fill in the omitted letter that is under the word (in color).

Manual (Nonelectric) Backspacing. Straighten the finger and reach to the backspace key with minimum hand motion.

Electric Backspacing. Reach with the little finger and make a light, quick stroke. Release the key quickly to avoid a double backspace. Hold the key down for repeat backspacing.

```
so so d c ld co d si e z al haz  fiz  seiz  st oke
      l  o     r    z  e       e     z    e    r
```

7D: New Key Location – g, n, and w (10)

DO: Find key on chart. | Locate key on keyboard. | Study reach diagram. | Type the drill.

REACH TECHNIQUE FOR G

Reach the *left first finger* to the right to type **g** without moving the other fingers from their home keys.

```
gg gf gf gg fgf gf gg fgf
gf go got fog rug jug rug DS
```

REACH TECHNIQUE FOR N

Move the *right first finger* down to type **n** without moving the other fingers from their home keys.

```
nn nj nj nn jnj nj nn jnj
nj an and an and hand can DS
```

REACH TECHNIQUE FOR W

Reach the *left third finger* up to type **w** without moving the hand forward or arching the wrist.

```
ww ws ws ww sws ws ww sws
ws we wit with wish which TS
```

(Job 1 continued)

four indicator parameters were measured at four intervals. These were, in general, 0, 240, 750, and 1,500 hours from the start of the test.

All tests were run by the suppliers, and the test results were keypunched on IBM data cards. Approximately 75,000 IBM cards of data were involved. A computer programmed analysis on an IBM 7094 was performed. One of the common programs involved: sorting, computing figures of merit, ranking of parameters and figures of merit, distribution analysis, and print-out in a variety of statistical presentations. The summarized data output was then reviewed by component engineers to provide the final reject decision. (Subsequent projects have made use of advanced computer programs to replace the component engineers.)

The best parts were rated as flight grade; the less than best but not reject were labeled as flight residual to be used only for nonflight service; and potentially unreliable items were rejected. The final results are summarized in the table below: *DS*

DEGRADATION PARTS ANALYSIS

	Grade Analysis			
Part	Total Quantity	Flight	Non-flight	Reject
Capacitors	5,291	3,758	957	576
Resistors	4,856	2,964	1,064	828
Diodes	5,032	3,872	1,003	157
Transistors	3,770	2,884	709	177
Miscellaneous	680	335	191	154
TOTALS	19,629	13,813	3,924	1,892

An analysis of these data shows that, on the average, 29 percent of all the parts (highest quality) purchased for Earlybird were not good reliability risks for use in flight hardware. Yet nearly 100 percent of this 29 percent reject were still within the specification limits and would be acceptable for use according to the usual quality criteria. *(Technical research report upon which this material is based was furnished by courtesy of the Hughes Aircraft Company, Culver City, Calif.)*

Job 2: Computer Report

Topbound manuscript	*1 carbon copy*
10 sp. ¶ indention; DS	*Number all pages*

Heading: BASIC COMPUTER PROGRAMMING (¶ 1) Who prepares the program that goes into the computer? Who types the data that are used with the program? What is done with the "print-out" of the computer? A computer is a general purpose tool like a truck. Answering these questions is as difficult as answering "Who drives a truck? Who loads a truck? What do you do with the material delivered by a truck?" The answers depend upon the environment: the nature of the problem, the type of equipment, and the organization that operates it. (¶ 2) Most application programs today are written within the framework of an Operating System. This is a body of procedures, programs, and human skills which enable the user with a problem to approach the computer in terms of that problem. The operating system acts as an intermediary, transforming the problem-oriented format into that required by the computer for solution. (¶ 3) The program is written in pencil by hand, using block printing in a standard style, on special forms specified by the system. The program is expressed in a synthetic, problem-oriented "compiler language" which must be learned by the programmer. The grammar and syntax of the compiler language are rigorous and must be strictly followed. The two most common compiler languages used in the United States are FORTRAN (FORmula TRANslator) and COBOL (COmmon Business-Oriented Language). Although the capabilities of the two languages largely overlap, FORTRAN is especially well suited for computational or scientific problems; while COBOL was designed for problems involving large amounts of data manipulation, file maintenance, and lengthy reports. Compiler languages are also known as "source languages," and the programs written for them are known as "source coding." (¶ 4) The source coding sheets must be keypunched on IBM cards in the format specified by the operating system. Usually the Computer Organization performs this service for the programmer. The resulting IBM cards are known as a "source deck." (¶ 5) The source deck is used as data by a program within the operating system called a "compiler." This program analyzes the source coding for errors in grammar, syntax, and logic; and it prints a "listing" of the source coding for the programmer, pointing out the errors it has found. If the source deck "compiles" successfully, the compiler translates the source coding into an "object program" in "machine language" which can later be used to solve the programmer's problem. The object program is printed and punched out by the computer on IBM cards. These cards are called the "object deck." (¶ 6) The data to be processed have to be prepared in a similarly rigorous manner, although the programmer has more latitude than he does in the format of his source coding. Usually the data are keypunched into IBM cards from handwritten special forms; however, other

7E: Stroking Technique Practice (15) *each line twice; DS between pairs; then type from dictation*

TECHNIQUE CUE	Wrists low. Fingers curved. Eyes on the copy as you type. Snap the finger slightly toward the palm of the hand as you release the key.

1 g `gf go got gold jug rug flag high right fight sight` *Space quickly*

2 n `nj an and hand lend tend sun run dun done zinc and`

3 w `ws with work wish show slow flow would worth world`

4 *Reinforcement* `tf nj cd ik ol rf ws nj gf uj gown town down crown` *Eyes on the copy*

5 *Sentence typing* `Gus and Zoe will walk down to see the town lights.`

7F: Continuity Practice (10) *each line twice*

CONTINUITY CUE	Read a letter; type it; then read another letter and type it without pausing.

1 *Space quickly* `an than zone then whiz land hand throw whose which` *Return quickly*

2 *Shift firmly* `Len went for a long walk.  He saw us in the crowd.`

3 `Gene works well.  He can work well with all of us.`

4 `Ken is a whiz at golf.  He will teach it to Franz.`

5 `Grace can go to town to get the long gown for Jen.`

....1....2....3....4....5....6....7....8....9....10

7G: Bonus (Extra-Credit) Typing *each line twice*

1 `dig end won row get cow now how new low worn sworn` *Wrists low*

2 `net gun run who new few zone size whiz glaze crown`

3 `Roz does this work well.  I like to do this drill.` *Hands quiet*

4 `Few of us can do this work as well as Zoe does it.`

5 `Joe King and Ed Wick will go for the food for Liz.`

....1....2....3....4....5....6....7....8....9....10

YOUR WORK STATION

Keep your work station free of unneeded books and papers. At the end of each period, pick up all waste paper; center the carriage of the typewriter. Push the chair to the desk as you leave the room.

Lessons 287, 288, and 289

Conditioning Practice (5′): Type 286A, page 411.

Sustained Skill Building (15′): Type a timed writing on 286C (¶s on page 412), using this plan:

Lesson 287: 10′ writing; circle errors; determine *gwam.*

Lesson 288: 10′ writing; correct errors as you type; proofread; add ½′ to 10 for each uncorrected error; use this total time to compute correct-words-a-minute rate (*cwam*).

Lesson 289: 10′ writing; circle errors; determine *nwam.*

Applied Typing (30′): Type the Jobs on pages 413–416. Use an eraser, when necessary, and your best correction techniques for acceptable work. *Additional time is provided in Lesson 290.*

Lesson 290

Conditioning Practice (5′): Type 286A, page 411.

Statistical Rough Draft (15′): Type 286B, page 411, as directed there.

Applied Typing (30′): Continue with the jobs you have been typing. At the end of the lesson, assemble all jobs you have completed, arrange them in job number order, evaluate each job as *acceptable* or *unacceptable,* and submit them to your teacher.

A typist in a business or a technical office performs a variety of typing activities. A skilled typist is expected to be able to move quickly from one kind of typing activity to another. The important standard to which all typed copy is subjected is one of accuracy and neatness, with due consideration for a reasonable degree of production speed.

Applied Typing: Lessons 287 – 290

Job 1: Technical Research Report

Leftbound manuscript (2″ top, first page)	*1 carbon copy*
5 sp. ¶ indention; DS	*Use judgment in arranging table*

Heading: DEGRADATION ANALYSIS SCREENING

All reliability screening is ultimately intended to provide a supply of reliable parts for manufacture into systems. All successful screening techniques are based on the same principles and physical laws. Whereas conventional quality screening is based on performance or functional parameters, reliability screening is based on indicator parameters.

Degradation Analysis Screening places major emphasis on screening tests using power aging after the parts have been manufactured and before they have been shipped from the supplier.

Degradation Analysis Tests

Parts can fail by suddenly ceasing to function (catastrophic failure) or they can fail by degrading in performance. The name Degradation Analysis should not be confused as applying only to the degradation failure. Degradation of the indicator parameters can reveal the incipiency of catastrophic failure as well as degraded performance.

Degradation testing consists of repeated measurement of selected parameters with power applied to determine the trends of parameter values under stress. Each item is serialized and each parameter measured is carefully identified with the item and the time and conditions of measurement.

The degradation test is usually from 1,000 hours to 1,500 hours on 100 percent of each lot. The parts are cycled power-on-off according to a normal use schedule. The load and temperature conditions are preferably set at the rated maximum for the parts. Less information is gained when typical average conditions only are used; however, some people prefer this milder test for fear of damaging the parts. The degradation test itself can be used to determine if the maximum conditions are too severe by plotting a mechanism curve of the failure data.

The important characteristic of degradation testing is that the exact values for each parameter existing at the start and finish of a test are not so important as the degradation path revealed by the repeated measurements. This degradation path in relation to the limits defines the part's inherent stability under stress and provides for reliability prediction based on curve fitting and curve extrapolation.

Case Application

Degradation analysis was used to screen all the parts used on the COMSAT "Earlybird" Satellite. A total of 19,000 parts (510 line items) in 143 part types were screened. A total of about 15 million part hours were achieved during the tests. From one to

(*Job continued, page 414*)

LESSON 8

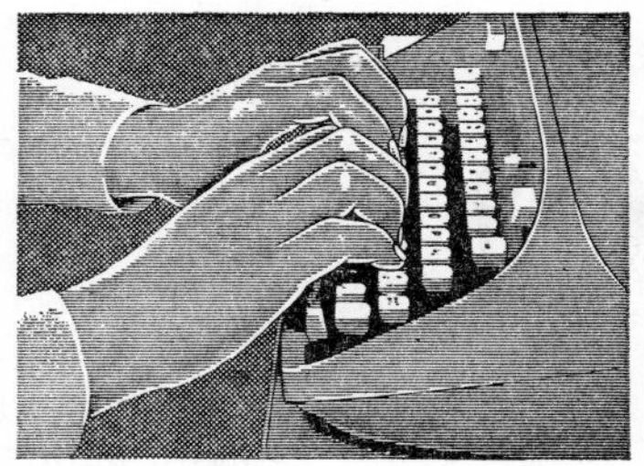

Full sheet | Single spacing
Left margin stop 25 spaces left of center; right stop to end of scale

NOTE: In this lesson and the remaining lessons of this unit, the time for the Conditioning Practice is changed to 8 minutes. In this time you are to make machine adjustments, get ready to type, and type the lines. The number of times each line of the practice is to be typed is changed to three beginning with Lesson 9. As your typing skill increases, more is expected of you. Work quickly.

8A: Conditioning Practice  *each line twice*

TECHNIQUE CUE	Sit up. Curve the fingers. Hold the eyes on the copy as you type. Space once after . used with an initial. (See Line 3.)

All letters and punctuation marks taught are used in the first line.

Begin slowly; speed up gradually

```
tfgf ol.l gfrf ujhj cded iknj wsza ;lkj asdf seize

grown wrong niece worth whose ground friend frieze

F. H. Craig would like to get Liz to sing for Joe.
....1....2....3....4....5....6....7....8....9....10
```

8B: Reinforcement Practice (15) *each line three times*

LINE 1: Train your eyes to see quickly and your fingers to type accurately vowel combinations, such as **ie** and **ei**.

LINES 2, 3, and 4: In words such as *truth*, *strung*, and *great*, make the direct reach from **t** to **r**, **u** to **n**, and **g** to **r** by moving the controlling finger from one key to the next without returning it to its home position.

LINE 5: Adjacent key controls, such as **lk**, **ds**, and **tr**, need special attention. Think each letter vigorously and make each motion precisely to type these combinations accurately.

1	ie | ei	nj ed ik then thin lie their friend freight height
2	tr | str	tf uj rf nj truth truce heart string strung struck
3	g | o | w | n	gf ol ws nj go gown grow crown wrong sought weight
4	gr	groan grind grain great gross grease ground Greece
5	lk | ds	walk silk talk stalk chalk leads sends finds winds
6	*All letters taught*	Roz could walk in the grounds with Frank and Jane.
		....1....2....3....4....5....6....7....8....9....10

All letters are used.

10′ GWAM

The space age is an exacting period. For example, an industry that 1 37
joins with others to build a rocket or a satellite must abide by strict 3 39
rules and regulations. The paper work, alone, is often impressive. To 4 40
manufacture a single steel pin requires a dozen different forms. Several 6 42
copies of each form must be typed. 6 43

The primary cause for this paper work is that every component part 8 44
which goes into the building of a space vehicle must be completely trace- 9 45
able from the gathering of raw materials to the placing of the part into 11 47
the vehicle. Then, when a malfunction occurs, experts can locate the 12 48
source of the trouble and discover the reason for failure. 13 49

Since a space vehicle has thousands of parts, there are a tremen- 15 51
dous number of traceability items that must be filed and kept at a 16 52
central storage area. Usual filing and retrieval procedures are not 17 53
adequate. Our new technology has found a solution. The files may be 19 55
kept on microfilm. This provides for quick access as well as a reduc- 20 56
tion in filing space. 20 57

Technical typists may be a valuable part of a space vehicle produc- 22 58
tion team. As an example, a technical report must be typed and proofread 23 59
with care. A single figure in a technical report, typed incorrectly, 25 61
may cause the report to be rejected. Extra time and effort must then 26 62
be used to correct the error. Such errors inflate production costs by 28 64
adding to an overhead burden. 28 64

To be an expert technical typist, you must first be a good typist. 29 66
A prime requisite is the ability to type statistical copy, or other 31 67
difficult copy, and to solve typing placement problems. The rewards 32 68
for such talent and skill will be in terms of a greater demand for your 34 70
services and higher salaries. Many of the new and exotic space indus- 35 71
tries will always employ the skilled technical typist. 36 72

10′ GWAM | 1 | 2 |

8C: Sentence Guided Writings (20)

1. **Type** each line twice without being timed; double-space between two-line groups.
2. **Type** each sentence for a guided half-minute writing; then for a one-minute guided writing.

All letters and punctuation marks taught are used.

		Words in Line	GWAM 30″ Guide
1	It is how we work that counts.	6	12
2	Jen said she would write our aunts.	7	14
3	The suit is a fit; it looks well on Zoe.	8	16
4	It is just our luck that he is to go with us.	9	18
5	Keith is in the lead in their fight for the right.	10	20

. . . . 1 . . . . 2 . . . . 3 . . . . 4 . . . . 5 . . . . 6 . . . . 7 . . . . 8 . . . . 9 10

8D: Tabulating Procedure (7)

TO CLEAR TAB STOPS:

1. Move carriage to extreme left.
2. Depress tab clear key **31** as you pull carriage all the way to the right to remove all tab stops.

Smith-Corona and Olympia typewriters have a Total Tab Clear Key that clears all stops at one time.

TO SET TAB STOPS:

Move the carriage to the desired position; depress tab set key **23**. Set other stops in a similar way.

GET READY FOR THE DRILL:

1. Clear all tab stops, as directed above.
2. Column 1 will begin at the left margin.
3. Tab for Column 2: 15 spaces beyond left margin.
4. Tab for Column 3: 15 spaces beyond *beginning* of Column 2.
5. Tab for Column 4: 16 spaces beyond *beginning* of Column 3.

TABULATING TECHNIQUE

Manual (Nonelectric). Depress and hold tab bar or key **24** down until carriage stops. Use the right first finger on the bar, the little finger on the tab key.

Electric. Flick the tab key lightly with the little finger. Return the finger to its home position quickly.

Type the words as shown, tabulating from column to column.

the —Tab→	and —Tab→	work —Tab→	with
sit	did	then	wish
end	due	when	turn

8E: Bonus (Extra-Credit) Typing *each line three or more times*

1	*Direct reaches*	It is true that Ed Grotz was in Greece for a week.	*Return quickly*
2	*Double letters*	Nell Hill will soon sell her house to Will Griggs.	
3	c	Charles cashed the checks for Dick and Jack Craig.	
4	*Left-hand words*	We were sad as we saw Grace was too scared to win.	

. . . . 1 . . . . 2 . . . . 3 . . . . 4 . . . . 5 . . . . 6 . . . . 7 . . . . 8 . . . . 9 10

LESSON 286

286A: Conditioning Practice (5) *each line three times*

Alphabet	We have justly criticized a query Webb & Fox are making on the report.	*Type with rhythm and continuity*
Figure-symbol	Please ship Model MRX 12–308–4759, Serial #158Z *, on or before May 26.	
One-hand	John referred an exaggerated union minimum wage case to me for action.	
Fluency	Remember: Past experience should be a guidepost, not a hitching post.	

| 1 | 2 | 3 | 4 | 5 | 6 | 7 | 8 | 9 | 10 | 11 | 12 | 13 | 14 |

286B: Statistical Rough Draft (15) *four 3′ writings: two for speed; two for control*

All letters and numbers used.

	3′ GWAM	
For convenient storage of technical reports, many firms are using	4	62
(sheet microfilm) (actual size: 4 1/2" X 5 3/4") what is known as microfiches. Each flat negative card can hold up to	12	70
60 pages--or frames. These postage stamp size frames be can viewed	17	74
through an ordinary desk-top reader.	26	84
¶ A virtue of this storage system is compactness--microfiches of 1,000	31	88
or documents # # technical reports of average length would fit into a regular shoe box.	36	94
rri Each negative card usually cailres an identifying code number as well	41	99
and date of publication as the title of the document. A code number such as M78-926-35789, for	48	105
example, might refer to a special technical report titled, Able-Star Gas	54	111
Jet Attitude Control System. ← Underline	57	115

If full-size copies of the report are needed, the report can be reproduced quickly and easily.

286C: Building Speed and Control (30) (*Use ¶s on page 412; follow directions below*)

1. **Speed.** Select a *speed goal* 4 to 8 *wam* above your average speed rate; type three 1′ guided writings on each ¶ at this goal rate. With each repetition try to eliminate any faulty typing patterns or other blocks to your speed.
   To reach a new speed level, do this:
   a. Keep carriage moving and your eyes on copy.
   b. Return carriage quickly and start new line.
   c. Keep fingers close to keys; use finger action.
   d. Hold wrists low and relaxed; hands quiet.
   e. Keep thumb on or near space bar; space quickly.
2. **Control.** Type two 1′ guided writings for *control* on each ¶. Select a *control rate* which is about 8 *wam* below your average speed rate.
   To improve your accuracy, do this:
   a. Type with continuity and without hurry.
   b. Concentrate on the copy as you type.
   c. Type with good stroking technique.

LESSON 9

Full sheet | Single spacing
Left margin stop 25 spaces left of center; right stop to end of scale

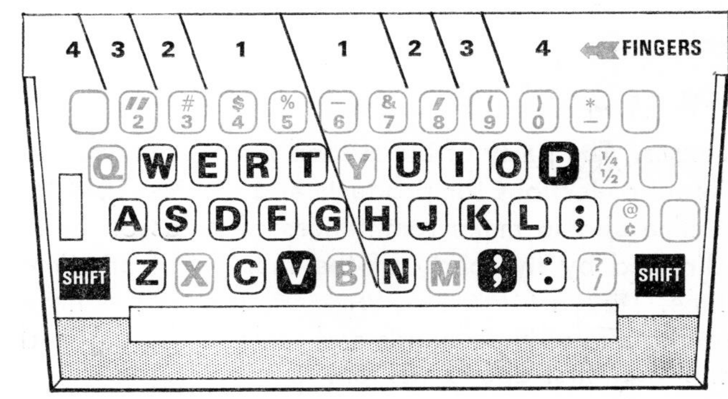

9A: Conditioning Practice (8) *each line three times*

TECHNIQUE CUE	Type with finger action. Hold the hands and arms quiet, almost motionless. Reach—don't hop—to the keys.

All letters taught — Jack Routh was a whiz of a lad at the age of nine. — *Keep your fingers curved*

g | n | w — Gene will go to town to get a white gown for Gwen.

Easy — I know it is how I think and what I do that count.

. . . . 1 . . . . 2 . . . . 3 . . . . 4 . . . . 5 . . . . 6 . . . . 7 . . . . 8 . . . . 9 10

9B: Drill on Tabulating (10) *twice with double spacing, tabulating from column to column*

MARGIN STOP	+ 15 sp. = TAB STOP	+ 15 sp. = TAB STOP	+ 16 sp. = TAB STOP
for	got	worn	when
dig	win	wing	down
rug	tow	town	sung
are	get	were	look
she	aid	than	torn

Return without looking up

9C: New Key Location – p, v, and , *(comma)* (10)

DO: Find key on chart. | Locate key on keyboard. | Study reach diagram. | Type the drill.

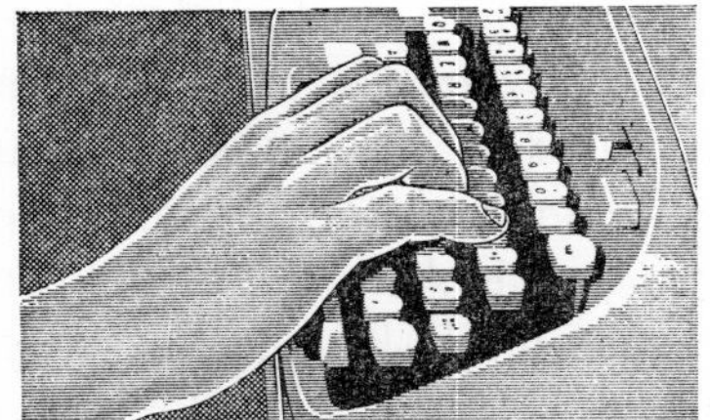

REACH TECHNIQUE FOR P

Straighten the *right fourth finger* and move up to type letter p. Avoid twisting the elbow out for the reach.

p; p ;p; pp ;p; p; pp ;p;

p; put pan lap tip gap up DS

REACH TECHNIQUE FOR V

Reach the *left first finger* down to type v. Hold the elbow in position and the hand in alignment.

vf v fvf vv fvf vf vv fvf

vf have five rove vf give DS

REACH TECHNIQUE FOR , (COMMA)

Reach the *right second finger* down to type , (comma). Space once after a comma in a sentence.

k, k, , k, Kit, Ken, Joe,

k, Ken, Kit, or I can go. TS

(Job 5 continued)

expenses. The party of the second part agrees also to make all collections for products and services sold by his office and to make remittances of funds on hand as directed by the party of the first part from time to time. (¶ 7) IN WITNESS WHEREOF, The parties have hereunto affixed their hands and seals on the day and in the year first above written.

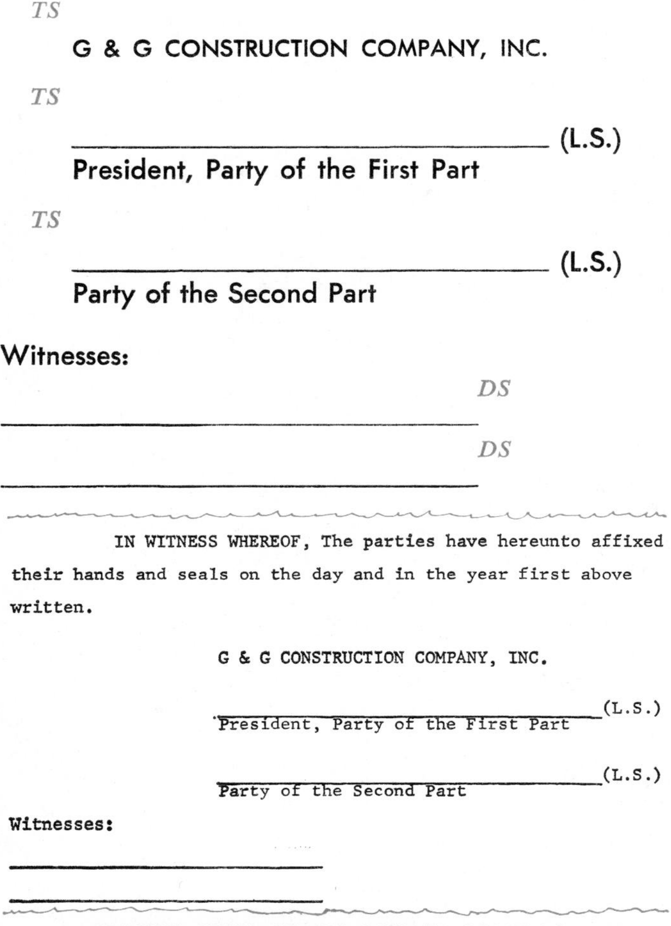

TS

G & G CONSTRUCTION COMPANY, INC.

TS

______________________________ (L.S.)
President, Party of the First Part

TS

______________________________ (L.S.)
Party of the Second Part

Witnesses:

________________________ *DS*

________________________ *DS*

IN WITNESS WHEREOF, The parties have hereunto affixed their hands and seals on the day and in the year first above written.

G & G CONSTRUCTION COMPANY, INC.

______________________________ (L.S.)
President, Party of the First Part

______________________________ (L.S.)
Party of the Second Part

Witnesses:

____

____

CLOSING LINES OF AN AGENCY CONTRACT

Job 6: Legal Letters

Modified block; mixed punct.	*Correct errors*
1 cc; center subjects	*Address envelopes*

Letter 1: March 10, 19— Mr. Robert Whitfield 3780 Bel Estes Drive San Jose, California 95124 Dear Mr. Whitfield: Whitfield vs. Jamison——File No. 6307 (¶ 1) The opposing counsel in your accident case wishes to take your deposition at 2:30 p.m. on Friday, March 17, at the offices of Burns & Reynolds, 420 Balfour Building, 351 California Street, San Francisco. (¶ 2) Please meet me in my office no later than 1:30 p.m. on that day so we can discuss your case at length before the deposition starts. Very truly yours, Wesley MacDonald Attorney-at-Law (68)

Letter 2: April 16, 19—— Mr. Robert Whitfield 3780 Bel Estes Drive San Jose, California 95124 Dear Mr. Whitfield: Whitfield vs. Jamison——File No. 6307 (¶ 1) Will you please send me a statement of all your doctor bills and other expenses relating to the above-named accident. I told the other attorney at the deposition that I would obtain this statement for him. The case cannot be properly evaluated or settled until you furnish this statement. (¶ 2) It appears that the possibility of this case going to trial is now quite certain. Your file has been referred to my associate, Dexter DeWitt. Mr. DeWitt is the trial specialist in our office. He is an excellent attorney in every respect; you will enjoy working with him. (¶ 3) Mr. DeWitt will contact you soon regarding this case. If you have any questions that you would like to take up with him, do not hesitate to call him. Also, remember that I am always available. Very truly yours, Wesley MacDonald Attorney-at-Law (151)

Letter 3: October 12, 19—— CERTIFIED MAIL Mr. Robert Whitfield 3780 Bel Estes Drive San Jose, California 95124 Dear Mr. Whitfield: File No. 6307 (¶ 1) Enclosed is our check No. 1150 in the sum of $973.14 which represents your net recovery from your recent accident case. (¶ 2) I am trying to obtain, as I told you I would, a Dismissal with Prejudice of the Cross-Complaint which was filed against you. The important thing at this point, however, is for you to notify in writing your insurance broker of the filing of this Cross-Complaint. Be sure to send a copy of the letter to me, and keep a copy for your files. (¶ 3) The suit was filed in the Superior Court of the State of California in and for the City and County of San Francisco, and is Action No. 502006. The Cross-Complaint was filed by Bryan Avery through his attorney, Charles Isaacs, and the prayer of the Cross-Complaint asks for the judgment of $673.00, plus costs. (¶ 4) It may well be that we will not succeed in our strategy of obtaining a Dismissal of the Cross-Complaint. In that event, your Insurance Company will have to defend this action for you. Very truly yours, Wesley MacDonald Attorney-at-Law Enc. (190)

9D: Stroking Technique Practice (12) *each line twice*

TECHNIQUE CUE	Make the reach to the letter **p** without moving the hand forward or swinging the elbow out.

SPACING REVIEW	Space twice after a . that ends a sentence, once after a . that ends an abbreviation within a sentence, and once after ; and , .

1 p — p; pen pan ;p; zip cup sip ;p; trip trap drop paid — *Curve the fingers*

2 v — vf vie vow fvf give five live fvf vote prove grove

3 , — Joe, Dick, and Hank can go; and Keith can go, too.

4 *Reinforcement* — gfnj ws.l p;vf za,k cdol vfp; za,k vice pace prove — *Hands and arms quiet*

5 *All letters taught* — Steve knows a good place to hear jazz for an hour.

6 *Continuity* — Vance will take the lead in a fight for the right.

9E: Continuity Practice (10) *each line twice*

TECHNIQUE CUE	Sit erect. Curve the fingers. Space quickly. Strike the key with a quick, sharp stroke; release it quickly.

All letters taught are used.

1 *Shift firmly* — Phil, Vince, and Pete will see this show at night. — *Eyes on copy*

2 Paul, I see, is right; and Zoe, I know, thinks so.

3 Dave, Paul, and Ed gained points, Pat Phelps said.

4 *Space quickly* — Eve Love got the pen as a prize for her good work.

5 Joe will lend a hand if he can to all who need it.

. . . . 1 . . . . 2 . . . . 3 . . . . 4 . . . . 5 . . . . 6 . . . . 7 . . . . 8 . . . . 9 10

9F: Bonus (Extra-Credit) Typing *each line three times*

1 *All letters taught* — Jen had the luck to win a prize at five dog shows. — *Think the letter*

2 Dave, Pat, and Eve Grove were in Spain and France.

3 I hope Steve and Pat are still in the French Zone.

4 It takes Vern hours to learn to do his work right.

5 To get to the top, Pat needs pep, poise, and push.

. . . . 1 . . . . 2 . . . . 3 . . . . 4 . . . . 5 . . . . 6 . . . . 7 . . . . 8 . . . . 9 10

☞ *It is your responsibility to leave your work station orderly and tidy for the next student who is to use it.*

Approximate 2" top margin for all pages

Center heading between ruled lines

10-space paragraph indention; double spacing; copy typed within marginal rules; testator's name in all caps

Introductory words in a paragraph usually typed in all caps; the words Last Will and Testament typed with initial caps

Type L.S. for seal

Single-space or double-space for acceptable paging

Approximate 1" bottom margin; if more than 1 page, page numbers centered ½" from bottom edge

LAST WILL AND TESTAMENT OF JOSEPH PHILIP LEAR

I, JOSEPH PHILIP LEAR, a resident of the City of Los Angeles, State of California, declare this to be my Last Will and Testament, and revoke all former Wills and Codicils.

FIRST: I direct that my just debts and funeral expenses be paid.

SECOND: I declare that I am married, and my wife's name is JOANNE DAVIS LEAR; I have two children now living, JOHN THOMAS LEAR and RALPH CHARLES LEAR.

THIRD: I give, devise, and bequeath all property, real and personal and wherever situated, to be divided into equal portions, one third to my wife, JOANNE DAVIS LEAR, one third to my son JOHN, and one third to my son RALPH. In the event my wife does not survive me, then her portion is to be divided equally between my sons.

FOURTH: I appoint as Executrix of my Will my wife, JOANNE DAVIS LEAR, to serve without bond. In the event she is unable or unwilling to serve, or to complete such service as Executrix, then it is my wish that CHRISTOPHER OWENS, a long-time friend of mine, shall be appointed as Executor.

This Will and Testament is subscribed by me on the sixteenth day of June, 19--, at Los Angeles, California.

________________________(L.S.)

The foregoing instrument, consisting of one page, was subscribed on the date which it bears, by the testator, JOSEPH PHILIP LEAR, and at the time of subscribing was declared by him to be his Last Will and Testament; and we, at the testator's request and in his presence and in the presence of each other, have signed such instrument as witnesses.

________________________residing at____________________

____

________________________residing at____________________

____

GENERAL FORM OF A WILL

LESSON 10

Full sheet | Single spacing
Left margin stop 25 spaces left of center; right stop to end of scale

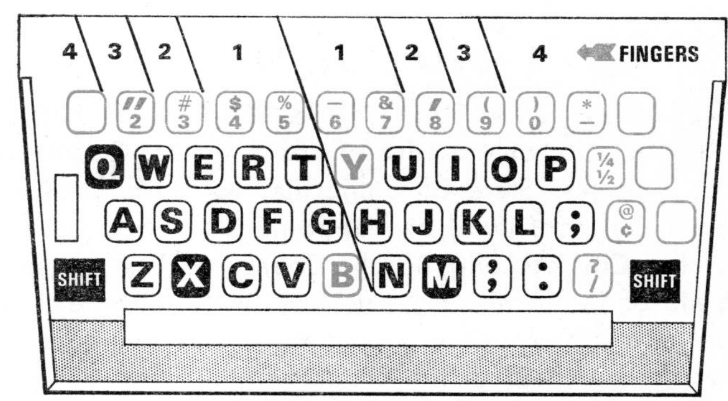

10A: Conditioning Practice (8) *each line three times*

SPACE-BAR TECHNIQUE	Use a quick, short down-and-in motion of the right thumb to space. Release quickly.

```
All letters taught   Phil and Jack Vance sought to win the first prize.
p | v | ,            Dave, Paul, and Vince were put up at a fine place.
Easy                 Our work is not done if it is not done just right.
                     ....1....2....3....4....5....6....7....8....9....10
```

10B: Drill on Tabulating (10) *twice with single spacing, tabulating from column to column*

MARGIN STOP + 15 sp. = TAB STOP + 15 sp. = TAB STOP + 16 sp. = TAB STOP

put	top	paid	pair
van	vow	give	vote
cup	lap	pent	pale
see	ill	want	noon
car	aid	work	well

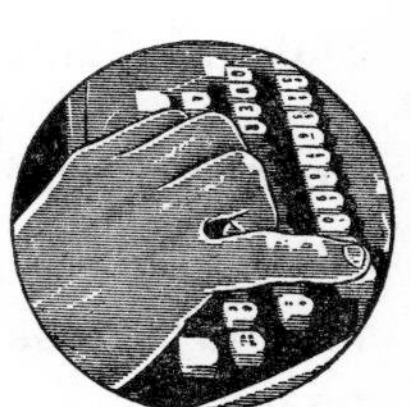

10C: New Key Location – q, m, and x (10)

DO: Find key on chart. | Locate key on keyboard. | Study reach diagram. | Type the drill.

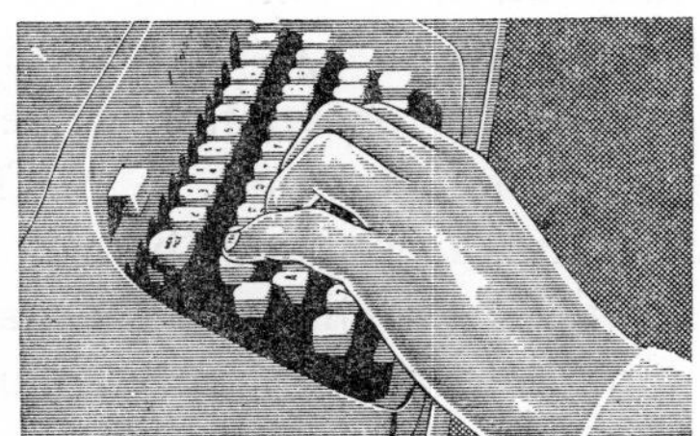

REACH TECHNIQUE FOR Q

Reach the *left fourth finger* up to type **q** without swinging the elbow out or arching the wrist.

```
qa q aqa qq aqa qa qq aqa
qa quit quiz qa quit quiz  DS
```

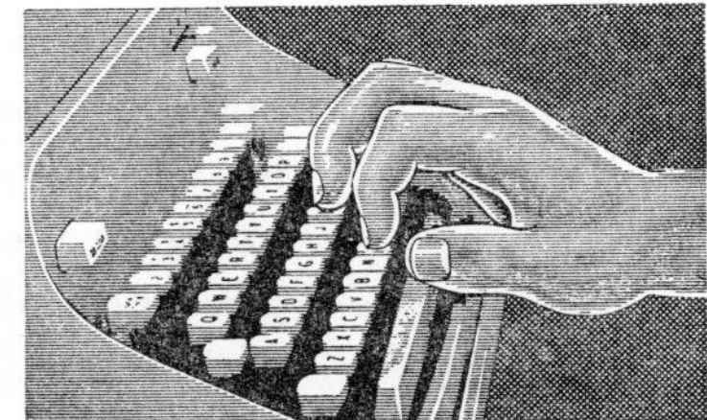

REACH TECHNIQUE FOR M

Reach the *right first finger* down to type **m**. Do not move the hand down or swing the elbow out.

```
mj m jmj mm jmj mj mm jmj
mj me map sum jam ham gum  DS
```

REACH TECHNIQUE FOR X

Reach the *left third finger* down to type **x** without moving the hand downward. Reach with the finger!

```
xs x sxs xx sxs xs xx sxs
xs fix six mix next sixth  TS
```

POWER OF ATTORNEY

(¶ 1) KNOW ALL MEN BY THESE PRESENTS, that I, ARTHUR GREENWOOD, of the City of Los Angeles, County of Los Angeles, State of California, by these presents do make, constitute, and appoint MELVYN B. KAMBEL, of the City of Long Beach, County of Los Angeles, State of California, my true and lawful attorney, for me and in my name, place, and stead to negotiate for the purchase of the property situated at the corner of Roycroft Avenue and Fourth Street, Long Beach, California, known as the Park View Property; and I hereby ratify and confirm all that my said agent or attorney will lawfully do, or cause to be done, in connection with this purchase. (¶ 2) IN WITNESS WHEREOF, I have hereunto set my hand and seal this __________ day of ____________, 19––.

TS

_________________________________(L.S.)

DS

Witnesses:

DS

____

DS

____

TS

State of California)
: ss.
County of Los Angeles)

(¶ 3) On *(current date)*, before me, a Notary Public, in and for said County and State, personally appeared ARTHUR GREENWOOD known to me to be the person whose name is subscribed to the within instrument and acknowledged that he executed the same. (¶ 4) WITNESS my hand and official seal.

DS

(Seal) ______________________________
Notary Public in and for said
County and State

Job 2: Typing a Will

Type the Will as shown on page 409; use legal-size paper; correct all errors; avoid errors on names, dates, and similar items

Job 3: Typing a Will

Retype the Will given on page 409. Make two carbon copies. **Goal:** To type the Will without error.

Job 4: Typing an Endorsement

Prepare a backing sheet with an endorsement for the Will typed as Job 3. (*See illustration, page 407.*) Staple materials; fold as shown.

Job 5: Agency Contract

Use legal-size paper (if available)	*10-space ¶ indention*
DS; current date	*Type closing lines as illustrated*
1 carbon copy	*Erase neatly all errors*

AGENCY CONTRACT

(¶ 1) This agreement, made and entered into on this, the ____________ day of ____________, 19––, by and between G & G CONSTRUCTION COMPANY, INC., a corporation of Anaheim, California, the party of the first part, and KENNETH BEDDOW, of Phoenix, Arizona, the party of the second part, (¶ 2) WITNESSETH: That, whereas, the party of the first part is about to open a branch office, to be located in Phoenix, Arizona, for the sale of its products and services, the said party of the first part hereby engages the services of KENNETH BEDDOW, the party of the second part, as manager of that office. (¶ 3) The party of the first part hereby agrees to pay to the party of the second part a monthly salary of One Thousand Two Hundred Dollars ($1,200), payable on the last day of every month, for a period of one year from the date of this contract. (¶ 4) The party of the first part hereby agrees to pay all reasonable office expenses, including rent and salaries of such help as shall be agreed upon from time to time between the parties hereto. (¶ 5) The party of the second part agrees to give his undivided time and attention to the business of the party of the first part and not to engage in any other business or occupation while in the employ of the party of the first part. (¶ 6) The party of the second part also agrees that he will be governed at all times by the instructions of the party of the first part with regard to all contracts entered into with third persons for the party of the first part; that he will render a report of each and every sale at the time of such sale, giving a detailed account of the products or services sold, the prices and the terms of the sale; and that he will submit each month to the party of the first part an itemized list of office

(Continued on page 410)

10D: Stroking Technique Practice (12) *each line twice*

LINE 1: Reach to **q** with the finger without moving the hand forward or swinging the elbow out.

LINE 2: Make a direct finger reach to **m** without moving the hand or changing its alignment with the keyboard.

LINE 3: Reach the finger down to type **x** without moving the hand downward. *Reach with the finger.*

1	q	qa quit quiz quite qa quiz quote quest queen quell	*Curve the fingers*
2	m	mj am jam sum ham firm form make come me men mends	
3	x	xs ax lax six fix tax fox wax six fix six tax next	
4	*Reinforcement*	qa mj xs p; za ol xs mj qa mj xs ik mix mixed quiz	*Keep the wrists low*
5	*All letters taught*	M. G. Pound will soon have the next quiz for Jack.	
6	*Continuity*	If Sam wants to have much more, he must work more.	

10E: Continuity Practice (10) *each line twice*

TECHNIQUE CUE	Type with your fingers; hold your arms and hands quiet. Get rid of jerks and pauses in your typing; just keep on.

All letters taught are used.

1	m	Mike makes much more right now than most men make.	*Eyes on copy*
2	x	Max Foxx placed their next quiz in this large jar.	
3	q	The queen was quite vexed with the quaint old man.	*Space quickly*
4		James will fix the tax form for Mr. and Mrs. Knox.	
5		Pam said that Mat will have Vince do all the work.	
		. . . . 1 . . . . 2 . . . . 3 . . . . 4 . . . . 5 . . . . 6 . . . . 7 . . . . 8 . . . . 9 10	

10F: Bonus (Extra-Credit) Typing *each line three times*

1	Quent fixed a queer mix of milk and malt for Milt.	*Quick return*
2	Jim will have Vance help with the next large deal.	
3	Mr. Quinn must mean for Max and me to see the man.	
4	Rex will have far more to do if Max Squires comes.	
5	Jack led for six games. He won a prize, and quit.	
	. . . . 1 . . . . 2 . . . . 3 . . . . 4 . . . . 5 . . . . 6 . . . . 7 . . . . 8 . . . . 9 10	

☞ *Remember to leave your work station in orderly condition.*

Typewritten Form. Most legal documents are typed with double spacing on legal paper 8½ by 13 or 14 inches with ruled left and right margins. Type within these vertical lines, leaving a space or two between the ruled lines and the typing. If the paper does not have vertical rulings, set the margin stops for a 1½-inch left margin and a ½-inch right margin. All pages should have a top margin of approximately 2 inches and a bottom margin of about 1 inch. Top and bottom margins are frequently modified to fit material to a page. The first page is not numbered; subsequent pages are numbered ½ inch from the bottom of the page with the number centered between the marginal rules.

Printed Legal Forms. Printed legal forms of affidavits, leases, deeds, wills, and other commonly used legal instruments are available. All the typist has to do with such forms is to type the appropriate information in the blank spaces provided on the form.

Backing Sheets. Legal documents may be bound in a manuscript cover or a blue backing sheet (legal back), a sheet somewhat heavier and about 1 inch wider and 1½ inches longer than the sheet on which the document is typed. The typed document is inserted under a 1-inch fold at the top of the backing sheet, and it is stapled in place.

In some law firms, a description (called the *endorsement*) of the legal paper is typed on the outside cover as illustrated below, or the backing sheet may have a printed endorsement (usually includes the name of the document and the name and address of the law firm). The completed document and the backing sheet are then folded in a special way for convenient storage in a safe deposit box or for filing in special filing containers. In modern legal practice, legal documents usually are stapled to a backing sheet and filed without folding and without an endorsement on the backing sheet.

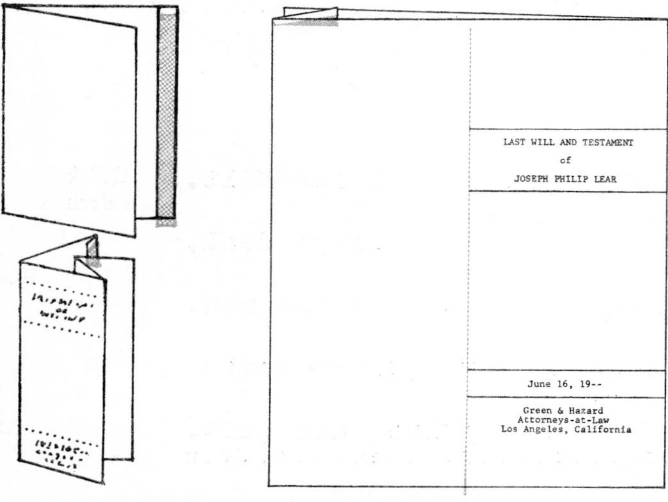

FOLDING A LEGAL DOCUMENT

ENDORSEMENT ON BACKING SHEET

Green & Hazard
Attorneys-at-Law
LONG BEACH, CALIFORNIA 90802

LAST WILL AND TESTAMENT OF JOSEPH PHILIP LEAR

I, JOSEPH PHILIP LEAR, a resident of the City of Los Angeles, State of California, declare this to be my Last Will and Testament, and revoke all former Wills and Codicils.

FIRST: I direct that my just debts and funeral expenses be paid.

SECOND: I declare that I am married, and my wife's name is JOANNE DAVIS LEAR; I have two children now living, JOHN THOMAS LEAR and RALPH CHARLES LEAR.

THIRD: I give, devise, and bequeath all property, real and personal and wherever situated, to be divided into equal portions, one third to my wife, JOANNE DAVIS LEAR, one third to my son JOHN, and one third to my son RALPH. In the event my wife does not survive me, then her portion is to be divided equally between my sons.

FOURTH: I appoint as Executrix of my Will my wife, JOANNE DAVIS LEAR, to serve without bond. In the event she is unable or unwilling to serve, or to complete such service as Executrix, then it is my wish that CHRISTOPHER OWENS, a long-time friend of mine, shall be appointed as Executor.

This Will and Testament is subscribed by me on the sixteenth day of June, 19--, at Los Angeles, California.

______________________(L.S.)

The foregoing instrument, consisting of one page, was subscribed on the date which it bears, by the testator, JOSEPH PHILIP LEAR, and at the time of subscribing was declared by him to be his Last Will and Testament; and we, at the testator's request and in his presence and in the presence of each other, have signed such instrument as witnesses.

______________________residing at______________________

______________________residing at______________________

LEGAL DOCUMENT WITH A BACKING SHEET

Job 1: Power of Attorney

A *power of attorney* is a formal written document authorizing another person to act as the attorney or agent of the person granting the power. **Note.** The letters "ss." are the abbreviation for the Latin word *scilicet* (namely).

Use 8½- by 11-inch paper	*10-space ¶ indentions*
Double spacing	*Current date*
SS the Notary Public statement at end of document	*2 carbon copies*
	Correct errors

(*Power of Attorney on page 408*)

LESSON 11

Full sheet | Single spacing
Left margin stop 25 spaces left of center; right stop at end of scale

COPY DIFFICULTY. The ease with which a paragraph can be typed is influenced greatly by three factors: 1—*Syllable intensity* (SI) or average number of syllables per word; 2—*Stroke intensity* or *average word length* (AWL); 3—Incidence of *high-frequency words* (HFW) or the percent of words used from among the thousand most-used words in business communication. Careful control of these three factors—SI, AWL, and HFW—enables us to indicate the difficulty of the copy selections in this book as easy (E), low average (LA), average (A), high average (HA), or difficult (D). The difficulty index at the right shows an SI of 1.0 syllables, an AWL of 4.5 strokes, and an HFW of 85 percent; a composite of E.

11A: Conditioning Practice (8) *each line three times*

Sit erect. | Hold the wrists low. | Type with easy, rhythmic stroking.
Think and type each letter and space. | Do not pause between strokes.

All letters taught	`Paul just picked Meg for the next five quiz shows.`	*Keep your eyes on the copy as you return*
q | m | x	`Max Quinn fixed the tax forms for Mr. Q. M. Munce.`	
Easy	`Sam should push for more speed in this next drill.`	
	. . . . 1 . . . . 2 . . . . 3 . . . . 4 . . . . 5 . . . . 6 . . . . 7 . . . . 8 . . . . 9 10	

11B: New Key Location – y, b, and ? *(question mark)* (10)

THIRD-ROW STROKING	When typing a key in the third (second from the top) row, reach with the finger without arching the wrist or moving the hand forward.

FIRST-ROW STROKING	When typing a key in the first (lowest) row make a direct finger reach without swinging the elbow out or changing the hand alignment with the keyboard.

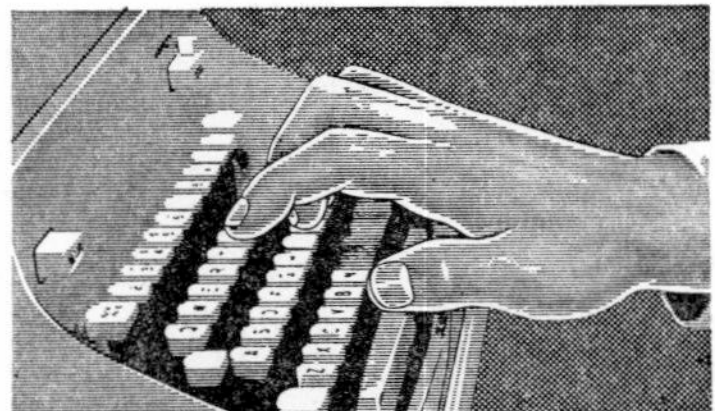

REACH TECHNIQUE FOR Y

Reach the *right first finger* up to type **y**. Do not arch the wrist or move other fingers from home keys.

```
yj y jyj yy jyj yj yy jyj
yj yet yj say jay hay jay
```
DS

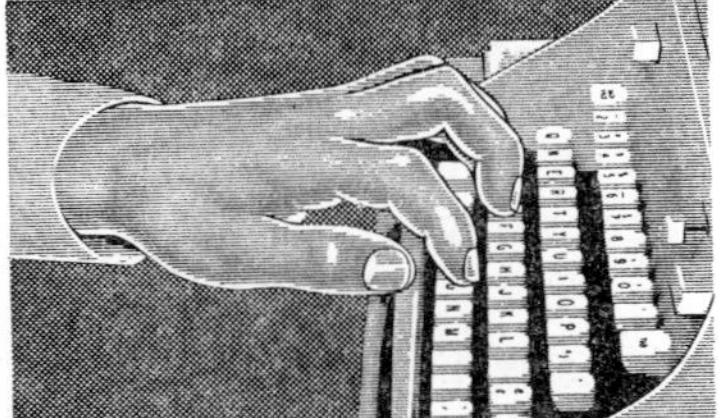

REACH TECHNIQUE FOR B

Reach the *left first finger* down to type **b** without moving the hand from its typing position.

```
bf b fbf bb fbf bf bb fbf
bf bid but bf big rub rob
```
DS

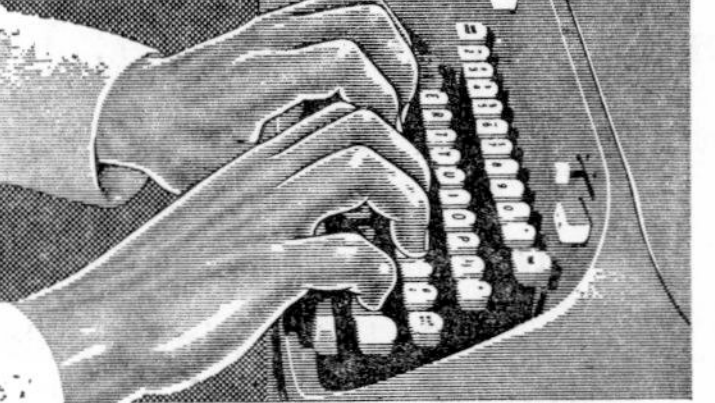

REACH TECHNIQUE FOR ?

Type **?** with the *right fourth finger*. Remember to shift to type **?**. Space twice after **?** at end of sentence.

```
?; ? ;?; ?; ;?; ?; ;?; ?;
?; ?; Is he?  Is he next?
```
TS

	10′ GWAM	
 Accuracy is expected of each employee in a law office. Careful	14	51
proofreading is a must for all typewritten work. Although an error	16	52
which occurs in straight text may be erased and corrected, complete	17	53
accuracy may be required in copy which includes names, figures, dates,	19	55
or other items. In such work, an erasure may cast doubt as to the	20	56
validity of the items.	20	56
 Another cardinal trait for the legal worker is that of objectivity.	22	58
By this is meant the ability to accept criticism and to gain from it.	23	59
Often office workers may not recognize the merit of constructive criti-	25	61
cism. They frequently take it as a personal affront, tension builds up,	26	62
and in the end it affects the quality of their output and their ability	28	64
to work well with others.	28	64
 The worker who possesses diligence is also highly valued in legal	29	65
offices. Diligence is the ability to give painstaking and concentrated	31	67
attention to assigned work. The diligent worker thinks about what he	32	68
is doing, and not about what he may be doing that night. The worker	34	70
who is industrious and attentive usually accomplishes much more in a	35	71
day than does the worker who is lost in a dream world.	36	72
10′ GWAM	1	2			

LESSONS 282-285

Lessons 282, 283, and 284

Conditioning Practice (5′): Type 281A, page 405.

Sustained Skill Building (15′): Type a timed writing on the ¶s of 281C, page 405 and this page, using this plan:

Lesson 282: 10′ writing; circle errors; determine *gwam*.
Lesson 283: 10′ writing; correct errors as you type; proofread; add ½′ to the 10′ writing time for each uncorrected error; use this total time to compute *cwam* (see page 401).
Lesson 284: 10′ writing; circle errors; determine *nwam*.

Applied Typing (30′): Type the Jobs on pages 407–410. Correct all errors. **Goal:** Acceptable work. (*Additional typing time is provided in Lesson 285.*)

Lesson 285

Use the following plan for Lesson 285:

Conditioning Practice (5′): Type 281A, page 405.

Typing for Accuracy (15′): Type two 1′ writings on each of the sentences of 281B, page 405.

Applied Typing (30′): Continue with the jobs you have been typing. At the end of the lesson, assemble all jobs you have completed, arrange them in job number order, evaluate each job as *acceptable* or *unacceptable*, and submit them to your teacher.

11C: Stroking Technique Practice (12) *each line twice*

TECHNIQUE CUE | Type with the fingers. Hold the arms quiet—almost motionless.

1	y	`yj yet jay say hay pay may coy they year hymn your`	*Space quickly*
2	b	`bf bid big bag but bit bar bug fib fob rib rob tub`	
3	?	`Did Bob go?  Has Bud quit?  Why did the boys quit?`	
4	*Reinforcement*	`yjyj bfbf ?;?; yj bf ?; qa mj xs yj vf ?; cd p; yj`	
5	*Alphabet*	`Max Beck gave Jay Quill the Zip Code for his town.`	*Curve the fingers; keep wrists low*
6	*Continuity*	`When a hard job comes your way, do you try or fly?`	

11D: Paragraph Typing (20)

DO: Clear tab stops; then set a stop for a 5-space paragraph (¶) indention. Use double spacing.

LEARN: Depress the tab bar or key to indent the first line of each paragraph (¶).

TYPE: The ¶s as shown; then type 1-minute writings on each ¶ as time permits. Type—but do not hurry!

All letters are used.

		Words in ¶	Total Words; 1' GWAM
1.0 E 4.3 96	Indent ➧ `It is how you type and not what you type now`	9	9
	`that means most.  You may not be a whiz just yet,`	19	19
	`but you will be some day.`	24	24
1.0 E 4.5 86	Indent ➧ `Use a quick stroke.  Type one key; move from`	9	33
	`it to the next one and type it.  Just go right on`	19	43
	`and you will type well in due time.`	26	50

. . . . 1 . . . . 2 . . . . 3 . . . . 4 . . . . 5 . . . . 6 . . . . 7 . . . . 8 . . . . 9 10

11E: Bonus (Extra-Credit) Typing *each line three or more times*

1	`Why did Fay and you say Ray may have to leave now?`	*Do not space after end-of-line punctuation*
2	`Jane fixed the door prize when Kay and Vince quit.`	
3	`Did Burt go?  Will Jay play?  Where does Bud live?`	
4	`May Dave and Bob Grubb stay for a day in New York?`	
5	`Have Bea and Burt Brown moved to Brooks, Ga., yet?`	

. . . . 1 . . . . 2 . . . . 3 . . . . 4 . . . . 5 . . . . 6 . . . . 7 . . . . 8 . . . . 9 10

☞ *Leave your work station in orderly condition.*

A Day in a Legal Office

LESSON 281

281A: Conditioning Practice (5) *each line three times*

Alphabet	A grizzly bear watched the excited fawns jump quickly over a snowbank.	Finger action; quiet hands
Figure-symbol	MODERN WORLD ENCYCLOPEDIA (12,890 pages) is listed at $34.75, less 6%.	
Long words	Electronics instrumentation engineers like aerothermodynamic research.	
Fluency	Typing with a sense of hurry will often cause you to make many errors.	
	| 1 | 2 | 3 | 4 | 5 | 6 | 7 | 8 | 9 | 10 | 11 | 12 | 13 | 14 |	

281B: Discovering Error Threshold – Progressive Difficulty Sentences (15)

1. Type each sentence once on the call of the 15″ guide; then the 12″ guide; then the 10″ guide.
2. Type a 1′ writing on each sentence; select a rate at which you can type without error.

			GWAM 15″	12″	10″
1	Balanced-hand	She may work with the auditor to amend or augment the endowment plans.	56	70	84
2	Combination	Be sure to send the letter with these statements to their new address.	56	70	84
3	One-hand	Jim drafted with great care a monopoly case as to minimum union wages.	56	70	84
4	Long words	Elaborate electronic equipment solved puzzling environmental problems.	56	70	84
5	Shift key	West & McNary, Inc., in East Orange is merging with J. B. Ames & Sons.	56	70	84
6	Figure-symbol	Earnings per share in 1965 were $3.80; in 1966, $4.85; in 1967, $5.20.	56	70	84
		| 1 | 2 | 3 | 4 | 5 | 6 | 7 | 8 | 9 | 10 | 11 | 12 | 13 | 14 |			

281C: Building Speed and Control (30) *(Use ¶s below and on page 406)*

1. **Speed.** Select a *speed goal* 4 to 8 *wam* above your average speed rate; type three 1′ guided writings on each ¶ at this goal rate.
2. **Control.** Type two 1′ *control* guided writings on each ¶. Select a *control rate* about 8 *wam* below your average speed rate of Step 1.

All letters are used.

	10′ GWAM	
What should be the pattern of studies for a legal secretary? She	1	37
may take the usual secretarial sequence that is taught in school. She	3	39
must be an expert typist. Exact skill in business English will be	4	40
needed. It is useful to have a knowledge of law. The highest paid	5	41
legal secretaries are usually college graduates.	6	42
A law secretary must have a host of ideal traits. One of these	8	44
vital traits is personality. A new client searching for a lawyer will	9	45
most often talk to the legal secretary first, either by phone or in	10	46
person. At this time a secretary must present herself in a pleasant	12	48
and agreeable manner. Initial impressions are of utmost importance.	13	49

(Continued)

LESSON 12

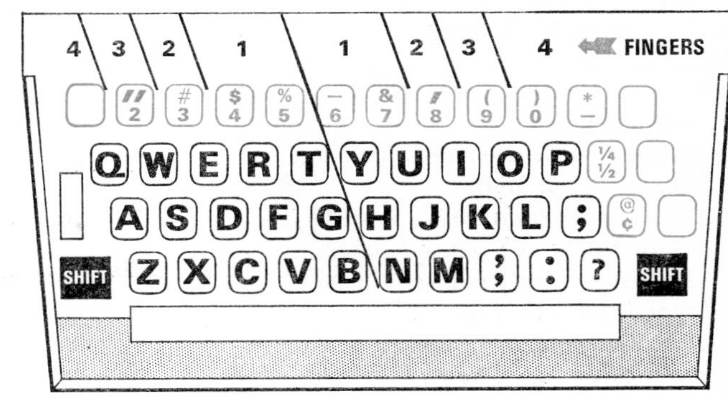

Full sheet | Single spacing
Left margin stop 25 spaces to left of center; right stop to end of scale

12A: Conditioning Practice (8) *each line three times*

LINE 1: Let the first typing be at a slow rate. Emphasize continuity of stroking. In the second and third writings, speed up a bit.
LINE 2: Strike the keys in rhythm; return the carriage quickly and without looking up. Improve your typing technique.

LINE 3: First, type the line at an appropriate rate of speed. Push for faster stroking.

Second, type at a slower pace to find the speed at which you can type with ease.

Third, type the sentence at a rate at which you can type with good control.

Alphabet	Zoe Clay just packed my box with five grown quail.	*Curve the fingers; keep wrists low*
y | b	You say my five boys may have to drive and strive?	
Easy	Think big, of course; but you must work hard, too.	
	....1....2....3....4....5....6....7....8....9....10	

12B: Reinforcement Practice (15) *each line three times*

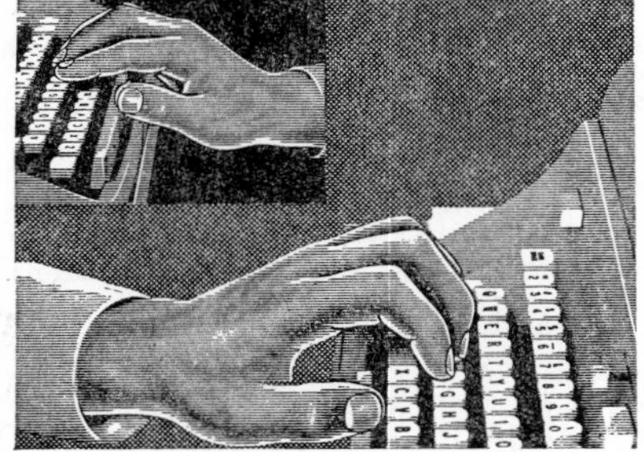

FINGERS: Curved, *not* Straight

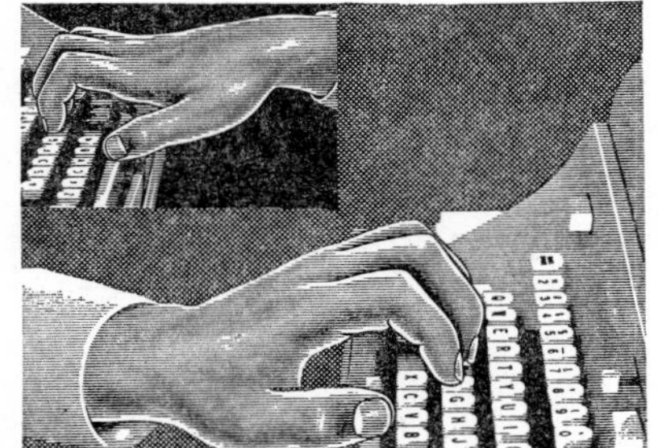

WRISTS: Low, *not* Arched

MOTIONS: Finger, *not* Hand

1	y | b	yjyjyj lay may they bfbfbf bug but rob bring brief	
2	m | q	mjmjmj met sum gum jam ham qaqaqa quit quick quote	*Return without spacing and without looking up*
3	x | p	xsxsxs mix six fox wax tax p;p;p; pay put par part	
4	v | n	vfvfvf vie vim five give njnjnj an and run sun won	
5	*Alphabet*	Dave Welp just picked the six men for my big quiz.	
6	*Easy*	Clay can give the men all the help they will need.	
		....1....2....3....4....5....6....7....8....9....10	

Job 4: Notice and Agenda of a Meeting

3 cc's; correct all errors; 1" margins all sides
Heading spaced and arranged as illustrated at right
SS items of agenda; DS after each item; indent sub-items 4 spaces; enclosure notation (if used) typed on 4th line below last line of agenda
Names of enclosed items indented 4 spaces; DS

```
                GENERAL SERVICES ADMINISTRATION
                                                DS
              NATIONAL ARCHIVES AND RECORDS SERVICE
                                                TS
       Notice of the first meeting of the Working Committee
                                                DS
          on the U.S. Government Correspondence Manual
                                                DS
September 6, 19--                                  9:30 a.m.
                                                DS
              Room 105, National Archives Building
                                                TS
                            AGENDA
                                                DS
1.  Description and background of the project
```

(*Heading—See Illustration*)

1. Description and background of the project | 2. Establishment of basic concepts for guidance of the Working Committee | a. Major contents of the manual | b. Permissive character of the manual | c. Format of the manual | 3. Review of detailed outline of subjects suggested for the manual | 4. Establishment of subcommittees and work schedules | Enclosures: | Condensed outline of manual | List of suggested subcommittees | Proposed schedule for the project

---

Job 5: Minutes of a Meeting

2 cc's; correct all errors; 1" margins all sides
Heading spaced and arranged as illustrated at right
Minutes typed in regular report form (See pp. 401–402)

```
                GENERAL SERVICES ADMINISTRATION
                                                DS
              NATIONAL ARCHIVES AND RECORDS SERVICE
                                                DS
   Minutes of the first meeting of the Working Committee on the
              U.S. Government Correspondence Manual
                                                DS
September 6, 19--                                  9:30 a.m.
                                                DS
              Room 105, National Archives Building
                                                DS
Chairman:  William Mitchell
                                                DS
Members present:  All members of the Working Committee were pres-
                  ent except William Winnett and Miriam Crandall
```

(*Heading—See Illustration*)

(¶ 1) 1. Background of the Project. The chairman explained the reasons for which the Special Commission recommended a standard correspondence manual for Government use. Its use would result in uniformity in correspondence practices; would require less training of typists; and would make it unnecessary for new agencies to develop their own manuals. (¶ 2) 2. Establishment of Basic Concepts. It was decided that the manual would be general in character. (Sub-¶ 1) a. Major Contents of the Manual. The Working Committee will concentrate on common areas of correspondence. (Sub-¶ 2) b. Permissive Character of the Manual. The chairman's suggestion that use of the manual be permissive was approved. (Sub-¶ 3) c. Format of the Manual. The Working Committee decided to issue the manual in loose-leaf form to simplify revision. (¶ 3) 3. Review of Detailed Outline of Subjects. The proposed outline of subjects was accepted after editing. (¶ 4) 4. Establishment of Subcommittees and Work Schedules. The Working Committee assigned members to subcommittees. The list of the members of each subcommittee is attached. The proposed schedule for the development of the manual will be discussed at the next meeting.

2 DS

A. B. Jones
Recorder

DS

Next meeting: October 6, 19––, 9:30 a.m.
Room 105, National Archives Building

12C: Stroking Checkup (12)

Type each sentence as a 1-minute writing, typing it as many times as you can until time is called.

Then, **type** Sentences 3 and 5 for 1 minute each and compare the *gwam* for the writings.

TECHNIQUE CUE	Type at a steady pace. Hold the hands and arms quiet. Center the stroking action in the fingers. Space quickly. Hold your eyes on the copy as you type.

All letters are used.

		Words in Line
1	Does the new boy like to play jazz?	7
2	Did you use a quick stroke at all times?	8
3	Is their work done as well as they can do it?	9
4	Jane and Vern must fix in mind the goal they seek.	10
5	Plan your work, and be sure to work the plan, too.	10
	. . . . 1 . . . . 2 . . . . 3 . . . . 4 . . . . 5 . . . . 6 . . . . 7 . . . . 8 . . . . 9 10	

12D: Paragraph Typing (15)

DO: Clear tab stops; then set a stop for a 5-space paragraph (¶) indention. Use double spacing.

LEARN: To remove a single tab stop without canceling all others, tabulate to the stop and operate the tab clear key.

TYPE: The ¶s as shown; then type 1-minute writings on each ¶ as time permits. Ignore the errors temporarily.

All letters are used.

		Words in ¶	Total Words
1.0 E 4.6 92	Indent ➧ This is a good time for you to take stock of	9	9
	what you have learned in just a few days. It may	19	19
	not seem to be much at first thought; still, what	29	29
	you have learned gives you a start.	36	36
1.0 E 4.5 90	Indent ➧ What should come next? If you quit now, you	9	45
	can have some skill to use, of course; but if you	19	55
	will keep on and do your best day by day, you can	29	65
	learn to type well; then you will have a skill to	39	75
	use and one to be prized.	44	80
	. . . . 1 . . . . 2 . . . . 3 . . . . 4 . . . . 5 . . . . 6 . . . . 7 . . . . 8 . . . . 9 10		

☞ *Is your work station in order for the next student who is to use it? That's your responsibility, you know.*

Federal Service Agency

WASHINGTON, D.C. 20001

Double-space

14 lines

December 13, 19--

In reply refer to:
OPD-X-3

Your reference:
CorMan-A

2 1/2 inches

AIRMAIL--CERTIFIED

Student Typewriting Service
Forest Park High School
Chatham Road and Eldora Avenue
Baltimore, Maryland 21207

Attention: Miss Susan Kazan

Gentlemen:

Subject: Standard format of Government letters

This letter shows the standard layout of a Government letter. No letter is likely to contain as many parts as are included here. The letter is intended to illustrate all the parts of a Government letter and to show their recommended placement.

1 inch — The address is always typed on the 14th line from the top of the page so that the letter can be sent in a window envelope. Items that follow the address, including the body of the letter, are moved up 2 lines each time an unneeded item is omitted. No attempt is made to center letters vertically on the page. — 1 inch

Enclosed is the U.S. Government Correspondence Manual you requested; other materials that may be of value to you are also enclosed or will be sent to you under separate cover.

Sincerely yours,

C. H. Alexander

C. H. ALEXANDER
Chief, Systems & Procedures
Division

Enclosures:
U.S. Government Correspondence Manual
The Seven Keys to Better Faster Typing

Separate cover:
United States Government Printing Office
Style Manual

cc:
Regional Commissioner
Public Information Officer

Adm-6:CJackson:ced 12-13---

1 inch

May not be needed

On agency copies only

FORMAT OF A GOVERNMENT LETTER

Unit 2 | Lessons 13-20

Improving Typing Motion Patterns

1. Arrange your work area for efficiency.
2. Adjust paper guide; insert full sheet.
3. Set the left margin stop 25 spaces to left of center for 50-space line; move right stop to end of scale.
4. Single-space drill lines; double-space and indent paragraphs.
5. *Bonus Typing:* Type selected lines of the Reinforcement Practices three times for extra credit.

LESSON 13

13A: Conditioning Practice (8) *each line three times*

FIRST WRITING: Type at an even pace, noting the awkward letter sequences. Practice these as time permits; try to smooth out awkward movements.

SECOND WRITING: Speed up the stroking slightly, but try to work out an improved stroking pattern for the awkward or difficult combinations.

THIRD WRITING: Push yourself a bit for increased stroking speed. Space quickly between words. Keep the carriage moving.

Alphabet	`Jack Foxe asked Verne to help on my big quiz show.`	*Eyes on the copy as you return*
Left hand	`As we said, a State Trade Tax Act set a fair rate.`	
Easy	`He and I may go with the men when they go to town.`	
	`....1....2....3....4....5....6....7....8....9....10`	

13B: Reinforcement Practice (12) *each line twice; then type from dictation*

1	*y*	`yjyjyj say may day jyj lay jay pay hay nay why you`	*Return without looking up*
2	*b*	`bfbfbf big but bog bad fbf boy buy rob rib rub tub`	
3	*?*	`?; ?; ?; May I go?  Did Rob pay?  Did you see Roy?`	
4	*All letters*	`he we up or on be my can lid tax jug ask five quiz`	*Space quickly*
5	*Continuity*	`May my boy go by bus?  Is the bus to be in by six?`	
		`....1....2....3....4....5....6....7....8....9....10`	

13C: Stroking Technique Practice – Direct Reaches (10) *each line three times*

TECHNIQUE CUE	When the same finger controls two keys in succession, as the first fingers control **mu** in **must** and **gr** in **group**, move the controlling finger directly to the second key. Type without pausing between strokes.

All letters are used.

1	`Must my group start for the great port in an hour?`	*Return quickly*
2	`Grace Kuhn found that much we said was but a myth.`	
3	`Liz Quinn just served the six men lunch on a tray.`	
4	`Ned tried to grasp the rail as he slipped on deck.`	
	`....1....2....3....4....5....6....7....8....9....10`	

Single-space the address; use block style. This placement is used for window envelopes. No line of an address should be longer than 4 inches. When runover lines are required, indent the second line 2 spaces from the left margin. (¶ 8) 7. Body of Letter. The following guides govern the spacing and paragraphing of letters: (Sub-¶ 1) a. Spacing. Begin the body of a letter a double space below the salutation or "Subject" line if one is used. Begin each paragraph flush with the left margin. Single-space the body of the letter; double-space between paragraphs. Double-space letters of one paragraph. (Sub-¶ 2) b. Paragraphing. Do not begin a paragraph near the end of a page unless there is room for at least 2 lines on that page. Do not continue a paragraph to the following page unless at least 2 lines can be carried over to that page. If this cannot be done, it is better to leave a deeper margin at the end of the preceding page. (¶ 9) 8. Complimentary Close. Type the complimentary close followed by a comma, a double space below the last paragraph, beginning approximately at the middle of the page. Except when specified, use the standard closing, "Sincerely yours." (¶ 10) 9. Typed Name and Title. When it is known who will sign the letter, type the name of the signer at least 4 lines below and flush with the complimentary close. Type the signer's title on the next line, flush with the name. If a runover line occurs in the title, indent the line 2 spaces. (¶ 11) 10. Enclosures. When an enclosure accompanying a letter is mentioned in the text, type the word "Enclosure" flush with the left margin, a double space below the line for the signer's title. For more than one enclosure, use the plural form and indicate the number of enclosures, as "Enclosures 3." If enclosures are not identified in the text, type the name of each enclosure on a separate line below the enclosure notation, flush with the margin. Example:

Enclosures:
Form Letters
Plain Letters

(¶ 12) 11. Distribution of Copies. When copies of a letter are sent to persons other than the addressee, show the distribution on copies retained in the agency. Indicate "carbon copy" by typing "cc:" flush with the left margin, a double space below the signer's title or any other preceding notation. Below "cc:" list the names or designations of the addressees, one below the other. (¶ 13) 12. Identification of Office, Writer, and Typist. Type only on copies retained in the agency the office symbol of the preparing office (if used), the writer's initials and surname, the typist's initials, and the date of typing. Place this information at the left margin, a double space below the signer's title or any other preceding notation. Do not type the notation on the original copy. Example:

OpRes:JLCarter:le 5–6–67

Secondary heading: B. Other Parts of Letters (¶ 1) For information as to placement of other special parts of letters, such as the "Attention" line or the "Subject" line, refer to the U.S. Government Correspondence Manual.

Job 2: Government Letters

1. Type the Government letter given on page 403 according to the general directions given in the report of Job 1, and the special directions shown in the illustration. Make 3 carbon copies; correct all errors.
2. Type the letter again, but address it to: **West Phoenix High School | 2910 N. 19th Avenue | Phoenix, Arizona 85015 | Attention: Mr. John McKenzie**

Job 3: Government Report

Type the following material in Government report form. Make one carbon copy; correct all errors.

BASIC AGREEMENT BETWEEN THE UNITED STATES AIR FORCE AND SPACE SYSTEMS, INC. (¶ 1) This agreement made this 1st day of March, 19––, has for its purpose simplification and increased efficiency in the negotiation and execution of Cost Reimbursement research and development contracts between the United States Air Force and Space Systems, Inc., a corporation incorporated under the laws of the State of California. (¶ 2) This basic agreement may be terminated in its entirety by either party upon thirty (30) days' notice in writing to the other party. (¶ 3) This agreement shall be reviewed, at a minimum, annually on the anniversary of its effective date and revised to conform with all requirements of the Armed Services Procurement Regulation and any additional provisions, including applicable provisions of the Air Force Procurement Instruction, as mutually agreed to by the parties. Such revisions shall be evidenced by Supplemental Agreements hereto. (¶ 4) In Witness Whereof, the parties hereto have executed this Basic Agreement as of the day and year first above written.

DS

THE UNITED STATES OF AMERICA

DS

By____________________

DS

SPACE SYSTEMS, INC.

DS

By____________________

13D: Guided Writings  *(Line: 50; Spacing: DS; ¶ indention: 5)*

TYPE:

1. Two 1-minute writings. Determine *gwam* on each, as directed at the right. Average the two *gwam* scores (total ÷ 2) to get your *base rate.* Then set new goal as directed in *To Set New Goal Rates* (Column 3).
2. Several ½-, 1-, and 2-minute writings, guided by the quarter-minute call of the guide.

TO DETERMINE GWAM:

1-minute: Superior dots and figures above the lines in ¶.

2-minute: First and second columns at right and scale beneath.

The paragraph (¶) is marked with the 4-word count shown in figures and with an in-between count of two words shown by a dot (.) to aid you in noting your goals.

TO SET NEW GOAL RATES:

Add 2 *gwam* to your *base rate* to get new 1-minute goal rate.

Use an even number for the goal. For example, if the rate is 15, make it 16 for ease in noting the check points.

Divide the new goal rate into quarter-minute segments. Note these in the copy.

¶	2' GWAM	
. 4 . 8 It has been said that no bird soars too high	4	28
. 12 . 16 . if it soars with its own wings, and so it is with	10	34
20 . 24 . 28 a man. He may rise just as high as he can by his	14	38
. 32 . 36 . own work; but if he soars by pull and not by work	20	44
40 . 44 . 48 well done, he will not keep the top job long.	24	48

2' GWAM | 1 | 2 | 3 | 4 | 5 |

LESSON 14

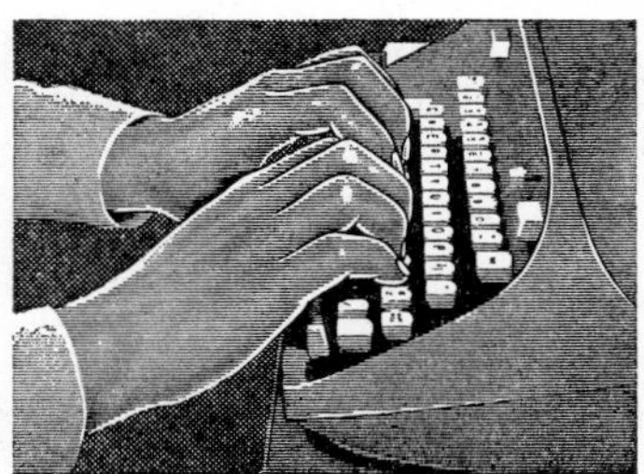

Full sheet; Line: 50; Spacing: SS

14A: Conditioning Practice (8) *each line three times*

Alphabet	Joyce Krumpf saw quite a big fox veiled in a haze.	*Return without spacing after* .
Right hand	Jim Polk said John Kuhn joined Lon on Mill Street.	
Easy	Did Pam sign her name on the work form with a pen?	
	. . . . 1 . . . . 2 . . . . 3 . . . . 4 . . . . 5 . . . . 6 . . . . 7 . . . . 8 . . . . 9 10	

14B: Building Typing Continuity (5) *(Line: 50; Spacing: DS; ¶ indention: 5)*

1. **Type** a 1-minute writing of 13D, above, without the guide call.
2. **Set** a new goal by adding 2 *gwam* for a new 1-minute goal.
3. **Type** two 1-minute guided writings at the new goal rate.

Lessons 277, 278, and 279

Conditioning Practice (5′): Type 276A, page 399, as directed there.

Sustained Skill Building (15′): Type a timed writing on 276C (¶s on page 400), using this plan:

Lesson 277: 10′ writing; circle errors; determine *gwam*.
Lesson 278: 10′ writing; correct errors as you type; proofread; add ½′ to the 10′ writing time for each uncorrected error; use this total time to compute correct-words-a-minute rate (*cwam*).
Lesson 279: 10′ writing; circle errors; determine *nwam*.

Applied Typing (30′): Type the Jobs on pages 401–404. Use an eraser, when necessary, and your best correction techniques for acceptable work. (*Additional time is provided in Lesson 280.*)

Lesson 280

Conditioning Practice (5′): Type 276A, page 399, as directed there.

Technique Evaluation (15′): As time permits, type each of the lines of 276B, page 399, as a 1′ writing. *Goal:* Good techniques and control.

Applied Typing (30′): Continue with the jobs you have been typing. At the end of the lesson, assemble all jobs you have completed, arrange them in job number order, evaluate each job as *acceptable* or *unacceptable*, and submit them to your teacher.

The following job assignments are designed to acquaint you with the recommended form to be used in typing Government correspondence, reports, and other materials.

Applied Typing: Lessons 277 – 280

General Information. Initial drafts of a Government report are double-spaced. The finished report is usually single-spaced with 1-inch margins on all four sides. The title (heading) of the report, typed in all capitals, is centered 1 inch from the top of the page. If there is a subtitle (secondary heading), it is centered a double space below the main title. The subtitle is usually typed with initial capitals only. Although practice may vary somewhat, the following report on the general format of letters will, when typed, illustrate the *general style* used in preparing reports in Government service. **Note.** Number second and subsequent pages in the upper right corner; type the number ½ inch (on the 4th line) from the top of the sheet, flush with the right margin. Continue the body on the 7th line (1 inch) from the top of the sheet.

Job 1: Typing Government Reports

Type a finished copy of the following report; 1″ margins on all sides; 1 carbon copy; correct errors
Center main and secondary headings; DS after each
Single-space report; type ¶s flush with left margin
DS after ¶s; use 4-space indention for first line of sub-¶s (see sub-¶ a, left column, page 402)

Main heading: PREPARATION OF CORRESPONDENCE
Secondary heading: A. General Format of Letters
(¶ 1) This brief report summarizes some of the general procedures followed in various Government offices in the preparation of letters. (¶ 2) 1. Use. Letters are used for correspondence with addressees outside the Government and for formal correspondence with officials of Federal agencies. (¶ 3) 2. Number of Copies. Prepare an official file copy of each letter. Make it the first or second copy so that it can be read easily. Keep other carbon copies to a minimum. (¶ 4) 3. Margins. Allow at least 1 inch for the left and right margins, and for the margin at the bottom of the page. Side margins may be increased to 2 inches for letters of not more than 10 lines. (¶ 5) 4. Date. Type the date a double space below the last line of the address in the letterhead, beginning 1½ inches from the right margin. Type the name of the month in full. Show the day and the year in numerals. (¶ 6) 5. Reference Lines. Reference lines are typed or printed a double space below the line for the date, and they are blocked at the same position. If "In reply refer to:" is printed on the letterhead, type the reference symbol of the originating office on a line with the phrase or below it. If the phrase is not printed but a reference is needed, type "In reply refer to:" a double space below the date. If an addressee's reference is not printed on the letterhead, you may type "Your reference:" a double space below the date (or a double space below the sender's reference if one is used). Example:

(Note: Start longest line 1½ inches from right margin.)

In reply refer to:
92DEP
Your reference:
Job Training

(¶ 7) 6. Address. Type the address at the left margin, on the 14th line from the top of the page.

14C: Reinforcement Practice (12)

1. **Type** each line twice with a quick stroke and key release.
2. **Cover** the page **and type** selected words as your teacher dictates.

1	q	qaqaqa quit quite qa quick quote quack queen queer	*Quick return*
2	m	mjmjmj me my may ham hum whom lump them harm charm	
3	x	xsxsxs ox box six fix wax mix next crux text fixed	
4	*All letters*	up and got job are why vex one clam quiz fast pick	*Space quickly*
5	*Shift keys*	Has Al gone? Did he go to York? Did Ted go, too?	
		. . . . 1 . . . . 2 . . . . 3 . . . . 4 . . . . 5 . . . . 6 . . . . 7 . . . . 8 . . . . 9 10	

14D: Guided Writings (15) *(Full sheet; Line: 50; Spacing: DS; ¶ indention: 5)*

1. **Type** two 1-minute unguided writings.
2. **Calculate** your base rate. Add 2 *gwam* to your base rate for a new 1-minute goal. Divide the goal into four equal segments.
3. **Type** ½-, 1-, and 2-minute writings, guided by the quarter-minute call, as time permits. Speed up your typing by passing from one word to the next quickly.

All letters are used.

	2' GWAM	
Win as if you have been used to it, and lose (4, 8)	4	28
just as if you like it for a change. This is the (12, 16)	10	34
way to show you are quite as big when you win the (20, 24, 28)	14	38
prize as when you lose it. The next time you win (32, 36)	20	44
the prize, win just as if you are used to it. (40, 44, 48)	24	48
2' GWAM	1	2	3	4	5			

14E: Learning to Proofread (10)

PURPOSE: To learn the first step in finding and correcting your errors.

DO:

1. Note the kinds of errors circled in the sample typed lines at the right.
2. Proofread and circle each error in a 1-minute writing of 14D.

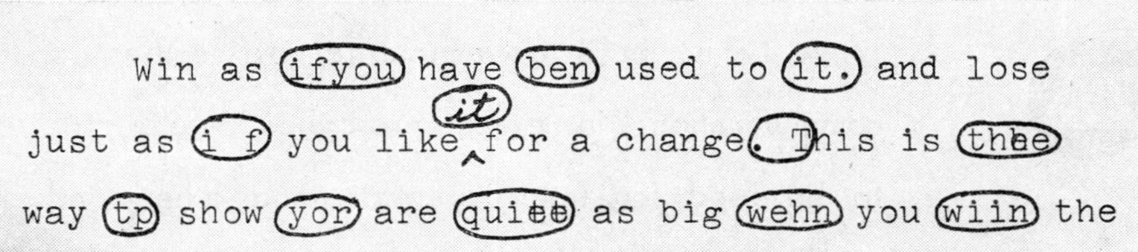

Line 1: (1) Failure to space; (2) omitted letter; (3) period for comma.

Line 2: (1) Faulty spacing; (2) omitted word; (3) incorrect spacing; (4) strike-over, only one error counted per word.

Line 3: (1) Misstroke; (2) misstroke; (3) strikeover; (4) transposition; (5) added letter.

All letters are used.

10′ GWAM

1.6 HA 5.8 70

In a democracy such as ours, the government exists as a servant of 1 37
the citizens; the citizens do not exist as servants of the government. 3 39
This democratic freedom must be guarded jealously in order properly to 4 40
guarantee that our "government of the people, by the people, for the 6 42
people, shall not perish from the earth." 6 42

1.6 HA 5.8 70

Service is a key word for any one who works for the government. 8 44
By this is meant service to the citizens of that government. This is 9 45
a primary responsibility and duty which should not be assumed lightly. 11 47
To be a civil servant denotes that duties and responsibilities shall 12 48
be carried out with a true devotion to this important principle. 13 49

1.6 HA 5.8 70

All our duties and privileges in a democratic form of government, 15 51
as we live it, grew out of and are secured by the Constitution. The 16 52
first ten amendments to the Constitution, as a point, are usually 17 53
phrased as the Bill of Rights. The first amendment grants a basic 19 55
right to freedom of religion, speech, and the press. It also implies 20 56
basic responsibilities. 20 56

1.6 HA 5.8 70

Neatness and accuracy are emphasized for all governmental work. 22 58
You are expected to be able to proofread carefully, and to erase and to 23 59
correct neatly the errors that you make in preparing all kinds of govern- 25 61
mental papers. Since papers may be typed with a variety of carbon copies, 26 62
accuracy is a requisite. As the number of copies typed increases, so 28 64
does the cost of an error. 28 64

1.6 HA 5.8 70

A typist in a governmental office has to learn to type written 29 65
communications in exact, prescribed ways. The specific form or style 31 67
to be used for letters, reports, and other kinds of written communica- 32 68
tions is outlined in a governmental correspondence manual. The typist 34 70
can look at this guide if there is any apprehension as to the exact 35 71
style to be used in preparing these or other kinds of copy. 36 72

10′ GWAM | 1 | 2 |

LESSON 15

Full sheet; Line: 50; Spacing: SS

15A: Conditioning Practice (8) *each line three times*

Sentence 1: Type at an even pace and at a speed you can maintain without breaks in continuity.

Sentence 2: Type at a slightly faster speed the second and third times the sentence is attempted.

Sentence 3: Experiment with different rates. Push for speed; then drop back in rate for control.

Alphabet Ev glazed my floors with wax when J. B. Peck quit. *Check finger posture*

Direct reaches You need great sums for the growth of the schools.

Easy Did Ken make the boys sign the form for the check?

. . . . 1 . . . . 2 . . . . 3 . . . . 4 . . . . 5 . . . . 6 . . . . 7 . . . . 8 . . . . 9 10

15B: Reinforcement Practice (12) *each line twice; then type from dictation*

TECHNIQUE CUE	Curve the fingers and hold them lightly in home position. Strike the key with a quick, firm, sharp stroke; then release it quickly and strike the next key without a pause. Keep the carriage moving steadily.

1 p p;p;p; up cup dip ;p; pen hope soap cope paid pain *Quick return without looking up*

2 v vfvfvf vet vim vex five have give love drive brave

3 , ,k,k,k Len, of course, must go. Tod, too, may go.

4 *All letters* buy wax glad hill faze jump crave monk start quote *Curve the fingers*

5 *Shifting* Is Pat, too, to go? Have Ted, Joe, and Paul left?

. . . . 1 . . . . 2 . . . . 3 . . . . 4 . . . . 5 . . . . 6 . . . . 7 . . . . 8 . . . . 9 10

15C: Stroking Technique Practice – Quiet Hands and Arms (10) *each line three times*

TECHNIQUE CUE	Hold the hands and arms quiet—almost motionless. Make the long reaches, such as **m** to **u** and **b** to **r**, with the finger—not by moving the arm forward or arching the wrist. Keep the typing action in the fingers.

All letters are used.

1 Brad is a whiz at bridge, I am told by Dick Munce.

2 Your Point Park Branch Bank cashed my large check.

3 Dr. Lon Myers said his next talk will be in Maine.

4 I feel the suit is just not quite right for Steve.

. . . . 1 . . . . 2 . . . . 3 . . . . 4 . . . . 5 . . . . 6 . . . . 7 . . . . 8 . . . . 9 10

Unit 49 | Lessons 276-280

A Day in a Government Office

LESSON 276

276A: Conditioning Practice (5) *each line three times*

Alphabet	Jack recognized the exquisite violet flowers strewn on the bumpy road.	*Fingers curved and upright*
Figure-symbol	Review of figures and symbols: 2″, 3#, $4, 5%, <u>6</u>, 7&, 8′, (90), @, ¢.	
	Electric 2@, 6¢ 8*, ′ ″	
Continuity	If it is possible to do so, he may go with us to the show in the city.	
Fluency	A formula for success can often be expressed in two words: hard work!	

| 1 | 2 | 3 | 4 | 5 | 6 | 7 | 8 | 9 | 10 | 11 | 12 | 13 | 14 |

276B: Technique Evaluation (15) *each line three times*

Finger position and key stroking — **CHECK**

Third row	Were you to quote our prices on their quiet typewriters, or were they? ✓	*Fingers curved and upright; finger action; wrists low; hands quiet*
First row	Can Aza Cobb and the six men do the many acrobatics at a civic affair?	
Fingers 3, 4	Five popular politicians were polled by the quaint but zealous voters.	
Long reaches	Many bright aluminum cymbals may be used at a big dedication ceremony.	
Figures	Bill Order #3109 for 265 shirts and 748 pairs of shoes by February 10.	

| 1 | 2 | 3 | 4 | 5 | 6 | 7 | 8 | 9 | 10 | 11 | 12 | 13 | 14 |

Response patterns

One-hand	After you rate the minimum area reserve, please refer the case to him. ✓	*Finger action*
Balanced-hand	The chairman also may wish to handle a quantity of field box problems. ✓	*Word response*
Combination	Be sure to check five cases of each kind before recording an increase. ✓	*Variable rhythm and continuity*
Combination	Do either of you have any ideas about the division of the area profit?	

| 1 | 2 | 3 | 4 | 5 | 6 | 7 | 8 | 9 | 10 | 11 | 12 | 13 | 14 |

Use of operative parts

Space bar	Can you pay the city chairman or any person for a map of such quality? ✓	*Quick spacing*
Shift key	Jan Q. McNeil and Paul W. O'Brien may visit Peter Ajax in Santa Clara. ✓	*Little finger reach*
Tab	(Set tab stops each 10 spaces) to do it is and the if they may do when it their work ✓	*No waste motion*
Carriage return	(Tab: 5)→ When you hear the bell, finish or divide the word you are typing; ✓ then make the return and start the line quickly with eyes on the copy.	*Quick return; eyes on copy*

| 1 | 2 | 3 | 4 | 5 | 6 | 7 | 8 | 9 | 10 | 11 | 12 | 13 | 14 |

276C: Building Speed and Control (30) (*Use ¶s on page 400; follow directions below*)

1. **Speed.** Select a *speed goal* 4 to 8 *wam* above your average speed rate; type three 1′ guided writings on each ¶ at this goal rate. With each repetition try to eliminate any faulty typing patterns or other blocks to your speed.

   To reach a new speed level, do this:

   a. Keep carriage moving and your eyes on copy.
   b. Return carriage quickly and start new line.
   c. Keep fingers close to keys; use finger action.
   d. Hold wrists low and relaxed; hands quiet.
   e. Keep thumb on or near space bar; space quickly.

2. **Control.** End your practice with two 1′ *control* guided writings on each ¶. Select a *control goal* about 8 *wam* below your average speed rate.

   To improve your control, do this:

   a. Type with continuity and without hurry.
   b. Concentrate on the copy as you type.
   c. Type with good stroking technique.

15D: Guided Writing (20) *(Full sheet; Line: 50; Spacing: DS; ¶ indention: 5)*

1. **Type** a 1′ writing of each ¶. Calculate average *gwam*. Set a new goal as instructed in the box at the right.
2. **Type** three 1′ writings of each ¶, guided by the quarter-minute call. Determine *gwam* for the fastest writing.
3. **Type** 3′ writings without the guide. Begin with ¶ 1 and type as much of ¶ 2 as you can.

> **TO CALCULATE BASE RATE:** Get average *gwam* of two writings.
>
> **TO SET NEW GOAL:** Add 2 or 3 words to your base rate for a new goal rate (even number).

4. Circle your errors. Determine *gwam* for one or more of the 3′ writings. Record *gwam* on your paper.

All letters are used.

You have heard it said that we should do all we do just as well as we can. As a rule, this is quite true; but at times we may have to work much too fast and do less than our best.

Most of us can do some things well, but some of us have to learn that at times we will have to work too fast to do a top job. There is no prize for the piece of work that is just next best, but it will get the job done.

2′ GWAM | 1 | 2 | 3 | 4 | 5 |
3′ GWAM | 1 | 2 | 3 | 4 |

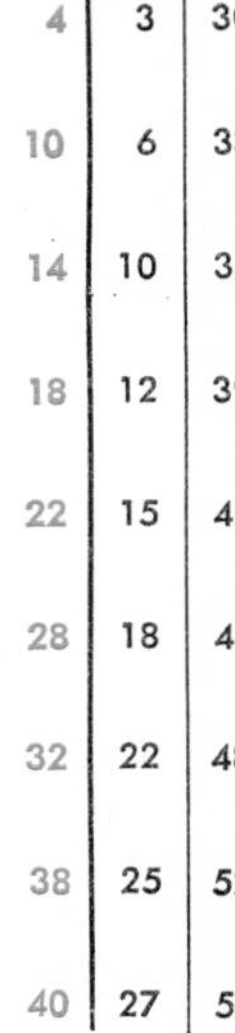

GWAM

2′	3′	
4	3	30
10	6	33
14	10	36
18	12	39
22	15	42
28	18	45
32	22	48
38	25	52
40	27	53

LESSON 16

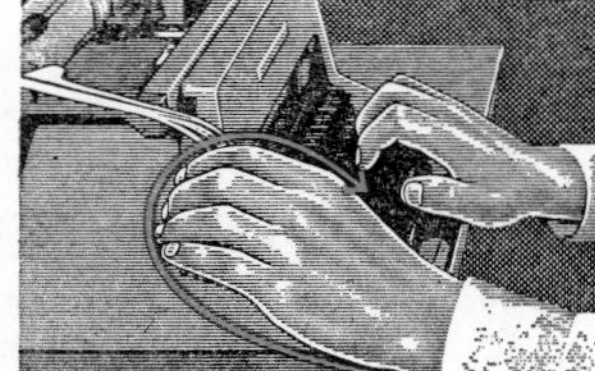

Full sheet; Line: 50; Spacing: SS

16A: Conditioning Practice (8) *each line three times*

Alphabet Jen said Vic and Liz Pfeil might quit work by six. *Eyes on the copy*

Shift keys Frank and Tom Spears will go to New York in March.

Easy When they go, the men may take this box with them.

. . . . 1 . . . . 2 . . . . 3 . . . . 4 . . . . 5 . . . . 6 . . . . 7 . . . . 8 . . . . 9 10

16B: Building Typing Continuity (5) *(Line: 50; Spacing: DS; ¶ indention: 5)*

1. **Type** a 1′ writing of ¶ 1, 15D, above, without the guide.
2. **Set** a new goal by adding 2 *gwam* for a new 1′ goal rate.
3. **Type** a 1′ writing of each ¶ at the new goal rate.

Job 5: Interoffice Memorandum (*half sheet; ¶ indention, 10*)

Words

TO: Charles R. Thornton, Personnel Director 8
FROM: James P. Wriston, Office Manager 15
DATE: April 15, 19–– 18
SUBJECT: Clerical Salaries 21

(¶ 1) A comparison of selected clerical salaries 30
for the years 1960 and 1965 is presented on the 39
attached sheet. You should find these data help- 49
ful in preparing your proposed salary increment 59
schedule for the next two or three years. (¶ 2) 67
You will note that some of the job classifications 77
have been changed slightly. For example, Gen- 86
eral Clerk––A has been changed to General 95
Clerk (Senior). Likewise, Stenographer––A has 104
been changed to Stenographer (Senior). (¶ 3) 112
If you are interested in studying the local figures, 123
I shall be glad to lend you the actual reports. 133
Attachment (*COMPANY MAIL envelope*) 135

Job 6: Table

Arrange the table attractively on a half sheet. →

			Job 6 Words	Job 7 Words
NATIONAL AVERAGE WEEKLY SALARIES *			7	7
				9
Job Classification	1960	1965	13 18	17 26
General Clerk (Senior)	$77	$ 92	25	33
General Clerk	62	74	29	38
Secretary A	93	109	32	42
Secretary	84	95	36	46
Stenographer (Senior)	76	89	41	52
Stenographer	69	80	45	56
Typist-Clerk	66	73	49	61
————————			52	64
* Source: AMS Directory of Office Salaries, 1960 and 1965–66.			62 64	74 76

Job 7: Expanded Table

Retype the salary table, adding a fourth column to show the *amount of increase* between the years 1960 and 1965: $15, 12, 16, 11, 13, 11, 7 →

Job 8: Invoice

Words

Sold To Lakeland Tile Company
1500 Central Avenue
Lakeland, Florida 33803

Terms 2/10, net 30

Date April 16, 19–– 7
Our No. RD–314920 13
Cust. Order No. 5627 19
Shipped Via Everglade Express Co. 24
Salesman Thompson 28

Quantity	Cat. No.	Description	Unit Price	Total	Words
240 tubes	T–21476	Tile Trim for 215 Display (2″)	.39	93.60	40
144 qts.	MX–475	High Resin	.83	119.52	48
48 gals.	M–111	Wall Adhesive	2.80	134.40	56
36 qts.	M–203	All-Purpose Cleaner	.45	16.20	65
12 ea.	M–22007	Trowels	2.00	24.00	71 73
				387.72	74

16C: Reinforcement Practice (12) *each line twice; then type from dictation*

1	g	gfgfgf go big cog rug rag rage gone girl give page	Curve the fingers
2	n	njnjnj an gun run can sun then than find send hunt	
3	w	wswsws we wed why sow now swim when whip what whom	
4	All letters	rub now just clay quiz pave hike mixed fight right	Quick, sharp stroke
5	Shifting	Did Ned leave? Ralph is right. We should all go.	
		....1....2....3....4....5....6....7....8....9....10	

16D: Stroking Technique Practice (10) *each line three times*

All letters are used.

1	Home row	Jake Pace led a dash for the flag as the lad fell.	Return without spacing
2	Top row	Ruth York wrote that you were quite right to quit.	
3	First row	Can Ben, Max, and Zeke drive back for the six men?	
4	Right hand	John Young knows you will look for him in my home.	
		....1....2....3....4....5....6....7....8....9....10	

16E: Sentence Guided Writings (15)

EXPLORATION LEVEL OF PRACTICE: When the purpose of your typing is to reach out into new speed areas, use the *exploration level of practice*. Take the brakes off your fingers and experiment with new stroking patterns and try out new speed areas.

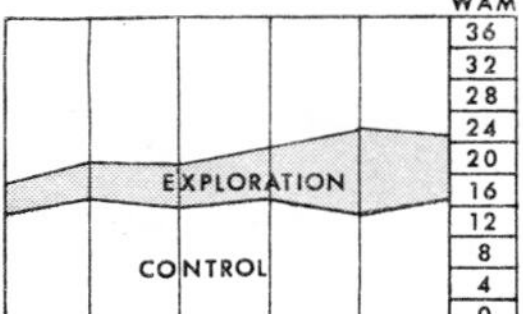

CONTROL LEVEL OF PRACTICE: When the purpose of your typing is to type with ease and control, drop back in rate and type on the *control level of practice*. This drop back should be 4 to 8 words below the exploration rate of typing.

TYPE: Each sentence for 1 minute, guided by the 20-second call. Type on the *exploration level*.

TYPE: Sentences 3 and 4 as two 1-minute writings, with the 15-second call, on the *exploration level*.

TYPE: Sentences 2 and 3 for 1 minute each, guided by the 20-second call, on the *control level*. Circle errors.

All letters are used.

		GWAM 20″	GWAM 15″
1	Mix the fruit juice in a large jar.	21	28
2	When did the five boys go to their work?	24	32
3	Put this queer box on the desk for Mrs. Kane.	27	36
4	The man who wants to win a prize must work to win.	30	40
5	Should the man lend a hand to those who work hard?	30	40
	....1....2....3....4....5....6....7....8....9....10		

Job 3: Page 2 of a Business Letter *(standard-size paper)*

Modified block, indented ¶s, mixed punctuation | Addressee: Mrs. R. C. Keller | Date: April 14

Words

(¶) Miss Roberta Peterson was very successful in handling the buffet at last year's 24
conference. You may want to ask her to take responsibility for the one listed for 41
May 30. Other possible assignments are listed below: 52

		Words
Invitations	Miss Kathryn Senneca	58
Program	Dr. Margaret McCullough	65
Room assignments	Mrs. Jeanne Lockland	72
Registration	Mr. Dewey Lambert	78

(¶) We want this year's conference to bring the maximum number of challenging and 94
motivating ideas to the secretaries who attend the national convention. With you 110
and Mr. Eldridge as cochairmen, I am sure we can achieve this goal. cordially 126
yours miss mildred simpson president 134

Job 4: Page 2 of Leftbound Business Report with Source Note

Words

(¶) Except in 1954, the average income of families increased each year from 1949 15
through 1964 (the latest year for which detailed information is available). In 1964, 33
the median family income was $6,556, compared to $4,167 a decade earlier. Accom- 49
panying this rise in average income was a shift toward higher incomes generally. 65
In 1964, about 65 percent of all families had money income of $5,000 or over, 81
compared to about 21 percent in 1949. At the lower end of the income scale, about 97
47 percent of all families in 1949 had income of less than $3,000 a year, as the 114
following table shows.[1] 119

FAMILY INCOME BY GROUPS 123

Total Money Income	Percent of Families				Words
	1949	1954	1959	1964	127 134 142
Under $3,000	47.5	31.7	22.7	17.6	148
$3,000 to $4,999	32.1	31.1	21.8	17.0	156
$5,000 to $6,999	12.5	20.4	24.2	19.8	163
$7,000 to $9,999	5.1	11.1	19.1	23.2	171
$10,000 and over	2.6	5.8	12.2	22.5	178 183
Total *	100.0	100.0	100.0	100.0	191

______________ 194

* Parts may not add to total because of rounding. 204

______________ 207

[1] U.S. Department of Commerce, Statistical Abstract of the United States (Washington: 232
U.S. Government Printing Office, 1966), p. 336. 242

LESSON 17

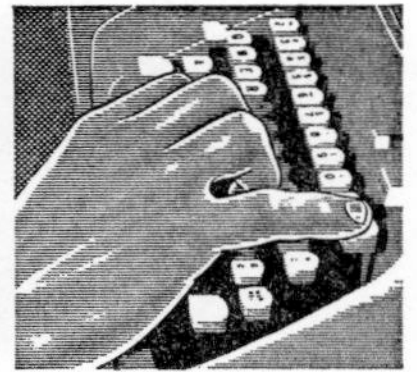

Full sheet; Line: 50; Spacing: SS

17A: Conditioning Practice (8) *each line three or more times*

Alphabet	Don Pugh will have Jay Black freeze my six quarts.	*Maintain control*
Drill on c	Checks cashed by Clay were all cleared by Charles.	
Easy	If the work is right, both men may sign the forms.	
	. . . . 1 . . . . 2 . . . . 3 . . . . 4 . . . . 5 . . . . 6 . . . . 7 . . . . 8 . . . . 9 10	

17B: Tabulating (7) *twice (See 8D, page 18, for explanation of tabulating procedure.)*

Eyes on the copy	cut	Tab	are	Tab	firm	Tab	care	Tab	them	*Return quickly*
	pen		one		form		milk		than	
	sir		bet		turn		cart		when	
	bid		ink		torn		join		hair	
KEY	3	8	3	8	4	8	4	8	4	

17C: Reinforcement Practice (15) *each line twice*

DO: Make pencil notation of the practice activities and page numbers given at the right. Place the notation at the side of your typewriter for easy reference. Use a full sheet for the typing.

13B, Page 27
14C, Page 29

17D: Typing for Control (20) *each ¶ once; control level*

DO: Use full sheet, 50-space line, double spacing, and 5-space ¶ indention. Make pencil notation of the practice activities and page numbers listed at the right. Place the notation beside your typewriter.

13D, Page 28
14D, Page 29
15D, Page 31

TYPE: Each ¶ once without being timed. Circle errors.

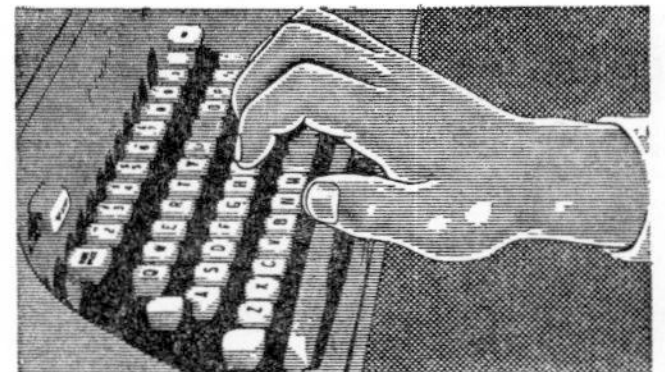

SPACE BAR TECHNIQUE

LESSON 18

Full sheet; Line: 50; Spacing: SS

18A: Conditioning Practice (8) *each line three or more times*

Alphabet	M. J. Gripz saved the six boys as Wynn Quick fell.	*Curve the fingers*
Adjacent keys	We said young Dan has as great poise as Brett has.	
Easy	If the pay is right, may Kit and I work with them?	
	. . . . 1 . . . . 2 . . . . 3 . . . . 4 . . . . 5 . . . . 6 . . . . 7 . . . . 8 . . . . 9 10	

Measuring Basic and Production Skills

LESSONS 274-275

274–275A: Conditioning Practice (5) *each line three times; then 1′ writings on Line 4*

Alphabet	Zahn Frakes quit his slow job and applied for a very big, complex one.	*Keep the hands and arms quiet*
Figure	50 .45 2.6 11.1 21.8 32.1 47.5 T3746 14 233 1959 2200 1966 30316 33612	
Figure-symbol	2/10, net 30 *Source #RI–67123–096 $3,000 $11 $4,999 MX-3720 $191.50	
Fluency	Len made an opportunity to explain the insurance statement to the men.	
	| 1 | 2 | 3 | 4 | 5 | 6 | 7 | 8 | 9 | 10 | 11 | 12 | 13 | 14 |	

274–275B: Measuring Basic Skill (15)

DO: Type a 10′ writing on the ¶s on 273C, page 394, in each lesson. Proofread, circle errors, and determine average *nwam* for the two writings, unless otherwise directed.

274–275C: Measuring Applied Typewriting Skill (30)

DO: Type for 30 minutes each day. Begin with Job 1 below and type as many jobs as you can. Prepare a carbon copy of each job. Correct any errors you make. At the end of Lesson 275, determine your *n-pram* (net production rate): acceptable words typed ÷ 60 minutes.

Job 1: Business Letter (*standard letterhead*)

Type the letter to the addressee listed below supplying the appropriate information in the blanks. ⟶

Modified block, indented ¶s, mixed punctuation; date: April 13, 19––; address envelope

To: **Mr. Peter R. Smythe, 1619 College Circle, Tampa, Florida 33612** (*supply appropriate salutation*) Policy: **#RI–67123–096** Coverage: **theft and collision** Premium: **$11.60** Payable: **on the first of each month** Agent: **Jarvis Associates**

Words

19

We take this opportunity to welcome you 27
into the select group of policyholders of the 36
Everglade Insurance Company. Your policy, 45
#_______________, is enclosed. We recom- 52
mend that you read it carefully to familiarize 62
yourself with the protection it provides. (¶) Page 71
2 of the policy outlines your protection in detail. 82
Since the insurance coverage in your policy gives 92
protection against _______________, you 102
should pay close attention to those sections. 111
Page 3 lists additional coverage and page 4 lists 121
exemptions. (¶) The premium for this policy is 130
$________, payable ____________. We will 142
send you a notice 15 days prior to due dates. 151
(¶) Our agent in your area, _______________, 160
is as near as your mailbox. Please contact us 169
anytime we can be of service to you. Sincerely 179
yours | EVERGLADE INSURANCE COMPANY | Royal 187
R. Richards | Vice-President | Enclosure 195/207

Job 2: Business Letter (*executive letterhead*)

Retype the letter as indicated below:

Modified block, open punctuation; date: April 13, 19––; address envelope

To: **Miss Patricia Towns, 2260 Newton Ave., S.E., Atlanta, Georgia 30316** (*supply appropriate salutation*) Policy: **#CQ–81526–475** Coverage: **fire, theft, and collision** Premium: **$67** Payable: **semi-annually, on January 15 and July 15** Agent: **Philip C. Clements**

18B: Reinforcement Practice (12) *each line twice; then type from dictation*

1	r	rfrfrf or for mar fir her corn worn farm true more	*Eyes on the copy; sit erect*
2	o	ololol own lot one owe old quote brown sworn pound	
3	z	zazaza zip haze size daze quiz faze doze zeal zinc	*Quiet hands*
4	*All letters*	was joy fixed queen prize black vexed might bright	
5	*Shifting*	Is Carl right? He thinks so, but what do you say?	

....1....2....3....4....5....6....7....8....9....10

18C: Stroking Technique Practice – One-Hand Words (10) *each line three or more times*

1	*Begin slowly*	A bad start on the set was caused by this old oil.	*Return quickly*
2		In fact, I was served well by the car at the base.	
3		The rate charged was far more than I cared to pay.	*Finger action*
4		At my age, I try to read a great deal of the time.	

....1....2....3....4....5....6....7....8....9....10

18D: Guided Writings (20) (*Line: 50; Spacing: DS; ¶ indention: 5*)

1. **Type** each ¶ for 1 minute on the *control level.* Average the two rates to determine your base rate; then add 2 *gwam* for a new goal rate.

2. **Type** each ¶ for two 1′ writings at your new goal rate on the *exploration level,* guided by the 15″ call; then 2′ and 3′ writings without the guide. Circle your errors.

All letters are used.

	GWAM 2′	GWAM 3′	
There are those who say that all is not well	4	3	30
with the young. It is said they do not want jobs	10	6	33
and have lost part of their zest for life; but is	14	10	36
this true? I am sure it is not so.	18	12	39
 If I had the quick wit and the drive some of	22	15	42
them do, I would try some big things. He who has	28	18	45
good wit and zeal will be the one to do the great	32	22	48
things that are to be done in the next few years.	38	25	52
What things will you do?	40	27	53

2′ GWAM | 1 | 2 | 3 | 4 | 5 |
3′ GWAM | 1 | 2 | 3 | 4 |

GWAM 1′ 10′

simply because he doesn't care; a person with bad judgment, though, does 86 19 83
so only because he doesn't know any better. Yet, to be clean and alto- 100 20 85
gether neat is a priceless quality we should all exemplify. 112 21 86

Giving proper attention to your apparel daily is very important to 13 23 87
work readiness. If a garment is kept clean and in press, it will last far 28 24 89
longer and retain a much better appearance. In addition, clothing tends 43 25 90
to restore itself to its original shape if it is properly stored for sev- 58 27 92
eral days between uses. Accordingly, you should use a rotation plan of 72 28 93
wearing and storing your clothes—shoes as well as other items. Items to 87 30 95
be worn tomorrow or next week ought to be carefully selected and in- 100 31 96
spected well in advance of the daily morning "dressing rush." Just 115 33 98
remember that an ounce of preparation is worth a pound of agitation. 128 34 99

To dress smartly or tastefully is not difficult to do. Moreover, it 14 35 100
can be done quite inexpensively if we will only exercise the proper care 28 37 102
in making our purchases. For example, if we pay attention to pattern, 43 38 103
colors, fabric texture, and accessories (jewelry, for instance), we can 57 40 104
make a few outfits do double duty because they can be "dressed up" or 71 41 106
"dressed down" to fit the occasion. 78 42 107

Simplicity of both apparel and coiffure is a basic quality. A haz- 13 43 108
ard many a person must overcome is the tendency to "dress up," to wear 28 45 109
high-style clothing, too many accessories, or way-out hairdos. Try to 42 46 111
"dress down," not up. An office is a work place, not a showcase. De- 56 47 112
velop your ability to make a good evaluation; then, look into the mirror. 71 49 114
High-cost items are not necessary, even though good taste is. Shy away 85 50 115
from extreme and unusual items. Rather, train yourself to recognize the 100 52 117
quality fabric and the classic style. Then, try to select accessories 114 53 118
that are suitable for and that harmonize with one or more basic outfits. 128 55 119

Exert a real effort to correct any item—of either apparel or per- 13 56 121
son—that may detract from a neat, pleasing appearance: gaudy colors, 27 57 122
extra jewelry, poorly cared for garments, run-over shoes, fingernails 41 58 124
that are improperly manicured, and so on. If you plan wisely and follow 56 60 125
the plan carefully, a long final look into a mirror will be sufficient 70 62 126
to give you a feeling of confidence that you can "pass inspection." Be 85 63 128
certain that your grooming and attire call attention only to you, not to 99 64 129
the clothing also. 103 65 130

1′ GWAM 1 2 3 4 5 6 7 8 9 10 11 12 13 14
10′ GWAM 1 2

LESSON 19

Full sheet; Line: 50; Spacing: SS

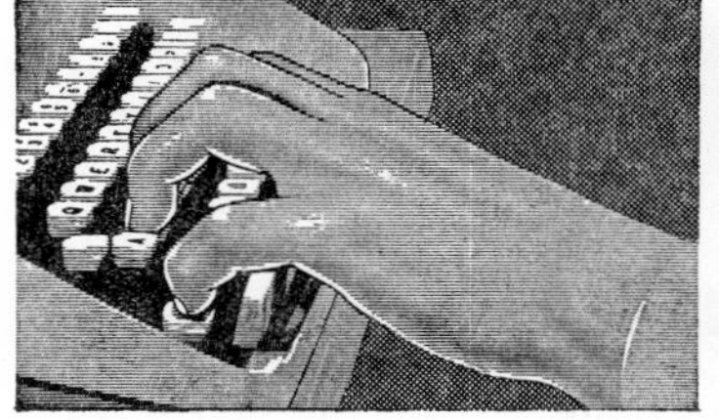

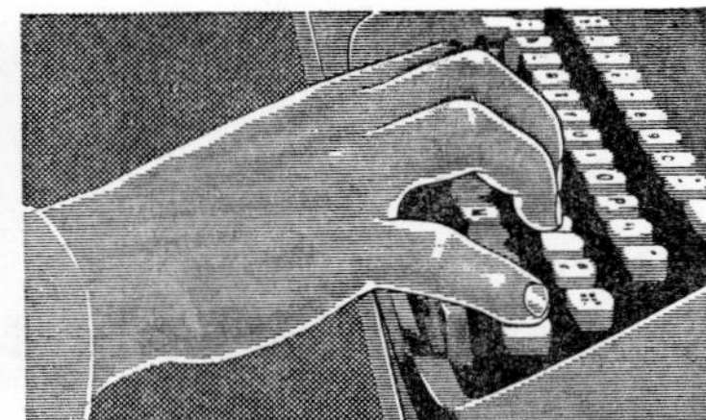

19A: Conditioning Practice (8) *each line three or more times*

Alphabet	Will Jim Bogg check Parts Five and Six of my quiz?	*Fingers well curved; wrists low*
One hand	Fred Kohn made a good case for his trade with Lon.	
Easy	The six men held that the right to work is theirs.	

. . . . 1 . . . . 2 . . . . 3 . . . . 4 . . . . 5 . . . . 6 . . . . 7 . . . . 8 . . . . 9 10

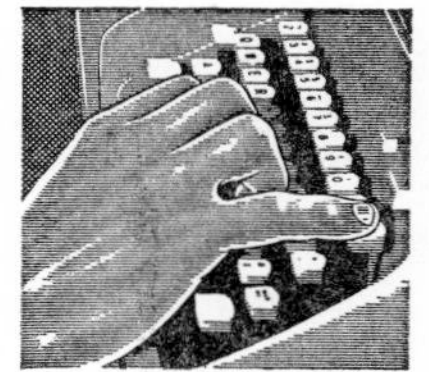

19B: Tabulating (5) *twice*

Tab across				
pay	few	both	card	lend
own	age	hand	hill	make
air	bad	town	case	born
end	oil	form	mill	span

KEY | 3 | 8 | 3 | 8 | 4 | 8 | 4 | 8 | 4 |

19C: Reinforcement Practice (12) *each line twice; then type from dictation*

Finger action; quiet hands

1 u ujujuj us use you just must plus hours house group

2 c cdcdcd cut can cent code stock check change church

3 i ikikik air fair like wire claim prize which signed

4 *All letters* at no be ox war ply dear quiz cave make just fight *Space quickly*

5 *Continuity* Can you cash my check? If not, Chuck or Mike may.

. . . . 1 . . . . 2 . . . . 3 . . . . 4 . . . . 5 . . . . 6 . . . . 7 . . . . 8 . . . . 9 10

19D: Stroking Technique Practice – Shift Keys (10) *each line three or more times*

TECHNIQUE CUE	**Reach** the little finger to the shift key; hold the key down until the capital has been typed and the key released. Keep the hand as near home position as you can.

All letters are used.

1 May Nat Hunt and Paul Lloyd go to Maine with Jack?

2 Eve Todd and Zoe Speer were in Fort Worth in June.

3 Clay Spahr flies to San Juan from New York in May.

4 Hal Flynn and Max Blye stayed at Queen Road, West.

5 Tom and Paul met Ruth Kahn and Beth James in Rome.

. . . . 1 . . . . 2 . . . . 3 . . . . 4 . . . . 5 . . . . 6 . . . . 7 . . . . 8 . . . . 9 10

LESSON 273

273A: Conditioning Practice (5) *each line three times; then 1′ writings on Line 4*

Alphabet	Della King or Pam Justin won six quarts of fancy guavas at the bazaar.	*Emphasize control first, speed second*
Figure	We traded in four typewriters: Nos. 4839206, 1592034, 204156, 562039.	
Figure-symbol	Get 60 reams of 17″ x 22″ Sheen-Coat litho @ $38.59 per cwt., less 4%.	
Fluency	The highlight of the day came when a new star was given a gold record.	
	| 1 | 2 | 3 | 4 | 5 | 6 | 7 | 8 | 9 | 10 | 11 | 12 | 13 | 14 |	

273B: Technique Mastery (15) *each line three times; then 1′ comparative writings on last three lines*

Shift keys	These members were there: P. C. App, A. H. Lambert, and J. A. Eppley.	*Emphasize quiet control of keys*
Shift lock	FOR SALE: 3-room lake cottage; FOR RENT: inboard-outboard houseboat.	
Ratchet release	Jensen and Haney,[5] as well as Whitmore,[6] give the same answer: H_2SO_4.	
Backspacer	He snapped, "Mind your <u>p's</u> and <u>q's</u>!" but they had reached their <u>xyz's</u>!	
Short words	I am, you are, she is, up to us, if you go, let the men, due a fee for	
Long words	outstanding opportunity, important application, employment requirement	
Awkward reaches	waxed eloquent, quasi-public, puzzled plumber, exaggerate, opinionated	
One hand	You get a minimum estate tax rate, I see; I started at a greater rate.	
Combination	Lend them my statement, amended by the union steward on the sixteenth.	
Balance hand	The chairman lent me a quantity of both forms to hand to the city men.	
	| 1 | 2 | 3 | 4 | 5 | 6 | 7 | 8 | 9 | 10 | 11 | 12 | 13 | 14 |	

273C: Growth Index (15) *10′ writing on the ¶s below and on page 395; proofread; determine* nwam

273D: Applied Typing (15) *complete the remaining Jobs (if time permits, redo selected ones)*

All letters are used.

	GWAM 1′	10′	
To be well groomed and to be dressed neatly and in good taste for	13	1	66
every occasion are vitally important, as each affects our self-confidence	28	3	68
and the kind of impression we make on the people with whom we associate.	43	4	69
Each quality is an index of our pride and of our judgment. Moreover,	57	6	71
we cannot avoid being evaluated at least partially on the basis of our	71	7	72
personal appearance. Co-workers, the "boss," and our friends and ac-	85	9	73
quaintances––all scrutinize the images we create in the minds of others.	99	10	75
Proper grooming and appropriate attire are attributes not to be had	14	11	76
just by wishful thinking, but neither one is very hard to achieve. On	28	13	78
the other hand, both demand a bit of planning and some homework. A lazy	42	14	79
person won't take the time or exert the effort needed for good grooming.	57	16	81
A person who is disinterested often dresses sloppily or inappropriately	72	17	82

1′ GWAM | 1 | 2 | 3 | 4 | 5 | 6 | 7 | 8 | 9 | 10 | 11 | 12 | 13 | 14 |
10′ GWAM | 1 | 2 |

(Continued)

19E: Guided Writings (15) *(Line: 50; Spacing: DS; ¶ indention: 5)*

1. **Type** each ¶ for 1 minute. Average the two rates for a base rate. Add 2 *gwam* to the base rate for a new goal.

2. **Type** each ¶ for 1 minute at new goal rate, guided by the 15″ call; then a 2- and a 3-minute writing without the guide. Circle errors.

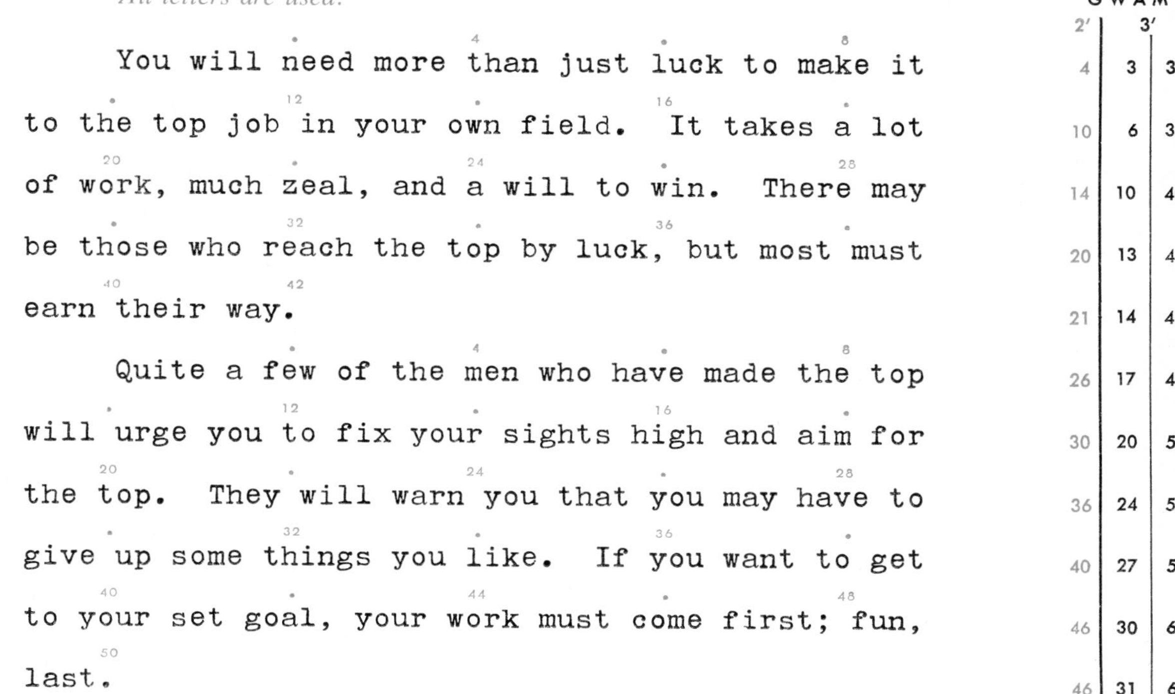

All letters are used.

		GWAM 2′	GWAM 3′	
1.0 E 4.5 87	You will need more than just luck to make it	4	3	34
	to the top job in your own field. It takes a lot	10	6	37
	of work, much zeal, and a will to win. There may	14	10	40
	be those who reach the top by luck, but most must	20	13	44
	earn their way.	21	14	45
1.0 E 4.5 87	Quite a few of the men who have made the top	26	17	48
	will urge you to fix your sights high and aim for	30	20	51
	the top. They will warn you that you may have to	36	24	54
	give up some things you like. If you want to get	40	27	58
	to your set goal, your work must come first; fun,	46	30	61
	last.	46	31	61

2′ GWAM | 1 | 2 | 3 | 4 | 5 |
3′ GWAM | 1 | 2 | 3 | 4 |

LESSON 20

Full sheet; Line: 50; Spacing: SS

20A: Conditioning Practice (8) *each line three or more times*

Alphabet	Zeke Riggs packed my box with five quail for Jane.	*Eyes on copy*
Double letters	Call Miss Booth to see if Nell is still in school.	
Easy	The men claim it is right for them to be paid now.	

. . . . 1 . . . . 2 . . . . 3 . . . . 4 . . . . 5 . . . . 6 . . . . 7 . . . . 8 . . . . 9 10

20B: Typing for Control (7) *(Line: 50; Spacing: DS; ¶ indention: 5)*

TYPE: A 1- and then two 2-minute writings of 19E, above, without the call of the guide. Type with easy, rhythmic stroking on the *control level.* Keep the carriage moving.

Job 7: Minutes of an Interdepartmental Meeting *(leftbound manuscript style; ss)*

BOOKCRAFTERS, INC.

Interdepartmental Meeting of April 14, 19--

<u>Time and Place of Meeting</u>

The regular monthly meeting of department heads of Bookcrafters, Inc., was held on Friday, April 14, 19--, in the Conference Room of the Company. The meeting was called to order at 10:30 a.m. by Mr. Norman C. Randolph, Executive Vice-President and presiding officer. Mr. Alex Chaldekas acted as recording secretary in the absence of Mr. Paul Morin, who was ill.

<u>Roll Call</u>

The following department heads were present: Messrs. Charles Duncan (Sales); Donald Evans (Accounting and Data Processing); Walter Nixon (Production); Barry Jackson (Shipping and Receiving); and Jay Simms (Office Services).

In addition, Mr. Chester Bielski (Office Manager) was present with the following special committee members: Miss Nancy Taylor (Food Service); Miss Julianne Johnson (Overtime Work); and Mr. George LeBlond (Recreational Activities).

<u>Approval of Minutes</u>

The minutes of the March meeting, which had been duplicated and distributed to all department heads, were approved as read.

<u>Reports of Special Committees</u>

<u>Food Service</u>. Miss Nancy Taylor presented a report comparing the selection, serving, and prices of foods and beverages of Vendomat, Inc., and VeriFresh Catering Company. After considerable discussion, Mr. Charles Duncan moved that a formal recommendation be made to discontinue Vendomat service and to contract with VeriFresh to operate the cafeteria. Mr. Donald Evans seconded the motion. The motion was carried.

<u>Overtime Work</u>. Miss Julianne Johnson reported her study of overtime for the month of March, indicating that more than the allowable overtime in a single day was being reported by certain employees and that more than the allowable overtime in any one week was being reported by others.

Mr. Bielski then reviewed the regulations regarding overtime for both plant and office employees and provided department heads with time sheets to simplify the recording and reporting of daily and weekly overtime.

<u>Recreational Activities</u>. Mr. George LeBlond reported the tentative formation of a men's and a women's softball league, subject to the written approval of an executive officer of each of the companies involved.

Mr. Barry Jackson moved that approval be granted. Mr. Jay Simms seconded the motion. The motion carried.

<u>Unfinished Business</u>

There was no unfinished business to be considered.

<u>New Business</u>

Mr. Chester Bielski presented a plan for expanded coverage under our group hospitalization insurance policy; he then answered questions raised by the department heads. Because the expanded coverage would be accompanied with a slight increase in premium rates to be borne partially by employees, the department heads were asked to discuss the plan with members of their respective departments before action is taken.

<u>Next Meeting</u>

The next Interdepartmental Meeting will be held on Friday, May 12, in the Conference Room at 10:30 a.m.

<u>Adjournment</u>

The meeting was adjourned at 11:45 a.m.

Respectfully submitted,

Alex Chaldekas
Acting Secretary

______________________________ ______________________________

Norman C. Randolph
Executive Vice-President

Date

20C: Stroking Technique Practice (10) *each line three or more times*

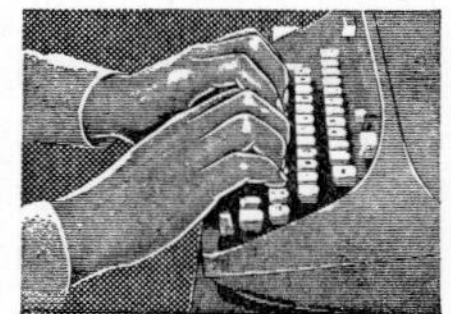

1	ei | ie	Their friends tried to ship eight bags by freight.
2	tr	Try to treat your true friends right at all times.
3	we	We were well paid; and when we left, we had a lot.
4	m | n	The men in the mines were numb from cold at night.
5	*Easy*	Six girls have quit the show Jack and Liz play in.

. . . . 1 . . . . 2 . . . . 3 . . . . 4 . . . . 5 . . . . 6 . . . . 7 . . . . 8 . . . . 9 10

20D: Growth Index (15) (*Line: 50; Spacing: DS; ¶ indention: 5*)

TYPE: Three 3-minute writings on the *control level.*

GOAL: A rate approximately 4 to 8 words slower than your base rate.

DO: Determine *gwam* for the best of the three writings. Circle errors.

All letters are used.

		GWAM 2′	GWAM 3′	
1.0 E 4.3 88	It is right for a man to know that he knows,	4	3	35
	but it is just as smart for a man to know when he	10	6	38
	does not know. When a man knows that he does not	14	10	42
	know, he can take steps to learn what he needs to	20	13	45
	know. How smart are you?	22	15	47
1.0 E 4.4 88	You can be glad for the things that you need	26	18	50
	to know. To learn, most of us must have the spur	32	21	53
	that comes from an urge to know more than we know	36	24	56
	just now. It is quite right to prize all we know	42	28	60
	so long as we do not quit. We must work on up to	46	31	63
	the next prize.	48	32	64

2′ GWAM | 1 | 2 | 3 | 4 | 5 |

3′ GWAM | 1 | 2 | 3 | 4 |

20E: Guided Writings (10)

TYPE: Three 1-minute writings of each paragraph of 20D, above, on the *exploration level.* Set a goal of 4 to 8 words more than your average *gwam* for 20D. Don't hurry, but speed up.

Job 4: Composing a Letter

Compose and type (with two cc's) a letter to Mr. David R. Dickson, 2127 Alps Road, Athens, Georgia 30604, to say that Mr. Duncan, the Sales Manager, will be in Atlanta at the Hotel Georgian Terrace until (*give date*). Tell Mr. Dickson that you have notified Mr. Duncan of his interest in the position of Assistant Sales Manager and that it is possible an interview will be arranged while Mr. Duncan is in Atlanta. Show an AIRMAIL notation. Sign your name as Secretary to Mr. Duncan. Add a cc notation and send a copy to Mr. Duncan.

Job 5: Executive Letter →

In Mr. Duncan's absence, you sometimes assist the secretary to Mr. Randolph, Executive Vice-President. Today, April 11, you have been asked to type a letter for Mr. Randolph, on his own executive-size stationery. He prefers modified block style with open punctuation. Prepare 3 cc's; address an envelope.

mrs. evelyn kennilworth john dewey high school 1400 south avenue springfield, missouri 65804 dear mrs. kennilworth (¶ 1) One of my associates has just written a booklet on the important subject of yearbook layout and preparation. It's called Tailor-Made Yearbooks and contains 64 pages of helpful guides to modern yearbook planning, illustration, and production. Each guide is liberally illustrated with contrasting models to show the effective and the not-so-effective uses of type, photographs, space, and other graphic elements. (¶ 2) Tailor-Made Yearbooks is designed to help you help us give you more attractive yearbooks with less effort on your part. I should like to send you a copy with my compliments to see if you find it as helpful as a review board of yearbook sponsors did. (¶ 3) Simply fill in and mail the enclosed card, and I'll see that the booklet reaches you promptly. Your comments will be welcome. sincerely yours norman c. randolph executive vice-president xx enclosure

Job 6: Agenda for an Interdepartmental Meeting

Prepare corrected copies of an agenda for Mr. Randolph's meeting on April 14 with all department heads. Make 5 cc's. Margins: top, 2"; side, 1"

```
                    Bookcrafters, Inc.
                            Interdepartmental
                    Agenda for^Meeting
                      April 14, 19--
                                                          C.
 1.  Call to order . . . . . . . . . . . . . . . .  Norman^Randolph
     #       and approval
 2. Reading^of the Minutes . . . . . . . . . . .  [Alex Chaldekas

 3.  Committee Reports
        Food Service  . . . . . . . . . . . . .   Nancy Taylro  tr
        Overtime Work . . . . . . . . . . . . .   Julianne Johnson
        Recreational Activities . . . . . . .     (Norman C. Randolph)
                                              tr
 4.  Unfinished busness . . . . . . . . . . . .   (George R. LeBlond)
                     i
     d
 5.6. Ajournment

 5. New Business
      Presentation of Proposal for
        Improved Hospitalization Plan . . .  Chester Bielski
```

Unit 3 | Lessons 21-30

Learning to Type Figures and Basic Symbols

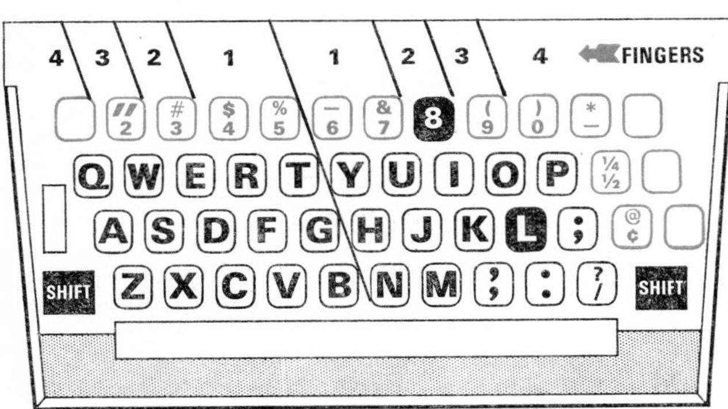

1. Arrange work area for efficient typing.
2. Adjust paper guide and insert full sheet.
3. Set left margin stop 30 spaces to left of center for a 60-space line; move right stop to end of scale.
4. SS drills; DS and indent paragraphs.
5. *Bonus Typing:* Type selected sentences from page 54 as directed.

LESSON 21

21A: Conditioning Practice (8) *each line three or more times*

Alphabet John Fox left my quiz show and gave back a prize he had won. *Sit erect*

y | v Did you say Fay and Van Favro lived in Vevey for five years?

Easy Fix in mind just what it is that you want; then work for it.

. . . . 1 . . . . 2 . . . . 3 . . . . 4 . . . . 5 . . . . 6 . . . . 7 . . . . 8 . . . . 9 . . . . 10 . . . . 11 12

21B: Figure Location – 8 and 1 (7)

DO: Find new key on chart, above. | Locate new key on keyboard. | Study reach diagram. | Type the drill.

REACH TECHNIQUE FOR 8

Reach the *right second finger* up to the top row to type **8**. Keep the wrist low.

i8k 8k 8k 8 k8k 88 k8k 888

Were 88 men on Flight 888? DS

USING LETTER l FOR FIGURE 1

If your typewriter does not have a special key for figure **1**, use the small letter *l* to type **1**.

> **Typing Double Figures**
>
> **Nonelectric.** Use a short, quick stroke and do not allow the full return of the key between strokes. **Electric.** Allow time for the key to return to normal position before typing it again.

1 11 111 11 1 11 111 11 11

Did 11 boys work 111 days? DS

REACH TO SPECIAL 1 KEY

If your typewriter has a special key for figure **1** located at the left of the keyboard, reach up to it with the *left fourth (little) finger.*

(*If the special key is located at the right of the keyboard, use the appropriate finger to type 1.*)

Before typing the reach drill, study *Typing Double Figures* at the left.

la l ala ll ala la lll ala

Did 11 boys work 111 days? DS

LESSONS 270-273

270–272A: Conditioning Practice (5) *each line three times daily*

Alphabet	Jack Wexler hopes to give quite a sizeable sum to your Fine Arts Fund.	Reach with the fingers, not the hands
Figure	My clerical and related staff totaled 350 in 1967; other workers, 248.	
Figure-symbol	9:00 a.m. 11:45 p.m. Flight 14 c/o April 12–15 806–721–2299 33480 2157	
Fluency	The work of the eight women was a tribute to the new program chairman.	

| 1 | 2 | 3 | 4 | 5 | 6 | 7 | 8 | 9 | 10 | 11 | 12 | 13 | 14 |

270–272B: Typing for Control (8) *5′ writing in each lesson on 269D, page 389; determine* nwam

270–272C: Applied Typing (37)

In this unit you will work for Mr. Charles A. Duncan, Sales Manager, and for Mr. Norman C. Randolph, Executive Vice-President, Bookcrafters, Inc.

Job 1: Itinerary

Mr. Duncan is leaving April 10 on a trip to Houston and Atlanta. Prepare in duplicate his travel and appointment schedule. →

2″ top margin; 1″ side margins; single-space individual entries; supply appropriate heading

MONDAY--April 10 (Washington to Houston)

8:00 a.m.	Leave Washington on Eastern Jet Flight 141. (All tickets in Eastern ticket envelope.)
10:03 a.m.	Arrive Houston. "Guaranteed-arrival" reservation at Hotel America.
12:30 p.m.	Lunch and interview with Mr. Ray Wallace about position as Assistant Sales Manager. (Application and related information and forms in Folder B.)

TUESDAY--April 11 (Houston to Atlanta)

11:05 a.m.	Leave Houston on Eastern Jet Flight 242.
2:28 p.m.	Arrive Atlanta. Confirmation of reservation at Hotel Georgian Terrace attached.
3:45 p.m.	Call Mr. Grayson (741–3069) for appointment schedule.

WEDNESDAY--April 12 (In Atlanta)

THURSDAY--April 13 (Atlanta to Washington)

3:00 p.m.	Leave Atlanta on Eastern Jet Flight 134.
4:21 p.m.	Arrive Washington. (Company chauffeur will meet you.)

Job 2: Letter in Personal Style

Mrs. Duncan is in Florida. Mr. Duncan has asked you to send her his revised itinerary. For such letters you use modified block, indented ¶s, mixed punctuation, and a personal style (the letter address placed at the left margin 5–6 lines below the title) as illustrated. →

Sincerely yours,

Adele Frazer

(Miss) Adele Frazer
Secretary to Mr. Duncan

Mrs. Charles A. Duncan
Palm Beach Biltmore Hotel
Palm Beach, Florida 33480

april 7, 19-- dear mrs. duncan Mr. Duncan's travel plans are changed slightly, and he has asked me to send you his correct itinerary. His travel schedule for next week is as follows: *(Copy the datelines; list flight data and hotels, omitting all other itinerary information in Job 1.)* (¶ 2) All of us here at the office hope you are finding your stay in Palm Beach restful and enjoyable. sincerely yours *(Your name)* secretary to mr. duncan mrs. charles a. duncan palm beach biltmore hotel palm beach, florida 33480

Job 3: Telegram

In the afternoon mail on April 10 a letter arrives from David R. Dickson, of Athens, Georgia. It includes an application for the position of Assistant Sales Manager. Wire Mr. Duncan in Houston that Mr. Dickson's data sheet is impressive and that he is free to come to Atlanta for an interview. Include Mr. Dickson's area code and telephone number (404–381–4427).

21C: Stroking Technique Practice (10) *each line three times*

1	8	Only 8 girls of a class of 88 made a grade of 88 on April 8.
2	1	The 11 boys and 111 men go to Spain by Flight 111 on May 11.
3	*Reinforcement*	8k8k 8 8k 11 18 181 818 88 188 118 k8k8 18k8 1881 1818 8k 81
4	*Continuity*	Their April 11 test will cover pages 11 to 18 and 81 to 188.
5	*Continuity*	Paul explained the June 8 quiz which covered pages 18 to 88.

. . . . 1 . . . . 2 . . . . 3 . . . . 4 . . . . 5 . . . . 6 . . . . 7 . . . . 8 . . . . 9 . . . . 10 . . . . 11 12

21D: Tab Mechanism Drill (7) *(Line: 60) twice as shown*

Clear and set:

	Margin	Tab	Tab	Tab	Tab	Tab	Tab	Tab
	for	the	wit	big	pay	are	end	with
	and	but	may	pen	got	you	aid	work
	all	111	ill	888	now	188	not	1818
	see	181	ink	881	has	818	how	8181

DS as you return

KEY | 3 | 5 | 3 | 5 | 3 | 5 | 3 | 5 | 3 | 5 | 3 | 5 | 3 | 5 | 4 |

21E: Building Control (18) *(Line: 60; Spacing: DS; ¶ indention: 5)*

1. **Type** a 1′ *exploration-level* writing.
2. **Type** three 1′ *control-level* writings. Determine best *gwam.* Circle errors.
3. **Type** 2′* and 3′ writings at your controlled speed. Circle errors and determine *gwam* for best 3′ writing.

All letters are used.

E 1.1 4.5 88

	GWAM 1′	3′	
The copy you have typed up to now has been typed line	11	4	39
for line as shown in the book, and the lines have ended at	23	8	43
the same point. For the most part, you will still type line	35	12	47
for line in this and the next unit of lessons, but the lines	47	16	51
may not be the same length. When copy is not in just the	59	20	55
form in which it is to be typed, you may have to divide words	71	24	59
at the end of some lines; so you must be quick to note the	83	28	63
ringing of the bell as the cue to end the line. You must	94	31	67
know the size word you may divide and how to divide it.	105	35	70

1′ GWAM | 1 | 2 | 3 | 4 | 5 | 6 | 7 | 8 | 9 | 10 | 11 | 12 |
3′ GWAM | 1 | 2 | 3 | 4 |

*Your 2-minute rate will be half the 1-minute *gwam* given in the first column at right, above.

GWAM 1' 10'

1.6 HA 5.8 70

Competition in a free enterprise system aids society in many vital 13 23 88
ways. To attract consumers away from other distributors or sellers, a 28 24 90
firm must try to improve the quality of its products, to develop new 41 26 91
products, and to operate efficiently in order to keep its prices down-- 56 27 92
that is, in line with those of main competitors. Thus, competition 69 29 94
serves to insure that consumers will get at fair prices the kinds of 83 30 95
products they want. 87 30 96

1.6 HA 5.8 70

Competition aids a society as a whole as well as the individuals 13 32 97
who comprise it in that it tends to make firms use the scarce productive 28 33 98
resources efficiently. If a business does not work efficiently, it will 42 35 100
fail, for consumers will buy lower-priced or higher-quality items from 56 36 101
a firm which operates more efficiently. Furthermore, the factor of 70 37 103
competition in our economy provides a chance for the person with ini- 84 39 104
tiative to enter business for himself and to try to share in the profits 98 40 105
being made by those already in business. 106 41 106

1.6 HA 5.8 70

One type of competition involves the price of goods. Price compe- 13 42 108
tition means getting volume away from rivals by lowering of price. Now, 28 44 109
though, more and more competition takes the form of nonprice rivalry. 42 45 110
For instance, customers may be attracted away from a seller by firms 56 47 112
which offer items that have superior features or that add to an item a 70 48 113
feature that a rival has not provided--an automatic eraser on a type- 84 49 115
writer, for one. Or consumers may be attracted by the packaging of an 93 51 116
item, such as a clean-hands cartridge for a typewriter ribbon. An ex- 112 52 117
tensive sales campaign aimed at convincing the buyer that a specific 126 54 119
type of a product is superior to others is also vital in nonprice 139 55 120
competition. 141 55 120

1.6 HA 5.8 70

Pure competition is the opposite of pure monopoly. A monopoly 13 56 122
exists when there is just one seller, or just a few sellers, and the 26 58 123
seller is able to avoid most of the elements of zealous rivalry. For 40 59 124
instance, if a seller does not have to compete with other sellers for 54 61 126
the consumer's dollars, he can boost his profit by selling his product 69 62 127
for a higher price. A critical field of government intervention in busi- 83 63 129
ness operations is devised to maintain competition and to avoid the 97 65 130
practice of monopoly. 101 65 130

1' GWAM | 1 | 2 | 3 | 4 | 5 | 6 | 7 | 8 | 9 | 10 | 11 | 12 | 13 | 14 |
10' GWAM | 1 | 2 |

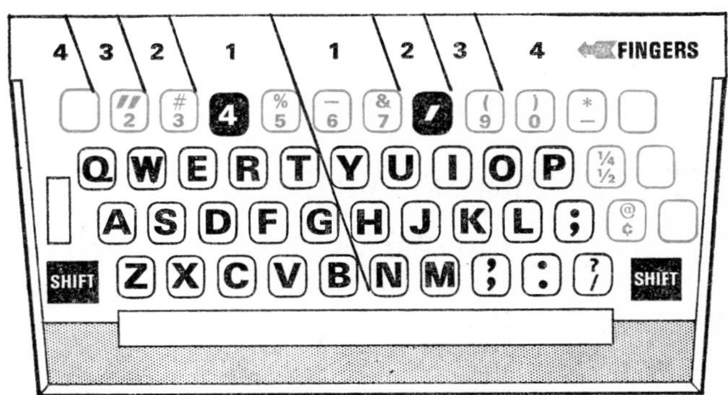

LESSON 22

60-space line | Single spacing

22A: Conditioning Practice (8) *each line three or more times*

Alphabet — Did Burt Jackson say Liza wove queer hex signs for Mr. Depp?

q | m | x — Max Quimby quickly fixed 18 quarts of the mixture for Mamie.

Easy — The ancient jewels at the downtown shop were worn by queens.

. . . . 1 . . . . 2 . . . . 3 . . . . 4 . . . . 5 . . . . 6 . . . . 7 . . . . 8 . . . . 9 . . . . 10 . . . . 11 12

22B: Symbol | Figure Location – ' (*apostrophe*), ! (*exclamation*), and 4 (7)

APOSTROPHE '

Nonelectric. Type ' (the shift of **8**) with the *right second finger*. Type the following drill:

8k 8k'k 8k'k 'k 'k 8k'k 'k

Isn't my pad on Ed's desk? DS

Electric. The ' is to the right of ; and is typed with the *right fourth finger*. Type the drill:

;'; '; '; '; ';'; ';'; ';'

Isn't my pad on Ed's desk? DS

EXCLAMATION !

Type the ' and backspace; then type the period (!). (If your typewriter has a special ! key, move the finger to it without moving the elbow outward.

Spacing Rule: Twice after ! at end of sentence; once after ! within sentence.

Type the following drill:

Fine! I spelled it right!

Eyes front! Type with me! DS

REACH TECHNIQUE FOR 4

Reach the *left first finger* to the top row to type **4**. Hold the other fingers over their home keys. Type the following drill:

r4f 4f 4f 4 f4f 44 f4f 444

I flew 444 miles on May 4. TS

22C: Stroking Technique Practice (10) *each line three times*

All letters, figures, and all symbols taught are used.

1 ' (Apostrophe) — Mrs. O'Neil can't or won't pay for her son's trip to Brazil.

2 ! (Exclamation) — Try! Don't fly! You can win if you think you can! Try it!

3 Reinforcement — 4f4f 4f 44 8k8k 8k 48 148 184 841 — Nonelectric: 8k'k 8k' / Electric: ';'; ';' — Isn't this great!

4 Continuity — Did the 14 boxes Joe shipped on May 14 weigh 44 pounds each?

5 Continuity — Haven't 14 experts from Quincy quizzed 148 boys and 184 men?

. . . . 1 . . . . 2 . . . . 3 . . . . 4 . . . . 5 . . . . 6 . . . . 7 . . . . 8 . . . . 9 . . . . 10 . . . . 11 12

LESSON 269

269A: Conditioning Practice (5) *each line three times; then 1′ writings on Line 4*

Alphabet	Bart Thomas finally quit working the puzzle just because he was vexed.	Work for quiet control of numbers and symbols
Figure	4-qt., 58 lbs., 16 gal., 30 doz., 9 x 12 ft., 17 oz., 25 yds., 110 in.	
Figure-symbol	2 P–900 @ $48.95 ea., less 15%; terms: 2/10, net 30; freight, $11.76.	
Fluency	When it is possible to take a cash discount for prompt payment, do so.	
	| 1 | 2 | 3 | 4 | 5 | 6 | 7 | 8 | 9 | 10 | 11 | 12 | 13 | 14 |	

269B: Statistical Typing – Script (10) *each sentence as a 1′ writing with 10″ or 12″ call*

	GWAM 12″	GWAM 10″
Acme Sales offers terms of 2/10, net 30.	40	48
Order 25# of Hill & Dale grass seed at $1.69.	45	54
Enter Jack 'n Jill's check for $147, $150 less 2%.	50	60
Get a copy of Bey's BEACON TO PROGRESS, $8.50 less 20%.	55	66
Request the proceeds of the note: $1,000 less $65, or $935.	60	72
The wire read: "Rush a 50# drum of C-2840 R & Z Compound C.O.D."	65	78

269C: Growth Index (15) *one 10′ writing on the ¶s shown below and on page 390*

269D: Applied Typing (20) *complete the remaining Jobs*

All letters are used.

	GWAM 1′	GWAM 10′	
Each person is involved in problems related to his efforts to get	13	1	67
the goods and services he wants. Every society faces the challenge of	27	3	68
trying to satisfy the wants of its citizens. Even though all societies	42	4	69
have this same problem, many different systems have been devised to pro-	56	6	71
duce and use the goods and services. The body of knowledge which relates	71	7	72
to producing and using the goods and services that satisfy human wants	85	9	74
is called "economics." "Business" is a term used to identify the efforts	100	10	75
of a group of people or of a single person to produce and distribute use-	115	11	77
ful goods or services.	119	12	77
The American economy is most often referred to as capitalism or a	13	13	78
free enterprise system. In such a system the producers or sellers try	27	15	80
to earn a profit by supplying economic goods, and the buyers try to ac-	42	16	81
quire a maximum amount of quality goods at the lowest prices. This con-	56	17	83
flict of interests between buyers and sellers is resolved to the good of	71	19	84
the society by a device known as competition. We should think of com-	85	20	86
petition as the rivalry among sellers for the customer's dollars.	98	22	87

(Continued)

1′ GWAM | 1 | 2 | 3 | 4 | 5 | 6 | 7 | 8 | 9 | 10 | 11 | 12 | 13 | 14 |
10′ GWAM | 1 | 2 |

22D: Tab Mechanism Drill (7) *once as shown (Line: 60)*

TECHNIQUE CUE	Hold your eyes on the copy as you tabulate from column to column. Reach to the tab key or bar with minimum hand motion and hold your other fingers in their home position. Control the tab mechanism with precision.

Margin	Tab	Tab	Tab	Tab	Tab	Tab	Tab
of	was	the	far	and	saw	can	can't
by	his	but	has	now	you	won	won't
as	few	men	not	had	car	its	isn't
88	188	141	144	441	814	414	81414
44	448	184	148	481	418	844	84184
84	841	481	844	488	884	814	48414
in	see	you	set	nil	fed	lop	sweet
up	him	get	nun	car	ilk	egg	joint
we	red	kin	wed	mum	sad	lip	bread

DS as you return

KEY | 2 | 5 | 3 | 5 | 3 | 5 | 3 | 5 | 3 | 5 | 3 | 5 | 3 | 5 | 5 |

22E: Guided Writings (18) *(Line: 60; Spacing: DS; ¶ indention: 5)*

1. **Type** each ¶ as a 1′ writing. Circle errors. Determine *gwam* for each writing. Average the two *gwam* scores (total ÷ 2) for a *base rate.*
2. **Add** 2 *gwam* to base rate for a new goal rate. Note checkpoints for quarter-minute guide.
3. **Type** each ¶ for two 1′ *exploration-level* writings, guided by the quarter-minute call.
4. **Type** each ¶ as a 2′ *control-level* writing without the call of the guide.
5. **Type** 3′ writings without the guide. Circle errors. Determine *gwam* for best writing.

NOTE. Copy containing figures or symbols is not classified "easy" (E) even though the words themselves are well within the SI, AWL, and HFW controls for easy copy.

All letters are used.

	3′ GWAM	
(1.1 / 5.0 / 89) Just how big the world is was not known in 1484; but by	4	33
1884, men had explored far and found paths across the seas.	8	37
Life could never be the same again, for great change has come	12	41
between 1884 and now.	13	43
Most of the things we have today were not thought of in	17	46
(1.1 / 4.9 / 89) 1484 and just a few were known by 1884. The size of the world	21	51
has shrunk and things have increased; and man now soars into	25	55
space with the boldness of a bird, as his mind conquers all!	29	59

3′ GWAM | 1 | 2 | 3 | 4 |

Job 9: Typing a Balance Sheet *(placed sideways)*

SUMMIT SALES COMPANY, INC.

Balance Sheet

March 31, 19––

ASSETS

Current Assets:			
Cash		$ 64,455	
Accounts and notes receivable	$2,360,932		
Less: Allowance for doubtful accounts	50,808	2,310,124	
Inventories, at lower of cost or market		1,418,056	
Prepaid insurance, advertising, etc.		9,808	$3,802,443
Fixed Assets:			
Property, plant, and equipment		$ 612,500	
Less: Accumulated depreciation		392,300	220,200
Total Assets			$4,022,643

LIABILITIES AND STOCKHOLDERS' EQUITY

Current Liabilities:			
Accounts and notes payable		$ 454,486	
Estimated liability for income taxes		57,500	$ 511,986
Capital Stock:			
Common stock, par value $1 per share	$1,500,000		
Capital paid-in in excess of par value	917,500	$2,417,500	
Earnings Retained for Use in the Business		1,093,157	$3,510,657
Total Liabilities and Stockholders' Equity			$4,022,643

Job 10: Typing an Income Statement *(placed sideways)*

SUMMIT SALES COMPANY, INC.

Comparative Income Statement

For the Years Ended March 31, 19–– and 19––

			Increase (Decrease)	
	19––	19––	Amount	%
Net Sales	$575,682	$506,342	$69,340	13.6
Cost of Sales	368,416	310,046	58,370	18.8
Gross Profit on Sales	207,266	196,294	10,970	5.6
Controllable Expenses:				
Salaries and wages	$ 14,675	$ 13,025	$ 1,650	12.6
Operating supplies	6,846	5,680	1,166	20.5
Advertising	4,232	4,919	(687)	(13.9)
Delivery	3,811	3,708	103	2.7
Uncollectible accounts	936	681	255	37.4
Miscellaneous	4,062	3,083	79	1.9
Total controllable expenses	$ 34,562	$ 31,996	$ 3,940	12.3
Fixed Expenses:				
Utilities	$ 11,201	$ 11,556	$ (355)	(3.0)
Insurance	3,090	2,842	248	8.7
Taxes and licenses	5,707	5,172	535	10.3
Interest	481	596	(115)	19.3
Depreciation	7,643	8,062	419	5.1
Total fixed expenses	$ 28,122	$ 28,228	$ 732	2.5
Total operating expenses	$ 62,684	$ 60,224	$ 4,672	7.5
Net Income	$144,582	$136,070	$ 6,298	4.6

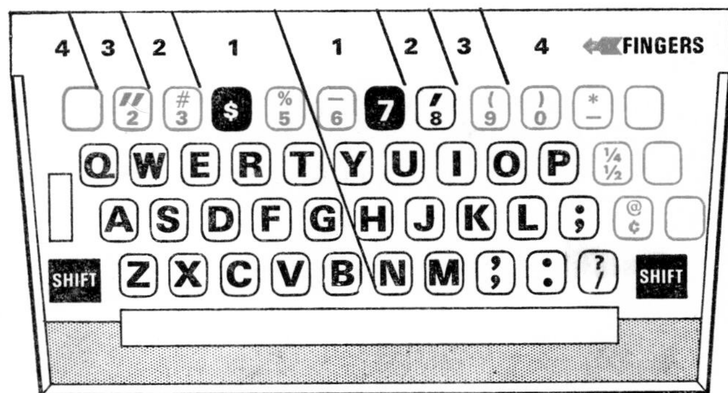

LESSON 23

60-space line | Single spacing

23A: Conditioning Practice (8) *each line three or more times*

Alphabet	Pam was quite excited when Jack Fyle bought the bronze vase.	*Quick return*
Figure-symbol	Mr. O'Neil will be 84 years old on July 14. Isn't he great!	
Easy	Type one key at a time; then go to the next key and type it.	

. . . . 1 . . . . 2 . . . . 3 . . . . 4 . . . . 5 . . . . 6 . . . . 7 . . . . 8 . . . . 9 . . . . 10 . . . . 11 12

23B: Symbol | Figure Location – $ and 7 (7)

REACH TECHNIQUE FOR $

You learned to type **4** with the *left first finger*. Since **$** is the shift of the **4** key, the same finger will move up to type **$**. Depress right shift key, then make a low finger reach to the top row to type **$**.

4f 4f$f 4f$f $f $f 4f$f $f

$14 $148 $1.44 $18.48 $814 DS

REACH TO 7

NOTE: Do not space between **$** and the following figure. Use **.** (period) to type the decimal point.

REACH TECHNIQUE FOR 7

Reach the *right first finger* up to type **7** without moving the other fingers from their home position. Keep the wrists low. Make a direct reach to **7** without swinging the elbow out. Don't let the hand "leap" forward.

u7j 7j 7j 7 j7j 77 j7j 777

Tod will be 17 on July 17. TS

23C: Stroking Technique Practice (10) *each line three times*

All figures and all symbols taught are used.

1 Vance Burke owed $144 on March 14 and paid $44 on August 14.

2 Ned and I have read 77 of the 177 pages assigned for June 7.

3 4f$f $f $f 7j7j 7j 7j 77 47 147 741 $14 $7 $74 $174 $471.77.

4 The 17 boys, 44 girls, and 18 men left for Peru on March 17.

5 Ned's May 7 check should have been for $748 instead of $478!

. . . . 1 . . . . 2 . . . . 3 . . . . 4 . . . . 5 . . . . 6 . . . . 7 . . . . 8 . . . . 9 . . . . 10 . . . . 11 12

23D: Typing from Dictation (7) *twice from dictation; then 1′ writings*

Clear and set tabs

									1′ GWAM
11	77	44	88	14	47	74	84	148	6
87	78	48	47	41	41	71	18	184	11
47	74	47	84	48	41	14	71	178	17
81	18	84	87	78	78	48	47	187	22
14	41	17	71	18	18	81	74	478	27

KEY | 2 | 5 | 2 | 5 | 2 | 5 | 2 | 5 | 2 | 5 | 2 | 5 | 2 | 5 | 2 | 5 | 3 |

Job 7: Filling in Form Letters

Fill in First Reminder letters for the seven customers in Job 3 whose accounts are between 15–30 days overdue. Fill in Second Reminder letters for the five customers whose accounts are between 31–45 days overdue. Address an envelope for each letter. Insert the letters into the envelopes.

Job 8: Typing Invoices (*in duplicate*)

Sold To Central Gift Shop
Central City
CO 80427

Date April 1, 19––
Our No. MA–59274
Cust. Order No. 1328
Shipped Via Continental Express
Salesman Mulligan

Terms 2/15, net 60

Quantity	Cat. No.	Description	Unit Price	Total
5	12D	Genuine Alligator Billfold	18.75	93.75
4	16D	Water Buffalo Pocket Secretary (Black)	3.75	15.00
2	26D	Ladies' Organizer (Blue Cowhide)	3.75	7.50
10	29D	French Purse and Key Case Set (Blue)	7.00	70.00
6	T–351	Men's Semi-Fitted Dressing Case	8.75	52.50
4	G–62	16″ Gusseted Zipper Case	19.50	78.00
2	2412P	Ladies' 25″ Pullman Case (Blue)	24.00	48.00
				364.75

Sold To Academy Appliances, Inc.
3030 N. Chestnut Street
Colorado Springs, CO 80907

Date April 1, 19––
Our No. MA–59286
Cust. Order No. 2740
Shipped Via Mile-High Freight Co.
Salesman Franklin

Terms 2/15, net 60

Quantity	Cat. No.	Description	Unit Price	Total
3	1050X	Men's Speedshaver	14.95	44.85
5	1063X	Ladies' Selectric Shaver	11.68	58.40
2	609DL	Vanitime Battery Clock	7.75	15.50
4	102C	Commodore III Travel Lamp	5.50	22.00
3	100A	Meteor Purse Flashlight	4.00	12.00
2	R770J	Travel Alarm Clock Radio	18.95	37.90
2	TB–1	Cordless Automatic Toothbrush	9.41	18.82
				209.47

23E: Building Control (18) *(Line: 60; DS; ¶ indention: 5)*

1. **Type** a 1′ writing on the *exploration level.* Push for speed.
2. **Type** three 1′ *control-level* writings. Drop back for control.
3. **Type** a 2′ and a 3′ writing at your own control rate. Circle errors. Determine 3′ *gwam* and use as the base rate for 24B, below.
4. **Type** 1′ control writings as time permits.

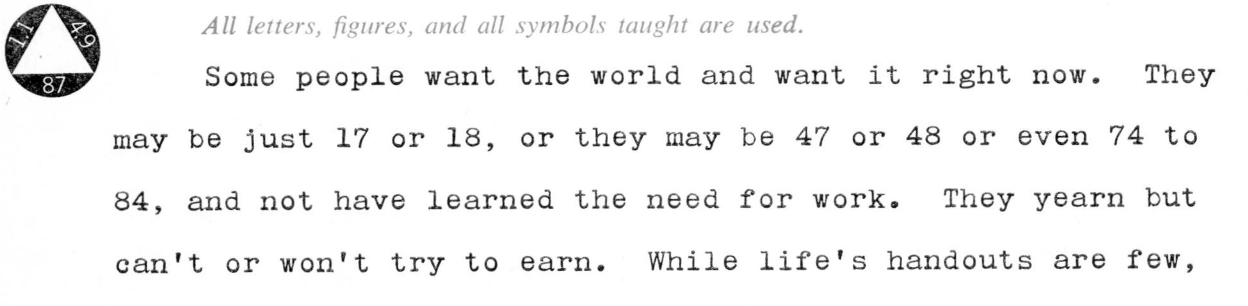

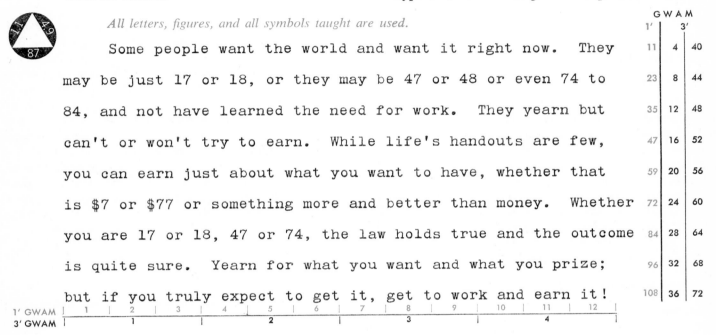

All letters, figures, and all symbols taught are used.

	GWAM 1′	3′	
Some people want the world and want it right now. They	11	4	40
may be just 17 or 18, or they may be 47 or 48 or even 74 to	23	8	44
84, and not have learned the need for work. They yearn but	35	12	48
can't or won't try to earn. While life's handouts are few,	47	16	52
you can earn just about what you want to have, whether that	59	20	56
is $7 or $77 or something more and better than money. Whether	72	24	60
you are 17 or 18, 47 or 74, the law holds true and the outcome	84	28	64
is quite sure. Yearn for what you want and what you prize;	96	32	68
but if you truly expect to get it, get to work and earn it!	108	36	72

1′ GWAM | 1 | 2 | 3 | 4 | 5 | 6 | 7 | 8 | 9 | 10 | 11 | 12 |

3′ GWAM | 1 | 2 | 3 | 4 |

LESSON 24

60-space line | Single spacing

24A: Conditioning Practice (8) *each line three or more times*

Alphabet	My job was to check liquids expressed by Zion's freight van.
Figure-symbol	George Jenkin's weekly pay is $74, but Paul's is $78 to $87.
Easy	Men of ancient times claimed they could foretell the future.

. . . . 1 . . . . 2 . . . . 3 . . . . 4 . . . . 5 . . . . 6 . . . . 7 . . . . 8 . . . . 9 . . . . 10 . . . . 11 12

24B: Building Speed (5) *(Line: 60; Spacing: DS; ¶ indention: 5)*

DO: Set a goal of 4 words more than your 3′ *gwam* for 23E, above.

TYPE: A 3′ writing of 23E, above, on the *exploration level,* at the new goal rate.

Job 4: Duplicating Collection Letters

1. Prepare a model copy of each of the following letters: 5½" x 8½" sheets, 1" letterhead; modified block, indented ¶s, mixed punctuation.
2. Leave room for the date and a 3-line address before the salutation. Type **Gentlemen** and **Past Due:** on the same line; position *Past Due:* so longest dollar amount ends at right margin.
3. Cut stencils and run 10 copies.

First Reminder

Gentlemen Past Due:

(¶ 1) When you opened this letter, it reminded you of a good intention, of something you forgot to do – (¶ 2) It was to send us your check for the amount shown above and now past due. (¶ 3) The statement of your account was probably just overlooked. If, however, there is some other reason for nonpayment, please let us know by jotting a note on the back of this sheet and mailing it in the enclosed envelope. (¶ 4) If your check is already in the mail, please disregard this reminder. Sincerely yours J. Harvey Calton Credit Department

Stronger Reminder

Gentlemen Past Due:

(¶ 1) As of our second billing date, shown on the enclosed itemized statement, your payment of the amount now past due had not been received. Probably your check is already on its way. If you have overlooked mailing it, however, please send it along now. (¶ 2) You have already discovered that Summit Sales offers not only unique gifts but outstanding values as well. Our unusually low prices are possible partly because our customers help us keep billing costs down by prompt payment (within 60 days after the invoice date). (¶ 3) Will you help us by mailing the amount shown above? Please use the return envelope enclosed to send us your payment now. Sincerely yours J. Harvey Calton Credit Department

Job 5: Typing a Discussion Collection Letter

Type the following "form" letter (8½" x 11" letterhead) to any addressee on your list of delinquent accounts whose account is between 46–60 days past due. Insert the dates March 1 and March 15 in the blanks. Date the letter March 31.

Gentlemen Past Due:

(¶ 1) Can you help us out? Will you tell us frankly just what the difficulty is? Seven weeks have now gone by since your account itemized on the enclosed statement became due. To our notices of __________ and __________, calling attention to the evident oversight, we have had no answer. (¶ 2) As you have not written to the contrary, we feel confident that the items you purchased have proved satisfactory, that our records are correct, and that you are indebted for the amount indicated. You know that our association has been mutually cordial. You also know that we want you to enjoy your credit privilege fully. But to make it possible for us to offer such a privilege, we must have equal cooperation, in the form of prompt payment, from our customers. (¶ 3) You have already enjoyed a liberal extension of time. As a matter of fair play and justice to other customers, however, we cannot permit a longer delay in payment than you have had unless you explain the extraordinary circumstances that have caused the current condition of your account. (¶ 4) By all means, maintain your past good credit standing with us. To do so, send your check now––while there is still time. Very truly yours Benjamin J. Eaton Credit Manager

Job 6: Typing an Urgency Collection Letter

Type the following "form" letter to any addressee on your list of delinquent accounts whose account is more than 60 days past due.

Gentlemen Past Due:

(¶ 1) We really tried to prevent this . . . (¶ 2) But since you have not replied to our previous reminders and our appeal for an explanation, we have no choice but to turn your long-overdue account over to our attorney for collection. (¶ 3) If you wish to have your attorney handle this action for you, I suggest that you send us his name and address. Or, if you desire to avoid this unpleasant and costly step by sending us your payment, mail your check directly to me. (¶ 4) It may be difficult for you to make your payments within the terms of our sales agreement; and yet, by allowing us to proceed with legal action, you are obligating yourself to pay not only for your full balance, but for all court costs and attorney fees as well. (¶ 5) Regretfully, unless we receive your check for at least half the past-due amount within the next seven days, we have no choice but to have our attorney take whatever steps are necessary to collect the amount due. Very truly yours Benjamin J. Eaton Credit Manager

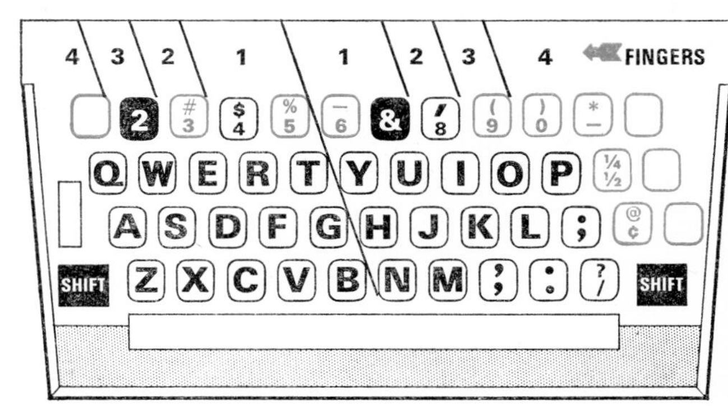

24C: Symbol | Figure Location – & (*ampersand*) and 2 (7)

REACH TECHNIQUE FOR & (*and*)
You typed **7** with the *right first finger.* As **&** is the shift of **7**, type it with the same finger.

7j 7j&j 7j&j &j &j 7j&j &j

Lang & Lee owe Kane & Orr. DS

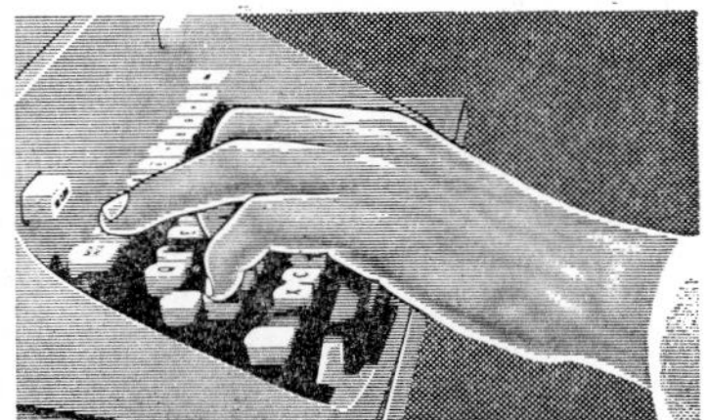

REACH TECHNIQUE FOR 2
Reach the *left third finger* up to type **2** without moving the elbow outward.

w2s 2s 2s 2 s2s 22 s2s 222

Are 22 boys on Flight 222? TS

24D: Stroking Technique Practice (10) *each line three times*

1 Lane & Hall merged with Park & North to form Park & Lane Co.

2 Steven will be 22 years 2 months and 22 days old on July 22.

3 *Reinforcement* 7j&j &j &j 2s2s 2s 2s 22 122 127 721 $2 $2.27 $12.72 7j&j &j

4 Of 22 typists 2 typed 72 words, 8 typed 47, and 12 typed 42.

5 Hall & Quick's note to Zahn & Fox, due March 2, is for $728.

. . . . 1 . . . . 2 . . . . 3 . . . . 4 . . . . 5 . . . . 6 . . . . 7 . . . . 8 . . . . 9 . . . . 10 . . . . 11 12

24E: Typing from Dictation (5) *twice from dictation; then type a 1′ writing if time permits*

Clear and set tab stops

									1′ GWAM
22	77	44	88	12	14	27	28	228	6
72	82	21	24	42	71	74	78	272	11
48	17	84	11	81	87	41	47	282	17
18	87	27	72	28	82	24	42	227	22

KEY | 2 | 5 | 2 | 5 | 2 | 5 | 2 | 5 | 2 | 5 | 2 | 5 | 2 | 5 | 2 | 5 | 3 |

24F: Building Speed – Sentence Guided Writings (15)

TYPE: Each sentence as two 1-minute writings, once guided by the 20″ or 15″ call; and once by the 15″ or 12″ call; then type Sentence 5 as a 1-minute writing without the guide call.

All letters, figures, and all symbols taught are used.

		GWAM 20″	15″	12″
1	Fine clips just $27 at Jung's! Buy now!	24	32	40
2	Didn't the 124 men walk off this job quickly?	27	36	45
3	Lon Zahl shipped 22 cases of peas and 27 of beans.	30	40	50
4	Joe's sale of 284 shares of Lynn & Orr stock was at 72.	33	44	55
5	Mat may lend Rod $27 to pay on his last month's bill of $84.	36	48	60

. . . . 1 . . . . 2 . . . . 3 . . . . 4 . . . . 5 . . . . 6 . . . . 7 . . . . 8 . . . . 9 . . . . 10 . . . . 11 12

Job 2: Typing a Trade-In Schedule

Arrange the table sideways on an 8½″ x 11″ sheet, spaced as indicated.

SUMMIT SALES COMPANY, INC.

March 31, 19--

Center

EQUIPMENT AND FURNITURE TO BE TRADED IN

	Number	*Net Cost*	1957	1959	1961	1963	1965
			Date Purchased				
TYPEWRITERS							
IBM *Selectric*	4050212	*$*419.15				X	
Olympia Standard	1174834	228.00			X		
Underwood Electric	13E8610325	371.00		X			
CALCULATING MACHINES							
Burroughs *Posting Machine*	F6849P	850.00 *	X				
Monroe Adding Machine	36939 *tr*	325.80		X			
SCM Marchant Calculator	606566	842.70				X	
OFFICE FURNITURE							
~~Clerical~~ *Secretarial* Desk	7560 *T*	125.00 *					X
Secretarial Chair	604	45.00		X			
Executive Desk	JC800W	237.50 *	X				
Executive Chair	*J90*	97.50			X		

**Reconditioned*

Job 3: Typing a Table of Delinquent Accounts

Summit Sales receives from a local data processing center a weekly list of overdue accounts, like the one below. Customers whose accounts are overdue between 15–30 days are sent a First Reminder; those whose accounts are overdue between 31–45 days are sent a Stronger Reminder; and those whose accounts are overdue more than 45 days are sent a Discussion or Urgency letter. Type (sideways on an 8½″ x 11″ sheet) a copy of the computer print-out, using the heading DELINQUENT ACCOUNTS and the subheading For the Week Ending March 31. As columnar headings, use: Name; Street Address; City, State, ZIP; Amount Overdue; Days Overdue. Use caps and lower case except for all-cap state abbreviations; DS the table.

A TO Z GIFT SHOP	ONE E. FIRST STREET	RENO, NV 89501	114.50	17
BOULDER INN	ROUTE 287, SOUTH	BOULDER, CO 80302	38.75	26
THE ELECTRIC SHOPPE	5000 CENTRAL AVENUE, S.E.	ALBUQUERQUE, NM 87108	146.25	34
EVANS DRUG CO.	1846 FAIRMOUNT	WICHITA, KS 67208	72.80	48
FOREVER YOURS GIFTS	AMES PLAZA AT 56TH	OMAHA, NB 68104	35.25	29
THE GIFTGIVER, LTD.	11TH AVENUE AT ROSE	REGINA, SASKATCHEWAN	121.50	16
JACKS AND JILLS	301 N. 27TH STREET	BILLINGS, MT 59101	62.45	54
KEEPSAKE GIFTS	P. O. BOX 1155	ENID, OK 73701	112.00	68
KIMBALLS, INC.	1414 AVENUE J	LUBBOCK, TX 79405	29.50	19
LA BOUTIQUE	112 1/2 MAIN STREET	HURON, SD 57350	178.40	72
PUEBLO CURIO SHOP	2100 HIGHWAY 50, E.	PUEBLO, CO 81001	66.75	34
RED ROCKS GIFT SHOP	655 BROADWAY	DENVER, CO 80203	100.00	18
TRIVETS AND TRINKETS	729 SEVENTH STREET	GREELEY, CO 80631	75.95	32
TWIN CITIES ANTIQUES	161 ST. ANTHONY AVENUE	ST. PAUL, MN 55103	78.45	37
UNIQUE GIFT SHOPPE	1600 W. LINCOLNWAY	CHEYENNE, WY 83001	111.00	25
WASHITA VALLEY GIFTS	P. O. BOX 250	VERDEN, OK 73092	72.50	44

LESSON 25

60-space line | Single spacing

25A: Conditioning Practice (8) *each line three or more times*

Alphabet	Must Van Hopkins and Jack Wexler face a big grand jury quiz?	*Eyes on copy*
Figure-symbol	Susan paid Lloyd & Marsh $72 on her June 24 bill of $284.72.	
Easy	Faith, hope, and hard work will help a man to win much more.	
	....1....2....3....4....5....6....7....8....9....10....11....12	

25B: Symbol | Figure Location – " *(quotation)* and 6 (7)

REACH TECHNIQUE FOR " *(quotation)*

Nonelectric. The " is the shift of **2** and is typed with the *left third finger.*

2s 2s"s 2s"s "s "s 2s"s "s

I said, "He can and will."

Electric. The " is the shift of the ' and is typed with the *right little finger.*

'; ';"; ';"; "; "; ';"; ";

I said, "He can and will." DS

NOTE. If the controlling finger is short, move the hand forward just slightly. Curve the other fingers and keep them over their home keys as you *reach* with the first finger.

REACH TECHNIQUE FOR 6

Reach up to **6** with the *right first finger* straightened slightly. Keep the wrist low. Try not to move the hand forward.

Although **6** on some machines may seem nearer the left first finger, use the *right* first finger to type it because the left hand already has a bigger work load than the right.

y6j 6j 6j 6 j6j 66 j6j 666

Read pages 6, 66, and 166. TS

25C: Stroking Technique Practice (10) *each line three times*

1 Ken is mixed on "choose" and "chose" and "loose" and "lose."

2 My 66 pupils had a speed range of 16 to 66 on the last test.

Nonelectric 2s"s "s "s

3 6j6j 6j 61 616 26 46 86 761 Burt said, "Type it!"

Electric ';"; "; ";

4 W. J. Fox drove Mr. Mazur and Mr. Squibb 462 miles on May 6.

5 Mat's check to Parker & Owen, dated July 16, is for $276.48.

....1....2....3....4....5....6....7....8....9....10....11....12

25D: Typing from Dictation (7) *twice from dictation; then type 1' writings*

									1' GWAM
88	22	77	44	66	12	14	16	166	6
26	46	61	62	64	67	68	76	126	11
21	24	27	28	41	42	46	47	466	17
81	84	86	87	82	71	72	74	761	22

KEY | 2 | 5 | 2 | 5 | 2 | 5 | 2 | 5 | 2 | 5 | 2 | 5 | 2 | 5 | 2 | 5 | 3 |

Lessons 265 and 267

Use the following plan for Lessons 265 and 267. Retain all completed Jobs until Lesson 269.

Conditioning Practice (5′): Type 264A, page 382, as directed there.
Statistical Typing (15′): Type two 1′ guided writings on each ¶ of 264B, page 382, then type a 5′ writing on all ¶s. Determine *gwam.*
Applied Typing (30′): Type the Jobs given below and on pages 385–388. Correct all errors.

Lessons 266 and 268

Use the following plan for Lessons 266 and 268. Retain all completed Jobs until Lesson 269.

Conditioning Practice (5′): Type 269A, page 389, as directed there.
Basic Skill Building (15′): Type two 1′ writings on each of the ¶s on page 383, one for speed and one for control; then type a 5′ writing using all the ¶s. Determine *gwam.*
Applied Typing (30′): Continue typing the Jobs.

Applied Typing: Lessons 265–269

In this unit you are to work in the financial division of Summit Sales Company, Inc., a wholesale firm engaged in selling gift items to specialty stores. Your work will consist primarily of preparing collection correspondence and financial reports. Use extreme care in proofreading and correcting your completed work, for errors in financial data can have serious consequences. Use your initials for reference and supply enclosure notations where appropriate.

Job 1: Preparing a Section for the Division Manual

Leftbound manuscript style with 1″ top margin; number the pages 63 and 64

SECTION 10

TRAVEL EXPENSE REPORTS

A travel expense report (Form SS 1984) must be prepared (either handwritten in ink or typewritten) before it can be submitted to the General Accounting Section.

A travel expense report should be prepared immediately upon the completion of each trip. If an employee travels every week, he should submit three reports a month covering the periods through the 10th, the 20th, and the last day of each month. Every blank of the travel expense report should be completed. (See page 65 for a properly completed form.)

All transportation ticket duplicates, receipted hotel bills, approvable restaurant check stubs, and any other pertinent receipts should be stapled to the report. The person who submits the report, as well as the person who authorized the charges to the employee's budget account, must sign the expense report.

Any time unusual circumstances arise or any time a traveling employee has questions, he should call on the General Accounting Section for the information he needs. (It is easier to ask before typing the report than to make corrections later.)

Employees who travel are provided advance funds. These funds are of two types: permanent advances and temporary advances.

A permanent advance is available to any employee whose duties require weekly travel. Such an advance is replenished, upon submission of an approved travel expense report, at the end of each trip. The amount of the advance must be indicated on the expense report to enable the General Accounting Section to determine the correct amount to replenish. If the traveling employee leaves the Company or is transferred to another department or division, he must repay the full amount of the advance.

A temporary advance is available to an employee who has no permanent advance but who is required to travel occasionally and temporarily on Company business. An employee may receive both a permanent and a temporary advance if an imminent trip he is to take requires a larger expenditure than is covered by his permanent advance.

To obtain a temporary advance, an employee must fill out Form SS 1987 as shown on page 66. The employee who requests the advance must complete and sign the form in triplicate; he must then have it approved by a person authorized to approve charges to the employee's budget account, by a representative of the General Accounting Section, and by a representative of the Treasurer's Office.

In the event an employee must reimburse the Company for the unused portion of his travel advance, he should attach a check for the appropriate amount to the expense report and take the report to the Summit Sales cashier. The expense report will be stamped to show that the balance due has been paid. The expense report should then be sent to the General Accounting Section in the usual manner.

25E: Building Control (18) *(Line: 60; Spacing: DS; ¶ indention: 5)*

1. **Type** a 1′ writing on the *exploration level.* Push for speed.
2. **Type** three 1′ writings on the *control level.* Drop back for control.
3. **Type** a 2′ and a 3′ writing at your controlled speed. Circle errors. Determine 3′ *gwam* and use as base rate for 26B, below.
4. **Type** 1′ control writings as time permits.

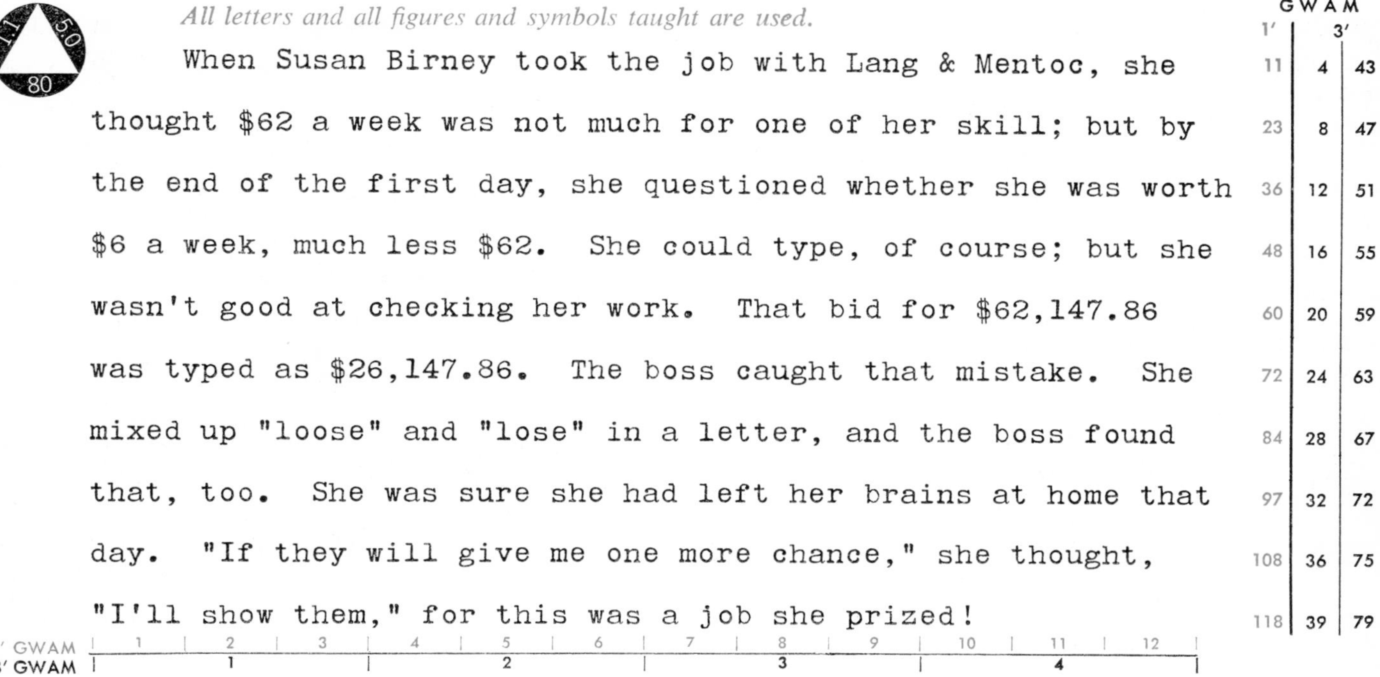

All letters and all figures and symbols taught are used.

	GWAM 1′	3′	
When Susan Birney took the job with Lang & Mentoc, she	11	4	43
thought $62 a week was not much for one of her skill; but by	23	8	47
the end of the first day, she questioned whether she was worth	36	12	51
$6 a week, much less $62. She could type, of course; but she	48	16	55
wasn't good at checking her work. That bid for $62,147.86	60	20	59
was typed as $26,147.86. The boss caught that mistake. She	72	24	63
mixed up "loose" and "lose" in a letter, and the boss found	84	28	67
that, too. She was sure she had left her brains at home that	97	32	72
day. "If they will give me one more chance," she thought,	108	36	75
"I'll show them," for this was a job she prized!	118	39	79

1′ GWAM | 1 | 2 | 3 | 4 | 5 | 6 | 7 | 8 | 9 | 10 | 11 | 12 |
3′ GWAM | 1 | 2 | 3 | 4 |

LESSON 26

60-space line | Single spacing

26A: Conditioning Practice (8) *each line three or more times*

Alphabet Will G. S. and J. B. Maxor plan to leave quickly for Zurich?

Figure-symbol Moore & Lane's Order 612 reads, "26 boxes of K74 at $18 ea."

Easy Think right and type right and gain the prize of good skill.

. . . . 1 . . . . 2 . . . . 3 . . . . 4 . . . . 5 . . . . 6 . . . . 7 . . . . 8 . . . . 9 . . . . 10 . . . . 11 12

26B: Building Sustained Typing Power (10) *(Line: 60; Spacing: DS; ¶ indention: 5)*

TYPE: Two 3′ writings of 25E, above, pausing briefly between writings to relax. Goal: 2 *gwam* more than base rate for 25E, above. Circle errors. Determine *gwam* for the better writing.

264C: Skill Comparison – Straight Copy (20)

DO: Type one 5′ and one 10′ writing on the ¶s. Determine *gwam* for each writing. Compare these rates with the average *gwam* on 264B. **Note:** The 10′ *gwam* = 5′ *gwam* ÷ 2.

	GWAM 1′	5′	
All letters are used.			
 The term "credit" generally refers to one's potential ability to	13	3	92
borrow money or to buy goods on time. It also represents the belief one	28	6	95
individual or firm has in another's intention as well as ability to set-	42	8	97
tle his debts. The consumer often buys on credit simply because he finds	57	11	100
it easier to remit for numerous purchases at one future time than to pay	71	14	103
now for each item separately. Furthermore, the consumer frequently buys	86	17	106
on credit because he does not have money readily available to pay now.	100	20	109
Thus, buying on credit or on the installment plan is a convenience, a	114	23	112
privilege, and a service. In general, consumer credit refers to those	129	26	115
debts that are incurred by the consumer for goods or services to be used	143	29	118
or consumed by himself and his family.	151	30	119
 As we view credit or installment purchases, we often think in terms	14	33	122
of the final consumer. But businesses "buy on time" just as individuals	28	36	125
do. The very nature of the sales of manufacturers and wholesalers to	42	39	128
retailers makes some kind of credit vital. Requiring a retailer to make	57	42	131
his purchases in cash would be most inconvenient. Thus, wholesalers	71	44	133
usually sell on time to retailers who have proved worthy of an extension	85	47	136
of credit. The granting of credit by a wholesaler permits a retailer to	100	50	139
buy goods and to sell at least part of them before he is expected to pay	114	53	142
the wholesaler. Usually the retailer is extended credit for thirty or	129	56	145
sixty days before payment is demanded.	136	57	146
 Credit has a number of advantages to a seller as well as to a buyer,	14	60	149
but it adds considerably to the cost of sales and, as a consequence, to	28	63	152
the price a consumer pays for the goods or services that he buys. A	42	66	155
principal added cost is a result of the clerical work required in record-	57	69	158
ing the sales and collecting overdue amounts and of the interest on the	71	72	161
funds that are invested or have been borrowed in order to extend credit.	86	75	164
Still other costs result from occasional losses due to bad debts and a	100	77	166
tendency of credit buyers to return goods for exchange or refund. To	114	80	169
avoid such losses, firms, regardless of size, must extend credit wisely	128	83	172
and follow tested credit policies and procedures. A businessman must	142	86	175
employ consistent and persistent procedures also for collecting overdue	157	89	178
amounts.	158	89	178

1′ GWAM | 1 | 2 | 3 | 4 | 5 | 6 | 7 | 8 | 9 | 10 | 11 | 12 | 13 | 14 |
5′ GWAM | 1 | 2 | 3 |

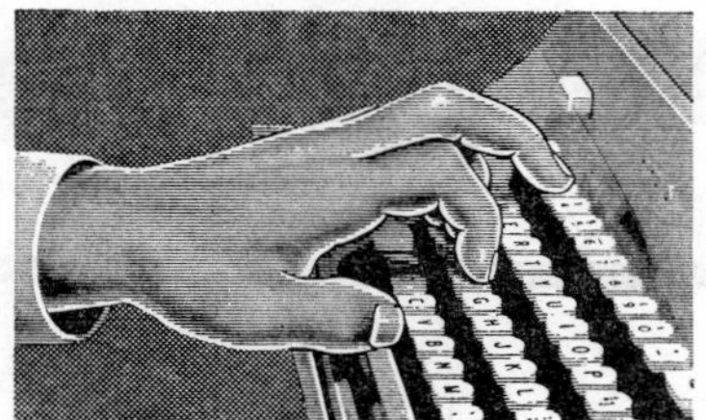
REACH TO 3

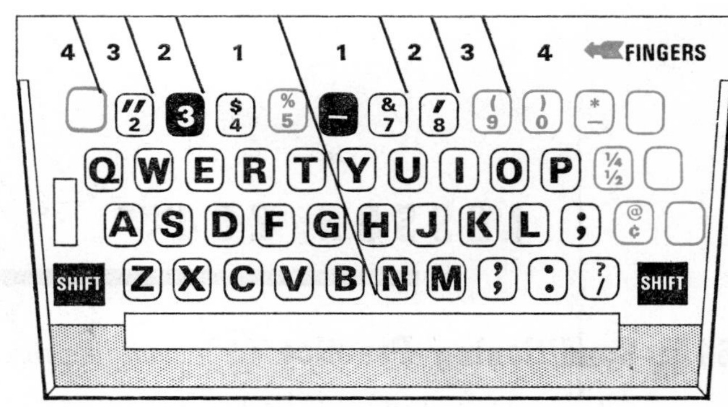

26C: Symbol | Figure Location _ (*underline*) and 3 (7)

REACH TECHNIQUE FOR _ (*underline*)
Nonelectric. Type _ (the shift of **6**) with the *right first finger*. Hold the wrist low; *reach* with the finger.

Electric. Type _ (the shift of the end key in the top row) with the *right fourth finger*. **Note.** To type a line, hold underline key down for length line desired.

REACH TECHNIQUE FOR 3
Reach up to **3** with the *left second finger* without arching the wrist or changing the hand position.

e3d 3d 3d 3 d3d 33 d3d 333

6j 6j_j 6j_j _j _j 6j_j _j DS p_; p_; _; _; p_; _; _; _; DS The 33 men sent 333 cards. TS

26D: Stroking Technique Practice (10) *each line three times*

To Underline: Backspace (or move the carriage by hand) to the first letter of the word. Type the underline once for each letter in the word.

To Underline Several Words: Depress the shift lock **29** and type an unbroken line. To release the shift lock, depress the shift key.

All letters and all figures taught are used.

1 Use a quick stroke. Hold your eyes on the copy as you type.

2 Just 33 of the 333 boys had read pages 33 to 333 by March 3.

Nonelectric 6j_j _j _j
3 3d3d 3d 3d 33 36 73 83 43 23 $3 $3.18 Don't rush!
Electric _;_; _; _;

4 If you think before you act, you won't be sorry how you act.

5 Fritz Maxwell may have missed Questions 33, 36, 63, and 134.

. . . . 1 . . . . 2 . . . . 3 . . . . 4 . . . . 5 . . . . 6 . . . . 7 . . . . 8 . . . . 9 . . . . 10 . . . . 11 12

26E: Building Speed – Sentence Guided Writings (15)

TYPE: Each sentence as two 1-minute writings, once guided by the 20″ or 15″ call and once by the 15″ or 12″ call; then type Sentence 5 as a 1-minute writing without the guide call.

All letters and all figures and symbols taught are used.

		GWAM 20″	15″	12″
1	The words "I can" will bring good power.	27	36	45
2	If "right makes might," they have real might.	27	36	45
3	Let's help all the men when we can and all we can!	30	40	50
4	Flight 146 from Quito to Brazil has 78 people on board.	33	44	55
5	The 33 boys earned $333 on June 23 working for Kean & Nixon.	36	48	60

. . . . 1 . . . . 2 . . . . 3 . . . . 4 . . . . 5 . . . . 6 . . . . 7 . . . . 8 . . . . 9 . . . . 10 . . . . 11 12

Unit 46 | Lessons 264-269

Typing in a Finanical Division

LESSON 264

264A: Conditioning Practice (5) *each line three times; then 1′ writings on Line 4*

Alphabet	Alex Jackson quickly taped a zesty show for a big festival next month.	*Begin slowly, speed up gradually*
Figure	T1040 No. 5359 C506 142M1539 RS4520 67C1014 1051X2679 M501 12-154W3150	
Figure-symbol	7½# @ $1.50, 4-slice, AC/DC, 60-cycle, 110—120 volts, ½-mile beam, $20	
Fluency	The man who buys on the installment plan pays a fee for the privilege.	

| 1 | 2 | 3 | 4 | 5 | 6 | 7 | 8 | 9 | 10 | 11 | 12 | 13 | 14 |

264B: Skill Comparison – Statistical Copy (25)

1. Type four 1′ guided writings on each ¶: two for speed, two for control.
2. Type two 5′ writings using both ¶s. Determine average *gwam*.

All letters and all figures are used.

GWAM 5′

1.6 5.8 70

Some firms sell on a cash basis alone; other firms sell "on account" 3 50
or "on credit" as well. Consumer credit offers a vital lift to an econ- 6 53
omy. For example, installment credit in 1965 amounted to $68,565,000,000, 9 56
a mammoth increase of $38,659,000,000 (137.17%) in the 10-year span since 12 59
1955. In 1965 noninstallment credit (single-payment loans, charge ac- 14 61
counts, and service credit) amounted to $19,319,000,000, a fast jump of 17 64
$9,395,000,000 (94.67%) since 1955. Such a pace is amazing in view of 20 67
the terrific expense of making credit purchases. 22 69

1.6 5.8 70

Some firms set commodity prices sufficiently high to stand the cost 25 72
of maintaining charge customers' accounts; other firms use one price for 28 75
cash purchases, another for purchases on account. Let's assume that a 31 77
TV set is marked at $159.95 cash or $164.95 if charged, payable in 30 33 80
days. The actual cost of charging the TV to a customer's account is 36 83
$5.00. In truth he is paying $5.00 to use $159.95 for 30 days, a fee 39 86
equivalent to a yearly interest rate of 37½%! Likewise, carrying charges 42 89
on installment purchases are typically in the neighborhood of 16% a year, 45 92
even though the nominal percent is quoted as only 6%. 47 94

5′ GWAM | 1 | 2 | 3 |

LESSON 27

60-space line | Single spacing

27A: Conditioning Practice (8) *each line three or more times*

Alphabet Did Max give J. B. Lowe's check to Fran Quinby as the prize?

Figure-symbol Pam's Check 361 to Howe & Neff for $738.46 is dated July 23.

Easy If you don't know the right way to loaf, don't try to do it!

. . . . 1 . . . . 2 . . . . 3 . . . . 4 . . . . 5 . . . . 6 . . . . 7 . . . . 8 . . . . 9 . . . . 10 . . . . 11 12

27B: Symbol | Figure Location – # *(No., lbs.)* and 9 (7)

REACH TECHNIQUE FOR #

You learned to type **3** with the *left second finger*. As # is the shift of **3**, move the same finger up to type it.

3d 3d#d 3d#d #d #d 3d#d #d

Ship order #6131 for 174#. DS

REACH TO 9

REACH TECHNIQUE FOR 9

Reach the *right third finger* up to type **9** without swinging the elbow out. Keep the wrist low. *Reach.*

o91 91 91 9 191 99 191 999

Study pages 9, 19, and 99. TS

NOTE. Before a figure, # is the symbol for *No.*; after a figure, it is the symbol for *pounds*. See Line 2, above.

27C: Stroking Technique Practice (10) *each line three or more times*

All letters and all figures taught are used.

1 We shipped Order #634 on August 7; Order #637, on August 28.

2 Our building lease for 99 years will be up on June 19, 1999.

3 3d#d #d #9 9191 91 91 99 29 39 49 169 179 #89 #987 #469 #298

Reinforcement (lines 2–3)

4 Order #931 from Zenith & Weaver is for 196# of #9X Compound.

5 Type with a <u>quick</u> stroke, and hold the <u>hands and arms quiet</u>.

. . . . 1 . . . . 2 . . . . 3 . . . . 4 . . . . 5 . . . . 6 . . . . 7 . . . . 8 . . . . 9 . . . . 10 . . . . 11 12

27D: Typing from Dictation (5) *twice from dictation*

33 99 22 66 44 77 88 #12 #34 #46 #67 #78 #29 #39 #49 #69 #96

The check is #193. Ship Order #491. Pay Bills #29 and #89.

Lee's <u>fare</u> was $29. His <u>room</u> was $14. He spent $69 <u>in all</u>.

GWAM 1' 5' 10'

A partnership may be defined as "an association of two or more per- 13 41 21
sons to carry on as co-owners a business for profit." Such a relation- 28 44 22
ship is based on an agreement, in writing or oral, that is legal as well 42 47 23
as voluntary. Even though a typical partnership is bigger than compar- 56 50 25
able single-owner firms, most are quite small. The vast majority of 70 53 26
partnerships in the nation consist of two owners who share both the 84 55 28
responsibility and the profit as a prearranged plan directs. The 97 58 29
average number of owners for this type of business structure is almost 111 61 30
exactly two and a half. 116 62 31

The dominant type of business ownership in this country is the cor- 13 64 32
poration. Nearly all definitions of the word emphasize the point that 28 67 34
a corporation is a legal entity; that is, it is an artificial being with 42 70 35
the rights, duties, and powers of a person. The definition includes, 56 73 36
furthermore, the concept of many people united into one body that does 70 76 38
not change its identity with each change in owners, and one that could 85 79 39
have perpetual life. The number of owners of a corporate firm is seldom 99 82 41
fewer than three and is generally many more, frequently as high as sev- 113 84 42
eral hundred and often in excess of a thousand people. 124 87 43

The name of a firm does not in itself reflect the type of ownership. 14 89 45
Likewise, the type of activity engaged in does not often reveal the form 29 92 46
of structure. Typical of the sole owner form, however, are the small- 43 95 48
town cafe, the corner grocery, and the local bakery. The partnership 57 98 49
form is in common use by law and accounting firms, by local insurance 71 101 50
agencies, and by stock and real estate brokers. The corporate form is 85 103 52
usually chosen for big business ventures, but many corporations are as 99 106 53
small as or even smaller than the average single-owner or partnership 113 109 55
operation. 115 110 55

American business is carried on by firms that range in size from 13 112 56
the small concern in which a single person runs his own shop, such as a 27 115 57
shoe repair shop; through the medium-sized firm, such as a grocery whole- 42 118 59
saler or a paper box producer; to the industrial giant such as an auto- 56 121 60
mobile manufacturer or a food products processor whose sales volume may 71 124 62
amount to millions of dollars annually and who may employ thousands of 85 126 63
workers. Over ninety businesses out of a hundred in this nation can be 99 129 65
classified as small according to Congressional definition. 111 132 66

An individual who aspires to enter the business scene as either an 13 134 67
employee or an owner should be familiar with company structure. His 27 137 69
knowledge will help him to assume his rightful place in the business 41 140 70
world and to improve his position. 48 141 71

1' GWAM | 1 | 2 | 3 | 4 | 5 | 6 | 7 | 8 | 9 | 10 | 11 | 12 | 13 | 14 |
5' GWAM | 1 | 2 | 3 |
10' GWAM | 1 | 2 |

27E: Guided Writings (20) *(Line: 60; Spacing: DS; ¶ indention: 5)*

1. **Type** each of the following ¶s as a 1′ writing on the *exploration level* without the call of the guide.
2. **Set** a goal of 4 *gwam* more than you typed in Step 1. Note the checkpoints in each ¶ for the quarter-minute call.
3. **Type** each ¶ as two 1′ writings on the *exploration level*, guided by the call.
4. **Type** each ¶ as a 2′ writing on the *control level* without the guide call.
5. **Type** 3′ writings without the guide. Circle errors; determine *gwam* for best writing.

All letters and all figures taught are used.

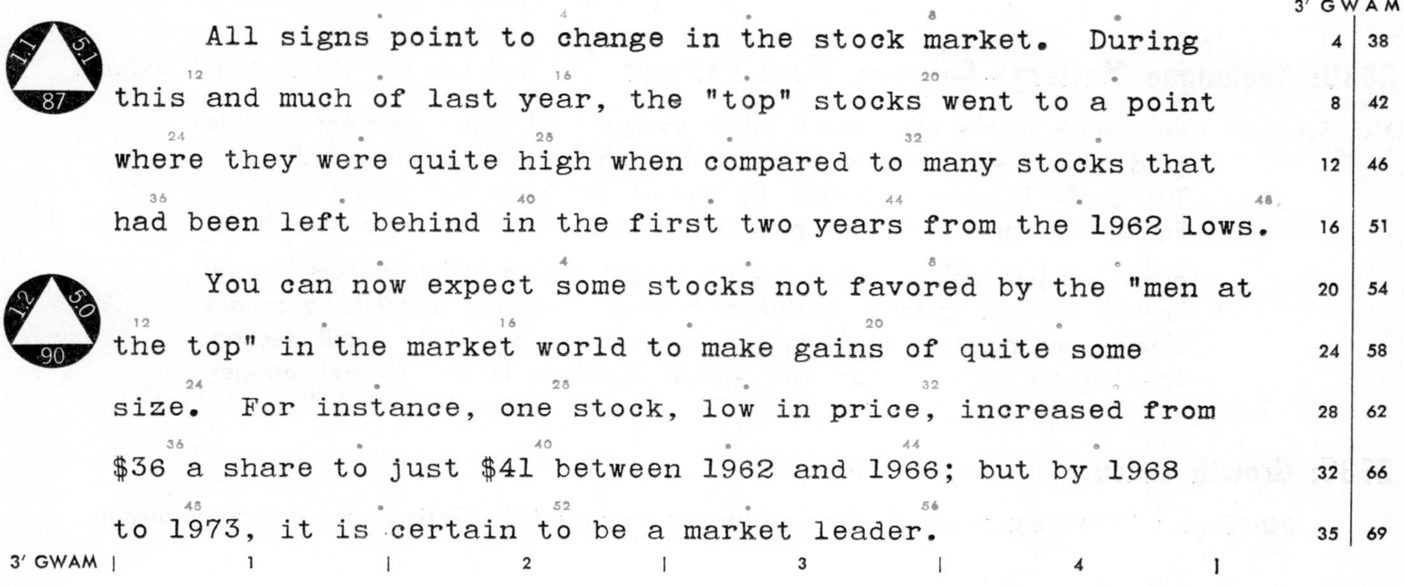

1.1 5.1 87

	3′ GWAM	
All signs point to change in the stock market. During	4	38
this and much of last year, the "top" stocks went to a point	8	42
where they were quite high when compared to many stocks that	12	46
had been left behind in the first two years from the 1962 lows.	16	51

1.2 5.0 90

	3′ GWAM	
You can now expect some stocks not favored by the "men at	20	54
the top" in the market world to make gains of quite some	24	58
size. For instance, one stock, low in price, increased from	28	62
$36 a share to just $41 between 1962 and 1966; but by 1968	32	66
to 1973, it is certain to be a market leader.	35	69

3′ GWAM | 1 | 2 | 3 | 4 |

LESSON 28

60-space line | Single spacing

28A: Conditioning Practice (8) *each line three or more times*

Alphabet Max Pavwor made quick jet flights to Zagreb on May 9 and 26.

Figure-symbol Kirk's order of April 29 to Long & Howe is for 436# of Q781.

Easy The good workman does his work better than just well enough.

. . . . 1 . . . . 2 . . . . 3 . . . . 4 . . . . 5 . . . . 6 . . . . 7 . . . . 8 . . . . 9 . . . . 10 . . . . 11 12

28B: Building Control (5) *(Line: 60; Spacing: DS; ¶ indention: 5)*

TYPE: A 3′ *control-level* writing on 27E, above. Circle the errors, but ignore your *gwam*. If time permits, retype the words in which errors occurred.

LESSON 263

263A: Conditioning Practice (5) *each line three times*

Alphabet	When Mr. Dexter buzzed for Jane, she gave a sigh and quickly reported.	Work for continuity in figure-symbol control
Figure	2956 48102 817 55103 2900 68124 2400 44702 1002 46828 3942 54307 60405	
Figure-symbol	G10, less 20%; K03 $.92 net; S90, $8.00; M728, $1.56; H169, $4.40 net.	
Fluency	If the city auditor addresses the chairman, I must be ready to report.	
	| 1 | 2 | 3 | 4 | 5 | 6 | 7 | 8 | 9 | 10 | 11 | 12 | 13 | 14 |	

263B: Technique Mastery – Common Word Patterns (10) *each line four times; then 1′ writings*

Near-balanced-hand words

that which thanks other thank might change total either payment provide
glad what claims profits perhaps through entitled original individual
The profit is always payable by special check during quality displays.
Furnish the gentlemen two price plans today for the future sale items.

Near-one-hand words

order number policy reason season longer station point pleases several
limited ordered greatly mortgage however increase certainly vacations
Please pay postage on certain units listed in my daily retail section.
The interest grows larger with annual increases in the federal budget.

| 1 | 2 | 3 | 4 | 5 | 6 | 7 | 8 | 9 | 10 | 11 | 12 | 13 | 14 |

263C: Growth Index (15) *one 10′ writing*

DO: Type a 10′ writing on the ¶s given below and on page 381. Circle errors; determine *nwam*.

263D: Applied Typing (20)

DO: Continue typing the jobs on which you have been working.

All letters are used.

	GWAM 1′	5′	10′
The ownership of a company usually assumes one of three basic	12	2	1
forms. These include the corporate form and two types that are not in-	27	5	3
corporated, the sole proprietorship and the partnership. When a company	41	8	4
is to be formed, the future owners or owner must decide which type of	55	11	6
structure best suits the purposes of the planned venture. A great many	70	14	7
factors may enter into the decision, and the eventual success or failure	84	17	8
of the firm may hinge upon the form of business ownership he chooses.	98	20	10
A sole proprietorship is a business owned by just one person and	13	22	11
operated for his gain. The owner, aided by only a few workers, con-	27	25	12
ducts a small business that, as a rule, caters to the consuming public.	41	28	14
The capital needed for running the firm is normally supplied by the	55	31	15
single owner from his own wealth, but is often augmented by borrowed	69	33	17
funds. The responsibility for all decisions is his, and he usually makes	83	36	18
them himself rather than delegate them to his employees. *(Continued)*	95	39	19

1′ GWAM | 1 | 2 | 3 | 4 | 5 | 6 | 7 | 8 | 9 | 10 | 11 | 12 | 13 | 14 |
5′ GWAM | 1 | 2 | 3 |
10′ GWAM | 1 | 2 |

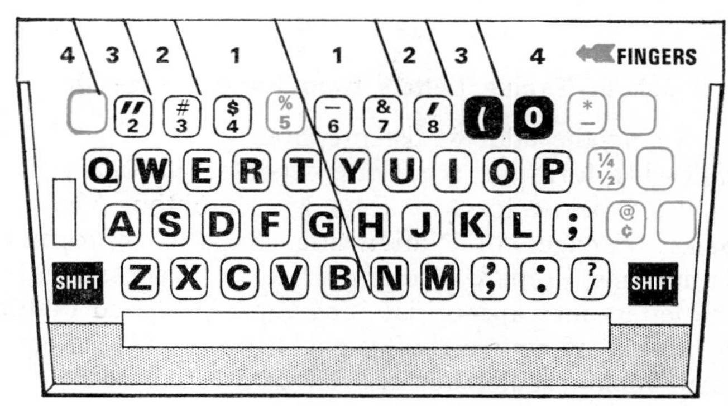

28C: Symbol | Figure Location – (*(left parenthesis)* and 0 (7)

REACH TECHNIQUE FOR (

You typed **9** with the *right third finger.* Since **(** is the shift of **9**, use the same finger to type it.

91 91(l 91(l (l (l 91(l (l

The (is part of a symbol. DS

REACH TO O

REACH TECHNIQUE FOR O

Reach the *right little finger* up to type **0** without moving the hand or swinging the elbow out.

p0; 0; 0; 0 ;0; 00 ;0; 000

Add 3, 30, 40, 60, and 70. TS

28D: Stroking Technique Practice (10) *each line three or more times*

All letters and all figures taught are used.

1 As (is the shift of 9, use the same finger to type (and 9.

2 Maxie will be 20 years 10 months and 20 days old on July 30.

3 91(l (l (l 3d#d #d #d 0;0; 0; 10 20 30 40 ;0 60 70 80 90 100

4 Monty Vaughn made a quick trip to Zurich on August 20, 1966.

5 My 12 men got $20 a day <u>each</u> for 10 days, a total of $2,400.

. . . . 1 . . . . 2 . . . . 3 . . . . 4 . . . . 5 . . . . 6 . . . . 7 . . . . 8 . . . . 9 . . . . 10 . . . . 11 12

28E: Typing from Dictation (5) *once from dictation*

10 20 30 40 60 70 80 90 100 200 300 400 600 700 800 900 1000

#d $f &j (l #20 $30 Hal owed $900. He paid $400 on July 20.

Ship Order #1690. Is Ned's bill $180? Pay Orr & Mead $200.

28F: Building Speed – Sentence Guided Writings (15)

TYPE: Each sentence for a 1′ writing, guided by the 20″, 15″, or 12″ call as your teacher directs; then type each sentence four times without the guide.

All letters and all figures and symbols taught are used.

		GWAM 20″	15″	12″
1	Jane's speed is 70; Bob's, 69; and Ken's, 64.	27	36	45
2	Rex cashed Zahl & Quincy's Check #890 for $173.62.	30	40	50
3	Is the (the shift of 9, and must you <u>shift to type it</u>?	43	57	71
4	"Well enough" is never good enough for "the man at the top."	36	48	60
5	Get on the track and keep going if you want to go somewhere!	36	48	60

. . . . 1 . . . . 2 . . . . 3 . . . . 4 . . . . 5 . . . . 6 . . . . 7 . . . . 8 . . . . 9 . . . . 10 . . . . 11 12

Job 8: Typing Letters from Form Paragraphs

Using the address list prepared as Job 2 and the following form ¶s, type letters (dated February 19) as listed below for Mr. John M. Hampton, Midwest Sales Manager of Nationwide. Supply appropriate salutations. Prepare 1 cc of each letter. Fold and insert the letters into appropriate envelopes prepared in Job 3, unless, of course, bulky enclosures (such as catalogs) make regular business envelopes unusable.

Letter 1: Address 2, ¶s 1–2, 2–2, 2–3, 4–2
Letter 2: Address 5, ¶s 1–3, 2–1, 2–3, 4–1
Letter 3: Address 3, ¶s 1–1, 2–2, 3–2, 4–1
Letter 4: Address 9, ¶s 1–3, 2–1, 2–2, 2–3, 2–4, 3–2, 4–1
Letter 5: Address 4, ¶s 1–2, 2–2, 2–3, 4–2
Letter 6: Address 8, ¶s 1–1, 2–1, 2–4, 4–1
Letter 7: Address 1, ¶s 1–3, 2–5, 2–6, 3–1, 4–1
Letter 8: Address 10, ¶s 1–3, 2–4, 2–6, 3–1, 4–2

1–1. Thank you for your recent letter. We are sending today in a separate mailing the material you requested so that you may examine it for possible adoption in your classes.

1–2. Thank you for your recent request for examination copies of our publications. A complimentary copy of each item you asked for is enclosed. Please examine these materials carefully and consider stocking them in your store.

1–3. Thank you for your recent request for examination copies of some of our teaching materials. We are sending today for the consideration of your teachers the items you requested. Enclosed with each book is a brochure describing in detail the special features of that publication.

2–1. OFFICE EMPLOYEES REFERENCE MANUAL by Koch and Kendall is a helpful guidebook that every business student should have. It is an excellent supplement for typewriting, shorthand, and office practice classes. It provides ready reference material that will be valuable for all office employees. It is a book that will be just as helpful on the job as while the student is in school.

2–2. LETTERHEADS AND BUSINESS FORMS may be used in typewriting, office practice, and transcription classes. The stationery and forms in this pad are bound at the bottom so that smooth edges are available at the top and at the left for easy insertion into the typewriter. Twelve different two-color letterheads and four different business forms are included, and each appears five times. Thus, there are 80 sheets in all.

2–3. WORD DIVISION GUIDE by Goldsmith is a useful supplement for typewriting, shorthand, office practice, English, and spelling classes. The basic word list is a handy reference for the correct spelling and acceptable division of the words commonly used in business communication (over 12,000 of them).

2–4. CLERICAL AND CIVIL SERVICE TRAINING by Gibson and Nicholas is a combination textbook-workbook. It is recommended as a review of the basic skills that are necessary for positions in business and government offices: grammar, punctuation, capitalization, spelling, arithmetic, and business procedure. The materials include a pretest, study and practice activities, periodic achievement tests, and a final examination.

2–5. APPLIED AUTOMATION by Kohler is designed to give the student an understanding of the basic automated data processing methods and procedures that should be understood by every prospective office worker. The textbook and practice set may be completed in five or six weeks. They are designed for use in any class in which typewriters are available. The practice set provides the student with realistic projects using some of the tools of automation such as punched cards, mark-sensed cards, checks, deposit tickets printed in magnetic ink, and work-flow diagrams.

2–6. SORTER AND TABULATOR TRAINING by Kells, consisting of a textbook, 48 control panel diagrams, and 50 blank cards, is designed to teach the operation of an IBM 82 sorter and an IBM 402 accounting machine.

3–1. For many of our publications we provide time-saving teaching aids. Those that correlate with the books you adopt for classroom use will be sent to you upon request.

3–2. Our latest catalog is enclosed for your convenience in ordering. The prices quoted are subject to our usual educational discount.

4–1. Thank you for this opportunity to be of service. We shall be most pleased to fill your order. You may be sure that we shall do whatever we can to merit your continued use of our materials.

4–2. Thank you for giving us this opportunity to submit these materials for your consideration. We shall be pleased to fill your order.

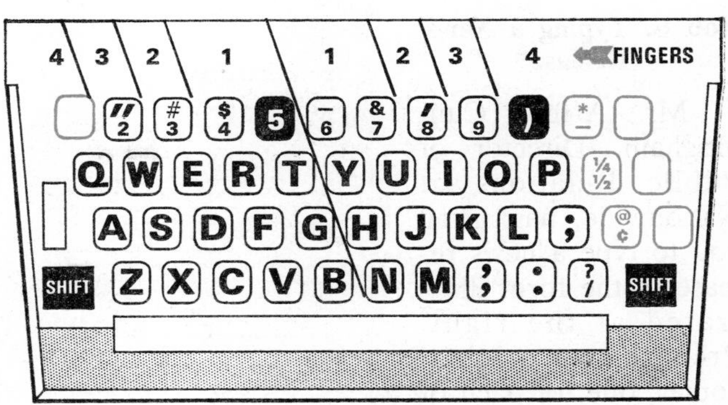

LESSON 29

60-space line | Single spacing

29A: Conditioning Practice (8) *each line three or more times*

Alphabet Dot Quayle will have Chuck Geizler fix Jen's big map for us.

Figure-symbol Can Paul type 9 and (with ease? Isn't Check #230 for $478?

Easy Claud Clayborn showed us the lovely old house he had bought.

....1....2....3....4....5....6....7....8....9....10....11....12

29B: Symbol | Figure Location –) (*right parenthesis*) and 5 (7)

REACH TECHNIQUE FOR)

The **)** is the shift of **0**, and both are typed with the *right little finger*. Hold the elbow in position—reach to **0** and **)**.

0; 0;); 0;););); 0;););

The ")" is the shift of 0. DS

REACH TO 5

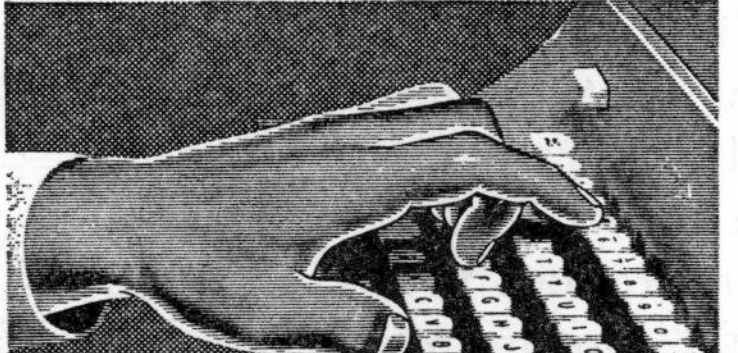

REACH TECHNIQUE FOR 5

Type **5** with the *left first finger* without moving the other fingers from their home keys or moving the hand forward. Low wrist.

t5f 5f 5f 5 f5f 55 f5f 555

Are 55 boys on Flight 155? TS

29C: Stroking Technique Practice (10) *each line three or more times*

All letters and all figures taught are used.

1 As) is the shift of 0, use the <u>same finger</u> to type 0 and).

2 Was Judge Young's talk to 15 men, 55 women, and 55 children?

Nonelectric 8k'k 8k 2s"s "s "

3 0;););); 3d#d #d 7j&j &j 4f$f $f 91(l (l

Electric ';'; '; ';"; "; "

4 Type 0 and) with the same finger (<u>the right fourth finger</u>).

5 B. J. Weaver sent Check #850 for $675.25 to Zelox & Squires.

....1....2....3....4....5....6....7....8....9....10....11....12

29D: Typing from Dictation (5) *once from dictation*

All figures taught are used.

12 13 14 15 16 17 18 19 20 21 22 23 24 25 26 27 28 29 30 500

Hall & Mill owe us $625. They can't pay <u>now</u>. Shall we sue?

He said, "Type it right!" Check #590 is for $150. Send it.

Job 6: Typing a News Release

Mr. Arthur Cunningham, Director of Public Relations at Nationwide, has asked you to type a news release in the form illustrated at the right. Prepare two original copies, one for each of two newspapers. Center and type *(more)* at the bottom of page 1; center and type 2 an inch from the top of page 2; center # to indicate end of release on page 2.

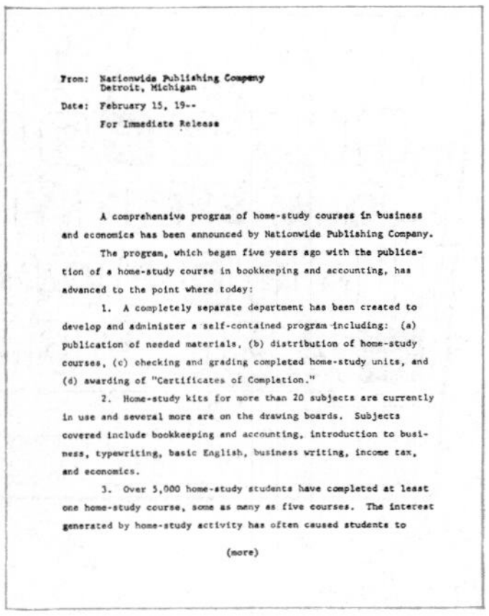
From: Nationwide Publishing Company
Detroit, Michigan

Date: February 15, 19--

For Immediate Release

A comprehensive program of home-study courses in business and economics has been announced by Nationwide Publishing Company.

The program, which began five years ago with the publication of a home-study course in bookkeeping and accounting, has advanced to the point where today:

1. A completely separate department has been created to develop and administer a self-contained program including: (a) publication of needed materials, (b) distribution of home-study courses, (c) checking and grading completed home-study units, and (d) awarding of "Certificates of Completion."

2. Home-study kits for more than 20 subjects are currently in use and several more are on the drawing boards. Subjects covered include bookkeeping and accounting, introduction to business, typewriting, basic English, business writing, income tax, and economics.

3. Over 5,000 home-study students have completed at least one home-study course, some as many as five courses. The interest generated by home-study activity has often caused students to

(more)

From: Nationwide Publishing Company *SS*
Detroit, Michigan *DS*
Date: February 15, 19— *DS*
For Immediate Release
1½"

(¶ 1) A comprehensive program of home-study courses in business and economics has been announced by Nationwide Publishing Company. (¶ 2) The program, which began five years ago with the publication of a home-study course in bookkeeping and accounting, has advanced to the point where today: (¶ 3) 1. A completely separate department has been created to develop and administer a self-contained program including: (a) publication of needed materials, (b) distribution of home-study courses, (c) checking and grading completed home-study units, and (d) awarding of "Certificates of Completion." (¶ 4) 2. Home-study kits for more than 20 subjects are currently in use and several more are on the drawing boards. Subjects covered include bookkeeping and accounting, introduction to business, typewriting, basic English, business writing, income tax, and economics. (¶ 5) 3. Over 5,000 home-study students have completed at least one home-study course, some as many as five courses. The interest generated by home-study activity has often caused students to enroll later in advanced teacher-directed classes offered by vocational-technical schools, private business schools, and junior colleges. (¶ 6) 4. A sizable percentage of the students who complete one or more home-study courses use their new knowledge or skill to obtain gainful employment or to upgrade themselves in the companies in which they have been working. (¶ 7) 5. Students from 15 states are "enrolled" in Nationwide's home-study program. The addition of more student-contact offices promises to enlarge the area served by this study-at-home plan.

Job 7: Typing a Form Letter with Changes

Type the following form letter (modified block, open) to addressees 1, 3, 6, 7, and 8 of the address list you prepared in Job 2. In ¶ 1, supply the correct representative's name as indicated below. Prepare a carbon copy of each letter. Fold and insert the letters into appropriate large business envelopes from those prepared in Job 3. Nationwide typists show the appropriate number after *Enclosures.*

Letter 1: Mr. Jacobs
Letter 2: Mr. Allen
Letter 3: Mr. Higgins
Letter 4: Mr. Marshall
Letter 5: Mr. Arnold

February 17, 19— *(Supply address and appropriate salutation)* (¶ 1) Improvement of communication skills is one of the most crucial needs of our time. Our part in the improvement program is to provide materials that will help you to develop students' speaking and writing skills for application in business and related situations. Your local Nationwide representative, Mr. __________, has suggested that you be asked to help us reach some major decisions regarding the revision of English for Business, Fifth Edition, by Dr. Millard J. Dunning and Dr. Nelda B. Morris. (¶ 2) To make it easy for you to give us your viewpoint and recommendations on several strategic issues, we have prepared the enclosed questionnaire. The questionnaire requires only that you check appropriate reactions or suggestions. Room is provided, however, for you to make amplifying or explanatory comments about each item. In addition, we invite you to include on a separate sheet of paper any other items about which you have suggestions for improving the book. (¶ 3) About fifty of the top teachers in the country are being asked to help us plan the new Sixth Edition. Your ideas, along with those of others in this group, will be carefully considered by a review board consisting of the authors, the editors, and selected members of our consulting team. The result will undoubtedly be a substantial improvement in an already effective teaching-learning instrument. (¶ 4) Please use the enclosed postage-free reply envelope to send us your completed questionnaire. We hope to receive it by March 17. Your cooperation will be appreciated by us and will be of great value to your future students. Sincerely yours Market Research Section *(No initials)*

29E: Building Control – Guided Writings (20) *(Line: 60; Spacing: DS; ¶ indention: 5)*

The letter E (denoting easy copy) is purposely not shown in the difficulty indicators of the following paragraphs. The number of shifted characters and figures, as well as the number of words outside the high-frequency group, makes the copy more difficult than it appears. Other instances in which an overall difficulty index is not given are rough draft, script, and statistical copy. Such copy is "designed" to increase your ability to handle not-so-easy stroking combinations.

1. **Type** a 1′ *control-level* writing of each ¶ without the guide. Determine average *gwam.*
2. **Set** a goal of 4 words *fewer*. Note the check points in each ¶ for the quarter-minute call.
3. **Type** each ¶ as two 1′ *control-level* writings guided by the quarter-minute call.
4. **Type** each ¶ as a 2′ *control-level* writing without the guide call.
5. **Type** 3′ writings without the guide. Circle errors. Determine *gwam* for best writing.

	3′ GWAM	
(1.2 / 4.8 / 81) Do not be ashamed of having brains, but do be ashamed if	4	44
you do not use them to the fullest. Not many of us overtax	8	48
our mind by asking too much of ourselves. In this sense it	12	52
is not true that "all men are born equal"; and the longer they	16	56
live and learn, the less so they become!	19	59
(1.2 / 4.8 / 82) When Leroy was 15 or 16, he could have been a "brain," I	22	62
know, had he not been lazy. He got by, but that is about all.	27	67
When he applies for a job now, he alibis that he was not "dumb"	31	71
but didn't want to be "too brainy." He is in night school now	35	75
and not ashamed that he has brains, only that he hasn't used	39	79
them fully.	40	80

3′ GWAM | 1 | 2 | 3 | 4 |

LESSON 30

60-space line | Single spacing

30A: Conditioning Practice (8) *each line three or more times*

Alphabet Was Jim Glick quizzed by Mr. Verick on part of his tax form?

Figure-symbol Did Mr. Marshall's March 25 Order #563 come to $789 or $987?

Easy Have faith in yourself and put that faith to work right now.

. . . . 1 . . . . 2 . . . . 3 . . . . 4 . . . . 5 . . . . 6 . . . . 7 . . . . 8 . . . . 9 . . . . 10 . . . . 11 12

30B: Building Control (10) *(Line: 60; Spacing: DS; ¶ indention: 5)*

TYPE: Two 3′ *control-level* writings of 29E, above. Check the number of errors made but ignore the *gwam.* As time permits, practice the words in which you made errors.

Job 5: Typing a Portion of a Report for Duplication (*top-bound manuscript form*)

Mr. James Couzins, Sales Manager of Nationwide, has asked you to type model copy for two sections of a report he is helping to prepare. From the model copy, a spirit duplicator master or a stencil will be typed. Number the pages 3 and 4. Use double spacing. Prepare a carbon copy.

SECTION II

THE CHALLENGE OF LEADERSHIP

This year, over 20,000 junior and senior high schools, private business schools, junior colleges, and four-year colleges and universities selected Nationwide Publishing Company to supply instructional materials for classroom use. They gave us this opportunity because they knew we were well qualified to furnish them with a product of the highest quality. In other words, they had confidence in our ability. This customer confidence is not acquired automatically. It's something that can't be purchased, borrowed, or manufactured. The only way you really achieve it is to earn it.

We're proud of our leadership in the textbook industry, and we realize that our position is built upon the confidence of our many school friends. We feel we understand the responsibilities of being Number One--we know that leadership is gained through serving our customers' needs and is retained by continuously improving the quality of our products, services, and facilities.

Over the years, Nationwide Publishing Company has introduced many innovations and improvements. Nationwide authors have a reputation of farsighted innovation growing out of classroom and laboratory experimentation. The men and women who produce Nationwide instructional materials are the finest craftsmen in the industry. Many of the standard production techniques of today began as an idea with a Nationwide employee.

New techniques, increased service, and pride in craftsmanship--all lead to better textbooks in the hands of our customers. It's part of the challenge we gladly accept and a responsibility we proudly assume.

SECTION III

CHANGES IN LEADERSHIP

During the past fiscal year, several important appointments were made in the top management of the company. President W. L. Johnson, Jr., became Chairman of the Board and President. He has been a member of the Board since 1949, having served as Executive Vice-President and Secretary. Mr. Johnson was named Chairman of the Board upon the death of Mr. W. L. Johnson, Sr., in August.

Richard E. Weeks, a member of the company's management group from 1951, was named Senior Vice-President. Mr. Weeks previously held several key positions in the company, including that of Sales Manager. He was elected a Vice-President and member of the Board of Directors in 1965.

J. Edward Houck joined the company as Vice-President of Finance in March of this year. Mr. Houck came to Nationwide Publishing Company from the Lindy Pen Company, of Jacksonville, Florida, where he served as Corporate Controller.

REACH TO HYPHEN

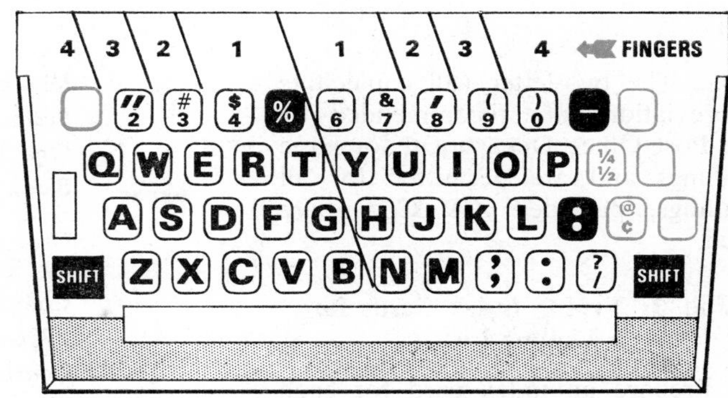

30C: Symbol Location – % *(percent)*, – *(hyphen)*, and : *(colon)* ⑦

REACH TECHNIQUE FOR %

You typed **5** with the *left first finger*. As **%** is the shift of **5**, type it also with the *left first finger. Do not use % for c/o (In care of).*

```
5f 5f%f 5f%f %f %f 5f%f %f
Charge Ed 5% for the loan.
```
DS

REACH TECHNIQUE FOR – (hyphen)

Reach the *right little finger* up to type – without swinging the elbow out. Keep the wrist low. *Use two hyphens to make a dash: ––.*

```
p-; -; -; - ;-; -- ;-; -;-
It is an out-of-date list.
```
DS

CONTROL OF : (colon)

Type the **:** (shift of **;**) with the *right little finger. Do not space before or after a* **:** *when it separates hours and minutes. Space twice after a* **:** *in other uses.*

```
;: ;: : ;: 6:15 8:30 10:25
Train 59 left at 6:15 p.m.
```
TS

30D: Stroking Technique Practice ⑩ *each line three or more times*

```
1                     Change the 5% rate on Wirtz & Lang's note (due May 5) to 4%.
2                     Were the up-to-date plans mailed to the out-of-town speaker?
3  Reinforcement      p-p; -p; -; 5f%f %f %f 0;); ); 91(l 7j&j 5f%f 4f$f 3d#d -;-;
4  Dash is --         Flight 585 left at 6:25 and got in at 8:45--a 950-mile trip.
5  Space twice after :  FOR RENT:  Two 6-room houses at 954 and 957 West 36th Place.
                      ....1....2....3....4....5....6....7....8....9....10....11....12
```

30E: Growth Index ⑮ *(Line: 60; Spacing: DS; ¶ indention: 5)*

TYPE: Three 3′ writings on the *control level*. Circle errors. Determine *gwam* for the best writing. If time permits, type a 1′ *exploration-level* writing on each ¶.

All letters used.

E 1.2 4.7 92

	GWAM 1′	3′	
It is right to "try, try again" if those first efforts do	12	4	39
not bring success; but if you try and "fail and fall," it is	24	8	43
foolish to keep on and on in that same old way. Rather, try	36	12	47
to experiment with some other way to do what you have to do.	48	16	51
If your first effort does not bring success, do not quit	11	20	55
and just let it go at that. Begin again in a new way to do	23	24	58
the work or gain more insight into the problem. When you	35	28	63
realize why you must do more than just try, try again, you	47	32	67
can then work with a purpose to be sure of success.	57	35	70

E 1.2 4.7 92

1′ GWAM | 1 | 2 | 3 | 4 | 5 | 6 | 7 | 8 | 9 | 10 | 11 | 12 |
3′ GWAM | 1 | 2 | 3 | 4 |

Note. The two-letter (all cap) state abbreviations are recommended by the Post Office Department for large mailings and are permitted for all mailings, provided ZIP Codes are used.

Job 2: Typing Index Cards for a Mailing List

Prepare an index card for each of the addresses given at the right. Type the name of the school or bookstore on the horizontal rule and use the name to keep the cards arranged alphabetically. Number the cards from 1 to 10.

Job 3: Chain Feeding Envelopes

Chain feed and address 10 small business envelopes using the back-feed method; then chain feed and address 10 large business envelopes using the front-feed method. Use the address list prepared in Job 2. Keep the envelopes for use in Jobs 7 and 8.

Miss Eleanor Grissom, Director
Business Training Institute
One 16th Street
Sioux City, IA 51103

Miss Jean C. Hamilton
Rockford Community College
2300 Easton Road
Rockford, IL 61107

Mr. R. D. Hicks, Mgr.
Campus Bookstore
2956 Academy Street
Dearborn, MI 48124

Dr. Robert Van Orman, Jr.
Department of English
Technical Secretarial College
Fort Wayne, IN 46805

Mrs. Elizabeth Steuffer
Joliet School for Girls
1375 Wisconsin Avenue
Joliet, IL 60432

Dr. Austin J. Vanderveer
Tri-State Junior College
5600 Country Day Lane
St. Louis, MO 63134

Mr. Evan K. Leeds, Mgr.
Nicolet Bookstore
1002 Marquette Avenue
Green Bay, WI 54304

Mr. Michael Ogden, Director
Wexford School of Business
2950 Quarry Road
St. Paul, MN 55111

Mr. James K. McCain, Principal
Omaha Vocational-Technical School
Omaha, NB 68102

Zanesville College of Business
First National Bank Building
Zanesville, OH 43701

Job 4: Filling in Order Acknowledgment Cards

Using workbook forms or duplicated cards supplied by your teacher, prepare order acknowledgments from the following data. Use the acknowledgment form illustrated at the right. Align the fill-ins so that the down-stem strokes almost touch (do not cut through) the underlines. Supply an appropriate salutation. Address each card as noted below, using your mailing list for appropriate addresses.

February 12, 19--

Dear Mr. Glenn

Thank you for your Order No. C-41735.
Shipment will be made on February 14 via Interstate Freight Company.

We appreciate this opportunity to be of service. Please call on us again whenever our publications can fulfill the needs of your students.

NATIONWIDE PUBLISHING CO.

Card 1, Address 10

Date of Acknowledgment: February 16, 19--
Customer's Order No.: C-31270
Promised Shipping Date: February 17
Shipped Via (Carrier): Gateway Trucking Co.

Card 2, Address 1

Date of Acknowledgment: February 16, 19--
Customer's Order No.: A-7456
Promised Shipping Date: February 18
Shipped Via (Carrier): Midwest Motor Express

Card 3, Address 9

Date of Acknowledgment: February 16, 19--
Customer's Order No.: ST 82143
Promised Shipping Date: February 20
Shipped Via (Carrier): Central Van Lines

Card 4, Address 2

Date of Acknowledgment: February 16, 19--
Customer's Order No.: M-11200
Promised Shipping Date: February 18
Shipped Via (Carrier): Motor City Transfer

Card 5, Address 5

Date of Acknowledgment: February 16, 19--
Customer's Order No.: BH 29473
Promised Shipping Date: February 19
Shipped Via (Carrier): Thru-Way Express Co.

Card 6, Address 4

Date of Acknowledgment: February 16, 19--
Customer's Order No.: R-72104
Promised Shipping Date: February 19
Shipped Via (Carrier): REA Express

BONUS TYPING FOR EXTRA CREDIT

DO: Set the left margin 30 spaces to the left of the center of the paper; move the right margin to the end of the scale. Set the line-space regulator on "1" for single spacing.

TYPE: Selected lines three to five times each: first for technique improvement, next for speed of stroking, and then for more precise control of finger motion patterns.

High-Frequency Words

All 107 *different* words that are used in the following drills are among the 400 most-used words in the English language. In a study of over 300,000 words in a large number of letters, memos, and reports, these 107 words accounted for more than 40 percent of all word occurrences. Thus, they are important to you in perfecting your typewriting skill. Practice them diligently and frequently.

Balanced-hand words of 2 to 5 letters

```
1  of to is it or by if us an do so me he am go the and for may
2  but sir pay due own men did box with they them make than when
3  work such form then wish paid name held both their city also
4  right field, of it, it is, for us, with them, both of, or me,
5  and the, may go to, due the men, to do it, and do so, by them
6  He may pay the six men for the work they did by the big box.
7  They did the work right and paid the dues on the city field.
   ....1....2....3....4....5....6....7....8....9....10....11....12
```

One-hand words of 2 to 5 letters

```
8  we in be on as no at up my are you was get him tax few set
9  dear were best only date card area upon case ever rate fact
10 after great state rates, get at, you were, tax him, after my
11 rate card, tax case, in no, we are, at only, as in, are ever
12 As you are on my state tax case, get a few tax rates set up.
13 Only a few tax rates were ever set in my area after my case.
   ....1....2....3....4....5....6....7....8....9....10....11....12
```

Double-letter words of 3 to 5 letters

```
14 all see too will been good need full well call feel soon week
15 free book less keep fill bill shall three offer books issue
16 still small, all too soon, too small, all will, shall still,
17 feel well, need less, three books, will call all, shall see,
18 The three books will fill the need; so issue the offer soon.
19 He will keep all books, too; do feel free to issue the bill.
   ....1....2....3....4....5....6....7....8....9....10....11....12
```

Balanced- and one-hand and double-letter words of 2 to 5 letters

```
20 of we to in or on is be it as by no if at us up an my he am
21 and all him for see you men too are may get but was pay tax
22 work will best then been rates such good were wish need only
23 right small state field offer rates their three great after
24 it is up to all, if you are free, he is less, offer to state
25 it was too soon, for all the men, he may call for, do keep it
26 It was then up to him to set the book rate on the small box.
27 On the rate card he saw the due date, the date he is to pay.
   ....1....2....3....4....5....6....7....8....9....10....11....12
```

Applied Typing: Lessons 258–263

In this unit you will work in the Sales Department of Nationwide Publishing Company. You will get a variety of experiences that are typical of those encountered in on-the-job situations.

As you complete the various job assignments, work quickly, efficiently, and carefully. Correct your errors neatly so that all completed work is usable. Be sure to indicate enclosures where appropriate.

Job 1: Typing an Interoffice Memorandum

Type the following memorandum for the guidance of new Nationwide typists (including you). Use 1″ margins and double spacing. If a photocopy machine is available, copy the illustrations at the right to accompany the memorandum.

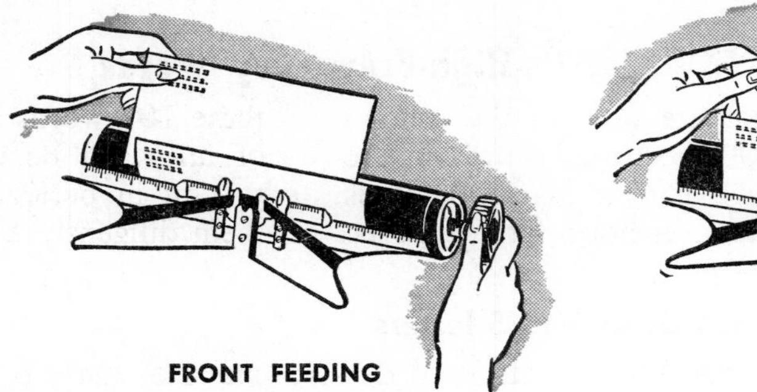

FRONT FEEDING

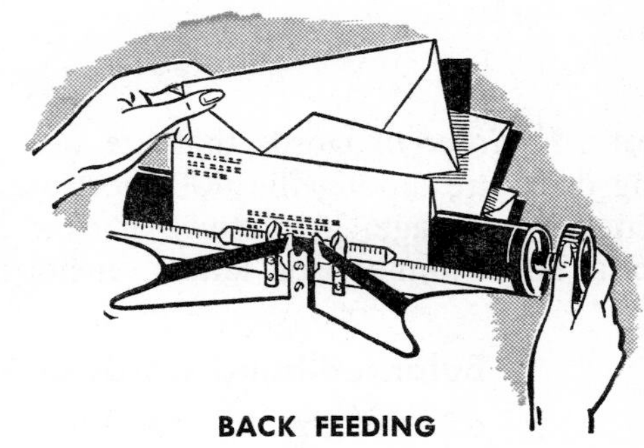

BACK FEEDING

TO: **All Typists and Stenographers**
FROM: **R. B. Smith, Training Director**
DATE: **February 14, 19––**
SUBJECT: **Chain Feeding**

When mass mailings are bieng prepared it is more efficient and economical to chain feed the necessary envelopes (or cards). The steps for two methods of chain feeding are given in this memo. New typists and stenographers should experiment withboth methods to select for thier own use the methods that is easier and faster.

Method 1: Front Feed. In the front feed method, the envelopes are fed into the machine from in front of the platen. Follow these steps:

1. Stack envelopes face down, flap toward you, on the left side of the typewriter.
2. Address the first envelope; then turn it back until a half inch shows above the alignment scale.
3. Insert the next envelope from the front placing it between the first envelope and the platen.
4. Turn the cylinder back to remove the first envelop andto position the second one. Continue the chain by feeding all envelopes from the front of the cylinder.

Method 2: Back feed. In the back-feed method the envelopes are fed into the typewriter from behind the cylinder. Follow th4se steps:

1. Stack the envelopes face up the on left sied of the typewriter.
2. Insert the envelope to typing position and place a second envelope behind the cylinder in the "feed" position.
3. Address the first envelope. As you pull the first one out of the machine with the right hand, feed another envelope in the "feed" position with the left.
4. As the first envelope is removed the second envelope will be moved into typing position. Continue the chain by placing a new envelope in the feed position each time the addressed envelope is removde.

Unit 4 | Lessons 31-34

Typing Special Symbols and Statistical Copy

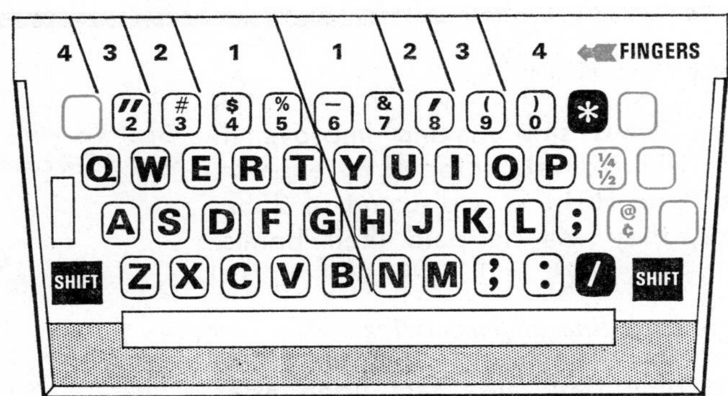

1. Arrange work area for efficient typing.
2. Adjust paper guide and insert full sheet.
3. Set left margin stop 30 spaces to left of center for a 60-space line; move right stop to end of scale.
4. Use single spacing unless otherwise directed.
5. *Bonus Typing:* Type selected lines from page 54 as directed.

LESSON 31

31A: Conditioning Practice (8) *each line three times*

Alphabet	Mr. V. W. Krugh quickly explained the job fire hazard to us.
Figure	Frank set the tab stops as follows: 25, 36, 48, 59, and 70.
Figure-symbol	Howe & Roth's long-term bonds (due in 1988) pay 4% interest.
Easy	It is right to be cautious, but it is foolish to be fearful.

. . . . 1 . . . . 2 . . . . 3 . . . . 4 . . . . 5 . . . . 6 . . . . 7 . . . . 8 . . . . 9 . . . . 10 . . . . 11 12

31B: Symbol Location – / (*diagonal*) and * (*asterisk*) (7)

REACH TECHNIQUE FOR /

Type / (end key in first row) with the *right fourth finger*. Make a direct reach. *Space between a whole number and a fraction typed with the diagonal (/).*

;/; /; 2/3 5/8 6 2/3 7 5/8

Use / to type 2/3 and 5/8. DS

REACH TECHNIQUE FOR *

Nonelectric. The * is the shift of – (hyphen) and is typed with the *right little finger*. Make the reach to * without moving the elbow in or out.

-; -;*; -;*; *; *; -;*; *;

Type * with this footnote. DS

Electric. Type * (shift of **8**) with the *right second finger*. Reach up to type * without moving the elbow in or out. Keep the wrist low as your finger moves up to type *.

8k 8k*k 8k*k *k *k 8k*k *k

Type * with this footnote. TS

31C: Stroking Technique Practice (10) *each line three or more times*

1 My stock (bought on July 19 at 36 5/8) sold today at 47 2/3.

2 Type * for a single footnote and ** for the second footnote.

3 *Reinforcement* 4f$f $f 7j&j &j 5f%f %f 91(l (l 0;);); /;?; ?; Nonelectric -;*; *; -;*; / Electric 8k*k *k 8k*k

4 Item 89-V, page 265, refers to *** (Three-Star) Market List.

5 Order #890 for Royal "WQ" totals $567.21 (less 2% discount).

. . . . 1 . . . . 2 . . . . 3 . . . . 4 . . . . 5 . . . . 6 . . . . 7 . . . . 8 . . . . 9 . . . . 10 . . . . 11 12

Unit 45 | Lessons 257-263

Typing in a Sales Department

LESSON 257

257A: Conditioning Practice (5) *each line three times; then 1′ writings*

Alphabet	Liz justified the margin quickly, but Don Evans saw Maxine improve it.	*Operate shift keys with a 1-2 count*
Figure	Order Nos. RD 12700, CD 236495, and CR 183462 were shipped by express.	
Figure-symbol	Ship Order #47239 for 135 copies of H60 and H811 at a discount of 25%.	
Fluency	When both make the quantity I paid for, they will be paid their bonus.	
	1 | 2 | 3 | 4 | 5 | 6 | 7 | 8 | 9 | 10 | 11 | 12 | 13 | 14	

257B: Technique Mastery – Response Patterns (5) *each line at least twice*

Stroke	are you get him set oil dear were best only date area fact upon after extra serve taxes refer start regret average opinion greater minimum I get an average tax rate in my opinion; you get a greater estate tax.
Combination	than were form best wish date world extra profit start chairman average members program statement workers within factory endorsement casement Workers on both programs will profit from their endorsement statement.
Word	also than form then wish paid name held city hand down town pays half field world visit profit handle chairman problems quantity amendment Go with them to the firm to sign the right work form for the chairman.
	1 | 2 | 3 | 4 | 5 | 6 | 7 | 8 | 9 | 10 | 11 | 12 | 13 | 14

257C: Typing for Speed and Accuracy (25) *1′ and 5′ writings; circle errors; determine* gwam

DO: Type two 1′ writings on each of the first four ¶s on page 373: one for speed, one for control.

DO: Type two 5′ writings using all ¶s on page 373. Determine *gwam*: 10′ *gwam* × 2.

257D: Skill Comparison Writing (15) *one 10′ writing*

DO: Type a 10′ writing using all ¶s on page 373. Circle errors; determine *nwam*.

DO: Compare the rate and number of errors with your performance in Lesson 256, page 372.

LESSONS 258-262

Lessons 258, 260, 262

Use the following plan for Lessons 258, 260, and 262. Retain all completed Jobs until Lesson 263.

Conditioning Practice (5′): Type 257A, above.

Technique Mastery (7′): Type the sentence of each group in 257B, above, as a 1′ skill-comparison writing. Determine *gwam*. As time permits, repeat the sentence on which you made the lowest rate.

Speed Typing (8′): Type five 1′ speed writings on selected ¶s on page 373. Determine *gwam* for each.

Applied Typing (30′): Type the Jobs on pages 375–379. Correct all errors neatly.

Lessons 259, 261

Use the following plan for Lessons 259 and 261. Retain all completed Jobs until Lesson 263.

Conditioning Practice (5′): Type 263A, page 380.

Technique Mastery (7′): Type the first two lines of each group in 257B, above. Work for precision of motion and direction.

Control Typing (8′): Beginning with ¶ 1, page 373, type each paragraph in turn until you can type it without error. *You are not expected to complete all ¶s in each lesson.*

Applied Typing (30′): Continue typing the Jobs.

31D: Typing from Script (7) *each sentence for 1′ writings; circle errors*

SCRIPT: Copy written with pencil or with pen and ink.

	Words
Check Haskell & Sims's Report #14, page 512.*	9
Evans & Cole shipped 17 carloads to us on 3/29/66.	10
"Watch your typing speed go up as your errors go down."	11

31E: Statistical Typing – Memorandum (18)

2 half sheets	Block style
60-space line	2-inch (12-line)
Single spacing	top margin

TYPE: Twice on half sheets; then 1′ writings on each ¶ as time permits.

LEARN: Lines to a half sheet; characteristics of block style.

Line 13

	Words
You are to use a half sheet of paper (8 1/2 by 5 1/2 inches)	12
and the block style to type this copy. In the block style,	24
all lines begin flush with the left margin and are typed in	36
single-spaced form, with double spacing between paragraphs.	48
DS	
When a full-size sheet of paper is folded from top to bottom,	12
you have half sheets of 33 lines each. You can use the four	25
sides of the folded paper, or you can cut it at the fold and	37
have two sheets 8 1/2 inches wide and 5 1/2 inches long.	48
....1....2....3....4....5....6....7....8....9....10....11....12	

LESSON 32

60-space line | Single spacing

32A: Conditioning Practice (8) *each line three times*

Alphabet	Judge Quimby awarded fine prizes to experts in Houck Valley.
Figure	We checked Items 23, 45, 67, and 89 on pages 129-30 and 156.
Figure-symbol	Use * for a footnote and / for made fractions; as, 2/3, 7/8.
Easy	Don't stop trying if you fail once--just try some other way!
	....1....2....3....4....5....6....7....8....9....10....11....12

32B: Typing from Script (7) *each sentence for 1′ writings; circle errors*

	Words
Item 48* on page 156 costs $90 (less 2% for cash).	10
Dodson's check is for $2,137.85, but he owes $2,173.85.	11
Use * for a single reference note; use / for made fractions.	12

GWAM 1' 10'

All letters are used.

Our type of capitalism reflects an economy in which the owners and 13 1 51
laborers work together under competitive conditions to produce goods 27 3 52
and services for the public to consume, with private gain as a principal 42 4 54
goal. The goods or services move from producer to consumer by a scheme 56 6 55
of exchange (or sales) in which the common medium of payment is usually 71 7 57
money or a useful substitute for it, such as credit. 81 8 58

Pure capitalism can exist only in a nation where the most eminent 13 9 59
condition is freedom of choice. This type of economy is called "laissez 28 11 60
faire," a term that means that the government does not interfere in the 42 12 62
conduct of business. American business at one time typified it, but in 57 14 63
recent years the restraint on business by government has grown so much 71 15 65
that our economy is now referred to as "modified capitalism." 83 16 66

An essential characteristic of capitalism is its freedom of private 14 18 67
property, meaning that businesses as well as individuals in the society 28 19 69
have a right to buy, own, and sell property of all kinds: land, build- 42 21 70
ings, machinery, equipment, and tools, to mention only a few. It also 56 22 71
implies that a businessman has the privilege of owning the goods he pro- 71 23 73
duces and of keeping any profit that may accrue as an outcome of the 85 25 74
sale of those goods. 89 25 75

Still another essential factor of capitalism is its freedom of pri- 13 27 76
vate enterprise. Most business ventures in this country are owned by a 28 28 77
person (not by a unit of government) who has invested personal funds in 42 29 79
an operation of his own selection, from the running of which he hopes to 57 31 80
reap profit for himself. This is true without regard to the size of the 71 32 82
firm. Even if a business must undergo specific routine steps in order 86 34 83
to receive permission to operate a corporation, it is still a private 100 35 85
enterprise. 102 35 85

A final characteristic that is essential for capitalism is the ex- 13 38 86
tent to which everyone affected by it has, to a considerable degree, 27 38 88
freedom of choice in his economic actions. The businessman is free to 41 40 89
choose the area of activity in which he will engage and to manipulate 55 41 90
the factors of land, labor, capital, and management as he sees fit in 69 42 92
order to achieve the highest measure of profit. Employees are at lib- 83 44 93
erty to select the jobs they wish, in the trades or callings they prefer, 98 45 95
and in the companies that offer them the best returns for their efforts. 113 47 96
Consumers are singularly free in their choices of the goods and services 127 48 98
they wish to buy within the limits of their financial resources. 140 49 99

1' GWAM | 1 | 2 | 3 | 4 | 5 | 6 | 7 | 8 | 9 | 10 | 11 | 12 | 13 | 14 |
10' GWAM | 1 | 2 |

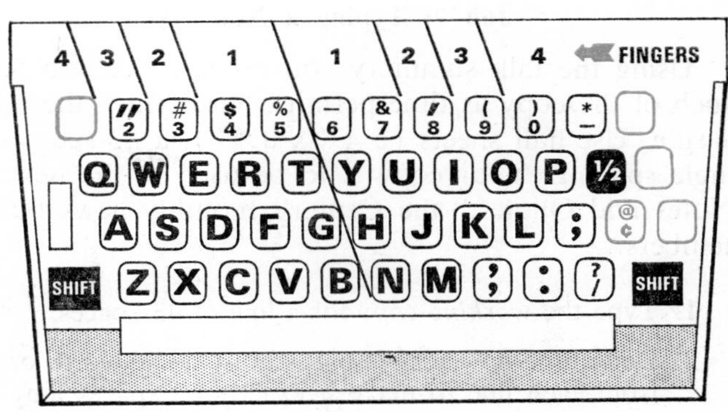

32C: Symbol Location – ½ and ¼ (7)

REACH TECHNIQUE FOR ½

Reach the *right fourth finger* up to type ½ without swinging the elbow out. Keep the wrist low.

;½; ½;½; ½;½; ½; ½;½; ½;½;

I typed ½, 2½, 3½, and 4½. DS

REACH TECHNIQUE FOR ¼

The ¼ is the shift of ½ and is typed with the *right fourth finger*. Remember: Shift to type ¼.

;½; ½;¼; ½;¼; ¼; ½;¼; ½;¼;

We used ¼, 3¼, 4¼, and 5¼. DS

Spacing Rules. Type a whole number and a "key" fraction (as, **6½**) without spacing between them. Type a whole number and a "made" fraction (made with /) with a space between (as, **6 2/3**).

Type 1/2, not ½, with 3/4. TS

32D: Stroking Technique Practice (10) *each line three or more times*

1 The interest rate on my $500 note is changed from 5% to 4½%.

2 Type fractions in the same way: 1/4 and 2/3--not ¼ and 2/3.

3 Reinforcement 3d#d #d 7j&j &j 4f$f $f /;?; ?; ½;¼; ¼; ½;¼; ¼;
Nonelectric -;*; *; 2s"s
Electric 8k*k *k ';";

4 Ed wired: "Offer 200 Lobox at 90½ and 100 Square Z at 68¼."

5 Dr. Jelk moved to 261½ West 78th Street, Newark, New Jersey.

. . . . 1 . . . . 2 . . . . 3 . . . . 4 . . . . 5 . . . . 6 . . . . 7 . . . . 8 . . . . 9 . . . . 10 . . . . 11 12

32E: Statistical Typing – Memorandum (18)

2 half sheets	Block style
60-space line	2-inch (12-line)
Single spacing	top margin

TYPE: Twice on half sheets; then 1′ writings on each ¶ as time permits.

LEARN: Vertical lines to full and half sheets; spaces to horizontal inch.

Words

SOME FACTS TO KNOW: A full sheet (8½ by 11 inches) has 66 — 12
lines. Each line has 102 elite or 85 pica spaces. A half — 24
sheet (8½ by 5½ inches) has 33 lines. — 31

DS

Your typewriter probably has 6 lines to a vertical inch, but — 12
some machines used in offices do not. To check the lines to — 24
an inch on your typewriter, type 1 to 6 in a single-spaced — 36
column; then remove the paper, turn it sideways, and measure — 48
the lines with a ruler or the margin scale. — 57

. . . . 1 . . . . 2 . . . . 3 . . . . 4 . . . . 5 . . . . 6 . . . . 7 . . . . 8 . . . . 9 . . . . 10 . . . . 11 12

Job 7: Typing a News Item

Using the talk summary you prepared as Job 5, type as much of the copy as time permits, "justifying" the right-hand margin. Use half sheets (5½" x 8½"), a 43-space line, and single spacing. Your copy is to be used in the next issue of "Notes and Quotes," the Center's monthly news bulletin for members.

1. Type the *working copy* for a line of 43 spaces.
2. Determine how many spaces must be added to or removed from each line to make it exactly 43 spaces long.
3. Distribute the spaces needed to "justify" the margin.
4. Retype the copy in "justified," corrected form.

FIVE BASIC STEPS

TO PHYSICAL AND MENTAL FITNESS

by

Allen G. Zaring, III

Man is both body and soul, a thing of///
both flesh and spirit. Whatever our per-//
sonal definition of soul, it is quite clear
that our minds and bodies are intricately//
interrelated. The health of the one affects
the well-being of the other. Let us look,/
then, at some ways of "keeping body and soul
together"--healthfully.

The basic steps to physical and mental//
fitness listed here are few and, with a bit
of self-discipline, not difficult to take.

1. Consume the right kinds and amounts of food and drink.
2. Engage daily in appropriate forms of bodily exercise.
3. Relax the mind and body with plenty of sleep.
4. Keep yourself clean--from the inside out.
5. Engage in a wide variety of activi- ties.

Consume the right kinds and amounts of//
food and drink. Most of us eat too much of
too few different kinds of food. We gorge/
ourselves with double-decker sandwiches,///
French fries, and pizza, washing them down/
with coke and other carbonated sugar waters.
We eat more than we need and "justify" it//
with "Waste not, want not." It is far better for food to go to waste than for it to/

FIVE BASIC STEPS

TO PHYSICAL AND MENTAL FITNESS

by

Allen G. Zaring, III

Man is both body and soul, a thing of
both flesh and spirit. Whatever our personal definition of soul, it is quite clear
that our minds and bodies are intricately
interrelated. The health of the one affects
the well-being of the other. Let us look,
then, at some ways of "keeping body and soul
together"--healthfully.

The basic steps to physical and mental
fitness listed here are few and, with a bit
of self-discipline, not difficult to take.

1. Consume the right kinds and amounts of food and drink.
2. Engage daily in appropriate forms of bodily exercise.
3. Relax the mind and body with plenty of sleep.
4. Keep yourself clean--from the inside out.
5. Engage in a wide variety of activi- ties.

Consume the right kinds and amounts of
food and drink. Most of us eat too much of
too few different kinds of food. We gorge
ourselves with double-decker sandwiches,
French fries, and pizza, washing them down
with coke and other carbonated sugar waters.
We eat more than we need and "justify" it
with "Waste not, want not." It is far better for food to go to waste than for it to

LESSON 256

256A: Conditioning Practice (5) *each line three times; then 1′ writings on Line 4*

Alphabet	Apex with its big trucks shut down the job as my five men lazily quit.	Begin slowly; speed up gradually
Figure	0 0 1 2 00 101 10 202 12 303 19 404 50 535 20 606 11 787 30 838 15 989	
Figure-symbol	10 lbs. CR–274 @ $2.48; 5 doz. ND–830 @ $5.99; 3 gal. CC–7214 @ $6.50.	
Fluency	The busy chairman may spend the usual profit, but the theory is right.	

| 1 | 2 | 3 | 4 | 5 | 6 | 7 | 8 | 9 | 10 | 11 | 12 | 13 | 14 |

256B: Technique Mastery: Stroking (10) *each line three times; then 1′ writings*

Direct or long reaches	Art tried to buy a large columnar pedestal from the huge art treasure. Vaughn brought Nancy by my office on Wednesday to do the TV rehearsal.	Try to reduce waste motions
Adjacent keys	Where can we buy a used calliope––in top condition––to awe the crowds? I hope you asked her whether she typed the last three words correctly.	
Outside reaches	Please don't quip when you are next quizzed about my project progress. Quote a top price at the outset; give Rex a prize for prompt purchase.	
Opposite-hand reaches	If he runs the van through that dark field, I will owe him for trying. I try to seize the seine; but when I rush down the slick bank, I slip.	
Shift keys	Route the memo to Epstein, Patrick, Fisher, Jacobs, Quentin, and Karl. Ask him to use the abbreviations N., S., E., and W. as the directions.	Use a 1-2 shift-key count
Rhythmic stroking	Their statement was worked out with great care; still it is not right. The efficiency of the eighteen girls took all of us by surprise today.	

| 1 | 2 | 3 | 4 | 5 | 6 | 7 | 8 | 9 | 10 | 11 | 12 | 13 | 14 |

256C: Growth Index (15) *one 10′ writing*

Type a 10′ writing on the ¶s given on page 373. Circle errors. Determine *nwam*.

256D: Applied Typing (20)

Continue with the jobs you have been typing. At the end of the period, assemble all the jobs you have completed, arrange them in order of job number, and submit them to your teacher.

LESSON 33

60-space line | Single spacing

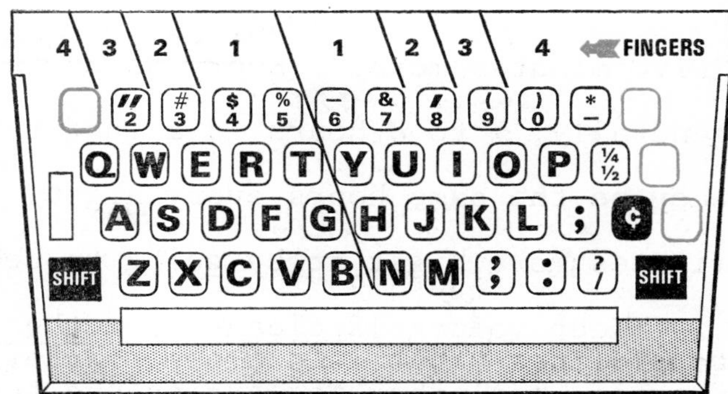

33A: Conditioning Practice (8) *each line three times*

Alphabet	Jim Rae did exceptionally quick engraving work for Buz Shaw.
Figure	What is the total of 23 and 45 and 67 and 89 and 90 and 100?
Figure-symbol	He sold 200 of Rank & Mann 3½% Pfd. (bought 4/17/65) at 89¼.
Easy	Advice: something the wise don't need and fools won't heed.
	. . . . 1 . . . . 2 . . . . 3 . . . . 4 . . . . 5 . . . . 6 . . . . 7 . . . . 8 . . . . 9 . . . . 10 . . . . 11 12

33B: Symbol Location – ¢ *(cent or cents)* and @ *(at)* (7)

REACH TECHNIQUE FOR ¢ and @
(Nonelectric)

Reach the *right fourth finger* to the right to type ¢. The shift of ¢ is @. Make the reach to ¢ and @ without moving the other fingers from their home keys.

;¢; ¢; ¢;@; ¢;@; ¢;@; ¢;@;

I sold 2 dozen @ 69¢ each. TS

REACH TECHNIQUE FOR ¢ and @
(Electric)

The ¢ is the shift of the figure **6** and is typed with the *right first finger.* The @ is the shift of the figure **2** and is typed with the *left third finger.*

6j 6j¢j ¢j 2s@s @s 2s@s ¢j

I sold 2 dozen @ 69¢ each. TS

SPACING RULES

1. Space before and after typing @.
2. Do not space between ¢ and the figure it follows.

These spacing directions apply when the symbols are used in a sentence or in typing bills, but not when used in reach-stroke drills such as the first line of the symbol-location drill.

33C: Stroking Technique Practice (10) *each line three or more times*

1 John paid 98¢ for the ball-point pen and 16¢ for the pencil.

2 Dorothy bought 10 7/8 yards @ $4.75 and 9 3/4 yards @ $5.25.

3 Reinforcement Nonelectric 2s"s "s 6j_j _j 8k'k 'k -;*; *; ¢;@; @; ¢;@; ½;¼; ¼; /;?; ?;
Electric ';"; "; -;_; _; 8k*k *k 6j¢j ¢j 2s@s @s ¢j@s

4 Vera sold a pen @ 98¢, pad @ 36¢, and 24 pencils @ 15¢ each.

5 The * before Item 29, page 306, indicates a decrease of 68¢.

. . . . 1 . . . . 2 . . . . 3 . . . . 4 . . . . 5 . . . . 6 . . . . 7 . . . . 8 . . . . 9 . . . . 10 . . . . 11 12

33D: Typing from Script (7) *each sentence for 1' writings; circle errors*

	Words
Is Order #495 (dated 6/30) for 12 doz. @ 87¢ each?	10
The full sheet of paper (8½ by 11 inches) has 66 lines.	11
The half sheet of paper (8½ by 5½ inches) has only 33 lines.	12

"Five minutes more." Everyone doesn't require the same amount of sleep; but generally, 7 to 8 hours is a good rule of thumb. It is necessary, too, that they be the same hours every night. If you are one of those who need "five minutes more," get it by going to bed earlier instead of getting up.

Keep yourself clean--from the inside out. Cleanliness may not be next to godliness, but it's close. Water, soap, dentifrice, antiperspirant, shampoo, and other toiletries are too inexpensive not to be used by everyone as insurance against being personally offensive. And don't put off the frequent trip to the laundry, the cleaners, and the shoe shop. Clothes do not make the man; but clean, well-pressed clothes reflect his self-concern.

Engage in a wide variety of interests. With todays increasing leisure time, we are no longer concerned with the "all work and no play" adage. But we are concerned with the kinds of liesure activity people ingage in. Too many of us are spectators rather than participants. We overuse one or two kinds of recreation: TV or movies or reading or records. Diversify your recreational interests and activities. Develop some that require you to do, especially for as well as with others.

Job 6: Typing Voucher Checks

Type in duplicate voucher checks 251–254 (dated February 27, 19––) for the signature of the secretary-treasurer of EHRC. Calculate total amounts, being sure to deduct invoice amounts marked CR which are credits to the EHRC account.

Eastern Hills Recreation Center
7285 Wooster Pike, Plainville, Ohio 45227   February 27, 19--   No. 250   13-34/420

Pay to the Order of Swift Lithographing Company, Inc. $ 25.10

Twenty-five and 10/100---------------------- Dollars

SOUTHWESTERN BANK & TRUST CO.
Fourth and Vine Streets, Cincinnati, Ohio 45201

Harvey B. Lockwood
Secretary-Treasurer, Eastern Hills Recreation Center

⑆0420⑈0034⑆ 797⑈550⑈

Detach this stub before cashing check

IN PAYMENT OF THE FOLLOWING INVOICES:

TO Swift Lithographing Company, Inc.
4530 Montgomery Road
Norwood, Ohio 45212

Date	Invoice	Amount
February 11	LP-00221	19.50
13	C-1145 CR	4.00
22	LP-00248	9.60
		25.10

Eastern Hills Recreation Center
7285 Wooster Pike, Plainville, Ohio 45227

TO: Evans Athletic Supply Company
316 Ludlow Avenue
Cincinnati, Ohio 45220

Date	Invoice	Amount
February 1	TH–1300	212.50
12	Q–214 CR	15.20
15	TH–1364	74.25
21	TH–1413	13.00

TO: Couzins Laundry & Cleaners
3200 Brotherton Road
Oakley, Ohio 45209

Date	Invoice	Amount
February 3	ST–2025	37.50
10	AC–1202 CR	4.95

TO: Mr. Fixit Lumber Company
Madison and Stafford Roads
Madisonville, Ohio 45227

Date	Invoice	Amount
February 17	ND–19103	67.50
18	ND–19196	11.25

TO: Jiffy Cleaning Products, Inc.
6936 Madisonville Road
Mariemont, Ohio 45227

Date	Invoice	Amount
February 16	RD–2417	15.30
23	RD–2523	8.40

33E: Statistical Typing (18) *(2 half sheets; Line: 60; Spacing: SS; ¶ indention: 5)*

1. **Type** the following paragraphs with a 1½-inch (9-line) top margin. The copy will be above the exact center of the half sheet (in "reading position").
2. **Type** the paragraphs again with a top margin of 11 lines for exact-center placement.
3. **Compare** the two writings. Which placement of the copy do you prefer?

Words

Do you have a 1914 or a 1931 one-cent piece, a 1915 10
nickel, or 1921 or 1931 dime, in your pocket? If so, you 22
have a coin that is worth more than its face value. This 34
is true for the 1919 or the 1924 quarter, too--and for many 46
other coins. 48

The 1914-D Lincoln cent is worth from $20 to $50; the 11
1919-S Liberty standing quarter, from $10 to $20. Do not 22
expect to find these or other coins of more than face value 34
in great use; but when you realize their worth, you might 46
just spot one the next time you count your change. 56

....1....2....3....4....5....6....7....8....9....10....11....12

LESSON 34

60-space line | Single spacing

34A: Conditioning Practice (8) *each line three times*

Alphabet Joe Bair quickly wrote the zoology exam for advanced pupils.

Figure Their address will be 867 South 19th Street after March 25.

Figure-symbol Tod's Order #541 (3/27/66) is for 8 doz. ** Pens @ 90¢ each.

Easy Your sure way to win is to work hard; to lose, to loaf much.

....1....2....3....4....5....6....7....8....9....10....11....12

34B: One-Minute Writings for Control (7) *(Line: 60; Spacing: DS; ¶ indention: 5)*

TYPE: Four 1′ writings on the *control level.* Circle errors. Determine *gwam* for best writing.

All letters are used.

E 1.2 4.9 85

1′ GWAM

You won't get to be a whiz in typing just by wanting to 11

excel in your daily practice. You must build typing power on 24

the very best techniques. The worker who is "slow but sure" 36

will get the work done sometime; but if he takes too much time, 48

he may find he has lots of time--to look for another job! 60

....1....2....3....4....5....6....7....8....9....10....11....12

Job 5: Typing a Summary of a Talk

Dr. Allen G. Zaring, Executive Director of the Center, has prepared the following summary of a talk he is to give to the Future Office Workers Club of Eastern Hills High School. Type the summary in double-spaced, unbound manuscript form (with three carbon copies).

FIVE STEPS TO PHYSICAL AND MENTAL HEALTH
by
Allen G. Zaring

Man is both body and mind, a thing of both flesh and spirit. Whatever our personal definition of soul it is quite clear that our minds and bodies are intri-cately inter related. The health of the one affects the well being of the other. Let us look then at some ways of "keeping body and soul together"--healthfully.

The basic guides to physcial and mental fitness here listed are few and with a bit of self-discipline, not difficult to master.

1. Eat the right kinds and amounts offood and drink.
2. Engage daily in appropriate forms of bodily exercise
3. Relax the mind and body with plenty of rest.
4. Keep yourself clean.
5. Engage in a wide variety of interests.

<u>Consume the right amounts of food and drink.</u> Nearly all of us eat too much of too few different kinds of foods. We gorge ourselves on double-decker sandwiches, french fries,and pizza, washing them down with cok and carbonated sugar waters. We eat more than we need and justify it with the old saw "Waste not, want not." It is far better for foodto go to waste than for it to go to waist! Make a game of eating: Try a different food every week and learn to choose those that are rich in protein and minerals and to shun those that are high in fats and carbohydrates. <u>Engage in appropriate forms of exer-cise.</u> Office workers are notoriously a sedentary lot. The only exercise most of us get in a day is the short walks we take to and from coffee breaks and lunch. Worsestill, our at-home exercise consists of little more than trips to the refrigerator and TV control knobs. Most people say they cant afford to join a health club but the truth of the matter is, office workers can't afford <u>not</u> to. Unless you discipline yourself to a <u>daily</u> exercise similar to those outlined in the popular physical booklets, you must discipline your pocketbook to a health club membership. <u>Relax the mind and body with plenty of sleep.</u> How much sleep does the working person require? Someone has said,

FIVE BASIC STEPS TO PHYSICAL AND MENTAL FITNESS
by
Allen G. Zaring, III

Man is both body and soul, a thing of both flesh and spirit. Whatever our personal definition of soul, it is quite clear that our minds and bodies are intricately interrelated. The health of the one affects the well-being of the other. Let us look, then, at some ways of "keeping body and soul together"--healthfully.

The basic steps to physical and mental fitness listed here are few and, with a bit of self-discipline, not difficult to take.

1. Consume the right kinds and amounts of food and drink.
2. Engage daily in appropriate forms of bodily exercise.
3. Relax the mind and body with plenty of sleep.
4. Keep yourself clean--from the inside out.
5. Engage in a wide variety of activities.

<u>Consume the right kinds and amounts of food and drink</u>. Most of us eat too much of too few different kinds of food. We gorge ourselves on double-decker sandwiches, French fries, and pizza, washing them down with coke and other carbonated sugar waters. We eat more than we need and "justify" it with "Waste not, want not." It is far better for food to go to waste than for it to go to waist! Make a game of eating: Try a new food each week and learn to select those that are rich in protein, vitamins, and min-erals and to avoid those that are high in fats and carbohydrates.

<u>Engage daily in appropriate forms of bodily exercise</u>. Office workers are a sedentary lot. The only exercise many of us get

34C: Statistical Typing Checkup (15) *(Full sheet; Line: 60; Spacing: DS; ¶ indention: 5)*

1. **Type** two 3′ writings on the *control level.* Circle errors. Determine *gwam* for better writing.
2. **Type** a 1′ writing on each ¶ on the *exploration level.* Note *gwam* for each writing.
3. **Type** a 1′ writing on each ¶ on the *control level.* Determine *gwam* and circle errors.

All letters and figures are used.

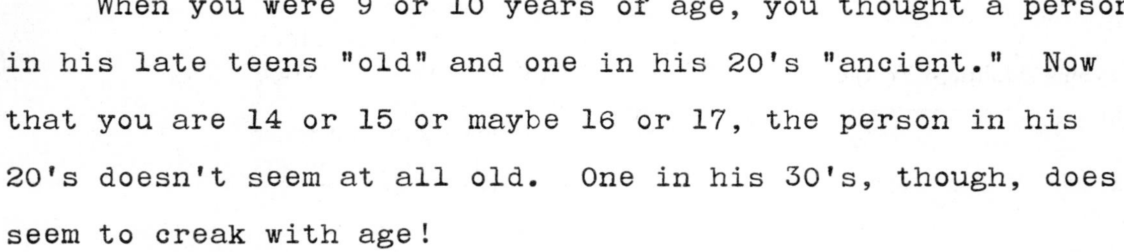

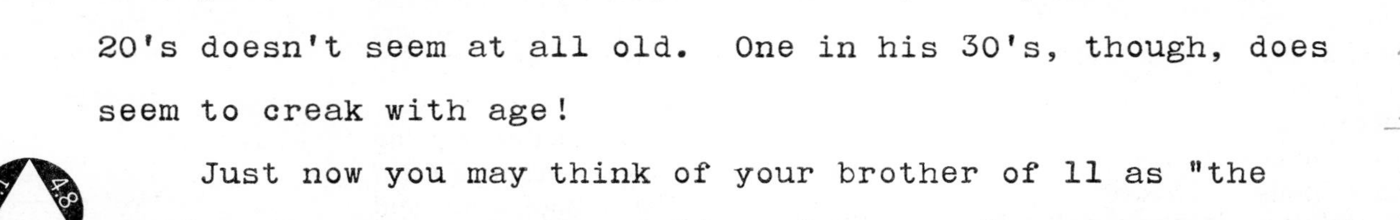

		GWAM 1′	3′	
1.1 / 4.8 / 83	When you were 9 or 10 years of age, you thought a person	11	4	41
	in his late teens "old" and one in his 20's "ancient." Now	23	8	45
	that you are 14 or 15 or maybe 16 or 17, the person in his	35	12	49
	20's doesn't seem at all old. One in his 30's, though, does	47	16	53
	seem to creak with age!	52	17	55
1.1 / 4.8 / 85	Just now you may think of your brother of 11 as "the	11	21	58
	brat" and of your sister of 13 as "the pest" and say you can't	23	25	62
	expect much of them; but when you are 18 or 19, the youngsters	36	29	67
	will be about the age you are now, and you will be amazed that	48	33	71
	in some strange way they, too, have become quite grown up!	60	37	75

1′ GWAM 1 2 3 4 5 6 7 8 9 10 11 12
3′ GWAM 1 2 3 4

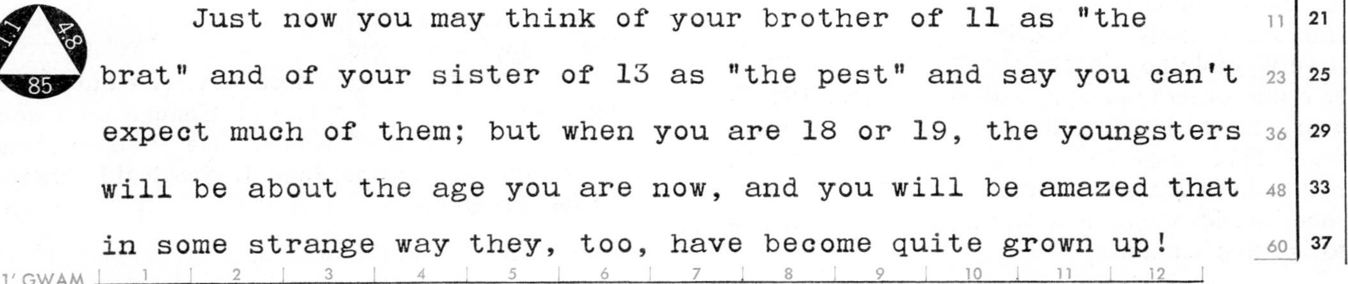

34D: Sentence Guided Writings (20) *(Full sheet; Line: 60; Spacing: SS)*

1. **Type** each sentence of Group 1 as a 1′ writing guided by the 15″ or 12″ call and once guided by the 20″ call.
2. **Type** the sentences of Groups 2 and 3 three times each without being timed.

All letters, figures, and symbols are used.

		GWAM 20″	15″	12″
Group 1	All of us have the wish to excel in our work.	27	36	45
	What do you hope to be next year or in five years?	30	40	50
	Care enough and share enough, and all will have enough.	33	44	55
	Much of what was written in ancient times has meaning today.	36	48	60
Group 2	Howard shipped 1450# @ 9½¢ a pound.	21	28	35
	On July 23, 1966, the stock sold at 78¼.	24	32	40
	Roger wears a size 7 3/8 hat and likes black.	27	36	45
	Jerry Mazell had 24 out-of-town boys at his party.	30	40	50

. . . . 1 . . . . 2 . . . . 3 . . . . 4 . . . . 5 . . . . 6 . . . . 7 . . . . 8 . . . . 9 . . . . 10 . . . . 11 12

Group 3
We paid 49¼, sold at 56½, and made $725!
He read Conquest, a book on "power politics."
The * refers to Sample Quiz 6 on page 90 of TESTS.
Pay Kerr & Orr's bill of $89.75 (less 10%) by the 20th.

In this unit you will get "work experience" by typing selected job assignments for several members of the staff of Eastern Hills Recreation Center. Prepare carbon copies when directed to do so, envelopes when appropriate. Correct any errors you make. Strive to make to-be-mailed items mailable, within-the-office items usable.

Job 1: Typing Mailing-List Index Cards

Type an address card, similar to the one illustrated at the right, for each new EHRC member listed below. Number the cards consecutively (in the upper right corner), starting with the number 191. If necessary, review the procedure suggested in the paragraphs of 251C, page 367. After typing all the cards, arrange them in alphabetic order by surnames. If two surnames are identical, arrange the two cards according to the first names.

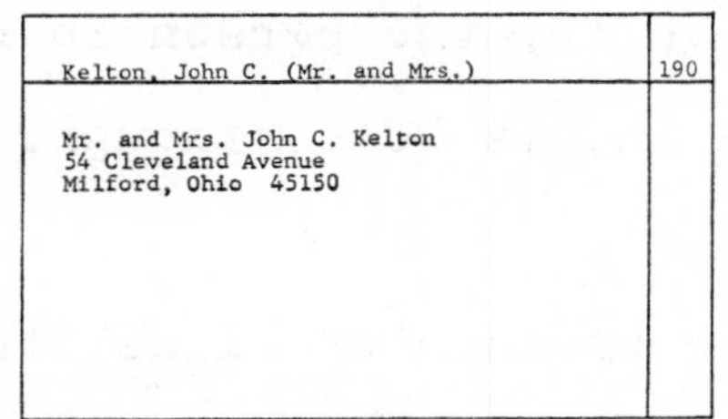

Kelton, John C. (Mr. and Mrs.) 190

Mr. and Mrs. John C. Kelton
54 Cleveland Avenue
Milford, Ohio 45150

Mr. Kenneth M. Gray
2846 Beechmont Avenue
Mt. Washington, Ohio 45226

Mr. Zahn Q. Fischer, Jr.
1293 Coolidge Avenue
Mt. Washington, Ohio 45230

Miss Virginia L. Lunt
R. R. 1, Box 68
Milford, Ohio 45150

Miss Cathy Kensington
Oxford House, Apt. 10
3720 Center Street
Mariemont, Ohio 45227

Miss Zoe Ann Fischer
6840 Main Street
Newtown, Ohio 45244

Mr. Quentin J. Lancaster
7839 Laurel Avenue
Madeira, Ohio 45243

Dr. and Mrs. Dean Hunter
546 Homewood Road
Fairfax, Ohio 45227

Mr. and Mrs. Alex B. Koch
389 Red Bud Place
Terrace Park, Ohio 45174

Mrs. Alma Jean Foster
3846 Walton Creek Road
Plainville, Ohio 45227

Mr. Richard S. Grayson
Overlook Apartments, #23
8360 Indian Hill Road
Indian Hill, Ohio 45227

Job 2: Typing Folder Labels

To open a correspondence folder for each new member, you are to type a label, similar to the one illustrated below, from each of the index cards you prepared in Job 1. If necessary, review the procedure suggested in the paragraphs of 251D, page 368.

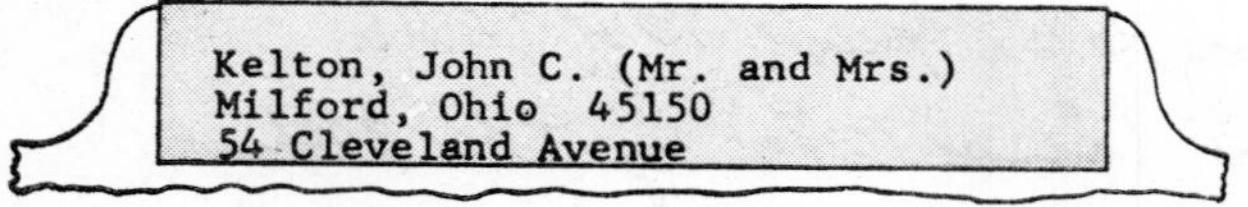

Kelton, John C. (Mr. and Mrs.)
Milford, Ohio 45150
54 Cleveland Avenue

Job 3: Typing Form Letters

Type the following "form" letter (with a carbon copy) to new members whose card numbers are 191–196. Use half-sheet stationery (5½" x 8½"), modified-block style, and open punctuation.

Telephone 271-4849
Eastern Hills Recreation Center
7285 Wooster Pike, Plainville, Ohio 45227
February 18, 19--

Miss Dorothy Dolbey
6582 Madison Road
Madisonville, Ohio 45227

Dear Miss Dolbey

Here is your "RC" Membership Card. You should bring it along each time you visit the Center. This card identifies you as a member in good standing and is your entre' to all regular and special teen activities.

You have joined a stimulating group of boys and girls. I'm sure "RC" membership will mean a lot to you, as it has to so many other young people. Do take full advantage of it during the coming year. Use the enclosed "Activity Schedule" to remind you of the wide variety of activities that await you at Eastern Hills Recreation Center.

I hope to see you here often. Why not stop by my office the next time you come in; perhaps I can answer any questions you may have about the programs we have planned for you.

Cordially yours

Lynn K. Shellenberg
Youth Director

xx

Enclosures

Then adapt the letter to young adult members 197, 198, 199, and 200 by making these changes: (1) If the letter is going to a couple, change *Card* to *Cards* and verbs and pronouns to plural form as necessary. (2) Substitute *young adult* for *teen* in ¶ 1. (3) Change *boys and girls* to *young men and women.* (4) Prepare *these* letters for the signature of **John J. Archibald Director, Adult Programs**

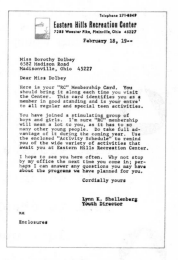

February 18, 19–– *(Address and Salutation)* (¶ 1) Here is your "RC" Membership Card. You should bring it along each time you visit the Center. This card identifies you as a member in good standing and is your entree to all regular and special teen activities. (¶ 2) You have joined a stimulating group of boys and girls. I'm sure "RC" membership will mean a lot to you, as it has to so many other young people. Do take full advantage of it during the coming year. Use the enclosed "Activity Schedule" to remind you of the wide variety of activities that await you at Eastern Hills Recreation Center. (¶ 3) I hope to see you here often. Why not stop by my office the next time you come in; perhaps I can answer any questions you may have about the programs we have planned for you. Cordially yours Lynn K. Shellenberg Youth Director (xx) Enclosures

Job 4: Typing Form Messages on Postal Cards

Send the following postal card message to new members 191–194 who are members of the Swim Club.

February 25, 19–– *(Salutation)* (¶ 1) Buckeye Memorial Pool at EHRC will be closed March 12–14 for facelifting repairs to assure you of more enjoyable swimming. Please bear with us during this period. (¶ 2) We'll be "back in the swim" on March 16. See you then. Pat Thornton, Physical Director

Centering; Word Division

1. Arrange work area for efficient typing.
2. Adjust paper guide and insert full sheet.
3. Use 60-space line and single spacing, unless otherwise directed.
4. *Bonus Typing:* Select drills from page 54.

LESSON 35

35A: Conditioning Practice (10) *each line three times; Line 4 for 1′ writings*

Alphabet	`This exquisite zircon will be put in my ring by Jack Vedorf.`	*Quick return*
Figure	`Mark's box is 6 by 9 feet and weighs from 275 to 300 pounds.`	
Symbol-figure	`Does Mr. Link's $5,000 Policy #24-789 expire on May 6, 1973?`	
Easy	`Always think each problem through before you try to type it.`	
	`....1....2....3....4....5....6....7....8....9....10....11....12`	

35B: Technique Practice – Shift Lock (10) *each line three times (Save for use with 35D)*

LEARN: The four steps in adjusting machine for typing a line in centered form.

1	*Use shift lock for ALL CAPS*	`Make FOUR machine adjustments before starting the centering.`
2		`FIRST STEP:  Move the margin stops to the ends of the scale.`
3		`SECOND STEP:  Clear all your tab stops that have been "set."`
4		`THIRD STEP:  Move the carriage to exact center of the paper.`
5		`FOURTH STEP:  Set tabulator stop at the center of the paper.`
		`....1....2....3....4....5....6....7....8....9....10....11....12`

35C: Drill on Horizontal Centering (10) *drill sheet; DS; repeat if time permits*

DO:
1. **Move** left margin stop to 0, right stop to end of scale.
2. **Clear** tab stops; then set a stop at center of paper.
3. **Tabulate** to center of paper and backspace from that point to center each line of the drill.

HOW TO CENTER: From center point of paper, backspace *once* for each *two* letters, figures, spaces, or punctuation marks in the line. Do not backspace for an odd or leftover stroke. Start to type where the backspacing ends.

```
                HORIZONTAL CENTERING
                                      TS
            Set tab stop at center of paper

              Backspace "once for two"

   In backspacing, disregard odd or leftover stroke

         Begin to type where backspacing ends
```

251D: Guided Writing for Control (10) *three 1′ guided writings on each ¶ at an appropriate speed*

All letters are used.

Text	GWAM 3′	5′	
The names used to file letters, memos, and reports are typically	4	45	85
typed on gummed file folder labels that are later affixed to the folders	9	48	88
themselves. Labels may be purchased in various styles, continuous rolls	14	51	91
and separate or folded strips being among the most common. The most ef-	19	54	94
ficient procedure is to insert a strip or a roll--not a single label--	24	57	96
quickly into the machine. It is possible, however, to type separate	28	60	99
labels by using a pleated sheet of paper to hold them in typing position.	33	63	102
Folder labels may be typed in a variety of styles, according to the	38	65	105
preference of the office supervisor. It is essential, nevertheless, that	42	68	108
the style selected be consistently applied. Every line begins just two	47	71	111
or three horizontal spaces from the left edge of the label, the first one	52	74	114
being positioned on the second line space from the top (or score line).	57	77	116
Individual or company names appear on the first line; city and state	62	80	119
names on the second; street addresses, if used, on the third.	66	82	122

3′ GWAM | 1 | 2 | 3 | 4 | 5 |
5′ GWAM | 1 | 2 | 3 |

251E: Sustained Skill Building (15) *two 5′ timed writings; determine average* nwam

Begin with the ¶s of 251C, page 367; continue with the ¶s of 251D, above. If necessary, repeat the ¶s of 251D, above. *The 5′* gwam count *begun on page 367 is continued for the ¶s of 251D.*

LESSONS 252-255

Lessons 252 and 254

Use the following plan for Lessons 252 and 254. Retain all completed Jobs until Lesson 256.

Conditioning Practice (5′): Type 251A, page 367, as directed there.

Technique Mastery (7′): Use each of the last three lines of 251B, page 367, as two 1′ speed writings.

Speed Typing (8′): Type two 3′ speed writings on 251C, page 367. Determine *gwam*.

Applied Typing (30′): Type the Jobs on pages 369–372. Use an eraser, when necessary, and your best correction techniques for usable work.

Lessons 253 and 255

Use the following plan for Lessons 253 and 255. Retain all completed Jobs until Lesson 256.

Conditioning Practice (5′): Type 251A, page 367, or use 256A, page 372.

Technique Mastery (7′): Use each of the first three lines of 251B, page 367, for two 1′ control writings.

Control Typing (8′): Type a 1′ guided writing on each ¶ of 251D, above; then type a 3′ control writing on both ¶s. Determine *nwam*.

Applied Typing (30′): Continue typing the Jobs.

35D: Problem Typing – Centered Announcement (10) *half sheets; DS; 1½" (9-line) top margin*

1. Place the typed copy of 35B, page 61, beside your typewriter for easy reference.
2. Get ready to type as directed in 35B, page 61. **Note.** To leave a 9-line top margin, begin typing on Line 10.
3. Center and type each line of the announcement at the right as directed in HOW TO CENTER, page 61.
4. Type the announcement a second time to fix in mind the procedure for horizontal centering.

```
FUTURE BUSINESS LEADERS OF AMERICA

will hear

Jerry Marshall, Former Peace Corpsman

speak on

"The Peace Corps:  Promises and Problems"

SCIENCE LECTURE HALL

Friday, the 26th, 3:45 p.m.
```

35E: Tabulated Drill (10) *twice as shown (Line: 60; SS; 15 spaces between columns)*

Learn to align columns of figures at the right. Space forward or backward as necessary. Set a tab stop for the digit in each column that requires the least forward and backward spacing. Do not consider fractions a part of the column; let them extend into between-column space.

	Margin	Tab	Tab	Tab
	901	1432	670	8145
Space forward →	53	175	123	267
	234	90 5/8	45 2/3	80
	604	6090	2350	9102
KEY	3 | 15	4 | 15	4 | 15	4

LESSON 36

60-space line | Single spacing

36A: Conditioning Practice (10) *each line three times; Line 4 for 1' writings*

Alphabet Ford G. Jenkins will have the zeal to become expert quickly. *Eyes on copy*

Figure I am just 16, but Paul is 19 years 3 months and 27 days old.

Symbol Burt Phillip's short-term policy has a pay-as-you-go clause.

Easy Your mind will manage your fingers if you will let it do so.

. . . . 1 . . . . 2 . . . . 3 . . . . 4 . . . . 5 . . . . 6 . . . . 7 . . . . 8 . . . . 9 . . . . 10 . . . . 11 12

36B: Horizontal Centering (10) *half sheets; DS; 2" (12-line) top margin; center each line*

Drill 1.

```
THE CAREFUL WRITER

A Modern Guide to English Usage

by

Theodore M. Bernstein

19--
```

Drill 2.

```
DRAMATICS CLUB MEMBERS

are invited to

Oklahoma Auditions

Wednesday, the 15th, 3:15 p.m.

The Little Theater
```

Unit 44 | Lessons 251-256

Typing in a General Service Office

LESSON 251

251A: Conditioning Practice (5) *each line three times; then 1′ writings on Line 4*

Alphabet	Lex Jory saw Van Biggs quickly catch a high foul to dazzle my top men.	*Work for quiet control of keys*
Figure	157 826 395 647 1205 7392 4036 5829 1400 02155 45227 90024 15213 45101	
Figure-symbol	February 26, J–4805, $1,412.75; March 5, C–9364 CR, $226.50; $1,186.25	
Fluency	Their statement for the six big fixtures should be paid by noon today.	

| 1 | 2 | 3 | 4 | 5 | 6 | 7 | 8 | 9 | 10 | 11 | 12 | 13 | 14 |

251B: Technique Mastery – Stroking (10) *each line four times; then 1′ writings*

Home row	Alf Gallo had an ad made; ask Jake Kallan to flash the ad at his sale.	*Keep the action in the fingers; down-and-in space-bar strokes*
Third row	Were you told to quote the prices of those tires to the two young men?	
Bottom row	The men can use five big zinc buckets to mix that brackish concoction.	
Double letters	Do you possess the supplies needed to write the letter of application?	
One-hand	My rate contract was referred to a union steward at the staff address.	
Balanced-hand	The auditor may sign the eight forms and pay the girls for their work.	

| 1 | 2 | 3 | 4 | 5 | 6 | 7 | 8 | 9 | 10 | 11 | 12 | 13 | 14 |

251C: Typing for Speed (10) *three 1′ speed writings on each ¶*

All letters are used.

	GWAM 1′	3′	5′	
All index cards in a card file should be typed in identical form,	13	4	3	45
for uniformity of style makes filing and finding faster and easier.	27	9	5	48
Personal as well as firm names are begun three spaces from the left	41	14	8	51
edge of the card and only slightly above the printed rule. Personal	54	18	11	54
names, however, are typed in transposed order; that is, surname first,	69	23	14	56
first name or initial second, and middle name or initial last. Per-	82	27	16	59
sonal or professional titles––such as Mrs. or Dr.––and seniority indi-	96	32	19	62
cators––such as Jr. or Sr.––are typed in parentheses after the name.	110	36	22	65
For a mailing list purpose, the name and address of a person or	13	41	24	67
company are typed in postal sequence a triple space beneath the horizon-	27	45	27	70
tal rule of an index card. A mailing address consists of a personal or	42	50	30	73
professional title (if appropriate) and name in the sequence usually	55	55	33	76
written; the house number and street name; the city and state names;	69	59	36	78
and, today vital, the postal ZIP Code. The address is ordinarily typed	84	64	39	81
with single spacing in horizontal alignment with the first word on the	98	69	41	84
printed rule of the index card.	104	71	43	85

1′ GWAM | 1 | 2 | 3 | 4 | 5 | 6 | 7 | 8 | 9 | 10 | 11 | 12 | 13 | 14 |
3′ GWAM | 1 | 2 | 3 | 4 | 5 |
5′ GWAM | 1 | 2 | 3 |

36C: Building Speed (10) *(Line: 60; DS; ¶ indention: 5)*

1. **Type** two 1′ writings on the *exploration level.* Determine average *gwam.*
2. **Type** 2′ writings on the *exploration level.* Try to maintain your average 1′ *gwam.*

All letters are used.

	GWAM 1′	2′	
Do you make full use of your practice time in learning	11	6	36
to type? You are the only one who can give an exact answer	23	12	42
to this vital question. Others may judge your practice	34	17	47
method and rate it as good, but is it quite right for you?	46	23	53
You must realize that how you type means more now than what	58	29	59
you type.	60	30	60

1′ GWAM | 1 | 2 | 3 | 4 | 5 | 6 | 7 | 8 | 9 | 10 | 11 | 12 |
2′ GWAM | 1 | 2 | 3 | 4 | 5 | 6 |

36D: Problem Typing – Syllable Identification (15) *(twice on half sheets; SS; 1½″ top margin)*

1. Begin Column 1 at left margin of 60-space line; set tab stops for Columns 2, 3, and 4 according to the *Key* beneath the list.
2. Center and type the heading; then TS.
3. Type first word in Column 1; tabulate to Column 2 and type the first word with the hyphen to show division between syllables; tabulate to Column 3 and type the first word; and tabulate to Column 4 and type the first word of Column 3 but *with the hyphen between syllables.*
4. Type the remaining words in a similar manner.
5. Verify syllable identification with the dictionary or with your teacher. Make pencil corrections. Retype the problem if time permits.

SYLLABLE IDENTIFICATION

TS

				Words
				5
backspaced	back-spaced	bookstands	book-stands	14
centered	cen-tered	knowledge		22
children	chil-dren	practiced		30
described	de-scribed	preferred		38
mentioned	men-tioned	progressed		47
possessed	pos-sessed	questioned		56
published	pub-lished	sentence		64
students	stu-dents	transfer		71
scheduled	sched-uled	transcript		80
thousands	thou-sands	transcribe		89

KEY | 10 | 6 | 11 | 6 | 10 | 6 | 11 |

36E: Typing Long Words (5)

TYPE: The words in Column 1 (above) in two lines (5 words per line), then the words in Column 3 (in the same manner). Type as fast as you can and as slow as you must to type *accurately.* Experiment with stroking patterns that will help you keep the carriage moving.

Problem 2: Invoice

				Words
Sold To:	Castle Gift Shoppe	Date	October 15, 19––	10
	2102 Prince Boulevard	Our No.	B–2514OP	18
	Wilmington, Delaware 19816	Cust. Order No.	WX–1703	29
Terms:	4/10, N/30 E.O.M.	Shipped Via	REA	38
Checked By:	*(Your initials)*	Salesman	Robinson	45

Quantity	Description	Cat. No.	Unit Price	Price	Words
					54
8 doz.	Goblets, 9-oz., Style 8A	G987	5.40 doz.	43.20	65
6 doz.	Parfait Glasses, 5-oz., Style 8	PG43	4.80 doz.	28.80	77
10 doz.	Cocktail Glasses, 4-oz., Style 3	CG62	6.10 doz.	61.00	89
4 doz.	Cordial Glasses, 1-oz., Style 7	CG6S	4.25 doz.	17.00	101
12 doz.	Tumbler Glasses, 4-oz., Style 1	TG19	3.90 doz.	46.80	114
6 doz.	Sherbet Glasses, 6-oz., Style 4	SG30	5.35 doz.	32.10	127
				228.90	128

Problem 3: Report of Inventory *(full sheet; DS data)*

	Words
PERRY AND ADDAMSON DEPARTMENT STORE	7
Report of Inventory, December 31, 19––	15
Appliances Department	24

Stock Number	Item	Recorded Balance	Warehouse Count	Difference	Words
					29 / 44
86 B 45818	Blender, 6-Speed, 38 oz.	102	102	0	53
86 CO 45320	Can Opener, Electric, Stand	223	222	−1	64
86 CO 45321	Can Opener, Electric, Deluxe	319	319	0	74
86 G 46050	Griddle, Teflon-Coated, 12″	92	92	0	84
89 EK 45620	Knife, Electric	137	138	+1	92
89 EK 45621	Knife, Electric, Cordless	64	64	0	101
90 M 2001	Mixer, Hand, 3-Speed	142	140	−2	110
90 M 45750	Mixer, Stand, 12-Speed	23	23	0	119
94 P 2809	Percolator, Automatic, 8-Cup	36	36	0	128
94 P 45403	Percolator, Automatic, 10-Cup	23	20	−3	138
96 S 45609	Skillet, Automatic, Aluminum	68	68	0	147
96 S 45100	Defroster, Electric	21	20	−1	156
96 T 45215	Toaster, 2-Slice	79	82	+3	163
96 T 45240	Toaster, 4-Slice	19	19	0	170
96 W 2361	Waffle Iron, Automatic	47	41	−6	179

LESSON 37

60-space line | Single spacing

37A: Conditioning Practice (10) *each line three times; Line 4 for 1′ writings*

Alphabet	Will Mrs. P. B. Jacks study very hard for the long tax quiz?
Figure	Leonard drove 570 miles in about 12 hours on April 23, 1966.
Figure-symbol	The 4½% rate on Frank's $3,750 note (dated 9/28/66) is fair.
Easy	Even if work is done well enough, it may not be good enough.

. . . . 1 . . . . 2 . . . . 3 . . . . 4 . . . . 5 . . . . 6 . . . . 7 . . . . 8 . . . . 9 . . . . 10 . . . . 11 12

37B: Technique Practice – Long Words (10) *each line twice; underline as shown*

LEARN: Words printed in italics should be underlined when typed. Words underlined in typed copy sent to the printer will be set in italics by the typesetter.

LEARN: A solid underline is preferred for titles and related word groups; a broken underline, for isolated or unrelated words: A Manual of Style; syllable identification; dots and hyphens.

		Words
1	Syllable identification is your first step in word division.	19
2	Careful pronunciation is a guide to syllable identification.	16
3	When in doubt, use a dictionary or the Word Division Manual.	18
4	Old dictionaries identify all syllables by dots and hyphens.	15
5	Newer dictionaries indicate only acceptable division points.	14
6	Learn and follow the basic guides for correct word division.	14

37C: Problem Typing – Syllable Identification (15) *(twice on half sheets; SS; 1½″ top margin)*

1. Begin Column 1 at left margin of 60-space line; set tab stops for Columns 2, 3, and 4 according to the *Key* beneath the list.
2. Center and type the heading; then TS.
3. Type the first word in Column 1; tabulate to Column 2 and type the word with the hyphens; then type Column 3; and in Column 4, type the words of Column 3 *with the hyphen between syllables.*

SYLLABLE IDENTIFICATION — Words 5

TS

				Words
beginning	be-gin-ning	accordance	ac-cord-ance	14
committee	com-mit-tee	commercial		23
condition	con-di-tion	commission		32
continued	con-tin-ued	conference		42
customers	cus-to-mers	connection		51
different	dif-fer-ent	convenient		60
personnel	per-son-nel	management		69
procedure	pro-ce-dure	provisions		78
reference	ref-er-ence	purchasing		88
relations	re-la-tions	successful		97

KEY: 9 | 6 | 11 | 6 | 10 | 6 | 12

LESSON 250

250A: Conditioning Practice (5) *each line three times; then 1′ writings*

Alphabet	Vic Brent told the group of women six quite zany jokes about his trip.	*Begin slowly, speed up gradually*
Figure	Table 214 on page 60 shows that 5,783 more workmen were hired in 1964.	
Figure-symbol	The interest due on September 19 is $25.67 ($3,850 for 60 days at 4%).	
Fluency	As soon as you have studied the papers carefully, give me your report.	
	| 1 | 2 | 3 | 4 | 5 | 6 | 7 | 8 | 9 | 10 | 11 | 12 | 13 | 14 |	

250B: Production Typing (45)

DO: Type the following problems for 30 minutes. Prepare a carbon copy for each problem. Correct errors as you type. When time is called, check your work carefully and determine *n-pram.*

Problem 1: Interoffice Memorandum (*cc on plain paper*)

Words

TO: Frank L. Powers, Vice-President DATE: March 17, 19–– 9
FILE: O–163PA 11
FROM: John A. Fitzpatrick, President SUBJECT: Expansion of Operations 22

On March 15, the Board of Directors voted to explore the possibility of expanding 38
the operations of the company to the southeastern part of the United States, 54
specifically in the states of Tennessee, North Carolina, Mississippi, Alabama, 70
Georgia, South Carolina, and Florida. 77

You are appointed as the chairman of a committee to determine the feasibility 93
of initiating operations in these states. The committee will consist of the following 110
individuals from the departments indicated: 119

Name	Department	
Howard C. Mensch	Marketing	131
Paul T. O'Brian	Purchasing	136
Sidney M. Samios	Personnel	142
Martin B. Klein	Controller	147
William R. Smith	Production	153

(Header row: 125)

The committee will prepare for presentation to the Board of Directors at its meet- 169
ing in June a detailed analysis of the proposal. The report will include the 184
following data: (1) Projected sales potential in the area for a 5-year period; 200
(2) Anticipated production for a 5-year period; (3) Sources of necessary raw 216
materials and component parts; (4) Potential sites for the location of new plant 232
facilities; and (5) Projected costs and potential return on capital investment for a 249
5-year period. 252

Will you please let me have an interim report of the committee's findings not 268
later than April 30, 19––. 273

37D: Building Control (10) *(Line: 60; DS; ¶ indention: 5)*

1. Type two 1′ *control-level* writings. Circle errors. Determine average *gwam.*
2. Type two 1′ writings at a rate 2 to 4 *gwam* less than your average *gwam.* Circle errors. Determine average *gwam.*

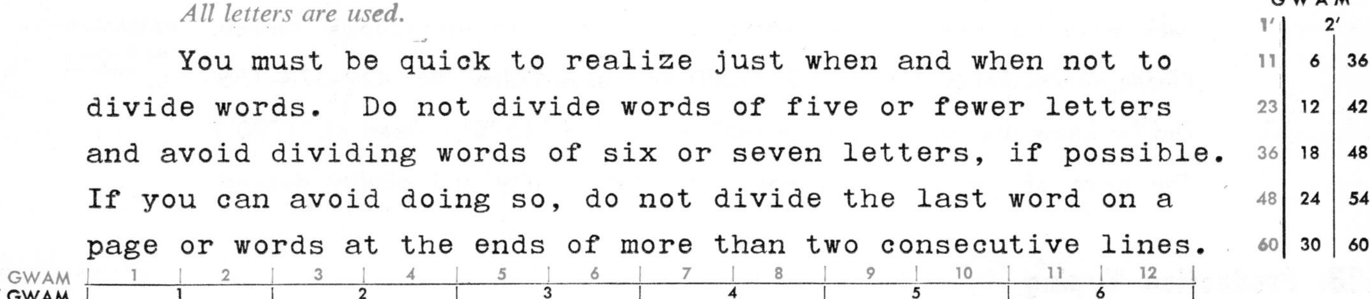

All letters are used.

	GWAM 1′	2′	
You must be quick to realize just when and when not to	11	6	36
divide words. Do not divide words of five or fewer letters	23	12	42
and avoid dividing words of six or seven letters, if possible.	36	18	48
If you can avoid doing so, do not divide the last word on a	48	24	54
page or words at the ends of more than two consecutive lines.	60	30	60

GWAM | 1 | 2 | 3 | 4 | 5 | 6 | 7 | 8 | 9 | 10 | 11 | 12 |
2′ GWAM | 1 | 2 | 3 | 4 | 5 | 6 |

37E: Bell Cue (5)

1. Set the right margin stop for an exact 60-space line (center + 30).
2. Type the sentence below slowly and *stop typing* as soon as the bell rings; then type the figures 1, 2, 3, etc., (instead of the remainder of the sentence) until the machine locks. The last figure typed is the number of spaces the bell on your typewriter rings before it locks. REMEMBER THIS NUMBER.
3. Subtract 3 from the number of *bell cue spaces* (Step 2) and move the right stop to the right that far (exact line ending + 5 or more).
4. Type the sentence three or more times to check the accuracy of the setting of the right stop.

Set stop for bell to ring 3 spaces before desired line ending.

LESSON 38

60-space line | Single spacing

38A: Conditioning Practice (10) *each line three times; Line 4 for 1′ writings*

■ In this lesson and those that follow, set the right margin stop 5 or more spaces beyond the desired line ending to compensate for the early ringing of the bell. (See 37E, above.)

Alphabet	P. X. Lantz will drive Mrs. Klung to Quebec for July Fourth.
Figure	By 9:45 a.m., 6 of the 18 men and 20 of the 37 boys arrived.
Figure-symbol	The * (page 123) refers to Document 456-78-90 dated 10/7/66.
Easy	Their auditor may make a claim for the goods that were lost.

. . . . 1 . . . . 2 . . . . 3 . . . . 4 . . . . 5 . . . . 6 . . . . 7 . . . . 8 . . . . 9 . . . . 10 . . . . 11 12

38B: Drill on Typing Outside the Margins (5)

1. Depress the margin release **25** and backspace 5 spaces into the left margin.
2. Type the 72-space sentence (below) three times, typing until the carriage locks (ignore the ringing of the bell); then depress the margin release and complete typing the sentence.

Set the right stop 5 to 8 or more spaces beyond the desired line ending.

LESSON 249

249A: Conditioning Practice (5) *each line three times; then 1′ writings*

Alphabet	Jack gave Liz many fine awards at the banquet for exceptional service.	*Reach with the fingers*
Figure	Please cancel Policy No. 159–267–380 and issue Policy No. 429–378–156.	
Figure-symbol	Did he know that Master Card #3462 was coded "1578" instead of "1790"?	
Fluency	The price of the item will depend on the quantity and quality desired.	
	1 | 2 | 3 | 4 | 5 | 6 | 7 | 8 | 9 | 10 | 11 | 12 | 13 | 14	

249B: Production Typing (45)

DO: Type the following problems for 30 minutes. Prepare a carbon copy for each problem. Correct errors as you type. When time is called, proofread your work carefully and determine *n-pram.*

Problem 1: Block Letter with Open Punctuation

Words

April 23, 19–– National Department Stores, 9
Inc. 4500 Michigan Avenue Chicago, Illinois 18
60615 Attention Mr. John L. Schmitt, Purchasing 27
Officer Gentlemen (¶ 1) Thank you for your 35
order for 5,000 of our Model T6145 transistor 44
radios to be marketed under your brand name, 53
"NATCO." We know you will find our transistor 62
radio a quality item that will please your cus- 72
tomers. (¶ 2) In our conversation last week, you 80
indicated that you were satisfied with the terms 90
of sale we offered with the exception of the 99
delivery schedule. After discussing this matter 109
with our Chief of Production, I am pleased to 118
say that we can deliver the radios on the follow- 128
ing schedule: 131

		Words
July 1	500	133
August 15	500	136
September 1	1,000	139
October 15	1,500	143
November 15	1,500	146

(¶ 3) Our production plans are almost completed, 156
and we will begin producing the radios as soon as 165
we receive the design of the crest you wish to 174
have embossed on the carrying case. (¶ 4) It 182
has been a great pleasure working with you on 192
this order. We hope that it marks the beginning 201
of a mutually satisfactory and profitable associa- 211
tion. Sincerely yours Ralph C. Henderson Direc- 221
tor of Marketing (181) 224

Problem 2: Modified Block Letter with Mixed Punctuation

Words

January 23, 19–– Mr. Donald York 1548 8
Maple Street Wilmington, Delaware 19805 16
Dear Mr. York (¶ 1) Your letter of January 16 24
addressed to our main office in Chicago has 33
been forwarded to me for reply. (¶ 2) Com- 40
plete repair services for your SUNBURY Electric 49
Mixer are available in our Philadelphia Store 59
which is located on the corner of Broad and 67
Vine Streets. The store is open Monday through 77
Friday from 8:00 a.m. until 5:00 p.m. and on 86
Saturday from 8:00 a.m. until 1:00 p.m. If you 96
do not wish to visit our store personally, you 105
may mail your SUNBURY mixer to us. We will 114
repair it promptly and return it to you free of 123
charge. (¶ 3) We hope that we will have the 131
pleasure of serving you in the very near future. 141
Sincerely yours Alexander C. Billingsley Man- 150
ager (122) 151

Problem 3: Business Report

DO: Type the paragraphs on page 363 as a report to be bound at the top. Use FORMS OF BUSINESS OWNERSHIP as a main heading and the following side headings preceding the ¶s indicated:

¶ 1 Private Ownership of Business
¶ 2 The Sole Proprietorship
¶ 3 The Partnership
¶ 4 The Corporation

38C: Problem Typing – Word Division (15) *twice on half sheets (Line: 60; SS; 1" top margin)*

1. Type the main heading centered horizontally.
2. After typing the first line of Item 2, reset the left margin stop 4 spaces to the right. To type the numbers for the following items, move the carriage outside the left margin. (See 38B, page 65.)
3. Circle errors; make corrections in form, if needed; and retype the problem.

Words

"DO NOT" AND "AVOID" GUIDES FOR WORD DIVISION 9

TS

1. Do not divide a word of five or fewer letters. 19

2. Do not divide from the remainder of the word: 30

Reset margin → a. A one-letter syllable at the beginning or end of a 41
word; as, <u>around</u>, <u>steady</u> 48

b. A syllable without a vowel; as, <u>wouldn't</u> 59

c. A two-letter syllable at the end of a word; as, 69
<u>greatly</u> 72 *(2 spaces)*

DS

3. Avoid dividing after a two-letter syllable at the begin- 84
ning of a word. Try to divide elsewhere in the word; as, 95
<u>express-ing</u>. 100

Use margin release; then backspace

4. Avoid dividing initials, proper names, numbers, or abbre- 113
viations. Initials or a given name may be separated from 124
a surname when necessary. 129

38D: Vertical Centering – Backspace-from-Center Method (20) *twice on half sheets (Line: 44; SS)*

LEARN: Triple-space after main heading.

DO:
1. Center drill vertically (follow Basic Rule at right).
2. Center horizontally and type main heading. Type remaining lines in block style.
3. Circle errors.
4. Retype from textbook copy.

TIPS FOR SAFE DRIVING

TS

Adjust seat belts.
Pull into traffic carefully.
Drive "defensively"––expect the unexpected.
Stick to your lane, except when passing.
Watch out for pedestrians.
Match your speed to road conditions.
Observe the legal speed limit.
Never pass on a hill or blind curve.
Dim your lights when car comes toward you.
Avoid fatigue; on long drives, stop to rest.
Slow down after dark.

VERTICAL CENTERING—BACKSPACE-FROM-CENTER METHOD

Basic Rule. From vertical center of paper, roll platen (cylinder) back once for each two lines, two blank line spaces, or line and blank line space. Ignore odd or leftover line.

Steps in Vertical Centering

1. To insert paper to vertical center, start spacing down from *top edge of paper*—
   - a. *Half sheet:* Down 6 TS — 1 SS (to Line 17).
   - b. *Full sheet:* Down 11 TS + 1 SS (to Line 34).
2. From vertical center—
   - a. *Half sheet,* SS or DS: Follow Basic Rule (back 1 for 2).
   - b. *Full sheet,* SS or DS: Follow Basic Rule (back 1 for 2); then back 2 SS for *reading position.**

NOTE: The mathematical method of vertical centering is taught on page 98.

* Approximately 2 line spaces above actual vertical center.

All letters are used.

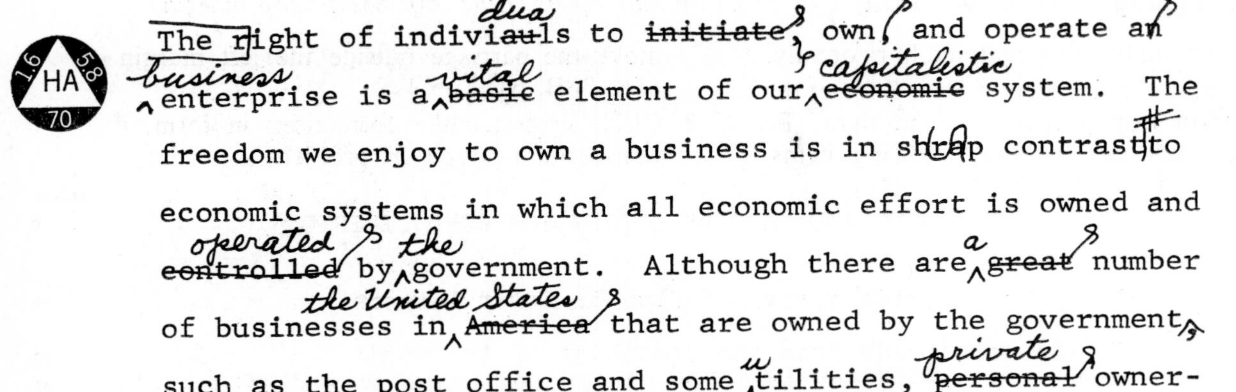

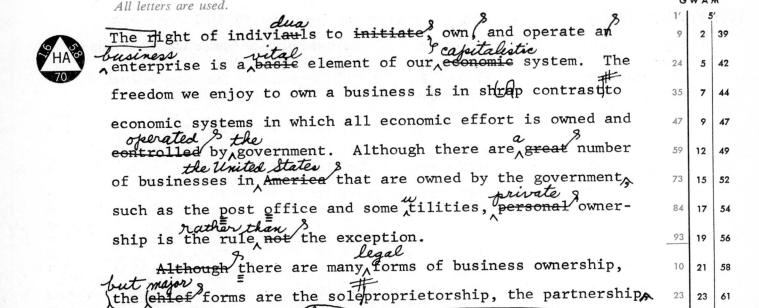

	GWAM 1'	5'	
The right of indivi~~au~~[dua]ls to ~~initiate~~, own, and operate an	9	2	39
[business] enterprise is a [vital] ~~basic~~ element of our [capitalistic] ~~economic~~ system. The	24	5	42
freedom we enjoy to own a business is in shrap contrast to	35	7	44
economic systems in which all economic effort is owned and	47	9	47
~~controlled~~ [operated] by [the] government. Although there are [a] ~~great~~ number	59	12	49
of businesses in [the United States] ~~America~~ that are owned by the government,	73	15	52
such as the post office and some [u]tilities, [private] ~~personal~~ owner-	84	17	54
ship is the rule [rather than] ~~not~~ the exception.	93	19	56
~~Although~~ there are many [legal] forms of business ownership,	10	21	58
[but major] the ~~chief~~ forms are the sole proprietorship, the partnership,	23	23	61
and the corporation. A business owned by one person, the	28	24	62
sole proprietorship, is the oldest and most common [form]. ~~In~~ [Under] this	49	28	66
form, the [owner] ~~proprietor~~ has the [utmost] ~~most~~ freedom in his actions,	60	30	68
and he owns all the earned profits. It is [limited] ~~small~~ in size,	72	33	70
scope, and [capital] ~~assets~~, how ever, and many sole owners [fail to] ~~do not~~	83	35	73
[earn] ~~make~~ a profit beduase of a lack of [managerial ability] ~~business skill~~.	94	37	75

	GWAM 1'	5'	
A partnership is an association of two or more persons who	12	2	32
agree, orally or in writing, to engage in a business for profit.	25	5	35
Though it adds financial strength and managerial skill to a	37	7	37
business, the partnership is the least popular form of business	50	10	40
ownership. The prime drawback of the partnership is that each	62	12	42
partner is personally liable for all the debts of the business.	75	15	45
A corporation is a legal entity with the rights, duties,	11	17	47
and powers of a person. It ranks first in terms of goods made,	24	20	49
workers hired, and profits won. By issuing stocks and bonds,	37	22	52
it can acquire capital easily from a number of individuals, and	49	25	54
it is unlimited in size and scope. Despite legal controls and	62	27	57
high taxes, the corporation dominates our business scene.	73	30	59

LESSON 39

60-space line | Single spacing

39A: Conditioning Practice (10) *each line three times; Line 4 for 1′ writings*

Alphabet Hal F. Jacolby is spending a quiet week in Veracruz, Mexico.

Figure The 15 girls and 8 boys typed Lessons 39 and 40 on March 26.

Figure-symbol Paul's bill read: "12 pads @ 25¢ each; 48 pens @ 79¢ each."

Easy Pause briefly if you make an error; then type without hurry.

. . . . 1 . . . . 2 . . . . 3 . . . . 4 . . . . 5 . . . . 6 . . . . 7 . . . . 8 . . . . 9 . . . . 10 . . . . 11 12

39B: Drill on Vertical Centering (10) *(Half sheets; Line: 40; once SS; once DS)*

TIPS FOR TYPISTS

TS

Head up; eyes on copy; feet flat on floor
Wrists relaxed and low; fingers curved
Hands poised lightly near keyboard
Thumb on or close to space bar
Quick key stroke and release
Quiet forearms and elbows

39C: Problem Typing – Guides for Word Division (15) *full sheet (Line: 60; SS)*

1. Center the problem vertically (reading position) on a full sheet.
2. Type the main heading centered horizontally.
3. After typing the first line of Item 1, reset the left margin stop 4 spaces to the right.
4. To type the numbers for the following items, backspace into the left margin. (See 38B, page 65).
5. Circle errors. Make needed corrections in form. Retype the problem if time permits.

Words

GUIDES FOR WORD DIVISION 5

TS

1. Divide a word between syllables only. Type a hyphen at 17
Reset margin → the end of the line to indicate the division. Type the 28
rest of the word on the succeeding line. 37

2. Divide after a one-letter syllable within a word, as sepa- 50
rate, unless the word ends with able, ible, or ical (the 65
two-syllable endings you must keep as a unit); as, depend- 78
able. If two one-letter syllables come together, divide 90
between the vowels; as, gradu-ation. 100

Use margin release; then backspace

3. When dividing words, type cial, tial, cion, sion, or tion 117
as a unit; as, impar-tial, impres-sion. 130

4. If the final consonant in a word is doubled when adding 142
a suffix, divide between the double letters; as, control- 155
ling; but when a syllable is added to a word that ends in 167
double letters, divide after the double letters; as, express- 181
ing, unwill-ing. 187

	GWAM 1′	10′	
Although the majority of the transactions on an exchange involve	13	18	73
stock transfers, an exchange is also a marketplace for bonds. A share	27	19	74
of stock represents ownership in a corporation; a bond is a form of	41	20	75
promissory note that represents capital lent to an enterprise. People	55	22	77
invest funds in stocks with the expectation of sharing in the company's	69	23	78
profits which are paid as dividends to stockholders. A person who buys	84	25	80
bonds lends his money for a specified period on the condition that the	98	26	81
money will be repaid with interest. The two basic types of stock are	112	28	82
common and preferred. Owners of common stock normally have the right to	127	29	84
vote for the directors of the enterprise and to share in any dividends.	141	30	85
One who owns preferred stock may not have the privilege of voting, but	155	32	87
he is usually paid dividends at a fixed percent before owners of common	170	33	88
shares earn any dividends.	175	34	89
Almost all corporate securities are sold to the public initially	13	35	90
by an investment banking house. When long-term or fixed capital is	27	37	91
sought by a new corporation or capital for expansion is desired by an	41	38	93
established corporation, it is usually obtained through the sale of	54	39	94
stocks or bonds. Since it would take quite a bit of time and effort for	69	41	96
a corporation to sell enough bonds or shares of stocks to individuals	83	42	97
to raise the funds, they turn to an investment banker or one who is a	97	44	98
specialist in raising the capital desired to begin or expand a business.	112	45	100
If the investment banker decides that the venture is a sound one, he	125	46	101
buys the stocks or bonds from the corporation at the market value less	140	48	102
a sum which serves as his commission for marketing the securities. The	154	49	104
securities are sold, in turn, directly to individual investors or to	168	51	106
banks, insurance companies, and mutual funds. In this fashion, people	182	52	107
from all walks of life have contributed to the amazingly rapid growth	196	53	108
of the American economy by helping to finance our industrial expansion.	210	55	110

1′ GWAM | 1 | 2 | 3 | 4 | 5 | 6 | 7 | 8 | 9 | 10 | 11 | 12 | 13 | 14 |

10′ GWAM | 1 | 2 |

248D: Skill Index – Rough Draft and Script (15)

1. Type a 5′ writing on paragraphs 1 and 2, page 363. Determine *gwam* and errors. Compare your score with the score recorded for 228B, page 336.
2. Type a 5′ writing on paragraphs 3 and 4, page 363. Determine *gwam* and errors. Compare your score with the score recorded for 229B, page 338.

39D: Drill on Word Division (15) *(1 full, 1 half sheet; Line: 60; DS)*

1. Center the drill vertically (reading position) on a full sheet; DS. (See page 66.)
2. Center and type the heading horizontally.
3. Tabulate from column to column.
4. When typing the Column 4 words, type the hyphen to indicate preferred divisions. If a word can't be divided, type it whole.
5. Center and type the drill on a half sheet; DS.

WORD DIVISION — Words 3

TS

				Words
announcement	announce-ment	instruction	instruc-tion	13
stretched	stretched	impression		22
educates	edu-cates	switched		29
initiates	ini-ti-ates	problems		37
expendable	expend-able	paragraph		46
syllables	syl-la-bles	continuing		56
insinuates	insinu-ates	physical		64
insinuation	insinu-ation	commercial		74
attention	atten-tion	exclusion		82
compelling	com-pel-ling	expelling		91
compressing	com-press-ing	telegrams		101
manuscript	manu-script	explosion		109
KEY 12	4 13	4 11	4 12	

LESSON 40

60-space line | Single spacing

40A: Conditioning Practice (10) *each line three times; Line 4 for 1′ writings*

Quick, snap stroke

Alphabet Was Len Grove quizzed by Ed Jackson on part of his tax form?

Figure Of the 789 who sailed on May 23, 54 left the ship on July 6.

Symbol Shift to type " (quotation), % (percent), and _ (underline).

Easy An idea is a funny little thing that won't work unless I do.

. . . . 1 . . . . 2 . . . . 3 . . . . 4 . . . . 5 . . . . 6 . . . . 7 . . . . 8 . . . . 9 . . . . 10 . . . . 11 12

40B: Building Figure Control (10) *(Line: 60; DS; ¶ indention: 5)*

1. Type three 2′ *control-level* writings. Circle errors. Determine average *gwam.*
2. Type 1′ writings at your average 2′ rate, as time permits. Try to type without error.

	GWAM 1′	2′	
For a goal of 32 words, the quarter-minute guides will	11	6	34
be 8, 16, 24, and 32. If the goal is 36 words, your guides	23	12	40
will be called at 9, 18, 27, and 36. For a goal of 40, the	35	18	46
guides will be called at 10, 20, 30, and 40. A call of the	47	24	52
guide can aid you to type at a specific rate.	56	28	56

1′ GWAM 1 2 3 4 5 6 7 8 9 10 11 12
2′ GWAM 1 2 3 4 5 6

Unit 43 | Lessons 248-250

Measuring Basic and Production Skills

LESSON 248

248A: Conditioning Practice (5) *each line three times*

Alphabet	Did Jack realize we expected to have Vera Quinby at the staff meeting?	*Return quickly*
Figure	The urban population rose from 1,347,398 in 1950 to 2,574,260 in 1961.	
Figure-symbol	In Lot #647A, 180 units (25%) were rejected at a total cost of $2,390.	
Fluency	Does the original study show the total quantity of materials required?	
	1 | 2 | 3 | 4 | 5 | 6 | 7 | 8 | 9 | 10 | 11 | 12 | 13 | 14	

248B: Technique Mastery (15) *each line four times; then 1′ writings*

Double letters	William keeps all his college books and business letters in my office.
Direct reach	If the country is to survive, great and sweeping changes must be made.
Right hand	In my opinion, they will pump a minimum of one million gallons of oil.
Left hand	I read that water rates are greater in my area than the state average.
Third row	I will type with fewer errors if I keep my eyes on the copy as I type.
Balanced-hand	When the work is done right, both workmen will be paid for their time.
	1 | 2 | 3 | 4 | 5 | 6 | 7 | 8 | 9 | 10 | 11 | 12 | 13 | 14

248C: Growth Index (15)

TYPE: One 10′ writing on ¶s below and on page 362. Circle errors. Determine *nwam*.

All letters are used.

	GWAM 1′	10′	
A stock exchange is a marketplace where securities are bought and	13	1	56
sold. Although there are numerous exchanges in the United States, the	27	3	58
oldest, busiest, and best known is the New York Stock Exchange. The	41	4	59
sales and prices of securities bought and sold on the New York Stock	55	6	60
Exchange are quoted on television and radio broadcasts and in almost	69	7	62
every daily newspaper. An exchange provides a marketplace for the sale	83	8	63
of securities in somewhat the same fashion that a retailer establishes	97	10	65
a market for the sale of articles of food or clothing. There are some	112	11	66
fundamental differences, however. A retailer owns the items he offers	126	13	67
for sale, and he establishes the prices to be paid. An exchange does not	141	14	69
own the securities traded on the exchange nor does it influence in any	155	15	70
way the prices at which they may be traded. *(Continued)*	163	16	71

1′ GWAM | 1 | 2 | 3 | 4 | 5 | 6 | 7 | 8 | 9 | 10 | 11 | 12 | 13 | 14 |
10′ GWAM | 1 | 2 |

40C: Growth Index (15) *(Full sheet; Line: 60; DS; ¶ indention: 5)*

1. Type a 3′ *control-level* writing. Circle errors. Determine *gwam.*
2. Type a 1′ *exploration-level* writing on each ¶.
3. Type a 1′ *control-level* writing on each ¶. Circle errors.
4. Type a 3′ *control-level* writing. Circle errors. Determine *gwam*; compare with first 3′ rate.

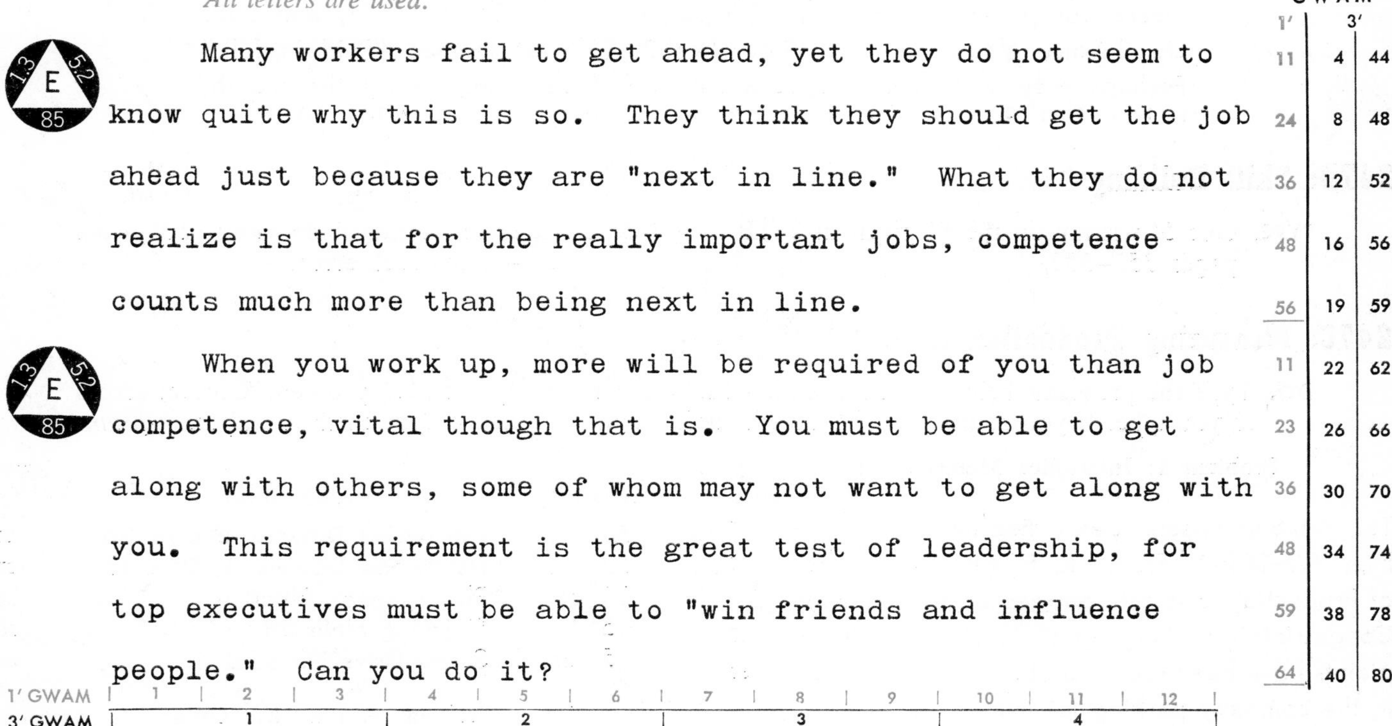

All letters are used.

E 1.3 5.2 85		GWAM 1′	3′	
	Many workers fail to get ahead, yet they do not seem to	11	4	44
	know quite why this is so. They think they should get the job	24	8	48
	ahead just because they are "next in line." What they do not	36	12	52
	realize is that for the really important jobs, competence	48	16	56
	counts much more than being next in line.	56	19	59
E 1.3 5.2 85	When you work up, more will be required of you than job	11	22	62
	competence, vital though that is. You must be able to get	23	26	66
	along with others, some of whom may not want to get along with	36	30	70
	you. This requirement is the great test of leadership, for	48	34	74
	top executives must be able to "win friends and influence	59	38	78
	people." Can you do it?	64	40	80

1′ GWAM | 1 | 2 | 3 | 4 | 5 | 6 | 7 | 8 | 9 | 10 | 11 | 12 |

3′ GWAM | 1 | 2 | 3 | 4 |

40D: Word Division Check (15) *(Full sheet; Line: 60; DS)*

1. Center the drill vertically (reading position), double spaced. Follow the directions given in Step 2. ⟶
2. Type the heading centered horizontally; then type the words in Columns 2 and 4 with the hyphen to indicate preferred divisions.

		WORD DIVISION		Words
		TS		3
available	avail-able	certificate	cer-tifi-cate	12
community	com-munity	convenience		22
conferred	con-ferred	convenient		31
equipment	equip-ment	especially		39
hesitates	hesi-tates	excellent		48
medicine	medi-cine	experiment		56
mentioned	men-tioned	facilities		65
modified	modi-fied	merchants		73
mortgage	mort-gage	operations		81
president	presi-dent	performance		91
problems	prob-lems	preferring		99
shipping	ship-ping	recommends		108
situation	situ-ation	regulations		117
standards	stan-dards	suggestions		127

KEY | 9 | 6 | 10 | 6 | 11 | 6 | 13 |

LESSON 247

247A: Conditioning Practice (5) *each line three times*

Alphabet	My five tricky questions were answered by the zoology experts in June.	*Fingers curved*
Figure	Please correct the errors found on pages 53, 64, 80, 92, 117, and 258.	
Figure-symbol	Our Invoice #4807 for $1,539.60 (less 20%) was stamped "Paid in full."	
Fluency	Perhaps they will have a special sale on these items during the month.	
	| 1 | 2 | 3 | 4 | 5 | 6 | 7 | 8 | 9 | 10 | 11 | 12 | 13 | 14 |	

247B: Skill Building (8)

TYPE: One 5′ writing on the ¶s given in 241B, pages 351–352.

DO: Circle errors. Determine *nwam*: (10′ *gwam* × 2) – 1 for each error.

247C: Measuring Production Skill (37)

DO: Type the problems below for 30 minutes. Make a carbon copy of each problem. Correct errors as you type. If you complete the problems before time is called, retype them. Compute *n-pram*.

Problem 1: Interoffice Memorandum

Words

To: All Supervisors Date: February 17, 19–– 7
File: PD–389–1 From: R. F. Alberts, Director 13
of Production Subject: Suggestion for Relieving 21
Congestion in Parking Lot (¶ 1) Numerous com- 28
plaints have been received about the congestion 38
in the company parking lot immediately before 47
and after working hours. To alleviate this situ- 57
ation, it has been suggested that the working 66
hours of the various shops be staggered as 74
shown below: 77

Shop	Begin Work	End Work	Words
			87
A	7:45 a.m.	4:45 p.m.	91
B	8:00 a.m.	5:00 p.m.	95
C	8:15 a.m.	5:15 p.m.	100

(¶ 2) Please study the effect of this suggestion 108
on your operations, discuss the proposal with 118
your employees, and let me have your comments 127
and recommendations not later than March 1. 136

Problem 2: Purchase Requisition

Words

Deliver to: M. L. Carlson Location: Repair Shop 5
Job No.: 1601 Requisition No. 753 Date: 7
June 8, 19–– Date Required: June 30, 19–– 12

Quantity	Description	Words
50 ea.	Hardwood Dowels, 1/8″ x 36″	20
50 ea.	Hardwood Dowels, 1/4″ x 36″	27
10 qts.	Plastic Wood Filler	33
5 lbs.	Finishing Nails 2d	38
5 lbs.	Screw Drive Nails 7d	44

Problem 3: Purchase Order

Words

Ordered from: Kraft Wholesale Hardware Co. 6
630 Main Street Tulsa, Oklahoma 74102 14
Order No.: RE–46168 Ship Via: Rapid Deliv- 18
ery Service Date: June 10, 19–– Terms: 2/10, 24
n/30 (*Use quantity and description of items given* 25
in Problem 2 above).

Cat. No.	Unit Price	Amount	Words
43180	.08 ea.	4.00	36
43181	.10 ea.	5.00	48
L9135	1.32 qt.	13.20	58
N2410	.33 lb.	1.65	67
N2473	.35 lb.	1.75	77
		25.60	79

Problem 4: Invoice

Type Invoice No. **H–3715A** dated **June 15, 19––**, and addressed to the Hart Manufacturing Co., 5893 Sperry Drive, Vinita, Oklahoma 74301, for the items listed in the Purchase Order in Problem 3; SALESMAN: **Sherman**

Unit 6 | Lessons 41-47

Announcements; Personal Notes; Postal Cards

LESSON 41

1. Arrange work area for efficient practice.
2. Adjust paper guide and paper-bail rolls.
3. Insert full sheet and adjust paper bail.
4. Unless otherwise directed: use a 60-space line; SS drills; DS and indent ¶ writings.

41A: Conditioning Practice (10) *each line three times; Line 4 for 1′ speed writings*

Alphabet	James Gibson will quickly explain what Dave made for prizes.
Figure	Rooms 210, 536, and 947 have been reserved for September 28.
Figure-symbol	Is the rate 6% or 5 3/4% on Howe & North's note for $26,000?
Easy	The men are skeptical about the authenticity of the records.

. . . . 1 . . . . 2 . . . . 3 . . . . 4 . . . . 5 . . . . 6 . . . . 7 . . . . 8 . . . . 9 . . . . 10 . . . . 11 12

41B: Problem Typing – Announcements (20)

Problem 1
(*Half sheet; Line: 50; SS*)

1. Set margin and tab stops for typing the ¶s *and* the list of names *before* starting the actual typing. Note the *Key* beneath the problem.
2. Center the problem vertically (see page 66, 38D); center the heading horizontally (see page 61, 35C). →

	Words
BAND REHEARSAL	3
TS	
The rehearsal scheduled for Friday afternoon, the	13
10th, has been postponed until Tuesday, the 14th.	23
The rehearsal will be held in the Music Room.	32
DS	
The following members of the Band are to report to	42
Mr. Novenski in Room 201 at 4:15 p.m. on Monday, the	53
13th, for instructions for their special program to	63
be given at the PTA meeting next Thursday:	72
Marquand Andrews Frank Nowak	78
Arthur Dawson Karl Schreiber	84
Michael Huemrich Max Sodini	90

KEY | 5 | 16 | 10 | 14 | 7 |

Problem 2
(*Half sheet; DS*)

Center the problem vertically (DS); center each line horizontally. →

	Words
THE ACADEMIC HONORS SOCIETY	6
announces	8
Free Tutoring for Juniors and Seniors	15
in	16
Physics and Mathematics	21
Wednesdays and Fridays	25
3:45 to 5:15 p.m.	29
Rooms 103 and 105	32

245C: Production Typing – Statistical Table (20)

DO: Type the following statistical table. Center the table horizontally and vertically in the reading position. Double-space the columnar entries. Correct errors as you type.

				Words
FARNSWORTH–ANDERSON DEPARTMENT STORE				7
Monthly Sales by Department for Year Ending December 31, 19––				20
(in thousands of dollars)				25
MONTH	DEPARTMENT A	DEPARTMENT B	DEPARTMENT C	34
January	21.9	23.8	27.7	39
February	20.6	23.7	27.6	43
March	25.3	32.0	36.8	47
April	30.1	34.1	39.0	52
May	27.1	35.2	44.9	56
June	21.5	35.1	46.3	60
July	25.2	29.6	39.6	64
August	29.9	29.6	38.9	68
September	34.4	34.3	47.6	73
October	33.7	44.0	58.1	78
November	37.1	40.9	49.0	82
December	41.9	51.3	66.4	87
TOTAL	348.7	413.6	521.9	92

LESSON 246

246A: Conditioning Practice (5) *each line three times*

Alphabet Has Max gone to Quebec and Japan instead of Norway and Czechoslovakia? *Shift quickly, but firmly*

Figure The stock rose today from 39 7/8 to 40 1/2 based on 5,160 shares sold.

Figure-symbol Earnings of Horner & Jones increased 7.2% in 1966 to $35.8 (millions).

Fluency The president praised each individual for his outstanding workmanship.

| 1 | 2 | 3 | 4 | 5 | 6 | 7 | 8 | 9 | 10 | 11 | 12 | 13 | 14 |

246B: Sustained Production Typing (45)

TYPE: A 30′ writing on the following:

Page 354, 242B
Page 356, 243C
Page 357, 244B, Problem 1
Page 358, 245B, Problem 1

Make one carbon copy. Correct errors as you type. If you complete the problems before time is called, retype them. When time is called, check your work carefully and determine *n-pram*.

41C: Centering on Special-Size Paper (10)

LEARN: To determine the center of special-size paper (or card), follow these steps:

1. Read and add the numbers from the cylinder scale at the left and right edges of the paper.
2. Divide the sum by 2. The resulting number is the center of the paper.

DRILL 1: 1. Insert a half sheet (5½″ x 8½″) with the long edge at the left.

2. Use double spacing and a 2½″ top margin.
3. Determine the center of the half sheet. Set tab.
4. Center horizontally each line of the announcement typed as Problem 2, page 70.

DRILL 2: 1. Fold the half sheet used in Drill 1 from bottom to top.

2. Insert the folded sheet, creased edge at left.
3. Use double spacing and a 1½″ top margin.
4. Center horizontally each line of the announcement typed as Problem 2, page 70.

41D: Building Control (10) *(Line: 60; DS; ¶ indention: 5)*

TYPE: A 1′ writing and three 2′ writings on the *control level.* Circle errors.

1.3 5.4 80

All letters are used.

	GWAM 1′	2′	
The technique for typing long or difficult words is to	11	5	40
type one stroke at a time without pausing between strokes.	23	11	46
Don't freeze to the last letter of a word. Don't stop to	35	17	52
see the errors you make as you type, but just type the next	47	23	58
word. Type carefully and move quickly from one letter to the	59	29	64
next. This is the technique for typing difficult words.	70	35	70

1′ GWAM | 1 | 2 | 3 | 4 | 5 | 6 | 7 | 8 | 9 | 10 | 11 | 12 |
2′ GWAM | 1 | 2 | 3 | 4 | 5 | 6 |

LESSON 42

42A: Conditioning Practice (10) *each line three times; Line 4 for 1′ speed writings*

Alphabet	Didn't Zoe quickly mix the very big jar of paste for Newton?	*Low wrists*
Figure	Item 10, page 263, priced at $4.97 must be changed to $6.58.	
Figure-symbol	John sold 230 paperback books @ 40¢ each and 169 @ 75¢ each.	
Easy	The usual title to the visual aids will be held by the firm.	
	. . . . 1 . . . . 2 . . . . 3 . . . . 4 . . . . 5 . . . . 6 . . . . 7 . . . . 8 . . . . 9 . . . . 10 . . . . 11 12	

42B: Building Speed (5)

TYPE: Three 1′ *exploration-level* writings on 41D, above. Determine *gwam* of best writing.

LESSON 245

245A: Conditioning Practice (5) *each line three times*

Alphabet	Judge Leroy Willoughby asked them five amazing and explicit questions.	*Low wrists; quiet hands*
Figure	The total work force of 13,280 employees includes 4,357 hired in 1966.	
Figure-symbol	The net amount due on Invoice #3591A is $624 ($780 less 20% discount).	
Fluency	The next payment that is due on the loan must be made within six days.	
	| 1 | 2 | 3 | 4 | 5 | 6 | 7 | 8 | 9 | 10 | 11 | 12 | 13 | 14 |	

245B: Production Skill Building – Business Forms (25)

DO: Type a 10′ writing on each of the following forms. If you complete the problem before time is called, start over. Determine *g-pram.*

Problem 1: Bill of Lading

Words

Shipper's No. **304750** Carrier **Freedom Transport Service, Inc.** From **Modern** 9
Furniture Manufacturing Company Date **October 16, 19––** at **Dearborn,** 21
Michigan Consigned To **Keystone Furniture Company** Destination **1520 Broad** 31
Street City **Harrisburg** County **Dauphin** State **Pennsylvania** Routing **Via** 39
Interstate Truck Lines, Detroit, Michigan Vehicle or Car Initial **OYT** No. **6472** 50

Packages	Description	Weight	Words
6	Folding Tables, Plastic Top	324#	57
2	Folding Chairs, Tubular Steel	300#	64
10	Toy Chest, Unpainted	230#	70
5	Bookcase, 3-shelf, Unpainted	145#	77
8	Cabinet, 2-drawer, Unpainted	185#	84

Shipper **Modern Furniture Manufacturing Company** Permanent Address 92
of Shipper **960 North Huron Street, Dearborn, Michigan 48120** 102

Problem 2: Statement of Account

Words

Date **October 31, 19––** To **Keystone Furniture Company, 1520 Broad Street,** 13
Harrisburg, Pennsylvania 17101 19

Date		Items	Debits	Credits	Balance Due	Words
October	1	Balance			569.00	24
	2	Invoice #74208	1,304.30		1,873.30	31
	10	Invoice #75316	401.60		2,274.90	38
	15	Payment on Account		569.00	1,705.90	45
	16	Invoice #80021	519.40		2,225.30	52
	23	Credit Memorandum #3610		105.20	2,120.10	61
	29	Payment on Account		1,304.30	815.80	68

1" Top margin

Words

October 16, 19-- 3

Operate return mechanism 4 times for 3 blank line spaces between date and salutation

Salutation

Dear Midge: DS

What a birthday party I had! Everything was just 16
about perfect, except that you couldn't be here. 26
The scarf you sent is beautiful. It does something 36
for my drab personality! Thank you for it. I'll 46
wear it often, and always with pleasure. DS 55

Hal Russell wants to take you to the Prom the first 65
weekend of next month. Stay the weekend with me, 75
please. That will make both Hal and me happy. DS 85

Again, thanks for the lovely scarf. Do write soon. 95
DS

Complimentary close

Sincerely, 97

Sandra

PERSONAL NOTE IN BLOCK STYLE

42C: Problem Typing – Personal Notes (25) *(Half sheet; Line: 50; SS; 1" top margin)*

Problem 1

LEARN: *Mixed punctuation* requires a colon after the salutation and a comma after the complimentary close.

TYPE: The model personal note illustrated above.

Problem 2

TYPE: Using the current date and directions in Problem 1, type the personal note given at the right.

* Three words (15 strokes) are counted for the date.

Words

3*

Dear Mike: 5

The big Tech-Roosevelt game will be played here on 16
the 25th. I have four seats at the 50-yard line. 26
I hope you'll come for the game and spend the week- 36
end with me. Kay will get a date for you. 45

Several parties are to be given after the game. 55
We'll let Kay and your date decide which we'll 64
attend. All of them should be fun. 72

Be sure to come for the game. Let me know your 81
flight schedule. I'll be on hand to meet you. 91

Yours, 92

42C continues on page 73.

244B: Production Skill Building – Business Forms (25)

DO: Type a 10′ writing on each of the following problems. If you complete the problem before time is called, start over. Determine *g-pram*.

Problem 1: Purchase Order

				Words
Ordered From:	New Century Electronics, Inc.	Order No.	EM–57289	13
	1200 West Street	Date	March 8, 19––	20
	Sheridan, Illinois 60551	Ordered by	Research Laboratory	32
Ship To:	King Manufacturing Co.	Terms	Net	41
	2430 Brimson Avenue	F.O.B.	Duluth	48
	Duluth, Minnesota 55801	Ship by	Air Express	56

Quantity	Cat. No.	Description	Price	Total	Words
100	HOF1350A	Semiconductors	14.40	144.00	72
500	PNP2N1038	Power Transistors	2.80	1,400.00	81
250	ARA63F2207	Stroboscopic Tubes	6.34	1,585.00	91
500	SQ2535	Cadmium-Sulfide Photocells	1.37	685.00	103
				3,814.00	105

(Header row: 64 words)

Problem 2: Invoice

				Words
Sold To:	Ace Hardware Store	Date	November 16, 19––	11
	2400 Jefferson Road	Our No.	R–4826–S	18
	Alexandria, Virginia 22316	Cust. Order No.	FT–38571	29
		Shipped By	Graylines Transport	35
Terms:	2/10, n/30	Salesman	Pierpont	43

Quantity	Cat. No.	Description	Price	Total	Words
400	47206	Duplex Receptacle, T Slot, 4″ Cover	.33	132.00	63
200	47276	Porcelain Receptacle	.24	48.00	71
150	29816	Porcelain Ceiling Receptacle	.42	63.00	81
50	47219	50 Amp 3-Wire Range Receptacle	1.13	56.50	92
				299.50	93

(Header row: 51 words)

244C: Production Typing – Business Forms (20)

DO: Type the following interoffice memorandum. Correct errors as you type.

Words

To: M. B. Kennedy, Purchasing Officer Date: 7
March 8, 19–– File: PO–145–67 From: H. W. 13
Wells, Comptroller Subject: Purchase of Special 21
Electronic Supplies (¶ 1) The following special 29
supplies are required for Project XB 1470 at the 39
earliest possible date: (*list items in Problem 1* 44
above; show all columns except the Total column) 74
(¶ 2) These supplies can be purchased from 82
New Century Electronics, Inc., 1200 West Street, 92
Sheridan, Illinois 60551, under the emergency 101
procedures established by Paragraph 301.9 of 110
the Manual of Standard Operating Procedures. 119
(¶ 3) Please arrange to have these items shipped 128
by Air Express and delivered to the Research 137
Laboratory immediately upon arrival. Please 146
advise when delivery has been made. 154

Problem 3: Personal Note

1. Insert a half sheet, long edge at left.
2. Determine center (see page 71, 41C).
3. Set stops for a 40-space line.
4. Use block style and mixed punctuation.
5. Type the date on Line 13 or 14, followed by three blank line spaces.
6. Girls type Problem 1, boys Problem 2, from page 72. Sign your own name.

42D: Bell Cue (10) *(Line: 60; DS; ¶ indention: 5)*

1. Type the ¶ with the full 60-space line. The line endings will not be the same as in the copy. Be guided by the bell cue for the return. *One* word should be divided.
2. Use a 70-space line and 5-space ¶ indention. Retype the ¶, dividing *no* words.
3. Type 1′ writings.

	1′ GWAM
Just as no two people are exactly alike, so	9
no two typewriters are exactly the same. This means	19
that it is necessary for each typist to learn the	29
peculiarities of the typewriter he will operate if	40
he is to make maximum use of it.	46
....1....2....3....4....5....6....7....8....9....10	

LESSON 43

43A: Conditioning Practice (10) *each line three times; Line 4 for 1′ speed writings*

Alphabet	Brevity and quick wit must be highly prized by Jay F. Dixon.	*Quick return*
Figure	I moved from 735 East 46th Ave. to 810 Dow Street on May 29.	
Figure-symbol	The out-of-town speaker wired, "Flight 210 arrives at 4:35."	
Easy	It is the duty of the girls to handle the quantity of forms.	
	....1....2....3....4....5....6....7....8....9....10....11....12	

43B: Building Control (5) *(Line: 60; DS; ¶ indention: 5)*

1. Type the ¶ without timing, with a goal of errorless typing. *Be guided by the bell cue for the return.*
2. Type two 1′ writings. Circle errors. Determine *gwam* of the better writing.

All letters are used.

	1′ GWAM
You can adjust to the operation of different	9
typewriters by learning the most effective manipu-	19
lation of the operative parts and the best stroking	29
technique to use. You can expect the change to cut	40
your speed for a few days, but you can compensate	50
for the loss by emphasizing accuracy and continuity.	60
....1....2....3....4....5....6....7....8....9....10	

Problem 2: Telefax Message

DO: Type the Telefax message below to be sent as a night letter. Correct errors as you type.

	Words
TXL Charge to: Browning Research Institute St.	8
Louis, Missouri August 17, 19–– Lyman Elec-	16
tronics Industries 7800 McClelland Drive San	25
Francisco, California (¶) Analysis of data regard-	34
ing new processing methods proposed for Oak-	43
land Plant will be completed August 15. David	52
Stevenson, Research Analyst, can meet with you	62
on August 17. Please advise if these arrange-	71
ments are satisfactory. James W. Reed, General	80
Manager	81

243C: Tabulation Skill Building – Timed Writing (25) *(DS the columnar items)*

1. Type a 10′ writing using the mathematical method to determine horizontal placement. Begin on Line 7. Determine *g-pram.*
2. Type a 10′ writing using the backspace-from-center method to determine horizontal placement. Begin on Line 7. Determine *g-pram.*

			Words
TEMPLEMAN–BARNES FURNITURE MANUFACTURING CORPORATION			11
Final Results of United Fund Drive			17
Department	Representative	Amount Pledged	33
Plant B	Barnes	$1,849.00	38
Plant A	Patterson	1,762.50	44
Plant C	Schermer	1,753.00	49
Administration	Richards	962.00	55
Personnel	Gordon	851.50	60
Training	Hanson	820.00	64
Sales	Breckinridge	780.75	70
Purchasing	Hayden	739.50	75
Quality Control	Clark	726.00	80
Legal	Turner	710.25	84
Accounting	Weaver	656.25	89
Marketing	Purcell	648.00	94
Maintenance	Kempt	591.25	99
Transportation	McKnight	586.75	106
Advertising	Watson	530.75	111
Public Relations	Ziegler	395.50	117
Research	Wozniak	372.50	122

LESSON 244

244A: Conditioning Practice (5) *each line three times*

Alphabet	After five months, Janice G. Badley was quite an expert pretzel maker.	*Space quickly*
Figure	In May, 4,958 units were manufactured; in June, 5,172; in July, 6,302.	
Figure-symbol	Sales in 1967 (based on final reports) rose $284,553 or 20% over 1966.	
Fluency	They plan to take a special inventory today of certain items in stock.	

| 1 | 2 | 3 | 4 | 5 | 6 | 7 | 8 | 9 | 10 | 11 | 12 | 13 | 14 |

43C: Typing from Script (10) *(Line: 60; SS)*

1. Type each sentence twice without error, untimed. (7′ limit)
2. Type 1′ writings on selected sentences, guided by the call. (3′)

		GWAM 15″	12″	10″
1	The city authority will handle the amendment.	36	45	54
2	Civic leaders will make their formal visit in May.	40	50	60
3	With good will and good skill, Jane can handle the job.	44	55	66
4	The height of the chair is not quite right for the chairman.	48	60	72
5	Our theory is the risk of a penalty may make them work hard.	48	60	72

43D: Problem Typing – Personal Notes (15) *(Half sheets; Line: 50; SS; Style: block, mixed; Date: Line 7)*

Problem 1

■ *The | in the copy indicates the end of the 50-space line, or other special line. Do not type it; but when you come to it, make the return without looking up and continue typing.*

TYPE: The note given at the right, double-spacing between single-spaced ¶s. Be guided by the symbol | to return the carriage.

	Words
October 18, 19-- | *(Operate return mechanism 4 times)* Dear Sandra:	6
| *DS* *(¶ 1)* Maybe I won't need to go to heaven now that I live | in	17
Winter Park! Everything so far has been fine, | especially the weather.	31
If this keeps up, it may | get monotonous, but I think I can stand it! |	45
(¶ 2) My address is 720 Via Lugano. The ZIP Code is | 32789. Please	58
encourage all in our group to write | me. I miss you more than you may	72
believe. | *(¶ 3)* Write soon and tell me what you do, where you go, |	84
and all about school. | *DS* Sincerely,	90

Problem 2: Alertness Training

When copy is marked for alertness training, you must be alert to note the planned "traps" for *un*thinking typists. In some later lessons, not all problems and drills will be *marked* for alertness training; nevertheless, you will be expected to check the accuracy of what is to be typed as well as what you type.

1. Insert a half sheet with long edge at the left.
2. Determine horizontal center (see page 71, 41C).
3. Set margin stops for a 40-space line.
4. Use block style and mixed punctuation.
5. Type the date on Line 13 or 14, followed by 3 blank line spaces. Type the note of Problem 1, but write it to **Sallie.**

43E: Drawing Horizontal Lines at the Typewriter (10)

Place the pencil point through the cardholder **12** (or on the type bar guide **36** above the ribbon), holding it firmly against the paper, and depress the carriage-release lever to draw the carriage across to make the line.

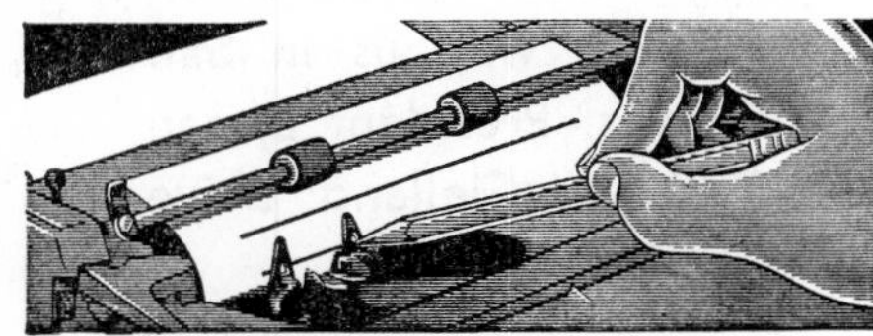

PRACTICE DRILLS

1. Center and type the following sentence:

   `My play is quite good.`

2. Draw a pencil line under the sentence, leaving a little white space between the bottom of the letters with down stems and the pencil line. *Operate the variable line spacer 3 to make room for the line below the letters.*
3. Note the relationship of the line to the type before you do Drills 4 and 5.
4. Draw an approximate 4″ pencil line; then center and type the sentence of Drill 1 on the line. *Be sure the letters with down stems do not cut through the line.*
5. Draw an approximate 3″ pencil line; then center and type your name above the line.

Words

4. If the column heading is the longest item, remember to set your tab stop so 338
that the longest item in the column is centered below the heading. 351

5. Main and secondary headings should be centered by the backspace-from-center 367
method even when the mathematical method is used to center columns of material 383
horizontally. 386

242C: Mathematical Tabulation (30)

1. Center each problem below on a half sheet of paper. Follow steps in 242B, p. 354 and this page. Insert paper with the *short* edge at the left.

Problem 1

CLAREMONT CLOTHING STORE		Words
Sales for Quarter Ending June 30, 19––		5 / 13
Department	Sales	19
Clothing	$37,462.50	23
Shoe	13,791.75	26
Hat	7,988.33	29

2. Center each problem below on a half sheet of paper. Follow the instructions in 1 except insert the paper with the *long* edge at the left.

Problem 2

WILLSTON DEPARTMENT STORE			Words
Monthly Sales Compared with Previous Year			5 / 14
Month	Last Year	This Year	23
January	$55,280	$62,740	28
February	48,730	50,940	33
March	57,820	60,220	37

LESSON 243

243A: Conditioning Practice (5) *each line three times*

Alphabet	Major Wright quickly explained the fighting hazards to Vince and Bill.	*Wrists low; reach to the number keys*
Figure	The chart shows that 7.68 squared is 58.9824; its reciprocal, .130208.	
Invoice terms	2/10 as of August 15; 5/10/E.O.M.; 4/15, prox.; 2/30/R.O.G.; 2/15–60X.	
Fluency	In the future, please send all payments on this loan to the City Bank.	
	| 1 | 2 | 3 | 4 | 5 | 6 | 7 | 8 | 9 | 10 | 11 | 12 | 13 | 14 |	

243B: Production Typing – Business Forms (20)

Problem 1: Telegram

DO: Send the following regular telegram charged to the sender, **Lyman Electronics Industries,** whose address and telephone number are to be transmitted. Correct errors as you type.

Words

San Francisco, California August 6, 19–– Mr. 15
James W. Reddinger, General Manager Brown- 23
ing Research Institute 3570 Boothwyn Boulevard 32
St. Louis, Missouri (¶) Imperative that all data 41
regarding new processing methods proposed for 51
Oakland Plant be presented to our Board of 59
Directors at earliest date. Please advise when 69
your representative can meet with us in San 78
Francisco. Michael J. Graves, President Lyman 87
Electronics Industries 7800 McClelland Drive 96
(415) 232–6400. 100

LESSON 44

44A: Conditioning Practice (10) *each line three times; Line 4 for 1′ control writings*

Alphabet	J. W. McVey explained the process of quick freezing to Bart.	*Curved fingers*
Figure	Certificates CA-4125 and ST-4789 are dated October 30, 1966.	
Figure-symbol	Your invoice reads, "2% discount in 10 days or 30 days net."	
Easy	A formal audit may be made of the books of the civic groups.	
	. . . . 1 . . . . 2 . . . . 3 . . . . 4 . . . . 5 . . . . 6 . . . . 7 . . . . 8 . . . . 9 . . . . 10 . . . . 11 12	

44B: Building Speed and Control (12) *(Line: 60; DS; ¶ indention: 5)*

1. Type a 1′ *control* writing. Determine *gwam*.
2. Type a 2′ *exploration* writing with the 15″ call to guide you at your 1′ controlled rate.
3. Type two 3′ *control-level* writings without the guide. Circle errors. Determine errors and *gwam* of better writing.

All letters are used.

	GWAM 2′	3′	
Some workers are too tired to maintain the quality of	5	4	30
their work at the height of a busy day in an office though	11	8	34
they may hold themselves to the quantity of work expected	17	11	38
of them. They may not realize it, but how well the work is	23	15	42
done ranks higher than how much is done even under pressure	29	19	46
for quantity output. Try to find out now just how well you	35	23	50
can work when much is to be done in a short time.	40	27	53

2′ GWAM | 1 | 2 | 3 | 4 | 5 | 6 |
3′ GWAM | 1 | 2 | 3 | 4 |

44C: Problem Typing (20) *(Half sheet, 2 postal cards)*

Problem 1: Memorandum with Subject Line

Use half sheet, 50-space line, SS, and block style for the memorandum at the right. Type the current date on Line 10, followed by 3 blank line spaces.

Be guided by | to return at the line endings.

	Words
Current date | *(3 blank line spaces)* SUBJECT: Typing a Postal Card |	9
DS (¶ 1) A postal card is 5½ by 3¼ inches and has a total | of 19 lines.	22
Since the top and bottom margins | take 2 or 3 lines each, there will be	36
just 12 to | 14 lines for typing. | *(¶ 2)* Each line has 55 pica or 66 elite	49
spaces, but the | left margin will take 3 or 4 spaces and the right |	63
margin 2 or 3 spaces. The writing line, then, is | limited to 48 to 50 pica	78
or 59 to 61 elite spaces.	83

44C continues on page 76.

Unit 42 | Lessons 242-247

Tabulated Reports and Business Forms Production

LESSON 242

242A: Conditioning Practice (5) *each line three times*

Alphabet	Quite sizable tax rebates were given to the Jenkins & Lawford Company.	*Read carefully; eyes on the copy*
Figure-symbol	Invoice #387 shows: Debits, $6.92; Credits, $17.59; Balance, $403.58.	
Invoice terms	2/30, n/60--45 extra; 4/30, prox.; 6/10, 90X; 4/30/R.O.G.; 3/10/E.O.M.	
Fluency	Please make the check for the special order payable to either of them.	
	| 1 | 2 | 3 | 4 | 5 | 6 | 7 | 8 | 9 | 10 | 11 | 12 | 13 | 14 |	

242B: Production Skill Building – Business Forms (15)

DO: Study the model interoffice memorandum on page 268.

TYPE: A 5′ writing on the interoffice memorandum below. Determine *g-pram*.

TYPE: A 5′ writing beginning with Item 1 as page 2 of an interoffice memorandum. Determine *g-pram*.

				Words
TO:	All Clerical Personnel	DATE:	November 1, 19––	8
		FILE:	OP–145K	10
FROM:	R. E. McMinn, Office Manager	SUBJECT:	Mathematical Centering	20

Many typists whose work is interrupted frequently by telephone calls or questions 36
prefer to use a mathematical method of centering horizontally material in columns. 53
This can be done by following these steps: 62

1. Count the strokes in the longest item in each column. (Remember, the heading may 79
need to be considered the longest item.) Determine the total strokes used in typing 96
the longest line in each column, as if it were one continuous line. 110

2. Subtract total strokes used (Step 1) from 85 (pica) or 102 (elite), or from the 127
horizontal spaces available for use on sheets of other sizes; divide the 141
remainder by the <u>number of columns plus one</u> to find the spaces in the margins 162
and between columns. Leave any extra spaces in the margins. <u>OR</u> 175

   Determine the number of spaces to be left between columns by judgment. <u>Add</u> the 190
total for Step 1 and the total spaces between columns; subtract this sum from 205
85 or 102, or from the horizontal spaces available; divide the remainder by 2 221
to find the number of spaces in each margin. 230

3. To determine the tab stops, add the number of spaces in the left margin to the 247
sum of the spaces required for the first column and the number of spaces 261
between the first and second columns. This will be your first tab stop. To 277
this number, add the sum of the spaces required for the second column and 292
the spaces between the second and third columns. This will be your second 307
tab stop. Continue in this manner for each additional column to be typed. 322

(*Continued*)

November 15, 19-- TS

Dear Linda: DS

Our Music Club has 40 tickets for the opera FAUST
for Friday, December 16, priced at $2.30 each.

You like opera, I know; so join us on December 16,
won't you? I'll hold a ticket for you. DS

Sincerely, TS

Maria Bueno

Secretary, Music Club

Problem 2: Message Typed on a Postal Card

1. Use 2 postal cards (or paper cut to the size of a 5½- by 3¼-inch card); 48-space line (to determine center, see page 71, 41C).
2. Type the message as illustrated above; then on the second card, type the same message, but use the salutation **Dear Suzanne:**

Problem 3: Addressing Postal Cards

LEARN: 1. Type the writer's name and/or return address in the upper left corner of the card on the address side: Begin on Line 2 from the top edge and 2 or 3 spaces from the left edge of the card.

2. DS a 3-line address; SS an address of 4 or more lines.

3. Space twice between state name (or abbreviation) and the ZIP Code. The state name, as well as *Avenue*, *Boulevard*, and other street designations, *may* be abbreviated to lend balance to the address lines.

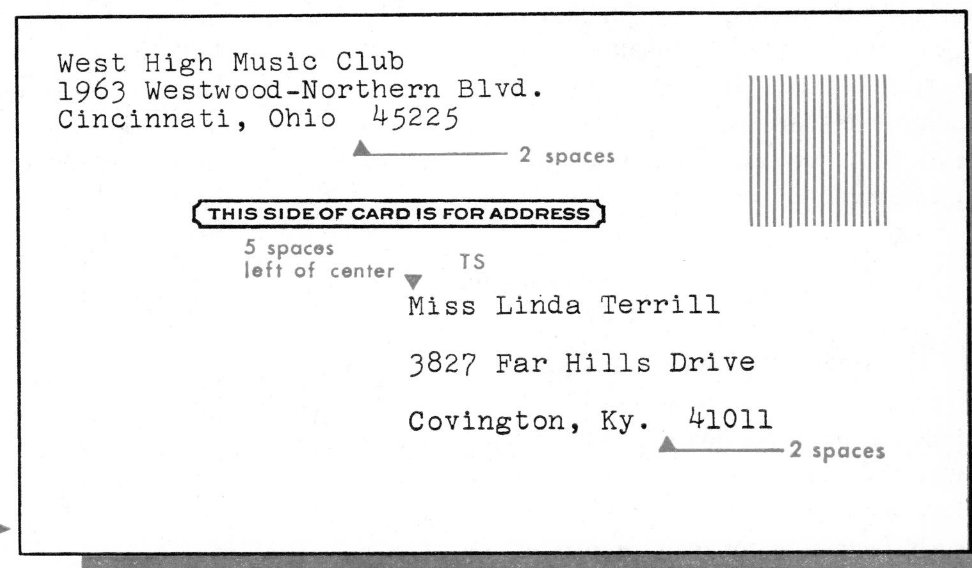

West High Music Club
1963 Westwood-Northern Blvd.
Cincinnati, Ohio 45225
2 spaces
THIS SIDE OF CARD IS FOR ADDRESS
5 spaces left of center
TS
Miss Linda Terrill
3827 Far Hills Drive
Covington, Ky. 41011
2 spaces

DO: 1. Insert the first card typed as Problem 2, above, and type the address side of the card as illustrated.

2. Insert the second card typed as Problem 2, above. Address the card to:

Miss Suzanne D'Alessandro
382 Taylor Mill Road
Newport, Kentucky 41075

241C: Measuring Production Skill (30)

Type the reports in the manuscript form indicated (20′). Prepare one carbon copy. Correct errors. List the enumerated items in Problem 1 in single-spaced form, indented 5 spaces from both margins, double-space between items. Determine *n-pram*: acceptable words typed ÷ 20.

Problem 1: Leftbound Report

Words

REORGANIZATION OF THE PERSONNEL AND 7
TRAINING DIVISION 11

(¶ 1) Effective July 1, the Personnel and Train- 19
ing Division will be redesignated as the Person- 28
nel Division. On the same date, the Training 38
Division will be established as a staff agency 47
under the direction of H. Carl McKinney, Vice- 56
President in Charge of Training. The Personnel 66
Division will retain responsibility for all activities 77
currently assigned as enumerated in the com- 85
pany's Manual of Organization and Functions, 94
except for those functions transferred to the 104
Training Division. It shall be the responsibility 114
of the Training Division to: 1. Plan, organize, 124
and administer a comprehensive training pro- 132
gram. 2. Establish objectives, policies, and pro- 142
cedures necessary to the accomplishment of the 152
training program. 3. Conduct an orientation 161
program for all new employees. 4. Coordinate 170
all training activities within the company. 5. Ad- 181
vise and assist line officials in the conduct of 190
on-the-job training. 6. Establish and conduct 200
special courses of instruction that may be re- 209
quired. (¶ 2) Changes in personnel and job 217
assignments necessary to effect this reorganiza- 226
tion will be announced in an interoffice 234
memorandum. 236

Problem 2: Unbound Report

INDEX NUMBERS 3

(¶ 1) The index number is one of the most com- 11
mon statistical measures used in business. An 20
index number is a measure of the <u>relative change</u> 33
that has taken place over a period of time. It is 43
invaluable in measuring trends and evaluating 52
such factors as prices, production, costs, and 62
sales. In its simplest form, an index number is 71
nothing more than a percentage. A year or 80
period in the past is selected as the base 89

Words

(100%), and any subsequent change is expressed 98
as a percentage of the base period. For exam- 107
ple, the cost of an item in 1956 (the base year 117
selected) was $50 (100%); in 1960, the cost of 126
the same item was $75 or one and one half 134
times its cost in 1956. In terms of a percentage, 145
the cost of the item in 1960 is 150% of the cost 154
of the item in 1956; thus, the index number 163
would be 150. Index numbers are used be- 171
cause it is usually simpler and easier to under- 181
stand percentages than it is to understand the 190
original statistical data, and the relative change 200
is readily apparent when it is stated as a per- 209
centage. (¶ 2) One of the most widely published 218
indexes is the Consumer Price Index computed 227
by the U.S. Bureau of Labor Statistics. Exam- 236
ples of this index are shown below: 243

Year	Index	247
1961	104.2	250
1962	105.4	252
1963	106.7	254
1964	108.1	256

(¶ 3) This is a much more complicated index than 265
the previous example. It reflects the changes in 275
prices paid by urban wage earners and clerical 284
workers in 46 representative cities throughout 294
the United States for a long list of goods and 303
services as compared with the prices paid in the 313
base period of 1957–1959. Although the com- 321
putation of the price index is a complex statisti- 331
cal process, the interpretation of the index is 341
relatively simple. It is easy to see that, based on 351
the factors measured by the index, the cost of 361
living in 1964 was 8.1% higher than in the base 370
period of 1957–1959. 374

Problem 3: Topbound Report

Type the material in Problem 1 in the form of a report to be bound at the top.

44D: Drawing Vertical Lines at the Typewriter (8)

Operate the line finder **6** (ratchet release). Place the pencil point through the cardholder (or on the type bar guide) above the ribbon. Turn the platen forward (away from you) for the length of line desired. Return the line finder to its normal position.

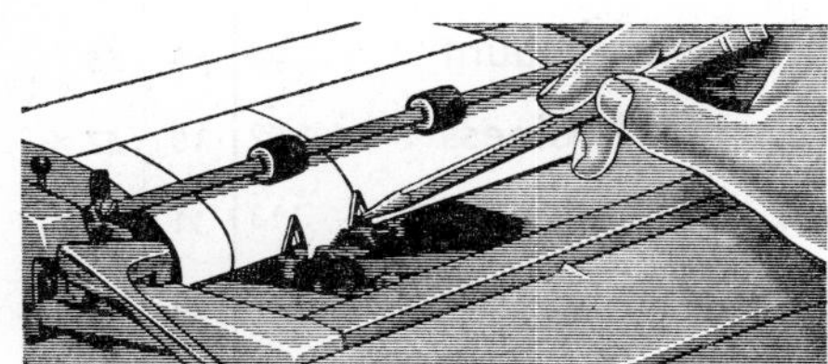

PRACTICE DRILLS

1. Draw two vertical pencil lines about 2″ long and about 4″ apart. (Return line finder to normal position.) Center (see page 71, 41C) and type near the top of the space between the lines the following words:

   Typing Headings

2. Draw a pencil line under the heading typed as Drill 1. Have a little white space between the bottom of the letters with the down stems and the line.
3. Draw two vertical pencil lines about 2″ long and about 2½ to 3″ apart. (Return the line finder to normal position.) Center (see page 71, 41C) and type your name near the top of the space between the lines; then DS and center and type the current date.
4. Draw a pencil line under the typed lines of Drill 3.
5. Type a 2″ underline; remove the paper; reinsert it; align, center, and type your name in proper position on the underline.

LESSON 45

45A: Conditioning Practice (10) *each line three times; Line 4 for 1′ control writings*

Alphabet	Jean Fox and Zona Voight typed quickly but with many errors.	*Quiet hands*
Figure	Ned bought 200 shares of Pacific at 74 3/8 on March 5, 1966.	
Symbol	"The doctor (Dr. Fixell)," the patient said, "is wonderful."	
Easy	Make a right turn at the first downtown light for the Arena.	
	. . . . 1 . . . . 2 . . . . 3 . . . . 4 . . . . 5 . . . . 6 . . . . 7 . . . . 8 . . . . 9 . . . . 10 . . . . 11 12	

45B: Centering Headings Between Vertical Lines (5)

1. Draw two vertical pencil lines about 2″ long and about 4″ apart. (Refer to 44D, above, for the procedure to follow.)
2. Center and type the name of your school between the lines; DS; center and type your own name.

45C: Information Recall (10) *each line three times, control level (Line: 60; SS)*

		Words
1	This postal card is 5½ by 3¼ inches and has 19 lines in all.	12
2	You can type on just 12 to 14 of the lines on a postal card.	12
3	Leave 3 or 4 spaces in the left margin when typing a card.	12
4	Have 2 or 3 spaces in the right margin when typing a card.	12
5	Typing line length: 48 to 50 pica or 59 to 61 elite spaces.	12

All letters are used.

	GWAM 1′	10′	
Reports are indispensable tools in the efficient operation of any	13	1	48
business enterprise. Modern managers thrive on a continuous flow of	27	3	50
data in the form of reports about such vital functions as sales, finance,	42	4	51
research, production, and purchasing. These reports may vary greatly	56	6	53
in length and scope. A report may be merely a tick mark made on a data	70	7	54
card in a fraction of a second or it may be a lengthy technical account	85	8	56
of a complex process which took days or weeks to prepare. No business	99	10	57
of any size will survive for very long without reports of many kinds.	113	11	58
Few people who are employed in the field of business escape the task of	127	13	60
writing or compiling reports, particularly those who hold office or	141	14	61
administrative positions.	146	15	62
The managers of a business utilize reports for numerous purposes.	13	16	63
They are one of the best means by which busy executives at all levels	28	17	64
of an enterprise keep well informed. Reports also establish a double	42	19	66
channel of communication through which data essential to the efficient	56	20	67
conduct of the business can flow. These vital data can be used to assess	70	22	69
results, to solve a wide variety of problems that arise, and to make	84	23	70
any changes that seem to be required. Plans made for the future must	98	24	72
be based on more than mere guesswork or vague ideas. The factual matter	113	26	73
that is found in business reports forms the basis for accurate, precise	127	27	74
decisions. Since such decisions may well decide the success or failure	142	29	76
of an enterprise in the months and years ahead, the value of timely,	155	30	77
accurate reports can be readily seen.	163	31	78
The quality of the plans and decisions that are made on the basis	13	32	79
of the data found in a report depends to a large extent on how well the	28	34	81
report is written. A poorly prepared report is likely to lead to poorly	42	35	82
formed plans and decisions. A good report is a thorough and completely	57	37	84
objective summary of all the facts and figures obtainable. It should be	71	38	85
skillfully organized and developed so that all the essential information	86	39	87
is presented in a logical sequence. The language of the report must be	100	41	88
clear, concise, and forceful. The appearance of the report should give	115	42	89
the reader a favorable impression. The data must be typed neatly, free	129	44	91
from untidy erasures, and arranged attractively on the page. A report	143	45	92
that is well prepared and well typed reflects favorably on the typist	158	47	94
as well as the writer.	162	47	94

1′ GWAM | 1 | 2 | 3 | 4 | 5 | 6 | 7 | 8 | 9 | 10 | 11 | 12 | 13 | 14 |

10′ GWAM | 1 | 2 |

45D: Problem Typing (15) *(2 postal cards; half sheet; block ¶s; SS)*

Problem 1: Postal Cards

1. Find the horizontal center of the postal card (see page 71, 41C); then set the margins for a 48-space line, a tab stop for center.
2. Beginning on Line 3, type the announcement given below and sign your name with a pen as the Secretary.
3. Type the announcement again on a second postal card. Use the directions given in Steps 1 and 2.

	Words
October 18, 19-- | *TS* *(¶ 1)* The FBLA meeting on Thursday, the 26th,	11
will be | held at 3:45 p.m. in Room 102. Mr. Max Lowell | will speak	25
on | *DS*	25
(Center) AUTOMATION AND OFFICE WORK | *DS*	31
(¶ 2) You can't afford to miss this expert's informa- | tive discussion of	44
YOUR future work. | *(Operate return mechanism 4 times)* Secretary	49

Problem 2: Addressing Postal Cards

Address the cards typed as Problem 1. Type the name of your school and the city, state, and ZIP Code in return address position. Address the cards to:

```
Mr. Gustave Applegate          Miss Arlene Fairchild
10253 Hunt Club Drive          21945 Beverly Street
Detroit, Mich.  48236          Detroit, Mich.  48237
```

Problem 3: Half Sheet Announcement

Type the message of Problem 1, above, as an announcement for posting on the bulletin board. Line: 50; SS; Date: Line 10, followed by 3 blank line spaces. Omit the signature and the title "Secretary."

45E: Aligning and Typing Over Words (10) *(Line: 60; SS)*

LOCATE: Aligning Scale **33**; Variable Line Spacer **3**.

1. **Type** the following sentence but do not make the return:

    `I think I can align this copy.`

2. **Move** the carriage so the word *think*, *align*, or *this* is above the scale. Note that a white line points to the center of the letter *i* in the word.

3. **Study** the relation of the top of the scale to the bottom of the letters with down stems.

    It is important for you to get an eye picture of the exact relation of the typed line to the top of the scale so you will be able to adjust the paper correctly to type over a word with exactness.

4. **Remove** the paper; reinsert it. Gauge the line so the bottoms of the letters are in correct relation to the top of the aligning scale. Operate the variable line spacer **3** if necessary to move the paper forward or backward. Operate the paper release **16** to move the paper to the left or right if necessary when centering the letter *i* over one of the white lines on the scale.
5. **Check** the accuracy of your alignment by setting the ribbon control **22** for stencil position and typing over one of the letters. If necessary, make further alignment adjustments. *Return the ribbon control to typing position.*
6. **Type** over the words *think*, *align*, and *this* in the sentence, moving the paper forward or backward, to the left or right, as necessary for correct alignment.
7. **Repeat** Steps 1, 3, 4, 5, and 6.

LESSON 240

240A: Conditioning Practice (5) *each line three times*

Alphabet	Vic Waxler disturbed the quiet room by telling zany jokes to Pam Ford.	*Sit erect*
Figure-symbol	The customer's bill for $765.98 was paid by Check #432 (dated May 10).	
Bottom row	A maximum of seven cubic inches of zinc can be moved in this size box.	
Fluency	The only way you can be certain your work is right is by proofreading.	

| 1 | 2 | 3 | 4 | 5 | 6 | 7 | 8 | 9 | 10 | 11 | 12 | 13 | 14 |

240B: Technique Improvement (10) *each line four times; then 1′ writings*

TECHNIQUE CUE | Make quick, sharp, snappy strokes.

Double letter	I feel that his appeal against the excessive rates will be successful.
Adjacent key	Please record the correct weight of the item on the front of the form.
Left hand	If Rex is ready, we can start our search for water in the vast cavern.
Balanced-hand	You may find that he does not have enough votes to pass the amendment.
Fluency	This theatrical performance is the outstanding activity of the season.

| 1 | 2 | 3 | 4 | 5 | 6 | 7 | 8 | 9 | 10 | 11 | 12 | 13 | 14 |

240C: Sustained Production (35)

DO: 1. Type a 25′ writing on the following reports. Make one carbon copy. Correct errors.

Page 347, 237B
Page 348, 237C
Page 350, 239C

2. If you complete the reports before time is called, start over.
3. When time is called, proofread, correct any errors you may have missed, and find *n-pram.*

LESSON 241

241A: Conditioning Practice (5) *each line three times*

Alphabet	The expert amazed the farm show judge by milking five cows so quickly.	*Quiet hands and arms*
Figure	Telephone Mr. Wiggins at 236–4089 on Thursday, April 17, at 10:15 a.m.	
One-hand	Fred Beggs can start the drive for greater tax rates on water in July.	
Fluency	Some of the items on display may not be sold during this special sale.	

| 1 | 2 | 3 | 4 | 5 | 6 | 7 | 8 | 9 | 10 | 11 | 12 | 13 | 14 |

241B: Growth Index (15) *one 10′ writing*

TYPE: A 10′ writing on the ¶s given on page 352. Proofread; circle errors; determine *nwam.*

LESSON 46

46A: Conditioning Practice (10) *each line three times; Line 4 for 1′ control writings*

Alphabet	`An expensive chintz would be quite too much for Jen Kingsly.`	*Low wrists*
Figure	`Ed paid` $20\frac{1}{2}$ `for the stock in 1966 and sold it for` $37\frac{1}{4}$ `today.`	
Figure-symbol	`Order #803-C for 145# of *** "K" was shipped by` <u>`Air Express`</u>`.`	
Easy	`Their girls have to handle a quantity of formal invitations.`	
	. . . . 1 . . . . 2 . . . . 3 . . . . 4 . . . . 5 . . . . 6 . . . . 7 . . . . 8 . . . . 9 . . . . 10 . . . . 11 12	

46B: Aligning and Typing Over (5)

1. Remove the paper on which you typed 46A; then reinsert it; gauge the line and letter (see page 78, 45E); and type over the first and last words in the last typed line.
2. Remove the paper; reinsert it; gauge the line and letter; and type over the first and last words in the first typed line.
3. If time permits, repeat for Lines 2 and 3.

46C: Word Division (10) *(Half sheet; Line: 60; SS)*

1. Clear tab stops. Using the *Key* beneath the columns, set tab stops for the 4-column list. *You are to supply Column 4.*
2. Center the problem vertically, single-spaced (see page 66).
3. Type the words in Column 4 with a hyphen to show preferred division when the bell rings on the third letter of each word in Column 3.
4. Check your divisions (pages 66 and 67); make corrections; then retype if time permits.

WORD DIVISION

TS

				Words
WORD DIVISION				3
aligned	aligned	division	divi-sion	10
assumed	assumed	experiment		18
briefly	briefly	explosive		25
couldn't	couldn't	immovable		33
detained	detained	impression		41
expressed	expressed	measured		49
expressing	express-ing	modifying		58
included	included	necessary		65
referring	refer-ring	selection		74
shouldn't	shouldn't	television		83
unlikely	unlikely	transcribe		91
unwanted	unwanted	uncovered		98
verify	verify	violated		105
withhold	with-hold	yachtsman		113
wrapping	wrap-ping	zoology		120

KEY | 10 | 6 | 11 | 6 | 10 | 6 | 11 |

LESSON 239

239A: Conditioning Practice (5) *each line three times*

Quiet keyboard control

Alphabet	Will the five puzzled jurors hear my expert questioning of Paul Black?
Figure-symbol	Change line 5 of Invoice #417 to read, "26 gals. Tyrofoam @ $3.98 ea."
Home row	Gloria made the fresh salad for all of us; Jack said he made the cake.
Fluency	Did he thank both men for the fine work they did today on these plans?

| 1 | 2 | 3 | 4 | 5 | 6 | 7 | 8 | 9 | 10 | 11 | 12 | 13 | 14 |

239B: Production Skill Building – Business Report (20)

DO: Study in the Reference Guide, page ix, the style and spacing for a manuscript to be bound at the top.

DO: Type the report in 237B, page 347. Follow the instructions given, except you are to prepare the report for top binding.

239C: Production Typing – Annual Report of Research and Engineering (25)

DO: Type the following report in the form of a manuscript to be bound at the top. Correct errors.

DO: Beginning with ¶ 2, type the report as the second page of a manuscript to be bound at the top. Correct errors.

Words

CONTINENTAL MANUFACTURING CORPORATION 8

Annual Report of Research and Engineering 16

Since its inception, Continental has been a 25
research-oriented organization. New processes 34
and new engineering concepts are constantly 43
being devised in a never-ending drive to create 53
new products, to improve and broaden the appli- 62
cation of existing products, and to cut costs. We 72
also seek new and better materials and explore 81
any phase of science that may lead to techno- 90
logical progress. Currently, we are spending 99
approximately $2,000,000 annually on this 108
vital work. 110

During this fiscal year, our investment in prod- 120
uct development and product improvement was 129
well rewarded by several noteworthy accom- 137
plishments. Our new multipurpose cam enjoyed 146
great initial acceptance. We introduced a new 155
friction-free roller joint that offers new solutions 166
to the slip joint friction problems of many manu- 176
facturers. Our sales of this item have reached 185
a substantial figure, and we look for an increase 195
of at least 50% next year. The mechanical com- 204
ponents of our universal gear were completely 214
redesigned to provide greater efficiency, longer 223
life, and reduced production costs. A revolu- 232
tionary new transmission is showing highly satis- 242
factory "test-in-use" performance, and we feel 251
certain that its ultimate completion will increase 261
our sales and earnings. 266

The engineers and scientists in our labora- 275
tories work very closely with our plant and field 285
engineers. In the United States, more than 200 294
Continental field engineers, with many years of 304
experience in the design and use of our prod- 313
ucts, work directly with users to help them utilize 323
more effectively the unique properties of Con- 332
tinental products. This customer service will soon 343
be made available to major users of our products 352
abroad. 354

Although we currently enjoy a significant 363
lead in our field, we must continue to increase 372
this lead. This can be done only if continuing 382
efforts are directed toward finding and perfect- 391
ing new and better products and processes to 400
meet the rapidly changing needs of our cus- 409
tomers. This is the challenge which faces re- 418
search and engineering in the year to come. 426

46D: Building Control (10) *(Line: 60; DS; ¶ indention: 5)*

1. Type a 1′ writing at a rate slightly less than your top speed. Determine *gwam.*
2. Type a 1′ *control-level* writing at about 4 *gwam* less than your first writing. Be guided by the call of the guide. Circle errors.
3. Type a 2′ and a 3′ *control-level* writing at approximately the rate you believe to be your best *control* speed. Circle errors.
4. As time permits, practice the words in which you made errors. Include the word preceding and the one following the circled word.

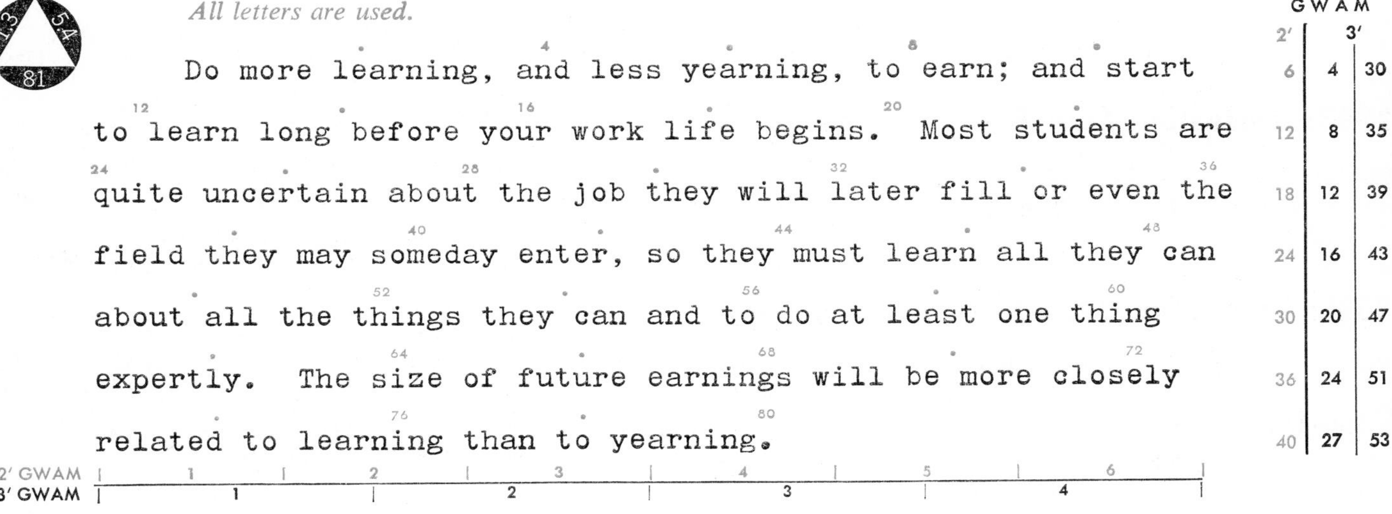

1.3 SI 5.4 AWL 81 HFW

All letters are used.

	GWAM 2′	3′	
Do more learning, and less yearning, to earn; and start	6	4	30
to learn long before your work life begins. Most students are	12	8	35
quite uncertain about the job they will later fill or even the	18	12	39
field they may someday enter, so they must learn all they can	24	16	43
about all the things they can and to do at least one thing	30	20	47
expertly. The size of future earnings will be more closely	36	24	51
related to learning than to yearning.	40	27	53

2′ GWAM 1 2 3 4 5 6
3′ GWAM 1 2 3 4

46E: Problem Typing Skill Building (15)

1. Make pencil notations of the following information and place it on the desk for easy reference: Page 72, Problem 1
   Page 75, Problem 1
2. Type two 3′ *exploration-level* writings on each problem. Determine *gwam* for better writing (Words ÷ 3). *Use the directions given for the problems on pages 72 and 75.*

LESSON 47

47A: Conditioning Practice (10) *each line three times; Line 4 for three 1′ control writings*

Alphabet	The quick jumping of the five or six young men dazzled Webb.	*Space quickly*
Figure	Jim must be in Newark, New Jersey, by 5:30 p.m. on April 29.	
Figure-symbol	The 2% discount on Penn & Horton's Invoice #1463-S is $7.58.	
Easy	Ruth Langhorn said she will vote by proxy for the amendment.	

. . . . 1 . . . . 2 . . . . 3 . . . . 4 . . . . 5 . . . . 6 . . . . 7 . . . . 8 . . . . 9 . . . . 10 . . . . 11 12

47B: Building Control (5)

TYPE: Three 1′ *control-level* writings on 46D, above. Try to type each writing without error.

LESSON 238

238A: Conditioning Practice (5) *each line three times*

Alphabet	Jim King was required to have nine large-sized boxes for play scenery.	*Work for continuity of stroking*
Figure-symbol	All $5,000 4½% bonds (Series 9) were sold on March 17, 23, 26, and 29.	
Top row	We were required to pay for our tour four weeks before the trip began.	
Fluency	If both of them ask for a loan on the same day, we may have a problem.	
	| 1 | 2 | 3 | 4 | 5 | 6 | 7 | 8 | 9 | 10 | 11 | 12 | 13 | 14 |	

238B: Production Skill Building – Business Report (20)

DO: Study in the Reference Guide, page ix, the style and spacing for a manuscript to be bound at the left.

DO: Type the report in 237B, page 347. Follow the instructions given, *except* you are to prepare the report for left binding. Correct errors.

238C: Production Typing – Advertising Copy (25)

DO: 1. Type the following rough draft of advertising copy in the form of a manuscript to be bound at the left. Correct not only the errors indicated but also any errors you may make as you type.

2. Beginning with ¶ 1, type the advertising copy as the second page of a manuscript to be bound at the left. Correct not only the errors indicated but also any errors you may make as you type.

Words

An Invitation to Luxurious Living 7
in an O'Brian home in WEST PARK ACRES 14

You will enjoy the atmosphere and raelity of lovely living 23
in a lovely O'Brian colonial home on a wooded lot in WEST PARK 41
ACRES. Here you will find a community developed especially to 54
satisfy the needs and desires of todays fastmoving executives. 67
WEST PARK ACRES is a planned community for space and privacey. 80
Yet, schools, transportation, shopping areas, and recreation 94
areas are but a few minute's away. Here are just a few of the 107
custom features you will find an O'Brian house: 117

Family-style kitchen with build-in appliances 126
Paneled family room with a huge fire place 135
Patio for informal entertainment 141
Two and one-half tiled baths 147
Central air conditioning 152
Four spacious bed rooms 157

Open Sundays from 1:00 p.m. until dark. Inspection on week days 169
is by appointment only. WEST PARK ACRES is located just one 186
mile from exit 13 of the Parkway West. Telephone, 465-7675. 194

47C: Growth Index (15) (*Full sheet; Line: 60; DS; ¶ indention: 5*)

1. Type two 3′ *control-level* writings. Determine errors and *gwam* for better writing.
2. Type a 1′ *exploration-level* writing on each ¶. Circle errors. Determine errors and *gwam*.
3. Type a 1′ *control-level* writing on each ¶. Circle errors. Determine errors and *gwam*.
4. As time permits, retype words in which you made errors.

All letters are used.

	GWAM 1′	3′	
Have a set time and place for studying. Place the books	11	4	44
and papers within easy reach. It will help you to understand	23	8	48
and remember what you read if you will outline it or underline	36	12	52
each key statement. Most of all, read for meaning and not just	49	16	56
to cover so many pages in the book.	56	19	59
Many students have real learning difficulties and don't	11	22	62
know why. The trouble may be that they do not use the best	23	26	66
study habits. When they realize this, they should ask for	35	30	70
help at once, and they may be led to acquire the exact study	47	34	74
habits that can lead to good work while still in school and	59	38	78
fine success on the job.	64	40	80

1′ GWAM 1 2 3 4 5 6 7 8 9 10 11 12
3′ GWAM 1 2 3 4

47D: Problem Typing (20)

Problem 1: Half Sheet Announcement

(*Line : 50; SS; 1½″ top margin*)
Center the heading horizontally.

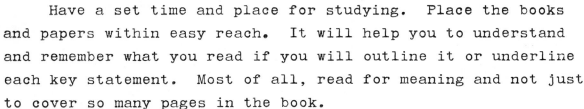

```
DINNER DANCE, DECEMBER 6
                TS
The French Club of St. Catherine Academy will have
a Dinner Dance for the benefit of the Scholarship
Fund on December 6.

You will dance to the music of M. Jonois and his
Orchestra and dine to the melody of Mlle. d'Aquin's
magic violin.

You can dine and dance with French "joy of life"
on December 6 for $10 a couple.  What a bargain!
Don't miss it.
```

Problem 2: Personal Note

(*Line: 40; SS; date on Line 13*)

Insert a half sheet with the long edge at the left. Type the announcement of Problem 1 as a personal note making the changes indicated at the right. Be alert to any needed punctuation. (See page 72.)

Date: November 10, 19––
Salutation: Dear Knox
Message: ¶s of Problem 1 (*omit heading*)
Complimentary close: Sincerely yours

Line endings will differ from those in the announcement.

Problem 3: Postal Card

Use a card or 5½″ by 3¼″ paper.
Center the problem vertically, double-spaced.
Center each line horizontally.

THE FRENCH CLUB OF ST. CATHERINE ACADEMY | Scholarship Fund | Dinner Dance | December 6 | Music by M. Jonois and Orchestra | Mlle. d'Aquin and Her Magic Violin | Ten Dollars a Couple |

Return address: 3026 Napoleon Avenue | New Orleans, La. 70115 |

Address: Mr. Randolph Budreaux | 10 Audubon Place | New Orleans, La. 70118 |

Words

Advertising and Sales Promotion 366

Continued and consistent use of all advertising media--newspaper, radio, 380
television, direct mail, and magazine advertising--will continue. The budget for 397
television will be increased by 10%, but expenditures for other media will remain 413
at approximately the same level as last year. Increased efforts must be made to 430
maintain liaison with the editorial staffs of all news media to increase the favor- 446
able news coverage about the corporation, its employees, and the industry. 461

Research and Engineering 471

Expenditures for research and engineering will be doubled next year. To 486
meet the expected vigorous competition, we must develop new products and improve 502
our existing products and production methods. Expansion of the Applied Research 518
Center at Akron will continue, and two new laboratories will be established in 534
Alabama to study the demands of nuclear power and space exploration. 547

237C: Production Typing – Report of Sales (25)

DO: 1. Type the following Report of Sales in the form of an unbound manuscript. Correct errors.

2. Beginning with ¶ 1, type the report as the second page of an unbound manuscript. Correct errors.

Words

NATIONAL ENGINEERING PRODUCTS CORPORATION 8

Actual Sales and Sales Adjusted for Changes in Prices 19

(Millions of Dollars) 24

Although sales reached an all-time high during the past year, a comparison 39
of the dollar value of actual net sales with net sales adjusted for changes in 54
the prices of products during the year reveals some areas of weakness. Sales 70
last year totaled $26,674,000 as compared with $33,809,000 this year. At first 86
glance, this appears to be an increase of 26%. As shown below, however, much 102
of this increase came as the result of higher prices. After adjustment for price 118
changes, sales actually rose less than 14%. 127

SALES DISTRICT	NET SALES	ADJUSTED NET SALES	136
Detroit	3.464	3.150	140
Houston	4.090	3.930	144
Philadelphia	4.336	2.830	149
Dallas	4.121	4.080	153
Chicago	4.350	4.070	157
San Francisco	4.198	3.810	162
Boston	4.457	4.327	166
Baltimore	4.793	4.411	170

These figures also reveal that net sales do not reflect the true comparative 185
position of the Districts. Although Baltimore and Boston retained first and 201
second places respectively, Philadelphia dropped to eighth place and Dallas 216
rose from sixth to third place. On the basis of net sales, the Philadelphia 231
District showed an increase in sales over last year, but the adjusted net sales 247
figure indicates that there was actually a decrease. 258

Unit 7 | Lessons 48-49

Inventory and Measurement

1. Arrange work area for efficient typing.
2. Adjust paper guide and paper bail rolls.
3. Set control to type on upper part of ribbon.
4. Use full sheet; Line: 60; SS drills and sentences; DS and indent timed writings.

LESSON 48

48A: Conditioning Practice (10) *each line three times; Line 4 for 1′ control-level writings*

Alphabet	John Wilcox quickly paid Tom for this big house in Veracruz.
Figure	Set your tab stops at these points: 29, 38, 47, 56, and 70.
Figure-symbol	A well-to-do man bought the ancient gem for $1,750, less 2%.
Easy	The authority with which you speak depends on what you know.
	. . . . 1 . . . . 2 . . . . 3 . . . . 4 . . . . 5 . . . . 6 . . . . 7 . . . . 8 . . . . 9 . . . . 10 . . . . 11 12

48B: Inventory of Manipulative Skills (20) *(Read each sentence before doing what it directs.)*

DO: Type as directed in each item. DS between items. Ignore misstrokes in the typing.

Do not type the numbered statement or the reference page number (given in parentheses).

DO: Refer, if necessary, to each reference page for the explanation of the *process* used in the typing.

1 Center horizontally and type **BASIC SKILLS** as a main heading on Line 7 of a full sheet. (p. 61)
2 Type the figures 1 through 10 correctly aligned in a column at the left margin. (p. 62)
3 Type the sentence: **How do you type words that are *printed in italics*?** (p. 64)
4 Draw a horizontal pencil line approximately 5 inches long. (p. 74)
5 Draw two downward vertical lines approximately 2 inches long to connect with the beginning and the end of the horizontal line drawn as directed in 4. (p. 77)
6 Center and type on the horizontal pencil line: **PROJECTED POPULATION BY 1980** (p. 71)
7 Type the sentence with correct spacing: **“ Ship 2 doz. # 9 Notebooks @24 ¢ ea.”** (pp. 48 and 58)
8 Remove the paper. Fold it lengthwise to give a sheet 4¼″ wide. Reinsert the sheet with the folded edge at the left. Center horizontally and type your name in caps on Line 13. DS; then center and type the current date. (p. 71)
9 Remove the paper; reinsert it; gauge line and letter for correct spacing. Type over the date of 8. (p. 78)
10 Remove the paper; unfold to have a full sheet; then fold from bottom to top; insert with the folded edge at the left. Center **MANIPULATIVE SKILLS** with a 2″ top margin. (p. 71)

48C: Discovering Speed Range with Maximum Accuracy (10) *(Line: 60; DS; ¶ indention: 5)*

1. **Type** 46D, page 80, as three 2′ writings: at 20 to 25, 25 to 30, and 30 to 35 *gwam* (or other appropriate speeds).
2. **Determine** the rate at which you maintain your best accuracy. Use this rate in typing 48D, below.

48D: Inventorying Basic Skill (10) *(Line: 60; DS; ¶ indention: 5)*

1. **Type** two 3′ writings of 47C, page 81, pausing briefly between writings to relax.
2. **Circle** errors and **determine** *gwam* for the better writing.

Unit 41 | Lessons 237-241

Business Report Production

LESSON 237

237A: Conditioning Practice (5) *each line three times*

Alphabet	A famous zoology expert did the job using a very well-known technique.	*Shift quickly but firmly*
Figure-symbol	The price index (base, 1958–1959) rose 42% in 1967––from 130 to 184.6.	
Roman numerals	Eliminate Units III, IV, IX, and XIII; add Units X, XV, XI, LX, and C.	
Fluency	If the quality of the product is high, both men may make a big profit.	
	| 1 | 2 | 3 | 4 | 5 | 6 | 7 | 8 | 9 | 10 | 11 | 12 | 13 | 14 |	

237B: Production Skill Building – Business Report (20)

DO: 1. Study the style and spacing for an unbound manuscript in the Reference Guide, page ix.

2. Type a 5′ writing on the following report, using unbound manuscript form. Determine *g-pram.*

3. Type a 5′ writing beginning with ¶ 2 (including the side heading) of the report as the second page of an unbound manuscript. Determine *g-pram.*

Words

NATIONAL ENGINEERING PRODUCTS CORPORATION 8

Annual Forecast of Operations 14

The past year was a phenomenal one in terms of expansion and progress. It 29
was a year marked by new record highs in production, sales, and earnings. These 46
achievements reflect, in part, the vigorous economic growth and prosperity of 61
the nation. Primarily, however, the progress made was the result of careful 77
planning and hard work. We can and should take pride in our accomplishments; at 93
the same time, we must realize that the records set pose significant challenges 109
and opportunities in the year ahead. We must continue to improve if we are to 125
remain a profitable and growing company. This general forecast of operation is 141
based on the knowledge that all divisions and all employees of the corporation 156
will expend every effort in the year to come to break all previous records. 172

<u>Equipment, Facilities, and Production</u> 187

The acquisition and construction of new capital equipment and facilities 201
valued at more than a million dollars will permit us to expand our operations in 218
Delaware and to add new production facilities in New York and Maryland. With the 234
early completion of these facilities, production during the coming year should 250
rise to a minimum of 20% over that of last year. 260

<u>Anticipated Domestic and Foreign Sales</u> 275

Domestic sales of our products are expected to rise approximately 6%. This 290
relatively small increase in domestic markets will be offset by the encouraging 306
trend in our foreign business. If we actively pursue business overseas in those 323
areas where we have technological advances, we should be able to double our 338
foreign sales. The net result will be an overall increase in sales of 25%. 353

(*Continued*)

LESSON 49

49A: Conditioning Practice (10) *each line three times; Line 4 for 1′ control-level writings*

Alphabet	Was K. D. Oxnam expecting to leave for quiet Zurich by July?	*Shift firmly*
Figure	Our firm had 7 clerks in 1960; 43, in 1965; and 82, in 1967.	
Figure-symbol	Do not space between the figure and these symbols: # ¢ % $.	
Easy	Hope and faith, mixed with hard work, will aid a man to win.	

. . . . 1 . . . . 2 . . . . 3 . . . . 4 . . . . 5 . . . . 6 . . . . 7 . . . . 8 . . . . 9 . . . . 10 . . . . 11 12

49B: Growth Index (10) *(Line: 60; DS; ¶ indention: 5)*

1. **Type** two 3′ control-level writings, pausing 20 to 30 seconds between writings to relax.
2. Determine *errors* and *gwam* for the better writing.

All letters are used.

E 1.3 5.2 85	GWAM 1′	3′	
People must get along with others because they live in a	11	4	44
community and "no man is an island." It is important, though,	24	8	48
for all people to have a place of solitude, an island, where	36	12	52
they can be still enough and alone long enough for the tensions	49	16	56
of their life to drain out of them.	56	19	59
E 1.3 5.2 85 The island all people need can't be found on known maps.	12	23	63
Exploring it must be just in thought, not in fact. It must be	24	27	67
a place where people can be still. It may be found in the home,	37	31	71
the school, the office, or wherever quiet hours can be known.	50	35	75
Those who find their island can realize the restoring power	62	39	79
of silence.	64	40	80

1′ GWAM | 1 | 2 | 3 | 4 | 5 | 6 | 7 | 8 | 9 | 10 | 11 | 12 |

3′ GWAM | 1 | 2 | 3 | 4 |

49C: Technique Practice – Direct Reaches (10) *each line three times on control level*

1 Cedric Briggs brought home many hungry young men on July 19.

2 My Aunt Myna Hunter and her brother brought lots of luggage.

3 Ruth Treen's 54 pupils have a speed range of 45 to 67 words.

4 Why must Mr. Muncie send his checks to the Sweet Briar Bank?

5 Robert Decik is a quiz whiz, and he may win tonight's prize.

. . . . 1 . . . . 2 . . . . 3 . . . . 4 . . . . 5 . . . . 6 . . . . 7 . . . . 8 . . . . 9 . . . . 10 . . . . 11 12

GWAM

1′ | 10′

All letters are used.

Less than fifty years ago, the typical American family bought very 13 1 48
few items on credit or on the installment plan. Many families assumed 28 3 49
mortgages to buy homes, but the use of credit to secure other goods and 42 4 50
services, particularly luxuries, was frowned upon. In that era, credit 56 6 52
had not yet become "respectable." Today, the consumer who does not use 71 7 53
credit or procure goods on the installment plan is rare indeed. A recent 86 9 55
poll shows that nine out of ten American families rely on credit of some 100 10 56
sort. Without a doubt, consumer credit has become a vital part of our 114 11 58
economy. 116 12 58

Credit has played an essential role in the industrial and financial 14 13 59
growth of our nation. Most of us are not able to pay cash for expensive 28 14 61
wares such as automobiles and refrigerators. This monetary barrier was 43 16 62
broken into small, periodic payments by the use of credit. As a result, 57 17 64
the market for durable goods grew rapidly. The enormous demands of the 72 19 65
consumer enabled producers to exploit the economies of mass production 86 20 66
which led to lower prices and goods of better quality. The high standard 101 22 68
of living we enjoy today is due in no small measure to the use of credit. 115 23 69

People use credit for numerous reasons. Credit saves time in paying 14 25 71
bills and makes it unnecessary to carry large sums of cash. Credit is 28 26 72
especially welcome in a crisis when we are faced with a serious illness, 43 27 74
unexpected household repairs, or other unforeseen financial troubles not 57 29 75
covered by insurance. Primarily, however, most of us use credit so that 72 30 77
we can buy more costly items on a small income and enjoy them as we are 86 32 78
paying for them. Homes, cars, radios, stereo sets, appliances, and furs 101 33 79
are but a few of many items that may be bought on the installment plan. 115 35 81

As a consumer, you should learn to utilize credit wisely. Although 14 36 82
credit is a valuable asset, there is always a danger that you may go too 28 37 84
deeply into debt. You must learn to exercise reasonable restraint and to 43 39 85
resist the temptation to buy that expensive convertible when you really 57 40 87
cannot afford to do so. By careful budgeting, you can decide exactly how 72 42 88
much money you can afford to allocate monthly for installment purchases. 87 43 90
Prudent planning will help keep you out of financial difficulty and will 102 45 91
aid you to get more of the many things you want in life—through credit. 116 46 92

1′ GWAM | 1 | 2 | 3 | 4 | 5 | 6 | 7 | 8 | 9 | 10 | 11 | 12 | 13 | 14 |
10′ GWAM | 1 | 2 |

49D: Problem Typing – Measurement (20) *each problem as directed*

Problem 1: Personal Note

Half sheet; Line: 50; SS
Style: block, mixed
Current date on Line 7, followed by 3 blank line spaces

Current date

Dear Clyde:

Believe it or not, I survived the Qualifying Round for the City Golf Championship. You can't be more surprised than I am or half as happy.

The semifinals are scheduled for two weeks from Saturday. I'd like to have you come over to cheer me on. The finals will be the following Saturday, but I may not be lucky enough to qualify for them.

Can you come for the weekend of the semifinals? That's when I need your support!

Yours,

Al Donaldson

Problem 2: Postal Card

Line: 50; SS
Style: block, mixed
Current date on Line 3
Be guided by the bell to return the carriage

Current date

TS

Dear Joe: DS *(Type ¶ 1 of Problem 1, above, as the first ¶ for the postal card message; then DS and type the following sentence as the closing ¶:)*

Hope you'll send some good thoughts my way when I play in the semifinals two weeks from Saturday.

Problem 3: Addressing a Postal Card

Return address: *Your name*
Your personal address
Your city, state, and ZIP Code

Card address: Mr. Joe W. Simmons

1203 South Charles St.

Seattle, Wash. 98144

Problem 4: Centered Announcement

(Half sheet; DS; center problem vertically, each line horizontally)

Announcing the Publication Date
of
AUTOMATION AND COMMUNICATION
Implications for Office Education
by
Patrick Drummond O'Shea
April, *(Next year)*
The McIntyre-O'Donovan Company

49E: Bonus (Extra-Credit) Typing *(Line: 60; SS) three times; correct spacing as you type*

		Words
1	We think the sentences provide excellent alertness training.	12
2	Type with accuracy --maximum accuracy-- in today's timed test.	12
3	They wired us, "Can ship 1,000 # 348 immediately @ 92 ¢ each."	12
4	Your $750 note (due 9/26) bears interest at the rate of 5 ¼ %.	12
5	These students are absent: Enid Korch, Mary Robb, Joe Lane.	12

LESSON 235

235A: Conditioning Practice (5) *each line three times*

Alphabet	That lazy carpenter quit his job six days ago to avoid working for me.	*Begin slowly, speed up gradually*
Figure-symbol	Deliver the chairs (Order #57326) to 1480 Maple Drive before 9:00 a.m.	
Double letters	Tell Anne to send all letters for Bill to the school office next week.	
Fluency	Now is the time for us to make special plans for our trip to the city.	
	| 1 | 2 | 3 | 4 | 5 | 6 | 7 | 8 | 9 | 10 | 11 | 12 | 13 | 14 |	

235B: Sustained Production (45)

1. Type with 1 cc the following letters for 30 minutes:

   Page 343, 232B, Problem 3
   Page 343, 233B, Problem 1
   Page 344, 233B, Problem 2
   Page 344, 233B, Problem 3

2. Retype as many of the letters as possible if you finish all of them before time is called.
3. Correct errors as you type; proofread each letter before you remove it from the typewriter; correct errors you may have missed. Figure your *n-pram*: acceptable words typed ÷ 30.

LESSON 236

236A: Conditioning Practice (5) *each line three times*

Alphabet	Major Robertson quickly explained several of the new fighting hazards.	*Quiet hands and arms*
Figure-symbol	The balance ($582.39) was paid by Ray & Blos on June 6 by Check #4170.	
Shift key	Jo, Ray, Peg, and I won't arrive in San Juan until 9:00 p.m. on May 9.	
Fluency	If the work is done right, the downtown apartment may open on March 1.	
	| 1 | 2 | 3 | 4 | 5 | 6 | 7 | 8 | 9 | 10 | 11 | 12 | 13 | 14 |	

236B: Technique Improvement (15) *each line four times; then 1′ writings*

TECHNIQUE CUE	Make short, direct reaches.

Third row	Please put a new ribbon on your typewriter before you type the report.
Home row	When the glass dish broke, Jack's dad had his salad plate in his hand.
Bottom row	Rex may use my new Wizzard Vacuum Cleaner if he cannot find the broom.
Left hand	Water rates in my area are greater than the average rate in the state.
Right hand	In my opinion, the milk commission should set a minimum price on milk.
Balanced-hand	Did she make both men pay for the original work she did on the manual?
	| 1 | 2 | 3 | 4 | 5 | 6 | 7 | 8 | 9 | 10 | 11 | 12 | 13 | 14 |

236C: Growth Index – Straight Copy (30)

TYPE: A 10′ writing on the ¶s on page 346. Strive for rapid stroking. Determine *gwam*.

TYPE: A second 10′ writing on the ¶s, working for control. Proofread and determine *nwam*.

Personal and Business Letters

1. Arrange work area for efficient performance.
2. Adjust paper guide and paper bail rolls.
3. Set ribbon control to type on upper part of ribbon.
4. Use full sheet; Line: 70; SS for drills and sentence typing; DS for timed writings on paragraphs.

LESSON 50

50A: Conditioning Practice (10) *each line three times; Line 4 for 1′ exploration-level writings*

Alphabet	Zero winds quickly exhausted Mr. Fred Jeffrey, but he did not give up.	*Sit erect; eyes on copy*
Figure	What is the sum of 9 and 12 and 39 and 40 and 48 and 57 and 60 and 93?	
Figure-symbol	The amount I paid is $25,640.78, with 3% sales tax and 15% excise tax.	
Easy	Some men will learn from experience, but others never recover from it.	
	| 1 | 2 | 3 | 4 | 5 | 6 | 7 | 8 | 9 | 10 | 11 | 12 | 13 | 14 |	

NOTE: Remove the paper; reinsert it; gauge the line and letter; then type over the first line. (See page 78.)

50B: Technique Practice – Typing Response (10)

Your early typing was by *stroke (or letter) response*, the response pattern used when you see, think, and type letter by letter.

When you see, think, and type short, simple, and easy words as *word wholes*, you type by *word-recognition response*, a quicker and higher form of response than stroke response.

Much of your typing must be by *combination response*, for most copy has some easy and some difficult combinations.

	Response	
1	*Stroke*	Ed had incisively penetrating psychological insights into my problems.
2	*Stroke*	With mixed punctuation, type the comma after your complimentary close.
3	*Combination*	If you want to succeed, always keep fun and work in right perspective.
4	*Combination*	That man proves he has maturity who carries his work responsibilities.
5	*Word-recognition*	The man who knows he is right will usually speak with quiet authority.
		| 1 | 2 | 3 | 4 | 5 | 6 | 7 | 8 | 9 | 10 | 11 | 12 | 13 | 14 |

50C: Problem Typing (20)

Problem 1: Style Letter (Page 86)

(*Full sheet; Line: 50; Style: modified block; Punctuation: mixed; tab stop at center; return address on Line 18*)

Type the letter as shown on page 86.

Problem 2: Alertness Training

Type the letter of Problem 1 again, but address it to **Director of Admissions | Sweet Briar College | Sweet Briar, Va. 24595 |**

Change Line 2 of ¶ 1 from **Swarthmore** to **Sweet Briar**.

Problem 3: Postal Card (*or 5½″ x 3¼″ paper*)

Review page 76 on procedure for typing postal cards; then:

Address side of card: Use return address from Problem 1 and the following card address: **Director of Admissions | Goucher College | Baltimore, Md. 21204 |**

Message side of card: Using a 50-space line, type on Line 3 the date from Problem 1, then TS. Type the salutation, the first ¶ (changing **Swarthmore** to **Goucher**), and the complimentary close from Problem 1. Then space forward 3 times and type the name.

Problem 2: Modified Block Letter with Indented ¶s and Mixed Punctuation

Words
The Shaffer Metals Company 6100 Bayside Road 12
Austin, Texas 78719 Gentlemen (¶ 1) Yesterday, 21
our production line came to an almost complete 30
halt for several hours. The cause of the delay 40
was your CX–720 1 5/8" x 1 5/8" coupling. 47
Our workmen discovered that this coupling 55
would not fit properly in our 62V18 assembly, 64
and work was stopped to determine the reason. 74
(¶ 2) Tests made by our Quality Control Division 82
revealed that your couplings measure 1 5/8" x 91
1 11/16". A spot check of 20,000 of these 100
couplings received under your shipment FN– 108
49683 indicates that all of them are of the 117
incorrect size. The specifications under which 127
the couplings were ordered, as shown in our 136
order #76590–Z, provided for 1 5/8" x 1 5/8" 145
couplings with a tolerance of not more than 153
1/320". (¶ 3) Will you please give this matter 162
your immediate attention. Fortunately, we have 171
sufficient couplings of the proper size to continue 182
production for several months. In the meantime, 192
we hope you will take action to replace the 200
defective couplings. Sincerely yours A. Harvey 210
Dickinson Purchasing Officer (187) 216

Problem 3: AMS Simplified Letter

Words
Century Industries, Inc. 2800 Allegheny Street 12
Pittsburgh, Pa. 15215 EXECUTIVE LIFE INSUR- 21
ANCE (¶ 1) What would happen if several of 28
your key executives were lost in an automobile 38
or airplane accident tomorrow? This is a pos- 47
sibility that none of us likes to think about––but 57
it IS a possibility. (¶ 2) Almost all successful 66
companies include key executives who have spe- 75
cial abilities, executives whose loss would pose 85
a serious financial hardship to the firm. Although 95
nothing can replace completely the loss of execu- 105
tive talent, prudent companies today can allevi- 114
ate the monetary loss through executive life 123
insurance. Your key executives can also be 132
insured under one of our special group life 141
insurance plans at a cost that is surprisingly low. 151
(¶ 3) We have made a thorough study of the 159
executives of your company and have developed 168
an insurance plan that is tailored especially for 178
them. It will take only a few minutes to describe 188
this plan––a few minutes that may be worth 197
thousands of dollars to your company. Won't 206
you have your secretary call me today for a 214
conference at your convenience? Frank B. Fields, 224
Account Executive (200) 228

LESSON 234

234A: Conditioning Practice (5) *each line three times*

Alphabet	Grace Jeffries had the murky brown liquid analyzed by several experts.	Reach with the fingers
Figure	In 1963, net sales totaled $4,918.7 million; earnings, $270.6 million.	
Figure-symbol	"Business News" (Pamphlet #5) shows that Z & L stock rose 7½% in 1964.	
Fluency	Your production will go up as errors go down if you type with control.	
	| 1 | 2 | 3 | 4 | 5 | 6 | 7 | 8 | 9 | 10 | 11 | 12 | 13 | 14 |	

234B: Sustained Production (45)

1. Type with 1 cc the following letters for 30 minutes:

   Page 341, 231B, Problem 2
   Page 342, 232B, Problem 1
   Page 342, 232B, Problem 2

   Retype the letters if time permits.

2. Correct errors as you type; proofread each letter before you remove it from the typewriter; correct errors you may have missed. Figure your *n-pram*: acceptable words typed ÷ 30 minutes.

Tabulate to center point to type return address, date, and closing lines

		Words in Parts	Total Words
Return Address	3726 Rosemont Drive	4	4
	Wilmington, Del. 19804	9	9
Date on Line 20	January 15, 19--	12	12
	Operate return 4 times		
	Director of Admissions	17	17
Letter Address	Swarthmore College	21	21
	Swarthmore, Pa. 19081	25	25
	DS		
Salutation	Dear Sir:	2	27
	DS		
	Please send me an application form for admission to	13	38
	Swarthmore. I am to be graduated in June and hope	23	48
	to enter college in September.	29	54
	I shall appreciate information about scholarships		64
	that are available and the procedure to follow in		74
Body	applying for one. Some financial aid is needed if		84
	I am to attend college in September, as I most		94
	earnestly hope will be possible.		100
	If a personal interview is desired, when should I	10	110
	plan to come to the campus and what records should	20	120
	I bring with me?	23	123
	DS		
Complimentary close	Sincerely yours, *Operate return 4 times*	27	127
Signature	Anabel M. Riley		
Typed name	(Miss) Anabel M. Riley	31	131

This letter is typed in the *modified block style with block paragraphs.* In this style, the return address, date, complimentary close, and writer's name are typed at the horizontal center of the paper; the inside address, salutation, and lines of the paragraphs are begun at the left margin.

With mixed punctuation, used in this letter, a colon follows the salutation and a comma follows the complimentary close. Marks are not required after the return address or the letter address unless an abbreviation followed by a period is used. It would be equally acceptable to use *open punctuation*, omitting the colon and the comma.

Style Letter 1: Modified Block with Mixed Punctuation

Problem 3: Modified Block Letter with Mixed Punctuation

Words
Mr. Thomas Atwood 3952 Grand Avenue Macon, 12
Georgia 31204 Dear Mr. Atwood (¶ 1) Thank 19
you very much for taking the time to write us 28
about the difficulty you are having with the 37
Argo Power Mower you purchased at our store 46
last month. We take great pride in our reputa- 55
tion for high-quality merchandise, and reports 65
such as yours help us maintain that reputation. 74
(¶ 2) You may recall that the Argo Power 81
Mower you purchased was one of several floor 90
models we had on special sale. The mowers 99
were sold "as is" at greatly reduced prices with 109
the understanding that there would be no war- 118
ranty or guarantee on our part. However, in 127
view of the difficulties you described, we have 136
contacted the local representative of the Argo 146
Power Mower Company. He has agreed to 154
inspect your mower within the next few days 162
and to determine what adjustments can be made. 172
(¶ 3) We regret very much the inconvenience 180
you have experienced. We value your patron- 188
age very much and hope that the Argo Company 197
will resolve your difficulties to your complete 207
satisfaction. If they do not do so, please let me 217
know immediately. Sincerely yours John M. 225
Gulbranson Director of Customer Relations (203) 235

LESSON 233

233A: Conditioning Practice (5) *each line three times*

Alphabet	Many knights were quite brave and fought jousts with exceptional zeal.	*Eyes on the copy*
Figure-symbol	The 4% wage tax (levied on April 15 by PL 1398) will yield $2,760,000.	
Direct reach	As a result of the report of graft and bribes, they made many changes.	
Fluency	It is true that the man who works hard and does his best profits most.	
	| 1 | 2 | 3 | 4 | 5 | 6 | 7 | 8 | 9 | 10 | 11 | 12 | 13 | 14 |	

233B: Problem Skill Building – Letters (45) *(Plain sheets)*

DO: Follow the instructions given in 232B, page 342, for the letters below and on page 344.

Problem 1: Modified Block Letter with Indented ¶s and Open Punctuation

Words
Miss Eileen Rochebrune 4312 Sixth Street Hamil- 12
ton, Ohio 45011 Dear Miss Rochebrune (¶ 1) Did 21
you ever have one of those days when nothing 30
seems to go right? We had one several weeks 39
ago when, in the midst of changing offices, your 48
letter was inadvertently misplaced. Please accept 59
our apology for the delay in our reply. (¶ 2) 67
The questions you raised concerning the benefits 77
we provide our employees are answered in de- 85
tail in the enclosed copy of our "Employee Hand- 95
book." On page 47 you will find a list of the 104
services we offer for the well-being of our 113
employees on the job. "Fringe" benefits, such 122
as paid vacations, sick leave, and retirement 131
plans are described beginning on page 50. 140
Please note our unusual profit-sharing plan on 149
page 53. We believe it is unique in American 159
business. After you have studied the benefits 168
our employees enjoy, I am sure you will under- 177
stand why we have achieved more than 40 years 186
of harmonious labor relations. (¶ 3) Thank you 195
for your interest in our company. If you would 204
like to have any additional information, do not 214
hesitate to write us. Next time, we promise a 223
more prompt reply. Sincerely yours W. E. Den- 232
nison Personnel Officer Enclosure (207) 239

50D: Composing and Typing – Sentence Completion (10) *(Line: 50; ¶ indention: 5; SS)*

1. **Type** complete sentences by filling in the needed information. The line endings will not be the same as those in the copy. Ignore the errors you make as you type.
2. When you have completed the typing, remove the paper, make pencil corrections, and retype the material on a half sheet with an appropriate top margin.

My name is *(type your name)*. I live in *(city or town and state)*, and I am a student at *(name of your school)*. My homeroom is *(use figures)*, and the homeroom teacher is *(use appropriate personal title with name)*. The name of the typewriter I am using is *(name of typewriter)*. My approximate *gwam* is *(state in figures)*. The name of my typewriting textbook is *(underline the title of the book)*. It is published by *(use name of publisher from title page)*. My chief difficulties in building accuracy are: *(list some difficulties)*.

LESSON 51

51A: Conditioning Practice (10) *each line three times; Line 4 for 1′ exploration-level writings*

Fingers curved; wrists low

Alphabet	Judge Bingham was quite vexed when C. K. Zuegendorfer failed to reply.
Figure	Mr. Robb owes a total of $3,475, of which $620 must be paid by July 9.
Figure-symbol	On May 9, Horton & Todd offered Special "Q" @ 78½¢ a lb. in 500# lots.
Easy	Going on a wild goose chase is a rather poor way to feather your nest.
	| 1 | 2 | 3 | 4 | 5 | 6 | 7 | 8 | 9 | 10 | 11 | 12 | 13 | 14 |

51B: Problem Typing – Letters (20) *(Line: 50; SS; Style: modified block, mixed; Address: Line 18)*

Problem 1: Modified Block Letter

	Words
Exeter Military Academy | Peachtree Road |	8
Asheville, N.C. 28803 | January 17, 19–– |	16
Return: 4	
Dr. Bryan N. LaSalle, Jr. | Director of Admis-	24
sions | Rollins College | Winter Park, Fla.	33
32789 | *DS*	34
Dear Dr. LaSalle: *DS*	38
(¶ 1) I am in my junior year at Exeter Military	46
Academy. | For the first two years of work, my	55
grade average | has been B. I believe I can	64
maintain or improve | this grade average from	73
now on. |	74
(¶ 2) My concern now is with the entrance re-	82
quirements | for your College of Liberal Arts.	91
Our school | counselor has suggested that I write	101
to you for | information about your required	109
course sequences. |	113
(¶ 3) As my study program for next year must	121
be made soon, | I shall appreciate an early re-	130
sponse from you. | *DS* Sincerely yours, |	137
Return: 4	
Anthony Duwalder	140

Problem 2: Speedup in Typing Letters

Type a 1′ writing on each of the following parts of the letter of Problem 1:

1. Return address, date, and letter address
2. Salutation and ¶ 1
3. ¶ 3 and closing lines

Problem 3: Alertness Training

Type Problem 1 again, but make the following changes as you type: (1) Use your personal return address; (2) in ¶ 1, use the name of your school; (3) type your name as the writer of the letter. *Circle all errors you make.*

LESSON 232

232A: Conditioning Practice (5) *each line three times*

Alphabet	Bruce and Jackie Page often won luxury items on television quiz shows.	Begin slowly, speed up gradually
ZIP Code	78605 13432 92075 89314 69045 61832 70452 17608 39164 29587 43902 58716	
Date	December 9 February 13 July 20 September 4 January 8 July 5 November 7	
Fluency	Although he did not file the claim today, he will do so in the future.	
	| 1 | 2 | 3 | 4 | 5 | 6 | 7 | 8 | 9 | 10 | 11 | 12 | 13 | 14 |	

232B: Problem Skill Building – Letters (45) *(Plain sheets)*

DO: For each of Letters 1, 2, and 3:

1. Study the appropriate style letter in the Reference Guide, page v.
2. Use margins and a date-line position appropriate for the letter length indicated.
3. Type a 1′ writing on the opening lines, beginning with the current date.
4. Type a 3′ writing on the body of the letter.
5. Type a 1′ writing on the closing lines.
6. Type a 5′ writing on the entire letter. Determine *gwam*.
   If time permits, type additional 5′ writings, trying to improve your performance.

Problem 1: Block Letter with Open Punctuation

Words

Mrs. Kenneth Marshall 1302 Mansion Drive 11
Duluth, Minnesota 55801 Dear Mrs. Marshall 20
(¶ 1) As a charge customer, you are one of 27
our SPECIAL people. To show you how much 36
we appreciate your patronage, we are offering 45
you and our other charge customers a unique, 54
money-saving opportunity. Through a special 63
purchase, we can offer you a wide selection of 72
leather casual coats at prices that can't be beaten. 83
These casual coats come in many classic styles 93
that will look good on you––and they won't go 102
out of fashion. (¶ 2) Won't you come in next 110
week and see these coats? You will find that 119
they are not only stylish but also practical for 129
driving, shopping, and all your leisure activities. 139
They never need costly dry cleaning––dirt and 149
stains come clean with a damp cloth and a little 158
mild detergent. (¶ 3) Remember, this offer is for 167
our charge customers ONLY. This opportunity 176
will NOT be offered to the general public. Just 186
show this letter to a sales clerk, and she will give 197
you an exclusive showing. We have only a lim- 206
ited number of these coats, so please don't take 216
a chance by waiting too long. Sincerely yours 225
J. N. Ray, Sales Manager (201) 230

Problem 2: Modified Block Letter with Mixed Punctuation

Words

Mrs. C. K. Wolfendon 1601 Chestnut Street 11
Minneapolis, Minnesota 55403 Dear Mrs. Wol- 20
fendon (¶ 1) If we could only make this letter 28
smile, you would see the paper crinkle from 37
corner to corner. That would show you how 45
happy we were to receive your order which 54
arrived today. Our records show that this is the 64
second order you have sent us in recent months 73
––an indication, we hope, that you are satisfied 83
with our merchandise. Thank you very much, 92
Mrs. Wolfendon. (¶ 2) There will be a slight 100
delay in filling your order for the personalized 110
stationery. This has been an extremely popular 119
item and, at the moment, it is out of stock. We 129
will promptly send the remaining items you 138
ordered and will ship the stationery as soon as 147
it is received from our print shop––probably 156
within a week or ten days. (¶ 3) A copy of our 165
latest catalog will be mailed to you within the 174
next few days. We hope that you will find many 184
items of interest in it so that we may have the 193
pleasure of serving you again very soon. Sin- 202
cerely yours C. Joseph Lewiston Sales Manager 212
(180)

51C: Building Speed and Control (10) *(Line: 70; DS; ¶ indention: 5)*

Type two 3′ writings; DS twice between them. Set the pace in typing easy ¶ 1; maintain the rate in typing ¶ 2, which is of average difficulty. Determine *gwam* for the better writing.

All letters are used.

It is all right for a colt to run and kick up his heels in the field before he is old enough for work responsibilities. But when he gets to be a big horse, he has to be made to know that we expect him to carry a work load that is in keeping with his strength.

It is quite necessary for people, young and old, to have fun. It is just as necessary for them to realize that having fun is of secondary importance when they have work obligations. The people who put fun and work in right perspective are the ones who have developed a maturity that will lead to success and happiness.

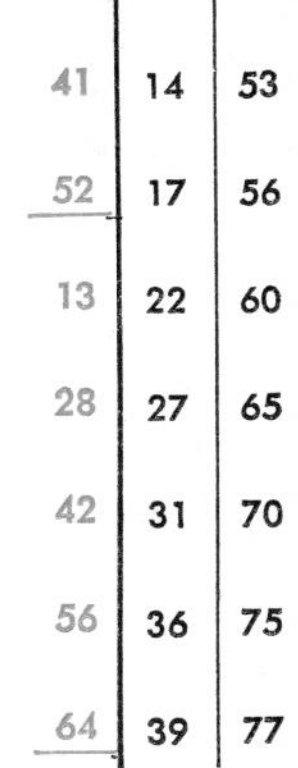

GWAM 1′	3′	
13	4	43
27	9	48
41	14	53
52	17	56
13	22	60
28	27	65
42	31	70
56	36	75
64	39	77

1′ GWAM | 1 | 2 | 3 | 4 | 5 | 6 | 7 | 8 | 9 | 10 | 11 | 12 | 13 | 14 |
3′ GWAM | 1 | 2 | 3 | 4 | 5 |

51D: Composing and Typing – Sentence Completion (10) *(Line: 60; ¶ indention: 5; DS)*

Type complete sentences. Make pencil corrections. Retype on half sheet with appropriate top margin.

In addition to typewriting, I am taking *(name subjects)*. My teacher of English is *(give name)*. My teacher of *(subject)* is *(name)*; of *(subject)*, *(name)*. *(Type similar sentences for all subjects.)* On my last report, I made *(grade)* in typewriting, *(grade)* in English, *(grade)* in *(complete the listing of grades and subjects)*.

LESSON 52

52A: Conditioning Practice (10) *each line three times; Line 4 for 1′ exploration-level writings*

Alphabet Mary planned to have exquisite views of John Zelesnick's big art show. *Space quickly; shift firmly*

Figure Paul must study Section 2, pages 75–190, and Section 3, pages 246–380.

Figure-symbol Waggoner & Glynn's 10/14 Order #1937 was for 2 5/8-inch pine flooring.

Easy Are we working on the solution of our problem, or are we a part of it?

| 1 | 2 | 3 | 4 | 5 | 6 | 7 | 8 | 9 | 10 | 11 | 12 | 13 | 14 |

52B: Building Speed (10)

1. **Type** three 1′ exploration-level writings of ¶ 2 of 51C, above. Type rapidly, but do not type carelessly.
2. **Type** three 1′ exploration-level writings of ¶ 1 of 51C, above. Speed up, but don't lose control of your fingers.

Problem 2: Timed Drills on Business Letter

TYPE: 1. The following letter as a 5′ writing in straight-copy form, beginning with the date. Use a 70-space line. Determine *gwam*.

2. Two 3′ writings in *letter form*, using block style with open punctuation. Determine margins and date line position, based on 350 standard 5-stroke words. Determine *gwam*.

3. Two 3′ writings in *letter form*, using block style with open punctuation, beginning with ¶ 3. Begin 1″ from top edge of paper, supplying an appropriate second-page heading. Determine *gwam*.

4. A 5′ writing in *letter form*, using block style with open punctuation. Determine *gwam* and compare it with your straight-copy speed.

	GWAM 3′	GWAM 5′
September 28, 19—— Mrs. Alexander Strawcutter 8419 Meadowview Lane	4	3
Evanston, Illinois 60201 Dear Mrs. Strawcutter	8	5
Welcome! We were extremely pleased to hear that you have decided to	12	7
make your home in our community. You will find our city to be modern and	17	10
progressive; our people, friendly and energetic.	20	12
May we help you establish your new home? After the confusion of	25	15
moving is over, you will no doubt find that there are many items you	29	18
need for your family and your home. When this time arrives, be sure to	34	21
visit WHEELERS, the largest and most convenient department store in town	39	23
for all your shopping needs. Under one roof, you will find departments	44	26
filled with dependable, quality merchandise for your home, your family,	49	29
your car, and even your dog or cat at prices to fit your budget. Free	53	32
parking, free delivery, and dependable repair service are just a few of	58	35
the little "extras" we provide our customers.	61	37
A charge account at WHEELERS has been opened for your convenience.	5	39
The enclosed credit card with your name and address embossed on it is your	10	42
key to savings and shopping convenience. You may prefer the thirty-day	14	45
payment plan, for which there is no charge, or you can take advantage of	19	48
our revolving charge account which includes a small monthly service charge.	24	51
For our records, will you please complete the credit application enclosed	29	54
and mail it to us. Better still, bring it with you on your first shopping	34	57
trip so that we may have the pleasure of greeting you personally.	39	60
We are looking forward to serving you. A special gift certificate	43	63
which entitles you to a credit of $2.50 on your first month's account is	48	66
yours when you make your first purchase. To receive your certificate,	53	68
just present this letter to me or to any of our friendly sales clerks.	58	71
Sincerely yours Jonathan M. Buckingham Sales Manager Enclosures 2	61	73

3′ GWAM | 1 | 2 | 3 | 4 | 5 |
5′ GWAM | 1 | 2 | 3 |

52C: Problem Typing – Letters in Modified Block Style (20)

Problem 1

Line: 50; SS
Style: modified block; mixed punctuation
Return address on Line 18

Words

9120 Boundbrook Street | Dallas, Texas 75231 | 9
(Current date followed by 3 blank line spaces) 12
Reservations Manager | Sheraton–Charles Hotel | 21
New Orleans, La. 70103 | *DS* Dear Sir: |
28

(¶ 1) Please reserve two connecting single rooms, 36
each | with bath, for the five days of Mardi 45
Gras, Thursday | through Monday, February 53
23–27. I shall have Miss | Marilyn McFarland 62
as my guest. | 65

(¶ 2) If possible, reserve rooms at the front 73
of the | hotel. If this is not possible, is there 82
a balcony | from which we can watch the 90
parades? | 92

(¶ 3) Let me know the charge for the rooms and 100
the date | a deposit should be made to hold the 109
reservation. | 112

Very truly yours, | (Miss) Monalee DeArmond 120

Problem 2

Use the directions, return address, and date of Problem 1, followed by 3 blank line spaces before typing the salutation. (*The letter address is omitted in this letter.*)

Words

12

Dear Marilyn: | 15

(¶ 1) What a Christmas gift I am to have! My 23
parents | are giving me five days at Mardi Gras, 32
and I am to | take a guest of my own choosing. 41
I choose you. | Mother says she will write the 51
formal invitation | later, but I couldn't wait to 60
tell you how much I | hope you will go with me 69
to New Orleans. | 73

(¶ 2) A family friend is Captain of the Krewe 81
of Comus. | He says he will ask for invitations 90
to some of the | Balls for us and will see that 99
we have escorts. | 103

(¶ 3) All hotel rooms will be reserved early, so 111
I have | written for reservations at the Sheraton– 121
Charles. | All I need now is to know you will go 131
to Mardi Gras | with me, and we'll have a 139
Ball! | Sincerely, | 142

52D: Composing and Typing (10) *(Line: 60; ¶ indention: 5; DS)*

1. **Compose** and type a short ¶ to tell what the line "Good fences make good neighbors" (from a Robert Frost poem) means to you.
2. **Proofread** your composition, circling all errors. Make pencil corrections; then retype the paragraph in good form.

LESSON 53

53A: Conditioning Practice (10) *each line three times; Line 4 for 1′ control-level writings*

Alphabet	Mr. Ed Byron did exceptionally good work for the Java quartz industry.	*Quick return*
Figure	Our class has read 15 plays, 36 books, and 40 articles since April 29.	
Figure-symbol	The new rate on Morrison & Richard's $2,850 note (due 6/19/73) is 4½%.	
Easy	A man is at his best when he is doing his best at work he can do best.	
	| 1 | 2 | 3 | 4 | 5 | 6 | 7 | 8 | 9 | 10 | 11 | 12 | 13 | 14 |	

NOTE: Remove the paper; reinsert it; gauge the line and letter; and type over the first line. (See page 78.)

Unit 40 | Lessons 231-236

Business Letter Production

LESSON 231

231A: Conditioning Practice (5) *each line three times*

Alphabet	Jeff organized the complex keyboard and quickly reviewed its function.	Improve shift and number control
Date	April 17 October 29 May 14 November 30 March 25 June 8 August 6 July 7	
ZIP Code	03126 14592 24718 36738 45069 50859 60178 72329 84701 93645 98301 24576	
Fluency	This manual shows both the cost and the quantity of the items on hand.	
	| 1 | 2 | 3 | 4 | 5 | 6 | 7 | 8 | 9 | 10 | 11 | 12 | 13 | 14 |	

231B: Problem Skill Building (45)

Problem 1: Drill on Letter Parts

DO:
Type the letter parts below as directed at the left. Use margins of 1½″. Space, capitalize, and punctuate the lines as you type.

Assume that the line on which you complete Step 1 is the top of the page for beginning Step 2 and that the line on which you complete Step 2 is the top of the page for beginning Step 3.

TYPE	LETTER PARTS
1 **Date, Address, and Salutation.** Use block style and open punctuation. Letter length: 200 words.	august 31 19–– mrs paul franklin 4511 camden avenue akron ohio 44306 dear mrs franklin
2 **Date, Address, and Salutation.** Use modified block style and mixed punctuation. Letter length: 300 words.	november 12 19–– republic metals corporation 4800 louisville pike albany kentucky 42602 gentlemen
3 **Date, AIRMAIL Notation, Address, and Salutation.** Use block style and open punctuation. Letter length: 250 words.	april 2 19–– mr r t boyd president fine & gilmore inc 643 kramer building minot north dakota 58701 dear mr boyd
4 **Date, SPECIAL DELIVERY Notation, Address, and Salutation.** Use modified block style and mixed punctuation. Letter length: 150 words.	september 14 19–– mr william scarborough director of public relations general products corporation 403 richmond road portland maine 04103 dear mr scarborough
5 **Closing Lines.** Use block style, open punctuation, and your initials.	sincerely yours francis e herald general manager
6 **Closing Lines.** Use modified block style, mixed punctuation, and your initials.	yours very truly kimball manufacturing company j e loman president
7 **Closing Lines.** Use modified block style, mixed punctuation, your initials, and an enclosure notation.	sincerely yours mark j lambert director of public relations
8 **Closing Lines.** Use modified block style, open punctuation, your initials, and a notation which indicates 3 enclosures.	very truly yours maxwell transportation company arthur benton traffic coordinator

53B: Problem Typing – Business Letters (20)

Problem 1: Modified Block Style

Letterhead (or full sheet) | Line: 50; SS
Set tab at center; indent for date and closing lines
Date on Line 15 followed by 3 blank line spaces

	Words
June 20, 19–– | Mr. Thomas J. Briggs | West High School |	10
6809 Franklin Blvd. | Cleveland, Ohio 44102 | Dear Mr.	21
Briggs: | (¶ 1) If you have several competent typists who are	32
ready | for office work, ask them to call for an interview | with	44
me. | (¶ 2) Before the interview, each applicant should com-	55
plete | an application form in ink. If the writing is neat | and	67
legible, I am impressed. If it has "messy" | corrections, I am	79
prejudiced against the applicant | even before the interview	91
is begun. | (¶ 3) Our Employment Test includes English, spell-	102
ing, | arithmetic, and typewriting. Competence in these | areas	114
is necessary, but we consider attitudes just | as important	126
as aptitudes and use the job interview | to evaluate the appli-	138
cant's attitudes. | (¶ 4) We expect to have two or three positions	150
open for | beginning office workers early next month. | Sin-	161
cerely yours, | *Return: 4* Albert N. Tomasson | Personnel	170
Director | *DS (Your initials)*	172

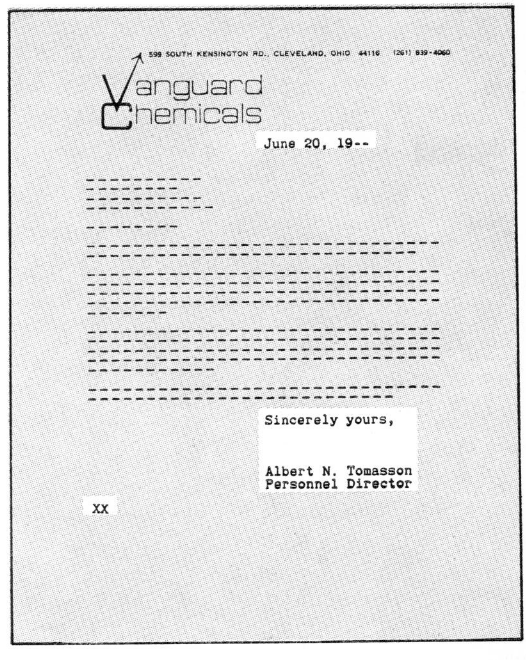
599 SOUTH KENSINGTON RD., CLEVELAND, OHIO 44116 (261) 839-4060
Vanguard Chemicals
June 20, 19--
Sincerely yours,
Albert N. Tomasson
Personnel Director
xx

Problem 2: Speedup in Typing Letters

Type two 1′ writings of each of the following parts of the letter of Problem 1, above: (1) date and other opening lines; (2) salutation and ¶ 1; and (3) final ¶ and closing lines.

53C: Rough Draft (10) *each line three times*

Rough Draft: Copy corrected with pencil or pen and ink is called rough draft.

Correction Symbols (Proofreaders' Marks)

Symbol	Meaning	Symbol	Meaning
^	means insert	#	means add space
Cap. or ≡	means capitalize	♂	means delete
⁀	means close up	tr or ∽	means transpose

		Words
1	Cap. ~~Grace~~ Miss Kumpf said to john Polk, "you sh ould put yourbest foot for wards."	14
2	Cap. What did the last speaker mean by "birds of a feather ~~will~~ flock together"?	14
3	Cap. The teacher said, "he is liek a truck that won't turn with one wheel."	14
4	~~We~~ you can reach for the moon as wellas the to p of ~~a~~ the fence if ~~we~~ you ~~will~~ try.	14
5	Don ~~says~~ thinks that quite people arenot the only ones who don't ~~talk~~ say ~~very~~ much.	14

53D: Composing and Typing (10) *(Line: 60; ¶ indention: 5; DS)*

1. **Compose** and type a three- or four-line ¶ telling what each quotation in the first two sentences of 53C, above, means to you. Ignore typing errors in this first draft.
2. **Make** pencil corrections in your typed copy; then retype the ¶s, using an appropriate top margin and line length. Type at a rate you can maintain with accuracy. Circle errors.

229C: Report Manuscript Inventory (30)

Problem 1: Unbound Manuscript with Footnote

Type ¶s 2 and 3 of the rough draft in 228B, page 336, as the body of an unbound manuscript. Use as a main heading: THE CREDIT UNION—AN EMPLOYEE SERVICE. Add as the final sentence of the last paragraph of the manuscript: **The mutual benefits to be derived from the credit union by employers and employees have been summarized by Chruden and Sherman in these words:**

> Its existence provides additional security to the employees of the company without management becoming involved in such detailed matters as approving or disapproving loans and enforcing payments on loans, which would not only be time-consuming but often embarrassing.[1]

[1] Herbert J. Chruden and Arthur W. Sherman, Jr., Personnel Management (2d ed.; Cincinnati: South-Western Publishing Co., 1963), p. 634.

Problem 2: Leftbound Manuscript with Footnote

Type the copy in 229B, page 338, as a leftbound manuscript. Use the following headings: Main heading: AN ECONOMIC VIEWPOINT; side heading preceding ¶ 1: *The Eighth Marvel of the World*; side heading preceding ¶ 2: *Individual and Economic Freedom*; side heading preceding ¶ 3: *Competition, Profit, and the Consumer*. Add to ¶ 3 of the manuscript: **To those who feel that this concept of profit and competition no longer applies to the American economy, Glos and Baker make this reply:**

> This is obviously a simplification of this part of our economic system, as there are many factors operating to offset and supplement this more or less purifying competitive movement. But it is still basically true in a large segment of our economic life . . . .[1]

[1] Raymond E. Glos and Harold A. Baker, Introduction to Business (6th ed.; Cincinnati: South-Western Publishing Co., 1967), p. 15.

LESSON 230

230A: Conditioning Practice (5) *each line three times*

Alphabet	Jack bought the required number of yellow hoops in sizes five and six.	*Work for quiet control*
Figure	Sales in 1958 totaled 327,490 units; in 1966, 563,482 units were sold.	
Figure-symbol	Read pages 284–370 in Automation by Boyd & Wray (Third Edition, 1965).	
Fluency	The quality of the work done is much more important than the quantity.	
	1 | 2 | 3 | 4 | 5 | 6 | 7 | 8 | 9 | 10 | 11 | 12 | 13 | 14	

230B: Skill Transfer – Straight Copy to Statistical, Rough Draft, and Script Copy (45)

TYPE: A 5′ writing on the straight copy in 226C, page 334. Find *gwam*. Then, type a 5′ writing on each of the following: (1) the statistical copy in 227B, page 335; (2) the rough draft in 228B, page 336; and (3) the script copy in 229B, page 338. Find *gwam* for each. Compare these speeds with your straight-copy speed as shown under GOALS. If time permits, type additional 5′ writings on selected copy to increase your percent of transfer.

GOALS: Compute the percent of transfer in your speed from straight copy by dividing the *gwam* attained on the statistical copy, rough draft copy, and script copy *by* your straight-copy speed. Evaluate your scores on the basis of the following chart which shows an acceptable percent of transfer:

Statistical Copy	66% to 75%
Rough Draft	68% to 85%
Script Copy	75% to 90%

LESSON 54

CARBON COPIES

To make one or more carbon copies as you type, place a carbon sheet (glossy side down) on a thin sheet of paper. If more than one copy is to be made, place another carbon sheet on a thin sheet; then place the letterhead or plain paper on top of that. Insert the "carbon pack" with the glossy side of the carbon sheet toward you. After the carbon pack has been partly inserted so the feed rolls grip the pack firmly, operate the paper release and return it to position before typing. This will release any air pocket and allow equal pressure from the feed rolls, which will help to avoid unsightly streaks on the carbon copy. The inserted carbon pack should have the dull side of the carbon sheet toward you.

54A: Conditioning Practice (10) *each line three times; Line 4 for 1′ control-level writings*

Reach with the fingers

Alphabet	Knox W. Heckler amazed us by endeavoring to qualify for the high jump.
Figure	Jane studied pages 95–170 of Section 2 and pages 184–260 of Section 3.
Figure-symbol	This Invoice #890-Y for 4/4 C&B Oak is for $723.56 (less 2% for cash).
Easy	Boredom is not in the work we do, but in ourselves as we do that work.
	| 1 | 2 | 3 | 4 | 5 | 6 | 7 | 8 | 9 | 10 | 11 | 12 | 13 | 14 |

NOTE: Remove the paper; reinsert it; gauge the line and letter; and type over the last line.

54B: Problem Typing – Business and Personal Letters (20)

Problem 1: Alertness Training

Type the letter of Problem 1, page 90, as directed:

Set a tab stop at center point for use in tabulating to position to type the date and closing lines. Make a carbon copy. Use modified block style and mixed punctuation. Use the following date and address:

Line 15: June 24, 19-- *Space 4 times*

Address: Mrs. Eloise M. Coleman
Business Teacher
Lakewood High School
Lakewood, Ohio 44107

Problem 2: Personal Letter

Carbon copy | *Line: 50* | *SS*
Style: modified block, mixed
Return address: Line 15

Words

260 Ridge Road | Cleveland, Ohio 44102 | 8
June 24, 19-- | *Return: 4* 10

Mr. Thomas J. Briggs | Business Teacher | West 19
High School | Cleveland, Ohio 44102 | Dear 27
Mr. Briggs: | *DS* (¶ 1) Now I know how un- 33
prepared I was for the job inter- | view you sent 42
me on a few days ago. I hadn't given | enough 51
thought to my real interests and even less | to 60
my job competence. | (¶ 2) I didn't have a rec- 68
ord of my school marks or the | names and 76
addresses of my references. I didn't have | my 85
social security card or number. Because I 94
didn't | have these with me for the interview, 103
I was at a | disadvantage from the start. | (¶ 3) 111
The test went fairly well, I think; but I need to | 121
review my English, spelling, and arithmetic 130
and must | practice my typing before another 139
interview. I'll | do this, too. | (¶ 4) I won't let 147
you down when I go for the next inter- | view, I 156
promise. | Sincerely, | Earle Caldwell 164

229B: Skill Transfer – Script (15)

TYPE: Two 5′ writings. Record average *gwam* and average errors.

All letters are used.

Script	GWAM 1′	5′	
The American people enjoy the highest standard of living	11	2	65
of any society in the history of civilization. We earn better	24	5	68
salaries, own better homes, buy more goods and services, and have	37	7	71
more leisure time than any other people on the earth. With less	50	10	73
than ten percent of the world's population, we produce almost	63	13	76
half of the world's goods. Is there any wonder why the American	76	15	78
economy has been named "the eighth marvel of the world"?	87	17	81

Script	GWAM 1′	5′	
The amazing economic success we have gained is built on the	12	20	83
basic concept of individual liberty and economic freedom in a	24	22	85
capitalistic society. Based on this concept, it is our right to	37	25	88
own property, invest in an enterprise of our choice, select our	50	27	91
life's work, and enjoy the fruits of our efforts with a minimum	63	30	93
of government control. There is ample evidence to confirm the	76	33	96
belief that an economic system that is based on free enterprise	88	35	98
and the profit motive, though far from perfect, will produce	101	38	101
greater profits for our nation than will any other system yet	113	40	103
to be devised.	116	41	104

Script	GWAM 1′	5′	
It has been said that competition is the balance wheel of	12	43	106
our economy and that profit is the mainspring. Business works	24	45	109
to earn maximum profits, but competition for customers forces	37	48	111
producers continually to seek greater efficiency. The result	49	50	113
is better quality as well as lower prices. The consumer is the	62	53	116
keystone of our economy because his demands dictate what shall	74	55	119
be produced. Since the producer who fails to provide the public	87	58	121
with goods it wants will soon fade from the scene, the fate of	100	61	124
any company rests to a large extent in the hands of the consumer.	113	63	126

54C: Rough Draft (10) *each line three times*

LEARN: In quoted matter, type the period or comma inside the ending quotation mark.

Correction Symbols (Proofreaders' Marks)

lc means lower-case letters (not caps)
[means move left] means move right

			Words
1	lc	If the Problem is once thought through, it wi l be quiet easy to do.	14
2	lc	The finest endow ment each can have is not Money but Brains.	14
3	Cap.	Kirk quoted the proverb, "a rolli ng stone gathers not moss."	14
4	lc	Our Typing Teacher told us, "Worry, Hurry, and Flurry cause most typing errors."	14
5	Cap.	Dr. Bragdon siad, "luck is a good word if you before it put a P."	14

54D: Composing and Typing (10) *(Line: 60; ¶ indention: 5; DS)*

1. **Compose** and type a short ¶ for each quotation in Sentences 3, 4, and 5 of 54C, above, to tell what it means to you. Ignore errors.
2. **Make** pencil corrections in your ¶s to have the wording more to your liking. Retype the ¶s in correct form. Circle errors.

LESSON 55

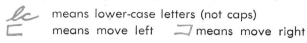

55A: Conditioning Practice (10) *each line three times; Line 4 for 1' control-level writings*

Alphabet	Did Jean Glick get Stewart Phelps to fix my map of Mozambique for Eve?	*Keep your eyes and your mind on the copy*
Figure	The information is given in Figure 26 of Part 3, Chapter 19, page 458.	
Figure symbol	Order 1 punch @ $5.40; 72 pencils @ 8¢ each; and 37 erasers @ 9¢ each.	
Easy	Perhaps money does talk, but it usually goes without saying very much.	
	| 1 | 2 | 3 | 4 | 5 | 6 | 7 | 8 | 9 | 10 | 11 | 12 | 13 | 14 |	

NOTE: Remove the paper; reinsert it; gauge the line and letter; and type over the last line.

55B: Rough Draft (8)

1. **Type** each sentence once to familiarize yourself with the correction symbols.
2. **Type** each sentence as two 1' control-level writings. Determine *gwam*.

		Words
lc	The teacher said, " To know to Wait is their secret."	14
Cap.	A well-know saying "knowledge is power," was usde by Lord Ba con.	14
	"Isn't typing accuracy as mcuh men tal as it is physical," she asked.	14

228C: Business Forms Inventory (30)

Problem 1: Purchase Order

			Words
To: Jacktown Plumbing Supply Company	Order No.	PS–2083X	12
1402 Wyandotte Avenue	Date	September 14, 19––	21
Cheyenne, Wyoming 82001	Terms	2/10, n/30	31
	Ship via	Trailway Express	36

Quantity	Catalog No.	Description	Price	Total	Words
12 ea.	WN–42310	Gas Water Heaters, 30 gal.	43.00	516.00	56
12 ea.	VN–36012	Double-Wall Vent Kits	7.40	88.80	66
24 ea.	GC–59870	Gas Connectors, 12-inch, Brass	1.24	29.76	79
				634.56	80

(Words for header row: 45)

Problem 2: Invoice

			Words
Sold To Benton Variety Store	Date	February 23, 19––	11
287 Market Street	Our No.	BV–3815–P	18
Ashtabula, Ohio 44004	Cust. Order No.	TA–74183	28
	Shipped Via	Parcel Post	33
Terms 2/15, n/30	Salesman	Carlson	40

Quantity	Catalog No.	Description	Unit Price	Total	Words
6 doz.	HCB–432	Hose Coupling, Brass, 3/8″	20.40 doz.	122.40	62
4 doz.	LA–714	Ladle, Aluminum, 7 1/4″	9.08 doz.	36.32	73
1 doz.	ROA–8	Rack, Oven, Aluminum, 8″	16.20 doz.	16.20	85
				174.92	86

(Words for header row: 50)

Problem 3: Interoffice Memorandum

TO: Theodore Cwierz, Employee Relations DATE: May 2, 19–– FILE: PD 58630–R FROM: P. D. Castle, Director of Personnel SUBJECT: Establishment of an Employee Credit Union (¶ 1) Use ¶ 1 of the rough draft in 228B, p. 336. (¶ 2) Line supervisors report that many of our employees have expressed an interest in establishing a credit union. Please investigate all aspects of this idea and report your findings at our next monthly staff conference.

LESSON 229

229A: Conditioning Practice (5) *each line three times*

Use down-and-in space-bar technique

Alphabet	Pam made the objective of the exercises clear by giving a weekly quiz.
Figure	Based on 7,243,500 shares, the stock average rose 16 points to 863.19.
Figure-symbol	Lot #658 (300 sheets, 8 3/4″ x 6 1/2″) will cost 90¢ per unit or $270.
Fluency	Make eight copies of the special report for the Chairman of the Board.

| 1 | 2 | 3 | 4 | 5 | 6 | 7 | 8 | 9 | 10 | 11 | 12 | 13 | 14 |

55C: Problem Typing Review (20)

Supplies needed 2 full sheets; 1 letterhead; 1 carbon sheet; 1 second (thin) sheet

DO: List the problems to be typed; ➧ place the list beside your machine; type the letters as directed.

Page 85, Problem 1
Page 90, Problem 1
Page 91, Problem 2

55D: Addressing Envelopes and Folding and Inserting Letters (20)

TO ADDRESS A SMALL ENVELOPE: Type the return address in the upper left corner (unless an envelope with a printed return address is used). Begin on the second line space from the top edge and 3 spaces from the left edge.

Type the first line of the address at or slightly below vertical center of the envelope. Start about 5 spaces to the left of the horizontal center of the envelope. Use block style.

Type a 3-line address with double spacing, but use single spacing for an address of 4 or more lines. Space twice between state name (or abbreviation) and the ZIP Code.

Note. In letter and envelope addresses, direction names (North, South, East, and West) may be abbreviated (N., S., E., and W., respectively).

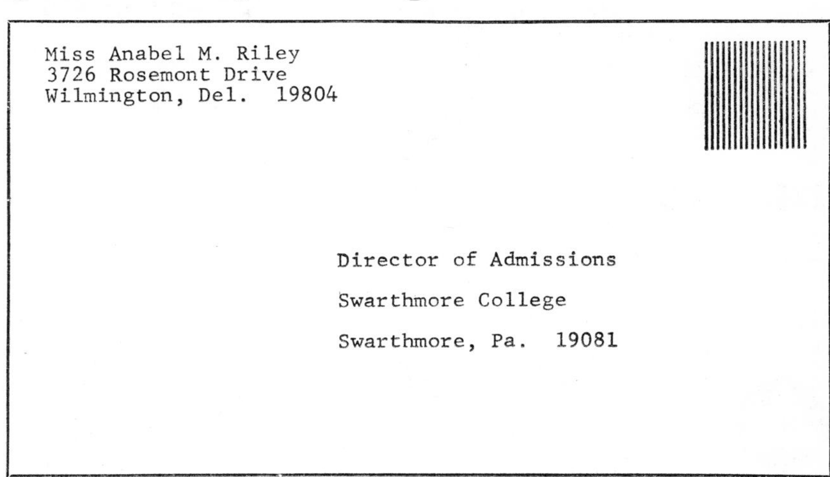

Miss Anabel M. Riley
3726 Rosemont Drive
Wilmington, Del. 19804

Director of Admissions

Swarthmore College

Swarthmore, Pa. 19081

FOLDING AND INSERTING LETTERS INTO SMALL ENVELOPES

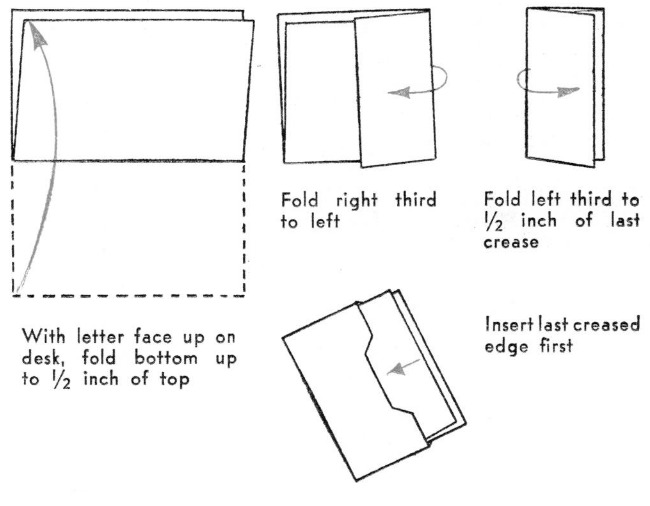

With letter face up on desk, fold bottom up to ½ inch of top
Fold right third to left
Fold left third to ½ inch of last crease
Insert last creased edge first

Problem 1: Addressing Envelopes

Address an envelope for each letter typed as 55C: Problem Typing Review (above). If a printed return address is not supplied, use your own return address.

Problem 2: Folding and Inserting Letters

Study the illustrations and directions for folding and inserting letters given at the right; then fold each letter typed as 55C and insert it into its addressed envelope. Hand the carbon copies to your teacher.

Problem 3: Skill Building

Address three envelopes as indicated at the right; then fold blank full-size sheets (as substitutes for typed letters) and insert one into each envelope.

A return address is given for the first envelope; for Envelopes 2 and 3, assume that an envelope with a *printed* return address is used.

1

Return address
Anthony Duwalder
Exeter Military Academy
Peachtree Road
Asheville, N.C. 28803

Letter address
Dr. Bryan N. LaSalle, Jr.
Director of Admissions
Rollins College
Winter Park, Fla. 32789

2

Mrs. Eloise M. Coleman
Business Teacher
Lakewood High School
Lakewood, Ohio 44107

3

Miss Janice L. Deveraux
364 W. 20th Street
Sioux City, Iowa 51104

LESSON 228

228A: Conditioning Practice (5) *each line three times*

Alphabet	Gary Shell will make very frequent trips to Mexico and Brazil in June.	Use a 1-2 shift-key count
Figure	His telephone number was changed from 463–8571 to 293–6082 on July 15.	
Figure-symbol	Order #6279 (dated June 13) read: "Buy C & N Common stock at 40 5/8."	
Fluency	The stock exchange provides a market for the sale of stocks and bonds.	
	1 | 2 | 3 | 4 | 5 | 6 | 7 | 8 | 9 | 10 | 11 | 12 | 13 | 14	

228B: Skill Transfer – Rough Draft (15)

TYPE: Two 5′ writings. Record average *gwam* and average errors.

All letters are used.

	GWAM 1′	5′	
¶The ~~development~~ *establishment* of credit unions *by* ~~for~~ employees appaers to be	12	2	50
one of the most *popular* ~~recent~~ trends in *industry* ~~business~~. A recent *survey* ~~poll~~	21	5	52
indicates that credit unions in the natoin have more than	36	7	54
twelvemillion members and that their assets have *topped the* ~~reached~~	48	10	57
six billion *mark*. Surveys show also that the credit union	60	12	59
~~is gaining~~ *has gained almost* universal approval and that it is rated by *many* ~~some~~	73	15	62
workers as the top employee serivice in industry.	83	17	64
The credit union is a coöperative *venture* ~~operation~~ operated	10	19	66
by the *employees* ~~men~~ ofa business under *federal* ~~national~~ and state laws topro-	23	21	68
vide financial ~~help~~ *aid* for union members. Union funds obtained	36	24	71
by the sale of share to members are used for loans, to members,	49	26	74
usually without *security* ~~collateral~~. The rate of interset paid on funds	61	29	76
invested is *higher* ~~greater~~ than that normally paid by *many* ~~most~~ banks,	73	31	78
whereas the interest rate on loans is usually lower.	83	33	80
¶Employers raelize that a worker is much less *efficient on the* ~~effective at his~~	12	36	83
~~work~~ *job* when he is worreid about over due debts or other *financial* ~~money~~	25	38	85
~~matters.~~ *problems* the credit union has proved to be a *far* ~~much~~ better	36	40	88
solution to these *problems* ~~matters~~ than advances pay onloans made by the	50	43	90
~~firm.~~ *Company* Thus, employers will often provide space, *equipment,* and clerical	65	46	93
help for the credit union.	70	47	94

LESSON 56

56A: Conditioning Practice (10) *each line three times; Line 4 for 1′ control-level writings*

Alphabet	Jane Peyton was quite lax about the exact zone marking for deliveries.	*Quick, sharp stroking*
Figure	Flight 690 with 74 men was due at 10:50 p.m. and arrived at 12:34 a.m.	
Figure-symbol	The $1,000 Dwyer Water Authority 4¼% bond, due 6/20/87, sold for $953.	
Easy	There are many problems that need to be thought through to a solution.	

| 1 | 2 | 3 | 4 | 5 | 6 | 7 | 8 | 9 | 10 | 11 | 12 | 13 | 14 |

NOTE: Remove the paper; reinsert it; gauge the line and letter; and type over the last line.

56B: Growth Index (10) *(Line: 70; DS; ¶ indention: 5)*

Type two 3′ control-level writings. Circle errors. Determine *gwam* for the better writing.

All letters are used.

1.3 E 5.2 85

Text	GWAM 1′	3′	
Quiet people are not the only ones who don't say much. Most of	13	4	46
what is called conversation is just a lot of idle chatter. While no	27	9	50
one expects us to talk of world problems or discuss the books of the	41	13	55
most popular authors all the time, these should have our attention	54	18	59
now and then, to say the least.	60	20	61

1.3 E 5.2 85

Text	GWAM 1′	3′	
There are dozens of problems that need to be thought through to a	13	24	66
solution, yet we just idly chatter away. "Silence is golden," it is	27	29	70
said; but we are off the gold standard too much of the time. If we	41	33	75
keep quiet except when we have something very important to say, there	55	38	79
will be a great many quiet people in the world!	64	41	83

1′ GWAM | 1 | 2 | 3 | 4 | 5 | 6 | 7 | 8 | 9 | 10 | 11 | 12 | 13 | 14 |
3′ GWAM | 1 | 2 | 3 | 4 | 5 |

56C: Rough Draft (10) *each line three times on the control level*

			Words
1	lc	My Brother Robert (has) decided to train (many) Great Danes for the trade.	14
2	Cap.	Will miss Betty Booth miss all of the (good) books that she left at school?	14
3		Sam pounds hard on the fact that we (must) ponder how poise comes promotes power.	14
4	Cap.	Buzz Beckman's excess of zeal amazes me, but can he excel max Manning?	14
5		We try to treat (top) executives always as we treat (our) other men customers.	14

227B: Skill Transfer – Statistical Copy (15)

TYPE: Two 5′ writings. Record your average *gwam* and average errors.

All letters are used.

	GWAM 1′	5′	
The past decade has been an era of enormous expansion in American	13	3	59
industry. The annual reports of the Kalizar Leather Company, makers	27	5	61
of quality luggage for 26 years, reflect a pattern of growth which would	42	8	64
be impressive in any era. Less than 10 years ago, the Kalizar Company	56	11	67
employed 1,189 persons in 9 plants located in 7 states, primarily in the	70	14	70
eastern part of the country. Today, the payroll totals 5,267 employees	85	17	73
in 23 plants, strategically located in 18 states to serve the people	99	19	76
from coast to coast. Net sales of the company provide an even more	112	22	79
impressive picture. In just 10 years, net sales have risen from a total	127	25	81
of $28,062,976 to $113,515,265, a gain of more than 400%!	138	28	84
The consolidated net income of the Kalizar Leather Company for the	13	30	86
fiscal year which ended July 31 was $4,712,360. This was equal to $3.32	28	33	89
a share on 1,373,175 shares of common stock outstanding as of the end of	43	36	92
the fiscal year after payment of $609,608 in annual dividends on 60,959	57	39	95
shares of preferred stock owned by 1,026 shareholders. The corporate	71	42	98
profit for the period represented a yield of 4.2% based on net sales.	85	45	101
Net profit for the current period increased $1,123,754 or 31% over the	99	48	104
previous year. Corporate gains this year are equal to $1.92 a share on	114	50	106
all outstanding stock. The Kalizar Company has declared a cash dividend	128	53	109
for 39 consecutive years, a record equaled by few other corporations.	142	56	112

1′ GWAM | 1 | 2 | 3 | 4 | 5 | 6 | 7 | 8 | 9 | 10 | 11 | 12 | 13 | 14 |
5′ GWAM | 1 | 2 | 3 |

227C: Business Letter Inventory (30) *(Plain sheets)*

Problem 1: Block Letter with Open Punctuation

Words

May 31, 19–– Miss Betty Foresman 3196 Ogel- 8
thorpe Street Burlington, Vermont 05401 Dear 18
Miss Foresman (For ¶s 1 and 2, use ¶s 2 and 3 20
of the straight copy in 226C, page 334.) (¶ 3) 217
Learn how you can increase <u>your value</u> and <u>your</u> 229
<u>pay</u> by developing your communication skills in 239
just a few minutes each day. Send for your free, 249
introductory booklet, "Word Power Is Earning 258
Power," without delay. Sincerely yours Alfred 268
E. Bankhead Assistant Director *(For this letter and* 274
all remaining letters in Part 4, be sure to use your own reference initials.) (242)

Problem 2: Modified Block Letter with Mixed Punctuation

Words

August 18, 19–– Mr. Robert Klein 306 Geyser 9
Avenue Billings, Montana 59101 Dear Mr. 17
Klein (¶ 1) Thank you for your letter of August 26
14 requesting information about the financial 35
status of the Kalizar Leather Company. (¶ 2) 43
(Use ¶ 2 of the timed writing in 227B, above.) 185
(¶ 3) We appreciate your interest in our com- 193
pany. If you would like any additional data, 210
please do not hesitate to write us. Sincerely 236
yours C. B. Waters Director of Public Relations 272
(190)

56D: Problem Typing – Measurement (20) *each problem once; circle errors*

Line: 50; modified block style; mixed punctuation; SS; date on Line 18, followed by 3 blank line spaces; address envelope; fold and insert letter [The boldface figure at the end of the word count column includes the word count for the envelope address.]

Problem 1

Words

October 28, 19–– | Mr. Wallace L. Aki | 448 8
North Wakea Avenue | Kahului, Maui, Hawaii 16
96732 | Dear Mr. Aki: | (¶ 1) You must take 23
a physical examination and complete | Form 32
F 9401 to obtain our Major Medical coverage. | 41
The form was sent to you on October 10. Fill 50
in | the white copy of the form yourself and 59
have your | doctor fill in the yellow copy. | (¶ 2) 67
Your insurance will become effective on the 76
first | day of the month following the date of 85
acceptance | of your application by the insur- 94
ance company. | (¶ 3) Write me if you have 101
questions about Form F 9401. | Sincerely yours, | 110
Return: 4 H. C. Muehlenberger | Secretary- 116
Treasurer | *(Your initials)* **118/132**

Problem 2

Words

Mr. Jose Morales | Products Manager | Univer- 11
sal Cyclops, Inc. | Venice, Calif. 90291 | Dear 20
Mr. Morales: | (¶ 1) We build supersonic wind 28
tunnels and are engaged | in aerodynamic re- 36
search under Government contract. | We employ 45
60 engineers to design and develop our | proj- 54
ects. A large part of the work is original | 63
design and requires a search for new materials, | 72
methods, and products. | (¶ 2) Our catalog file 81
will be more valuable if we have | technical 89
information about your products. May | we 97
have a copy of your catalog for our library. | 107
Very truly yours, | Hans G. Fischer | Engineering 116
Librarian | *(Your initials)* **118/132**

Problem 3

Words

October 30, 19–– | Mr. B. J. Dahlen, President | 9
Dahlen Investments, Inc. | Monessen, Pa. 18
15062 | Dear Mr. Dahlen: | (¶ 1) At a meeting 26
of stockholders held on October 25, | you were 35
elected a Director of this Company for a | 43
three-year term beginning on December 1. | 51
(¶ 2) Please be present at the reorganization 59
meeting to | be held at 1:30 p.m. on November 68
15 to take your | oath of office. | (¶ 3) It will 76
be a pleasure to have you on our Board. | Sin- 85
cerely yours, | H. C. Muehlenberger | Secretary- 94
Treasurer | *(Your initials)* **95/117**

Problem 4

Use the same directions, but type the letter of Problem 3 with the following changes:

Letter address	Mr. Elwood N. Bauer | Vice President McKeown, Wakefield & Co. Pittsburgh, Pa. 15219
Saluta-tion	Supply one that is appropriate.
Change	¶ 1 from *three*-year term to *one*-year term

Take time to proofread all letters again and circle any error not found in your first reading. Double-check the accuracy of your typing on the envelopes. Begin now to verify the accuracy of your problem typing, too, especially of names and numbers. Your proofreading grade will be determined by your accuracy in finding all the errors you have made in your typing. Since error detection is the first step in error correction, this evidence of your thoroughness in finding errors is important and must be demonstrated before you begin the practice of erasing and correcting errors, as you will be taught to do in later lessons.

226C: Straight-Copy Skill Evaluation (35)

TYPE: Three 1′ speed writings on each ¶. Three 1′ control writings on each ¶.

TYPE: Two 5′ writings. Record average *gwam* and average errors.

All letters are used.

	GWAM 1′	5′	
Have you ever considered what we would do without words? Language	13	3	62
is so commonplace we take it for granted. As children, we learn quickly	28	6	65
to make meaningful sounds. Our capacity to communicate increases as we	42	8	68
grow older; we acquire the ability to read and to express complex ideas	57	11	70
orally. Rarely, however, do we stop to consider that language is the	71	14	73
vital tool of man's intellect. Without words, our perceptive power	84	17	76
would be of no value and civilization as we know it would not exist.	98	20	79
Do you realize that the merit of office employees is rated often on	14	22	81
the basis of communication skills? The number of positions for typists	28	25	84
continues to grow rapidly, but the demand is for typists who can do more	43	28	87
than merely copy data. Business requires many secretaries, particularly	57	31	90
those who can take the ideas of the boss and express them correctly.	71	34	93
Accountants are also in great demand, but they must be able to do more	85	37	96
than just enter figures in the proper columns; they must be able to	97	39	98
explain clearly and concisely the figures on financial statements.	112	42	101
 Business places a premium on the employee who is adept in the use	13	45	104
of language. Those who are trained as clerks, typists, secretaries, or	28	48	107
bookkeepers can earn good salaries; but those who have also developed	42	50	109
an ability to express ideas vividly and concisely will gain success more	56	53	112
rapidly. If you are proficient in the art of communication, there is no	71	56	115
doubt that you will find your efforts rewarded in terms of higher pay.	85	59	118

1′ GWAM | 1 | 2 | 3 | 4 | 5 | 6 | 7 | 8 | 9 | 10 | 11 | 12 | 13 | 14 |
5′ GWAM | 1 | 2 | 3 |

LESSON 227

227A: Conditioning Practice (5) *each line three times*

Alphabet	Jaywalkers vex policemen who fight quite zealously against bad ideals.	*Eyes on copy*
Figure	Listed in order, the test scores are: 19, 32, 46, 57, 68, 70, and 83.	
Figure-symbol	Line 1 of Order #3850 should read, "274 @ 6½¢" instead of "971 @ 6¼¢."	
Fluency	It pays to work for both quantity and quality in all that you must do.	

| 1 | 2 | 3 | 4 | 5 | 6 | 7 | 8 | 9 | 10 | 11 | 12 | 13 | 14 |

Unit 9 | Lessons 57-64

Simple Tabulated Reports

1. Arrange work area for efficient performance.
2. Adjust paper guide and paper-bail rolls.
3. Set control to type on upper part of ribbon.
4. Use full sheet; Line: 70; SS, unless otherwise directed.

LESSON 57

57A: Conditioning Practice (8) *each line three times; Line 4 for 1′ speed writings*

Alphabet	C. J. Downey asked to be given a week to reply to their tax quiz form.	*Eliminate waste motions*
Figure	Pages 210–239, Section 4, of Volume XIV (6/17/58) covers these points.	
Figure-symbol	Their price is 75¢ a copy (less 20% discount on orders of 36 or more).	
Easy	The chairman claims that a majority of the members like the amendment.	
	| 1 | 2 | 3 | 4 | 5 | 6 | 7 | 8 | 9 | 10 | 11 | 12 | 13 | 14 |	

57B: Tabulating Drills (10)

Drill 1. Leave 12 spaces between words (columns). Set margin and tab stops (Guides 1, 2, and 3). 

advantageous   extemporaneous

Drill 2. Leave 8 spaces between groups of figures (columns). Set margin and tab stops (Guides 2 and 3). *Note:* Space forward or backspace to align figures at the right-hand side.

123,456	45,789	10,090	7,630
90,765	4,320	2,091	16,419

GUIDES FOR HORIZONTAL PLACEMENT OF COLUMNS

1. Preparatory Steps

a. Clear margin stops by moving them to extreme ends of the scale.
b. Clear all tab stops.
c. Move carriage to center of paper.
d. Decide spacing between columns —preferably an even number of spaces (4, 6, 8, 10, etc.).

2. Set Left Margin Stop

From center of paper, backspace 1 space for each 2 letters, figures, symbols, and spaces in longest line of each column and for each 2 spaces left between columns. *Set the left margin stop at this point.* If an extra space occurs at the end of the longest line of a column when backspacing, carry it forward to the next column.

3. Set Tab Stops

From the left margin, space forward once for each letter, figure, symbol, and space in longest line in the first column and for each space to be left between first and second columns. *Set tab stop at this point for second column.* Follow similar procedure when additional columns are to be typed.

57C: Problem Typing – Two- and Three-Column Tabulations (20)

Problem 1

Half sheet; SS; 10 spaces between columns
Center: the problem vertically (page 66)
the heading horizontally (page 61)
the columns (Guides 2 and 3, above)

WORDS FREQUENTLY MISSPELLED		Words
	TS	6
collateral	believable	10
commitment	consensus	14
discrepancy	extraordinary	19
independence	justifiable	24
maintenance	manageable	29
miscellaneous	occasionally	34
KEY 13	10	13

PART 4

Applied Office Typewriting

You are now in the last semester of typewriting. In addition to making a final push to attain production proficiency on correspondence, reports, and forms, you will put your skill to work in a variety of office-like situations. Along with the typing of familiar papers, your job assignments will include the preparation of: single and mass mailings, financial papers, medical reports and records, legal documents, executive papers, technical reports, and government communications.

Unit 39 | Lessons 226-230

Basic and Problem Skills Inventory

LESSON 226

226A: Conditioning Practice (5) *each line three times*

Alphabet	Dave F. Erby, the well-known singer, excels at composing "quiet" jazz.	*Type with continuity*
Figure	On June 19 and 20, Ray flew 3,267 miles by jet in 5 hours, 48 minutes.	
Figure-symbol	Wasn't invoice #795 from Fen & May for $3,820 (less 6%) paid on May 1?	
Fluency	Sign both forms for the sale of the special stock and mail them today.	
	| 1 | 2 | 3 | 4 | 5 | 6 | 7 | 8 | 9 | 10 | 11 | 12 | 13 | 14 |	

226B: Technique Evaluation: Stroking (10) *each line four times; then 1′ writings*

TECHNIQUE CUE | Strike each key quickly and sharply.

		CHECK
Shift key	Send the "Report of Operations" to Mr. J. R. Pugh in Ocean City, N. J.	✓ *Minimum motion*
Top row	To improve your typing power, you must use proper stroking techniques.	✓ *Finger action*
Left hand	The tax rate on estates will be increased after the first of the year.	✓ *Fingers curved*
Right hand	In my opinion, you should not plan to join the group in the Yukon now.	✓ *Fingers upright*
Direct reach	My brother has decided he will need a much larger truck for this trip.	✓ *Quiet hands*
	| 1 | 2 | 3 | 4 | 5 | 6 | 7 | 8 | 9 | 10 | 11 | 12 | 13 | 14 |	

Problem 2

Half sheet; SS
8 spaces between columns
Center: the problem vertically
the heading horizontally
the columns horizontally

Technique Cue: Reach to the tab bar or key without moving the hand out of position. Tabulate from column to column without looking up from the copy.

WORD DIVISION
TS

			Words
	WORD DIVISION		3
against	accurate	accu-rate	8
driver	business	busi-ness	13
imply	cordially	cor-dially	19
opened	delegate	dele-gate	24
Paulsen	judgment	judg-ment	29
spaces	opening	open-ing	34
steady	problems	prob-lems	39
they're	programmed	pro-grammed	46
until	strenuous	strenu-ous	51
unique	transferred	trans-ferred	57
whether	unanimous	unani-mous	63
zephyr	verbally	ver-bally	68

57D: Composing and Typing (12) *(Full sheet; Line: 60; ¶ indention: 5; DS)*

1. Assume that the bell rings on typing the first letter of each word in Column 1 of Problem 2, above. Compose and type explanations of why each word is typed without being divided. You may begin as in the paragraph suggested at the right.
2. Correct your copy by the guides on page 66; then retype it with a 2-inch top margin.

Do not separate a one-letter syllable at the beginning or end of a word, as in "against" and "steady," from the rest of the word.

(Complete your explanation for the other words of Column 1.)

LESSON 58

58A: Conditioning Practice (8) *each line three times; Line 4 for 1' speed writings*

Improve your techniques

Alphabet	With superb form, five or six good ski jumpers whizzed quickly by Nan.
Figure	The store moved from 3948 North 56th Street to 1270 Degas Place, West.
Figure-symbol	Your Policy #NY13967–946–21 (issued February 5, 1960) expires in 1973.
Easy	To build skill, they take three or four short timed writings each day.
	| 1 | 2 | 3 | 4 | 5 | 6 | 7 | 8 | 9 | 10 | 11 | 12 | 13 | 14 |

58B: Drill on Spacing the Main and Secondary Headings (10)

SPACING MAIN AND SECONDARY HEADINGS: Double-space between main and secondary headings, if both are used; triple-space between last line of heading (whether main or secondary) and first line of columns (or columnar headings).

DO: Have 10 spaces between columns. Set margin and tab stops (see page 96). Center headings horizontally.

TYPE: Drill as given at right.

Main heading THE SMALLEST AND THE LARGEST STATE
DS
Secondary heading Land Area (Sq. Mi.) and Capital
TS

Rhode Island	1,214	Providence
Alaska	586,400	Juneau

225C: Tabulation Production Measurement (38)

Time Schedule

Get ready to type	3′
Timed production	30′
Proofread; compute *n-pram* . .	6′

Type the following four tables for 30′ when directed to begin. Make 1 cc for each. Correct errors as you type. If time permits, start over. Mark uncorrected errors. Compute *n-pram*.

Problem 1 *Full sheet 1 cc Reading position* DS *body Spread heading*
Space 16 between columns 1 and 2; 6 between 2 and 3

			Problem 1 Words	Problem 3 Words
U N I T E D S T A T E S P O P U L A T I O N[a]			10	10
July 1, Selected Years 1955–1964			17	17
(Thousands)			19	19
				29
	Total	Residing in	23	32
Year	Population	United States	33	38
				48
1955	165,276	164,309	41	52
1956	168,225	167,310	48	57
1957	171,278	170,375	56	61
1958	174,154	173,332	63	65
1959	177,208	176,513	70	69
1960	180,684	179,992	78	73
1961	183,756	183,057	85	78
1962	186,656	185,890	93	82
1963	189,375	188,616	100	86
1964	192,072	191,334	107	90
______			111	94
(a) Includes armed forces overseas			118	101
Source: Department of Commerce, Bureau of the			128	110
Census			129	111
				122
		+ *Vertical lines: pica*		30/152
		elite		35/157

Problem 2 *Half sheet 1 cc Center vertically* SS
4 spaces between columns Type lines

				Words
UNITED STATES POPULATION				5
BY AGE GROUPS *				8
(Millions)				10
				19
Age Group	1975	1980	1985	24
				33
Total	230.4	252.1	275.6	39
Under 5 years	37.3	30.6	33.0	44
5–19 years	65.9	72.8	82.0	50
20–44 years	72.7	82.4	92.6	55
45–64 years	43.4	43.2	43.0	60
65 years and over	21.2	23.1	25.0	67
				76
Source: Department of Commerce, Bureau of				85
the Census				87

Problem 3 *Retype Problem 1, omitting leaders 1 cc*
Box table, typing horizontal and 4 vertical lines
Group by 5s; leave 10 spaces between columns

Problem 4 *Correct rough draft of table Half sheet 1 cc*
Center vertically 8 spaces between columns

				Words
all caps → Sex Ratio of U. S. Population #				6
(Ratio Represents Males Per 100 Females)* →				14
Age	1950	1960	Total	22
Under 15 years	103.7	103.4	103.7	29
15 to 24 years	79.8	98.3	99.8	35
25 to 45 years	96.5	95.7	95.8	41
45 to 64 years	100.2	95.7	93.6	47
65 and over #	89.7	82.8	77.6	53
All Ages (lc)	98.7	97.1	96.4	57
				61
*Estimated for (as of) July 1				66
Source: Department of Commerce,				72
Bureau of the Census				76

VERTICAL CENTERING: MATHEMATICAL METHOD

1. Count the lines and blank line spaces needed to type the problem. (Count 2 for triple-space after main or secondary heading and 1 for double-space between lines.)
2. Subtract lines used from 66 for full sheet or 33 for half sheet.
3. Divide by 2 to get top and bottom margins. If fraction results, disregard it. Space down from top edge of paper *1 more than number of lines to be left in top margin.* For READING POSITION, which is above exact vertical center, subtract 2 from exact top margin.

58C: Problem Typing – Tables with Main and Secondary Headings (20)

Problem 1

Full sheet; DS
Center: the problem vertically (see above)
the headings horizontally
the columns (see page 96)

Solution:

Lines available:	66
Lines used:	24
For top and bottom margins:	42

42 ÷ 2 = 21; therefore, start heading on Line 22

Alertness Cue: Space forward (last two numbers in middle column) from the tab stop to keep the column of figures aligned at the right.

Problem 2

Type Problem 1 again, but place it in *vertical reading position.* Use the machine adjustments already made for typing Problem 1.

TEN LARGEST STATES

DS

Land Area (Sq. Mi.) and Capital

TS

			Words
TEN LARGEST STATES			4
Land Area (Sq. Mi.) and Capital			10
Alaska	586,400	Juneau	15
Texas	267,339	Austin	19
California	158,693	Sacramento	25
Montana	147,138	Helena	29
New Mexico	121,666	Santa Fe	35
Arizona	113,909	Phoenix	40
Nevada	110,540	Carson City	45
Colorado	104,247	Denver	50
Wyoming	97,914	Cheyenne	55
Oregon	96,981	Salem	59

58D: Drill on Special Symbols (12)

1. **Practice** typing the symbols of Column 3 as directed in Column 2. Type each twice.
2. **Center** columns horizontally with 6 spaces between (Guides, page 96). **Type** drill twice.

SPECIAL SYMBOLS

TS

			Words
SPECIAL SYMBOLS			3
Caret	Diagonal (/); roll platen back one line	next my/day.	15
In care of	Small c; diagonal; small o	c/o	23
Carbon copy	Small letter c typed twice	cc	32
English pound	Capital L; backspace; f	£	40
Equals	Two hyphens, one slightly below the other	=	50
Plus	Diagonal; backspace; hyphen	⌿	58
Division	Colon; backspace; hyphen	÷	65
Subscript	Letter; cylinder forward slightly; figure	H_2O	72

Problem 3: Bill of Lading *(2 cc's)*

	Words
Shipper's No. 251407 Carrier Midwest Valley Transit	6
From National Steel Foundries, Inc. Date January 19, 19––	16
at Cleveland, Ohio Consigned to Dey Hardware Supply Company	24
Destination 7296 Cumberland Road Street Warwick City Kent County	31
State Rhode Island Routing Scranton – Hartford Vehicle or Car Initial XR No. 751340	40

Packages	Description	Weight	
8	Galvanized 1/2″ Pipe in 10′ pieces	68#	48
4	Threaded Coupling for 1/2″ pipe	2#	56
2	Piston Pumps	140#	60
12	Galvanized Steel Building Frame	360#	68

Shipper National Steel Foundries, Inc.	74
Permanent address of shipper 3905 Carnegie Avenue Cleveland, Ohio 44115	83

Problem 4: Invoice for Problem 3 *(2 cc's; SS body)*

				Words
Date	January 19, 19––	Sold	Dey Hardware Supply Company	9
Our Order No.	251407	To	7296 Cumberland Road	15
Cust. Order No.	AL–436790		Warwick, Rhode Island 02886	22
Terms	Net 30 days	Shipped Via	Midwest Valley Transit	29

Quantity	Description	Unit Price	Total	
8	Galvanized Steel Pipe in 10′ pieces	$ 1.43	$ 11.44	40
4	Threaded Steel Couplings	.14	.56	48
2	Piston Pumps	79.85	159.70	54
1	Galvanized Steel Building Frame	193.50	193.50	65
			$365.20	66

LESSON 225

225A: Conditioning Practice (5) *each line at least three times*

Curved, upright fingers

Alphabet; shift	John Waltz with Felix Maqua staged hit plays at a camp by Beaver Lake.
Figure-symbol	Order #2390 amounted to $456.78 and was paid by check #678 on July 19.
Long words	We can do much with interest, determination, and average intelligence.
Fluency	The little things in life are the ones that often seem to be so large.
	| 1 | 2 | 3 | 4 | 5 | 6 | 7 | 8 | 9 | 10 | 11 | 12 | 13 | 14 |

225B: Skill Building (7) *1′ writings on selected ¶s from pages 326–327*

LESSON 59

59A: Conditioning Practice  *each line three times; Line 4 for 1′ writings*

Alphabet	G. P. Winlock plans to drive Elizabeth Jeffries to Quebec next May 30.	*Make your fingers do the work*
Figure	My car license is B6–890 and my Social Security number is 185–26–4379.	
Figure-symbol	Their Invoice #85309, dated 12/18, totals $621.30, less 2% in 10 days.	
Easy	It is your duty to find a remedy for each of your typing difficulties.	

| 1 | 2 | 3 | 4 | 5 | 6 | 7 | 8 | 9 | 10 | 11 | 12 | 13 | 14 |

59B: Drill on Typing "Spread" Headings 

TO TYPE A "SPREAD" HEADING: Space once between letters and three times between words.

TO DETERMINE WHERE TO START A "SPREAD" HEADING: Backspace from center once for each letter *except the last letter in the line*, and once for each 2 spaces to be left between words (ignoring extra spaces).

DO: Use double spacing. Type each title as a "spread" heading. The first heading is shown in "spread" form.

W O R D   D I V I S I O N

COMPOSING AND TYPING
ROUGH DRAFT
PROMOTION COSTS

59C: Problem Typing – Tables with "Spread" Headings (20)

Problem 1

Half sheet; DS; center vertically and horizontally

Set tab stop for the digit in the second column that requires the least forward and backward spacing.

P R O M O T I O N C O S T S		Words
	TS	6
Advertising Index	$ 9,761.35	12
Circulars	13,247.59	16
Direct Mail	10,451.20	20
Exhibits and Dues	5,832.40	26
Samples	24,850.00	29
Miscellaneous	639.81	33

Problem 2

Half sheet; DS; center vertically and horizontally

Alertness Cue: If you are using an electric machine, release the shift lock to type the apostrophe.

Center { L A D I E S ' W E A R DS		Words
First Quarter Departmental Sales		5
	TS	11
Blouses and sweaters	$ 640.90	18
Coats and Suits	6,067.25	23
Dresses and Lingerie	3,591.25	29
Furs	2,976.48	31
Handbags and Gloves	876.40	37
Hats	603.50	39
Jewelry	2,901.00	43
shoes	1,372.75	45

59D: Composing and Typing – Letter (12)

Use your return address
Current date on Line 18
Modified block style; mixed (see page 86)

1. Address your letter to **Director of Admissions** | (*Name of college of your choice, city, state, and ZIP Code, if known*).
2. Compose and type a personal letter to ask for an application form for admission to the college. Ask about the possibility of getting part-time work. Mention your typing skill.
3. Proofread your letter; make corrections; then retype the letter with a carbon copy.

LESSON 224

224A: Conditioning Practice (5) *each line at least three times*

Alphabet; shift	Jim Paxon and Higley Wirtz were varsity halfbacks at quiet Ball State.	*Wrists low; hands quiet*
Figure-symbol	Jerry's Policy #918-657-402 for $3,000 was stamped "To be reinstated."	
Long words	The intramural basketball rivalries instigated much scholastic fervor.	
Fluency	A champion is the man who always keeps trying to break his own record.	
	| 1 | 2 | 3 | 4 | 5 | 6 | 7 | 8 | 9 | 10 | 11 | 12 | 13 | 14 |	

224B: Typing from Script and Rough Draft (7) *each line at least three times for speed*

		Words
(1)	*Typing is a skill that is applied in many helpful ways.*	11
(2)	*Need for office workers grows even greater rather than less.*	12
(3)	It is ~~difficult~~ *hard & for us* to keep ~~abreast of~~ *pace with* increassing knowle dge ~~of our~~ *stet* wrold.	14
(4)	As ~~the~~ world popualtion increases, Sceintists ~~search for~~ *seek other* sources of food.	14

224C: Special Office Form Production Measurement (38)

Type the following four problems for 30′ when directed to begin. Make 1 cc for each, unless directed otherwise. Correct errors as you type. If time permits, start over. Mark uncorrected errors. Compute *n-pram.*

Time Schedule	
Get ready to type	2′
Timed production	30′
Proofread; compute *n-pram* . .	6′

Problem 1: Interoffice Memo

COMPANY MAIL envelope

	Words
To: H. C. Webb, Division Manager J. R.	7
Miller, Foundry Foreman Date: *(current)* File:	15
AL–55629–A From: John M. Fuller, Vice-Presi-	22
dent Subject: Production Reorganization (¶ 1)	28
Our study of our production load, equipment,	37
and organization has revealed specific weak-	46
nesses in our present production organization,	55
resulting in excessively high costs in production.	66
We are, therefore, submitting detailed recom-	75
mendations for updating some of our equipment	84
and revising some of our production procedures.	94
A copy of our report is enclosed. (¶ 2) These	102
recommendations should be evaluated carefully.	111
When you complete your study of the report, I	121
shall be interested in receiving your reactions to	131
our proposals and additional suggestions and	140
proposals that you will wish to present. (xx)	149
Enclosure *+ Envelope*	151/166

Problem 2: Business-Reply Message

2 cc's with message; 1 cc with response
COMPANY MAIL envelopes

	Words
To: Mr. Alfred D. Hill Area Sales Manager	8
Suite 42–B Capitol Plaza Date: *(current)*	16
(¶ 1) As you suggested, a meeting of the district	24
sales managers will be held at 1:30 p.m. on	33
February 11 in the Company's Board Room. The	42
major purpose of the meeting will be to discuss	52
the promotion plans for the two new products	61
we will be introducing. Will you please be	70
ready to present at that time the sales data you	80
have been preparing? If you finish your presen-	89
tation in about an hour, we can use the second	98
hour for discussion. Richard Van Horn, Vice-	107
President *+ Envelope*	109/124

Reply: *(current date)* (¶ 1) I shall look forward	7
to presenting at the February 11 meeting the	16
sales data I have been preparing and also a	25
couple of suggestions for promotion of the new	34
products. An hour should be adequate for the	44
presentation. Alfred D. Hill *+ Envelope*	49/59

LESSON 60

60A: Conditioning Practice (8) *each line three times; Line 4 for 1′ control writings*

Alphabet	Six experts from Brazil drove quickly away from John Greggory's place.	*Shift firmly; space quickly*
Figure	Ed paid a $72.90 premium on his $5,000 insurance policy dated 8/13/64.	
Figure-symbol	Terms on Hendrick & Babson's order dated 4/6 for $879.50: 2/10, n/30.	
Easy	Now is the time to stop pushing for high speed and drive for accuracy.	
	| 1 | 2 | 3 | 4 | 5 | 6 | 7 | 8 | 9 | 10 | 11 | 12 | 13 | 14 |	

60B: Drill on Centering Columnar Headings (12)

TO DETERMINE CENTER OF COLUMN: From point at which column begins, space forward once for each two letters, figures, or spaces in the longest line (the line that requires the most strokes to type).

TO TYPE COLUMNAR HEADING: From center of column, backspace once for each two spaces in heading. Begin to type where backspacing ends.

DO: Type the two drills given at the right. Use double spacing. Center drills horizontally.

Drill 1. Spaces between columnar items: 10

Name	Date
Andrew Wellington	September 27, 19--

Drill 2. Spaces between columnar headings: 8

Above Average Growth	Population Growth
California	6,119,000

60C: Problem Typing – Tables with Columnar Headings (20)

Problem 1

Half sheet; SS; exact center
8 spaces between columns

stet means "Let it stand" or "Ignore correction."

Problem 2

Full sheet; DS; reading position

B U I L D I N G F U N D (Center)

DS → stet ~~Contributions~~ Gifts Received in First Quarter

TS →

DS →

Name	State	Contribution	Words
			5
			12
			20
Marie O. Andrews	Ohio	$ 500.00	27
Rita Bennetts	Pennsylvania	705.00	33
Marilyn Cleveland	Massachusetts	10,000.00	42
Mrs. John E. Dexter	New Jersey	7,150.00	51
Dora W. Evrett	Virginia	1,000.00	58
Mrs. Ida Horton	Ne w Jersey	250.00	65
[Roberta Johnstone	Ohio	1,425.75	72
Alice Manningtor	[Texas	15,750.00	79
Mrs. C. H. Stuarte	Iowa	175.00	85
Lucy B. Underhill	Pennsylania	1,000.00	93
Ann Jean Woods	Iowa	150.00	99
Mrs. H. O. ~~Wilma~~ Ziegler	Rhode island	325.00	108
TOTAL		$38,475.75	112

Problem 2: AMS-Style Letter

Capitalize and punctuate special lines as necessary

Words

(Current date) Mr. Donald K. Erhard Sales 8
Manager Voka Adhesive and Wood Products 16
Company 5603 Covington Avenue Bethlehem, 25
Pennsylvania 18017 POLICY ON ADJUST- 32
MENT (¶ 1) Will you please notify all salesmen 40
that from now on we will enforce strictly the 49
policy outlined below for making adjustments 58
on complaints from the users of our wood and 67
adhesive products: 71

1. Any complaint should be referred back to 80
the distributor from whom the product was 89
bought. The referral letter to the customer 98
should show adequate interest in customer 106
welfare. 108

2. Any complaint should be reported to us 117
through the distributor from whom the ad- 125
hesive or wood product was purchased. 132

3. After the complaint is made to us in writing, 142
we should, within 15 days' time after the 151
complaint is received, inspect the job on 159
which our product is alleged to have been 168
used. 169

4. Within two days after the inspection has 178
been made, a formal report in writing 186
should be submitted and samples of the 193
product used should be included for further 202
inspection. 205

5. The decision about the complaint should be 214
sent to the distributor from this office. 223

(¶ 2) Adjustments are costly in time and money. 231
However, if adjustments are not handled 239
promptly and effectively, they may be even more 249
costly in goodwill. In addition, many complaints 259
provide a basis for improvement of our product. 269
Therefore, complaints must be handled in close 278
relationship to the work of this office. CHARLES 288
W. JOHNSON – ADMINISTRATIVE ASSISTANT 296
(xx) cc Mr. Ronald T. Conwell Assistant Sales 304
Manager (254) *+ Envelope* 306/331

Problem 3: Government-Style Letter

Use government-size stationery
Modified block, mixed *1" side margins*

Words

(Current date) AIRMAIL Mrs. Mildred Kulas 8
3629 Plymouth Avenue Waterloo, Iowa 50702 17
Dear Mrs. Kulas (¶ 1) Thank you for your 24
thoughtful and thought-provoking letter and re- 34
sponse to the questions contained in my public 43
opinion poll. Specific suggestions such as yours 53
help to make my work easier and more mean- 61
ingful in carrying out the wishes of the people 71
that I represent. (¶ 2) A revision such as that 79
which you suggested was rejected twice by a 88
large margin in the Ways and Means Committee. 98
A bill recently approved by the House would 106
provide expanded medical assistance through 115
programs operated essentially by the states. 124
(¶ 3) I am appreciative of your concern regard- 132
ing school financing and expansion. To main- 141
tain effective schools in an area where the 150
population is growing rapidly, your government 159
representatives have had to push for increases 169
in property tax to the extent that many citizens 179
feel this tax to be a serious burden. Therefore, 189
we have felt much pressure recently for increased 199
Federal financial assistance. If an adequate pro- 208
portion of Federal tax collections were returned 218
to the states in which they are collected, this 228
money could be used for medical and educa- 236
tional purposes within the states. (¶ 4) I appre- 245
ciate your comments. I hope you will find the 254
enclosed summary of opinion-poll responses of 263
interest. Sincerely yours Kenneth H. Heckman 273
Financial Policy Committee *(Reference initials on* 279
file copy only.) Enc. (244) *+ Envelope* 280/292

Problem 4: Page 2 of Two-Page Letter

To: **Mr. Jacob Weirton** *Modified block, mixed*
Use horizontal style heading; retype in vertical style
(See Reference Guide, page vii)

Words

Heading 8
the kinds of benefits that will have permanence 18
rather than short-lived advantages, for we be- 27
lieve these will be of most benefit to our workers. 37
(¶ 3) We believe, too, that fringe benefits should 46
be consistent with our total fiscal policy. The 56
enclosed copy of our tentative proposals will 65
support this belief. Very sincerely yours R. D. 75
Crown Executive Vice-President (xx) Enclo- 83
sure 84

60D: Drill on Erasing (10)

Type the sentences as they are shown below; do not type the numbers. Then study the guides for erasing given at the right. Erase and correct each error in your typescript.

1 We ahve to eat to live.

2 Stop gorging adn start movign.

3 We sit too much adn wakl too little.

4 Never dampen eth eraser.

5 Erase thoroughyl; retype the wrod lightly.

GUIDES FOR ERASING

1. Use a plastic shield and a typewriter (hard) eraser.
2. Lift the paper bail.
3. Turn the paper forward if the error is on the upper two thirds of the page or backward if it is on the lower third.
4. Move the carriage to the left or right as far as you can so the eraser crumbs will not fall into the typewriter mechanism.
5. Erase lightly—don't "scrub" the error. Blow eraser particles away as you erase.
6. Return the paper to writing position and type.

LESSON 61

61A: Conditioning Practice (8) *each line three times; Line 4 for 1′ control writings*

Concentrate on the copy

Alphabet	Jackson, Fieldor & Quigley will build their plant in Veracruz, Mexico.
Figure	We sold 72 English, 36 bookkeeping, and 60 typewriting books on May 8.
Figure-symbol	On Line 16, type "On 4/18 ship Ward & Sons 72 pens @ $3.90, less 5½%."
Easy	It is a part of the work of a proficient typist to proofread the work.
	| 1 | 2 | 3 | 4 | 5 | 6 | 7 | 8 | 9 | 10 | 11 | 12 | 13 | 14 |

61B: Drill on Erasing (7)

Erase and correct all errors made in typing 61A: Conditioning Practice. Follow the guides of 60D, above, when you erase. (If you did not make any errors, repeat the drill of 60D.)

61C: Problem Typing – Letters with Tables (20)

Problem 1: Letter with Tabulated Items

Line: 50; SS
Modified block style; mixed
Current date on Line 16 followed by 3 blank spaces
Errors erased and corrected

	Words
Mrs. Zelda Belknap Moore | 64 Grand Boule-	11
vard | Bedford, Ohio 44014 | Dear Mrs.	18
Moore: | (¶ 1) In the first quarter we received	26
contributions from | our Ohio alumnae as shown	35
below: |	37

Name	Amount	Words
Name	Amount	39
Marie O. Andrews	$ 500.00	44
Roberta Johnstone	1,425.75	50

	Words
(¶ 2) Alumnae from eight states contributed	57
$38,475.75 to | the Building Fund in the first	66
quarter of the year. | We are grateful for this	76
continued support of our | Development Program.	85
I hope you will make it pos- | sible for us to add	94
your name and generous gift to | the Ohio Honor	104
Roll. | Sincerely yours, | Luther E. Martin | Vice-	113
President | *(Dictator's and your initials, as LEM: mts)*	116

Before you remove the letter from the typewriter, proofread it and correct any error you may have missed.

LESSON 223

223A: Conditioning Practice (5) *each line at least three times*

Alphabetic	Ed Key and Jinx Rahe won five prizes at a racquet club in Palm Groves.	*Uniform key stroking*
Figure-symbol	Handy & Kent 4½% bonds (due May 20, 1987) sold at 103 to 106 on May 5.	
Long words	The demand for extreme accuracy will increase as automation increases.	
Fluency	Luck is generally nothing more than tough work that has been rewarded.	
	| 1 | 2 | 3 | 4 | 5 | 6 | 7 | 8 | 9 | 10 | 11 | 12 | 13 | 14 |	

223B: Skill Comparison (7) *1′ writing on each line; compare results; then repeat*

Easy	The many fine houses built by the firm pleased most of the new buyers.
Average	All classes appreciated the excellent progress reported by committees.
Difficult	American manufacturers submitted payroll statistics to research teams.
	| 1 | 2 | 3 | 4 | 5 | 6 | 7 | 8 | 9 | 10 | 11 | 12 | 13 | 14 |

223C: Letter Production Measurement (38)

Type the following four problems for 30′ when directed to begin. Make 1 cc and address an envelope for each. Correct errors as you type. If time permits, start over. Mark uncorrected errors. Compute *n-pram.*

Time Schedule	
Get ready to type	2′
Timed production	30′
Proofread; compute *n-pram* . .	6′

Problem 1: Letter with Tabulation

Modified block, mixed

Words

(Current date) Mr. Walter P. DuBois General Construction Company 310 Wedgewood Road 17
Charleston, South Carolina 29407 Dear Mr. DuBois (¶ 1) At a meeting held during this past week 35
by our Council, bids submitted for our proposed construction projects were reviewed and compared. 55
Of the bids offered for consideration, we are pleased to tell you that two of your bids were lower 74
than those of competing contractors. You submitted the low bid on the highway overpass project 94
and on the new traffic control tower for the airport. (¶ 2) The following list indicates the four projects 114
for which your bids were in excess of those submitted by other bidders: 129

YX–2697	Community Center	$32,815.40	136
BK–3548	Warehouse Addition	19,236.75	144
LR–1796	Park Shelter House	7,145.00	151
MN–2487	Equipment Storage Facilities	3,987.35	160

(¶ 3) The figures listed above represent those which, in each case, represented the lowest bid for 179
the project named. It was the decision of the Council that all contracts be awarded to the lowest 199
bidder for each job. (¶ 4) We wish to negotiate with you as soon as possible on the two projects 217
for which your firm submitted low bid. Our Legal Department will draw up the contracts and draft 237
other legal papers required within the next few days. They will then contact you for completion of 257
legal details required before the projects can be started. Very truly yours Charles J. MacClintock 277
City Controller (xx) (241) + *Envelope* 280/301

Problem 2: Alertness Training

Type the letter of Problem 1, page 101, but address it to **Miss Leah Myerson | 2408 Doehne Road, Harrisburg, Pa. 17110** | Use modified block style, mixed punctuation. Use the tabulated items for Pennsylvania from 60C: Problem Typing, page 100.

61D: Building Sustained Typing Power (15) *(Line: 70; DS; ¶ indention: 5)*

Type each ¶ below for one or two 1′ writings; then type two 3′ writings on the *control level.* Circle errors. The copy is more difficult than you have been using, but keep typing!

All letters are used.

	GWAM 1′	3′	*5′
Not all adults are adult. Some have grownup bodies and childish	13	4	3
minds, yet it requires maturity to adjust to others without expecting	27	9	5
them to do all the adjusting. No one lives without coming in contact	41	14	8
with others; so conflicts come and will keep on coming until all men	55	18	11
realize that they must work for the solution of the problems instead	69	23	14
of being the chief cause of them.	75	25	15

	GWAM 1′	3′	*5′
Problems come to all of us eventually. How we attempt to solve	13	29	18
them is a clue to our maturity or lack of it. Whether young or old,	27	34	20
our immaturity is showing when we try to solve difficulties through	40	38	23
flight or fight. We may run away from some problems and fight back	54	43	26
at some critics, but this is the immature way of handling difficulties.	68	48	29

1′ GWAM | 1 | 2 | 3 | 4 | 5 | 6 | 7 | 8 | 9 | 10 | 11 | 12 | 13 | 14 |
3′ GWAM | 1 | 2 | 3 | 4 | 5 |
5′ GWAM | 1 | 2 | 3 |

*The 5′ GWAM will be used when typing 62B, below.

LESSON 62

62A: Conditioning Practice (8) *each line three times; Line 4 for 1′ control writings*

Alphabet	The audience was quite amazed by the report J. F. Knox gave on July 6.	*Reach to the top-row keys*
Figure	Mark had 190 at the 3-, 5-, and 7-day Workshops on July 8, 14, and 26.	
Figure-symbol	Does Mr. Chambord's Policy #163045 for $7,500 expire on June 29, 1978?	
Easy	To be proficient in office work, you must find and correct all errors.	

| 1 | 2 | 3 | 4 | 5 | 6 | 7 | 8 | 9 | 10 | 11 | 12 | 13 | 14 |

62B: Building Sustained Typing Power (15)

Type two 5′ writings of the ¶s of 61D, above, and the ¶ on page 103. When you have typed the two ¶s above, flip the page, indent for the ¶, and continue typing until time is called. If you type the three ¶s before time is called, retype the single ¶ on page 103. The figures in the 5′ columns give the *gwam* for the ¶s on pages 102 and 103. *Control level; errors circled.*

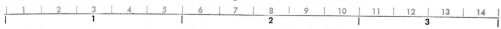

	GWAM 1′	5′
 What is this strange phenomenon that suddenly, without warning,	13	55
turns your world, or at least a small part of it, topsy turvey? What is	27	58
this mysterious law, and how does it operate? It is truly the law of	41	61
frustration that besets every individual at times. Like the law of	55	63
gravity, the law of averages, the law of supply and demand, it's a	68	66
peculiarity of nature, and not brought about by the specific intention	83	69
of man. It's the law that causes your shoestring to break when you are	97	72
already late getting started for work. It's the law that places you	111	75
immediately behind a truck that breaks down or travels at a snail's pace	125	77
in a long line of traffic, especially when you are in the greatest hurry.	140	80
Have you experienced it? Of course you have. Have you ever been	13	83
exactly one person too late in line? Has your alarm been bewitched not	28	86
to ring when you needed it very urgently? Has that special company ever	42	89
appeared when you looked your worst instead of arriving with you looking	57	92
your best? Have you anytime hunted vexedly for items that must still be	71	95
exactly where you put them, but aren't? The run in your stocking just	86	98
as you go out the doorway, your car key locked in the car, and the	99	100
obstinancy of some new apparatus as you are attempting to show it off	113	103
are illustrations of this unbelievably diabolic plot. You thought you	127	106
merely slid on some slippery wax or liquid that day with all the people	142	109
watching? No, that was again McClellan's law operating.	153	111
 McClellan's law harasses all persons in different fashion, but	13	113
there's no denying that it does beset everybody. How can we find protec-	27	116
tion against it? Can we deny or ignore it? Should we repeal it? Is	41	119
there some quality of craft, or cunning, or strategem we can utilize	55	122
against it? No, we can in no way vanquish it; and we cannot renounce,	69	125
revoke, or appeal to any source to any avail. We are "stuck with it,"	83	128
as the saying goes. Therefore, the only sensible procedure we can follow	98	131
regarding McClellan's law is to adjust to it in the best manner possible.	113	134
It might even be so that to adapt to it is the single method to win	127	136
against it.	129	137
 How can that adjustment come about? When you see your companion	13	139
frowning because he has just had another encounter with McClellan's law,	28	142
you know that he has not won, but has been defeated in his little skir-	42	145
mish with the law of frustration. The thwarting brought about by a con-	56	148
flict with this law is frequently of little duration and may be forgotten	71	151
within a day or even in briefer time. A happy frame of mind tends many	85	154
times to make possible a faster solution to the situation that has arisen	100	157
than does a feeling of angry frustration. So smile, give a raspberry	114	160
sound of contempt to the law of McClellan, and forget the whole thing!	129	162
Seek ideas about the brighter spots of your day! Still, wouldn't it be	143	165
great if we could enact a law against McClellan's law!	154	168

1′ GWAM | 1 | 2 | 3 | 4 | 5 | 6 | 7 | 8 | 9 | 10 | 11 | 12 | 13 | 14 |
5′ GWAM | 1 | 2 | 3 |

(To determine 10′ *nwam*, divide 5′ *gwam* by 2; then subtract 1 for each error.)

222D: Skill Building – Straight Copy (12) *2′ speed writings on selected ¶s of 222C*

(To determine 2′ *gwam*, divide 1′ *gwam* by 2)

62B: Building Sustained Typing Power *(continued)*

All letters are used.

	GWAM 1′	5′	
We should think less about how difficult our problems are and more	13	31	45
about how to solve them. We can't expect them to leave just because	27	34	48
we won't recognize them. So, we must face them squarely and strive	41	37	50
to solve them promptly if we are to gain the benefits that come from	55	40	53
problem solving, which can lead us from immaturity toward maturity.	68	42	56

1′ GWAM | 1 | 2 | 3 | 4 | 5 | 6 | 7 | 8 | 9 | 10 | 11 | 12 | 13 | 14 |
5′ GWAM | 1 | 2 | 3 |

62C: Errorless Typing (7)

Type each line three times without error, typing on the *control level* with rhythmic continuity. For extra credit, type each line three times *in succession* without error.

CONTROL HINTS	Sit erect, feet on floor. Fingers curved. Space quickly with down-and-in motion. Eyes on copy. Begin at a slow, even pace. Increase stroking rate gradually.

Type with ease. Hold the arms still. Let your fingers do their work.
Just hold on to the right set of mind, and you can handle the big job.
The worker ranks appreciation of his good work as of first importance.
| 1 | 2 | 3 | 4 | 5 | 6 | 7 | 8 | 9 | 10 | 11 | 12 | 13 | 14 |

62D: Tabulating Skill Review (20)

Make pencil notations of each page and drill. Study the *explanation of the process* as given on the appropriate page; then type each drill once as directed.

Page 97, 58B
Page 99, 59B
Page 100, 60B

LESSON 63

63A: Conditioning Practice (8) *each line three times; Line 4 for 1′ control writings*

Alphabet	Joe's high quiz marks excelled Frank McGow's low marks by five points.	*Fingers curved; wrists low*
Figure	The next quiz will be on March 26 and covers pages 35–149 and 168–170.	
Figure-symbol	She read the article "Reach for Skill," but not the book Typing Power.	
Easy	Len found that the elements of the problem are difficult to determine.	
	| 1 | 2 | 3 | 4 | 5 | 6 | 7 | 8 | 9 | 10 | 11 | 12 | 13 | 14 |	

63B: Building Control (7)

Type each line of 62C, above, once without error; then type the ¶ at the top of the page with as few errors as you can. Type with continuity—keep the carriage moving.

Unit 38 | Lessons 222-225

Measuring Basic and Production Skills

LESSON 222

222A: Conditioning Practice (5) *each line at least three times*

Alphabet; shift	Fred Printz or Jack Craver may exhibit quaint wares at the Art League.	*Quick, snap stroke*
Figure	The population of Washington was 437,571 in 1920; and 802,180 in 1960.	
Long words	Some job experiences are interesting and some of them are bewildering.	
Fluency	To succeed, a business must have workers who are sincere and diligent.	
	| 1 | 2 | 3 | 4 | 5 | 6 | 7 | 8 | 9 | 10 | 11 | 12 | 13 | 14 |	

222B: Skill Comparison (8) *1′ writing on each line; compare results; then repeat*

Easy	Some of the old tires were placed on the junk list for early disposal.
Average	We asked that exceptional staff to assist with records of application.
Difficult	Our correspondence concerning vital specifications was examined daily.
	| 1 | 2 | 3 | 4 | 5 | 6 | 7 | 8 | 9 | 10 | 11 | 12 | 13 | 14 |

222C: Growth Index  *two 10′ writings from the ¶s on pages 326–327*

All letters are used.

	GWAM 1′	5′
 There ought to be a law against the law of frustration, sometimes	13	3
referred to as McClellan's law. Of all the controls that have ever	27	5
operated in some way on the behavior of man, McClellan's law is probably	41	8
the one we can best manage without. If we were to gain the opportunity to	56	11
vote on its repeal, the decision would without doubt be unanimous to do	71	14
away with this law of frustration. Every individual is influenced by it	85	17
at times; every person is sometimes frustrated by it. It has been known	100	20
to thwart, to outwit, to foil, to baffle, to discourage, and to defeat	114	23
even the brightest and the most optimistic of individuals. Nobody has	128	26
yet discovered a way to win a fight against it.	138	28
 The day is sunny, with not a cloud in the sky. Vacation is near.	13	30
There is not a reason in the world for a touch of gloom. At least you	28	33
believe there isn't, but then you see your usually cheerful working	41	36
colleague come in with a frown that forebodes drastic trouble. But don't	56	39
worry; he'll recover. He has only been vexed by McClellan's law. Your	70	42
kindly boss has mentioned much to indicate approval and a higher salary,	85	45
but you suddenly receive a threat of very early and unwanted retirement.	100	48
Have you entirely lost your working ability and value? No, your	113	50
employer has only had a sudden bout with McClellan's law.	124	52

(Continued)

1′ GWAM | 1 | 2 | 3 | 4 | 5 | 6 | 7 | 8 | 9 | 10 | 11 | 12 | 13 | 14 |
5′ GWAM | 1 | 2 | 3 |

63C: Growth Index (15) *(Line: 70; DS; ¶ indention: 5) type a 3′ and a 5′ control-level writing*

All letters are used.

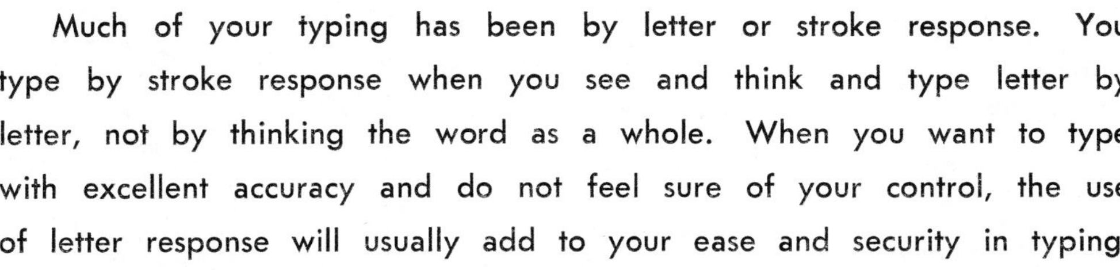

Text	GWAM 3′	5′	
Much of your typing has been by letter or stroke response. You	4	3	45
type by stroke response when you see and think and type letter by	9	5	48
letter, not by thinking the word as a whole. When you want to type	13	8	50
with excellent accuracy and do not feel sure of your control, the use	18	11	53
of letter response will usually add to your ease and security in typing.	23	14	56
To type a short and easy word, think the word and type it as a	27	16	59
whole. This is the way to type by word-recognition response, which is	32	19	61
a higher form of typing than the letter response you used in the early	36	22	64
practice. Recognize and type short and easy words as words, and just	41	25	67
type without thinking the letters of the words. This will lead to a	46	27	70
higher and quicker form of stroking.	48	29	71
Some of the typing will be by combination response, which is the	52	31	74
way to type when the copy has some hard and some easy words. The right	57	34	77
response will come if you will use the right practice procedures and	62	37	79
try to adapt your typing response to the level of difficulty you find	66	40	82
in the copy to be typed. Type right, and type in the right way.	71	42	85

3′ GWAM | 1 | 2 | 3 | 4 | 5 |
5′ GWAM | 1 | 2 | 3 |

63D: Problem Typing Review (20)

Make pencil notations of the assignments at the right. Place the notations on the desk. Type each problem once. Correct errors.

Page 98, 58C, Problem 1 *(full sheet; reading position)*
Page 100, 60C, " 1 *(half sheet; exact center)*
Page 101, 61C, " 1 *(letterhead or full sheet)*

LESSON 64

64A: Conditioning Practice (8) *each line three times; Line 4 for 1′ control writings*

Alphabet	Fred Lowery just gave a quick report on Africa that amazed Boyd Nixon.	*Quick return*
Figure	The 150 to 200 young men worked from 4:15 to 6:30 p.m. on May 8 and 9.	
Figure-symbol	Hunter & Muncy's check for $697.80 (Check #1435) was cashed on July 2.	
Easy	The problem is big, but a man of determination can certainly solve it.	
	| 1 | 2 | 3 | 4 | 5 | 6 | 7 | 8 | 9 | 10 | 11 | 12 | 13 | 14 |	

64B: Building Sustained Typing Power (15)

Type two 5′ control writings of 63C: Growth Index, above. Circle errors. Determine *gwam* for better writing.

Problem 1: Interoffice Memo

Type an original copy for each individual named below

Words
Brad C. Parks, Treasurer 5
S. T. Headley, Controller 5
J. W. Terry, Chief Accountant 6

Words
TO: *(Insert name and title)* FROM: S. W. Turner, 8
Financial Vice-President DATE: October 3, 19–– 16
SUBJECT: Report of Change in Accounting Pro- 23
cedures (¶ 1) It has been the practice of the 31
company during the past to capitalize all re- 40
search and development costs and to amortize 49
them over a period of five years. Beginning 58
with the next fiscal year, this procedure will be 68
changed. At that time, research and develop- 77
ment costs will be charged immediately to ex- 85
pense, except for those costs already capitalized 95
which will continue to be amortized over the 104
remaining period of time. This change has been 114
approved by the Internal Revenue Service and 123
our Executive Board. (¶ 2) Please let me have 131
a detailed plan for implementing this change in 141
accounting procedures not later than October 150
17. Your plan should include recommendations 159
for specific changes in current operating and 168
reporting procedures. 173

Problem 2: Table

Full sheet *Reading position* *DS body*

Words
ANATCO MANUFACTURING COMPANY 6

Report of Absenteeism for April, 19–– 13

Department	Man-Days Lost	Rate *	Words
			25
Administration	17	2.1%	30
Engineering	29	3.5%	34
Finance	14	1.8%	37
Purchasing	21	2.2%	41
Marketing	30	2.9%	44
Personnel	16	1.7%	48
Production:			51
Shop A	59	2.9%	54
Shop B	72	4.1%	57
Shop C	61	2.8%	60
Shop D	67	3.0%	63

——————— 66

*Computed by dividing the number of man- 74
days lost by the average number of employees 83
times the number of workdays (100). 91

Problem 3: Unbound Report

Words
ANATCO MANUFACTURING COMPANY 6

Projects Pending as of April 30, 19–– 13

Project 141–66, Reclassification of Salaried 31
Positions 35

Of the 1,320 salaried positions within the 44
company, 967 have been reclassified on the 52
basis of complete job analyses. This project 61
is on schedule and will be completed by June 15. 71

Project 157–66, Renovation of the Facilities 89
in Cafeteria A 95

All major construction work has been com- 103
pleted and the kitchen equipment has been in- 112
stalled. The project has been delayed two weeks 122
because the vendor failed to deliver the tables 131
and chairs on the date requested. This furniture 141
is scheduled to arrive within one week and the 151
opening of the new cafeteria facilities has been 160
rescheduled for May 15. 166

Words
Project 193–67, Establishment of the Sloan 183
Research Laboratories 191

This project was completed on April 5 and 200
the Sloan Research Laboratories are now fully 209
operational with a staff of more than 100 engi- 218
neers, designers, draftsmen, technicians, and 227
research managers. Formal dedication of the 236
laboratories will be held on Wednesday, May 2, 246
at 1:00 p.m. 248

Project 201–67, Development of Ultra-Service 266
Aluminum 270

The purpose of this basic research project 278
is to develop an ultra-service aluminum with a 287
minimum yield strength of at least 100,000 296
pounds per square inch. The new pressure 304
chamber in the Sloan Laboratories will facilitate 314
the completion of this project. Only 10% of the 324
proposed experiments have been completed, 333
however, and there are no significant findings to 343
report at this time. 347

64C: Problem Typing Measurement (20) *(Half sheet; SS; 10 spaces between columns)*

Problem 1: Table

To center the columnar headings:

1. To find center of column: space forward 1 for 2 in the longest line of column.
2. To center columnar heading: from center of column, backspace 1 for 2 in heading.
3. Type heading where backspacing ends.

Spacing cue: Do not space after a period within an abbreviation.

SOME BUSINESS ABBREVIATIONS

TS

		Words
		6
Name	Abbreviation	12
	DS	
Bill of lading	B/L	16
Cash (collect) on delivery	C.O.D. (c.o.d.)	25
Free on board	F.O.B. (f.o.b.)	31
Freight	frt.	33
Horsepower	H.P. (h.p.)	38
Hundredweight	cwt.	42
Merchandise	mdse.	45
Miscellaneous	misc.	49
That is	i.e.	52

Problem 2: Letter with Tabulated Items

Letterhead; carbon copy; Line: 50; SS
Modified block, mixed; current date on Line 18
8 spaces between columns

Words

Mr. E. H. Stern | 7093 Saginaw Ave., S. | 11
Chicago, Ill. 60617 | Dear Mr. Stern: | 18

(¶ 1) We can reduce your fuel bills and prolong 27
the life | of your heating equipment for just 35
$9.75. Our ser- | vicemen will check and adjust 44
the thermostat and gas | valve of your furnace, 54
oil the motors and blowers, | and also do the 62
following: | *DS* 65

		Words
Clean	Check	67
Burner	Fuel chamber	71
Safety pilot	Flue	75
Filters	Motor mountings	80

(¶ 2) Please call 632–4758 for our immediate 87
expert ser- | vice. | Very truly yours, | Service 96
Manager | *(Your initials)* 98

Problem 3: Alertness Check

Type the letter of Problem 2, above, as directed, but address the letter to ⟶ Mrs. R. H. Gage | 2934 Roscoe Street, W. | Chicago, Ill. 60618 |

64D: Errorless Typing (7)

Type each line three times without error, typing on the *control level* with rhythmic continuity. For extra credit, type each sentence three times *in succession* without error.

CONTROL HINTS	Keep your eyes on the copy. Hold the shift key down firmly until the shifted character has been struck and released. Reach with the fingers.

Our principal said, "This principle of learning affects all students."

The effect of this law will affect all of us when we are 65 years old.

Are you all ready to go? Is it all right that Frank has already gone?

| 1 | 2 | 3 | 4 | 5 | 6 | 7 | 8 | 9 | 10 | 11 | 12 | 13 | 14 |

LESSON 220

220A: Conditioning Practice (5) *each line at least three times*

Alphabet	Judge Miles Benton quickly awarded seven prizes for the best exhibits.	Fingers upright
Figure	Of the 13,794 full-time employees, 2,758 are women and 11,036 are men.	
Figure-symbol	They ordered 26 of #50870 at a total cost of $36.14 (26 @ $1.39 each).	
Fluency	They expect to finish the work in the office by the end of this month.	

| 1 | 2 | 3 | 4 | 5 | 6 | 7 | 8 | 9 | 10 | 11 | 12 | 13 | 14 |

220B: Skill Comparison (7)

Type one 2′ writing on 216C, page 318; type one on 217C, page 320. Compute *gwam*; compare rates.

220C: Sustained Production Typing (38)

Time Schedule	
Get ready to type	3′
Timed production	30′
Proofread; compute *n-pram* . .	5′

Arrange supplies. Make a list of problems to be typed. Type for 30′ when directed to begin, following the instructions given for each problem. For each problem, prepare 1 cc. Correct errors as you type. Proofread each problem carefully before removing it from the typewriter. If you finish all problems before time is called, begin again. Mark uncorrect errors; compute *n-pram.*

Page 319, 216D, Problem 3
Page 320, 217D, Problem 1
Page 321, 217D, Problem 2
Page 322, 218D, Problem 2

Turn in problems arranged in the order in which they are listed.

LESSON 221

221A: Conditioning Practice (5) *each line at least three times*

Alphabet	Have Joe Maples fix the bad wiring and synchronize the clocks quickly.	Finger-action reaches
Figure	He sold 849,571 shares of Class A and 238,460 shares of Class B stock.	
Figure-symbol	Blanchard's social security tax for 1967 was $376.32 (6.4% of $5,880).	
Fluency	Ask her to visit with me in my office as soon as she is able to do so.	

| 1 | 2 | 3 | 4 | 5 | 6 | 7 | 8 | 9 | 10 | 11 | 12 | 13 | 14 |

221B: Growth Index (8) *one 5′ writing on the ¶s in 215D, page 317; compute* nwam

221C: Production Measurement (37)

Arrange supplies. Type the three problems on page 325 for 30′ when directed to begin. For each problem, prepare 1 cc. If time permits, start over. When time is called, mark uncorrected errors and compute *n-pram.*

Time Schedule	
Get ready to type	2′
Timed production	30′
Proofread; compute *n-pram* . .	5′

Unit 10 | Lessons 65-72

Outlines and Manuscripts

1. Arrange work area for efficient performance.
2. Adjust paper guide and paper-bail rolls.
3. Set control to type on upper part of ribbon.
4. Full sheet; Line: 70; SS, unless otherwise directed.

LESSON 65

65A: Conditioning Practice (5) *each line three times at a rate you can maintain with accuracy*

Alphabet	Mrs. Joyce Zublick is not quite finished with this expensive training.
Figure-symbol	Rhea & Lowen's Invoice #873 for $641.50 (less 2%) was paid on the 9th.
Roman numerals	Use capital letters for Roman numerals: I II IV V VI X XI XII XX XXI.
Easy	If you fall, get to your feet and climb before you skid to the bottom.
	| 1 | 2 | 3 | 4 | 5 | 6 | 7 | 8 | 9 | 10 | 11 | 12 | 13 | 14 |

Note. Remove the paper; reinsert it; gauge line and letter; type over the last line.

65B: Building Control (8) (*Use 63C, page 104, for a 5′ control writing. Circle errors. Determine* gwam.)

65C: Problem Typing – Outline (20) *each problem as directed*

Problem 1: Topic Outline

Full sheet
50-space line
Single spacing
Exact vertical center

1. **Space** forward once from margin to type Roman numeral I. Reset margin 4 spaces to the right of I for subtopics A and B.
2. **Set** the first tab stop in the fourth space to the right of **A**; second stop, in the fourth space to the right of **1**.

Operate margin release and backspace to type Roman numeral II

```
                    AUTOMATION
                                        TS
 I.  Economics of automation
                         DS
     A.  Investment and productivity
     B.  Impact on national economy
         1.  Productivity
         2.  Employment mobility
         3.  Earnings
                    DS
II.  Impact on employment and earnings

     A.  Effects of some innovations
         1.  Computers and clerical work
             a.  Decrease in clerical employees
             b.  Increase in earnings
         2.  Computer systems and data communication
     B.  Skills and education
         1.  Social background and education
         2.  Distinction between education and skills
             a.  Professional and technical workers
             b.  Craftsmen, foremen, and operatives
             c.  Laborers
```

LESSON 219

219A: Conditioning Practice (5) *each line at least three times*

Alphabet	Joel found that good executives were able to analyze problems quickly.	Fingers curved
Figure	Shop A produced 9,430 units; Shop B, 8,165 units; Shop C, 7,920 units.	
Figure-symbol	John's commission on Order #98453 will be exactly $96 (7½% of $1,280).	
Fluency	Is it true that many of the reports were not typed in the proper form?	
	| 1 | 2 | 3 | 4 | 5 | 6 | 7 | 8 | 9 | 10 | 11 | 12 | 13 | 14 |	

219B: Skill Comparison (7) *1′ writing on each sentence of 219A; compare rates*

219C: Skill Building – Statistical Copy (8) *repeat 218C, page 321*

219D: Production Typing (30)

Type the following two problems for 25′ when directed to begin. For each problem, prepare 1 cc. If time permits, start over. When time is called, proofread and compute *g-pram.*

Time Schedule	
Get ready to type	2′
Timed production	25′
Proofread; compute *g-pram* . .	3′

Problem 1: Financial Report

Type as unbound manuscript

			Words
FIRST NATIONAL BANK OF CENTRAL CITY			7
Financial Condition at the Close of Business December 31, 19––			20
Resources:			24
Cash and Due from Banks	$ 2,370,724.64		32
Loans and Discounts	14,355,026.99		39
U. S. Government Securities	5,053,076.05		47
Other Governmental Securities	663,057.70		56
Investment Securities	1,306,246.45		63
Fixed Assets	173,684.08		69
Other Assets	9,878.13		77
Total Resources		$23,931,694.04	89
Liabilities:			94
Capital Stock	$ 525,000.00		101
Surplus	525,000.00		105
Undivided Profits	561,403.61		110
Reserves	8,804.75		114
Unearned Discount	437,279.72		120
Deposits	21,874,205.96		128
Total Liabilities		$23,931,694.04	141

Problem 2: Monthly Progress Report

Type the report in 218D, Problem 1, page 322, in the form of a leftbound manuscript.

Problem 2: Topic Outline with Changes

Type the outline of Problem 1, page 106, with the following changes: (1) "Spread" the main heading (see page 99); (2) add a new first main topic: **I. Historical perspective**; (3) change Roman numerals I and II to II and III; (4) type the problem in reading position instead of vertical center (*Alertness cue:* See page 98 for rule to determine reading position.); (5) correct errors unless otherwise directed.

65D: Errorless Typing (7) *(Line: 70; SS) each line three times without error*

Line 1. A semicolon or colon follows, but a comma or period precedes, the quotation mark.
Line 2. Avoid dividing the last word on a page.
Line 3. In typing manuscripts, leave the bottom margin a line shorter or longer to avoid carrying a single line to the next page.

1 Len said, "Might makes right"; however, Sue said, "Right makes might."
2 Shorten or extend the final line on the page to avoid dividing a word.
3 Do not carry over to the next typed page a single line of a paragraph.
| 1 | 2 | 3 | 4 | 5 | 6 | 7 | 8 | 9 | 10 | 11 | 12 | 13 | 14 |

65E: Drills on Line Finder (Ratchet Release) (10)

LEARN:

When the automatic line finder **6** (ratchet release) is moved forward, the line spacing mechanism is disengaged. The line finder is located near the line-space regulator and should be used instead of the variable line spacer when a new line position is wanted temporarily.

To operate the line finder, pull the lever forward; then move the cylinder forward or backward to the desired writing position. When the lever is returned to its position after the typing, move the cylinder knob slightly to return it to the line of writing.

TYPE: Drill 1

1. Type a 2" line; then center and type your name on the line.
2. Operate the line finder (ratchet release), move the cylinder forward 3 or 4 lines, and type the current date centered under your name.
3. Return the lever to position, move the cylinder back to your name, and type over your name.

TYPE: Drill 2

1. Type "What is past is prologue."
2. *Without changing the position of the carriage:* operate the line finder, move the cylinder back (toward you) a half line space, and type the figure *2* as a superior footnote reference; as

"What is past is prologue."[2]

LESSON 66

66A: Conditioning Practice (5) *each line three times at a rate you can maintain without error*

Line 1. The title of a book, a booklet, or a magazine is usually underlined but may be typed in ALL CAPITALS.
Line 3. Use ' (apostrophe) for a quote within a quote and type the single mark before the final double quotation mark.

Alphabet Marnie sold a dozen copies of Harvey Dixon's new book, <u>Judge the Quiz.</u>
Figure-symbol Strikes in 1966 delayed delivery of 7,840 tons (25% of all shipments).
Single quote Emory said, "My teacher quoted, 'Poetry is the language of the soul.' "
Easy Should the good people of this town help Claud in this election fight?
| 1 | 2 | 3 | 4 | 5 | 6 | 7 | 8 | 9 | 10 | 11 | 12 | 13 | 14 |

66B: Building Accuracy with Speed (8) *1' errorless writings of each line of 65D, above*

218D: Production Typing (30)

Type the following two problems for 25′ when directed to begin. For each problem, prepare 1 cc. If time permits, start over. When time is called, proofread and mark errors. Compute *g-pram.*

Time Schedule	
Get ready to type	2′
Timed production	25′
Proofread; compute *g-pram* . .	3′

Problem 1: First Page of Topbound Report

Words

Severns Manufacturing Company 6
Progress Report for Month of March, 19-- 14
¶ Production. Average daily production for the month totaled 31
10,824 units. This represented an increase of 70 units over the 44
previous month but a decrease of 207 units based on production in 57
March of last year. This decrease can be attributed to the severe 70
snowstorm on March 25. Units rejected by Quality Control remained 84
below the 4% level. 88
¶ Sales. Orders for delivery in May, June, and July totaled 101
48,620 units as compared with the 41,000 units estimated for the 114
same period. A slight adjustment in production plans for April 126
will be necessary to meet the additional demand. 136
¶ Personnel. Worker productivity remained at approximately 150
the same level as February. The work force was relatively 162
stable during the month: 17 employees retired or resigned; 19 174
new employees were hired. Absenteeism rose 8.6%, primarily 186
because of the inclement weather. 193

Problem 2: Table

Full sheet *Reading position* *DS body*

Words

SEVERNS MANUFACTURING COMPANY 6
Productivity for the Previous Six Months 14

Month	Units Produced	Man-Hours	Productivity	Words
				31
October	10,900	16,700	.653	36
November	10,872	16,550	.657	42
December	10,361	16,410	.631	48
January	10,963	16,850	.651	53
February	10,757	16,300	.660	59
March	10,824	16,500	.656	63

66C: Improving Skill in Using the Line Finder ⑦ (*Type 65E, page 107, as directed*)

66D: Problem Typing – Outlines ⑳

Problem 1: Rough Draft of Topic Outline

Full sheet
60-space line; SS
Exact vertical center

1. **Space** forward once from margin to type Roman numeral I. Reset margin 4 spaces to the right of I for subtopics A and B.
2. **Set** the first tab stop 4 spaces to the right of **A**; second stop, 4 spaces to the right of **1**.

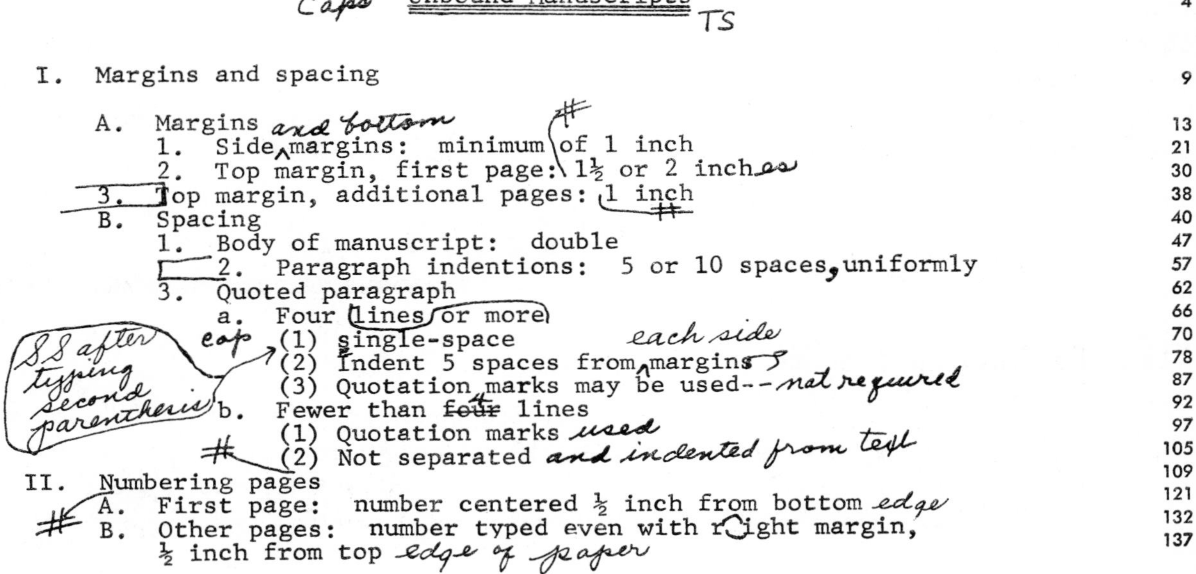

Words

Caps Unbound Manuscripts TS 4

I. Margins and spacing 9

A. Margins and bottom 13
1. Side margins: minimum of 1 inch 21
2. Top margin, first page: 1½ or 2 inches 30
3. Top margin, additional pages: 1 inch 38
B. Spacing 40
1. Body of manuscript: double 47
2. Paragraph indentions: 5 or 10 spaces, uniformly 57
3. Quoted paragraph 62
a. Four lines or more 66
(1) single-space 70
(2) Indent 5 spaces from margins each side 78
(3) Quotation marks may be used--not required 87
b. Fewer than four lines 92
(1) Quotation marks used 97
(2) Not separated and indented from text 105

II. Numbering pages 109
A. First page: number centered ½ inch from bottom edge 121
B. Other pages: number typed even with right margin, 132
½ inch from top edge of paper 137

SS after typing second parenthesis

Problem 2: Topic Outline with Changes

Type the outline of Problem 1, above, but (1) add as a final main topic: **III: Main heading centered**; (2) type problem in reading position; and (3) correct errors, unless otherwise directed.

66E: Page Line Gauge ⑩ (*Full sheet; SS*)

You can use a page line gauge as a guide when typing manuscripts, determining top and bottom margins, and placing footnotes correctly.

Make a page gauge: Type the figure *1* in the first line space below the top edge and near the right edge of a full sheet; then number the lines consecutively through 33. For the lower half of the page, type 33 down to 1 on consecutive lines.

Drill Using Page Line Gauge

Place the page gauge back of and extending slightly to the right of a full sheet; insert both into machine; space forward to Line 13 from the top. Center horizontally and type

A MAN OF IDEAS

as a main heading. Then space forward to Line 11 from the bottom and type

is richer for his having lived.

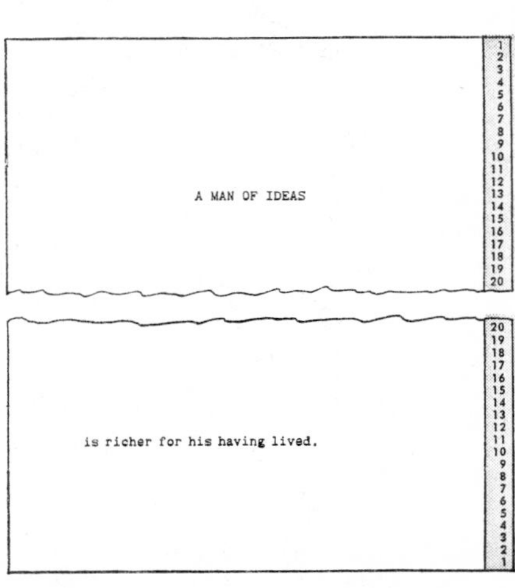

Problem 2: Interoffice Memo

Type an original copy to each person indicated at right →

	Words
M. A. Peters, Director of Personnel	7
R. L. Beggs, Vice President of Production	8
B. W. Spencer, Director of Finance	7

	Words
TO: *(Insert appropriate name and title)* FROM:	8
P. L. Meyer, Director of Industrial Relations	9
DATE: September 23, 19–– SUBJECT: Report of	15
Change in Union Contract (¶ 1) On September	23
20, a meeting was held with F. E. Crane, Busi-	32
ness Agent of Local 2793 of the Production	40
Workers Union under the provisions of Section	49
68 of our current union contract, which states	59
that minor changes in the contract may be made	68
by mutual agreement. (¶ 2) Mr. Crane and I	76
discussed paragraph 17a of the current agree-	84
ment which reads, in part: "The company shall	94
deduct from the pay of each union member <u>each</u>	103
<u>week</u> any dues assessed by the union. . . ." It	113
was agreed that this clause will be changed to	123
read: "The company shall deduct from the pay	132
of each union member <u>each</u> <u>pay</u> <u>period</u> any	143
dues assessed by the union. . . ." (¶ 3) This	151
change in the contract is effective immediately	161
and will permit the company to initiate the pro-	170
posed biweekly compensation plan for produc-	179
tion workers at the earliest possible date.	188

LESSON 218

218A: Conditioning Practice (5) *each line at least three times*

Type with continuity and rhythm

Alphabet	Vera's quartet was joined by six zany musicians who played folk songs.
Figure	I ordered 36 desks, 49 chairs, 15 tables, 80 lamps, and 72 file trays.
Figure-symbol	Premiums on Policy #51629 (with an 80% coinsurance clause) are $47.93.
Fluency	Did he make a change in the total quantity of items to be sold in May?
	| 1 | 2 | 3 | 4 | 5 | 6 | 7 | 8 | 9 | 10 | 11 | 12 | 13 | 14 |

218B: Skill Comparison (7) *1′ writing on each sentence of 218A; compare rates*

218C: Skill Building – Statistical Copy (8) *two 1′ writings and one 3′ writing; find* gwam

	GWAM 1′	3′	
The financial report shows that the company's financial condition	13	4	56
remains strong with assets exceeding $275,000,000. Net income for this	28	9	61
fiscal year totaled $12,950,000, or $3.48 per share, an increase of 20%	42	14	66
over the $10,800,000, or $2.62 per share, the previous year. The company	56	19	71
also added $6,587,416 to retained earnings. Net sales reached a new	70	23	75
record of $294,262,000 as compared with $263,842,000 last year. Export	85	28	80
sales accounted for 24% of the total sales or $59,822,880. Expenses	98	33	85
also increased, however. Production expenses included in the cost of	112	37	89
goods sold were $9,420,000, or 4.2% of sales. Administrative expenses,	127	42	94
including marketing costs, reached $29,719,000, or 10.8% of sales. Next	141	47	99
year, despite rising costs it is believed that income will increase 20%.	156	52	104

1′ GWAM | 1 | 2 | 3 | 4 | 5 | 6 | 7 | 8 | 9 | 10 | 11 | 12 | 13 | 14 |
3′ GWAM | 1 | 2 | 3 | 4 | 5 |

LESSON 67

67A: Conditioning Practice (5) *each line three times at a rate you can maintain without error*

Line 3. Do not space after a period used within an abbreviation, whether typed in capital or lower-case letters, but use normal spacing after the final period that punctuates the last letter of an abbreviation.

Line 4. Type the title of an article in quotation marks. The quotation mark does not change the normal spacing that follows a word or a punctuation mark with which the quotation mark is used.

Alphabet	Ron Plevin quickly amazed all of us by his exact knowledge of jujitsu.
Figure-symbol	Check prices on these items: #56, #234, and #789 (pages 129 and 140).
Abbreviations	The C.O.D. shipment to Reynolds & Lane, Inc., was sent f.o.b. Detroit.
Easy	A new article, "How to Win or Lose," tells how to win even if we lose.
	| 1 | 2 | 3 | 4 | 5 | 6 | 7 | 8 | 9 | 10 | 11 | 12 | 13 | 14 |

67B: Drill on Typing Superior Figure and Footnote (10) *(Side Margins: 1"; DS) twice*

Use a superior figure in the text for each footnote reference. To type a superior figure: (1) operate the line finder **6** (ratchet release); (2) move the cylinder back (toward you) a half space; (3) type the figure; (4) return the line finder and cylinder to position.

Note. Instead of using the line finder to position the carriage for typing the superior figure, you can roll the cylinder back a half space and hold it in position as you type the superior figure.

In planning the manuscript page, save 3 lines for the divider line and the spaces before and after it; 3 or 4 lines for each footnote to be typed on the page; and 6 lines for the bottom margin.

Type the footnote on the same page with the superior figure. After typing the last line of text on the page, single-space and type a 1½-inch divider line; then double-space and type the footnote with single spacing. If two or more footnotes are to be typed on the same page, double-space between them. Authorities differ on details of typing footnotes, but the illustrations are in acceptable form.

DO: Place your page gauge back of a full sheet with the line numbers extending to the right; insert the two sheets; then type the following drill, beginning on Line 13 from the bottom of the page. This placement will leave an exact 1-inch bottom margin.

Hard work was Edison's success secret. "Genius," he said, "is two per-

cent inspiration and ninety-eight percent perspiration."[1]

SS ________________

DS [1]"Edison--One of the World's Great Inventors," Compton's Pictured Encyclopedia, 1957 Edition, Vol. 4, p. 281.

Left Margin Stop = left edge + 12 elite left edge + 10 pica

Right Margin Stop = right edge — 12 elite right edge — 10 pica

67C: Problem Typing – Manuscript with Footnote (20) *(Margins: 1" side, 2" top; ¶ indention: 5; DS)*

DO: Type the manuscript as illustrated on page 110.

217C: Skill Transfer – Script (8) *two 1′ writings and one 3′ writing; compute* gwam

	GWAM 1′	3′	
The ownership of many modern corporations rests in the hands	14	4	48
of thousands of small stockholders who are usually widely scattered	26	9	53
geographically. Theoretically, the stockholders control the opera-	39	13	57
tion of the company through the election of the board of directors.	53	18	62
For most stockholders, however, the only contact with the company	66	22	66
is a periodic dividend check and the annual report. The annual	79	26	70
report includes a summary of the company's operations and progress	92	31	75
during the year, a financial statement, and plans for the future.	106	35	79
Annual reports are elaborately illustrated with charts, graphs, and	120	40	84
color photographs of the company's products and facilities.	132	44	88

217D: Production Typing (30)

Type the following two problems for 25′ when directed to begin. If time permits, start over. For each problem, prepare 1 cc on plain paper. When time is called, proofread and mark errors. Compute *g-pram*.

Time Schedule	
Get ready to type	2′
Timed production	25′
Proofread; compute *g-pram* . .	3′

Problem 1: Unbound Manuscript

	Words
Jefferson Self-Service Retail Stores, Inc.] *Center, all caps*	9
Selection of a ~~site~~ Site in Bakerstown	15
triple space Introduction	20
The (l.c.) Marketing Division, at the request of the Board of Directors,	33
made a ~~survey~~ *study* of four sites in Bakers town to determine the best ~~site~~ *location*	48
for a new Jefferson Retail Store. The ~~five~~ *major* factors ~~we studied~~ *considered* were	62
(1) siutability of ~~building;~~ *facilities;* (2) customer # traffic; (3) ease of accessa- *i*	76
bility; (4) compitition; *e* and (5) business establishments surrounding.	90
A map ~~indicating~~ *showing* the ~~place~~ *location* of each site is *included* in appendix A.	104
triple # Recommendation	110
¶ It is] recommended that Site #3 be ~~chosen~~ *selected* as the location of the	123
new retail store. On the bases *i* of the Factors (l.c.) studied, it is beleived that	137
that this Site (l.c.) is the best. A ~~summarization~~ *detailed analysis* of the advantages and	151
dis advantages ofeach # Site ~~is outlined~~ *will be found* in appendix B.	162

A MAN OF IDEAS

TS

(¶ 1) Scoffed at as impractical and rated by his teacher as "dull and backward," George Westinghouse proved to be a creative genius with a far-ranging mind.[1] He contributed as much to science as his better-known competitor, Thomas Alva Edison.

(¶ 2) Young Westinghouse joined the Army as a private when he was 17 years old. At the end of the Civil War, he enrolled at Union College but was soon asked to leave. He was then 19 years old. It was just a few months later that he was awarded his first patent for a rotary steam engine. His next patent was for a device by which a derailed train could be put back on its tracks in a matter of minutes, and every railroad in the country became his customer.

(¶ 3) George Westinghouse built an industrial empire. Near the end of his life, he lost control of his companies to his bankers; but he was more imaginative than those who rated him "dull and backward" and more practical than those who thought him impractical. And when he was found slumped in a wheelchair dead, he was surrounded by sketches for a motor to drive the chair.

A MAN OF IDEAS

Scoffed at as impractical and rated by his teacher as "dull and backward," George Westinghouse proved to be a creative genius with a far-ranging mind.[1] He contributed as much to science as his better-known competitor, Thomas Alva Edison.

Young Westinghouse joined the Army as a private when he was 17 years old. At the end of the Civil War, he enrolled at Union College but was soon asked to leave. He was then 19 years old. It was just a few months later that he was awarded his first patent for a rotary steam engine. His next patent was for a device by which a derailed train could be put back on its tracks in a matter of minutes, and every railroad in the country became his customer.

George Westinghouse built an industrial empire. Near the end of his life, he lost control of his companies to his bankers; but he was more imaginative than those who rated him "dull and backward" and more practical than those who thought him impractical. And when he was found slumped in a wheelchair dead, he was surrounded by sketches for a motor to drive the chair.

To the end of his days Westinghouse was a "man of ideas." He never lost the impelling urge to create. More than 400 patents were credited to him in his lifetime. The whole world is richer for his having lived.

[1]I. E. Levine, Inventive Wizard: George Westinghouse (New York: Julian Messner, Inc., 1962).

(¶ 4) To the end of his days Westinghouse was a "man of ideas." He never lost the impelling urge to create. More than 400 patents were credited to him in his lifetime. The whole world is richer for his having lived.

Note for elite type: *After last line of text, space down 6 line spaces before typing divider rule.*

[1]I. E. Levine, Inventive Wizard: George Westinghouse (New York: Julian Messner, Inc., 1962).

67D: "Squeezing" Letters (15)

1. If omission is at beginning or end of word: (a) Move the carriage a half space before or after the word; (b) hold carriage in position with hand; (c) type the omitted letter.

2. If the omission or addition is within word: (a) Erase word; (b) return cylinder to writing position; (c) operate paper release and move paper a half space to left or right; then

for omitted letter: type word so first letter is in half the space that follows the preceding word and the final letter is in half the space that follows the corrected word;

for added letter: retype word so that the first letter is 1½ spaces to right of last letter of preceding word.

Note. Omitted stem letters "i" and "l" can often be typed between two letters without erasing. Hold the carriage in position and type the letter.

Type the sentences as given; then make corrections.

Line 1: Squeeze "l" at beginning and end of words.
Line 2: Squeeze "t" at end of two words.
Line 3: Squeeze "i" in two words.
Line 4: Erase "ur" and type "scrub."
Line 5: Erase and correct two words.
Line 6: Erase and correct two words.

```
1 A 65-space ine wil be right.
2 Tha style is not righ  for this letter.
3 I do not lke the lne length.
4 Erase lightly--don't "scurb" the error.
5 When you erase, erase quiet lighty.
6 The men workd many horus for us.
```

Problem 2: Report Outline *(Reading position)*

Words

OUTLINE OF A FORMAL BUSINESS REPORT 7

I. The introduction 11

A. Title page 14
B. Preface or letter of transmittal 21
C. Table of contents 25
D. List of tables, charts, and other illustrations 36

II. The body of the report 41

A. Summary 43
B. Recommendations or conclusions 50
C. Body of report 54

III. Supplementary material 59

A. Appendix 62
B. Bibliography 65
C. Index 66

Problem 3: Interoffice Memo

Type an original copy to each person indicated at right →

Words

M. A. Saxton, Director of Personnel 7
B. T. Knowlton, Chief of Training 7
M. L. Bernard, Director of Administration 8

Words

TO: *(Insert name and title)* FROM: C. Daniel 9
Root, President DATE: July 13, 19–– SUBJECT: 15
Report of Action by Board of Directors (¶ 1) 23
At a special meeting on July 12, the Board of 32
Directors voted to establish a program to en- 41
courage our employees to develop executive 49
leadership through collegiate training. Under 59
this program, all salaried employees will be 68
encouraged to take undergraduate or graduate 77
courses in business, management, and economics 86
during off-duty hours. Those who successfully 96
complete approved courses will be reimbursed 105
for all costs, including tuition, books, supplies, 115
and travel. (¶ 2) Will you please study this pro- 123
posal carefully and be prepared to discuss the 133
policies and procedures necessary to implement 142
it at a meeting which will be held in the Con- 151
ference Room on July 19. 157

LESSON 217

217A: Conditioning Practice (5) *each line at least three times*

Alphabet	Jacqueline bought six patterns to help Ward make covers of many sizes.	*Thumb close to space bar*
Figure	The index for all items increased from 105.3 in 1962 to 114.8 in 1967.	
Figure-symbol	Profits (after taxes) were $835,240 in 1967––an increase of almost 8%.	
Fluency	Do you plan to attend the annual meeting of the Personnel Association?	
	| 1 | 2 | 3 | 4 | 5 | 6 | 7 | 8 | 9 | 10 | 11 | 12 | 13 | 14 |	

217B: Skill Comparison (7) *1′ writing on each sentence of 217A; compare rates*

LESSON 68

68A: Conditioning Practice (5) *each line three times at a rate you can maintain without error*

LEARN: *Line 3.* Use ' (apostrophe) as the symbol for minute and " (quotation) for second.

Alphabet	Dwight Jacobs frequently goes to visit the Phoenix Municipal Park Zoo.
Figure-symbol	Brown & Newton's C.O.D. Order #809-Y (dated 10/23) amounts to $746.59.
Minutes; Seconds	My class typed 45 <u>gwam</u> on a 2′ writing with the call of the 15″ guide.
Easy	I can handle problems of the chairman's formal visit in the usual way.

| 1 | 2 | 3 | 4 | 5 | 6 | 7 | 8 | 9 | 10 | 11 | 12 | 13 | 14 |

68B: Building Accuracy with Speed (15) *(Two 5′ control-level writings)*

All letters are used.

1.3 E 5.2 85

	GWAM 1′	5′	
There is more to job getting than I had thought. Since I can do	13	3	41
several things quite well and some things exceptionally well, I thought	27	5	44
all I had to do was to make my availability known. How wrong I was I	42	8	46
learned when I tried to get a summer job after school ended in June.	56	11	49
Neither my work skills nor my availability had much attention at first	70	14	52
from the world of business.	75	15	53
My first mistake was to telephone for an interview with the "chief	13	18	56
man for employment." I didn't get the Chief Man; rather, I got a tele-	27	21	59
phone turndown. For the next interview, I was there in person; but I	41	23	61
went in the late afternoon and was asked to come back the next morning.	56	26	64
I am not lazy, and I was there bright and early—well, early; but I	70	29	67
certainly wasn't at my best.	75	30	68
The job interview was my big problem. I was prepared to work but	13	33	71
unprepared for the interview. Once I learned how to get ready for the	27	36	74
interview, I got a job and learned a lot during the summer weeks.	40	38	76

1′ GWAM | 1 | 2 | 3 | 4 | 5 | 6 | 7 | 8 | 9 | 10 | 11 | 12 | 13 | 14 |
5′ GWAM | 1 | 2 | 3 |

68C: Footnote on Partially Filled Page and the Ellipsis (10) *(Side Margins: 1″; DS)*

Partially Filled Page with Footnote: Leave the space required between the last line of the text and the divider line to place the footnotes and to have an approximate 1″ (6-line) bottom margin. Use your page gauge for placing the divider line.

Ellipsis: Used to indicate omission of words from a quotation; shown by three alternating periods and spaces, or four if the end of a sentence is included in the omission.

(Continued on page 112)

216C: Skill Transfer – Rough Draft (8) *two 1′ writings and one 3′ writing; compute* gwam

	GWAM 1′	3′	
~~There is~~ a wide variety of reports in the business world. It is	14	5	48
not ~~unlikely you will~~ find daily reports on the ~~condition~~ of personell,	25	8	52
purchaseing, and ~~housecleaning~~. Reports may be made ~~each week~~ on the	38	13	56
progress acheived in ~~manufacturing~~ and sales. A ~~thorough~~ report of the	52	17	61
~~pecuniary~~ condition of a business is made once ~~year~~ year semi annually	70	23	67
or monthly. A report may be ~~just~~ a breif, informal memo or it may be	85	28	72
a formal, comprehensive technical manuscript. In wahtever form it maybe,	100	33	77
a business report is used to ~~provide data~~ which is used by exectuives as	118	39	83
a ~~maens of~~ planing, ~~solving~~ problems, and making decesions.	131	44	88

216D: Production Typing (30)

Time Schedule	
Get ready to type	2′
Timed production	25′
Proofread; compute *g-pram* . .	3′

Type the following three problems for 25′ when directed to begin. For each problem, prepare 1 cc on plain paper. If time permits, start over. Mark errors. Compute *g-pram.*

Problem 1: Interoffice Memo

Block enumerated items

Words

TO: All Chiefs of Departments DATE: July 15, 7
19–– FROM: C. W. Jenkins, Vice-President of 15
Administration SUBJECT: Preparation of Special 22
Reports. (¶ 1) Numerous decisions that have 30
far-reaching effects on the successful operation 39
of the company are made frequently on the 48
basis of information included in special reports. 58
In view of the importance of these reports, it is 68
vital that they be well written and properly pre- 78
pared. These points should be kept in mind 86
when you write reports: 1. Make them brief. 96
Reports should be no longer than is necessary 105
to present the essential points clearly and force- 115
fully. 2. Be objective. Overstatements, unsup- 124
ported assertions, and unqualified conclusions 134
should be avoided. 3. Use clear, forceful lan- 143
guage and proper English. 4. Organize the 152
report so that it can be read quickly and easily. 162
(¶ 2) The organization of a report demands spe- 170
cial attention. In general, there are three major 180
parts of a report: the introduction, the body, 190
and the supplementary material. The introduc- 199
tion includes a title page, a preface or letter 209
of transmittal that explains the general nature 218
of the report, a table of contents, and a list 228
of tables, charts, or other illustrations. (¶ 3) 236
The body of a report should begin with a sum- 245
mary of the entire report and any recommenda- 254
tions or conclusions. Although it may seem 263
strange to place this information at the begin- 272
ning of the report, busy executives prefer to 281
see the recommendations or conclusions <u>before</u> 292
they read the minute details. All data necessary 302
to substantiate the recommendations or conclu- 311
sions follow. Headings and subheadings are 319
used in the body of the report for clarity and 329
ease of reading. (See Section 14.1 of the Office 339
Procedures Manual for detailed instructions on 348
format.) (¶ 4) The supplementary part of a re- 356
port usually includes an appendix and a bibliog- 366
raphy. If considered necessary, an index may 375
also be added. Tables and exhibits that are not 385
absolutely essential in the body are included in 394
the appendix. A bibliography is provided so 403
that the reader may note the source of the data 413
found in the body of the report. 420

Type on Line 23 from bottom of page

Balsley and Robinson say, "Preparation . . . consists of . . . (1) pre-interview collection of information and (2) preinterview personal preparation."[1] This was my guide for getting my job for the summer, but I failed at first to follow its advice. As another writer said: "Looking for a job is a job."[2]

Space down as necessary to have a 1-inch bottom margin

———————— DS

[1]Irol Whitmore Balsley and Jerry W. Robinson, Integrated Secretarial Studies (Jubilee ed.; Cincinnati: South-Western Publishing Co., 1964), p. 369. DS

[2]M. Jean Herman, The Job Interview (New York: Alumnae Advisory Center, Inc., 1966), p. 4.

68D: Problem Typing (20) (*¶ indention: 5*)

Type the paragraphs of 68B, page 111, as a manuscript with the heading JOB HUNTING typed as follows: On Line 10 for pica type; Line 13 for elite. To complete ¶ 3, add the lines of 68C, above, beginning with *Balsley and Robinson say,* and typing the footnotes as indicated to have a 1-inch bottom margin.

LESSON 69

69A: Conditioning Practice (5) *each line three times at a rate you can maintain without error*

Alphabet	Four complex keyboard reviews were quickly organized by Patrick Johns.
Figure-symbol	Order #896 (File 54–2) must be shipped to Norris & O'Dell by April 30.
Feet; Inches	Use ′ for feet and ″ for inches. Sue bought a rug that is 18′9″ long.
Easy	Was the auditor skeptical of the authenticity of Mr. Lowe's signature?

| 1 | 2 | 3 | 4 | 5 | 6 | 7 | 8 | 9 | 10 | 11 | 12 | 13 | 14 |

69B: Drill on X-ing Out Words (5)

When composing and typing a first draft, strike the **x** and **m** alternately with the first or second finger of each hand to cross out unwanted words.

1. **Type:** Today the novel takes many forms.
2. **X-out** last three words; complete sentence to read: Today the novel is experimental.

69C: Composing and Typing (40) (*Line: 65; ¶ indention: 5; DS*)

State in three or four ¶s your qualifications for an office position. Tell how you will prepare for an interview. Use the quotation at the right and the first footnote of 68C, above. X-out words you want to change. Correct and retype with appropriate heading of your own choosing.

Balsley and Robinson say, "The purpose of an interview is to enable an employer to observe your appearance . . . and discuss your qualifications."[1]

215D: Growth Index (15) *two 5′ writings; circle errors; determine* nwam

	GWAM 1′	5′	
All letters are used.			
What data will you be asked to provide on an application form?	13	3	63
Most employers will ask you to give your name, address, social security	27	5	66
number, height, weight, and date of birth. Usually, there is a section	41	8	68
for education, one for skills you have acquired, and one for a detailed	56	11	71
history of any work experience. You may be asked to enter each job	70	14	74
you have held, the inclusive dates, your wages, and the name of the	84	17	77
employer. Almost all firms ask for a list of individuals to whom they	98	20	80
can refer for information about your character, ability, and attitude.	112	22	83
You may also be asked to list your hobbies, clubs, and other personal	126	25	85
interests. Some employers may ask you to compose a brief essay telling	140	28	88
why you applied for a job with them and stating the sort of duties you	154	31	91
would prefer.	157	31	91
 Although you may not realize it, the application form is a good	13	34	94
test of many of your qualities. It shows whether or not you have the	27	37	97
ability to comprehend and to follow simple instructions. The answers	41	40	100
you give will reflect your ability to write, to organize your thoughts,	55	42	103
and to present facts clearly and concisely. A check with your former	69	45	105
employers and the references you give may reveal how accurate or how	83	48	108
honest you are. Your penmanship may give a hint of how neat and orderly	98	51	111
your work will be. If you are well prepared and answer all questions	112	54	114
accurately and neatly, you should have no difficulty. If you do not	126	56	117
do so, you may be told that there are no job vacancies for anyone with	140	59	119
your qualifications.	144	60	120

1′ GWAM | 1 | 2 | 3 | 4 | 5 | 6 | 7 | 8 | 9 | 10 | 11 | 12 | 13 | 14 |
5′ GWAM | 1 | 2 | 3 |

LESSON 216

216A: Conditioning Practice (5) *each line at least three times*

Alphabet	Frank Black realized that Mavis Quigley would adjust the property tax.	*Fluent rhythm*
Figure	In 1966, they produced 243,875 units as compared with 200,473 in 1965.	
Figure-symbol	National security cost $58.4 million--42% of the $137.6 million spent.	
Fluency	Does he intend to invite us to visit the new plant in the near future?	

| 1 | 2 | 3 | 4 | 5 | 6 | 7 | 8 | 9 | 10 | 11 | 12 | 13 | 14 |

216B: Skill Comparison  *1′ writings on sentences of 216A; compare rates*

LESSONS 70-71

70A and 71A: Conditioning Practice (5) *each line three times in each lesson*

Alphabet	James Wexford gained amazing typing skill by improving his techniques.
Figure-symbol	Rothburn & McKeown's check dated 6/28 for $7,892.50 pays Invoice #134.
Special symbols	Use x for times and – for minus. What is the answer to 290 x 8 – 457?
Easy	Did he question the authority of those who make such profits possible?

| 1 | 2 | 3 | 4 | 5 | 6 | 7 | 8 | 9 | 10 | 11 | 12 | 13 | 14 |

Line 4: Squeeze the letter *s* to change each writing of the line to: Did she question (etc.).

70B and 71B: Errorless Typing (20) *each sentence five times, or three times without error*

1	*Easy*	You can be sure a man with both his feet on the ground won't fall far.
2	*ei | ie*	Keith and Harriet Weir went to see their friend, Mrs. Leigh Creighton.
3	*Adjacent*	Sam Frew has pointed out that truth has greater power than we believe.
4	*One-hand*	Lonny Hill was as sad as Fred Webster was at your team's great defeat.
5	*Easy*	Does the man who knows he is right usually speak with quiet authority?
6	*Long*	Use the operative parts of the typewriter efficiently and effectively.
7	*Alphabet*	Is V. J. Brahmford quite well known as an exceptional zoology student?
8	*Easy*	Mr. Cleland, the auditor, is right to make the men pay for the chairs.
9	*Adjacent*	Drew has said that Julia and Sadie Poindexter have done superior work.
10	*Easy*	The chairman said he may name both Elena and Claudia to the committee.

| 1 | 2 | 3 | 4 | 5 | 6 | 7 | 8 | 9 | 10 | 11 | 12 | 13 | 14 |

70C and 71C: Drill Review (25)

Make pencil notations of each page and drill listed at the right. Study the *explanation of the process* as given on the appropriate page; then type each drill once as directed.

Page 109, 67B
Page 110, 67D
Page 111, 68C
Page 100, 60B

LESSON 72

72A: Conditioning Practice (5) *each line three times at a rate you can maintain without error*

Note. To type the degree symbol (°) in Line 3, turn the cylinder toward you slightly and hold it as you type small o.

Alphabet	Mrs. Alex J. Preble's zeal very quickly influenced those good workmen.
Figure-symbol	Ship by C.O.D. express Order #541–2 for 8 2/3 doz. of #607 @ 89¢ each.
Degree	The freezing point of water is 32° F. and the boiling point is 212° F.
Easy	Do for your neighbor as you would like for your neighbor to do for you.

| 1 | 2 | 3 | 4 | 5 | 6 | 7 | 8 | 9 | 10 | 11 | 12 | 13 | 14 |

72B: Errorless Typing (15) *each sentence of 70B and 71B, above, as a 1' writing*

72C: Problem Typing Review (30)

Make pencil notations of each page and problem listed at the right. Type the problem once as directed. Correct all errors.

Page 108, 66D, 1
Page 109, 67C
Page 106, 65C, 1

Unit 37 | Lessons 215-221

Business Reports

LESSON 215

215A: Conditioning Practice (5) *each line at least three times*

Alphabet Jerry said that six quiz prizes will be given by the Franklin Company.
Figure Change Frank's social security number from 152–03–4697 to 141–02–4586.
Figure-symbol The property taxes in 1968 will be 4.253¢ per $1 (an increase of 7¼%).
Fluency You will note that they have planned no increases in prices this year.
| 1 | 2 | 3 | 4 | 5 | 6 | 7 | 8 | 9 | 10 | 11 | 12 | 13 | 14 |

Release keys quickly

215B: Technique Practice (10) *each line three times; then 1′ writings*

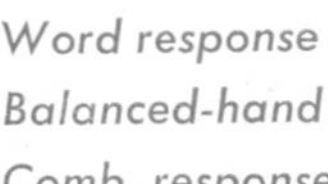

Word response The job could not be done then, but it could be done later in the day.
Balanced-hand The chairman may visit the men and they may then pay the quantity due.
Comb. response New automatic exhaust valves will be installed in the old incinerator.
Stroke response The astronaut encountered considerable body force during acceleration.
| 1 | 2 | 3 | 4 | 5 | 6 | 7 | 8 | 9 | 10 | 11 | 12 | 13 | 14 |

215C: Skill Building – Straight Copy (20)

1. Type three 1′ writings on each ¶ on the *exploration level.* Try to increase your speed with each writing.

2. Type three 1′ writings on each ¶ on the *control level.* Try each time to type with as few errors as possible.

All letters are used.

When you apply in person for a new job, your initial contact with a company will undoubtedly be the personnel office. Usually, you will be greeted by an interviewer whose duty it is to provide information about the firm and the current job openings and to aid you in filling out an application form. She may be authorized to interview applicants and to screen out the ones who do not appear to meet the company's standards. Thus, your first task is to win the approval of the receptionist.

It is only a matter of common sense to "put your best foot forward" when you seek a new job. You will want to dress appropriately and to be well groomed. Do not neglect your mental preparation, however. You can expect that the interviewer will ask you numerous questions about your education, experience, and personal history. You can be sure that if you give vague answers you will create a poor impression. You will avoid this if you are armed with all the essential data in advance.

GWAM 1′	5′	
14	3	42
28	6	45
42	8	48
57	11	51
71	14	54
85	17	56
98	20	59
14	22	62
28	25	65
43	28	68
57	31	70
71	34	73
86	37	76
98	39	79

1′ GWAM | 1 | 2 | 3 | 4 | 5 | 6 | 7 | 8 | 9 | 10 | 11 | 12 | 13 | 14 |
5′ GWAM | 1 | 2 | 3 |

Unit 11 | Lessons 73-75

Review and Measurement

LESSON 73

1. Arrange work area for effective performance.
2. Adjust paper guide and paper-bail rolls.
3. Set control to type on upper part of ribbon.
4. Full sheet; Line: 70; SS, unless otherwise directed.

73A: Conditioning Practice (7) *each line three times; Line 4 for two 1′ accuracy writings*

Typing + and = in Line 3: On some machines, special keys are used; on others the symbols are 'made":

To type + (plus), type the /; backspace; then intersect with the – (hyphen).

To type = (equal), type – (hyphen); backspace; move the platen forward slightly and hold it while you type – (hyphen) again. Return the platen to typing position.

Alphabet	Helvig d'Aquin visited Mexico, Brazil, and Peru for two weeks in July.
Figure-symbol	The price on Item #416 is given as $5.40 on page 392 of Catalogue B78.
Special characters	If 23 x 654 – 789 + 190 = 15,042, how much would 32 x 456 + 109 equal?
Easy	You can always do much more through push than you can do through pull.
	| 1 | 2 | 3 | 4 | 5 | 6 | 7 | 8 | 9 | 10 | 11 | 12 | 13 | 14 |

73B: Errorless Typing (10) *(each line three times without error)*

1	*b*	Bret Brown brought Robert Brier and his bride to join the bridge team.
2	*c*	Can Chief Clerk Cedric Chadworth cash the checks for Clay and Charles?
3	*m-n*	Many more men mentioned lack of memory as their main cause of concern.
4	*p*	Purposeful practice for typing power brought the opportunity to excel.
5	*q*	Quick wit is quite frequently required for those queer quiz questions.
6	*x*	Rex expects to stay at the Essex–Sussex Hotel for the next six months.
		| 1 | 2 | 3 | 4 | 5 | 6 | 7 | 8 | 9 | 10 | 11 | 12 | 13 | 14 |

73C: Problem Typing Review (33)

Make notation of the page and problem numbers listed at the right. Type as many problems as you can, making one carbon of each. Proofread and correct errors before removing the page.

Page 85,	Problem 1	(Also address envelope)
100,	2	
105,	3	(Also address envelope)
112,	68D	

LESSONS 74-75

74A and 75A: Conditioning Practice (5) *each line three times in each lesson*

Alphabet	Have we checked the six very old quill pens Jen bought from Ziegler's?
Figure-symbol	Order #514-B for 18 2/3 doz. of Item #607 @ 98¢ ea. was shipped C.O.D.
Direct-adjacent	Frederic Decker's many months in the jungle left him tired and hungry.
Easy	Stay on your toes, and you can then keep others from stepping on them.
	| 1 | 2 | 3 | 4 | 5 | 6 | 7 | 8 | 9 | 10 | 11 | 12 | 13 | 14 |

Problem 2 (*1 cc*)

Using **December 10** as the date, type the letter in modified block style, mixed punctuation to:

Mr. Evan K. Richardson
1930 Redondo Avenue
Salt Lake City, Utah 84108

Supply an appropriate salutation. In the closing lines use **Sincerely yours** and the name **Thomas W. Gibbons, Jr.** Mr. Gibbons is **Promotion Manager.**

Words

Heading and salutation 22
(¶ 1) Your comments on your experience with the new Lite-Line 33
models of Ultramatic typewriters were most gratifying. Both Miss 46
McCloskey and Mr. Sanate have reported similar reactions from 59
businessmen and teachers alike. (¶ 2) From many requests, we have 71
arranged the following schedule for display-demonstrations for you 84
for the week of January 15: 90

				Words
1/15	Reno	University of Nevada	9:30–11:30 a.m.	100
		Office Services, Inc.	2:30– 3:30 p.m.	108
1/17	Moscow	University of Idaho	10:00–11:15 a.m.	118
		Office Products Co.	1:30– 2:45 p.m.	125
1/19	Laramie	University of Wyoming	8:30– 9:30 a.m.	136
		Yellowstone Supply Co.	10:30–11:50 a.m.	145

(¶ 3) The foregoing time schedule is such that you can probably 157
work in one or two demonstrations on the 16th and the 18th with- 169
out crowding your travel schedule unduly. Enclosed is a list of 182
requests for demonstrations. Assuming that you might work a few 195
more programs into your schedule, I have checked those requests 208
that might be most worthwhile. Telephone numbers and addresses 221
are provided for your convenience. (¶ 4) Continued good luck in 233
demonstrating the Lite-Line series. I shall appreciate a report of pros- 247
pect reactions to the new models and to each of the programs you 260
conduct. (240) 262
+ Closing lines and envelope **270/284**

Problem 3 (*1 cc*)

Using **December 10** as the date type the letter in modified block style, mixed punctuation, to:

Miss Marilyn Kenney
Washington High School
2600 Harrison Boulevard
Ogden, Utah 84401

Supply an appropriate salutation and appropriate closing lines. Dictator is **Wm. C. Pohlmeyer**, who is **Sales Manager**.

Words

Heading and salutation 25
(¶ 1) Thank you very much for your inquiry about prices of the 36
new Lite-Line models of our Ultramatic typewriters. Since you were 50
present at the Weber College demonstration by Mr. Carel, I shall 63
not review the features of the new machines. I am enclosing a 75
descriptive brochure that does so, however, in order that you may 88
study it at your convenience. (¶ 2) Increased production costs have 101
compelled us to raise the prices on all Ultramatic machines. These 115
price changes will become effective on the first of March. Because 128
the new Lite-Line models will not be available for delivery before 142
then, the listed prices already reflect the increase in production 155
costs. This accounts for the difference in price between the current 169
and the new models as indicated below: 177

	Current	Lite-Line	184
Pacesetter	$ 255.00	$ 265.00	190
Champion	360.00	370.00	195
Rhythmatic	455.00	470.00	200

(¶ 3) Not to be overlooked, however, are the new and improved 211
features of the Lite-Line models––all these for a very slight increase 225
in price. I am asking our representative, Mr. Robert Elliott, to make 239
an appointment with you to discuss the savings you can enjoy by 252
outfitting entire classrooms with the new Lite-Line models at the 265
special school discount price. (247) 272
+ Closing lines and envelope **285/302**

Problem 4 (*1 cc*)

Retype the memorandum of Problem 1, page 313, but address it to **John E. Williams, Houston Branch Manager**. (*Total words: 295*)

74B and 75B: Growth Index (10) *5′ writing on control level in each lesson*

All letters are used.

	GWAM 1′	5′	
When the going gets tough, the tough get going and the weak drop	13	3	45
out. Just how does one man get to the top of his profession while	26	5	48
another with just about as much ability is not very successful? Is	40	8	51
it luck or pull or something else? Men at the top all have that "some-	54	11	53
thing else" that a quitter does not have––they have the kind of faith	68	14	56
required to overcome all problems.	75	15	57
The pipes to a fountain may be full of water, but the water won't	13	18	60
flow unless it is turned on. Just so it is with "that something" that	27	20	63
is in us. It won't work unless we make a demand on it. When we plan	41	23	66
intelligently, work efficiently, and believe mightily, the power will	55	26	69
express itself through all we do and help us to realize our utmost good.	70	29	71
When the going gets tough, as it will at times, be tough enough	13	31	74
to get going. First, plan intelligently; next, work efficiently; and	27	34	77
all the time believe mightily that you can do whatever you need to do	41	37	80
to solve the problems that come to you. This is the way to solve a	54	40	82
problem, large or small, and the sure way to find your highest good.	68	43	85

1′ GWAM | 1 | 2 | 3 | 4 | 5 | 6 | 7 | 8 | 9 | 10 | 11 | 12 | 13 | 14 |
5′ GWAM | 1 | 2 | 3 |

74C and 75C: Problem Typing (35) *(5′ to get ready; 20′ for typing; 10′ for proofreading and correcting)*

Problem 1: Manuscript with Footnote

Carbon copy
1″ side margins
¶ indention: 5; DS

2″ top margin
1″ bottom margin
Correct errors

	Words
THE LIBRARY AND THE CURRICULUM	6
(¶ 1) Some educators say the library is the heart	15
of the curriculum. For me and many others in	24
our school, we have a "heart" that does not	33
function. Why this is so is more important than	43
that it is so, and the why is simple––no one has	53
shown us how to use the library properly. And	62
we are not alone in our ignorance. (¶ 2) Accord-	70
ing to the results of a survey of 41,170 seniors	80
from 69 colleges and universities in 38 states,	90
most of them did not know how to use the	98
library either. Thirty-five percent were unable	108
to interpret a cross-reference in the Readers'	119
Guide to Periodical Literature; 60 percent did	134
not recognize the form or purpose of a subject	144
card in the card catalog; and 90 percent did not	153
know the meaning of a New York Times Index	166
citation.[1] The sad fact is that I don't know these	177
things either. For me and many other students,	186
the greatest potential source of education, the	196
library, is not functioning as the "heart of the	206
curriculum."	208
———————	212
[1]Ralph Perkins, The Prospective Teacher's	225
Knowledge of Library Fundamentals (New York:	241
The Scarecrow Press, Inc., 1965).	268

LESSON 213

213A: Conditioning Practice (5) *each line at least three times*

Alphabet; shift	We realized "gloomy old junk shops" can be full of expensive antiques.	*Finger-stroking action*
Figure	The serial number of this 1967 Model 274XV Transistor is 813–J1–90635.	
Outside reaches	As our mizzen-mast appeared on the horizon, 20 Indians held a pow-wow.	
Fluency	Think through a job before you begin it, and you have a map to follow.	
	| 1 | 2 | 3 | 4 | 5 | 6 | 7 | 8 | 9 | 10 | 11 | 12 | 13 | 14 |	

213B: Sustained Production Typing (45)

Time Schedule

Get ready to type	7′
Timed production	30′
Proofread; compute *n-pram* . .	8′

Make a list of the problems to be typed. Type for 30′ when directed to begin, following the instructions given for each problem. Make 1 cc for each problem. Correct all errors as you type. If time permits, start over. Proofread; mark uncorrected errors. Compute *n-pram*.

Page 310, 209D, Problem 1
Page 311, 210C, Problem 2
Page 312, 211D, Problem 1
Page 313, 212C, Problem 2

Turn in problems arranged in the order in which they are listed.

LESSON 214

214A: Conditioning Practice (5) *repeat 213A, above*

214B: Sustained Production Measurement (45) *if time permits, start over*

Time Schedule

Get ready to type	7′
Timed production	30′
Proofread; compute *n-pram* . .	8′

Problem 1 (*1 cc*)

Type an interoffice memorandum to **Joseph G. Nieman, San Francisco Branch Manager**, from **Thomas W. Gibbons, Jr., Promotion Manager**. Date the memo **December 10** and use as a subject line **New Lite-Line Ultramatic Display Booths.**

(*Problems 2–4 are on page 315*)

Words

Heading 35

(¶ 1) Here are the advance promotional materials highlighting the 47
major product features of the new Lite-Line series of Ultramatic 60
Office Machines. In addition, we are sending you color photographs 74
of several model displays that have been suggested by our promotion 87
section. To guide you in developing your own promotional displays, 101
the following size and cost data may be useful: 111

Display A	6′ x 6′ x 9′ (2-color)	$ 475.00	120
Display B	6′ x 9′ x 9′ (3-color)	650.00	128
Display C	6′ x 12′ x 9′ (4-color)	995.00	136
Display D	8′ x 12′ x 9′ (5-color)	1,650.00	145

(¶ 2) For most local shows and demonstrations, either Display A or 157
Display B should be adequate. Only for major regional or national 171
shows can we justify the expenditure required for Display C or 183
Display D. It is our plan to produce two of Display C, one to be 197
kept in the New York office, the other in the San Francisco office. 210
If some show demands the larger Display D, we believe we can add 223
two 2-foot mobile units (one for the front of each side of Display C) 237
without destroying its symmetry and unity. (¶ 3) After studying these 250
promotional materials and the suggested displays, submit to me your 264
proposals (with cost estimates) before contracting with anyone to 277
construct the display booths. *+ Envelope* 284/296

Problem 2: Manuscript with Two Footnotes (*Use directions of Problem 1, page 115*)

Words

BROTHERS OF THE SEA 4

(¶ 1) America's Ernest Hemingway and Rho- 11
desia's D. R. Sherman are, in many respects, 20
"brothers of the sea." Both have written of an 29
old man and a boy and the sea in simple, com- 38
pelling, and moving stories. The similarities in 48
their books are found in the sparse words and 57
simple sentences as well as in the main char- 66
acters. The differences are in the roles of the 76
old man and the boy. (¶ 2) The old man in 83
The Old Man and the Sea[1] embodies the basic 97
nobility in human striving. The giant fish is the 107
embodiment of what is noble in animate nature. 117
And the sea—la mar, which is what the people 127
call her in Spanish when they love her—was the 137
home of the great fish and the love of the old 146
man. This moving story expresses the basic 155
attitudes the author held toward life. (¶ 3) In 163
Brothers of the Sea,[2] the old man is a secondary 177
character. The battle is between the boy and 186
life. The story, in its great simplicity, is of a boy 197
who finds friendship with a dolphin and an 206
awakening interest in a girl. It is a touching, 216
poignant story, well told. (¶ 4) Reading these 224
books is a profound experience, like living a 233
tragedy which, at the last, emerges without grief 243
into beauty. 246

——————— 250

[1] Ernest Hemingway, The Old Man and the 261
Sea (New York: Charles Scribner's Sons, 1952). 272
[2] D. R. Sherman, Brothers of the Sea (Boston: 285
Little, Brown, and Company, 1966). 291

Problem 3: Tabulated List

Full sheet | 10 spaces between columns | DS | Reading position

			Words
SCHEDULED VISITS TO BUSINESS			6
Leaving at 1:30			9
Monday	Wednesday	Friday	18
Annamae Ashton	Leo Arthur	Ted Barbour	26
Elvin Dodson	Don Bixler	Carolyn Brink	34
Corwin Eichler	Ruth Charles	Steve Dodson	40
Grace Flaxton	Leah Harris	Cora Flynn	49
Nora Grayson	Sam Jenkins	Jane Glynn	56
Joe Llewellyn	Mary McCain	Jean Ishert	64
Nina McAlister	Nell O'Neill	Maud Lowen	72
Alice Nelson	Vera Ross	John McNeil	79
Barbara Nolan	Elona Spence	Sid O'Dell	86
Susan Parker	Gladys Upton	Mabel O'Hara	94
Clara Quiegley	Helen Vicker	Bruce Ryan	102
Martha Simmons	Liza Wolfex	Ned Roberts	110
George Turner	Jim Young	Mary Todd	117
Brenda Whitney	Mary Zeuger	Bell Yeager	124

Problem 4: Modified Block Letter

Full sheet | Line: 50 | Date at center on Line 18 | Envelope

Use the following portions of 74B, page 115, as the body of the letter: ¶ 1, omitting the first sentence, and ¶ 3. Address the letter to **Mr. Robert Baldhoff | 490 Rio Bravo | San Antonio, Texas 78213**. Use an appropriate salutation and complimentary close. The letter is to be signed by **Alexander C. Tiffin | Assistant Dean of Students | xx**

Problem 5: Outline in Rough Draft

Full sheet | Line: 42 | SS | Center in reading position

Words

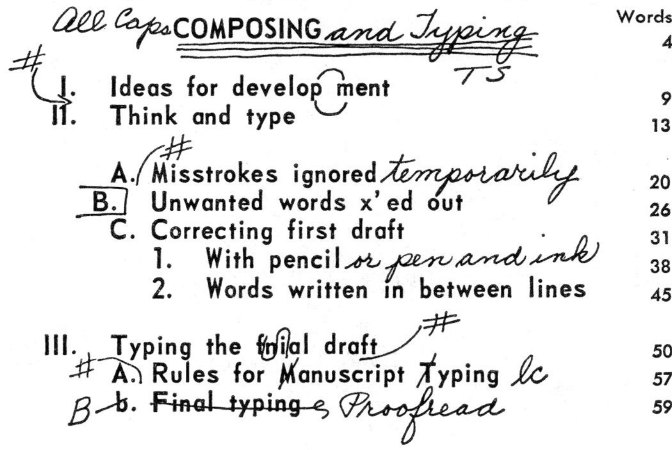

All Caps COMPOSING ~~and Typing~~ 4

I. Ideas for develop ment 9
II. Think and type 13

A. Misstrokes ignored temporarily 20
B. Unwanted words x'ed out 26
C. Correcting first draft 31
1. With pencil or pen and ink 38
2. Words written in between lines 45

III. Typing the finial draft 50
A. Rules for Manuscript Typing lc 57
B ~~b. Final typing~~ Proofread 59

Problem 6: Corrected Outline

Half sheet | SS | Exact vertical center

Make pencil corrections in your copy of the Problem 5 outline, then retype it in correct form on a half sheet, long side at top.

Problem 7: Composing and Typing

Make a reservation of a room with twin beds and a bath for your father and mother at Plantation Motor Inn, Raleigh, North Carolina, for Friday of week after next. Specify the exact date and ask that the reservation be held for 7 p.m. arrival. Your father will sign the letter. Use your home address and the style of letter you prefer. Address an envelope.

LESSON 212

212A: Conditioning Practice (5) *each line at least three times*

Alphabet; shift	Quinby Hall, the Executive Mansion, was razed; June fogs kept it damp.	*Quiet hands; quick, snap stroke*
Figure-symbol	Shipment #14837 from Elson & Gray arrived; #90625 from Mack's <u>did not</u>.	
Double letters	I will soon offer a good annuity for a planned deferred annual income.	
Fluency	What you learned today might well determine what you will be tomorrow.	
	| 1 | 2 | 3 | 4 | 5 | 6 | 7 | 8 | 9 | 10 | 11 | 12 | 13 | 14 |	

212B: Basic Skill Maintenance (10) *1′ writings on selected ¶s on pages 308–309; select a goal*

212C: Production Typing – Memorandums with Tabulations (35) *if time permits, start over*

Time Schedule	
Get ready to type	3′
Timed production	25′
Proofread; determine *g-pram* . .	7′

Problem 1 (*1 cc*) ⟶

Type the memorandum to **James S. Randall** from **Charles R. Jakob, Sales Manager**. Date it **January 18** and use the subject **Special Price Quotation for Heritage Hill Project**.

Words

Heading 23

(¶ 1) You are hereby authorized to quote the following prices as 35
your rock-bottom bid on the Heritage Hill apartment project, all 48
prices F.O.B. Arlington: 53

1125	Fold-Away Hood Fan (36″)	$39.65 ea.	62
1135	Fold-Away Hood Fan (42″)	41.09 ea.	70
SP–1725	Splash Plate (22″ x 36″)	9.99 ea.	78
SP–1736	Splash Plate (22″ x 42″)	11.36 ea.	87
MC–1683	Lighted Double Bathroom Cabinet	43.77 ea.	97
MC–1652	Lighted Single Bathroom Cabinet	22.47 ea.	107

(¶ 2) These special prices are based upon two important factors: 119
(1) the number of units involved, and (2) the promotion value that 132
would result from being able to say that Virginia-Made products 145
were chosen for the Heritage Hill project. These prices, therefore, 159
are applicable only to this one situation. *+ Envelope* 168/174

Problem 2 (*1 cc*) ⟶

Type the memorandum to **All Order Interpreters** from **Mr. Jakob**, using the date **January 18** and the subject **Prices for New Line of Chimes.**

Words: 26

Heading 20

(¶ 1) The following items have been added to our line of chimes. 32
The first price listed should be quoted to builders; the second, to 46
dealers. 48

L-26	"Regal" Door Chime	24.95	17.77	55
L-56	"Jefferson" Door Chime	26.95	18.87	63
L-14	"Fiesta" Door Chime	25.95	18.27	71
L-32	"Futura" Door Chime	17.95	12.57	78

(¶ 2) As the names imply, the "Regal" should be suggested for a 90
formal decor; the "Jefferson," for a colonial motif; the "Fiesta," for 116
a Spanish atmosphere; and the "Futura," for a modern setting. 104
+ Envelope 123

Problem 3 (*1 cc*)

Retype Problem 1, using the date **January 19** and substituting the items listed at the right.

Heading and ¶1 53

8010	Pull-Chain Wall Fan (8")	14.69 ea.	61
8110	Pull-Chain Wall Fan (10")	22.46 ea.	69
8070	Automatic Wall Fan (8")	17.36 ea.	77
8170	Automatic Wall Fan (10")	23.46 ea.	85

+ ¶ 2 and envelope 146/152

Building Typewriting Competence

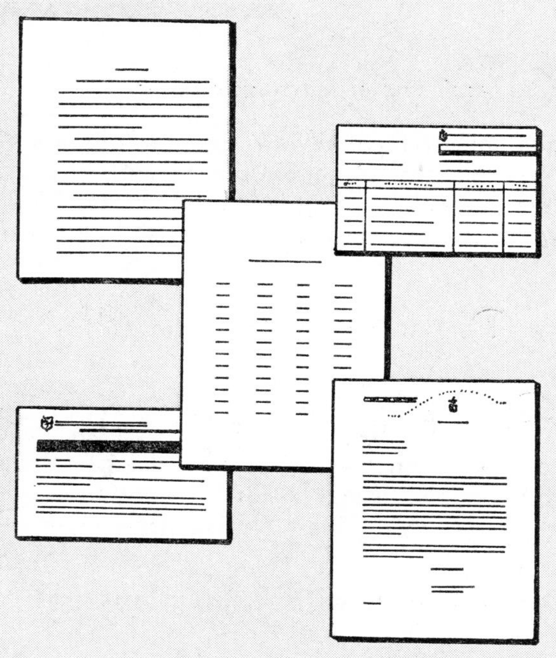

YOU HAVE A DUAL GOAL in completing the next 75 lessons of this book: (1) to attain basic skill proficiency and (2) to improve your ability to apply your basic skill in the preparation of personal and business papers.

YOU WILL INCREASE your typing speed and accuracy as well as your ability to apply related English as you type.

YOU WILL EXTEND your knowledge and skill in typing report manuscripts, letters with special features, and reports in tabular form.

AND YOU WILL LEARN to type often-used business forms, such as telegrams, invoices, interoffice memos, and voucher checks.

With purposeful, diligent effort as you type the practice materials, you will build typing competence for personal and business use.

Machine Checkup and Adjustments *for each lesson in Part 2*

USE:

1. A 70-space line and single spacing.
2. A 5-space indention for all paragraphs.
3. Double spacing for all timed writings of more than 1-minute duration.

CHECK:

1. Paper guide position.
2. Position of paper-bail rolls and the paper bail.
3. Position of ribbon control—set it for typing on upper portion of the ribbon.

2. Set paper rolls to divide paper into thirds.

1. Set the paper guide at 0 on most typewriters.

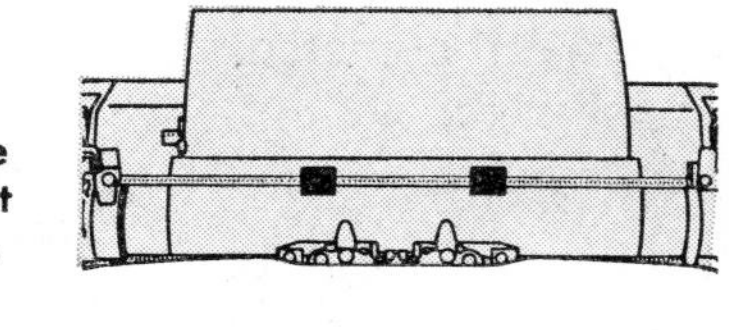

3. Set ribbon control for typing on upper portion of ribbon.

Bonus Typing

Practice is the key to skill growth, so do not waste time. Whenever you have free time (before, during, or after class), use the drills or problems given in the lessons. Type and *retype* them. Practice with a purpose, for the value of repetition lies in the purposefulness with which it is done.

As you type the drills or problems, work for speed, for accuracy, or for improvement of techniques, according to your own needs. Label all such work *Bonus Typing*. Extra credit will be given for it. Check your work and record at the top of each sheet the total lines typed (TLT), and the total errorless lines typed (TEL) if your goal was accuracy.

Key Skill-Building Factors

Here are the key factors that lead to expert typewriting skill:

1. **Good Typewriting Form.** Perfect your typewriting techniques by daily attention to *how* you type.
2. **Individual Effort.** Your success in developing typewriting skill depends on your own effort. *Try* to improve, and you *will* improve.
3. **Proper Practice.** *Purposeful* practice at appropriate *levels* of practice is essential (sometimes for speed, often for technique improvement, and at other times for control or accuracy).
4. **Alertness.** Be alert! Think about *what* you type and also *how* you type. Be alert to new ways to improve your typewriting skill.

LESSON 211

211A: Conditioning Practice (5) *each line at least three times*

Alphabet; shift	Gladys and Monique joined the Bellview Chapter of Zeta Kappa Xi today.	*Shift quickly*
Figure-symbol	Read "@" as "at"--425 pens @ (at) 70¢ each; 368 clips @ (at) 19¢ each.	
Direct reaches	Many young hunters have brought their brothers or father to the shoot.	
Fluency	You have to know by your own proofreading that the work is just right.	
	| 1 | 2 | 3 | 4 | 5 | 6 | 7 | 8 | 9 | 10 | 11 | 12 | 13 | 14 |	

211B: Basic Skill Maintenance (5) *1' writings on 211A above*

211C: Manipulative Preview (10) *Margins: 1"; SS; 4 spaces between columns*

Clear the tab stops; then set new stops for typing the tabulation in Problem 1 at the right below, using backspace-from-center method.

Type ¶ 1, the tabulation, and ¶ 2. If you finish the drill before time is called, space down 4 times and retype it.

211D: Production Typing – Memorandums with Tabulations (30) *if time permits, start over*

Time Schedule	
Get ready to type	3'
Timed production	20'
Proofread; determine *g-pram* . .	7'

Problem 1 (*1 cc*)

Using the machine adjustments of 211C above, type the memorandum given at the right. Address a COMPANY MAIL envelope.

Words

TO: Robert C. Flannigan, Credit Manager 7
FROM: Margaret Sparks, Credit Clerk 13
DATE: January 5, 19-- 16
SUBJECT: Delinquent Accounts 20

The accounts listed below (all of St. Paul) are more than 32
60 days past due. None of them has responded to the usual three 45
reminders. Each should therefore be sent one of our "discussion" 58
letters bearing your signature. 65

					Words
Mr. Donald R. Thomas	1247	DeSoto	55101	$67.50	74
Miss Greta Morgan	901	N. Dale	55103	24.95	83
Dr. Florence Markham	3302	Rice	55112	45.80	92
Mr. C. J. Dietreich	2658	Maywood	55117	79.65	101
Mr. Adam P. Logan	774	Lark Avenue	55109	92.70	110

Because each of these accounts has previously been 121
slow to pay, it is recommended that the Form 3 appeal be used in 134
the letter inasmuch as it indicates that a less-than-prompt payment 147
history is reflected in one's credit rating even when the individual 161
eventually pays his bill. (xx) *+ Envelope* 167/176

Problem 2 (*1 cc*)

Retype Problem 1 above, using the date **February 5**. In ¶ 1: Say that all addresses are in Minneapolis and that all are more than 3 months past due; in Sentence 2 add **and the discussion letter.** In the third sentence, change "discussion" to **urgency.** Substitute the list and the closing ¶ at the right.

Heading and ¶ 1 72

					Words
	Mr. Jay C. Beck	4500 Arden ave.	55424	$56.50	81
tr	Mr. Wm. C. Jaegre	104 Utica Rd.	55431	83.25	90
	Miss Anna Sloan	1607 Scott Ave.	55432	129.45	99

¶ It may be helpful to know that both Mr. Beck and Miss Sloan are 112
classified as "new" customers. Mr. Jaeger, ~~however,~~ on the other hand, has been a 127
credit customer for over ten years; ~~and~~ furthermore, this is the first time he 142
has been in credit trouble. *+ Envelope* 148/158

Unit 12 | Lessons 76-80

Technique Evaluation and Skill Inventory

LESSON 76

In this unit you will check and evaluate your own typewriting skill. Use this inventory as a guide to practice activities that will help improve your performance.

76A: Conditioning Practice 

DO: For all Conditioning Practices in Lessons 76–150.

1. **Type** each line three times as follows: first, at a slow, well-controlled pace as you give attention to good stroking technique; next for speed; and, finally, for accuracy with as much speed as is consistent with the goal of accuracy. *Double-space* after each three lines.
2. **Retype** selected lines as time permits. Select those lines that caused you difficulty; if none of the lines were difficult for you, retype each line once or twice.

Alphabet	Pecquoix Avenue was a bizarre jungle of many colored, blinking lights.	*Fingers curved*
Figure	Do Problems 6, 7, 8, and 9 on page 4, and Problems 2 and 3 on page 50.	
Fingers 3 and 4	A plucky polo player amazed us as he zigzagged crazily down the field.	
Speed	She may make the goal if she works with vigor and with the right form.	
	| 1 | 2 | 3 | 4 | 5 | 6 | 7 | 8 | 9 | 10 | 11 | 12 | 13 | 14 |	

76B: Finger Position Evaluation  *compare your finger position with the positions illustrated*

Chart 1

Proper Curve of Fingers in Home Position

(Sectional side view of right hand)

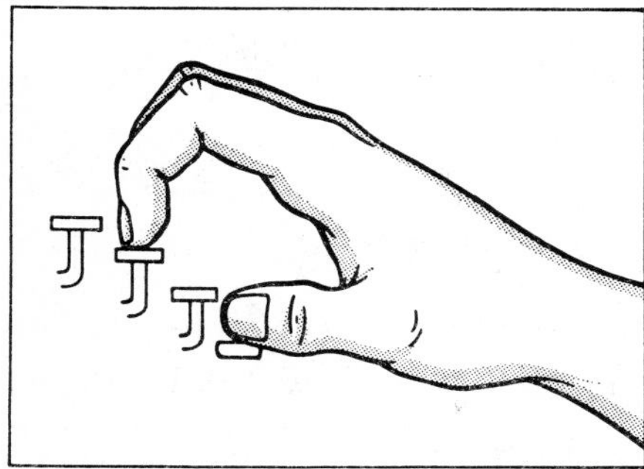

Points of Emphasis:

1. Each finger curved at first and second joints.
2. Little, if any, curve at the knuckle joint.
3. Thumb curved and resting lightly on the space bar.
4. Wrists low and relaxed.

Front sectional view of fingers of left hand in home position, illustrating right *and* wrong *finger positions*

Chart 2

Wrong: Fingers in improper alignment with *Home Keys* (slanting)

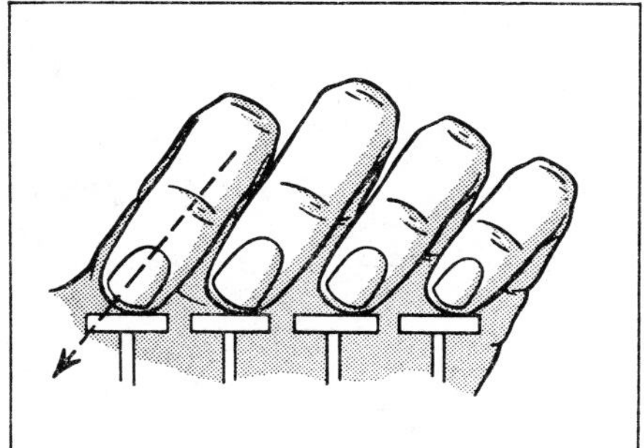

Result: Direction of stroke results in a glancing stroke causing clashing and jamming of keys. Turn hand inward to get proper finger alignment.

Chart 3

Right: Fingers in proper alignment with the *Home Keys* (upright)

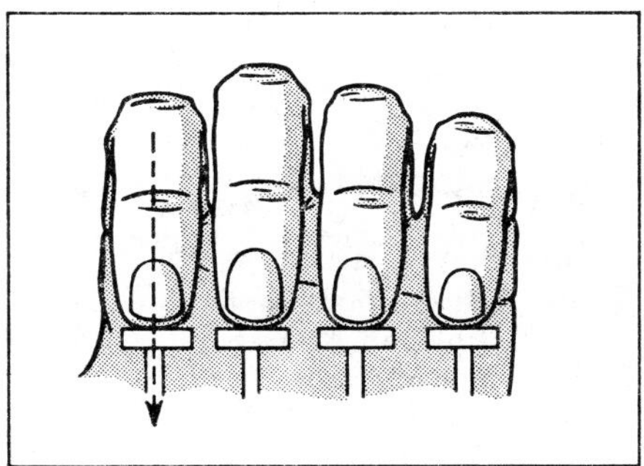

Result: Direction of stroke enables typist to strike keys with a direct, quick snap stroke with an immediate release of the key.

LESSON 210

210A: Conditioning Practice (5) *each line at least three times*

Alphabet; shift	A sizable tax rebate was quickly given to Jamal, Feldher & Parks, Inc.	*Finger-reach action*
Figure-symbol	Their July 28 quotation of $759.46, less 10%, includes a 3% sales tax.	
Long reaches	My summer activity involved a trip on Route 66--in a convertible, too!	
Fluency	There is no real job security except the security of good workmanship.	
	| 1 | 2 | 3 | 4 | 5 | 6 | 7 | 8 | 9 | 10 | 11 | 12 | 13 | 14 |	

210B: Basic Skill Maintenance (10) *1′ writings on selected ¶s on pages 308–309; force speed*

210C: Production Typing – Letters with Tabulations (35) *if time permits, start over*

Time Schedule

Get ready to type	3′
Timed production	25′
Proofread; compute *g-pram* . .	7′

Problem 1 (*1 cc*) ⟶

Using the date **January 15**, type the letter in modified block style, open punctuation, to:

Mr. J. D. Morgan, Purchasing Agent
Archibald Homes, Inc.
1846 K Street, N. W.
Washington, D. C. 20006

Supply an appropriate salutation and appropriate closing lines. Dictator is **Charles R. Jakob**, who is **Sales Manager**. Address an envelope.

Problem 2 (*1 cc*)

Using the directions of Problem 1, type the second letter shown at the right to:

Mr. Andrew T. Morenci
Kreyling Contracting
Company
1400 E. Madison Street
Charleston, WV 25312

Note postal code abbreviation for state name

Problem 3 (*1 cc*)

Retype Problem 1, but address it to:

Mr. Arnold C. Higgenbotham
1678 Beechwood Avenue
Baltimore, Maryland 21228

List only the first and last items and, since Mr. Higgenbotham is a *retail* customer, change the prices to $49.95 and $18.75, omitting the abbreviation ea. (*Total words: 142*)

Note. As a part of your daily alertness check, supply your initials for reference and an appropriate notation of enclosures, even though these items may not be listed in the closing lines of the problems.

Words

Heading and salutation 27

(¶ 1) We are pleased to quote as follows on the items listed in your 40
letter of January 10: 44

M–2040–1	Colonial 5-Light Chandelier	35.97 ea.	54
M–2054	Spanish Bronze Chandelier	62.70 ea.	62
M–2805	Castillian Foyer Candelabra	59.70 ea.	71
M–4101	Castillian Wall Sconce	26.97 ea.	79
M–4012	"Mother of Pearl" Ceiling Nestle	10.77 ea.	89

(¶ 2) Your interest in our products is appreciated. We hope that we 102
may have the privilege of supplying your requirements. Shipment 115
will be made immediately upon the receipt of your order. (¶ 3) For 127
your convenience a copy of our latest catalog is being mailed to you 141
today in a separate envelope. 147

+ Closing parts and envelope 157/178

Heading and salutation 26

(¶ 1) We are glad to have your letter asking for prices on some of 38
our products. The prices quoted below are F.O.B. Charleston: 51

M-5601-31	Empire Post Lantern	20.97 ea.	59
M-5232-31	Empire Wall Bracket	10.77 ea.	67
M-2635-31	Empire Sphere Pendant	29.97 ea.	75

(¶ 2) We have made frequent shipments to Huntington contractors 87
and will be glad to have an outlet in Charleston. 97
(¶ 3) Upon receipt of your purchase order, we can make immediate 109
shipment by Atlantic Trucking Company to Charlottesville and by 122
Inland Freight to Charleston on terms of 1/10, n/30. 132

+ Closing parts and envelope 142/161

76C: Technique Checkup – Key Stroking (10) *each line twice; 1′ writings on sentences, as time permits*

DO: Check, evaluate, and try to improve your key-stroking techniques as you type the lines.

CHECK

✓ *Curved, upright fingers; wrists low; hands quiet*

Home-Row Keys

jj jhj jag ask fad dad had half glad dash asks flash shall glass flags

add gas; all had hash; all glad lads shall; a lad has had half a glass

All lads and lasses from Dallas just ask sad dads to add cash for gas.

| 1 | 2 | 3 | 4 | 5 | 6 | 7 | 8 | 9 | 10 | 11 | 12 | 13 | 14 |

✓ *Quick, snap finger strokes with quick key release*

Third-Row Keys

aqua wise deed for got hay jug kid old pal try quite poppy typewriters

We wrote it; your typewriter; you were to try to quote it; your quips;

Were you aware that your quips are quite popular with your peer group?

| 1 | 2 | 3 | 4 | 5 | 6 | 7 | 8 | 9 | 10 | 11 | 12 | 13 | 14 |

✓ *Finger-action reaches; low, quiet wrists*

First-Row Keys

zinc six cod five box man lynx zoo view can curved numb number bonanza

five or six names, many men can mix the zinc, a number of men can fix,

Five or six men can line the box with zinc. Nan gave a lynx to a zoo.

| 1 | 2 | 3 | 4 | 5 | 6 | 7 | 8 | 9 | 10 | 11 | 12 | 13 | 14 |

76D: Basic Learnings Recall – Composition at the Typewriter (10)

DO: Number and type a short, but complete sentence answer to each of the following questions. Skip any question you cannot answer, but match answer and question numbers.

1. How many strokes can be typed in a *horizontal* inch when pica type is used? elite type?
2. How many *lines* can be typed in a *vertical* inch on most standard typewriters?
3. When 8½″ x 11″ paper is inserted into the typewriter with the paper guide at 0, what is the center point for a machine with pica type? elite type?
4. How many vertical line spaces are there on a sheet of 8½″ x 11″ paper?
5. How many vertical line spaces are there on a sheet of 8½″ x 5½″ paper?
6. When paper 5½″ wide by 8½″ long is inserted with the left edge at 0 on the scale, what is the horizontal center point for a machine with pica type? elite type?
7. How many vertical line spaces are there on a sheet of 5½″ x 8½″ paper?
8. Where, for most typing, should the paper guide be set on the paper-guide scale?
9. What is the function of the paper-release lever?
10. How many spaces should be added to the right margin to allow for the ringing of the bell?
11. How many blank lines are there between single-spaced lines? double-spaced lines? triple-spaced lines?
12. On 8½″ x 11″ paper, where should the left and right margin stops be set for 1-inch margins: pica type? elite type?

LESSON 209

209A: Conditioning Practice (5) *each line at least three times*

Alphabet; shift	Will Dan have experts make quick flights to Mexico and Brazil in July?	*Quick carriage return*
Figure-symbol	His May 12 letter clearly states, "We can ship 35 #974 lamps @ $8.60."	
Long words	Develop initiative, and familiarize yourself with production routines.	
Fluency	Do your best, and you will learn as you serve and earn as you deserve.	
	| 1 | 2 | 3 | 4 | 5 | 6 | 7 | 8 | 9 | 10 | 11 | 12 | 13 | 14 |	

209B: Basic Skill Maintenance (5) *1′ writings on selected ¶s on pages 308–309; force speed*

209C: Manipulation Preview (10) *Margins: 1½″; SS; indented ¶s; 4 spaces between columns*

Locate the tabulation in the letter of Problem 1, 209D, at the right below. Clear present tab stops; then set new stops for typing the tabulation, using backspace-from-center method. Type ¶ 1, the table, and ¶ 2. If you finish the drill before time is called, retype it.

209D: Production Typing – Letters with Tabulations (30) *if time permits, start over*

Time Schedule	
Get ready to type	3′
Timed production	20′
Proofread; compute *g-pram* . .	7′

Problem 1 (*1 cc*) ⟶

Using the machine adjustments of 209C, type the letter in modified-block style with indented ¶s, mixed punctuation. Address an envelope. Mark your errors.

Alertness Training. Use judgment in arranging the opening and closing lines; also supply needed punctuation.

Words

January 1, 19–– Lowry, Poland & O'Brien Attorneys-at-Law Suite 13
1102 Rand Tower Minneapolis, Minnesota 55402 Gentlemen 24
DELINQUENT ACCOUNTS (¶ 1) As attorneys for Hansen's, Inc., you are 36
requested to institute collection proceedings against the customers 50
whose names are listed below. All addresses are in the city of 62
Minneapolis. 65

Mr. Gary L. Richards	2917 Douglas Avenue	$243.85	75
Mrs. R. B. Stevenson	2521 Ivy Lane	138.96	83
Miss Judith Ames	6402 Laurel Avenue	97.60	92
Mr. J. B. Gregory	3700 East River Road	83.50	101

(¶ 2) The last payment on each of these accounts was made in 112
September. The fifth and final notice in the collection series was 125
mailed to each of these persons at the place of employment. We 138
have given every possible opportunity for them to pay in full or 151
in part what is owed us. (¶ 3) Since we have been unable to get 163
any response from five notices, we ask that you take immediate 176
action to collect the accounts. Sincerely yours Robert G. Flannigan 189
Credit Manager (xx) (167) + *Envelope* 193/211

Problem 2 (*1 cc*) ⟶

Retype Problem 1, using the date **February 1**. Say that all addresses are in the city of St. Paul. Use the substitute delinquent account list given at the right. In ¶ 2 change September to October.

Problem 1, through ¶ 1 65

Mr. Frank W. Hoevel	620 Aurora Avenue	$147.58	75
Mrs. W. B. Locke, Jr.	1681 Edgerton Street	93.60	85
Dr. John E. McCane	3121 Portland Avenue	247.35	94
Mr. Carl J. Meyers	2880 Patton Road	156.20	103
Miss Amanda Riede	101 Sunset Lane	86.00	111

+ *Problem 1, ¶s 2 and 3* 203/221

76E: Straight-Copy Skill Checkup (8) *5′ writing; determine* gwam; *proofread for errors*

All letters are used.

Text	GWAM 1′	GWAM 5′	
It is now time to make a personal inventory of your typewriting	13	3	51
ability. As you find weak points in your typing skill, make a list of	27	5	54
them. The first important step in building your performance is to give	41	8	56
consideration to the way you type, or the form you use as you type. Do	56	11	59
you sit directly in front of your machine in a comfortable, relaxed	69	14	62
position? Do you keep your fingers well curved, strike the keys with	83	17	65
the tips of your fingers, and let only your fingers do the work? Give	98	20	68
attention, too, to the sound of your typing. Are you able at all times	112	22	71
to type with rhythm and continuity?	119	24	72
What are a few of the other elements that are indispensable to good	14	27	75
technique? It is essential to keep the right thumb curved and close to	28	29	78
the space bar in order to space quickly after every word. Realize, also,	43	32	81
that you lose speed if you look away from the copy to the typewriter.	57	35	83
Make the return quickly at the end of every line; start the new line	71	38	86
without a pause. Try to read and type words, rather than typing just	85	41	89
letter by letter. In every lesson, then, make a genuine effort to im-	99	44	92
prove your technique. You will find that, almost like magic, every	112	46	94
refinement you make will lead to a higher skill.	122	48	96

1′ GWAM | 1 | 2 | 3 | 4 | 5 | 6 | 7 | 8 | 9 | 10 | 11 | 12 | 13 | 14 |

5′ GWAM | 1 | 2 | 3 |

76F: Centering Checkup (15)

Problem 1 Center poem, vertically and horizontally. Use a half sheet (8½″ x 5½″), long side up. Double-space all lines, except leave a triple space after the author's name.

Note. Center only the first line of the poem; start other three lines at this same point.

Problem 2 Center poem, vertically and horizontally. Use a half sheet (5½″ x 8½″), short side up. Same centering directions as used for Problem 1.

OUTWITTED

by

Edwin Markham

He drew a circle that shut me out--
Heretic, rebel, a thing to flout.
But Love and I had the wit to win:
We drew a circle that took him in!

	GWAM 1'	GWAM 5'

As you start from the room, you notice a member of your family 13 52
communicating by satelite facilities with a favorite aunt in Paris. 26 55
They are conferring visually and by written exchange, as well as by 40 57
voice. The aunt is transmitting a copy of a new French gourmet recipe. 55 60
You look at her again; she certainly never seems to age much; she does 69 63
not look a day older than her picture twenty years ago when she was 82 66
fifty. You retreat in a happy and productive mood, aided not only by 96 69
the very tantalizing flavor of the kelp seaweed at breakfast but also by 111 71
the weather control and those mood adjusters, designed especially for you. 126 74

After you accept your briefcase from the robot, you step through 13 77
the door of your plastic house. The robot then throws away the dishes 27 80
and goes to help other members of the family. You see the auto-door 41 83
close after you, and you quickly board the outdoor escalator to the 55 85
transportation that you will need for today. Since another member of 69 88
the family must have the air hovercraft, you might travel at a thousand 83 91
miles an hour by train or use the car on the underground automated 96 94
highway. Then, since your agenda indicated that you have a meeting on 111 97
another continent in an hour, you may fly with several hundred others 125 99
by supersonic plane or else go by ballistic rocket. Junior will have 139 102
to use individual propulsion to get to the urban school center. 151 105

It's a good thing your work schedule is only four hours daily for 13 107
three days a week. You didn't sleep quite your formula-guided quota of 28 110
hours last night because of viewing with your family yesterday the new 42 113
programs at the automated library of the urban school center. Also, you 56 116
want time to use the learning machine this afternoon to review history 71 119
of the days when the big cities were not closed in and were not weather 85 122
and aroma adjusted. Tomorrow you have a big international committee 99 124
meeting on economic problems. The next day you will be flying with 113 127
Junior's planet science group on a field trip to the moon by way of the 127 130
latest permanent space station. 133 131

Is the world described here one of science fiction? Possibly some 13 134
of it, but many of these ideas are in planning stages and some are 27 137
almost realities today. Tomorrow's world will doubtless be vastly 40 139
different from the one we inhabit now. There appears to be no end to 54 142
the variety of improvements the human mind can conceive. These changes 69 145
are not to be feared, however; they are for our benefit. To use and to 83 149
help develop them wisely, an individual tomorrow will need, even more 97 151
than is true today, to seek opportunities to learn. But also, chances 111 154
to learn and to select a vocation will be greater than ever, and there 125 156
is need for you. 129 157

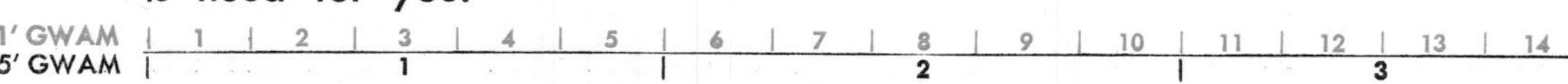

(To compute 10' nwam from 5' rate, divide 5' gwam by 2; then subtract 1 for each error.)

LESSON 77

77A: Conditioning Practice (5) *each line three times (as directed on page 118)*

Alphabet	Five kind doctors gazed jubilantly at the new hospital annex marquees.	*Fingers upright*
Figure	The inventory includes 96 pamphlets, 1,827 books, and 3,450 magazines.	
Adjacent key	That popular but wise aquanaut was not careless in water sports.	
Speed	The eight girls wish to go with me when I pay the firm for their work.	
	| 1 | 2 | 3 | 4 | 5 | 6 | 7 | 8 | 9 | 10 | 11 | 12 | 13 | 14 |	

77B: Skill Transfer Checkup – Statistical Copy (15)

1. **Type** a 5′ writing using the ¶s of 76E, page 120. Proofread; determine *gwam*.

   Goal: To exceed the rate you made when typing the paragraphs previously.

2. **Type** a 5′ writing on the statistical copy below. Proofread; determine *gwam*.
3. **Compute** *% of transfer*: statistical-copy rate divided by straight-copy rate.

All numbers are used.

	GWAM 1′	5′	
In a recent study of first-year beginning high school typing stu-	13	3	54
dents, the lowest quarter (0–25%) of a random sample of 3,072 students	27	5	57
typed 33 words a minute or less with 10 or more errors on a 5-minute	41	8	60
straight-copy writing of average difficulty. The top quarter (76–100%)	55	11	63
wrote 45 or more words a minute with from 0 to 3 errors. Some students	70	14	66
in this group wrote at rates of 80–90 words a minute. The average rate	84	17	69
was 38.5 words a minute with 7.8 errors. The rates on statistical copy	98	20	72
(again, on a 5-minute writing) ranged from a low of 17 words a minute	112	22	74
to more than 58 words a minute, with an average rate of 34.5 words a	126	25	77
minute with 7.5 errors.	131	26	78

	GWAM 1′	5′	
The rates on long writings varied according to the kind of copy.	13	29	81
As a case in point, on a 25-minute letter production writing (sample of	28	32	84
2,568 students), the lowest 25 percent wrote 21 words a minute or less	42	35	86
with 30 or more errors. The top 25 percent wrote 31 or more words a	56	37	89
minute with 0 to 13 errors. The mean rate was 25.2 words a minute with	70	40	92
23.5 errors. On a 15-minute, 3-column tabulation writing (sample of	84	43	95
2,639 students), the lowest 25 percent wrote 17 words a minute or less	98	46	98
with 19 or more errors; the top 25 percent wrote 25 or more words a	112	49	100
minute with 0 to 7 errors. The average rate was 20.7 words a minute	126	51	103
with 14.8 errors.	129	52	104

1′ GWAM \| 1 \| 2 \| 3 \| 4 \| 5 \| 6 \| 7 \| 8 \| 9 \| 10 \| 11 \| 12 \| 13 \| 14 \|
5′ GWAM \| 1 \| 2 \| 3 \|

Unit 36 | Lessons 208-214

Letters and Memorandums with Tabulations

LESSON 208

208A: Conditioning Practice (5) *each line at least three times*

Alphabet	I quickly organized a complex keyboard review for Jan Shimson to type.	*Quick, snap stroke*
Figure-symbol	A "#" can mean "pounds"; as, "Send 2,354# of #7698 sand on August 10."	
Long words	Electronic data processing, we must realize, demands extreme accuracy.	
Fluency	You can't stand still if you want to go places—you have to get going.	
	| 1 | 2 | 3 | 4 | 5 | 6 | 7 | 8 | 9 | 10 | 11 | 12 | 13 | 14 |	

208B: Skill Comparison (10) *1' comparison writings; practice slowest lines; repeat*

Easy	The main problem given the chairman was to make a profit for the firm.
Average	Their group was interested in the increases in federal mortgage rates.
Difficult	Regional experts examined declarations referring to excessive actions.
	| 1 | 2 | 3 | 4 | 5 | 6 | 7 | 8 | 9 | 10 | 11 | 12 | 13 | 14 |

208C: Growth Index (15) *10' writing on ¶s below and on page 309; determine* nwam

208D: Building Speed and Accuracy (20) *5' writings on the ¶s below and on page 309*

All letters are used.

	GWAM 1'	5'
There appears to be no end to the variety of discoveries and of	13	3
improvements that flow with increasing volume and speed from the minds	27	5
of mankind. Such changes tax the imagination of any who would try to	41	8
predict the manner of our lives five years from now or ten years from	55	11
now. To attempt to forecast life in fifty years or one hundred years	69	14
would truly put one "out on a limb." The world of work, the nature of	83	17
learning, the patterns of daily living, and our recreational activities	98	20
will be vastly different, we hear, even within a decade. Try to imagine	112	22
a tomorrow which you might experience about fifty years from today.	126	25
A computer-robot awakens you in a manner designed by your need for	13	28
news, music, or soothing sounds for a morning hater, or a roar for any	28	31
who might want to sleep longer. You go through the weather-adjusted	41	33
room into your morning shower, already set for a friendly warmth. The	56	36
robot selects and makes ready for you your synthetic apparel proper for	70	39
the day. It then draws into the house a facsimile-size morning paper,	84	42
places it near your breakfast service, and adjusts the no-bulb light-	98	45
ing. As you have your breakfast—ready in one second—you notice your	112	48
schedule for the day, shown by automation.	121	49

(Continued)

1' GWAM | 1 | 2 | 3 | 4 | 5 | 6 | 7 | 8 | 9 | 10 | 11 | 12 | 13 | 14 |
5' GWAM | 1 | 2 | 3 |

77C: Technique Checkup – Key Stroking (8) *each line twice; 1′ writings on sentences, as time permits*

DO: Check, evaluate, and try to improve your key-stroking techniques as you type the lines.

CHECK

✓ Finger-action reaches; quick snap stroke

First- and Third-Row Keys

quay azure wax economy rivet better many imply over quiz union minimum

He implied that many of the union men were employed at a minimum rate.

| 1 | 2 | 3 | 4 | 5 | 6 | 7 | 8 | 9 | 10 | 11 | 12 | 13 | 14 |

✓ Curved, upright fingers; wrists low; hands quiet

Third and Fourth Fingers

Aza Pap saw six plump polo ponies eating kumquats near the plum patch.

Azaleas, on poles in the plaza, slowly overlapped all extra low walls.

| 1 | 2 | 3 | 4 | 5 | 6 | 7 | 8 | 9 | 10 | 11 | 12 | 13 | 14 |

✓ Uniform key stroke; variable rhythm

Double Letters

A full-blooded Indian princess dazzled onlookers at all embassy balls.

Three little kittens tossed and rolled a cotton ball across the floor.

| 1 | 2 | 3 | 4 | 5 | 6 | 7 | 8 | 9 | 10 | 11 | 12 | 13 | 14 |

✓ Finger-action reach; hands quiet

Hyphen Key

They saw jack-in-the-pulpits and forget-me-nots near the right-of-way.

| 1 | 2 | 3 | 4 | 5 | 6 | 7 | 8 | 9 | 10 | 11 | 12 | 13 | 14 |

77D: Skill Application Inventory – Outline and Theme (22)

Problem 1: Outline in Unarranged Form

Full sheet	*Center heading*
60-space line	*Arrange in correct outline form*
1½-inch top margin	*Reference (if needed): page 106*

IMPORTANT TYPEWRITING TECHNIQUE
AND MOTION PATTERNS

I. Stroking Technique
A. Proper key stroke
1. Use quick, snap stroke; release key quickly
2. Strike key with fingertip; keep stroking action in fingers
3. Use uniform stroking pressure
B. Finger position
1. Keep fingers curved and close to keys
2. Keep fingers in upright position
3. Hold hands and arms quiet; wrists low and relaxed
II. Essential Motion Patterns
A. Control of carriage return
1. Throw or return carriage quickly at end of line; on manual machine use quick, flick-of-wrist motion
2. Start new line quickly
B. Control of shift keys
1. Reach to shift key with little finger; keep other fingers in typing position
2. Push shift key all the way down before striking letter key

C. Control of space bar
1. Keep right thumb curved and close to space bar
2. Strike space bar with quick, down-and-in motion (toward palm); release quickly
3. Make spacing stroke part of word; start next word without a pause or break

D. Other essential patterns
1. Keep fingers close to keys; avoid bouncing hands and arms
2. Type with continuity and rhythm; avoid breaks or pauses
3. Keep eyes on copy to be typed
4. Read copy properly for anticipation of stroking patterns

(Please turn to page 123 for Problem 2.)

Problem 1: AMS Simplified Letter

Words

May 3, 19-- Mrs. Melvin C. Watson 746 8
Third Street, Newport News, Virginia 23610 16
A THOR QUESTIONNAIRE (¶ 1) Will you do us a 24
favor? It is extremely important for us to know 34
how pleased you are with your new Thor Dryer. 43
Our designers and engineers are always seek- 52
ing ways to please you, the consumer, by im- 60
proving our product. You can help us help you 70
by telling us on the enclosed questionnaire what 80
you like and what you don't like about the Thor 89
Dryer. (¶ 2) This survey is completely anony- 97
mous and confidential. Your name was drawn at 106
random from the customer warranties on file in 116
our office by an independent research firm, 125
Hodges Associates. We do not know the iden- 133
tity of any person being questioned nor will 142
Hodges Associates tell us unless you ask them 151
to do so. Your reply is of vital importance, 161
though. The questionnaire has been sent to a 170
small sample of Thor owners and the accuracy 179
of the findings depends upon a 100 percent 187
return. (¶ 3) Please answer your questionnaire 196
now. It will only take a few minutes. Most of 205
the questions can be answered with a simple 214
check mark. A stamped, addressed envelope is 223
enclosed for your convenience in returning the 233
questionnaire. (¶ 4) We shall appreciate your 241
cooperation. CLIFTON C. ENGLESON – GENERAL 250
MANAGER (xx) Enclosure (219) + *Envelope* 254/267

Problem 2: Letter with Inverted ¶s

Words

May 3, 19-- Mr. Robert E. Slenker 3025 8
Guilford Street Greensboro, North Carolina 16
27409 Dear Mr. Slenker (¶ 1) APEX CREDIT 24
CARDS are passports to the finest things in life. 34
You don't need to carry large amounts of cash 43
when you have an Apex Credit Card nor do you 52
need any other credit card. With a multipurpose 62
Apex Credit Card, you can get practically any- 71
thing you need from soup to nuts and bolts! You 81
can throw away all those single-purpose credit 90
cards that have been cluttering your purse or 99
wallet when you get your Apex Credit Card. 108
(¶ 2) DO you plan to travel? With an Apex 115
Credit Card you can charge your accommoda- 124
tions, your meals, your gas, and even your sou- 133
venirs! Apex Credit Cards are honored at more 142
service stations, hotels, motels, shops, and res- 152

Words

taurants than any other credit card at home or 161
abroad. Flowers, theater tickets, airline tickets, 171
and gifts are just a few of the purchases you can 181
make with an Apex Credit Card. If, by chance, 191
you should need cash, you will have no diffi- 200
culty cashing a check with your Apex Credit 208
Card, since we guarantee your personal checks. 218
(¶ 3) MORE and more people are taking advan- 225
tage of the convenience and personalized ser- 234
vice that an Apex Credit Card provides. Why 243
don't you join them and enjoy the finest things 253
in life? Just fill out the enclosed application and 263
mail it today. You'll be glad you did. Cordially 274
yours James T. Harrison Director of Member- 282
ships (xx) Enclosure (250) + *Envelope* 286/301

Problem 3: Letter with Side Headings

Words

May 4, 19-- Mr. Martin Boles 1604 Avondale 9
Road Ridley Park, Pennsylvania 19078 Dear 17
Mr. Boles: (¶ 1) Enjoy a Seaside Vacation Enjoy 30
a memorable vacation by the sea at the STAR- 39
BOARD HOTEL on the boardwalk in Ocean Point, 48
New Jersey. Our efforts are devoted to provid- 57
ing true hospitality so that you may have an 66
enjoyable stay in a world of pleasure at the 75
ocean's edge. (¶ 2) Relax in Luxury Accommo- 86
dations at the STARBOARD HOTEL were designed 95
for gracious living. All rooms feature such con- 104
veniences as color television, large picture win- 114
dows, and air conditioning. Dining is delightful 124
in our BAROQUE ROOM overlooking the ocean. 133
Sauna baths, a heated swimming pool, and free 142
cabanas on our private beach are but a few of 151
the many "extras" we offer to make your visit 160
more enjoyable. (¶ 3) Try Fun Variety Ocean 171
Point offers recreation for every member of the 181
family. You can golf, play tennis, go deep-sea 190
fishing, bicycle on the boardwalk, or enjoy an 200
invigorating swim in the ocean. If this sounds 209
too energetic, you can just relax on a beach or 219
browse through the interesting shops on the 228
boardwalk. (¶ 4) Write now The enclosed color 236
brochure of the STARBOARD HOTEL includes infor- 245
mation on our rates and tells of our exciting 254
midweek specials for this season. Just fill out the 265
reservation application and you will have em- 274
barked on a new adventure in fun. Cordially 283
yours, Lewis M. Charles, General Manager (xx) 292
Enclosure (261) 293
+ *Envelope* 307

Problem 2: Arranging Material in Theme Form

Full sheet *60-space line*	*¶ indention: 5*	*Single-space* *1½" top margin*

Note. *Double-space after last line and start author's name at center point.*

	Words
Heading: I BELIEVE (¶ 1) I believe in the supreme	7
worth of the individual and in his right to life,	17
liberty, and the pursuit of happiness. (¶ 2) I be-	26
lieve that every right implies a responsibility;	36
every opportunity, an obligation; every posses-	45
sion, a duty. (¶ 3) I believe that the law was	54
made for man and not man for the law; that	62
government is the servant of the people and not	72
their master. (¶ 4) I believe in the dignity of	81
labor, whether with head or hand; that the world	90
owes no man a living but that it owes every man	100
an opportunity to make a living. (¶ 5) I believe	109
that thrift is essential to well-ordered living and	119
that economy is a prime requisite of a sound	128
financial structure, whether in government, busi-	138
ness, or personal affairs. (¶ 6) I believe that	147
truth and justice are fundamental to an enduring	156
social order. (¶ 7) I believe in the sacredness of	166
a promise, that a man's word should be as good	175
as his bond; that character—not wealth or	184
power or position—is of supreme worth. (¶ 8)	192
I believe that the rendering of useful service is	202
the common duty of mankind and that only in	211
the purifying fire of sacrifice is the dross of	220
selfishness consumed and the greatness of the	229
human soul set free. (¶ 9) I believe in an all-	238
wise and all-loving God, named by whatever	246
name, and that the individual's highest fulfill-	256
ment, greatest happiness, and widest usefulness	266
are to be found in living in harmony with His	275
will. (¶ 10) I believe that love is the greatest	283
thing in the world; that it alone can overcome	293
hate; that right can and will triumph over might. |	303
—John D. Rockefeller, Jr.	308

LESSON 78

78A: Conditioning Practice (5) *each line three times*

Alphabet	Fools won't likely adopt the unique economizing objectives of experts.	*Finger-action reaches*
Figure	I may buy 15 jackets, 289 blankets, 74 kits, 360 lamps, and 110 tires.	
Shift key	J. C. McNeil, Vice President of Roxy's, Inc., is now in New York City.	
Speed	They wish to go to the city with the chairman for the profit due them.	
	| 1 | 2 | 3 | 4 | 5 | 6 | 7 | 8 | 9 | 10 | 11 | 12 | 13 | 14 |	

78B: Technique Checkup – Control of Operative Parts (8) *each line three times*

DO: Check, evaluate, and try to improve your key-stroking techniques as you type the lines.

CHECK

Space-Bar Control

✓ *Quick, down-and-in motion with thumb*

and the and the (*repeat for full line; space quickly and keep carriage moving*)

Many a lovely maiden may dream of a wealthy man of charm and chivalry.

Shift-Key Control

✓ *Little finger reach; hands quiet*

Mr. Richard W. Parkhearst is employed by H. B. Richardson and Company.

J. B. Lane may visit Chicago, New York, Boston, New Haven, and Albany.

Carriage Return (*Manual: Use quick, flick-of-wrist motion; keep eyes on copy.*)

✓ *Quick return and start of line*

TAB: center + 10

Return the carriage quickly

and start the new line. —Tab→ (*Repeat as many times as time permits.*)

LESSON 206

206A: Conditioning Practice (5) *each line at least three times*

Alphabet	Jan Waxler memorized her part quickly, but Frank is having difficulty.	Finger action; quiet hands
Figure	As of February 5, membership increased 43,896 to a total of 1,022,798.	
Figure-symbol	Brent's Order #3970–Y (dated 4/18/67) was shipped by Z & L on March 2.	
Fluency	Do you know which of us will help the chairman make the special audit?	

| 1 | 2 | 3 | 4 | 5 | 6 | 7 | 8 | 9 | 10 | 11 | 12 | 13 | 14 |

206B: Building Speed and Accuracy (7)

Type a 5′ writing on the ¶s on pages 299 and 300.

206C: Sustained Production on Business Letters with Special Features (38)

Time Schedule	
Get ready to type	4′
Timed production	30′
Proofread; compute *n-pram*	4′

Arrange supplies. Make a list of the problems at the right and check them off as you complete them. Type for 30′, following instructions for each problem typed. Correct errors as you type. If you finish before time is called, start over. Mark uncorrected errors. Compute *n-pram.*

Page 302, 203C, Problem 3
Page 304, 204C, Problem 3
Page 305, 205C, Problem 2
Page 302, 203C, Problem 2
Page 303, 204C, Problem 2

Turn in problems arranged in the order in which they are listed.

LESSON 207

207A: Conditioning Practice (5) *each line at least three times*

Alphabet	Did Jack Quill or Rex Maby win a TV set as first prize in the drawing?	Quiet hands
Figure	I believe that between 1968 and 1970 we will need 2,534 new employees.	
Figure-symbol	The profit in 1966 was $54,728; it was $62,937 in 1967––a rise of 15%.	
Fluency	Does he plan to send the original copy to us by the end of this month?	

| 1 | 2 | 3 | 4 | 5 | 6 | 7 | 8 | 9 | 10 | 11 | 12 | 13 | 14 |

207B: Special Feature Letters Production Measurement (45)

Arrange supplies. Type the three problems on page 307 for 30′ when directed to begin. Make 1 cc and address an envelope for each. Correct errors as you type. If time permits, start over. Mark uncorrected errors. Compute *n-pram.*

Time Schedule	
Get ready to type	7′
Timed production	30′
Proofread; compute *n-pram*	8′

78C: Skill Transfer Checkup (15) *(Repeat 77B, page 121. Goal: Increased speed.)*

78D: Skill Application Inventory – Letters (22)

Problem 1: Personal Letter in Unarranged Form

Modified block style	*Mixed punctuation*
50-space line	*Reference: page 86*

Type the current date on Line 18, followed by 3 blank lines. Address an envelope.

	Words
(Current date) | *Letter address:* Director of Ad-	6
missions | University of California | 405 Hilgard	15
Avenue | Los Angeles, California 90024 | Dear	24
Sir: | (¶ 1) I am a sophomore at Birmingham	31
High School. It is | my hope to qualify for	40
admission to UCLA as a pre- | law student. |	48
(¶ 2) Are there any special courses that I must	56
take dur- | ing the next two years in order to	65
meet the entrance | requirements for prelaw	73
students? I plan to follow | the regular academic	83
program of our school, but I | also hope to take	92
some courses in business education. | (¶ 3) Any	101
information that you can give me will be very |	110
much appreciated. | Sincerely yours, | Jeffrey J.	119
Geren	120/140

Problem 2: Business Letter in Unarranged Form

Modified block style	*Mixed punctuation*
50-space line	*Reference: page 86*

Type the current date on Line 16, the address 3 blank lines below. Address an envelope.

	Words
Mr. Jeffrey J. Geren | 5145 Collett Avenue |	11
Encino, California 91316 | Dear Mr. Geren:	20
(¶ 1) I am glad to learn of your interest in	28
UCLA. I shall try to answer the questions you	37
raised in your letter. (¶ 2) To qualify for ad-	45
mission to UCLA, you must be a high school	54
graduate with at least a "B" average in all your	63
academic courses. In addition, you must have	73
completed the following program: 2 years of a	82
foreign language; 2 years of mathematics (alge-	91
bra and geometry, for example); 1 year of	100
American history; 3 years of English; 1 year of	109
a laboratory science taken in either the 11th or	119
12th grade; and 1 additional year's course in	128
mathematics, language, or science. (¶ 3) I would	137
recommend, too, that you take at least one year	146
of typewriting. You will find the typewriter an	156
invaluable aid in college. (¶ 4) I shall look for-	165
ward to meeting you when you enroll at UCLA. |	174
Sincerely yours, | J. W. Robson | Admissions	182
Officer | *(Use your initials for reference.)*	183/196

LESSON 79

79A: Conditioning Practice (5) *each line three times*

Alphabet	Quick, lively jazz and wailful blues excite the progressive music fan.	*Quick,*
Figure	Today he typed 40 letters, 15 reports, 369 orders, and 278 statements.	*snap*
Continuity	a;sldkfj *(Repeat this pattern for a full line without spacing; use quick, snappy strokes.)*	*stroke*
Speed	When he paid for the land, he also signed the audit form for the firm.	
	| 1 | 2 | 3 | 4 | 5 | 6 | 7 | 8 | 9 | 10 | 11 | 12 | 13 | 14 |	

79B: Technique Checkup – Response Patterns (High-Frequency Words) (7) *each line three times*

CHECK: ✓ *Fingers upright and close to keys* ✓ *Quick, finger action* ✓ *Hands and arms quiet*

Stroke response	in we on be no as up at you are dear date best only were was get state
Word response	of to is it or by if us an do so me the and for may but with they them
One-hand	Are you able to state only a best date for a review of the area cases?
Balanced-hand	If it is so, then I may go with them and make them do the work for us.
Variable rhythm	and the, and the date, for the case, after the fact, state the problem

205C: Typing Letters with Side Headings (40)

Preview side-heading letter style by reading the information in the Problem 1 letter and studying the illustration at the right. Then type the three side-heading style letters for 30′ when directed to begin. If time permits, start over. Mark errors. Compute *g-pram*.

Time Schedule	
Study problem; get ready . . .	7′
Timed production	30′
Proofread; compute *g-pram* . .	3′

Problem 1 *Letter with side headings* *1 cc*
Modified block, open *Envelope*

Words
April 24, 19–– Miss Ann T. Barry Brooks Sec- 9
retarial School 173 Ross Boulevard Bangor, 17
Maine 04401 Dear Miss Barry (¶ 1) Empha- 25
size Key Words A special letter style used 36
seldom except in sales promotion correspondence 46
is the letter with side headings. Although side 56
headings may be used with any basic letter style, 66
they are most frequently used with the modified 75
block style. In this side-heading letter style, key 86
words or phrases designed to catch the attention 96
of the reader are placed to the left of the para- 105
graphs to which they relate. These key words 115
may be underlined or typed in all capitals or in 124
color for special emphasis. Each side heading is 134
aligned horizontally with the first line of the 144
paragraph to which it applies. If the side head- 154
ing requires more than ten spaces, two or more 163
lines may be used for it. (¶ 2) Use One-Inch 173
Margins The side headings are usually consid- 184
ered part of the body of the letter in determining 194
side margins for the letter. With standard-size 204
paper, side margins should be at least one inch. 214
The date line, as in other letter styles, is placed 224
according to letter length. (¶ 3) Set Left Margin 236
To determine the starting point for the inside 245
address and body of the letter, space in from the 255
one-inch left margin the number of strokes re- 264
quired for the longest side heading, plus three 274
spaces. Set the margin stop at this point to type 284
the inside address and body. Move outside the 294
margin stop to the one-inch margin position to fill 304
in the side headings. (¶ 4) Try It Actually, typ- 314
ing a letter with side headings is not difficult. Try 325
it yourself to see how easy it is. Sincerely yours 335
Rose M. Taylor Communications Consultant (xx) 344
(309) + *Envelope* 360

HOMAN & HARDY
ADVERTISING
4222 Arlington Avenue
Lincoln, Nebraska 68502
hh

April 24, 19--

Miss Ann T. Barry
Brooks Secretarial School
173 Ross Boulevard
Bangor, Maine 04401

Dear Miss Barry

Emphasize Key Words — A special letter style used seldom except in sales promotion correspondence is the letter with side headings. Although side headings may be used with any basic letter style, they are most frequently used with the modified block style. In this side-heading letter style, key words or phrases designed to catch the attention of the reader are placed to the left of the paragraphs to which they relate. These key words may be underlined or typed in all capitals or in color for special emphasis. Each side heading is aligned horizontally with the first line of the paragraph to which it applies. If the side heading requires more than ten spaces, two or more lines may be used for it.

Use One-Inch Margins — The side headings are usually considered part of the body of the letter in determining side margins for the letter. With standard-size paper, side margins should be at least one inch. The date line, as in other letter styles, is placed according to letter length.

Set Left Margin — To determine the starting point for the inside address and body of the letter, space in from the one-inch left margin the number of strokes required for the longest side heading, plus three spaces. Set the margin stop at this point to type the inside address and body. Move outside the margin stop to the one-inch margin position to fill in the side headings.

Try It — Actually, typing a letter with side headings is not difficult. Try it yourself to see how easy it is.

Sincerely yours

Rose M. Taylor
Communications Consultant

ao

LETTER WITH SIDE HEADINGS

Problem 2 *Letter with side headings in caps* *1 cc*
Modified block, mixed *Envelope*

Words
April 10, 19–– Miss Patricia Conley 701 Pine 9
Drive Dallas, Texas 75209 Dear Miss Conley 18
(¶ 1) SURE-CHIC! Get in the swing of spring with 27
the latest fashions from Julie Lane. Our show- 36
room is ablaze with new season splendor for 45
discerning fashionables. (¶ 2) POW-COLORS! 52
Catch the action in gay-mood knits, chic prom- 61
enade suits, or gay casuals. Rival the sun in 71
colors of hot pink, Capri blue, or golden apricot. 81
We have the styles and colors to match any occa- 91
sion or mood. (¶ 3) GO-FASHIONS! See our 98
formals for that "special" event, our casuals for 108
just relaxing, our globe-trotter styles for travel. 118
Get in the swim with our seaside styles or have 128
fun in the sun in our lively playtime coolers. 138
Come to Julie Lane and add a new dimension 146
to your life this summer! Fashionably yours 155
Myra B. Massingale Fashion Consultant (xx) 163
(133) + *Envelope* 175

Problem 3

Type the letter of Problem 2 to **Miss Susan Keil 3529 Maple Street Dallas, Texas 75213**

(*Words: 11*)

79C: Skill Transfer Checkup – Rough Draft (15)

1. **Type** a 5′ writing using the paragraphs of 76E, page 120. Proofread; determine *gwam*.

   Goal: To type with a minimum of errors. Do this by starting slowly and typing with continuity.

2. **Type** a 5′ writing on the rough-draft copy below. Proofread; determine *gwam*.
3. **Compute** *% of transfer*: rough-draft copy rate divided by straight-copy rate.

CORRECTION SYMBOLS					
	¶ Paragraph	^ Insert	⁀ Close up	# Space	Transpose
	] Indent	≡ Capitalize	lc Lower case	Delete	

	GWAM 1′	5′	
in the business office			
Some]copy that you type ^ may be in rough-draft form, similar	17	3	57
to this copy. the copy will con⁀tain many kinds of correc-	28	6	59
In some cases,			
tions which usually will be handwritten. ^ These corrcetions	43	9	62
may be difficult to read they as may have been hurriedly	55	11	64
busy *as he studies and revises the copy.*			
written by a ~~business~~ person. Often, too, your employer may	73	15	68
or report			
aks you to type a letter ^ in rough form. When this request	87	17	71
is made, your empl⁀oyer maybe in a rush for the rough co⁀py;	99	20	73
therefore, he may tell you to strike-over or x-out any errors	111	22	75
you make. *If readable, the copy is satisfactory for use.*	123	25	78
The employer then uses the rough copy as a way to ~~study~~	10	27	80
or report.			
~~and~~ evaluate the content of the letter. He will make many	23	29	82
handwritten			
^ changes and other corrctions. When thecorrected rough draft	51	35	88
is returned to you, you will be expectd to make the correc-	63	37	90
As you type from this rough draft,			
tions indicated. ^ You will need to read the copy carefully	82	41	94
tobe sure you understand all corrections and to be sure that	94	43	97
draft			
the corrected ~~copy~~ makes good sense. As a final step, you	106	46	99
will need to proofread carefully the final draft that you	118	48	101
prepare from the rough draft. *When this has been done,*	129	50	104
before he returns the copy to you to be typed in its final form.			
the copy is ready to be submitted to your employer	139	52	106
for his final approval.	144	53	106

Words

of your car's spark plugs, points, carburetor, and 132
fan belt. We will also clean your motor. When 141
we finish, your motor will sound and look almost 151
like new. (¶ 3) BEST yet, we promise you one- 159
day service. You can bring your car in for a 169
tune-up any time before 10 a.m. and we will have 178
it ready for you by 4 p.m. Better still, let us 188
pick up your car in the morning and return it to 198
you in the evening. There is no extra charge 207
for this service. For pickup, just call 472–3916 217
the day before you want service. (¶ 4) SERVICE 226
has been our specialty for many years. Won't 235
you give us an opportunity to show you what 243
we can do for you and your car? Call us today. 253
We promise you won't be sorry. Sincerely 262
yours Michael A. Tompkins, Service Manager 270
(xx) (239) + *Envelope* 271/284

Problem 3 *Inverted ¶ letter, mixed punctuation* *1 cc*
Be alert to punctuation and date *Envelope*

Words

Mrs. Norman C. Nicholson 1562 Orchard Road 12
Charleston, South Carolina 29408 Dear Mrs. 20
Nicholson (¶ 1) BONNYMADE, specialists in syn- 28
thetic fabrics, offers you the world's largest se- 38
lection of draperies. The biggest department store 48

Words

could not duplicate the selection of sizes, styles, 59
and colors we offer. What's more, you save 68
money by buying direct from the manufacturer. 77
Since there is no middleman to add to the cost, 87
you can save up to 60 percent! (¶ 2) DRAPERIES 95
of the finest fabrics in solids, patterns, brocades, 106
boucles, or overall prints can be yours for the 115
lowest price you will find anywhere. We guar- 124
antee that we do have the exact size, color, and 134
texture to solve any decorating problem you 143
may have. (¶ 3) ARE you skeptical? Glance 151
through the colorful brochure enclosed. See for 160
yourself the wide variety of colors, sizes, and 170
fabrics we have to offer. The prices will prove 180
that BONNYMADE offers you a better value at 189
lower costs than you can get from any store. 198
(¶ 4) BEST of all, you send no cash with your 206
order. Select draperies in the size, color, and 215
texture to match your decor, mail your order, 225
and we will send your draperies immediately. 234
You may pay for them in four installments at no 243
extra charge. Don't miss out on this golden 252
opportunity to dress up every room in your 261
house. Send your order today. Sincerely yours 271
Dorothy Sue Jackson Decorator Coordinator 280
(xx) Enclosure (246) + *Envelope* 282/297

LESSON 205

205A: Conditioning Practice ⑤ *each line at least three times*

Alphabet	If Paul Hixon adjusts it, I believe we can energize my rocket quickly.	*Rhythmic stroking*
Figure	On May 14, 2,903 men enrolled; on May 15, 1,876; and on May 16, 1,479.	
Figure-symbol	She bought 1,320 units @ 60¢ ($792) and 1,940 units @ 57¢ ($1,105.80).	
Fluency	Do you know that they plan to order more stock for their special sale?	
	| 1 | 2 | 3 | 4 | 5 | 6 | 7 | 8 | 9 | 10 | 11 | 12 | 13 | 14 |	

205B: Technique Refinement ⑤ *each line at least three times*

Double letter	The committee will meet in his office next week to discuss the matter.
Shift key	Didn't Jen, Sue, Roy, and Hal attend the FBLA meeting at Tampa in May?
Long words	Profit maximization could lead to misrepresentation and malproduction.
Speed	Did she say that both men may go to work today if they sign the forms?
	| 1 | 2 | 3 | 4 | 5 | 6 | 7 | 8 | 9 | 10 | 11 | 12 | 13 | 14 |

79D: Skill Application Inventory – Tabulation (23)

Problem 1: Typing a Tabulation from Semiarranged Copy

Full sheet
Reading position
Heading lines properly spaced
Double-space data of columns
6 spaces between columns

Each figure is used a minimum of 10 times.

W. & J. SLOANE COMPANY

DS

Outstanding Accounts

TS

			Words
	W. & J. SLOANE COMPANY		5
	Outstanding Accounts		9
J. Kay Baird	434 W. 120 Street	$110.85	17
Sylvia Barrett	1739 Eastern Avenue	175.00	25
Lloyd Bartholome	2689 Mar Vista Drive	65.75	34
Colette Berman	23649 Thurston Circle	74.82	42
Margaret Halm	8366 Balboa Avenue	95.25	50
George Hammer	390 Riverside Drive	78.45	58
Jon Kauffer	4193 Sixth Street	170.62	66
Emmett Minski	8410 Winton Place	92.36	73
Ray Schroeder	780 Ocean Front Drive	59.82	82
John Seymour	3674 New Rochelle Lane	156.72	90
Rosalyn Solon	3489 Eighth Avenue	45.10	98
Gloria Wilson	2397 E. Phoenix Road	68.15	106

Problem 2: Typing a Tabulation from Semiarranged Copy

Retype Problem 1 with these changes:

Half sheet
Center vertically
Heading lines properly spaced
Single-space data of columns
10 spaces between columns

LESSON 80

80A: Conditioning Practice (5) *each line three times*

Uniform key stroke

Alphabet The queen and bogus knights vied with extra joy and zeal for crumpets.

Figure In 1967, 583 new employees were added. Read pages 20, 42, 92, and 98.

Double letters Lesson by lesson, the necessary effort will help you boost your speed.

Speed She may go with them to the town by the lake to do work for the widow.

| 1 | 2 | 3 | 4 | 5 | 6 | 7 | 8 | 9 | 10 | 11 | 12 | 13 | 14 |

80B: Technique Checkup – Number Reaches (5) *each line twice*

Each figure used a minimum of 15 times.

CHECK	✓ Fingers well curved ✓ Quick, snap stroke	✓ Finger-reach action ✓ Carriage kept moving	✓ Hands quiet ✓ Wrists low

1 10 12 23 34 45 56 67 78 89 90 19 98 87 76 65 54 43 32 20 26 37 48 50

11 127 384 651 590 930 846 727 263 485 190 564 372 139 805 204 678 901

1231 2342 3453 4564 5675 6786 7897 8908 9019 0120 9203 8465 9503 29576

204C: Typing Letters with Inverted Paragraphs (38)

Preview inverted ¶ letter style by reading the information in the Problem 1 letter and studying the illustration at the right. Then type the three inverted ¶ style letters for 25′ when directed to begin. If time permits, start over. Mark errors. Compute *g-pram*.

Time Schedule	
Study problem; get ready . . .	7′
Timed problem production . . .	25′
Proofread; compute *g-pram* . .	6′

Problem 1 *Inverted ¶ letter, open punctuation* *1 cc*
Be alert to punctuation *Envelope*

Words

September 18, 19–– Miss Sarah A. Klausing, 9
President Central City Business College Lin- 17
coln, Nebraska 68509 Dear Miss Klausing 25
(¶ 1) The letter with inverted paragraphs is a 34
special letter style that is not seen too often. In 44
this special letter style, all lines, except the first 55
in each paragraph, are indented five spaces. 64
This unusual arrangement is eye appealing and 74
is used most often in sales promotion correspon- 83
dence. (¶ 2) The letter with inverted para- 90
graphs is nothing more than a modification of 100
the modified block style letter. The date line, 109
the address, and the salutation are typed exactly 119
as you would in the modified block style. Mixed 129
punctuation is used most frequently, although 138
you may use open punctuation if you wish. 147
(¶ 3) You can use the letter placement table to 155
determine the margins for the letter. Unless the 165
letter is long, it is usually not necessary to adjust 176
the position of the date line to allow for the 186
indention of the lines in the left margin. Set 195
your margins initially so that the <u>first</u> line of 205
each paragraph is centered horizontally. (¶ 4) 213
After you have typed the first line of the first 223
paragraph, reset your left margin so that the 232
remaining lines of the paragraph will be in- 241
dented five spaces. For the first line of each 251
succeeding paragraph, it is necessary to depress 260
the margin-release key and to position the car- 270
riage at the original left margin. (¶ 5) The com- 278
plimentary close, the typed name, and the official 288
title are typed exactly as you would type them 298
in the modified block style. When you type your 308
initials and any enclosure notations, however, 317
be sure to position the carriage at the original 327
left margin. Sincerely yours John E. Homan, 336
Director (xx) (304) 338

+ Envelope 356

FIRST-CLASS LETTERS
1736 LLANFAIR STREET, BANGOR, MAINE 94401

September 18, 1967

Miss Sarah A. Klausing, President
Central City Business College
Lincoln, Nebraska 68509

Dear Miss Klausing

The letter with inverted paragraphs is a special letter style that is not seen too often. In this special letter style, all lines, except the first in each paragraph, are indented five spaces. This unusual arrangement is eye appealing and is used most often in sales promotion correspondence.

The letter with inverted paragraphs is nothing more than a modification of the modified block style letter. The date line, the address, and the salutation are typed exactly as you would in the modified block style. Mixed punctuation is used most frequently, although you may use open punctuation if you wish.

You can use the letter placement table to determine the margins for the letter. Unless the letter is long, it is usually not necessary to adjust the position of the date line to allow for the indention of the lines in the left margin. Set your margins initially so that the <u>first</u> line of each paragraph is centered horizontally.

After you have typed the first line of the first paragraph, reset your left margin so that the remaining lines of the paragraph will be indented five spaces. For the first line of each succeeding paragraph, it is necessary to depress the margin-release key and to position the carriage at the original left margin.

The complimentary close, the typed name, and the official title are typed exactly as you would type them in the modified block style. When you type your initials and any enclosure notations, however, be sure to position the carriage at the original left margin.

Sincerely yours

John E. Homan, Director

ao

LETTER WITH INVERTED PARAGRAPHS

Problem 2 *Inverted ¶ letter, mixed punctuation* *1 cc*
Be alert to punctuation and date *Envelope*

Words

Mr. Spencer M. Pennington 358 Freedom Road 12
Hamilton, Ohio 45011 Dear Mr. Pennington 20
(¶ 1) KELLER'S MOTORS announces with pride the 28
opening of its enlarged service facilities. We 38
have installed the most modern equipment avail- 47
able and hired additional factory-trained me- 56
chanics to service your car faster and better. No 66
repair job is too large or too small for us to 75
handle––and we guarantee efficiency and satis- 84
faction in all work we do. (¶ 2) FOR a limited 93
time only, we are offering a special motor 101
tune-up at the unbelievable price of only $6.95. 111
The tune-up includes an inspection and adjustment 121

(Continued)

80C: Skill Transfer Checkup (15) *(Repeat 79C, page 125. Goal: Improved Accuracy.)*

80D: Related Learnings Checkup (25)

Problem 1: Word Division and Vertical Centering Recall

Half sheet
Double spacing
Center vertically

Note the color underline under various letters of the words in the first column. Assume that the bell rings at this point as you are typing the word at the end of a line. In the second column show by use of the hyphen the first acceptable division point of the word after the underlined letter. The correct division of the first word is illustrated. If the word cannot be divided, type the complete word.

The first item illustrates the rule that hyphened compound words are divided only at the hyphen that separates the two elements of the compound.

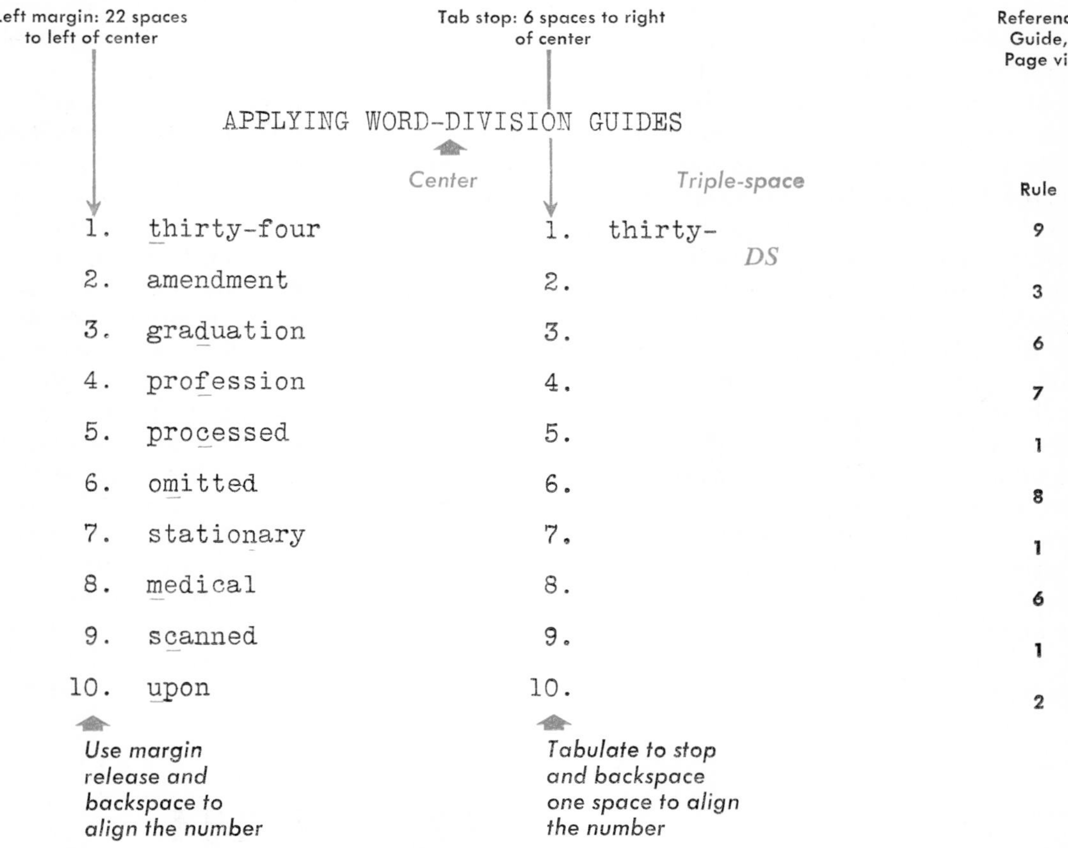

Problem 2: Composition Typing - Word-Division Rule Recall *(Full sheet; 60-space line)*

Using the same numbers as given for the words in Problem 2, type in your own words the word division rule that applies to the specified word. Single-space your answers with a double space after each answer. If you cannot recall the rules, refer to Reference Guide, page vii.

Problem 2 *1 cc Current Date Envelope*

Words

Martin's Hardware Store 1500 Delaware Avenue 12
Hackensack, New Jersey 07601 SERVICES FOR 21
KWIKGRO DEALERS (¶ 1) Welcome to the grow- 28
ing list of exclusive dealers for KWIKGRO. Your 37
Order No. 6497S for 250 cartons of KWIKGRO 46
has been received and we can assure you that 55
it is being processed right now. You can expect 65
delivery on your order within a few weeks. 74
(¶ 2) May we take this opportunity to remind 81
you of some of the many services we provide 90
our dealers. Yours for the asking are several 100
kinds of placards and signs that can be used 109
as attractive window or store displays. You may 118
also obtain copies of our colorful leaflet that 128
describes and illustrates the value of KWIKGRO. 138
For each carton of KWIKGRO ordered, you may 147
obtain 30 copies of the leaflet without charge. 156
Additional copies may be obtained for a nominal 166
sum. In addition, you may have any of the six 175
special advertising mats that have been prepared 185
by our advertising agency. All you need do is 195
add your name, address, and telephone number 204
to these mats and you will have an eye-appealing 214
newspaper advertisement. (¶ 3) The enclosed 222
pamphlet, "Services for KWIKGRO Dealers," de- 231
scribes in more detail the product. If we can 240
help you in any way in setting up point-of-sale 250
display material or in planning radio, television, 260
or newspaper advertising campaigns, please let 269
us know and one of our salesmen will visit you 279
at your convenience. CHARLES W. PARKINSON – 288
SALES MANAGER (xx) Enclosure (259) 293
+ Envelope 308

Problem 3 *1 cc Current Date Envelope*

Words

Mr. R. C. Brady, President Elkin Industries Inc. 13
75 Arno Road Newark, New Jersey 07111 21
MORE EFFECTIVE ADVERTISING (¶ 1) Are you get- 28
ting the most for your advertising dollar? Does 38
your ratio of advertising expenses to sales 47
continue to increase? Are you interested in 56
increasing your sales through more effective 65
advertising? (¶ 2) At Benton Associates, adver- 73
tising is our business; in fact, it is our <u>only</u> busi- 84
ness. Our expert staff specializes in squeezing 94
the most from each advertising dollar. We have 104
helped many clients to reduce the ratio of adver- 113
tising expenses to sales and to increase sales 123
through more effective advertising. We are con- 132
fident that we can do the same for you. (¶ 3) We 141
can develop a master advertising campaign 149
tailored to fit your specific needs to maintain 159
sales during "off-seasons" or to increase overall 169
sales at any time. We can prepare advertising 178
copy and presentations for all media including 188
newspapers, magazines, radio, television, direct 197
mail, and outdoor. We can also place your 206
advertising with the proper media at the most 215
appropriate time. Finally, we can make detailed 223
analyses of the effectiveness of your advertising 235
through the facilities of our consumer research 244
staff. (¶ 4) Won't you let us relieve you of your 253
advertising problems? We will be happy to 262
show you, in detail, exactly what we can do for 272
you. Just write or call us. It won't cost you 281
anything except a few minutes of your time. 290
R. T. BENTON – VICE-PRESIDENT (xx) (264) 297
+ Envelope 314

LESSON 204

204A: Conditioning Practice (5) *each line at least three times*

Alphabet	Bud wants to examine quickly just the freight elevators in Zelienople.	*Eyes on copy*
Figure	In 1967, Hartland won 20,983 votes; Marks, 14,562; and Raymond, 8,703.	
Figure-symbol	At the shareholders' meeting, 51,859 (36%) voted "no" on Proposal #72.	
Fluency	If he wants a good job with high pay, he must work with greater vigor.	
	| 1 | 2 | 3 | 4 | 5 | 6 | 7 | 8 | 9 | 10 | 11 | 12 | 13 | 14 |	

204B: Skill Comparison (7) *1' writing on each sentence of 204A; compare rates*

Unit 13 | Lessons 81-85

Speed and Accuracy Emphasis

You will make your greatest gains in speed and accuracy if you practice with the purpose of each drill or exercise in mind. In addition, you should always practice at an appropriate *practice level.*

Speed Level. Use the *exploration level (speed)*, indicated in the directions by (S), when you make a definite effort to force your speed. You do this by taking the "brakes" off your fingers, by letting your fingers do the work, and by typing with rhythm and continuity.

Control Level. Use the *control level*, symbol (C), when you are to emphasize accuracy—error reduction. Your goal should be to reduce errors to not over 1 a minute. To do this, reduce speed somewhat and find that rate at which you can type with the best control.

Technique-Emphasis Level. Use this level, symbol (TE), when the purpose is to refine technique patterns. First, reduce speed a bit and give attention to "how" you are typing; then try out your improved technique patterns at higher and higher speeds.

LESSON 81

81A: Conditioning Practice (5) *each line three times*

Alphabet	Just work for improved basic techniques to maximize your typing skill.
Figure	The shipment included 132 divans, 156 lamps, 48 desks, and 790 chairs.
Shift key	R. H. Dalton, of Ault, Moore & Wallace Company, is visiting in Newark.
Speed	The map of the ancient land forms may aid them when they work with us.

| 1 | 2 | 3 | 4 | 5 | 6 | 7 | 8 | 9 | 10 | 11 | 12 | 13 | 14 |

81B: Technique Improvement – Response Patterns (10)

TYPE: Each line three times. Use these practice levels: 1—TE; 2—TE; and 3—S.

TYPE: From dictation, as time permits, the lines which have the flag (|►) opposite them.

One-Hand Words (Stroke Response)

		EMPHASIZE
Left hand	tax few set date card area case ever facts rates great reserve average	*Finger action; uniform stroking*
Right hand	him oil pin upon join milk pump pink union nylon imply opinion minimum	
Left and right hands	minimum address million decrease monopoly referred immunity exaggerate	

Balanced-Hand Words (Word Response)

Think the word	|► he am sir pay due make than when also work such form their right field	*Finger reaches; speedy stroking; quick spacing*
Read and type in word groups	|► if it is | to do so | and the | with them | their work | such form | both men wish	
	|► and the | and then | and if they | and if they go | go to the | pay for | the work	

One- and Balanced-Hand Words (Combination Response)

One-hand	Your union staff is aware that the monopoly case has been exaggerated.	*Continuity of stroking*
Balanced-hand	Both men wish to do their work and then go with them to the field box.	

| 1 | 2 | 3 | 4 | 5 | 6 | 7 | 8 | 9 | 10 | 11 | 12 | 13 | 14 |

LESSON 203

203A: Conditioning Practice (5) *each line at least three times*

Alphabet	Kevin Bixby will equalize the temperature if you can adjust the gauge.	*Uniform stroking*
Figure	Read Lesson 39, page 64; Lesson 52, page 170; and Lesson 82, page 195.	
Figure-symbol	Mary found the data on pages 89–137 of World Facts (Vol. 50, No. 264).	
Fluency	Will he give us some idea of his plans for a visit to the city in May?	
	| 1 | 2 | 3 | 4 | 5 | 6 | 7 | 8 | 9 | 10 | 11 | 12 | 13 | 14 |	

203B: Skill Comparison (7) *1′ writing on each sentence of 203A; compare rates*

203C: Typing AMS Simplified Letters (38)

Preview Administrative Management Society letter style by reading the information in the Problem 1 letter and studying the illustration at the right. Then type the three AMS style letters for 25′ when directed to begin. If time permits, start over. Mark errors. Compute *g-pram.*

Time Schedule	
Study problem; get ready . . .	7′
Timed production	25′
Proofread; compute *g-pram* . .	6′

Problem 1 *AMS letter with 1 cc* *Envelope*

Words

September 11, 19—— Mr. F. W. Burbank, Office 9
Manager Highlands Manufacturing Company 17
5329 Harrison Street Newark, New Jersey 25
07108 AMS SIMPLIFIED LETTER STYLE (¶ 1) Your 33
letter of September 6 regarding the increasing 42
costs of producing business letters reflects the 52
concern of many businessmen today. The Ad- 61
ministrative Management Society has suggested 70
that the cost of letters can be reduced by the 79
adoption of a simplified letter style. In this 89
block style letter, the salutation and complimen- 98
tary close are omitted. To type this style, follow 109
these directions: 1. Type the address four lines 119
below the date. 2. Type the subject in capital 128
letters a triple space below the address. 137
3. Begin the body of the letter a triple space 146
below the subject line. 4. Type enumerated 155
items flush with the left margin; indent unnum- 164
bered listed items five spaces. 5. Type the 173
writer's name and title in capital letters at least 184
four lines below the body of the letter. 6. Type 194
the typist's reference initials, in lowercase letters, 205
a double space below the writer's name and any 215
enclosure notations a double space below the 224
reference initials. (¶ 2) The AMS simplified letter 233
style is both practical and attractive. If you want 244
to reduce your letter costs, we suggest you try 253
it. MICHAEL A. BURTON – PRESIDENT (xx) (222) 261
+ Envelope 284

7305 COMMERCE AVENUE, TRENTON, NEW JERSEY 08618

September 11, 19--

Mr. F. W. Burbank, Office Manager
Highlands Manufacturing Company
5329 Harrison Street
Newark, New Jersey 07108

AMS SIMPLIFIED LETTER STYLE

Your letter of September 6 regarding the increasing costs of producing business letters reflects the concern of many businessmen today. The Administrative Management Society has suggested that the cost of letters can be reduced by the adoption of a simplified letter style. In this block style letter, the salutation and complimentary close are omitted. To type this style, follow these directions:

1. Type the address four lines below the date.
2. Type the subject in capital letters a triple space below the address.
3. Begin the body of the letter a triple space below the subject line.
4. Type enumerated items flush with the left margin; indent unnumbered listed items five spaces.
5. Type the writer's name and title in capital letters at least four lines below the body of the letter.
6. Type the typist's reference initials, in lowercase letters, a double space below the writer's name and any enclosure notations a double space below the reference initials.

The AMS simplified letter style is both practical and attractive. If you want to reduce your letter costs, we suggest you try it.

MICHAEL A. BURTON - PRESIDENT

ao

AMS SIMPLIFIED LETTER

81C: Selected Goal Practice – Progressive-Difficulty Sentences (10)

1. Select a speed goal and type each sentence four times with the 20-, 15-, or 12-second call of the guide, as directed by your teacher. Pause briefly after each spurt writing to relax.
2. Type a 1′ writing on each sentence. Type on the *speed level* (S). Compare rates.

Note. *The figures above the copy indicate the 1′ rates in terms of the guide call.*

GWAM

20″ Guide . . .	3	6	9	12	15	18	21	24	27	30	33	36	39	42	High-
15″ Guide . . .	4	8	12	16	20	24	28	32	36	40	44	48	52	56	Frequency
12″ Guide . . .	5	10	15	20	25	30	35	40	45	50	55	60	65	70	Words Emphasized

Balanced-hand	Sign the forms so the chairman may pay both of the men for their work.
Combination	It is the opinion of their union man that this nylon work rate is low.
One-hand	Were you aware that the area water reserves are far below the average?

| 1 | 2 | 3 | 4 | 5 | 6 | 7 | 8 | 9 | 10 | 11 | 12 | 13 | 14 |

81D: Skill Building – Guided Writing (15)

1. **Type** a 3′ writing (at a controlled pace with good stroking techniques).
2. **Determine** *gwam.* To this rate add 8 *gwam.* Determine quarter-minute goals for 1′ writings at the new rate. For example, if the new rate is 48 *gwam,* type 12 words each quarter minute (guide figures 12, 24, 36, and 48).
3. **Type** two 1′ writings on ¶ 1 at the goal rate, your teacher calling the quarter-minute guides.
4. **Repeat** Step 3 with ¶ 2.
5. **Type** a 3′ writing, trying to equal your 1′ *gwam* for the 3 minutes. Determine *gwam.* Compare the rates of the two 3′ writings.

		GWAM 1′	3′	
¶ 1 1.3 SI	The office worker has to cope with many problems in the office.	13	4	50
	Not the least of these problems is the art of getting along with other	27	9	54
	workers. Part of the solution to the problem of getting along with	41	14	59
	others is to do your own work in the right way. This right way of	54	18	63
	working is one of the marks of the mature person.	64	21	67
¶ 2 1.4 SI	It has been said that the mature person is one who can face reality.	78	26	71
	A mature person is one who finds more satisfaction in giving than in	92	31	76
	getting. A mature person is one who can solve problems of life without	106	35	81
	"flipping his lid," who does not make the same mistakes again and again,	121	40	86
	and who will reason with another person instead of punching him in the	135	45	90
	nose.	136	45	91

1′ GWAM | 1 | 2 | 3 | 4 | 5 | 6 | 7 | 8 | 9 | 10 | 11 | 12 | 13 | 14 |
3′ GWAM | 1 | 2 | 3 | 4 | 5 |

81E: Typing for Accuracy (10)

TYPE: Selected sentences from Special Drills, page 136, repeating each one until you have typed it at least twice without error.

GOAL: Try to complete five sentences as directed. *Unless your teacher directs you otherwise, begin with Sentence 1 and work straight through.*

LESSON 202

202A: Conditioning Practice (5) *each line at least three times*

Alphabet	Pam Grove did the final exercise quickly when she realized its object.	*Keep carriage moving*
Figure	There were 2,834 responses from the 6,750 surveys mailed on August 19.	
Figure-symbol	Of the 1,340 items made by Shop #28 on June 9, 67 (5%) were defective.	
Fluency	She said they would like to change the size of the order they sent us.	
	| 1 | 2 | 3 | 4 | 5 | 6 | 7 | 8 | 9 | 10 | 11 | 12 | 13 | 14 |	

202B: Building Speed and Accuracy (30) *follow instructions given for 201C, page 299*

All letters are used.

	GWAM 2′		GWAM 5′	
It would be very difficult to find an employer who does not insist	7	80	3	60
upon having an interview with a job applicant before hiring him. Some	14	87	6	63
experts feel that the interview is one of the most important steps in	21	94	8	66
the selection of a new employee. Time may be taken during the interview	28	102	11	69
to verify the information given on the application form and to secure	35	109	14	72
any other data desired. The major aim of the job interview, though, is	42	116	17	75
to enable an employer to observe closely the person's poise, dress,	49	123	20	77
grooming, and use of language. The interview is also a good chance	56	129	22	80
for the interviewer to describe the jobs that may be open and for the	63	136	25	83
applicant to ask questions about the company, the jobs, and other topics	70	144	28	86
in which he may have an interest.	74	147	29	87
If you are invited to report for a job interview, you must realize	7	78	32	90
that your application form and test scores made a good impression on the	14	85	35	93
company. It is costly in both time and money to interview everyone who	21	92	38	96
applies for a job. For this reason, a company will not call anyone who	28	99	41	98
does not seem to possess the qualities desired. During the interview,	36	106	44	101
be alert and focus your attention on the questions that are asked.	42	113	46	104
Answer each query clearly and honestly. Let your voice, conduct, and	49	120	49	107
choice of words reflect your knowledge, attitude, and interest. Gain	56	127	52	110
confidence from the fact that you are but one step away from a job offer	64	134	55	113
and that the position will be yours if you "put your best foot forward."	71	142	58	115

2′ GWAM | 1 | 2 | 3 | 4 | 5 | 6 | 7 |

5′ GWAM | 1 | 2 | 3 |

202C: Sustained Skill Building (15)

Type a 10′ writing beginning with the ¶s given on page 299 and continuing with the ¶s above. If you complete all 4 ¶s, repeat the ¶s in 202B above. (To determine 10′ *nwam,* divide total 5′ *gwam* by 2; then subtract 1 for each error.)

LESSON 82

82A: Conditioning Practice (5) *each line three times*

Alphabet	Will Jim realize that excellent skill develops by refining techniques?	*Finger-action reaches*
Figure	Is American Flight 738 scheduled to arrive at 9:25 a.m. or 10:46 p.m.?	
Third-row	u uj r rf y yj t tf i ik e ed o ol w ws p p; q qa typewriter quote try	
Speed	I may work with them or their friends in the ancient city by the lake.	
	| 1 | 2 | 3 | 4 | 5 | 6 | 7 | 8 | 9 | 10 | 11 | 12 | 13 | 14 |	

82B: Technique Improvement – Response Patterns (10)

TYPE: Each line three times. Use these practice levels: 1—TE; 2—TE; and 3—S.

TYPE: From dication, as time permits, the lines with the flag (|►) opposite them.

			EMPHASIZE
		One-Hand Words (Stroke Response)	
Four-letter		dear pull were lump data look test jump gave hook best upon rate only	*Finger action; fingers upright*
Five-letter		union draft imply aware pupil staff nylon weave plump great jumpy react	
Left and right hands		I was asked to refer a minimum number of weavers to the union address.	
		Balanced-Hand Words (Word Response)	
Three-letter	|►	own men did box big end six she fit got aid via bid map key bit cut oak	*High-speed word response (think word— type word)*
Four-letter	|►	with paid name held city both hand sign busy firm kept half risk rush	
Five-letter		right world forms title eight firms spent usual spend corps civic visit	
Long words		profit handle formal bushel ancient problem chairman quantity amendment	
Balanced-hand		I may visit the chairman of the civic corps and sign the ancient form.	
Balanced-hand		Eight of the title firms may sign the amendment by the end of the day.	
		| 1 | 2 | 3 | 4 | 5 | 6 | 7 | 8 | 9 | 10 | 11 | 12 | 13 | 14 |	

82C: Selected-Goal Practice (10) *(Repeat 81C, page 129. Goal: Accuracy.)*

82D: Skill Building – Guided Writing (15)

1. **Type** two 1′ writings on ¶ 1, page 131. Force your speed to a new level by typing with continuity and without a sense of hurry.
2. **Type** two 1′ writings on ¶ 2, guided by your teacher's call of the quarter-minute guide. Try to maintain the ¶ 1 rate.
3. Type one 2′ writing on ¶ 1. At end of first minute, your teacher will call "one minute"; return the carriage and start again. **Goal:** To maintain your 1′ rate during the second minute. (Divide the 1′ rate by 2 to get the 2′ GWAM.)
4. **Repeat** Step 3 with ¶ 2.
5. **Type** a 3′ writing using both paragraphs. **Goal:** To maintain your 1′ rate on the 3′ writing. Determine *gwam.*

Unit 35 | Lessons 201-207

Business Letters with Special Features

LESSON 201

201A: Conditioning Practice (10) *each line at least three times; then 1′ speed writings*

Alphabet	Why did Rex Foyle object when Doctor Parkston gave him a tranquilizer?	*Fingers curved and close to keys*
Figure	Etna, a city of 30,497 people, is 15 miles from Clairton on Route 268.	
Figure-symbol	In 1964, cotton production increased 28.3% to 15.7 million 500# bales.	
Fluency	The men said they are entitled to be paid for the work they have done.	
	| 1 | 2 | 3 | 4 | 5 | 6 | 7 | 8 | 9 | 10 | 11 | 12 | 13 | 14 |	

201B: Skill Comparison (10) *1′ comparison writings; practice; repeat*

Easy	There are many folks who never try the things they want to do in life.
Average	New machines and procedures used greatly interested the new employees.
Difficult	Better pupils stated opinions concerning minimum state taxes on water.
	| 1 | 2 | 3 | 4 | 5 | 6 | 7 | 8 | 9 | 10 | 11 | 12 | 13 | 14 |

201C: Building Speed and Accuracy (30)

1. Type two 2′ writings on each ¶; find *gwam*.
2. Practice difficult words and phrases.
3. Type two 5′ writings for speed, using both ¶s; determine *gwam*.
4. Practice difficult words and phrases.
5. Type a 5′ writing for control; find *nwam*.

All letters are used.

	GWAM 2′		GWAM 5′	
Tests of many kinds are used in the world of business as a guide	7	70	3	54
in the selection of employees. These may range from achievement tests	14	77	5	56
to tests of aptitude, intelligence, and personality. The major purpose	21	84	8	59
of these tests is not only to describe the person but to predict what	28	91	11	62
he may be able to do on a job. Achievement tests are used to obtain a	35	99	14	65
measure of an applicant's skills and mental ability. An aptitude test,	42	106	17	68
on the other hand, is designed to determine how well an applicant may be	49	113	20	71
able to learn a new job. Tests of personality and of job interest are	57	120	23	74
also used, especially for clerical, secretarial, and other office jobs.	64	127	25	76
What kind of tests can you expect to take when you apply for a job?	7	71	28	79
The clerical proficiency test, the typing test, and the secretarial test	14	78	31	82
are those used most commonly for office positions. You will recognize	21	85	34	85
these tests easily since they are quite similar to the ones you take in	29	92	37	88
school. The clerical proficiency test consists of problems in English	36	100	40	91
and arithmetic. The typing test is usually a five- or ten-minute test	43	107	42	93
for speed and accuracy. In the secretarial test you will be asked to	50	114	45	96
take dictation and to transcribe it in mailable form. You will have no	57	121	48	99
trouble with any of these tests if you do all your work in school well.	64	128	51	102

2′ GWAM | 1 | 2 | 3 | 4 | 5 | 6 | 7 |
5′ GWAM | 1 | 2 | 3 |

		GWAM 1′	3′	
¶ 1 1.4 SI	One of the first ways by which you are usually judged is by your	13	4	52
	appearance. It is safe to say that the well-groomed person makes a much	28	9	57
	better impression on others than the one who is not. In addition, the	42	14	62
	well-groomed person is usually relaxed, and he creates an impression of	56	19	67
	a person who is competent, dependable, and sure of himself.	68	23	71
¶ 2 1.5 SI	Proper care of your hair, fingernails, and teeth has an important	81	27	75
	effect on your appearance. The clothes you wear need not be expensive;	96	32	80
	the important thing is that they are neat and clean, that they fit	109	36	84
	properly, and that they are appropriate for the occasion. Cleanliness,	123	41	89
	neatness, and a warm, friendly smile represent the winning combination	138	46	94
	that adds up to good appearance.	144	48	96

1′ GWAM | 1 | 2 | 3 | 4 | 5 | 6 | 7 | 8 | 9 | 10 | 11 | 12 | 13 | 14 |
3′ GWAM | 1 | 2 | 3 | 4 | 5 |

82E: Typing for Accuracy (10)

TYPE: Continue typing the sentences of the Special Drills, page 136, as time permits.

GOAL: To type each sentence until you have typed it at least twice without error.

LESSON 83

83A: Conditioning Practice (5) *each line three times*

Alphabet	Just strive for maximum progress by quickly organizing the daily work.	*Wrists low, hands quiet*
Figure	The zoo ordered 785 birds, 4 bears, 20 bisons, 9 lions, and 163 snakes.	
Third-row	Type upper-row keys properly by making quick reaches with the fingers.	
Speed	He may sign the usual form by proxy if they make an audit of the firm.	

| 1 | 2 | 3 | 4 | 5 | 6 | 7 | 8 | 9 | 10 | 11 | 12 | 13 | 14 |

83B: Skill Building (10)

TYPE: A 1′ writing on each sentence of 83A, above. Type for speed. Compare rates.

TYPE: Additional 1′ writings, as time permits, on the lines on which you made the lowest rates.

Problem 1: Company Mailing Brochure

1 cc 1" side margins; 2" top margin Omit ¶ numbers
DS body SS ¶ 7 list, but DS between items
Center headings; TS before subheads

Words

THAT FIRST JOB 3

1. Whatever you do in life, nothing will ever 12
surpass the excitement of getting that first job 22
and reporting for your first days of work. 31
Through this experience you have an opportunity 40
to learn a great deal that will help you through- 50
out your lifetime. If you plan carefully, the 60
entire experience should be a pleasant one 68
for you. (70) 70

<u>The Right Job Leads</u> 78

2. To be successful and happy in your work, 86
it is important that you and the job be compat- 96
ible. Therefore, you need to study carefully 105
your strengths and your weaknesses, your inter- 114
ests and your life goals, and employment en- 123
vironment and opportunity. Build a long-term 132
plan to overcome your weaknesses and to con- 141
tinue your education along the lines of your 150
greatest interests and abilities. (86) 156

3. After you determine the kind of work you 165
want to get and are competent to do, use a vari- 175
ety of job leads to obtain initial employment. 184
Your teacher will explain what your school will 194
do to help you, but do not depend upon the 202
school alone. Realize the value of many leads, 212
weed out the obviously poor leads, and follow 221
up the others quickly. (69) 226

<u>The Interview</u> 231

4. Typically an important step in obtaining that 241
desired position is the job interview. Like the 251
step of surveying job prospects, the interview 260
requires careful planning. Then always make an 270
appointment if you expect to have an interview. 279
Too many beginning workers do not realize that 289
this must be done. The main purpose of a job 298
interview is to help the employer determine the 308
sort of person you are and just what you can do 317
for the business and what you expect in return. 327
(101)

5. Take your social security card with you for 336
your interview. Also take a data sheet that lists 346
your school grades, an exact statement of your 356
skill, two or three references, and the names of 365
those with whom you have had part-time jobs. 375

Words

You may also have to answer questions about 383
your hobbies and personal habits and your plans. 393
(66)

<u>An Employment Test</u> 400

6. When you go for the interview for a new 409
job, be prepared to take a test to prove your 418
competence. No matter how expert the inter- 427
viewer is in interviewing you, he will probably 436
realize that he cannot be sure of the soundness 446
of his judgment without some test results to 455
aid in checking his appraisal of your work 464
competence. (73) 466

7. Will you get the job? That depends partly 475
on the following factors: 1. Your poise and 484
grooming 2. Your experience in activities of 493
leadership and of working with others 3. The 502
way you answer questions asked of you—both 511
the answers you give and the way you give them. 520
(55)

Problem 2: Letters from Form Paragraphs

Modified block, open 1 cc Envelope

Using the opening and closing ¶s given below for each letter and special ¶s from Problem 1 as indicated below, type a letter to:

(Current date—3 words)

	Words	Special ¶s
Mr. Michael A. Green 1123 Crest Avenue Birmingham, Alabama 35209	(13)	**1, 4, 5**
Miss Mary Jane Hill 532 East Capitol Avenue Jackson, Mississippi 39201	(14)	**2, 3, 4**
Miss Janet L. DuBois 720 Wedgewood Road Charleston, South Carolina 29407	(13)	**4, 5, 6**

(Salutation—3 words)

Opening ¶

Thank you for your most interesting letter in 9
which you asked questions about initial employ- 18
ment. We are pleased to send you suggestions 30
we have found to be helpful throughout our 39
experience of helping to bring together the 48
right person and the right job. (54) 54

Closing ¶

The services of our firm are at your disposal. 10
Call on us if we can be of further help to you. 19
Cordially SELECT EMPLOYMENT SERVICE Thomas 28
J. Brady President (xx) (32) 32

83C: Accuracy Index (10)

Accuracy hint: To type accurately, you must type at a rate at which you can maintain control; discover that rate in this practice.

TYPE: Two 1′ writings for speed. Subtract 8 words from the average of your two *gwam* rates. Determine quarter-minute goals for this new rate.

TYPE: 1′ writings at this new rate guided by your teacher's call of the quarter minute. **GOAL:** Not over 1 error—if necessary, vary the rate.

All letters

You quickly recognize the value of typewriting for your own personal use. A good typewriting skill, also, pays many job dividends in the employment market. Learning to typewrite well is worth the extra effort that it takes. Most of us can typewrite much faster than we do. The problem may be that we lack a desire to improve, or we fail to practice in the right way.

83D: Growth Index – Straight Copy (15) *two 5′ writings; determine* gwam; *proofread for errors*

All letters are used.

1.4 LA 5.4 80

Text	GWAM 1′	5′	
It is amazing how much work efficiency can be increased by careful	13	3	52
planning and organizing of all work to be done. This is as true of work	28	6	55
in class as it is of work in the business office. In the business office,	43	9	58
there is a trend toward work simplification and the use of time and motion	58	12	61
principles in all work. Office workers learn to increase their efficiency	73	15	64
by grouping similar jobs. They adjust their work pace to the difficulty	88	18	67
of the job. They try to check waste motions by having all materials that	102	20	70
they may need for the job they are to do within easy reach and arranged	117	23	73
for quick use.	120	24	74
In the typing classroom, you should plan all work and work in the	13	27	76
right way. In terms of using the typewriter, this right way of operat-	27	29	79
ing means that you type with good techniques, that you work for a fluent	42	32	82
key-stroking pattern with the reach action limited to the fingers only	56	35	85
so that you will be able to keep the hands quiet; that you eliminate	70	38	88
all unnecessary motions; and that you work for an increasing sense of	84	41	90
relaxation as your skill develops. Then, too, boys and girls who are	98	44	93
learning to type must make a real effort to improve. As is so for the	112	46	96
right way of working, a real effort to improve is an essential element	126	49	99
of success.	129	50	99

1′ GWAM | 1 | 2 | 3 | 4 | 5 | 6 | 7 | 8 | 9 | 10 | 11 | 12 | 13 | 14 |
5′ GWAM | 1 | 2 | 3 |

83E: Typing for Accuracy (10) (*Continue the drills on page 136: each line twice without error.*)

Problem 2: Bill of Lading

Words

Shipper's No. 194056 Carrier Midwest Transit 5
From Decatur Products Co. Date December 1, 19-- 12
At Decatur, Illinois Consigned to Jackson Builders, Inc. 20
Destination 226 Cheshire Street Eugene City Lane County Oregon State 27
Routing Portland 29
Delivering Carrier Midwest Transit Vehicle or Car Initial XL No. 4962 33

Packages	Description	Weight	Words
10	Sanding Discs	5#	38
6	Shelving Units	138#	42
8	Railing Sections	128#	47
3	Top-Mount Lavatory Faucets	13#	54

Shipper Decatur Products Co. 58
Permanent address of shipper 1916 Fairmont Drive, Decatur, Illinois 62526 67

Problem 3: Invoice

				Words
Date	December 1, 19--	Sold	Jackson Builders, Inc.	8
Our Order No.	EG-2294-C	To	226 Cheshire Street	14
Cust. Order No.	CL-15720		Eugene, Oregon 97401	20
Terms	2/10, n/30	Shipped Via	Midwest Transit	26

Quantity	Description	Unit Price	Total	Words
10 pkg.	7" Sanding Discs, 16-A	3.98	$ 39.80	34
6 ea.	40" x 36" x 12" Shelving Units	8.99	53.94	44
8 ea.	5' Railing Sections	5.55	44.40	51
3 sets	Top-Mount Lavatory Faucets	9.50	28.50	62
			$166.64	63

LESSON 200

200A: Conditioning Practice (10) *1' writings on selected ¶s on pages 293–294*

200B: Manuscript and Form Paragraph Production Measurement (40)

Time Schedule	
Get ready to type	3'
Timed production	30'
Proofread; compute *n-pram*	7'

Type the two problems on page 298 for 30' when directed to begin. Correct errors as you type. If time permits, start over. Proofread; mark uncorrected errors. Compute *n-pram*.

LESSON 84

84A: Conditioning Practice (5) *each line three times*

Alphabet	The kind queen received extra jewels from a dozen brave young pirates.	Curved, upright fingers
Figure	Order 75 pencils, 36 pens, 12 desk pads, 48 desk sets, and 90 erasers.	
First-row	m mj v vf n nj b bf , ,k c cd . .l x xs / /; z za / /; z za . .l xs .l	
Speed	Eight girls wish to go with them to the ancient city for the ornament.	
	| 1 | 2 | 3 | 4 | 5 | 6 | 7 | 8 | 9 | 10 | 11 | 12 | 13 | 14 |	

84B: Technique Improvement – Response Patterns (10)

TYPE: Each line three times at these practice levels: 1—TE; 2—S; 3—S.

TYPE: From dictation, as time permits, the lines with the flag (|►) before them. Work for a speedy typing response.

1. The color bar (———) under the words indicates word response. Read and type these words, word groups, or word parts as units.
2. The color dots (• • • • •) under the words indicate stroke response. Read and type these words or word parts stroke by stroke.

TECHNIQUE CUES	Fingers close to the keys; speedy finger action; uniform stroking; space quickly—down-and-in motion; work for rhythmic continuity

Word Response

1 |► and the | pay the men | for the work | if they go | and if they | the right sign |

2 |► the key city | spend the day | sign the form | the busy firm | the right title |

Combination Response

3 |► to the pin | for him | the pay | they were | their date | right union | hand weave |

4 their union | sight draft | right pupil | busy staff | firms react | usual weave |

5 a date, the date, for the case, when they restate, restate the problem

6 the address, and the address, for the address, refer to their address,

7 card, the card, to the union, at the address, gave the statement to the

Variable Rhythm

8 A date for the case will be agreed upon when they restate the problem.

9 They gave the statement to the union at the address shown on the card.

| 1 | 2 | 3 | 4 | 5 | 6 | 7 | 8 | 9 | 10 | 11 | 12 | 13 | 14 |

84C: Accuracy Index (10)

TYPE: Additional writings on the paragraph of 83C, page 132, using the same practice procedures.

GOAL: Control with a fluent rhythm pattern.

DO: After each writing, circle errors, try to determine reason for errors. If you type without error, increase your speed by 4 words a minute on new writings.

Problem 5: Telegram *(3 cc's; charge sender)*

Words

St. Louis, Missouri *(current date)* Dr. William A. 16
Phelps 34 West Monroe Street Phoenix Med- 24
ical Clinic Phoenix, Arizona (¶) Anesthetizing 32
equipment requested in your Order #1320 now 41
being assembled for testing. Shipment should be 51
released within the next 10 days. Other surgical 61
supplies shipped via express today. Melvin R. 70
Hayes Hayes Medical Supplies, Inc. (xx) 247 79
East Broadway Avenue 83

Problem 6: Telefax Night Letter *(3 cc's)*

TCY Charge to: Midwest Manufacturing Co. 6
Detroit, Michigan *(current date)* Jones Con- 14
struction Company 3974 Washington Street 22
Toledo, Ohio (¶) Order #8562 for 20 pcs., 8" 31
25-ft. "I" beams will be shipped within 10 days. 41
Other shipments will be released as designated 50
in contract. Leon L. Franks Production Man- 59
ager (xx) 60

Problem 7: Confirmation Letter, Block, Open

Words

(Current date) Jones Construction Company 8
3974 Washington Street Toledo, Ohio 43624 17
Attention Mr. Richard D. Jones Gentlemen 25
(¶ 1) We are happy to have your order for struc- 34
tural steel products to be used on the Consoli- 43
dated Oil Project. Your first shipment will be 53
ready within a few days. (¶ 2) I have just tele- 61
graphed you as follows: 66
(Insert Telefax message of Problem 6) 94
(¶ 3) We have arranged our production sched- 102
ules to meet your building plans, and all of 110
the processed items will be ready on time. We 120
anticipate no delays in getting our materials to 130
you. (¶ 4) Thank you for this opportunity to 138
supply your steel needs. The enclosed brochure 147
describes some of our plans to serve you better 157
as we take advantage of new technological de- 166
velopments. Sincerely Kenneth B. Heckman 174
(xx) Enclosure (123) *+ Envelope* 177/191

LESSON 199

199A: Conditioning Practice (10) *each line three times; then 1′ writings on selected lines*

Alphabet; shift Bev Hixon quizzed Jim Croquet for weekly guest shows at Park View Inn.
Figure 116 ft. Catalog No. TR 13474 at 2/10, n/30 Customer Order No. JC 58979
Figure-symbol $6,205.79 (Smith & Rout*) $4\frac{1}{2}$ x $8\frac{1}{4}$ Tom's 13% long-term 7 5/8" #69 @ 20¢
Fluency To succeed, a business must have workers who are sincere and diligent.
| 1 | 2 | 3 | 4 | 5 | 6 | 7 | 8 | 9 | 10 | 11 | 12 | 13 | 14 |

Quick, finger-action reaches

199B: Production Measurement on Business Forms (40)

Time Schedule

Get ready to type	3′
Timed production	30′
Proofread; compute *n-pram* . .	7′

Type the following three problems for 30′ when directed to begin. Make 2 cc's. Correct errors as you type. If time permits, start over. Proofread; mark uncorrected errors. Compute ***n-pram.***

Problem 1: Purchase Order

Words

Order No. CL–15720 2
Date November 30, 19–– 10
Terms 2/10, n/30 16
Ship Via Midwest Transit 24

To: Decatur Products Co.
1916 Fairmont Drive
Decatur, Illinois 62526

Quantity	Cat. No.	Description	Price	Words
10 pkg.	LR 28104	7" Sanding Discs, 16-A	$ 39.80	30
6 ea.	LD 62085	40" x 36" x 12" Shelving Units	53.94	40
8 ea.	KX 53726	5′ Railing Sections	44.40	49
3 sets	JD 62635	Top-Mount Lavatory Faucets	28.50	58
			$166.64	61

84D: Skill Building – Guided Writing (15)

1. **Select** *best control rate* you made on 1′ writings of 84C.
2. **Type** a 1′ writing on ¶ 1 at the goal rate; your teacher will call the quarter-minute guides. **Goal:** Not over 1 error.
3. **Type** another 1′ guided writing: Increase your rate by 4 *gwam* if you made your rate and goal of Step 2; if not, repeat Step 2.
4. **Type** two additional 1′ writings at increasing rates of 4 or 8 *gwam*. **Goal:** Not over 1 error.
5. **Repeat** Steps 2-4 for ¶ 2.
6. **Type** a 3′ writing, trying to maintain your best 1′ rate. **Goal:** No more than 3 errors. Determine *gwam*.

		GWAM 1′	3′	
¶ 1 1.5 SI	Practicing good manners whether you are at home or in school, with	13	4	55
	your family or your friends, will help you acquire poise and assurance.	28	9	60
	Being well-mannered means following the recognized rules of behavior which	43	14	65
	help to make your relationships with others more pleasant. The basis of	58	19	70
	good manners is kindness, thoughtfulness, and a deep concern for others.	72	24	75
¶ 2 1.6 SI	Courtesy and consideration are very important in making friends	85	28	79
	and in keeping them. Good manners are really a reflection of your own	99	33	84
	attitude toward others. You must like people, respect them, be inter-	113	38	88
	ested in them, and make the effort to get along with them. In school,	127	42	93
	do you make the effort to be pleasant by being considerate of your	140	47	97
	classmates, your teachers, and every school administrator?	152	51	101

1′ GWAM | 1 | 2 | 3 | 4 | 5 | 6 | 7 | 8 | 9 | 10 | 11 | 12 | 13 | 14 |
3′ GWAM | 1 | 2 | 3 | 4 | 5 |

84E: Typing for Accuracy (10) *(Continue the drills on page 136: each line twice without error.)*

LESSON 85

85A: Conditioning Practice (5) *each line three times*

Alphabet	Six women in the valley heard piercing squawks of dozens of blue jays.	*Rhythmic continuity*
Figure	I have read 127 books, 364 magazines, 50 newspapers, and 89 pamphlets.	
First-row	Six brave men helped Aza C. Bonman carry an excited lynx to a zoo van.	
Speed	She may pay the firm for the work when they sign the right audit form.	

| 1 | 2 | 3 | 4 | 5 | 6 | 7 | 8 | 9 | 10 | 11 | 12 | 13 | 14 |

85B: Technique Improvement (10) *(Repeat 84B, page 133. Goal: Improved rhythm pattern.)*

LESSON 198

198A: Conditioning Practice (10) *1′ writings on 197A, page 293*

198B: Special Communications Production Measurement (40)

Time Schedule	
Get ready to type	3′
Timed production	30′
Proofread; compute *n-pram* . .	7′

Type the following seven problems for 30′ when directed to begin. Make 1 cc unless more are specified. Address envelope except for telegrams. Correct your errors as you type. If time permits, start over. Proofread; mark uncorrected errors. Compute *n-pram*.

Problem 1: Business-Reply Message (*2 cc's*)

Words

Message to: Mr. Michael Lee Oscarson Vice- 6
President Main Office Date: *(current)* (¶ 1) 14
We are finding extensive shortages on board 22
feet of lumber from Feeder Mill No. 1. The 31
shortages have occurred on deliveries for each 41
of the last three weeks. (¶ 2) Will you please 49
send me instructions regarding action you wish 58
us to take? R. S. Davis Receiving Foreman 67
+ *COMPANY MAIL envelope* 80

Reply: Date: *(current)* (¶ 1) Will you please 86
visit the Feeder Mill right away, observe opera- 96
tions, talk with the foreman, and report back to 105
me. Describe the situation and make your 114
recommendations. (¶ 2) What is the situation on 122
deliveries from each of the other feeder mills? 132
Do we face serious shortages on raw material in 142
the near future? Michael Lee Oscarson 150
+ *COMPANY MAIL envelope* 158

Problem 2: Business-Reply Message (*2 cc's*)

Message to: Mr. John H. Caprell Broker Dahl- 6
berg Building Date: *(current)* (¶ 1) We will 14
have two carloads of the hand-split cedar fenc- 23
ing ready to ship out by the end of this week. 32
(¶ 2) We cannot have the next two carloads 40
ready before three weeks from this date. Will 49
this delivery date receive any strenuous objec- 58
tion from your buyer for this shipment? Michael 68
Lee Oscarson 71
+ *COMPANY MAIL envelope* 82

Reply: Date: *(current)* (¶ 1) The buyer agrees 88
to this delivery date. (¶ 2) How soon can you 96
have three additional carloads ready to deliver 106
to him? He is willing to pay one-half cent more 116
per picket for an early shipping date. John H. 125
Caprell 127
+ *COMPANY MAIL envelope* 139

Problem 3: Interoffice Memorandum (*3 cc's*)

Words

To: Howard Webb, Division Manager Norbert 8
E. Deering, Foundry Foreman Date: *(current)* 16
File: ER–62905–A From: John C. Fuller, Vice- 23
President Subject: Accident Prevention (¶ 1) 29
The recent outbreak of serious accidents in our 38
foundry disturbs me greatly. I am concerned 47
not only with the personal suffering and financial 58
loss sustained by our workers but also with the 67
disruptive effect these accidents are having on 77
our production schedules. This past month has 86
been especially costly because of man-hours lost 96
by some of our key men. (¶ 2) It is imperative, 105
therefore, that you take immediate steps to pre- 114
vent further accidents in your departments. By 124
the end of this week, I want each of you to 132
report to me personally on your proposals for 142
attacking this accident problem. (xx) cc David 151
C. Carter Labor Relations 156
+ *COMPANY MAIL envelope* 172

Problem 4: Interoffice Memorandum

To: W. H. Jones, Production Department Date: 7
(current) File: TR–41937 From: Vern T. John- 14
son, Controller Subject: Invoices––Report 21
T–31–36 (¶ 1) A statement from United Re- 28
tailers, Inc., Lincoln, Nebraska, in the amount of 38
$937.34, is enclosed. This statement, represent- 47
ing miscellaneous purchases covered by our 56
requisitions during the last month, should be 65
checked at the Job Office and paid from your 74
funds. (¶ 2) The reference to Purchase Order 82
No. 3894 on their statement is in error, since 92
that purchase order calls for mortar and cement 101
only. (¶ 3) Please tell your suppliers to send 110
only those invoices covered by purchase orders 119
from the Main Office to us and to send miscel- 128
laneous billings to your office. (xx) Enclosure 137
+ *COMPANY MAIL envelope* 147

85C: Selected Goal Practice – Right- and Left-Hand Words (12)

1. Select a speed goal and type each sentence three times with the 20-, 15-, or 12-second call of the guide, as directed by your teacher.

2. Type a 1′ writing on each sentence. Type on the *speed level.* Compare rates.

Speed Cue: *Finger-reach action; fingers upright.*

Left- and right-hand words are color underlined.

GWAM	3	6	9	12	15	18	21	24	27	30	33	36	39	42
20″ Guide . . .	3	6	9	12	15	18	21	24	27	30	33	36	39	42
15″ Guide . . .	4	8	12	16	20	24	28	32	36	40	44	48	52	56
12″ Guide . . .	5	10	15	20	25	30	35	40	45	50	55	60	65	70

Left hand Six dazed, sad referees, cast in savage waters, were saved extra fast.

Right hand In the lull of July the milk for the only plump mink was at a minimum.

Left hand A bad case of fear was detected as Reed stared weakly down the street.

Right hand The judge gave an opinion on a minimum number of union monopoly cases.

Right and left It is my opinion that you are the only test rater who can state facts.

| 1 | 2 | 3 | 4 | 5 | 6 | 7 | 8 | 9 | 10 | 11 | 12 | 13 | 14 |

85D: Growth Index – Straight Copy (15) *two 5′ writings; determine* gwam; *proofread for errors*

All letters are used.

LA 1.4 5.4 80

Text	1′	5′	
The glory of America is that more people have achieved the good	14	3	52
things of life than anywhere else in the world today or at any time in	27	5	55
history because of the opportunity that exists for the person who is	41	8	58
willing to work. A person's responsibility for his own life is basic	55	11	60
to a free, civilized society such as ours. In the world of work, your	69	14	63
own work skills and talents are the best guarantee that you can secure	83	17	66
a job when you need it. To an ever-increasing degree, work skills are	97	19	69
based on a sound education; and, because the problems of unemployment	111	22	72
are greatest for those with the least skill, a good education is the	125	25	74
best single investment that you can make in your own future.	137	27	77
In school, your teachers are concerned about you as a person and	13	30	79
as a student. In the world of work, an employer will be more concerned	27	33	82
about what you can produce in return for the wages that you earn. Your	42	36	85
opportunities for advancement in the world of work will be quickly en-	56	39	88
hanced if you will recognize that an advancement will necessitate a	69	41	91
determined attempt on your part. Employers want alert workers who can	84	44	94
get a task done when it needs to be done, who can work under pressure	98	47	96
when the need arises, and who can add a bit extra to the job.	110	49	99

1′ GWAM | 1 | 2 | 3 | 4 | 5 | 6 | 7 | 8 | 9 | 10 | 11 | 12 | 13 | 14 |

5′ GWAM | 1 | 2 | 3 |

85E: Typing for Accuracy (8) *(Complete the drills on page 136: each line twice without error.)*

	GWAM 1′	GWAM 5′
 A third reason that learning is on the mind of most of us is that	13	63
so many more groups are involved in the stimulation of learning and in	27	66
the aiding of learning, or are looking for ways to take part. It seems	42	69
that everyone wants to "get into the act" in some way. Not only do our	56	72
local, state, and national governments, by research and funding, help	70	75
educators to do a better job, but also private business firms are taking	85	78
an increasing share in the preparing of educational services, materials,	99	81
and aids. As giant leaps in technology take place, businesses and our	114	84
educators work together to seek ways of applying the advances to a	127	86
better education for more people.	134	88
 Still another reason, and a major one, for great interest today in	13	90
adding to our individual knowledge has to do with the gigantic strides	28	93
we are taking in bringing to light many more facts about the world in	42	96
which we live. A Rip Van Winkle of today would have to sleep no more	56	99
than five years to find almost unbelievable the queer world to which	70	101
he awakened. Today we enjoy the excitement of seeing history happen in	84	104
real or current time, before our very eyes. New scientific and techni-	98	107
cal findings, for instance, occur in our world with such speed that some	113	110
of them become outmoded almost before they can be put into use, as they	127	113
make possible even newer discoveries.	135	114
 Sources of power, heretofore unknown to man, are changing our mechan-	14	117
ical world. Cameras can bring a far place almost close enough to touch.	28	120
Space explorations have drawn the next planet as near to us in thought	43	123
as the next continent seemed a few years ago. Into the seas men go, not	57	126
only to walk the surface and find the secrets of the depths and to	71	129
search for valuable sources of food, but also to live there for days to	85	131
determine the adaptability of man to unfamiliar environs, under condi-	99	134
tions thought before this time to be entirely alien to man.	111	137
 One living in our world today cannot just drift, eventually going	13	139
into a career that might seem convenient at the time. Today we have	27	142
great selectivity in what we wish our world to become and what we want	41	145
our own lives to become. So learn. Follow up your interests with en-	55	148
ergy, and study hard in order to be able to live your life as you plan	69	151
it. There are many jobs to be done––going to the moon; eliminating	83	153
squalor, poverty, and ignorance; prolonging healthy life; learning more	97	156
about the human mind; rebuilding cities. Isn't it exciting to plan what	112	159
your part might be in enlarging our world of tomorrow?	122	161

1′ GWAM | 1 | 2 | 3 | 4 | 5 | 6 | 7 | 8 | 9 | 10 | 11 | 12 | 13 | 14 |
5′ GWAM | 1 | 2 | 3 |

197D: Skill Building (15) *10′ writing on ¶s on pages 293–294; compute* nwam

To compute 10′ nwam from 5′ rate, divide 5′ gwam by 2; then subtract 1 for each error.

SPECIAL DRILLS

Line	Letter Fixation	
1	a	Anxiously, Abdulla lay awake awaiting another angry wail from the auk.
2	b	The bright baby boys babbled with joy as the abbey cobbler hurried by.
3	c	Clear, iced coffee was critically acclaimed in the city of Cincinnati.
4	d	Dick decided on that dark dreary day to deliver a dog at this address.
5	e	Everyone needs to strive for excellence in every educational endeavor.
6	f	Fifteen flying fish were seen fifty feet from the ferry by this staff.
7	g	George saw the giggling girls engaged in playing the gigantic guitars.
8	h	They gave them their share of the cash which should pay for the house.
9	i	If it is possible, this trip I should like to visit Tahiti and Hawaii.
10	j	The judge enjoyed the jokes and jargon of the jolly jesters from Fiji.
11	k	The bookkeeper from Kankakee scratched his knee on the kinky oak bark.
12	l	The little child fell asleep while listening to Louis tell tall tales.
13	m	My most remarkable ambition is to aim for maximum mental performances.
14	n	Neither Ann nor Nancy noted the number ninety-nine on this new listing.
15	o	One of our most important efforts for formal recognition is good work.
16	p	A popular pitcher attempted to whip the ball past the opposing batter.
17	q	The question of giving equal value to quality and quantity was quoted.
18	r	Railroad tariff restriction rate reports are referred to a rate clerk.
19	s	Successful speed hints suggest snappy, sharp strokes with the fingers.
20	t	A typist used little effort to type the twenty-three business letters.
21	u	He refused to use the unusual vacuum cleaner with the huge dust tubes.
22	v	Five beaver, full of vim and vigor, eventually leveled five fir trees.
23	w	Wally saw the wind whipping the snow against the windows of the wharf.
24	x	The extra exercise provided by mixing the wax in a box may tax Xerxes.
25	y	Today you may improve yesterday's typing rate if you just keep trying.
26	z	Zestful, quizzical quiz kids dizzily zigzagged round a buzzing bazaar.
	Vowel Confusion	
27	ie, ei	A mischievous thief grabbed eight wieners and a stein of caffein brew.
28	ie, ei	He studied and weighed each piece of weird, foreign china he received.
	Adjacent Key	
29	m, n	Many more men and women may be named to a new international committee.
30	e, r, t	Robert's great try to aid the fort attracted attention to this treaty.
31	Various	Exactly at twelve noon, I shall ask you to name many popular factions.
	Long Words	
32		Some students are uninformed and passionately determined to remain so.
33		Self-discipline is essential to the effective exercise of originality.

| 1 | 2 | 3 | 4 | 5 | 6 | 7 | 8 | 9 | 10 | 11 | 12 | 13 | 14 |

Unit 34 | Lessons 197-200

Measuring Basic and Production Skills

LESSON 197

197A: Conditioning Practice (5) *each line at least three times*

Alphabet; shift	Yvonne Schultz will sing with Becky Marquis next June at Lofty Rapids.	*Quiet hands and arms*
Figure	90 lbs. Catalog No. DL 68005 at 2/10, n/30 Customer Order No. AC 36947	
Figure-symbol	$5,309.48 (Hayes & Fishel*) 1½ x 2¼ Bob's 67% <u>one-arm</u> 1 7/8'' #50 @ 63¢	
Fluency	It is helpful to recall that problems of others are much like our own.	
	| 1 | 2 | 3 | 4 | 5 | 6 | 7 | 8 | 9 | 10 | 11 | 12 | 13 | 14 |	

197B: Skill Comparison (10) *1' comparison writings; practice; repeat*

Easy	Most of the last order was sent to the stock clerk for close checking.
Average	Some of the men paid their own way to visit the other big city hotels.
Difficult	Service dealers requested data regarding greater real estate taxation.
	| 1 | 2 | 3 | 4 | 5 | 6 | 7 | 8 | 9 | 10 | 11 | 12 | 13 | 14 |

197C: Growth Index (20) *three 5' writings from the ¶s on pages 293–294*

All letters are used.

	GWAM 1'	GWAM 5'
Learning, undoubtedly one of the most stimulating activities in	13	3
which we might take part in our exciting world of today, is rapidly	26	5
taking more and more time of more and more people. This is so for	40	8
several reasons. One is a kind of awareness. In this almost science-	54	11
fiction world in which we live, people are becoming much more aware,	68	14
almost universally, of the importance of what we learn––importance to	82	16
our future success and to the improvement of the world in which we	95	19
live. Keeping up with the Joneses today does not mean that third car	109	22
or the television set for every room or the patio swimming pool; it	123	25
truly has more to do with explorations in knowledge.	133	27

	GWAM 1'	GWAM 5'
Another influence causing great numbers of people today to place	13	29
learning among the foremost of their leisure time pleasures is that of	27	32
our psychologists and researchers in learning, who are helping us become	42	35
aware that most of us use only a very small part of our learning poten-	56	38
tial. It is possible for each of us to learn a great deal more than has	71	41
ever in the past been thought possible. As researchers discover a fac-	85	44
tor that influences the amount people learn and the zest with which they	99	46
learn, they send these helpful ideas on to others, just as doctors make	114	49
known their findings, or as scientists disclose for the benefit of all of	129	52
us a discovery they make about the almost inconceivable magnitude of the	143	55
world in which we live. Thus as knowledge is added, so is understanding	158	58
of the ways in which we can gain that knowledge and make it useful.	171	61

(Continued)

1' GWAM | 1 | 2 | 3 | 4 | 5 | 6 | 7 | 8 | 9 | 10 | 11 | 12 | 13 | 14 |
5' GWAM | 1 | 2 | 3 |

Unit 14 | Lessons 86-90

Using the Typewriter for Learning

Practice Levels. In the lessons of this unit and those that follow, you will be directed from time to time to type on the *technique-emphasis* level (TE), *control* level (C), or *speed* level (S). Study again the explanations of these levels on page 128 and be guided by them in your practice.

LESSON 86

86A: Conditioning Practice (5) *each line three times*

Alphabet	The juke box music puzzled a gentle visitor from a quaint valley town.	*Curved, upright fingers*
Figure	In 1967, we had 83 office chairs, 40 office desks, and 52 work tables.	
Long words	Work for typing perfection through thoughtful and purposeful practice.	
Speed	They lent the ancient ornament to their neighbor by the big city dock.	
	| 1 | 2 | 3 | 4 | 5 | 6 | 7 | 8 | 9 | 10 | 11 | 12 | 13 | 14 |	

86B: Technique Improvement – Control of Operative Parts (10) *each line three times: TE, TE, S*

TECHNIQUE CUE	Keep your hands in typing position and make the reach to the shift key by extending the little finger. Work for good timing to avoid "floating caps."

Note. *Book titles may be typed in all caps or with the underline.*

Shift-key control

Ja Ja Ja Jack Jack Jack; F; F; F; Floyd Flynn; Paul McNaulty; Al Dyane
Jack, Frank, Paul, and Quinn read the book HOW TO SUCCEED IN BUSINESS.
Kate Sutton and Jane McNeil wrote the book <u>How to Succeed in Business.</u>

TECHNIQUE CUES	1. Right thumb in spacing position—on or close to the space bar. 2. Avoid up-and-down movement of right hand on words ending in **y**, **n**, **m**. 3. Reach with the finger. Space quickly: down-and-in motion.

Space-bar control

pay them when they pay them when they work pay them when they work
The grumpy little man managed a stern frown upon seeing the torn ream.
Jim may question many men and women as they try to leave the map room.

TECHNIQUE CUE	Manual Return: Quick, flick-of-the-wrist motion. Start new line quickly. Electric Return: Extend little finger and tap the return key.

Center + 10 = TAB

Carriage (or carrier) return

		and the *Return*
lake	Tab	and the
work	Tab	and the
lake	Tab	*Repeat as many times as time permits.*

LESSON 195

195A: Conditioning Practice (5) *each line at least three times*

Alphabet	Typing helped Jim Zabowsky to develop coordination and quick reflexes.	*Return carriage quickly*
Figure	Make these changes in Section 175, page 240, and Section 186, page 309.	
Figure-symbol	The interest on Frank's loan #347 ($825 at 6% for 90 days) was $12.38.	
Fluency	Perhaps the boy's health will change their plans for the trip to Erie.	

| 1 | 2 | 3 | 4 | 5 | 6 | 7 | 8 | 9 | 10 | 11 | 12 | 13 | 14 |

195B: Technique Practice (5) *each line at least three times*

Top row	Did Roy and Porter quarrel about the wire Roy put around his property?	*Type with continuity*
First row	Was Ben Zumbrosky the first naval commander to sink six enemy convoys?	
Shift keys	Wouldn't Joan and Bert take Al's package to the I. F. Mark's Building?	
Balanced-hand	Six of the girls may aid the chairman when he works for the town firm.	

| 1 | 2 | 3 | 4 | 5 | 6 | 7 | 8 | 9 | 10 | 11 | 12 | 13 | 14 |

195C: Skill Building – Straight Copy (15) *two 5′ timed writings*

Use 190D, page 286. Compute *nwam* for each 5′ writing. Determine average *nwam* to compare with *earlier* 190E results.

195D: Problem Typing (25) *continue with the problems on pages 288–291*

LESSON 196

196A: Conditioning Practice (5) *each line at least three times*

Alphabet	Bucking the tremendous waves of Lake Zephyr was quite an exciting job.	*Start new line quickly*
Figure	Flight 509 will depart at 12:38 p.m. from Gate 4; Flight 607 was late.	
Figure-symbol	Order #485: "Buy 670 shares of F & M (now at 31$\frac{1}{2}$) if it drops to 29."	
Fluency	The items for the special display of spring styles will be sent today.	

| 1 | 2 | 3 | 4 | 5 | 6 | 7 | 8 | 9 | 10 | 11 | 12 | 13 | 14 |

196B: Technique Practice (5) *each line at least three times*

Left hand	We feel that the great fear regarding the extra taxes was exaggerated.	*Rhythmic stroking*
Right hand	My opinion poll showed that numerous people dislike the milk monopoly.	
Long words	Intelligence and integrity are important qualifications of executives.	
Fluency	He may be able to help solve some of the problems which we have today.	

| 1 | 2 | 3 | 4 | 5 | 6 | 7 | 8 | 9 | 10 | 11 | 12 | 13 | 14 |

196C: Sustained Skill Building – Straight Copy (15)

Type a 10′ writing on the ¶s given on pages 285 and 286. To determine 10′ *nwam*, add 190C *gwam* to 190D results and divide by 2; then subtract 1 for each error.

196D: Problem Typing (25) *continue typing the problems on pages 288–291*

86C: Related Learnings – Number Guides (15)

Practice Plan—For best results, follow this *study-learn-apply* procedure for each rule:

1. **Study** explanatory guide or rule.
2. **Type** *Learn* sentence, noting rule application at color underlines. See *Note.*
3. **Type** *Apply* sentence, making all needed corrections; then DS. *Points that may need correction are noted by color underline.*

Machine Adjustments:

1. 70-space line; single spacing.
2. 1½″ top margin on first page of each series of guides (number, capitalization, etc.); 1″ margin on all other pages.
3. Bottom margin of about 1″ on all pages that are full.

After completing each series:

1. Assemble sheets in order.
2. Number all pages (except first) in upper right corner even with right margin ½″ from top of sheet.
3. Staple sheets in upper left corner and turn them in.

Note. *Use margin release and identify each pair of sentences by typing the guide number 4 spaces outside left margin. Retain sheet for next lesson.*

1. Spell numbers from one to ten except when used with numbers above ten.*
2. Always spell a number beginning a sentence even though figures are used later in the sentence.
3. As a general rule, spell the shorter of two numbers used together.
4. Spell isolated fractions in a sentence, but type a series of fractions in figures. Use the diagonal (/) for "made" fractions.

*A common practice in business, however, is to use figures for all numbers, except those which begin a sentence. This practice makes number recognition much easier and verification more sure.

(Center) SERIES 1: NUMBER GUIDE EXAMPLES

TS

1 *Learn* He ordered 72 books on English, 8 on mathematics, and 36 on geography. *SS*
Apply About 150 delegates, 225 observers, and seven guests were at the assembly. *DS*

2 *Learn* Eighty-six applications were received, but only 15 persons were hired. *SS*
Apply 8 of the men were here yesterday; the other 16 will come tomorrow.

3 *Learn* Order No. 1350 called for ten 50-gallon drums and 350 ten-gallon cans.
Apply We may need 340 3-pound boxes and 15 75-pound drums tomorrow.

4 *Learn* About two thirds of the work is done. Type 1/8, 1/2, 1/4, and 15 7/8.
Apply 1/3 of the work is completed. Add one half, 3/4, six 5/8, and 13 5/16.

86D: Skill Applications – Centering on Special-Size Paper (20)

Study illustration below: Note that center is found by using formula shown at right. Formula can be used, also, for finding center of a column or line.

Formula for Finding Center

Scale reading at left edge of paper	10
+ Scale reading at right edge of paper	70
Total ÷ 2 = Center Point	80 ÷ 2 = 40

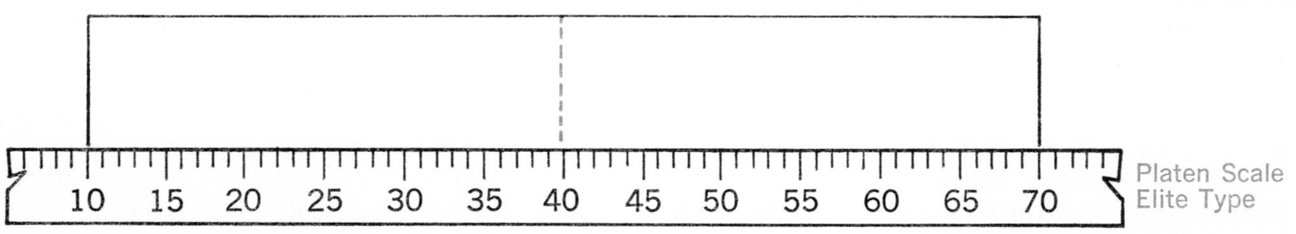

Problem 7: Model Copy of Itinerary

DO: Type a model copy of the itinerary below.

Words

UNIVERSAL TRAVEL AGENCY 5

Itinerary for Special European Tour 12

		Words
June 19	NEW YORK: Evening departure	19
	from Kennedy Airport.	24
June 20 – 24	LONDON: Sightseeing and special	33
	excursion to Stratford-on-Avon.	40
June 25 – 26	AMSTERDAM: City tour and excur-	49
	sion to Leiden.	52
June 27 – 30	COPENHAGEN: Land and water	60
	tour; trip to Royal Castles.	65
July 1 – 3	BERLIN: Tour of West and East	74
	Berlin.	76
July 4 – 9	VIENNA: City tour; excursion to	84
	Vienna Woods; special opera	90
	performance.	92
July 10 – 12	VENICE: Water tour of city.	101
July 13 – 17	ROME: City and Vatican tour; ex-	110
	cursion to Naples.	114
July 18 – 20	GENEVA: City tour; mountain	122
	climb.	123
July 21 – 25	PARIS: Special city tours; excur-	132
	sion to Versailles.	137
July 26	NEW YORK: Late afternoon arrival	145
	at Kennedy Airport.	149

Problem 8: Spirit Master from Model Copy

DO: Prepare a spirit master from the model copy of the itinerary you typed in Problem 7 above. Prepare the master according to the instructions given in Problem 6, page 290.

Problem 9: Topbound Manuscript

DO: Type the material below in the form of a manuscript to be bound at the top. Make 1 cc. Use the main heading PHOTO AND THERMAL COPIERS. Correct errors as you type.

Words

Main heading 5

(¶ 1) A number of machines have been devel- 12
oped in recent years that will copy typewritten 22
or printed material from an original copy. These 32
machines operate on a principle of xerography 41
or thermography; either light or heat is used 50
to transfer the material from the original copy 60
to special copy paper. Some of these machines 69
will produce, in black and white, material of 79
various colors. The machines used most com- 87
monly, however, will reproduce only originals 96
that have been typed or printed in black ink. 106
The photo and thermal copy machines are espe- 115
cially useful in making additional copies of in- 124
coming documents, such as customer's orders 133
and bills of lading. They may also be used when 143
additional copies of correspondence and reports 152
are required. Considerable time is saved by 161
reproducing copies from the original, and the 170
danger of errors which may be made when ma- 179
terial is retyped is eliminated. (¶ 2) Although 187
some copiers have been designed to reproduce 196
as many as 40 copies a minute, their use as 205
duplicators has been limited to a great extent by 215
the cost. If only 10 to 20 copies of typewritten 225
material are required, however, time and labor 235
may be saved by reproducing the copies re- 243
quired on a copy machine. This procedure 251
eliminates the necessity for making carbon copies 261
and frees the typist from the tedious task of 270
correcting errors on multiple carbon copies. 280
(¶ 3) The preparation of materials for copy ma- 288
chines is quite simple: 1. Be certain that your 297
type is clean and that your ribbon will produce 307
dark print. 2. Type the material to be copied 316
on bond paper unless special paper is required. 326
3. If you make an error, erase the error properly 336
and correct it. For some copy machines, it is 346
necessary to cover an error with special white 355
correction fluid. When this is necessary, use just 365
enough of the fluid to cover the error com- 374
pletely, let the fluid dry, and then retype the 383
material correctly. 387

Problem 10: Copy for Photo Reproduction

DO: Type the agenda below to be reproduced on a photo copier. Follow the instructions given for preparing copy for photo reproduction in Problem 9 above.

Words

THE MORTON MANUFACTURING COMPANY 7

Meeting of the Executive Board 13

(Current date) 16

1. President's report. (Mr. Homer) 23
2. Plans for the reorganization of the Produc- 32
tion Division. (Mr. Schlegel) 38
3. Report of new products under development. 48
(Mr. Crago) 50
4. Committee report on new legislation which 59
may affect company operations. (Mr. Schaef- 68
fer) 69
5. Report of personnel activities. (Mr. Hixon) 78
6. Summary of projected sales by territory for 88
the next fiscal year. (Mr. Barclay) 95
7. Report of Financial Committee on suggestions 105
for raising new capital. (Mr. Prokay) 112

DRILLS: Aligning and Centering

1. Type and underline your name, using a continuous (unbroken) underline.
2. Study relationship of typed letters to underline. Note that only a slight space separates the letters from the underline. Note, also, the relationship of typed letters and underline to the aligning or line-of-writing scale **33**.
3. Turn cylinder (platen) forward about an inch. Type an underline of 24 spaces; remove the paper.
4. Reinsert the paper. Center and type your name in proper relation to the underline.
5. *Evaluate your aligning skill:* Are the letters of your name typed in the same relative position to the underline as they were in Step 1? If not, repeat Steps 3 and 4.

PROBLEMS: Aligning, Centering, and Fill-In

1. *Center:* Vertically and horizontally, the following lines (double spaced). *Use:* four 5″ x 3″ cards (or slips of paper), long side up.

    STUDENT SERVICE AWARD

    to

    (Type 24-space underline)

    for

    OUTSTANDING STUDENT LEADERSHIP

2. On the cards prepared in Step 1, type the following names, correctly centered and in proper relation to the underline.

Evelyn Wong	Julian R. Siegel, Jr.
Linda Brownell	Allen Ziegler, III

LESSON 87

87A: Conditioning Practice (5) *each line three times*

Alphabet	The quiet king came forth to extend prizes to very bewildered jesters.	*Space quickly; down-and-in motion*
Figure	Jack typed 15 letters, 48 envelopes, 73 tags, 29 labels, and 60 cards.	
Double letters	A committee will meet the bookkeeping class to discuss current assets.	
Speed	They may use eight or more of the angle forms in order to do the work.	
	| 1 | 2 | 3 | 4 | 5 | 6 | 7 | 8 | 9 | 10 | 11 | 12 | 13 | 14 |	

87B: Technique Improvement – Stroking (10) *each line three times: 1 – TE; 2 – TE, 3 – S*

EMPHASIZE

Long, Direct Reaches

Quick reaches; finger action

ce ce ec ec br br un un nu nu mu mu ny ny my my num num rv rv ym ym ym

ec ce eccentric ny many num number br brief rv curve my myth ym symptom

My uncle will receive a bright uniform from the eccentric game umpire.

Third and Fourth Fingers

Fingers curved and upright; snap stroke

Paul saw six wasps as he ate apples and lollipops at the quaint place.

A poll of six zealous politicians was looked upon as a quick solution.

Paul was opposed to the use of lollipops to placate the quizzical lad.

Long Words

Fluent rhythm; continuity

Fan the spark of possibility within you into the flame of achievement.

Free men protect freedom by accepting the responsibilities of freedom.

The science of electroencephalography probes the mystery of the brain.

| 1 | 2 | 3 | 4 | 5 | 6 | 7 | 8 | 9 | 10 | 11 | 12 | 13 | 14 |

Problem 5: Fill-Ins on Form Letters

DO: Fill in a form letter for each of the individuals listed in Problem 4, page 289, using the copies duplicated in Problem 3. Try to match the color of ink by using a lighter or heavier stroke, as needed. Type the current date, name and address, salutation, and amount due as follows:

1. Set the left margin even with the left margin of the form letter.
2. Type the date on Line 12.
3. Type the address and salutation on the proper lines. Use a personal title with each name in the salutation. The ZIP Code for Haverford is 19041. Include it with each address.
4. Type the amount due in the appropriate space.

Problem 6: Leftbound Manuscript

DO: Type the manuscript for binding at the left. Make 1 cc. Use the main heading SPIRIT DUPLICATION. List in appropriate form the items in ¶ 3. Correct your errors as you type.

Words

Main heading 4

(¶ 1) The spirit duplicator is an inexpensive 12
means of making copies when a small number of 21
copies are required and the appearance of the 30
copy is not of primary importance. As many as 40
350 copies may be obtained from a spirit mas- 48
ter, although the usual number of copies from a 58
single master ranges from 10 to 150. (¶ 2) The 66
spirit master set consists of two basic parts: the 77
master sheet and a sheet of special carbon. A 86
backing sheet may also be used to obtain a bet- 95
ter consistency of type. If a specially prepared 105
master set is not available, simply place the 115
carbon paper between the master sheet and the 124
backing sheet, with the glossy side of the carbon 134
sheet toward you. When you type, the carbon 143
copy will be on the <u>back</u> of the master sheet. 152
(¶ 3) These suggestions will help you to make 160
better masters and better copies: 1. Prepare a 170
model copy of the material to be typed. Unlike 179
the stencil process, there are no guide marks 189
that must be followed. Check your model copy 198
for accuracy of form and typing. 2. When you 207
prepare the master, the type must be clean. The 217
ribbon should be thin (a heavy ribbon causes 226
broad type and filled-in characters). If the ribbon 236
is too heavy, the master may be typed with the 246
ribbon indicator in the "stencil" position. This 256
procedure makes it difficult to proofread the 265
copy, however. 3. Use a firm, even stroke on a 275
nonelectric machine. On electric typewriters, a 284
lower impression control adjustment usually pro- 294
vides better copies. 4. If you make an error, 303
scrape off the letter or word on the reverse side 313
of the master sheet with a razor blade or knife. 323
Then, rub a correction-pencil point over the 332
scraped area. 5. Before correcting the error, 342
tear off an unused portion of the carbon and 351
slip it under the part to be retyped; remove the 361
torn portion as soon as you have corrected 369
the error. 6. Before removing the master from 379
the typewriter, proofread the copy and correct 388
any errors you may have missed. 394

GUIDE FOR SPIRIT MASTER

87C: Related Learnings – Number Guides (End of Series 1) (10)

1. Reinsert sheet used for typing sentences of 86C, page 138.
2. Align copy properly and continue with Guide 5 sentences.
3. Follow *Practice Plan* outlined in 86C, page 138.

5. Numbers preceded by nouns are usually expressed in figures.
6. Express measures (also weights and dimensions) in figures.
7. The percent sign (%) is used when preceded by definite figures. Percent (spelled) is preferred with approximations and in formal writing.
8. Spell names of small-numbered avenues and streets (ten and under). Type house numbers in figures except for house number One.

5 *Learn* We found the exact quotation in Volume VIII, Section 4, pages 210–213. *SS*
Apply Rule six can be found in Monograph one, Chapter ten, page 136, Paragraph one.
DS

6 *Learn* The box I sent to Ralph measured 6 ft. 9 in. and weighed 72 lbs. 2 oz.
Apply James Kane, who is only 16 years old, is nearly six ft. three in. in height.

7 *Learn* This interest rate of $4\frac{1}{2}$% will be changed to $6\frac{1}{4}$% on your future loans.
Learn Approximately 50 percent of the students have completed all this work.
Apply Nearly 40 % of all mortgage loans last week were made at 6 3/8 percent.

8 *Learn* The factory is at 18 First Street; the store, at 164 West 59th Street.
Learn They moved their office from One Lexington Avenue to 270 Fifth Avenue.
Apply We plan to move our store from 264 4th Street to 3975 6th Avenue.

87D: Skill Applications (25)

Problem 1: Centering Columnar Headings (*Practice solution first; then center on half sheet.*)

Try the problem without referring to the solutions; then check your solution with those suggested.

1. Type the word *accommodate* in its three forms at the *stops* listed below.
2. Center, type, and underline the headings a double space above the words.

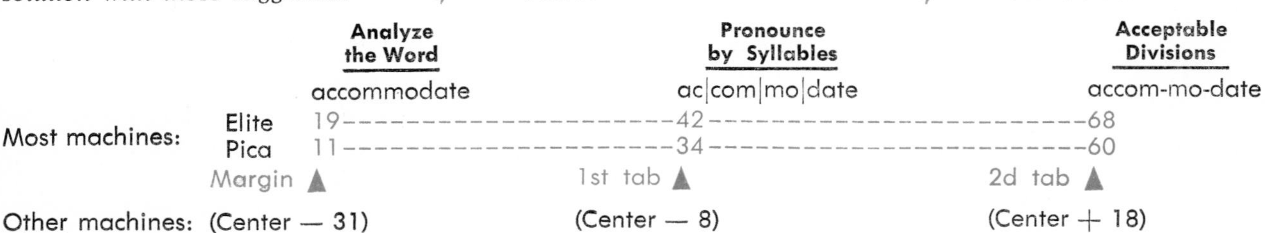

Analyze the Word
Pronounce by Syllables
Acceptable Divisions
accommodate
ac|com|mo|date
accom-mo-date
Most machines:
Elite 19 — 42 — 68
Pica 11 — 34 — 60
Margin
1st tab
2d tab
Other machines: (Center — 31)
(Center — 8)
(Center + 18)

Suggested Solutions:

1. Forward-space, backspace method. From the first letter of the word, space forward (→) one space for each two spaces in the word (or hyphened word), ignoring any extra letter at the end of the word. This is the center of the word or column.

Forward space →1→2→3→4→5 spaces
Illustration: `ac|co|mm|od|at`

From this point, backspace (←) once for each two spaces in the heading to be centered, again ignoring any odd or leftover letter.

Backspace ←1←2←3 spaces
Illustration: `An|al|yz`

From this point, type and underline the heading. It will be centered over the word.

2. Mathematical method. To the number on the cylinder (platen) or line-of-writing scale immediately under the first letter of the word, add the number shown under the space following the last letter of the word. Divide this sum by 2; the result will be the center point. From this point on the scale, backspace to center the heading. Type and underline the heading, and it will be centered.

Words

completely closed (such as a, d, o, p) must be 338
struck more lightly, whereas capitals and certain 348
letters such as "m" and "w" must be struck with 358
greater force. If you make an error, it can be 367
corrected easily with correction fluid. If there 377
is a film over the stencil, this must be detached 387
until you resume typing. Use a glass burnisher 397
or a paper clip to rub the surface of the error 407
on the stencil sheet. Place a pencil between the 417
stencil sheet and the cushion sheet and apply 426
a light coating of the correction fluid over the 436
error. Let it dry and then make the necessary 445
correction, using a medium touch. 452

Problem 2: Model Copy of Form Letter

DO: Type model copy in block style with open punctuation. Assume a letterhead depth of 1¾ inches. Omit date, address, salutation, and amount due. Leave space for these items (shown in Problem 4) to be filled in after the stencil has been run.

Words

(¶ 1) Mr. Randolph W. Laughlin, Club Manager, 8
has informed me that your account at the Colum- 17
bian Country Club is now two months overdue. 26
The records of the treasurer indicate that the 36
balance due on your account as of the first of 45
this month is $______. (¶ 2) The constitution of 54
our Club provides that members may have the 63
privilege of charging expenses incurred at the 72
Club but that this privilege will be withdrawn 82
if a member does not pay his account promptly. 91
The constitution further provides that a member 101
whose account is two months in arrears will be 110
notified in writing by the president. If no action 121
is taken by the member to pay his account 131
within three weeks of notification, his name is 139
posted on the Club bulletin board indicating the 149
amount owed. At the same time, the member 157
is not permitted to incur any additional charges. 167
If no action is taken within six weeks of the date 178
of notification, the individual's membership is 187
automatically canceled. (¶ 3) We feel certain 195
that your past-due account is an oversight. Will 205
you please give this matter your immediate atten- 215
tion so that you may remain a member in good 224
standing and enjoy the many benefits and privi- 233
leges of the Columbian Country Club. Send 242
your check for the amount due to the Club 250
Manager without delay. Sincerely yours Harry 259
M. Lyons President (254) 263

Problem 3: Stencil from Model Copy of Form Letter

DO: Prepare a stencil from the model copy of the form letter you typed in Problem 2. Follow the instructions for stencil duplication in Problem 1, page 288. Work rapidly, but carefully. Run fifteen copies. Problem 5, page 290, provides instructions for filling in the form letters.

Problem 4: Interoffice Memorandum

DO: Type the memorandum with 1 cc. Center the data at the end of the memorandum. Correct errors as you type.

Words

TO: Harry M. Lyons, President 5
FROM: Randolph W. Laughlin, Club Manager 12
SUBJECT: Report of Delinquent Accounts 18
DATE: *(Current)* 21

(¶ 1) Listed at the end of this memorandum are 30
the names and addresses of those Club members 39
whose accounts are now two months overdue. 48
Also shown is the amount owed by each member 57
as of the first of this month. All members listed 67
reside in Haverford. (¶ 2) Each member has 74
been notified twice of the amount due on his 83
account. No reply has been received to date 92
from any of these members. In accordance with 102
the provisions of the Club constitution, therefore, 112
form letters signed by you on the stencil notify- 122
ing the members of actions which may be taken 131
have been prepared and will be dispatched 139
tomorrow. 142

Name and Address	Amount Due	Words
		152
Edward R. Boyd, 232 Main Street	$141.20	160
Fred V. Dean, 1401 Iben Drive	236.50	168
Robert W. Leads, 30 Fifth Avenue	79.25	176
John S. McKean, 781 Pine Street	51.62	183
Cecil L. Printz, 14 Delaware Avenue	114.28	192
Elwood Roberts, 6901 Market Street	101.14	200
David U. Schuler, 847 White Avenue	274.90	209
Alfred K. Woods, 486 Maple Street	172.97	217

Problem 2: Typing Semiarranged Table (*Learning Recall*)

Type the following list of words in *two* columns. Maintain the alphabetic sequence in Columns 1 and 3.

Half sheet (short side up: 5½ x 8½)
Center vertically and horizontally
Single-space words in columns
2 columns, 10 spaces between

PLACEMENT LEARNING CUES:
Vertical center: Sheet is 8½″ deep.
Horizontal center: 86D, page 138.
Longest line each column: 10 spaces.

				Words
	WORDS OFTEN CONFUSED *TS*			4
accept	except	lose	loose	9
advice	advise	past	passed	14
affect	effect	peace	piece	20
coarse	course	principal	principle	26
compliment	complement	quiet	quite	33
council	counsel	stationary	stationery	41
desert	dessert	their	there	46
hear	here	threw	through	51
it's	its	weather	whether	56

LESSON 88

88A: Conditioning Practice (5) *each line three times*

Variable rhythm

Alphabet	The explorer quickly adjusted the beams as the freezing wave hit them.
Figure	Please notice Rule 36 on page 210 as well as Rule 85 on pages 479–482.
Adjacent key	Remember that courtesy is to human relations what oil is to machinery.
Speed	If they are to go with us to the big city, we shall be there at eight.
	| 1 | 2 | 3 | 4 | 5 | 6 | 7 | 8 | 9 | 10 | 11 | 12 | 13 | 14 |

88B: Technique Improvement (10) (*Repeat 87B, page 139*)

88C: Skill Applications (35)

Problem 1: Outline in Semiarranged Form (*Full sheet; Line: 60; Correct errors; Reference: p. 106*)

Heading: WRITING A REPORT

I. Selecting a Topic
A. Limit the topic
B. Select a major thesis or theme
C. Decide what information is needed
1. Check appropriate library sources
2. Make notes of research
D. Review and edit notes
1. Organize and refine notes
2. Decide if more information is needed
E. Prepare an outline from notes
1. Determine main ideas or divisions
2. Decide upon supporting subtopics

II. Writing the Report (*Be alert for form errors*)
A. Let outline be guide
B. Type First Draft from Notes
C. Edit and Revise first draft
1. Give special attention to grammar
2. Eliminate unnecessary details
3. Check for readability and interest
D. Type final draft in required Form
E. Proofread final draft for copying or typing errors
F. Prepare title page, table of contents (if needed), and bibliography
G. Assemble report for submission to Instructor

Problem 1: Unbound Manuscript

DO: Type manuscript with 1 cc and DS. Use STENCIL DUPLICATION as main heading. List in appropriate form the items in ¶ 2. Correct your errors as you type. Use careful stroking.

Words
Main heading 4
(¶ 1) Hundreds of copies of typed mate- 10
rial can be made in a short time through 19
the use of the stencil process of dupli- 26
cation. A stencil consists of three basic 35
parts: the stencil sheet, the backing 43
sheet, and the cushion sheet. When a 50
typewriter key strikes the stencil sheet, 59
it "cuts" an impression in the shape of 67
the type. The cushion sheet is placed 75
between the stencil and the backing 82
sheet to absorb the impact of the strik- 90
ing keys. A film sheet may be placed 97
on the top of the stencil sheet if darker 106
copies are desired. This film also pro- 113
tects the stencil sheet from letter cutout 122
when the type face is extremely sharp. 130
(¶ 2) Before typing the stencil, follow 137
these steps: 1. Type a model copy of 145
the material to be stenciled. Check it 153
for accuracy of form and typing. Be 160
certain that you place the copy on the 168
page so that it will be within the stencil 176
guide marks. 2. Clean the typewriter 184
type thoroughly. 3. Adjust the ribbon 192
lever to stencil position. 4. Insert the 200
cushion sheet between the stencil sheet 208
and the backing sheet. 5. Check the 216
touch control to see that it is set at a 224
point that will assure the sharpest out- 232
lines without cutting out the characters. 240
6. Place the top edge of the model 247
copy at the corner marks of the sten- 255
cil to see where to type the first line 263
of the copy. The scales at the top 270
and sides of the stencil will help 278
you position the copy correctly. (¶ 3) 284
Insert the stencil assembly into the 291
typewriter and align it properly, ex- 298
actly as you would a sheet of paper. 306
Use a firm, uniform, staccato touch as 314
you type. On some machines, the period 322
and comma keys and keys with parts 329

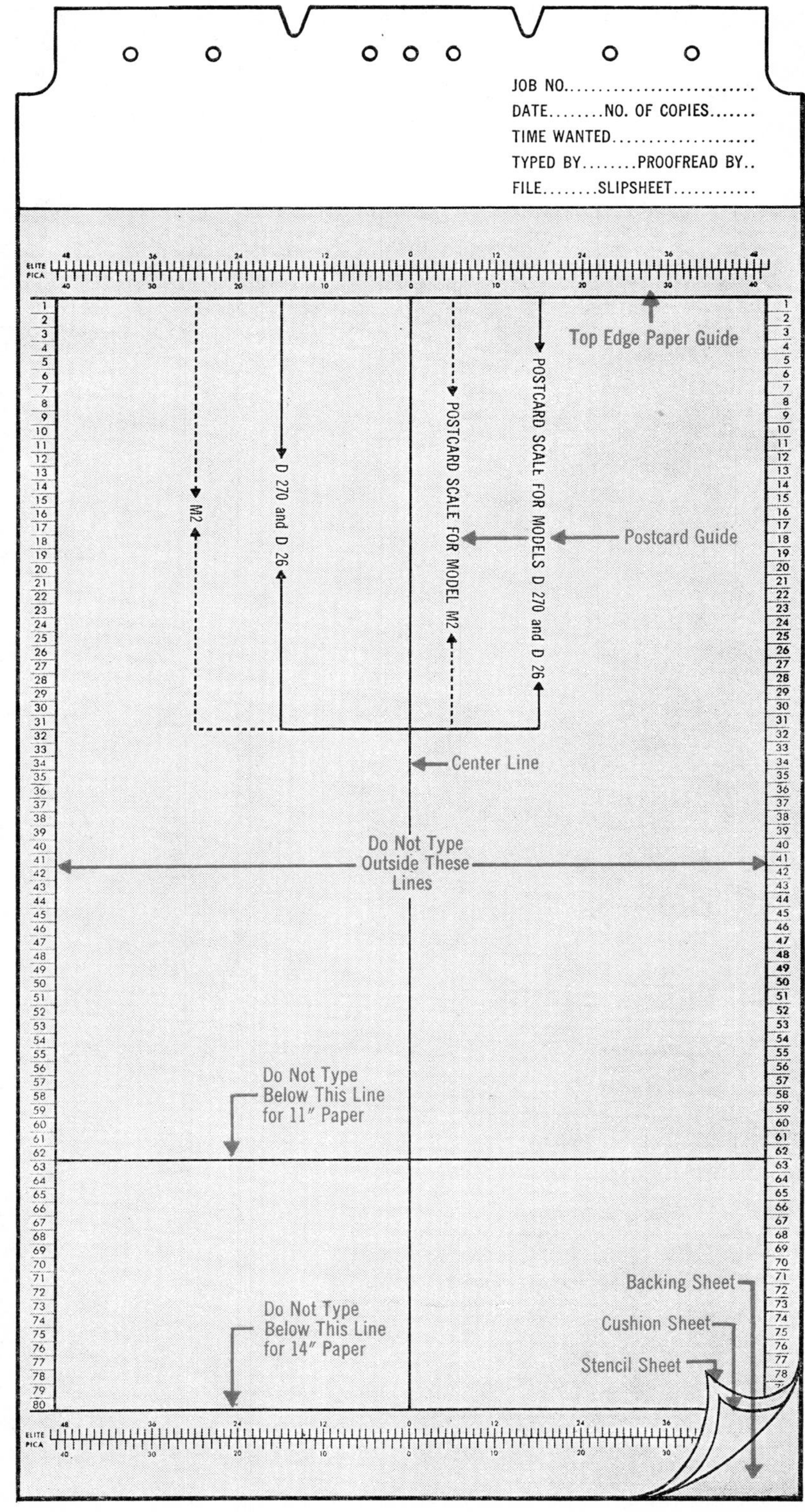

GUIDES FOR STENCIL

Problem 2: Library Cards

Type two 5″ x 3″ library catalog cards (or slips of paper of same size) from illustration of typical card at right. Space as directed on illustration.

```
1
2        BUSINESS  <-- General classification
                 DS
2 #'s   Author
651  Becker, Esther R.
B       Success and satisfaction in your  <-- Title
     office job, by Esther R. Becker and
     Richard L. Lawrence, Harper, 1954
Call number  149 pp.  DS   Publisher   Brief description
Indent: 3   The author "discusses the techniques
     for adjusting attitudes and developing
     personal traits that lead to satisfac-
     tion and success in one's job, . . . ."
        Other classifications where book is listed
     1. Business   2. Clerks   3. Secretaries
     Second line from bottom edge
```

Problem 3: Postal Cards

1. *Type* three postal cards (or use paper cut to 5½″ x 3¼″) in the form illustrated.
2. As each card is finished, address it to:

   Century Research Associates, Inc. *DS*

   5621 North Michigan Avenue *DS*

   Chicago, Illinois 60615
3. After cards are completed, type names and addresses below on the blank lines.

```
1
2
3 February 18, 19--
                  TS
-4-> Gentlemen:  DS

Please send me your free brochure, The Business
Letter Cost Index.  Will you also add my name to
your mailing list to receive the monthly, "Busi-
ness Communications Suggestions."  DS

Name____________________________________________
                                              DS
Address_________________________________________
                                              DS
City________________State_______Zip Code_______
```

Mr. Joseph M. Alvarez
4915 Hayvenhurst Street
Los Angeles, Calif. 90016

Miss Carol Yamaguchi
5461 Winnetka Avenue
Seattle, Wash. 98101

Mr. Dwight Nott
22 Old Army Road
Buffalo, N.Y. 14212

LESSON 89

89A: Conditioning Practice ⑤ *each line three times*

Alphabet	Visitors did enjoy the amazing water tricks of six quaint polar bears.	*Quick, snap stroke*
Figure	Will you enter machine Nos. 12–93–45 and 10–87–36 on the repair cards.	
Fingers 3 and 4	The plump squaw was coloring wax apples as the zany tourists appeared.	
Speed	If they do the work, they may go to the lake to fish and to dig clams.	
	| 1 | 2 | 3 | 4 | 5 | 6 | 7 | 8 | 9 | 10 | 11 | 12 | 13 | 14 |	

LESSONS 191-194

Lessons 191 and 193

A. Conditioning Practice (5′): Type 195A, page 292.

B. Technique Refinement (7′): Type two 1′ speed writings on each of the first three lines of 195B, page 292.

C. Speed Typing (8′): Type two 3′ speed writings on the difficult straight-copy ¶ below. Compute *gwam*. Try to increase your speed with each writing.

D. Problem Typing (30′): Type the problems beginning on page 288. After Lesson 191, continue typing each day at the point you left off the previous day.

Lessons 192 and 194

A. Conditioning Practice (5′): Type 190A, page 285.

B. Technique Refinement (7′): Type two 1′ control writings on each of the first three lines of 190B, page 285.

C. Control Typing (8′): Type two 3′ control writings on the statistical copy below. Compute *gwam*. Try to improve your accuracy with each writing.

D. Problem Typing (30′): Continue typing the problems on pages 288–291. If time permits, start over, trying for improved skill.

191C–193C: Straight Copy *type long words in syllables*

	GWAM 1′	3′	
The responsibilities assigned to an organizational segment of	12	4	48
a business must be specific, definite, and understood. When a major	26	9	53
organizational unit receives its assigned objectives in clear-cut,	40	13	57
unmistakable terms, it then has the responsibility to assure that the	54	18	62
subassignment of functions to subordinate units are of such a char-	67	22	66
acter that there is no question as to exactly what is expected. Vague	81	27	71
language of policies, procedures, memoranda, or directives which	94	31	75
prescribe the authority and responsibility of organizational units	108	36	80
with similar functions will result in overlappings, duplications,	121	40	84
and conflicts so extensive that confusion is inevitable.	132	44	88

1′ GWAM | 1 | 2 | 3 | 4 | 5 | 6 | 7 | 8 | 9 | 10 | 11 | 12 | 13 | 14 |
3′ GWAM | 1 | 2 | 3 | 4 | 5 |

192C–194C: Statistical Copy *emphasize figure-symbol accuracy*

	GWAM 1′	3′	
The Xanthate Chemical Company reports that on June 30 there were	13	4	51
15,680 shareholders who owned 10,373,664 shares of stock. Of the total	27	9	56
shareholders, 12,475 (79.5%) were individuals who owned 2,444,584 shares	42	14	61
of stock or 23.6% of the total. Of these individuals, 6,058 (38.6%)	56	19	65
were women who owned 1,200,392 shares or 11.6% of the total. A total	70	23	70
of 5,146 were men (32.8%) who owned 1,122,225 shares or 10.8% of the	84	28	74
shares. Joint accounts totaling 1,271 (8.1% of the shareholders) were	98	33	79
classified as individual shareholders. This group owned 121,967 shares	112	37	84
(1.2% of the total). The 3,205 remaining shareholders (20.5%) were	126	42	88
institutional investors with 10,373,664 shares or 20.5% of the total.	140	47	93

1′ GWAM | 1 | 2 | 3 | 4 | 5 | 6 | 7 | 8 | 9 | 10 | 11 | 12 | 13 | 14 |
3′ GWAM | 1 | 2 | 3 | 4 | 5 |

89B: Growth Index – Straight Copy (15) *two 5′ writings; determine* gwam*; proofread for errors*

All letters are used.

	GWAM 1′	5′	
There are two kinds of typists who never amount to much––those who	13	3	51
cannot do what they are told and those who do little else. One of the	28	6	54
important things all students must learn to do is to proofread quickly	42	8	57
and accurately every item of work they produce on the typewriter. A	56	11	60
letter or report with every error neatly corrected represents a pride	70	14	62
in work that reflects to the credit of the person who produced it.	83	17	65
Nearly all of us, now and then, need to be reminded that the work we	97	19	68
produce is our personal envoy in the eyes of others. Often, this work	111	22	71
may be the primary basis on which quality judgments are made.	123	25	73
It is important to find and correct all errors before the finished	13	27	76
work is given either to the teacher to grade or to the executive in the	28	30	79
office to use. Some typists fail to find their errors because they are	42	33	82
careless. They do not realize the effect an error may have on those who	57	36	85
see the finished job. In checking your work, be especially sure to verify	72	39	88
the accuracy of each date, figure, and amount. Check, too, to see if all	87	42	91
words are divided correctly at the ends of lines. Then read the copy	101	45	93
carefully to be sure that each word is spelled right and that each typing	115	48	96
error is corrected.	119	49	97

1′ GWAM | 1 | 2 | 3 | 4 | 5 | 6 | 7 | 8 | 9 | 10 | 11 | 12 | 13 | 14 |

5′ GWAM | 1 | 2 | 3 |

89C: Skill Applications (30)

Problem 1: Tabulation (*Spelling Emphasis*)

Half sheet; single-space data
Center vertically; triple-space after centered heading
6 spaces between columns

Type and arrange table in proper form. Note spelling of each word as it is typed.

SPELLING DEMONS

copied	copying	tried	trying
employ	employed	valley	valleys
gully	gullies	stop	stopping
confer	conferring	profit	profited
begin	beginning	useful	using
desire	desirable	courage	courageous
notice	noticeable	true	truly
argue	argument	brief	chief
either	neither	seize	leisure
weird	height	neighbor	weigh

KEY | 6 | 6 | 10 | 6 | 8 | 6 | 10 |

190D: Typing for Control (10) *two 1′ writings on each ¶; work for control*

	GWAM 1′	5′
All letters are used.		
Policies and procedures contribute to the efficient conduct of any	13	3
business. A policy is a guide or a rule of action that is utilized in	28	6
the solution of recurring problems. A procedure indicates the specific	42	8
steps that must be taken in implementing a policy. Thus, a policy may	56	11
set forth the number of days of sick leave employees may take each year	71	14
without loss of pay; the procedures tell what action is to be taken and	85	17
what forms are to be filled out when an employee takes sick leave. In	99	20
many industries, all procedures are published in a manual which is known	114	23
as the Manual of Standard Operating Procedures. This manual is issued	128	26
as a handbook for all personnel and often is used to train new employees.	143	29
 Policies are used by managers as aids in reaching decisions at all	13	31
levels of an enterprise. They promote efficiency because they save a	27	34
great deal of time, permit a more consistent solution to most of the	41	37
recurring problems, and allow a manager to do his job with more freedom	56	40
of action. To avoid confusion, all of the policies of a company must	70	42
be written clearly and concisely. At the same time, steps must be taken	84	45
to insure that each employee knows all of the policies and understands	98	48
the reason for each one. When this is done, a worker enjoys a greater	113	51
sense of security since he knows what to expect and he realizes that	126	54
each employee will receive equal treatment regardless of his job.	139	56
 Many of the duties performed by clerks, typists, and stenographers	13	59
in a business office are standard or routine in nature. For the sake of	28	62
efficiency, a company may specify a set method of doing such things as	42	65
typing letters, handling mail, receiving callers, filing, and preparing	57	68
reports. The steps or procedures to be followed in executing most of	71	71
these routine tasks are almost always found in an Office Procedures	84	73
Manual. When you first take a job, you may be asked to study this	98	76
manual and to use it as a guide until you know all of the procedures	112	79
well. If you learn the procedures quickly and apply the skill you have	126	82
acquired in school, you will be noted as an able and effective worker.	140	84

1′ GWAM | 1 | 2 | 3 | 4 | 5 | 6 | 7 | 8 | 9 | 10 | 11 | 12 | 13 | 14 |
5′ GWAM | 1 | 2 | 3 |

190E: Skill Building – Straight Copy (15) *two 5′ timed writings*

Use ¶s above. Compute *nwam* for each 5′ writing. Determine average *nwam* to compare with 195C.

Problem 2: Semiarranged Table (*Learning Recall and Spelling Suggestions*)

1. *Preview:* Drill paper; clear all stops; set margins as suggested at right, or use *backspace-from-center method*. Type longest word, or words, of each column (see |▶) in proper columnar position. Center and type columnar headings over these words. Use the *Mathematical Method*. Check solution by the *Forward-Space, Backspace Method*. Reference: 87D, page 140.
2. Type and arrange table in proper form. Use the *Forward-Space, Backspace Method* for centering the headings over the columns.

Full sheet	*Left margin and tab stops for columns*—Elite (Center 50): 19, 42, 68; Pica (Center 42): 11, 34, 60.
Center vertically	*Other machines (0 as center):*
TS after centered heading	Col. 1—Center — 31
DS after columnar headings	Col. 2—Center — 8
DS data; 12 spaces between columns	Col. 3—Center + 18

Note. *The color underline in Col. 1 shows part of word where misspellings most frequently occur. Do not type the underlines.*

SUGGESTED STUDY PROCEDURES
FOR WORDS OFTEN MISSPELLED ◀ *Type as two-line heading*

TS

Analyze the Word	Pronounce by Syllables	Acceptable Divisions	Words
			5
			11
Analyze	Pronounce	Acceptable	17
the Word	by Syllables	Divisions *DS*	29
knowledge	knowl-edge	knowl-edge	35
separate	sep-a-rate	sepa-rate	41
graduation	grad-u-a-tion	gradu-ation	49
enough	e-nough	Do not divide	54
planned	planned	Do not divide	60
government	gov-ern-ment	gov-ern-ment	68
candidate	can-di-date	can-di-date	75
attendance	at-tend-ance	attend-ance	82
difference	dif-fer-ence	dif-fer-ence	89
▶ accommodate	▶ ac-com-mo-date	accom-mo-date	97
misspell	mis-spell	mis-spell	103
recommend	rec-om-mend	rec-om-mend	110
referring	re-fer-ring	refer-ring	117
supersede	su-per-sede	super-sede	123
proceed	pro-ceed	pro-ceed	128
occurring	oc-cur-ring	occur-ring	135
foreign	for-eign	for-eign	140
absence	ab-sence	▶ Avoid dividing	147
teacher	teach-er	Do not divide	153
business	busi-ness	busi-ness	159
receive	re-ceive	Avoid dividing	165
quantity	quan-ti-ty	quan-tity	171
studying	stud-y-ing	study-ing	177

Problem 3: Typing from Dictation (*as time permits, with book closed*)

Full sheet; center vertically and horizontally
TS after centered heading: IMPROVING SPELLING
DS data of columns; assume longest line of each column has 12 spaces; 10 spaces between columns

1. Type the list of words in Problem 2 (Col. 1) in two columns from your teacher's dictation:

   Col. 1: Type word as it should be spelled.

   Col. 2: Type word and show, by hyphen, acceptable division points of word. If word can't be divided, type it whole.

2. Check your spelling and word division; circle each spelling or word-division error.

Unit 33 | Lessons 190-196

Reproduction Typing

LESSON 190

190A: Conditioning Practice (5) *each line at least three times*

Alphabet	Jack explained that Vi was frightened by the queer tale about zombies.	*Wrists low; hands quiet*
Figure	I moved to 3701 Market Street on May 28; my telephone is now 465-7920.	
Figure-symbol	He said, "Labor costs rose to $1,384,290 in 1967—an increase of 15%."	
Fluency	They may be authorized to vote in the election for the board chairman.	
	| 1 | 2 | 3 | 4 | 5 | 6 | 7 | 8 | 9 | 10 | 11 | 12 | 13 | 14 |	

190B: Technique Refinement (10) *each line three times; then 1' writings*

Direct reach	If my brother agrees to do the job, you can expect much more progress.	*Type with continuity*
Adjacent key	We asked three more experts for their opinion on population increases.	
Double letter	She suggested I call a meeting of the committee to discuss the matter.	
Balanced-hand	Civic and social problems of the town may form the theme of the panel.	
	| 1 | 2 | 3 | 4 | 5 | 6 | 7 | 8 | 9 | 10 | 11 | 12 | 13 | 14 |	

190C: Typing for Speed (10) *three 1' writings on each ¶; work for speed*

All letters are used.

Text	GWAM 1'	GWAM 5'	
Rules control almost all of our actions in life. Rules regulate	13	3	47
our activities in school and our behavior in the games we play. In our	27	5	50
personal relations with others, we are guided by the rules of etiquette	42	8	53
or good manners. Many local, state, and federal laws direct or control	56	11	56
the actions of individuals and groups in our society. Although these	70	14	59
laws limit our freedom of action, it is not possible to live or work	84	17	61
in any group without them. If there were no rules, there is no doubt	98	20	64
that confusion and strife would lead to the fall of our society.	111	22	67
You will find a great many rules and regulations when you enter	13	25	69
the business scene. There will be rules about the hours of work, wages,	27	28	72
absences, safety, and many other aspects of the work situation. Most	41	30	75
companies of any size publish these rules in an employee manual. Almost	56	33	78
all firms take the time and effort to explain the rules to employees	70	36	81
during the first day or week of work. Rules are just as essential to	84	39	83
the efficient conduct of business as they are to society. It is for	98	42	86
this reason that industries favor the employee who observes the rules.	112	45	89

1' GWAM | 1 | 2 | 3 | 4 | 5 | 6 | 7 | 8 | 9 | 10 | 11 | 12 | 13 | 14 |

5' GWAM | 1 | 2 | 3 |

LESSON 90

90A: Conditioning Practice (5) *each line three times*

Alphabet	Exquisite rings were made quickly by the jovial friends on the piazza.	*Return*
Figure	We received 129 chairs, 30 typewriters, and 75 desks on Order No. 648.	*carriage*
Fingers 3 and 4	The happy porpoise easily leaped through the loop and caught the ball.	*quickly*
Speed	If you do all your work in the right way, the work will be easy to do.	
	| 1 | 2 | 3 | 4 | 5 | 6 | 7 | 8 | 9 | 10 | 11 | 12 | 13 | 14 |	

90B: Skill Building – Straight Copy (15) *(Repeat 89B, page 143; Goal: Improved speed or accuracy)*

90C: Skill Applications (30)

Problem 1: Justifying the Right Margin (*Line: 32 pica, 39 elite; Spacing: SS; ¶ indention: 3*)

Copy may be typed with the right margin even (justified). School papers are often typed in this manner so the duplicated copies will have the appearance of a printed page. A stencil is typed from the master copy, and the desired number of copies are duplicated. A stencil is always typed with the ribbon disengaged.

Except for the last line of a paragraph, the words in each line are spaced so that the right margin will be even. This is done by adding extra spaces between words to fill out short lines, and using half spaces between words to squeeze words on lines.

You are to type the two ¶s at the left in two columns. Leave 4 spaces between columns; do not space between paragraphs. Do this:

1. Type the *work copy* with the / to show needed variable spacing for each line.
2. Retype the copy in two columns (count lines used and put half in each column), making the line endings uniform. Center heading, COPY WITH EVEN RIGHT MARGIN, a TS above the columns and about 1½″ from top edge.

Part of the *work copy* and *final copy* are shown in pica type. Lines 1, 2, and 4 require extra spacing. Line 3 is just right. To get the right margin even, the typist has to use judgment and distribute the spaces so they are least noticeable.

```
////////////////////////////////
   Copy may be typed with the///
right margin even (justified).//
School papers are often typed in
this manner so the duplicated///
copies will have the appearance/
```

WORK COPY

```
   Copy  may be  typed  with the
right margin  even  (justified).
School papers are often typed in
this   manner   so the  duplicated
copies will have  the appearance
```

COPY WITH EVEN RIGHT MARGIN

Problem 2: Manuscript on Changing Typewriter Ribbon (*DS; Margins: side 1″, top 2″; ¶ indention: 5*)

CHANGING THE TYPEWRITER RIBBON (*TS*)

(¶ 1) These are the basic steps to follow in changing the ribbon on most standard typewriters: (¶ 2) 1. Wind the ribbon on one spool. Adjust the ribbon-reverse lever and wind the ribbon on the right spool, unless the spools are interchangeable. Observe the direction of travel of the ribbon. (¶ 3) 2. Press down the shift-lock key, and move the ribbon-indicator lever to the position for typing on the lower portion of the ribbon. Depress any two central keys, such as y and u, and lock the two type bars in front of the printing point. This will raise and lock the ribbon carrier so that the old ribbon can be removed easily and the new ribbon inserted. Observe how the ribbon is threaded through the ribbon-carrier mechanism. (¶ 4) 3. Remove the ribbon from the carrier and remove both spools. Check the way each spool is attached to its hub, and how the ribbon is attached to the empty spool. (¶ 5) 4. Hook the new ribbon to the empty spool and wind several inches of the new ribbon on it. Be sure to wind this ribbon in the right direction. Place both spools on their holders and thread the ribbon through the ribbon carrier. (¶ 6) 5. Release the shift-lock key and return the ribbon indicator to the position for typing on the upper portion of the ribbon. Unlock the two type bars that were used to raise the ribbon carrier, and the typewriter will be ready for use.

Problem 2: Bill of Lading (*2 cc's*)

Words

Shippers No. Z–10952 Carrier Monarch Transport Company From Tri-State Steel Products Company 13
Date November 25, 19–– at Huntington, West Virginia Consigned to Hayes Construction Company 28
Destination 507 Jefferson Avenue Street Columbus City Franklin County State Ohio Routing 36
Portsmouth – Chillicothe Car Initial TY No. 94312 41

Packages	Description	Weight	Words
11	1 1/4-in. Galvanized Steel Pipe	24,291#	49
13	Automatic Baler Tie Wire	12,642#	58
9	3/8-in. x 6 Steel Machine Bolts	685#	67
7	1/2-in. x 36 Threaded Steel Rods	370#	76
10	3/16-in. x 1 1/2 Flat Head Bolts	135#	84
23	6 x 12 – 2/4 Welded Wire Mesh	8,165#	92

Shipper Tri-State Steel Products Company 99
Permanent address of shipper 2095 West Auburn Street, Huntington, West Virginia 25701 110

Problem 3: Invoice

2 cc's *SS body*

				Words
Date	November 25, 19––	Sold	Hayes Construction Company	9
Our Order No.	A–605173	To	507 Jefferson Avenue	15
Cust. Order No.	OK–98642		Columbus, Ohio 43215	21
Terms	Net 30 days	Shipped Via	Monarch Transport Company	29

Quantity	Description	Unit Price	Total	
3 ea.	Type 1432–M Decade Resistance Box	97.00 ea.	$ 291.00	41
7,945 lin. ft.	Reinforcing Steel Bent for Curbs	.08 lin. ft.	635.60	55
	(.68 lbs. per ft. of curb)			60
8,000 lbs.	Deformed Reinforcing Bars, #4 x 3–0	8.20 cwt.	656.00	73
50 gro.	1/4-in. x 2 1/2-in. Zinc-plated Carriage Bolts	3.63 gro.	181.50	90
			$1,764.10	91

Problem 4: Invoice

Address given in Problem 3 *2 cc's* *DS body*

Quantity	Description	Unit Price	Total	Words
16 ft.	1 1/2-in. Galvanized Steel Pipe	.27	$ 4.32	40
550 ft.	3/4-in. Butt-Weld Standard Pipe, Threaded	.24	132.00	52
10 sets	6 pc. Masonry Drills	7.40	74.00	62
			$210.32	63

Unit 15 | Lessons 91-98

Manuscripts and Reports

One of several acceptable ways of typing footnotes is illustrated in this unit. The lessons are designed to help you gain skill in arranging copy in manuscript or report form.

LESSON 91

91A: Conditioning Practice (5) *each line three times*

Alphabet	Liza picked several exquisite flowers which grew by the jungle swamps.	Start new line quickly
Figure	Please ship Order No. 750 for 36 typewriters, 49 desks, and 128 lamps.	
Long reaches	The unusual aluminum bridge is decorated with many bright nylon flags.	
Speed	The authenticity of the six amendments may torment the skeptical boys.	
	| 1 | 2 | 3 | 4 | 5 | 6 | 7 | 8 | 9 | 10 | 11 | 12 | 13 | 14 |	

91B: Related Learning – Capitalization Guides (10)

Practice Plan:

1. Study explanatory guide or rule.
2. Type *Learn* sentence, noting rule application.
3. Type *Apply* sentence, making all needed corrections; then DS. Reference: 86C, page 138.

Machine Adjustments:

1. 70-space line; single spacing.
2. 1½″ top margin first page; 1″ margin on all other pages; bottom margin of about 1″ on all pages that are full.

1. Capitalize the first word of every sentence and the first word of every complete direct quotation.
2. Do not capitalize fragments of quotations.
3. Do not capitalize a quotation resumed within a sentence. Note. Type the comma or period before the ending quotation mark.
4. Capitalize the first word after a colon if that word begins a complete sentence. Note. Space twice after the colon.
5. Capitalize first and last words and all other words in titles of books, articles, periodicals, headings, and plays, except words of four letters or less used as articles, conjunctions, or prepositions.

SERIES 2: CAPITALIZATION GUIDE EXAMPLES

Retain paper for use in next lesson.

1	*Learn*	She said, "There is no substitute for hard work in attaining success."
	Apply	kahlil Gibran once wrote, "i have learned silence from the talkative."
2	*Learn*	Among other things, he stressed the importance of "a sense of values."
	Apply	His basic thesis seemed to be that the teacher "Affects all eternity."
3	*Learn*	"When all else fails," a unique sign read, "try following directions."
	Apply	"I'll toot your horn", she said impatiently, "While you start my car".
4	*Learn*	These are the directions: Use a 5-space indention and double spacing.
	Apply	Do this daily: check the ribbon control and set the paper guide at 0.
5	*Learn*	Have you read the new book by Thomas Booth, The Value of an Education?
	Apply	The article "wonders of the space age" should be on your reading list.

LESSON 189

189A: Conditioning Practice (5) *each line at least three times*

Alphabet; shift	Rex Key and Jim Rahe won five prizes at a racquet club in Palm Groves.	*Uniform key stroke*
Figure	at 2 percent, 10 days, net 30, Cust. Order No. 9831543M for 6,792 sets	
Figure-symbol	$1,825.94 (Rice & Haly*) 9¼ x 3½ Bill's 6% <u>heavy-duty</u> 7 2/5'' #10 @ 16¢	
Fluency	The world of tomorrow will be won by those who are very well informed.	
	| 1 | 2 | 3 | 4 | 5 | 6 | 7 | 8 | 9 | 10 | 11 | 12 | 13 | 14 |	

189B: Technique Refinement (5) *1′ comparative writings*

Easy	One or two men should plan to spend a few days working on the program.	*Adjust stroking speed to copy difficulty*
Average	The secretary listed several basic reasons for not granting new loans.	
Difficult	Our correspondence concerning vital specifications was examined daily.	
	| 1 | 2 | 3 | 4 | 5 | 6 | 7 | 8 | 9 | 10 | 11 | 12 | 13 | 14 |	

189C: Selected Business Forms Production Measurement (40)

Arrange supplies. Type the following four problems for 30′ when directed to begin. Correct errors as you type. If time permits, start over. Mark uncorrected errors. Compute *n-pram*.

Time Schedule	
Get ready to type	4′
Timed production	30′
Proofread; compute *n-pram* . .	6′

Problem 1: Purchase Order

2 cc's — *SS body*

		Words
	Order No. 58905–D	2
To: Millar Electrical Supply Company	Date November 25, 19––	12
2507 East Lake Avenue	Terms Net 30 days	18
Cleveland, Ohio 44103	Ship Via Buckeye Transit, Inc.	28

Quantity	Cat. No.	Description	Price	
10 doz.	FB–41205	120-v, 20 amp, Fuseless 2-circuit Breakers	$228.00	41
8 ea.	AL–68937	Single-circuit Automatic Lighting Device	120.00	54
850 ft.	DC–20451	1/2-in. Galvanized Steel Conduit	56.95	65
3 coils	IW–87369	2-wire, #14 Electrical Cable	59.85	75
60 ea.	CF–14520	30-amp, Cartridge Fuses, Brass Ends	9.00	87
4 ctns.	DL–41306	Fluorescent Lamps	36.20	95
12 rolls	DF–30295	3/4-in. x 66 Electrical Tape	22.00	107
			$532.00	108

91C: Skill Building – Speed and Accuracy Emphasis (10)

1. **Type** two 1′ writings on ¶ 1 for speed. If you complete the ¶, start over.
2. **Type** two 1′ writings on ¶ 1 on the *control* level (not over 1 error in each writing).
3. **Repeat** Steps 1 and 2, using ¶ 2. *Goal:* Try to equal the rate you made on ¶ 1.

¶ 1
Alphabet

It is not easy for a lazy typist to improve, but there is a big difference between such a typist and a relaxed typist. A relaxed typist still keeps just the right amount of alert tension which forces the fingers to strike the keys quickly.

¶ 2
Statistical (all numbers used)

A watch has about 176 different parts. The tiny heart of a watch, the balance wheel, beats 18,000 times per hour. Pulsing back and forth, it travels 9 3/4 miles every 24 hours. This distance equals a journey of 3,558 3/4 miles in a year.

91D: Skill Application – Manuscript Without Footnotes (25)

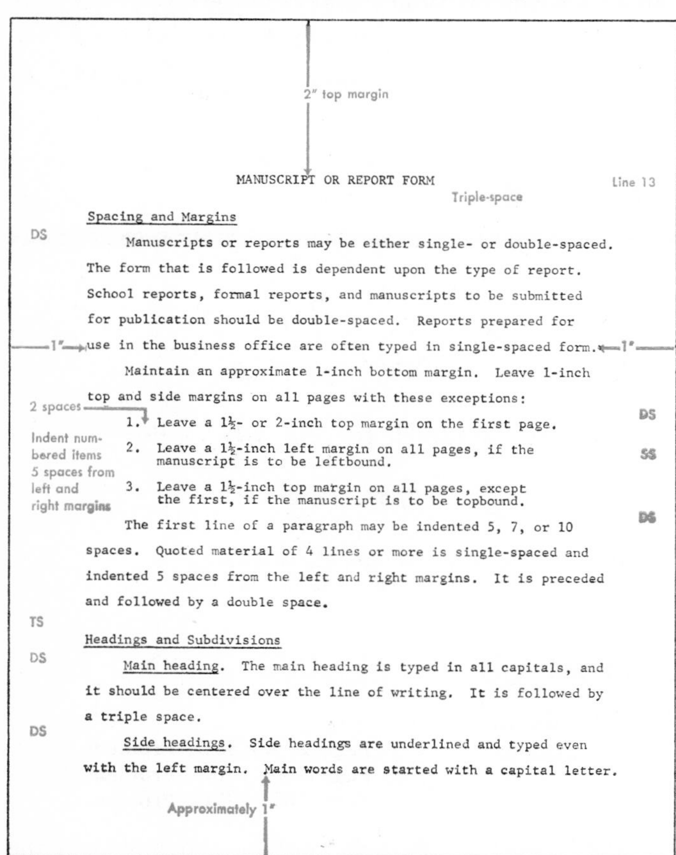

MANUSCRIPT OR REPORT FORM

Spacing and Margins

Manuscripts or reports may be either single- or double-spaced. The form that is followed is dependent upon the type of report. School reports, formal reports, and manuscripts to be submitted for publication should be double-spaced. Reports prepared for use in the business office are often typed in single-spaced form.

Maintain an approximate 1-inch bottom margin. Leave 1-inch top and side margins on all pages with these exceptions:

1. Leave a 1½- or 2-inch top margin on the first page.
2. Leave a 1½-inch left margin on all pages, if the manuscript is to be leftbound.
3. Leave a 1½-inch top margin on all pages, except the first, if the manuscript is to be topbound.

The first line of a paragraph may be indented 5, 7, or 10 spaces. Quoted material of 4 lines or more is single-spaced and indented 5 spaces from the left and right margins. It is preceded and followed by a double space.

Headings and Subdivisions

Main heading. The main heading is typed in all capitals, and it should be centered over the line of writing. It is followed by a triple space.

Side headings. Side headings are underlined and typed even with the left margin. Main words are started with a capital letter.

FIRST PAGE OF UNBOUND MANUSCRIPT WITHOUT FOOTNOTES

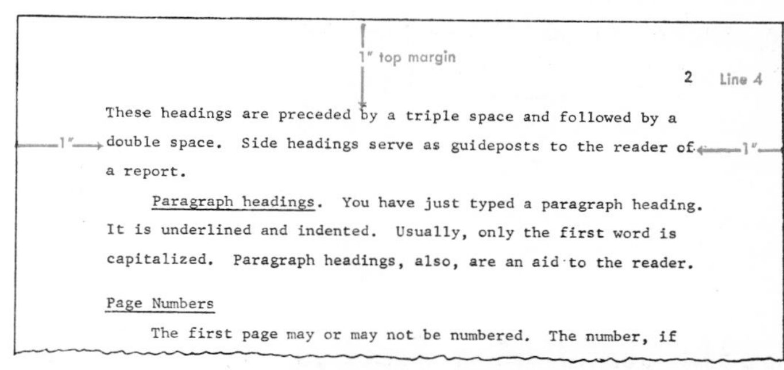

2

These headings are preceded by a triple space and followed by a double space. Side headings serve as guideposts to the reader of a report.

Paragraph headings. You have just typed a paragraph heading. It is underlined and indented. Usually, only the first word is capitalized. Paragraph headings, also, are an aid to the reader.

Page Numbers

The first page may or may not be numbered. The number, if

PARTIAL SECOND PAGE OF UNBOUND MANUSCRIPT

1. **Study** the illustrations here and the paragraphs on manuscript or report form, page 148.
2. **Type** the problem in unbound manuscript form as directed below. Indent the *enumerated items* 5 spaces from left and right margins and space as illustrated. *Note:* Make a light pencil mark at the right edge of the page about 1″ from the bottom edge (and again at 1½″) to remind you to leave a 1″ bottom margin.

Full sheet; DS; 5-space ¶ indention
Page 1: 2″ top, 1″ side, and 1″ bottom margins (approximately)
Do not number page
Page 2: 1″ top and side margins
Number page in upper right corner

Problem 2

Type invoice below as illustrated for Problem 1 on page 281 *2 cc's* *SS body*

				Words
Date	November 23, 19--	Sold	Custom Builders and Contractors	10
Our Order No.	A-605174	To	1057 East Broad Street	16
Cust. Order No.	XY-092350		Richmond, Kentucky 40475	24
Terms	Net 30 days	Shipped Via	Blue Grass Transit	30

Quantity	Description	Unit Price	Total	
9,780 lbs.	Reinforcing Steel Rods 5/8-in. x 16 ft.	8.24 cwt.	$ 805.87	44
4,625 lin. ft.	Contraction Joint Type D1	.78 lin. ft.	3,607.50	56
	(Sandplates required)			61
30 gro.	1 1/2 – 8 Zinc-Plated Sheet Metal Screws	1.90 gro.	57.00	74
241 sq. yds.	6 x 12 – 2/4 Welded Wire Mesh	.58 sq. yd.	139.78	89
			$4,610.15	91

Problem 3

Type an *invoice*; make 2 cc's on plain half sheets. Use the information that follows:

Words

Date March 17, 19-- Our Order No. 3
A-594061 Cust. Order No. 36821-C Terms 6
Net 30 days Sold To Hayes Construction Co. 13
507 Jefferson Avenue Columbus, Ohio 43215 22
Shipped Via Valley Transport 10 pr. Louvered 29
Shutters Unit Price $1.82 Total $18.20 | 12 34
sets Hand-Painted Wall Plates Unit Price $7.15 41
Total $85.80 | 4 sets Flower Boxes and Legs 48
Unit Price $7.35 Total $29.40 | Total $133.40 52

LESSON 188

188A: Conditioning Practice (5) *each line at least three times*

Quick, snap stroke

Alphabet; shift	Maxwell Quigley and Vern Jackson backed the new team of Gateway Plaza.
Figure	at 3 percent, 5 days, net 30 days, Our Order No. 8940632L for 217 yds.
Figure-symbol	$3,047.16 (Frank & Son*) 2½ x 5¼ John's 12% soft-focus 5 3/8" #6 @ 49¢
Fluency	You can acquire stimulating ideas by reading a variety of great books.
	| 1 | 2 | 3 | 4 | 5 | 6 | 7 | 8 | 9 | 10 | 11 | 12 | 13 | 14 |

188B: Sustained Production on Selected Business Forms (45)

Time Schedule

Get ready to type	7′
Timed production	30′
Proofread; compute *n-pram* . .	8′

Arrange supplies. Make a list of the problems at the right and check them off as you complete them. Type for 30′, following instructions given for each problem typed. Correct all errors as you type. If you finish before time is called, start over. Mark uncorrected errors. Compute *n-pram.*

Page 279, 185D, Problem 2
Page 280, 186C, Problem 2
Page 282, 187C, Problem 2

Turn in problems arranged in the order in which they are listed.

MANUSCRIPT OR REPORT FORM *TS*

Spacing and Margins *DS*

Manuscripts or reports may be either single- or double-spaced. The form that is followed is dependent upon the type of report. School reports, formal reports, and manuscripts to be submitted for publication should be double-spaced. Reports prepared for use in the business office are often typed in single-spaced form.

Maintain an approximate 1-inch bottom margin. Leave 1-inch top and side margins on all pages with these exceptions:

1. Leave a 1½- or 2-inch top margin on the first page.
2. Leave a 1½-inch left margin on all pages, if the manuscript is to be leftbound.
3. Leave a 1½-inch top margin on all pages, except the first, if the manuscript is to be topbound.

The first line of a paragraph may be indented 5, 7, or 10 spaces. Quoted material of 4 lines or more is single-spaced and indented 5 spaces from the left and right margins. It is preceded and followed by a double space.

TS

Headings and Subdivisions *DS*

Main heading. The main heading is typed in all capitals, and it should be centered over the line of writing. It is followed by a triple space.

Side headings. Side headings are underlined and typed even with the left margin. Main words are started with a capital letter. These headings are preceded by a triple space and followed by a double space. Side headings serve as guideposts to the reader of a report.

Paragraph headings. You have just typed a paragraph heading. It is underlined and indented. Usually, only the first word is capitalized. Paragraph headings, also, are an aid to the reader.

Page Numbers

The first page may or may not be numbered. The number, if used, is centered and typed one-half inch from the bottom edge. Other page numbers, as a general rule, are typed on the fourth line in the upper right corner so that they are approximately even with the right margin; however, if the manuscript or report is to be bound at the top, the page numbers are typed in the first-page position.

Other General Guides

As a general rule, avoid ending a page with one line of a new paragraph, or carrying one line of a paragraph to a new page. This general rule, however, is no longer strictly enforced, even in formal writing.

The regular word-division rules govern the division of words at the ends of lines. Avoid, if possible, dividing words at the ends of more than two consecutive lines, or at the end of a page.

LESSON 92

92A: Conditioning Practice (5) *each line three times*

Alphabet	These children were amazed by the quick, lively jumps of the gray fox.	Quiet hands and arms
Figure	Express measures in figures; as, 156 quarts, 284 gallons, 7,903 pecks.	
Third row	You were to quote your best prices on those typewriters, were you not?	
Speed	She may go with them down the lane to the shale rocks by the big lake.	
	| 1 | 2 | 3 | 4 | 5 | 6 | 7 | 8 | 9 | 10 | 11 | 12 | 13 | 14 |	

92B: Technique Improvement – Reading the Copy (10) *type three times; then, three 1′ speed writings*

	Words
Try to read | and type | this copy | in these | word groups. | Make a quick |	13
typing response | to each | word group. | Think the | word groups | as they |	27
are typed. | This is | another way | to force | your speed | to higher levels. |	41

Problem 3

Type a *bill of lading*; make 2 cc's on plain half sheets. Use the information that follows:

	Words
Shipper's No. 362801 Carrier Valley Trans-	4
port From Becker Building Supply Co. Date	10
March 16, 19–– at Toledo, Ohio 43624 Con-	17
signed to Hayes Construction Co. Destination	22
507 Jefferson Avenue Street Columbus City	28
Franklin County Ohio State Routing Marion –	32
Delaware Vehicle or Car Initial XL No. 75143	36
10 Louvered Shutters 19# | 12 Hand-Painted	44
Wall Plates 3# | 4 Flower Boxes and Legs 26#	53
Shipper Becker Building Supply Co. Perma-	58
nent address of shipper 3970 Washington	61
Street, Toledo, Ohio 43624	67

LESSON 187

187A: Conditioning Practice (5) *each line at least three times*

Alphabet; shift	Jinx Bevan played croquet with Dianne Pizor from the famous King Club.	*Finger-action reaches*
Figure	at 2 percent, 10 days, net 30 days, Our Order No. 3728413LJ for 596 ft.	
Figure-symbol	$6,370.29 (Bell & Muse*) 4¼ x 5½ Paul's 18% self-made 6 5/8" #42 @ 70¢	
Fluency	A student of high standing should try to be well versed in many areas.	

| 1 | 2 | 3 | 4 | 5 | 6 | 7 | 8 | 9 | 10 | 11 | 12 | 13 | 14 |

187B: Building Sustained Typing Power (13)

Type one 10′ writing from 183C, pages 275–276. Compute *gwam*; compare rate with 186B, page 279.

187C: Typing Invoices (32)

Time Schedule

Get ready to type . . . 2′
Timed production . 25′
Proofread and compute *g-pram* . . 5′

Type the following three invoices for 25′ when directed to begin. If time permits, start over. Mark errors. Compute *g-pram*.

Problem 1

Type invoice as shown at right
2 cc's *DS body*

INVOICE — 2095 West Auburn Street, Huntington, West Virginia 25701 — TRI-STATE STEEL PRODUCTS COMPANY

		Words
Date	November 23, 19--	4
Sold to	Buckeye General Contractors, Inc.	12
	1905 North Main Street	17
	Chillicothe, Ohio 45601	24
Our Order No.	A-605172	
Cust. Order No.	483950-K	
Terms	Net 30 days — Shipped Via Central Freight Lines	30

Quantity	Description	Unit Price	Total	Words
600 ft.	1/2-in. Flexible Copper Tubing	.29 ft.	$ 174.00	42
8,750 lbs.	Reinforcing Steel for Structures	8.35 cwt.	730.63	55
6,291 sq. yds.	6 x 6 - 6/6 Welded Wire Mesh	.42 sq. yd.	2,642.22	68
	For Slope Walls 5-0 x 150-0 Rolls			77
968 lin. ft.	Load Transfer Joint	1.35 lin. ft.	1,306.80	88
			$4,853.65	89

INVOICE

92C: Skill Application – Rough Draft of Manuscript Without Footnotes (25)

Full sheets; carbon pack
DS; 5-space ¶ indention
Margins: 1½" top; 1" side
Correct errors
Proofreading correction symbols: See page 125

1. Study copy on erasing errors.
2. Assemble carbon pack (original, carbon paper, and copy sheet).
3. Type problem in *unbound* manuscript form. Make corrections indicated in the copy.

Note. When enumerated items are in double-spaced form, they are typed as illustrated in the copy.

Total Words

Triple-space

CORRECTING ERRORS 4
ON ORIGINAL AND CARBON COPIES 10

and corrected. to follow
All typing errors should be erased. These are the steps in 26
making corrections: 31

or cylinder
1. Turn the platen forward a few spaces to prvoide working space; 46
a extreme
then move hte carrige to the right or left so the eraser crumbs 61
will not fall into the machine. 68

Move the paper bail out of the way.
2. Pull the ori ginal sheet forward and place a card 86
(5 x 3 inches, or slightly larger) in front of not behind the first 100
carbon. this protects thecopy from carbon smudges as the erasure 113
original
is made on the sheet. 119

Flip the original sheet back and or blow
3. Make the erasure with a hard eraser. Brush the eraser 139
off the paper.
crumbs ~~away from the typewriter~~. 144

4. Move the protective card to a positoin in front of the 156
second carbon, if more than one copy is being made. Erase the 168
error on the first carbon copy. Erase all other errors in a like 182
manner. 183

5. Remove the protective card and type the correction. 195

¶ When you erase, be carefull that your fingers do not smudge the 207
copy as you hold the paper. Most typists use an eraser shield 220
to protect the typing that is not to be erased. 230

If the erasure is to be made on the upper two thirds of the 242
paper, turn the cylinder forward; if on the lower third of the 254
the ward
paper, turn cylnider back so that the paper will not slip out of 269
the typewriter as you erase. 275

Problem 1 *Type bill of lading as shown* *2 cc's*

Words

UNIFORM STRAIGHT BILL OF LADING **Original—Not Negotiable—Domestic** **Shipper's No.** 815062 1

Monarch Transport Company **Carrier** Agent's No. 7

RECEIVED, subject to the classifications and tariffs in effect on the date of the issue of this Bill of Lading.

From Tri-State Steel Products Company **Date** November 22, **19** -- 16

at Huntington, West Virginia 21

the property described below, in apparent good order, except as noted (contents and condition of contents of packages unknown) marked, consigned and destined as shown below, which said company (the word company being understood throughout this contract as meaning any person or corporation in possession of the property under the contract) agrees to carry to its usual place of delivery at said destination, if on its own railroad, water line, highway route or routes, or within the territory of its highway operations, otherwise to deliver to another carrier on the route to said destination. It is mutually agreed, as to each carrier of all or any of said property over all or any portion of said route to destination, and as to each party at any time interested in all or any of said property, that every service to be performed hereunder shall be subject to all the conditions not prohibited by law, whether printed or written, herein contained, including the conditions on back hereof, which are hereby agreed to by the shipper and accepted for himself and his assigns.

Consigned to Hayes Construction Company 27

Destination 507 Jefferson Avenue Street Columbus City Franklin County Ohio State 36

Routing Portsmouth - Chillicothe 41

Delivering Carrier Vehicle or Car Initial TY No. 94312 42

No. Packages	Kind of Packages, Description of Articles, Special Marks, and Exceptions	* Weight (Sub. to Cor.)	Class or Rate	Check Column	
3	Stainless Steel 1/2-in. Wire	2,675#			50
7	Sheets, Galvanized Steel	6,749#			57
2	Butt-Weld Standard Pipe, 3/4-in.	1,242#			65
10	Rivet Tools, Heavy Duty	75#			72
3	Masonry Drills, 6 piece	45#			79

Subject to Section 7 of conditions, if this shipment is to be delivered to the consignee without recourse on the consignor, the consignor shall sign the following statement:

The carrier shall not make delivery of this shipment without payment of freight and all other lawful charges.

(Signature of Consignor.)

If charges are to be prepaid, write or stamp here, "To be Prepaid."

Received $ to apply in prepayment of the charges on the property described hereon.

Agent or Cashier

Per

(The signature here acknowledges only the amount prepaid.)

Charges Advanced:

$

* If the shipment moves between two ports by a carrier by water, the law requires that the bill of lading shall state whether it is "carrier's or shipper's weight."

NOTE—Where the rate is dependent on value, shippers are required to state specifically in writing the agreed or declared value of the property. The agreed or declared value of the property is hereby specifically stated by the shipper to be not exceeding

per

Tri-State Steel Products Company Shipper Agent, Per 85

Permanent address of shipper 2095 West Auburn Street, Huntington, West Virginia 25701 97

1

BILL OF LADING

Problem 2 *Type bill of lading below, as illustrated for Problem 1 above* *2 cc's*

Words

Shipper's No. 815063 Carrier Blue Grass Transit From Tri-State Steel Products Company Date 12
November 22, 19–– at Huntington, West Virginia Consigned to Custom Builders and Contractors 27
Destination 1057 East Broad Street Street Richmond City Madison County State Kentucky Routing 37
Morehead – Winchester Vehicle or Car Initial XL No. 86054 43

Packages	Description	Weight	
28	Contraction Joint, Type D1	10,142#	51
20	Reinforcing Rods 5/8-in. x 16 ft.	9,780#	62
5	Welded Wire Mesh, 6 x 12 – 2/4	275#	69
7	Sheet Metal Screws, 1 1/2 – 8	55#	77
15	Drain Augers for 1/4, 3/8-in. Drills	215#	86
9	5-Die Pipe Threader Sets	160#	92

Shipper Tri-State Steel Products Company 99
Permanent address of shipper 2095 West Auburn Street, Huntington, West Virginia 25701 111

92D: Related Learning – Capitalization Guides *(Cont.)* (10) *(Reinsert sheet used for 91B, page 146.)*

6. In footnotes used in manuscripts or reports, capitalize names of authors, first and last words and all other words in titles of books, articles, and pamphlets, names of magazines and newspapers, except words of four or fewer letters used as articles, conjunctions, or prepositions. Footnotes may be typed and capitalized as shown in the following examples.

6 *Learn*

Type the superior figure ½ space above line of writing

Footnote reference to a book:[1] *(title underlined)*

[1] Herbert W. Johnson, How to Use the Business Library (3d ed.; Cincinnati: South–Western Publishing Co., 1964), p. iii.

Footnote reference to a magazine or periodical:[2] *(title enclosed in quotes)*

[2] Bernice K. Konehue, "Use of Reference Materials in the High School," Education, Vol. 84, No. 4 (December, 1963), p. 218.

Footnote reference to a magazine or periodical with no author listed:[3]

[3] "Libraries as Important as Schools, Says Kennedy in NLW Message," Library Journal (May 15, 1963), p. 1962.

Footnote reference to a newspaper:[4]

[4] "New Math to Be Tried in Local Schools," Cincinnati Enquirer (December 3, 1965), p. 2.

LESSON 93

93A: Conditioning Practice (5) *each line three times*

Alphabet	The reporters quickly recognized the vexing problems of judging flaws.	Type with continuity
Figure	I ordered 720 pencils, 36 pens, 49 erasers, and 185 cardboard folders.	
Home row	J. Kagal asked a lad if he had added a dash of salt to a dish of hash.	
Speed	The six men may go down to the rifle field to fix the eight-day dials.	

| 1 | 2 | 3 | 4 | 5 | 6 | 7 | 8 | 9 | 10 | 11 | 12 | 13 | 14 |

93B: Alertness Training – Spelling (5) *each line twice; note spelling of words underlined*

EMPHASIZE Direct-reach finger action

1 She tried and they were trying to get copies of new copying process.

2 The picture portrayed beautifully many valleys and gullies in an area.

3 Either of you should receive the weird brief which the chief prepared.

4 I profited and benefited by conferring with him at a beginning caucus.

5 It would be desirable to avoid an argument with that courageous woman.

Problem 2 *Type purchase order* *2 cc's* *SS body*

			Words
	Order No.	58906–Y	2
To: Valley Plumbing Supplies, Inc.	Date	November 21, 19––	11
7564 South River Road	Terms	Net 30 days	18
Parkersburg, West Virginia 26101	Ship Via	Ohio Valley Transport	29

Quantity	Cat. No.	Description	Price	
550 ft.	RC–19047	3/8-in. Rigid Copper Tubing, Type C	$148.50	43
900 sq. ft.	XI –85623	4-mil., 3 ft.-wide, Flexible Vinyl Plastic	74.00	57
1 gro.	TM–06248	1 x 3/4 x 3/4 Malleable Reducing Tees	89.20	69
3 ea.	EH–79531	220-v, 60-c, AC Electric Water Heaters	241.85	81
2 doz.	FM–80567	3 x 3 x 1 1/2-in. Y Branch Copper Fittings	62.40	96
			$615.95	97

Problem 3

Type a *purchase order*; make 2 cc's on plain half sheets. Use the information that follows:

Words

To Becker Building Supply Co. 3970 Washing- 8
ton Street Toledo, Ohio 43624 Order No. 14
36821–C Date March 14, 19–– Terms Net 19
30 days Ship Via Valley Transport 10 pr. 26
Q–762 Louvered Shutters $18.20 | 12 sets 34
S–154 Hand-Painted Wall Plates $85.80 | 4 sets 43
X–202 Flower Boxes and Legs $29.40 | Total 51
$133.40 52

LESSON 186

186A: Conditioning Practice (5) *each line at least three times*

Fingers upright

Alphabet; shift	Barb Pfau sent quiet Judge Tazmore eleven sketches drawn by Cal Nixon.
Figure	2 doz. Our Order No. 103945 at 10 percent 5 days, net 30 Order No. 687
Figure-symbol	$8,204.95 (Boyd & Long*) 7½ x 6¼ Betty's 13% know-how 8 3/4" #65 @ 90¢
Fluency	There is much good to be gained by travelling both at home and abroad.
	| 1 | 2 | 3 | 4 | 5 | 6 | 7 | 8 | 9 | 10 | 11 | 12 | 13 | 14 |

186B: Building Sustained Typing Power (13)

Type one 10′ writing from 184B, page 277. Compute *gwam*; record rate to compare with 187B. (To compute *gwam* from 5′ rate, divide 5′ *gwam* by 2)

186C: Typing Bills of Lading (32)

Type the following three bills of lading on pages 280–281 for 25′ when directed to begin. If time permits, start over. Mark errors. Compute *g-pram*.

Time Schedule

Get ready to type	2′
Timed production	25′
Proofread; compute *g-pram*	5′

93C: Related Learning – Capitalization Guides *(Cont.)* (10) *study-learn-apply*

7. Capitalize an official title when it immediately precedes a name. When used elsewhere, type it without the capital unless it is a title of high distinction or it refers to a specific person.
8. Business or professional titles used without the name of the person are not usually capitalized.
9. Capitalize all proper nouns and their derivations.
10. Capitalize the names of the days of the week, months of the year, holidays, periods of history, and historic events.

7 *Learn* On Tuesday, President Fairbanks of the Ottawa Company will address us.
Apply John DeJur is the Executive Assistant to president James R. O'Connell.

8 *Learn* The doctor will be here at 10 a.m. The attorney is studying the case.
Apply The Dean will see him soon. Dr. Owen is the new Professor of history.

9 *Learn* John wrote an interesting report on European and American folk dances.
Apply They plan to attend the canadian Shakespearean Festival during August.

10 *Learn* Capitalize these words: Tuesday, May, Labor Day, and the Middle Ages.
Apply On friday, november 10, we will have a test on the restoration Period.

93D: Skill Application – Manuscript with Footnotes (30)

1. Study illustration and the paragraphs on footnote form.
2. Type the 1-page manuscript as directed below.

Full sheet; Center heading over line of writing
TS after heading; DS copy
Margins—
Left: 1½"; Right: 1"
Top: 1½"—if pica type is used
2"—if elite type is used
SS before and DS after the underline separating copy and footnotes

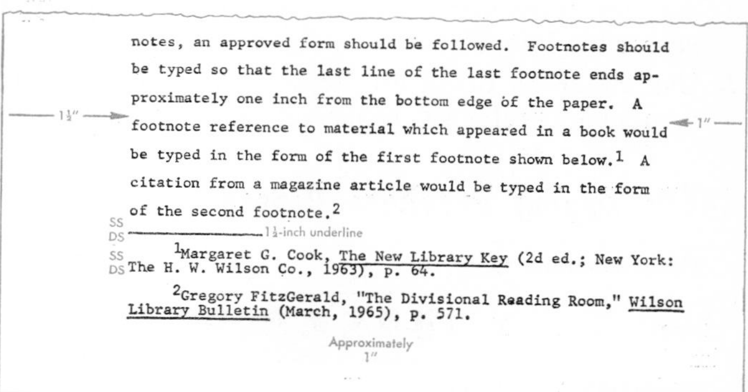
notes, an approved form should be followed. Footnotes should be typed so that the last line of the last footnote ends approximately one inch from the bottom edge of the paper. A footnote reference to material which appeared in a book would be typed in the form of the first footnote shown below.[1] A citation from a magazine article would be typed in the form of the second footnote.[2]

[1]Margaret G. Cook, The New Library Key (2d ed.; New York: The H. W. Wilson Co., 1963), p. 64.

[2]Gregory FitzGerald, "The Divisional Reading Room," Wilson Library Bulletin (March, 1965), p. 571.

FOOTNOTE PLACEMENT AND STYLE

FOOTNOTE FORM REVIEW

In school, you will often have to prepare themes, reports, or term papers which require library research. When you quote from the written material of others, or use ideas of an author, you must acknowledge the source of your information. This is usually done by means of a footnote reference with the footnote itself appearing at the bottom of the page on which the reference is made.

In this brief manuscript page, you will review the proper order and form of footnotes by typing the two footnotes listed below. Note that the footnotes are separated from the manuscript by a dividing line 1½ inches long. Footnotes are indented to the paragraph point, preceded without spacing by a reference figure raised one-half line space, and single-spaced with double spacing between footnotes. In typing footnotes, an approved form should be followed. Footnotes should be typed so that the last line of the last footnote ends approximately one inch from the bottom edge of the paper. A footnote reference to material which appeared in a book would be typed in the form of the first footnote shown below.[1] A citation from a magazine article would be typed in the form of the second footnote.[2]

---

[1] Margaret G. Cook, The New Library Key (2d ed.; New York: The H. W. Wilson Co., 1963), p. 64.

[2] Gregory FitzGerald, "The Divisional Reading Room," Wilson Library Bulletin (March, 1965), p. 571.

LESSON 185

185A: Conditioning Practice (5) *each line at least three times*

Alphabet; shift	Tom Peterson relaxed with Jack Zore by a quiet cove near the Gulf Inn.	*Fingers curved*
Figure	500 lbs. Our Order No. B 47122 at 30 days net, shipped October 8, 1969	
Figure-symbol	$4,965.02 (Jones & Young*) 3½ x 8¼ Sue's 17% one-half 6 3/4" #892 @ 7¢	
Fluency	There are many interesting places for people to visit in this country.	
	| 1 | 2 | 3 | 4 | 5 | 6 | 7 | 8 | 9 | 10 | 11 | 12 | 13 | 14 |	

185B: Basic Skill Maintenance (7)

Type one 5′ writing from 183C, pages 275–276. Proofread and compute *gwam*; compare rate with your 5′ *gwam* rate typed on 184B.

185C: Typing Selected Business Forms – Preview (3)

TIPS FOR TYPING SPECIAL FORMS—Purchase Orders, Bills of Lading, Invoices.

1. Set margin stops.
2. Set tab stops for frequent indentions, and type *across* the line, rather than vertically.
3. Use either DS or SS for items in the body. Some companies prefer DS, especially with few items.
4. When a listing requires more than one line, type the long entry with SS; then DS between items.
5. In the *price* or *amount* column, underline the last figure; then DS to type the total amount.
6. Purchase orders, bills of lading, and invoices are often mailed in window envelopes. For folding, see Reference Guide, page vi.

185D: Typing Purchase Orders (35)

Time Schedule

Get ready to type . . . 3′
Timed production . 25′
Proofread; and compute *g-pram* . . 7′

Type the following three purchase orders for 25′ when directed to begin. If time permits, start over. Mark errors. Fold the first two copies for a window envelope, to send to seller. Compute *g-pram.*

Problem 1

Type purchase order shown at right 2 cc's
DS items in body

HAYES — hayes construction company 507 jefferson avenue, columbus, ohio 43215 — purchase order

		Words
order no.:	58904-E	2
date:	November 21, 19--	12
to:	Tri-State Steel Products Company 2095 West Auburn Street Huntington, West Virginia 25701	17
terms:	Net 30 days	26
ship via:	Monarch Transport	29

quantity	cat. no.	description	price	Words
2,675 lbs.	ST-82051	CF Stainless Steel, 1/2-in. SS304 Wire	$1,263.94	44
6,749 lbs.	GY-97356	Sheet Steel, Galvanized and Hot Dipped	507.52	57
1,099 ft.	PS-48207	3/4-in. Butt-Weld Standard Pipe, Threaded	126.39	70
50 ea.	RS-36159	Heavy-Duty Rivet Tool, Interchangeable Jaws	732.50	84
25 sets	DN-82705	6 pc. Masonry Drills, Tungsten-Carbide Tips	162.50	100
			$2,792.85	103
Margin stop	Tab	Tab	Tab	

(fold here; DS)

purchasing agent

PURCHASE ORDER

LESSON 94

94A: Conditioning Practice (5) *each line three times*

Alphabet Six flying fish whizzed quickly over my jigs as a big tuna approached.
Figure Type 1 and 2 and 3 and 4 and 5 and 6 and 7 and 8 and 9 and 10 and 213.
First row Can Van Bonn mix the zinc? Nan coaxed a nimble zebra back to the zoo.
Speed The clansmen got into the dory by the shale rock and circled the lake.
| 1 | 2 | 3 | 4 | 5 | 6 | 7 | 8 | 9 | 10 | 11 | 12 | 13 | 14 |

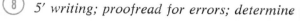

Quick, finger-action reaches

94B: Growth Index – Straight Copy (8) *5′ writing; proofread for errors; determine* gwam

All letters are used.

	GWAM 1′	5′	
What are some of the criticisms that are frequently made of the	13	3	50
new office employee? An executive of an insurance firm said that nearly	27	5	53
ninety percent of all the new workers they hired were poor spellers.	41	8	56
He stated, too, that most of these new employees had poor vocabularies.	56	11	59
Another common fault was that many young workers often did not do a fair	71	14	62
day's work for a fair day's wage. There is no secret to success. Success	86	17	65
is the result of doing more than is required by the immediate task. It	100	20	68
has frequently been said that the employee who never does any more than	114	23	71
he gets paid for, will never get paid for any more than he does.	127	25	73
Other employers said that many new typists did not know how to use	13	28	76
a dictionary, that they did not proofread all work carefully before	27	31	79
giving it to the employer, that they did not have good work habits, and	41	34	82
that they often did not take pride in a job well done. Employers stated,	56	37	85
too, that new typists had poor tabulating skills, and did not recognize	71	40	87
the need for good English skills. These men said that they did not	84	42	90
expect the young office employee to have all the qualities needed for	98	45	93
good job performance, but they would be happy if he had some of them.	112	48	96

1′ GWAM | 1 | 2 | 3 | 4 | 5 | 6 | 7 | 8 | 9 | 10 | 11 | 12 | 13 | 14 |
5′ GWAM | 1 | 2 | 3 |

94C: Skill Application – Manuscript with Footnotes * (37)

Margins—Top: 2″, first page
1″, all other pages
Left: 1½″, all pages
Right: 1″, all pages
Bottom: 1″ (approx.), all pages
Number all pages in proper position
Space properly between all parts
Correct errors
Manuscript Form Reference: 91D, pages 147–148

Type in manuscript form the report given on the following pages. The first page of the manuscript in pica type is shown in arranged form on page 153; other pages are shown in semiarranged form.

Number the footnotes as shown in the report. (Footnotes may be numbered consecutively or started anew on each page.)

Note. To save space for the footnotes and still leave an inch for the bottom margin, *do this:* Make a light pencil mark at the right edge of the sheet about 1″ from the bottom. As you type each footnote reference, place another pencil mark 3 or 4 spaces above the previous mark. This will reserve 3 spaces for typing each footnote. Erase these pencil marks when the page has been removed from the typewriter.

******You are not expected to complete the report in this lesson; additional time is provided in Lessons 95–98.*

184B: Skill Building – Speed and Accuracy Emphasis (30)

1. Type one 5′ writing on both ¶s. Compute *nwam*.
2. Type two 3′ writings on ¶ 1
   (a) Speed (exploration) level; (b) control level.
3. Repeat Step 2 procedure for ¶ 2.
4. Type one 5′ writing on both ¶s. Compute *nwam*. Record the better 5′ writing.

All letters are used.

	GWAM 3′		GWAM 5′	
Those who devote their time to a study of the society in which we	4	64	3	72
live tell us that this is a most virile period in our national life.	9	69	5	75
They cite figures to show that we are having growth at unequaled rates;	14	74	8	78
and they are quick to list many of the amazing signs of our political,	19	78	11	80
social, and economic progress. To capable students of world cultures,	23	83	14	83
however, these changes in our society are regarded as normal, rather	28	88	17	86
than unexpected, outcomes of our free way of life. They concede that	33	92	20	89
the fine things we enjoy are the fruits of an economic system that	37	97	22	92
encourages private initiative and that recognizes the right of each	42	101	25	94
person to secure a fair return on his investments, whether it be in	46	106	28	97
terms of new wealth or prestige. Ours is a unique system among all	51	111	30	99
nations of the world, and it merits our profound respect and support.	55	115	33	103
Few countries can boast of achievements so great or so diversified.	60	120	36	105

	GWAM 3′		GWAM 5′	
One of the vital premises upon which our competitive business	4	60	38	108
system functions is the principle that all people should share in the	9	65	41	110
products of our unique industrial capacity. The chief aim of those in	14	69	44	113
charge of our business enterprises is to provide goods and services at	18	74	47	116
a modest cost for all people in all walks of life. There is no finer	23	79	50	119
goal for our unusual business activities than to make worthy donations	28	83	53	122
to improving our way of life. To create new articles that can enrich	32	88	55	125
our existence, however, business is required to make huge investments	37	93	58	127
and must assume many risks. It is sound and just, then, for all who	42	97	61	130
invest in business to expect a proper return for the risks they take.	46	102	64	133
Each of us should try to assess the merits of business in terms of the	51	107	67	136
good it provides instead of unduly criticizing its leaders′ motives.	56	112	69	139

3′ GWAM | 1 | 2 | 3 | 4 | 5 |
5′ GWAM | 1 | 2 | 3 |

184C: Technique Refinement – Tabulator Controls and Rough Draft (10)

Use 183D, page 276; follow directions; compare results in this lesson with rates attained earlier in 183D.

USING THE LIBRARY

TS

Indent 5
DS

Do you remember the old story of Aladdin and his lamp? As the story goes, Aladdin had but to rub the lamp and a genie appeared who granted his every wish. All of us have learned that in today's world it is by working, not wishing, that we attain our goals; yet, it is nice to know that a modern-day Aladdin's lamp awaits our use. That lamp is represented by 1½" the vast power that the library has for us, if we are willing 1" to make the effort to learn to use the library.

The late President Kennedy emphasized the fact that "good libraries are as essential to an educated and informed people as the school system itself."[1] Further evidence as to the importance of the library is given in the following statement:

Indent 5 spaces from left and right margins SS

> . . . if all the libraries in the world were destroyed, all the important machines and ways of producing power, especially nuclear power, would soon be things of the past. Only library materials contain the records, formulas, blueprints, theory, and information that would enable the present production and utilization of machines and nuclear power to continue or increase.[2]

The resources of the library are grouped under such types of materials as books, periodicals, documents, manuscripts,

SS

DS

[1]"Libraries as Important as Schools, Says Kennedy in NLW Message," Library Journal (May 15, 1963), p. 1962.

DS

[2]Carter Alexander and Arvid J. Burke, How to Locate Educational Information and Data (4th ed.; New York: Bureau of Publications, Teachers College, Columbia University, 1958), p. 3.

Approximately 1"

1

FIRST PAGE OF MANUSCRIPT WITH FOOTNOTES—LEFTBOUND

	GWAM 3′		GWAM 5′	
Of all the problems faced by business, none is so great as the	4	59	39	109
choice of fine personnel. Those who are excited most over the ability	9	64	42	112
of office help admit to a real dearth of zealous workers who have an	14	68	45	114
interest in getting ahead. There are scores of folks who believe that	18	73	48	117
business can afford to pay them for just putting in time. They expect	23	78	50	120
maximum wages for minimum performance; and they fail to realize that	28	83	53	123
costs are affected by employee behavior. For all those having a real	32	87	56	126
desire to succeed, there are numerous openings in modern business. But	37	92	59	128
ambition must be alive with action if executives are to be attracted.	42	97	62	131
The goals of sizable salary increases and other worthy benefits can be	47	101	65	134
reached quickly by all those eager to acquire the type of skill and the	51	106	67	137
kind of attitude for which business is willing to pay.	55	110	70	139

3′ GWAM | 1 | 2 | 3 | 4 | 5 |
5′ GWAM | 1 | 2 | 3 |

183D: Technique Refinement – Tabulator Controls and Rough Draft (10)

1. Type one 3′ writing, making rough draft corrections. Do not erase your errors. At the end of 3′, circle your errors; then compute *g-pram*.
2. Type one 3′ writing, making rough draft corrections. Erase and correct your errors. At the end of 3′, compute your *n-pram*. Compare rates.

Full sheets	*1 cc*	*Reading position*
Body in groups of 3		*10 spaces between columns*

Words

all caps → Leading Bowlers — 3

DS

[← business and professional women's league — 11

TS

Name	Team	Three-Game ~~Average~~ Total	Words
DS →			
ss Susie Hess	~~Professionals~~ Medics	669	26
Cheryl Luke	Stenos	6~~00~~ 25	30
Kathy White	~~Majesties~~ Barristers	618	36
# Mary Myers	Executives	595	41
Ruby ~~Ruth~~ Taylor	Engineers	594	46
Wanda Duty	Journalists	591	51

LESSON 184

184A: Conditioning Practice (10) *each line at least three times; then 1′ comparative writings*

Type with continuity and rhythm

Alphabet; shift	Herb Fox saw Jim Quiling twice as they packed vases for Sam Therzon's.
Figure	826 yds. Shipper's No. 34219 at 15 days net on Cust. Order No. B 67805
Figure-symbol	\$9,258.63 (Burns & Copes*) 4¼ x 7½ Jane's 10% <u>one-way</u> 4 7/8" #89 @ 65¢
Fluency	It is a wise plan to become familiar with facts about foreign nations.

| 1 | 2 | 3 | 4 | 5 | 6 | 7 | 8 | 9 | 10 | 11 | 12 | 13 | 14 |

Note. *Ibid.* ("the same") may be used when the work referred to is the same as that in the immediately preceding footnote (see footnote 3).

The abbreviation *op. cit.* ("the work cited") may be used with the names of the authors of a work previously cited when there are intervening footnotes (see footnote 9).

pamphlets, pictures, films, recordings, maps, or newspapers. These in turn are usually cataloged by authors, titles, and subjects.[3] But these materials are of little value to us, unless we know where to look for them. Like the genie of Aladdin's lamp, the power of the library is at the instant service of anyone who knows how to use it. Johnson makes this point quite clear when he says that the library "is an institution of great value with possibilities far beyond the needs of the average individual, but the sources and tools it provides are no more effective than the skill of the user."[4] This comment is supported by the following statement:

> Self-contained ability to take advantage of the multiple services of a library assures the student a competency which permits him to accomplish the independent study and research required of him in his future as a scholar, or, where college experience is not his future, will qualify him to gain lifelong satisfactions through the public library, sometimes called "the people's university."[5]

Knowledge of how to locate information and other data is, then, the master key that will unlock the potential power of the library. Some suggestions for using the library follow.

TS

The Card Catalog

DS

The card catalog is the basic tool of any library. It is, as Cook has noted, the largest and most important detailed "index to the library's collection."[6] Depending upon the size of the particular library, the card catalog consists of one or more cabinets containing drawers of index cards arranged in alphabetical order, usually by author, title, and subject. One of two systems of subject classification is used by most libraries––the Library of Congress or the Dewey Decimal Classification. To the classification numbers derived from either of these two systems, large libraries add a further author refinement designation known as the "Cutter" number.[7] Anyone who uses libraries frequently should understand the basic nature of these systems. Most high school students, however, need

SS

DS

[3] Ibid., p. 4.

DS

[4] Herbert W. Johnson, How to Use the Business Library (3d ed.; Cincinnati: South–Western Publishing Co., 1964), p. iii.

[5] Bernice K. Konehue, "Use of Reference Materials in the High School," Education, Vol. 84, No. 4 (December, 1963), p. 218.

[6] Margaret G. Cook, The New Library Key (2d ed.; New York: The H. W. Wilson Co., 1963), p. 64.

[7] R. W. Murphey, How and Where to Look It Up (New York: McGraw–Hill Book Co., Inc., 1958), pp. 29–32.

Selected Business Forms

LESSON 183

183A: Conditioning Practice (5) *each line at least three times*

Alphabet; shift	Toby Heinz waved to Maxie Quill from a jagged cliff back of San Pablo.	*Thumb close to space bar*
Figure	25 sets Shipper's No. 260518 at 30 days net on Cust. Order No. 408976E	
Figure-symbol	$2,640.75 (Hall & West*) 3¼ x 9½ Joe's 18% <u>thirty-one</u> 6 3/8" #75 @ 90¢	
Fluency	This year I shall work with vigor to improve my skill in typing power.	
	| 1 | 2 | 3 | 4 | 5 | 6 | 7 | 8 | 9 | 10 | 11 | 12 | 13 | 14 |	

183B: Technique Refinement (5) *1' comparative writings*

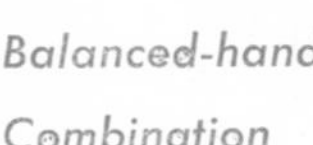

Balanced-hand	They may then make an audit of the downtown firms and fix the penalty.	*Adjust stroking speed to copy difficulty*
Combination	Do you recommend that we sign the amendment and get the case approved?	
One-hand	A water reserve saves him a decrease in stated acreage, in my opinion.	
	| 1 | 2 | 3 | 4 | 5 | 6 | 7 | 8 | 9 | 10 | 11 | 12 | 13 | 14 |	

183C: Skill Building – Speed and Accuracy Emphasis (30)

1. Type one 5′ writing on both ¶s. Compute *nwam.*
2. Type two 3′ writings on ¶ 1
   (a) Speed (exploration) level; (b) control level.
3. Repeat Step 2 procedure for ¶ 2.
4. Type one 5′ writing on both ¶s. Compute *nwam.* Record the better 5′ writing.

All letters are used.

The world of business is an intricate, dynamic place. While some people may think of it primarily as a big market arena where money is exchanged for wares produced, there is ever so much more to successful business activity than meets the eye. Basically, the area of business consists of many entities, some well organized and others not so well ordered, ranging in size from small units to giants of commerce. Vital to all business are matters of finance, ideas about the extent of new production, notations for the use of credit, devices for judging quality theories that relate to costs, and an array of other factors that help to decide profit or loss. It is easy to forget that company structure may be either quite complex or very simple and that the size of a firm does not normally connote the scope or severity of its problems. There is much to learn by careful study and analysis of a modern industry.

(Continued)

GWAM 3′		5′	
4	65	3	72
9	70	5	75
14	75	8	78
19	80	11	81
23	84	14	84
28	89	17	86
33	94	20	89
37	98	22	92
42	103	25	95
47	108	28	98
52	113	31	101
56	117	34	103
61	122	37	106

3′ GWAM | 1 | 2 | 3 | 4 | 5 |
5′ GWAM | 1 | 2 | 3 |

only familiarize themselves with the mechanics of the Dewey Decimal System since this particular system is the one generally used by high school libraries.

Let's assume that your assignment is to make a report on the career opportunities in the business office. How do you find some facts about such jobs? The first thing to do would be to look in the card catalog under such general headings as business, vocational guidance, occupations, or careers. In the card drawer containing the index cards on "Vocational Guidance," for example, you'll find listed on separate cards all the books in the library on this subject. Each card will give complete information about a book which deals with this subject––its title, author, date and place of publication, number of pages, and a brief description. Books which are listed on subject cards are, as a rule, listed also on an author card and on a title card. If you try to locate a specific book you already know about, you can find it faster by checking the author or title cards.

After you have located the specific reference card, the key to the location of the book in the library is the call number. This call number, located at the left edge of the card, is a combination of numbers and letters which identifies this book as separate from every other book in the library. For example, a book by E. R. Becker and Richard Lawrence, Success and Satisfaction in Your Office Job, has the call number 651B. This figure represents the Dewey Decimal Classification number and the first author's initial. To find this book, you would go to the area and shelf in the library identified with this specific number.[8]

TS

Special Reference Sources

DS

Most research needs of high school students are satisfied by using the materials found in the reference section of the library. Large libraries usually have a general reference room and a number of special reference rooms. Small libraries, which are typical of most high schools, have only one main room. Books found in the reference section of such libraries are generally limited to use in the library because of the constant demand for them. Typical types of reference books would include dictionaries, encyclopedias, yearbooks, indexes, biographies, and such materials as maps, charts, and atlases. These are important reference sources. Every student should become thoroughly acquainted with them.

---

[8] Gregory FitzGerald, "The Divisional Reading Room," Wilson Library Bulletin (March, 1965), p. 571.

Indexes

When you are seeking information on current affairs or problems, you may not be able to find the information you need in a book or in the special reference materials; however, there are sure to be magazine articles about almost any current issue. The place to find references to these magazine articles is the Readers' Guide to Periodical Literature. The Readers' Guide uses many abbreviations because it presents a great deal of information in a limited space. A list of abbreviations and their meanings is given at the front of the Guide. The Readers' Guide will give you such information as, (1) magazine articles published on a given subject within stated dates; and (2) length and format (whether illustrated or not) of an article, the date on which it appeared, and the pages on which the article can be found.

A number of other indexes are available in most libraries. Perhaps one of the most useful for high school students is the Cumulative Book Index. It lists all books published in the English language by author, subject, and title. In addition, it gives the name of the publisher of the book. Similarly, the other indexes contain much useful information.

Summary

There are three important rules to remember when seeking information in the library. The first rule is to be specific; the second, to be accurate; and the third, to help yourself.[9] Decide what your research problem is and how much and what type of information you want; then begin your study by (1) looking through the card catalog to see what is readily available in the library; (2) consulting the encyclopedias, almanacs, and yearbooks; and (3) checking the various periodical and book indexes. Finally, learn to use your library in the best and most efficient way. You will soon discover that it is indeed a modern-day Aladdin's lamp!

---

[9] Cook, op. cit., p. 43.

Note. On a partially filled page, the divider line and footnote are usually placed at the bottom of the page.

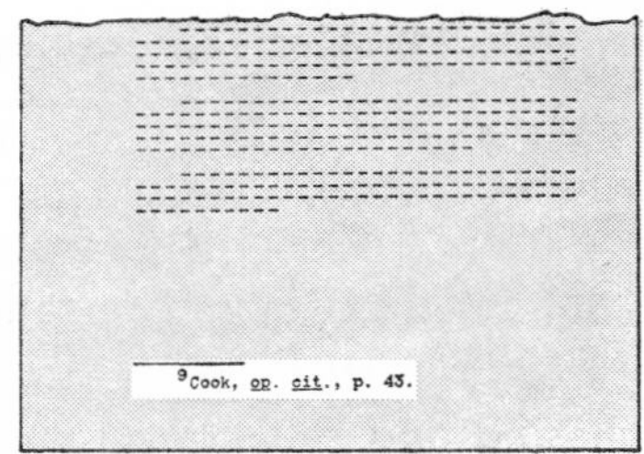

[9]Cook, op. cit., p. 43.

Problem 3: Telefax

2 cc's   Send as night letter   SS

Words

Call letters: TCS Charge to: Industrial Solvents, 5
Inc. Chicago, Illinois *(current date)* Blue Grass 15
Equipment Company 1905 West Broadway 22
Avenue Louisville, Kentucky (¶) Interested in 31
purchase of 24 executive-size (60" x 30" x 29") 40
double-pedestal desks for delivery Bloomington 50
plant. Prefer wood finish. Send description, de- 59
livery date, prices, terms. Leonard Liguori Pur- 69
chasing Agent (xx) 72

Problem 4: Letter of Confirmation

Modified block, mixed   1 cc   Envelope

Date: *(current)* Mr. James F. Murphy Senior 8
Consultant Murphy Structural Engineers, Inc. 17
1095 Washington Avenue Gary, Indiana 46402 26
Dear Jim: (¶ 1) We just wired you as follows: 35

(Insert message of Problem 2) 88

Plans for an additional building to be constructed 98
adjacent to Civic Concert Hall have caused the 107
site owners and managers to modify their plans 117
for the right-wing entrance to Civic Concert Hall. 127
Changes are proposed in order to provide a 136
larger amount of usable space in the adjacent 145
building and to present an attractive, comple- 154
mentary view in relation to the two buildings. 164
(¶ 2) I am enclosing duplicate copies of the 171
modifications requested. May I ask that you and 181
a colleague with whom you have worked on this 190
project give it your attention soon. Then when 200
we confer––Monday, if possible––we shall be 209
able to make some definite decisions regarding 218
the requested modifications. Cordially, Lester 228
Steidl, Director Architectural Engineers, Inc. 237
(xx) Enclosures: Two copies of requested modifi- 246
cations for Civic Concert Hall (195) 252
+ Envelope 275

Problem 5: Business-Reply Message

2 cc's   SS   COMPANY MAIL envelope

To: Mrs. Dixie Patterson Buyer for Beauty 8
Equipment Commerce and Industry Building 16
Date: *(current)* (¶ 1) To coordinate our pur- 23
chasing and sales program effectively, we need 33
to decide now which merchandise will receive 42
special promotion next spring. (¶ 2) Will you 50
please identify for me soon those items which 59
you feel will generate buyer interest and which 69
you are planning to "push" next season. We 77
shall then forward this material to the Advertis- 87
ing Department and request early preparation 96
of suitable publicity material. Warren Caster, 106
Vice President *+ Envelope* 108/127

Problem 6: Response to Message

1 cc   SS   COMPANY MAIL envelope

Reply: *(current date)* (¶ 1) Since many travel- 7
minded women look for devices that will en- 15
hance rapid grooming and hair styling, we plan 24
this year to promote a line of luggage-style hair 34
dryers with power-operated manicure sets. Also, 44
our fast-color machine should be a big-sell item 54
this year. (¶ 2) Each dryer will have two handy 63
finger-tip heat controls, providing at least four 73
different heat levels. Each will have the beehive- 83
style bonnet for swift drying. The beehive bon- 92
net will be a feature on the fast-color machine, 102
too, but women will look especially at the fea- 111
tures of time saving and of soft color toning. 121
Dixie Patterson *+ Envelope* 124/132

Problem 7: Message; Response

2 cc's for business-reply message; 1 cc for response
SS   COMPANY MAIL envelopes

Message to: **Mrs. Martha Nelson, Manager** 6
Beauty Services and Supplies Date: *(current)* 15
Send same message as for Problem 5. 104/118

Reply: *(current date)* (¶ 1) The easy-to-care- 124
for style that can go sophisticate for evening will 135
be the big news in hair style for this coming 144
spring. Therefore, we shall be promoting fast- 154
and easy-care items as well as health-care items. 164
(¶ 2) With more and more women seeking fast 171
but healthful hair-color change, the fast-color 181
machine and luggage-style hair groom kits and 190
hair dryers should promote especially well. 199
Women will be traveling, lying on the beach, 208
and water skiing in larger numbers than ever 217
before, but they'll still hope for that hair-beauty 228
miracle. Martha Nelson *+ Envelope* 232/241

LESSON 95

95A: Conditioning Practice (5) *each line three times*

Alphabet	Jack found seven quaint game boxes at the new little bazaar in Waypol.	*Wrists low and relaxed*
Figure	Jack and Jim labeled 12,967 illustrations, 450 tables, and 38 figures.	
Third row	Jerry Pettie won't quote you a good price on any of those typewriters.	
Speed	The authenticity of the ancient amendment may help them gain clemency.	
	| 1 | 2 | 3 | 4 | 5 | 6 | 7 | 8 | 9 | 10 | 11 | 12 | 13 | 14 |	

95B: Related Learning – Capitalization Guides (End of Series) (10) *study-learn-apply*

11. The seasons of the year are not capitalized unless personified.

12. Capitalize geographic regions, localities, and names. Points of the compass are not capitalized when used to indicate direction or when used in a descriptive sense.

13. Capitalize such words as street, avenue, company, etc., when used with a proper noun.

14. Capitalize names of organizations, clubs, and their derivatives.

15. Nouns preceding a figure are usually capitalized, although common words, as line, page, and sentence, are not.

11	*Learn*	This winter seems very cold; the icy fingers of Winter are everywhere.
	Apply	Each of the four seasons––Fall, Winter, Spring, Summer––has its charm.
12	*Learn*	I live in the East, but I plan to move west to Squaw Valley next year.
	Apply	At one time Andrew lived in the south; he now lives on the west coast.
13	*Learn*	Is 123 Fifth Street or 123 Fifth Avenue the address of Dowe & Company?
	Apply	Is this the Street where you live, or do you live on Tennessee avenue?
14	*Learn*	The Boy Scouts will meet at the Commercial Club at 4 p.m. on Saturday.
	Apply	The future business leaders of america may meet at the fairmont hotel.
15	*Learn*	He read Judge Baxter's decision in Volume III, Section 123, page 1049.
	Apply	J. D. Morgan & Company uses style 34 as shown on Page 12 of catalog 5.

95C: Skill Application – Manuscript with Footnotes (35) *(Continue 94C, pages 152–155.)*

LESSON 96

96A: Conditioning Practice (5) *each line three times*

Alphabet	Jerome quickly realized that six lively polliwogs would soon be frogs.	*Fingers curved and close to keys*
Figure	The test for April 8 will cover pages 64–75, 98–130, 152–239, and 402.	
Fingers 3 and 4	Was it Polly who saw Paul quizzing Wally about eating all the loquats?	
Speed	The town chairman is delighted to learn that he will get an endowment.	
	| 1 | 2 | 3 | 4 | 5 | 6 | 7 | 8 | 9 | 10 | 11 | 12 | 13 | 14 |	

181B: Sustained Production on Special Business Communications (45)

Time Schedule	
Get ready to type	7′
Timed production	30′
Proofread; compute *n-pram* . .	8′

Arrange supplies. Make a list of the problems at the right and check them off as you complete them. Type for 30′, following instructions given for each problem typed. Correct all errors as you type. If you finish before time is called, start over. Mark uncorrected errors. Compute *n-pram*.

Page 269, 178C, Problem 3
Page 270, 179C, Problems 2, 4, 5
Page 272, 180C, Problem 2
(last message)
Page 272, 180C, Problem 3
(last reply)

LESSON 182

182A: Conditioning Practice (5) *each line at least three times*

Alphabet; shift	Jim Quincy and Max Azen hiked for long hours to view stately Big Peak.	*Fluent rhythm*
Figure	Last spring I sold 304 rakes, 86 hoes, 172 spades, and 59 lawn mowers.	
Figure-symbol	Smith & Moore's bill #826307 for 195# @ 46¢ a lb. amounted to $90.68.	
Fluency	There is little to taking a test for those who are very well prepared.	
	| 1 | 2 | 3 | 4 | 5 | 6 | 7 | 8 | 9 | 10 | 11 | 12 | 13 | 14 |	

182B: Special Communications Production Measurement (45)

Arrange supplies. Type the following seven problems for 30′ when directed to begin. Correct errors as you type. If time permits, start over. Mark uncorrected errors. Compute *n-pram*.

Time Schedule	
Get ready to type	7′
Timed production	30′
Proofread; compute *n-pram* . .	8′

Problem 1: Interoffice Memo

1 cc   1″ side margins   COMPANY MAIL envelope

Words

To: Gerald G. Green Production Manager 7
Date: *(current)* File: MD–19675–CL From: 12
H. W. Adams, President Subject: Market Ex- 19
pansion (¶ 1) Dave McKelvey, Executive Vice 26
President, has just returned from Latin America 36
and from the Caribbean Area where he has been 45
for several months. While he was there, he 54
studied economic conditions and discussed with 63
a number of leading merchants the possibility 73
of marketing several of our products. He reports 83
eager interest; therefore, he is highly optimistic 93
that mutually profitable relationships can be 102
established. (¶ 2) Since there are special finan- 111
cial problems relating to international opera- 120
tions, it will take some time to study the pos- 129
sibilities and to plan and prepare negotiations 138
on Mr. McKelvey's proposals. Will you please 148
meet with me early next week to discuss requests 157
for possible product modification. These re- 166
quests come from some potentially large cus- 175
tomers in the areas Mr. McKelvey visited. (xx) 184
+ Envelope 193

Problem 2: Full Rate Telegram

2 cc's   SS   Charge sender

Information in printed heading 6
Indianapolis, Indiana *(current date)* Murphy 15
Structural Engineers, Inc. 1095 Washington 23
Avenue Gary, Indiana (¶) Received today 31
urgent request to modify drawings for right- 39
wing entrance to Civic Concert Hall. Will need 49
to discuss with you immediately effect of several 59
aspects of proposed changes on cost estimates, 68
as well as on performance schedules. Can you 77
see me Monday? Lester Steidl, Director Archi- 86
tectural Engineers, Inc. (xx) 41 Audubon 94
Road 95

96B: Speed Emphasis – Progressive-Difficulty Sentences (12)

Type: Two 1′ writings on each sentence for speed. **Goal:** Try to equal sentence 1 rate on 2, 3, and 4.

		High-frequency words emphasized	**EMPHASIZE**
1	*Balanced hand*	The field chairman may make them do their work and then sign the form.	*Word response*
2	*Combination*	Will you deliver the statement and the contract to them for signature?	*Variable rhythm*
3	*One hand*	I regret that you gave only a minimum opinion on the extra water case.	*Quiet hands*
4	*Numbers*	A customer ordered 123 boxes, 456 metal forms, 78 books, and 90 desks.	*Finger reaches*
		| 1 | 2 | 3 | 4 | 5 | 6 | 7 | 8 | 9 | 10 | 11 | 12 | 13 | 14 |	

96C: Skill Application – Manuscript with Footnotes (33) *(Continue 94C, pages 152–155.)*

LESSON 97

97A: Conditioning Practice (5) *each line three times*

Alphabet	With amazing dexterity, the jovial squaws plucked the big white fowls.	*Keep carriage moving*
Figure	They sold 40 watches, 128 rings, 93 clips, 56 tie pins, and 27 clocks.	
Shift key	H. A. McLain and P. T. Hall are employed by the Adams & Brown Company.	
Speed	If they pick the eight fowls for the widow, she will pay them in cash.	
	| 1 | 2 | 3 | 4 | 5 | 6 | 7 | 8 | 9 | 10 | 11 | 12 | 13 | 14 |	

97B: Accuracy Emphasis (12) *(Repeat 96B but with emphasis on accuracy: not over 1 error each 1′)*

97C: Skill Application – Manuscript with Footnotes (33) *(Continue 94C, pages 152–155.)*

LESSON 98

98A: Conditioning Practice (5) *each line three times*

Alphabet	The unique weave of the blue-gray jacket pleased many zealous experts.	*Uniform stroking*
Figure	Was Order 943 for 56 typewriters delivered to 12078 E. Twelfth Street?	
Double letters	The difference between success and luck may well be a matter of pluck.	
Speed	Pay the man for the form and ask the auditor to make the usual checks.	
	| 1 | 2 | 3 | 4 | 5 | 6 | 7 | 8 | 9 | 10 | 11 | 12 | 13 | 14 |	

98B: Skill Building – Straight Copy (15) *two 5′ writings on 94B, page 152; Goal: Improvement*

180C: Typing Business-Reply Messages (35)

Type the following three problems for 25′ when directed to begin. If time permits, start over. Mark format and typescript errors. Compute *g-pram.* **Goals:** Efficient procedure and good format.

Time Schedule	
Get ready to type	5′
Timed production	25′
Proofread; compute *g-pram* . .	5′

Problem 1 *Copy message and reply as shown in illustration on page 271* *SS*

Problem 2 *Type 3 business-reply messages* *2 cc's* *SS* *Address envelopes; COMPANY MAIL on envelopes*

Words

To: Mr. Joseph H. Young Transportation Offi- 8
cer Rutherford Building Date: *(current)* (¶ 1) 16
Use copy from ¶ 1, Problem 1, illustration, 72
p. 271. (¶ 2) Please investigate the details of 79
shipping and send me a report of your follow-up 89
with the carriers. Warren Caster, Vice President 99
+ *Envelope* 113

To: Mr. David L. Hanson Controller and Budget 8
Officer Administration Building Date: *(current)* 18
(¶ 1) It has come to my attention that we have 26
probably overstocked the electric hairbrush, 35
Model XP–3075, which we bought for our fall 44
promotion. (¶ 2) Will you examine the inven- 52
tory control records and let me know how many 61
units we now have in stock, as well as the cost 70
per unit. We may consider further discounts to 80
move this item. Warren Caster, Vice President 89
+ *Envelope* 106

To: Mr. L. R. Oscarson Plant Foreman Bodie 8
Canyon Plant Date: *(current)* (¶ 1) Will you 15
please investigate our present control procedures 25
on materials reaching and leaving the plant and 35
make recommendations as to whether present 44
controls should be maintained or tightened. 53
Warren Caster, Vice President 58
+ *Envelope* 71

Problem 3 *Type replies to Problem 2 messages* *1 cc* *SS* *COMPANY MAIL on envelopes*

Words

Reply to message sent to Joseph H. Young:

Date: *(current)* (¶ 1) Shipment #809572 for 7
the Adkins Beauty Salon, Nashville, left our 16
docks via Thruway Carriers. At Chattanooga the 26
cartons were unloaded and placed in the Thru- 35
way terminal storage area. Two days later the 44
order was shipped to Nashville. There is no evi- 54
dence that the merchandise was inspected when 63
it reached or left the terminal storage area. 72
(¶ 2) It is probable that there was damage in 80
transit. Do you want all papers setting forth the 91
details? Joseph H. Young + *Envelope* 96/104

Reply to message sent to David L. Hanson:

Date: *(current)* (¶ 1) As of nine o'clock this 8
morning, we had 725 cases of the Model 16
XP–3075 electric hairbrush in stock. Each case 25
contains 24 brushes, making the item count 34
17,400. Sales last week totaled 237 brushes, a 44
drop of almost 300 from the week before. (¶ 2) 52
Our cost per brush was $3.65; our retail price is 62
$8.75. David L. Hanson + *Envelope* 67/75

Reply to message sent to L. R. Oscarson:

Date: *(current)* (¶ 1) The enclosed Procedural 8
Report No. 1 is from our organization manual 17
and indicates our present control procedures on 26
incoming and outgoing products. Report No. 2 36
presents my recommendations for change. (¶ 2) 44
I shall be pleased to meet with you to discuss my 54
recommendations. L. R. Oscarson Enc. 2 61
+ *Envelope* 70

LESSON 181

181A: Conditioning Practice (5) *each line at least three times*

Alphabet; shift	Max Hazel drove Jack Quinn to Big Springs for one week of easy living.	*Release keys quickly*
Figure	The auto dealer moved 395 tires, 64 rims, 82 wheels, and 107 hub caps.	
Figure-symbol	Order #3652 for $1,798.40 was sent by Young & Weston on July 15 or 16.	
Fluency	Tabulated reports that have been ruled neatly give a smart appearance.	
	| 1 | 2 | 3 | 4 | 5 | 6 | 7 | 8 | 9 | 10 | 11 | 12 | 13 | 14 |	

98C: Skill Applications (30)

Problem 1: Manuscript with Footnotes (*Complete report, 94C, pages 152–155*)

Problem 2: Manuscript Bibliography

Margins—Top: 2"; Left: 1½"; Right: 1"
Center heading over line of writing
Start first line of each entry at left margin; indent second and succeeding lines 5 spaces
SS with DS after each entry

Type the following bibliography which is a listing of the references used in the preceding problem. The entries as shown illustrate one form that may be used in typing a bibliography.

Number this page to follow the last page of the report.

Entry 1: Book reference with two authors.
Entry 2: Book reference, one author.
Entry 3: Magazine reference.
Entry 4: Book reference.
Entry 5: Magazine reference.
Entry 6: Article with no author listed—alphabetized according to title.
Entry 7: Book reference.

BIBLIOGRAPHY

TS

Alexander, Carter, and Arvid J. Burke. How to Locate Educational Information and Data, 4th ed. New York: Bureau of Publications, Teachers College, Columbia University, 1958.

Cook, Margaret G. The New Library Key, 2d ed. New York: The H. W. Wilson Co., 1963.

FitzGerald, Gregory. "The Divisional Reading Room," Wilson Library Bulletin. (March, 1965), pp. 565–566, 571.

Johnson, Herbert W. How to Use the Business Library, 3d ed. Cincinnati: South–Western Publishing Co., 1964.

Konehue, Bernice K. "Use of Reference Materials in the High School," Education. Vol. 84, No. 4 (December, 1963), pp. 217–220.

"Libraries as Important as Schools, Says Kennedy in NLW Message," Library Journal. (May 15, 1963), p. 1962.

Murphey, R. W. How and Where to Look It Up. New York: McGraw–Hill Book Co., Inc., 1958.

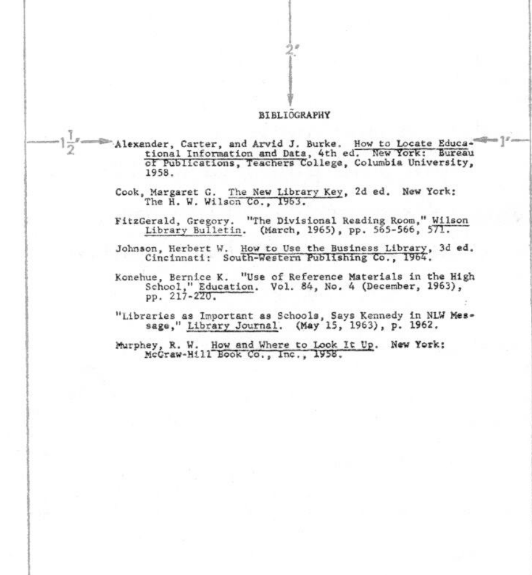

Problem 3: Manuscript Title Page

Type a title page for the report you prepared as Problem 1:

1. Center the title USING THE LIBRARY 2½" from the top of the page.
2. Type your name 2½" below the title; DS and type the name of your school.
3. Type the current date 2½" below the name of your school.

Note. The typing on the title page may be arranged in many ways. The important thing is that it be attractively and neatly arranged. Since the report is to be leftbound, center the title over the *line of writing*.

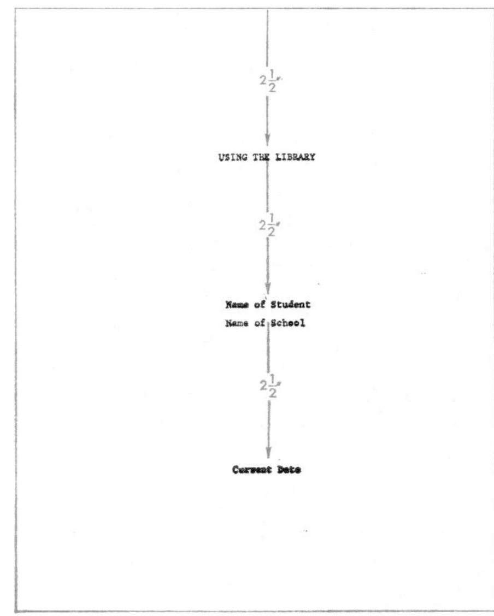

LESSON 180

180A: Conditioning Practice (10) *each line three times; then 1′ speed writings on Lines 1 and 2*

Alphabet; shift	Max Zerner played five big sets with Phil Quigley at new Camp Jackson.	*Fingers close to keys*
Figure	He judged 97 horses, 83 cows, 410 pigs, and 652 sheep at a state fair.	
Figure-symbol	Brown & Tomer's Invoice #8290, dated September 24, totaled $14,372.35.	
Fluency	Some big firms use special-size stationery for their business letters.	
	| 1 | 2 | 3 | 4 | 5 | 6 | 7 | 8 | 9 | 10 | 11 | 12 | 13 | 14 |	

180B: Business-Reply Messages – Preview (5)

Features and Procedures to Study:

1. A two-way, within-company, communication, requiring a reply to be typed on the same page as the original message.
2. Sender types message in left-hand column, keeps the second copy (yellow), and forwards others (white and pink) to addressee.

Note: Signatures of both parties may be typed and then initialed, or handwritten.

3. Addressee types reply in right-hand column, keeps third copy (pink), and returns original copy (white) to sender.
4. The type of envelope and form of address to be used depends upon whether the message travels through U. S. Postal channels or through COMPANY MAIL.
5. To insert in envelope, fold from bottom to top, creasing horizontally at the center of the page.

REPLY–O–GRAM 1056 PEACHTREE STREET, N. W. ATLANTA, GA. 30301

Beauticians' Equipment and Supply Company

MESSAGE	REPLY	Words— Message	Words— Reply
TO ⌐	DATE (current)		3
Mr. John P. Jaczesko	The Adkins shipment (#809572)	4	9
Warehouse Manager	met all of our qualifications before	8	17
Rutherford Building	leaving the warehouse. All hair	12	23
	dryers were inspected for perform-		30
	ance and soundness; they were		36
DATE November 29, 19--	packed with proper padding in suit-	15	43
Howard Green, our agent for the Nash-	able cartons marked "Fragile." All	23	50
ville area, reports major damage to six	boxes were inspected at the time of	31	57
cartons included in the shipment to Adkins	sealing by Supervisor Frank Hogan.	39	64
Beauty Salon. The bases for all hair dry-	Thus, when the order left our docks,	47	72
ers sustained sufficient damage to require	there was no evidence of either	56	78
factory overhaul; and all six hoods for	damage or breakage. I am sending	64	85
the dryers were damaged beyond repair.	copies of all inspection reports.	72	92
Please check shipping data on this		79	
order and let me know who certified the		87	
shipment when it left our warehouse.		95	
BY Warren Caster, Vice-President	SIGNED John P. Jaczesko	100	95

BUSINESS-REPLY MESSAGE

Unit 16 | Lessons 99-100

Evaluation: Review and Measurement

LESSON 99

Lesson 99, which reviews previous learnings and helps you evaluate your typing skill, will prepare you for the measurement activities in Lesson 100.

Both lessons require that you make notes of work to be done, that you locate references (if needed), and that you place a marker in your book to guide you back to these lessons.

99A: Conditioning Practice (5) *each line three times*

Alphabet	The new Zula and Jaguar sports cars were moved quickly from a box car.	*Space quickly; down-and-in motion*
Figure-symbol	These contributions of $389, $156.75, $12.73, and $4.50 total $562.98.	
Fractions	Type the following fractions and mixed numbers: ½, ¼, 5¼, 7½, and 9¼.	
Speed	If they give him a key to the office, he might finish the work for us.	

| 1 | 2 | 3 | 4 | 5 | 6 | 7 | 8 | 9 | 10 | 11 | 12 | 13 | 14 |

99B: Number Practice (6) *1′ writing on each sentence*

Please ship Order No. 205 for 9 divans, 164 desks, and 378 desk lamps.

Was a discovery made on July 10, 1963? May 24, 1965? or June 18, 1967?

Type these amounts in a column: 47.52, 43.19, 468.90, 423.65, 417.80.

Write checks for these amounts: $4.56, $7.13, $89.20, $75.62, $34.89.

| 1 | 2 | 3 | 4 | 5 | 6 | 7 | 8 | 9 | 10 | 11 | 12 | 13 | 14 |

EMPHASIZE *Finger-reach strokes*

99C: Skill Building – Statistical Rough Draft (9) *three 2′ writings*

Copy (handwritten corrections: set apart; as; #; below zero; It has the biggest trees and the oldest trees.; in a single season.)	2′ GWAM	
California is by nature a land of contrsats. Since 1769, forex-	8	56
ample, the Ca lifornia-Nevada arrea has had an average of 5,000	14	62
earth quakes a year. Mt. Lassen had had temperatures of 56 de-	20	69
grees; death valley has had 134 degrees in the shade. California	28	76
the is sunniest and foggiest state. It has no snow in some areas,	39	88
yet tamarack in the high sierras has had as much as 842 inches of	46	94
snow in a single season.	48	97

99D: Review of Related Learnings and Basic Skill Applications (30)

1. *Correct It as You Type.* The sentences at the top of page 160 are in problem form. To type them correctly, you must recall basic number and capitalization guides. The appropriate guide code is given at the left of each sentence.

If you are uncertain about a problem sentence, the code will guide you to the correct rules in preceding lessons. For example, 1–2:138 refers to Guides 1 and 2, page 138.

Note. A color underline indicates a *possible* (not necessarily *required*) point of correction. It is used to "cue" you to a *possible* correction and to test your ability to make "correct decisions" as you type. Make only *required* corrections.

179C: Typing Telegrams, Telefax Messages, and Confirmation Letter (35)

Time Schedule

Get ready to type . . . . . . 5′
Timed production . . . . . . 25′
Proofread; compute *g-pram* . . 5′

Type the following five problems for 25′ when directed to begin. If time permits, start over. Mark format and typescript errors. Compute *g-pram*.

Goals: Efficient procedure and good format.

NOTE: Desk-Fax is a special machine used by Western Union in businesses having a large volume of telegraph messages. The form used with Desk-Fax is called Telefax, illustrated below:

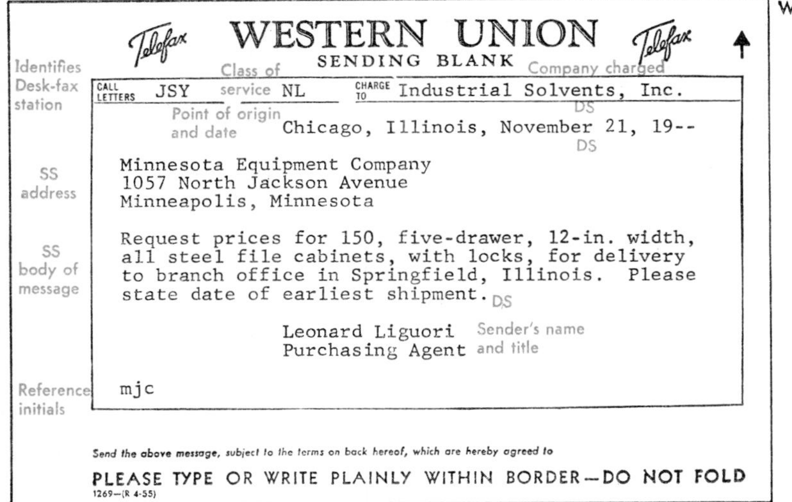

Words

Telefax WESTERN UNION Telefax
SENDING BLANK

Identifies Desk-fax station — Class of service — Company charged

CALL LETTERS JSY   service NL   CHARGE TO Industrial Solvents, Inc. 7
DS
Point of origin and date   Chicago, Illinois, November 21, 19-- 14
DS

SS address
Minnesota Equipment Company 20
1057 North Jackson Avenue 26
Minneapolis, Minnesota 29

SS body of message
Request prices for 150, five-drawer, 12-in. width, 40
all steel file cabinets, with locks, for delivery 50
to branch office in Springfield, Illinois. Please 60
state date of earliest shipment. DS 67

Leonard Liguori   Sender's name 70
Purchasing Agent   and title 73

Reference initials   mjc 74

Send the above message, subject to the terms on back hereof, which are hereby agreed to

PLEASE TYPE OR WRITE PLAINLY WITHIN BORDER—DO NOT FOLD
1269—(R 4-55)

TELEFAX MESSAGE

Problem 1: Full Rate Telegram

3 cc's   SS   Charge sender
Send company name

Words
Information in printed heading 6
Indianapolis, Indiana, October 12, 19–– Faris 15
Mechanical Engineering Company 5702 West 23
Union Street Evansville, Indiana (¶) Final hear- 32
ings on bids for Westside Shopping Center 40
will be held in our Executive Board Room 49
November 13, 19––. All bids must be received 58
at least 15 days prior to hearing date. Please 67
get your bids to me as soon as possible. Lester 77
Steidl, Director Architectural Engineers, Inc. 87
(xx) 41 Audubon Road 90

Problem 2: Night Letter

3 cc's   SS   Charge sender

Information in printed heading 6
Indianapolis, Indiana, October 21, 19–– Hayes 15
Electrical Contractors, Inc. 107 Northcliff Ave- 25
nue Ft. Wayne, Indiana (¶) Request you send 33
representative to final hearings November 13, 42
19––, on bids for Westside Shopping Center, 51
bids to be received at least 15 days prior to 60
hearing date in order to be considered. Your 69
bid received yesterday. Meeting to be held in 78
our Executive Board Room. Architectural Engi- 87
neers, Inc. (Lester Steidl:xx) 41 Audubon Road 96

Problem 3: Telefax

As shown in illustration at top of page

Problem 4: Full Rate Telefax

1 cc   SS   Call letters and charge as above

Words
Information in printed heading 7
Chicago, Illinois, November 21, 19–– Badger 15
Office Equipment, Inc. 9065 Wisconsin Avenue 24
Milwaukee, Wisconsin Please give date of ear- 33
liest shipment of 50 desks, Stock No. 728, at 42
same price as your November 7 shipment, for 51
delivery to branch office in Springfield, Illinois. 62
Leonard Liguori Purchasing Agent (xx) 69

Problem 5: Letter of Confirmation

1 cc   Modified block, open punctuation

November 21, 19–– Mr. L. E. Keller Sales 8
Manager Minnesota Equipment Company 1057 16
North Jackson Avenue Minneapolis, Minnesota 25
55411 Dear Mr. Keller (¶ 1) Thank you for 33
your advance information on expected price 41
increase on office equipment. Today we wired 50
you as follows: 54
(Insert message of Problem 3) 91
(¶ 2) We are considering immediate purchase 99
of equipment for our Milwaukee branch. We 107
shall probably order from 150 to 200 additional 117
filing cabinets this week. Sincerely yours Leon- 126
ard Liguori Purchasing Agent (xx) (92) 133
+ Envelope 155

Number and type the sentences in correct form; use a 74-space line.

1–2:138 **1.** 5 of the 126 checks on out-of-town banks were returned to the firm.

3:138 **2.** Did Order No. 15 call for one hundred ten-gallon cans or 10 100-gallon drums?

4:138 **3.** Only 1/2 of the work is done. Add 1/8, three fifths, 1/4, 1 1/2, and 5/6.

6:140 **4.** Jerome Johnson is five feet 9 in. in height, and he weighs 165 lbs. 14 oz.

5, 8:140 **5.** Please send your check to 1350 5th Avenue, New York, by December fourteen.

1:146 **6.** heed well Samuel Johnson's advice, "what is easy is seldom excellent."

2:146 **7.** i was impressed by what she said about "A dedication to quality work."

3:146 **8.** "if at first you do succeed," he said, "Try something more difficult."

4:146 **9.** this is what the sign said: take the santa ana freeway to disneyland.

5:146 **10.** i have just finished the book by lewis, how to read better and faster.

7:151 **11.** i understand that president kerr is scheduled to speak at the meeting.

8–9:151 **12.** a scientist gave an interesting report on roman and grecian mythology.

8–9:151 13:156 **13.** the editor will meet now with the attorney from smith & brown company.

10:151 11:156 **14.** i announced that school would open on monday, september 11, this fall.

12–14:156 **15.** the century club is on sixth street, just east of the new civic plaza.

15:156 **16.** check lines 14, 16, and 29, on page 37, in volume v, for the solution.

Alertness check: Did you remember to align numbers at the right?

2. *Centering and Aligning.* Follow these steps:

a. On a half sheet, type an underline from 10 to 50 on the line-of-writing or cylinder scale.

b. Center and type your name on the underline. Study position of letters to the underline.

c. Remove paper. Reinsert paper; align it so you can type your name directly over the previous typing. *Cue:* Move ribbon control lever to stencil position. Tap a key or two to check alignment. When alignment is satisfactory, return ribbon control to normal position. Type your name.

d. Evaluate the retyping. If the letters are not exactly over the previous letters, repeat Steps a-c.

e. Move the paper forward about an inch (6 lines). Type your name again. Now type the columnar heading *My Name* so that it is centered a double space above your name.

3. *Footnote Review.* Retype 92D, page 150: center copy vertically (reading position); full sheet; heading: FOOTNOTE REVIEW

LESSON 100

100A: Conditioning Practice (5) *each line three times*

Alphabet	The quiet, still life was movingly executed on canvas by Jack Z. Parr.	*Eyes on copy*
Figure-symbol	Write checks for these amounts: $41.44, $53.26, $178.90, and $414.45.	
Shift key	Jack Brown and Don Hutson will visit Chicago, New York, and St. Louis.	
Speed	The eight men handled the historical ornament with the utmost caution.	

| 1 | 2 | 3 | 4 | 5 | 6 | 7 | 8 | 9 | 10 | 11 | 12 | 13 | 14 |

Problem 3

Words

To: Angelo Fergerson Director of Personnel 8
Date: *(current)* File: TI–301966 From: H. W. 14
Adams, President Subject: Personnel Needs 21
(¶ 1) We are encouraged by our construction 28
engineers to believe that we may be able to 37
move into our new annex within six months. 46
Barring unforeseeable delays, we should be 54
operational soon thereafter. (¶ 2) You will recall 64
that at the last meeting of our Executive Board 73
you were asked to prepare a report on personnel 83
requirements needed to expand operations in 92
the new building. We need now to discuss your 101
recommendations. (¶ 3) Will you plan to meet 109
with the Board next Tuesday afternoon at two 118
o'clock to give your report, including cost figures 128
on which you are working with the Finance 137
Department. I should like to have you lead the 146
discussion regarding your report and elicit ques- 156
tions from those present. (xx) *+ Envelope* 162/172

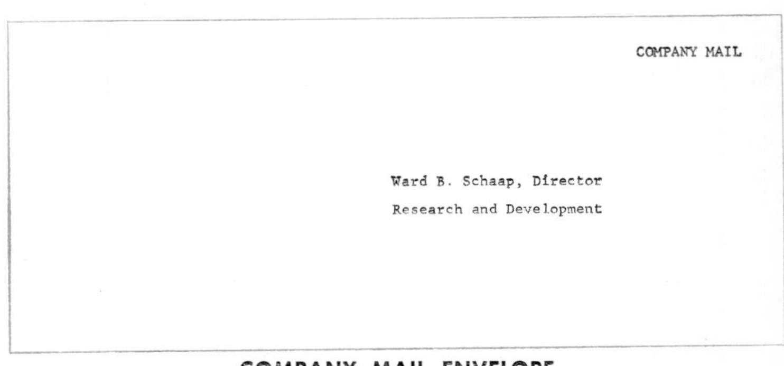

COMPANY MAIL

Ward B. Schaap, Director
Research and Development

COMPANY MAIL ENVELOPE

Problem 4

Words

Retype Problem 3, but make these changes:
To: **Ronald L. Nelson Production Engineer** 7
File: **TI–301955** *Subject:* **Production Needs**
Substitute the word *production* for *personnel* in
the second ¶. Add to ¶ 3: **I shall be free to talk** 166
with you tomorrow afternoon regarding new 174
equipment. (xx) *+ Envelope* 177/187

LESSON 179

179A: Conditioning Practice (5) *each line three times; then 1′ speed writings on Lines 1 and 2*

Alphabet; shift	Jack Seizdorf met Gwen Havner by the big exotic plant in Quebec Manor.	*Finger-stroking action*
Figure	He will print 85 blotters, 173 cards, 29 leaflets, and 406 newspapers.	
Figure-symbol	Smith & Powers paid Invoice #8936 totaling $740.25, less 10% discount.	
Fluency	We should learn well those skills needed in all good business offices.	
	| 1 | 2 | 3 | 4 | 5 | 6 | 7 | 8 | 9 | 10 | 11 | 12 | 13 | 14 |	

179B: Telegrams and Desk-Fax Messages (10)

Features to Review: Telegram

1. Special lines: type and class of service (type X) and account billed.
2. Sender's address and date a TS below account billed.
3. Addressee and his address a DS below date and at the left margin; SS name and address.
4. Sender's name aligned with sender's address, a DS below body. If sent, address and telephone number typed under name; otherwise, under reference initials.
5. Reference initials at left, a DS below sender. Include dictator's name or initials if company name is typed as part of the telegram.

Special Features: Telefax (See illustration at top of 270.)

1. Call letters typed to identify Desk-Fax Station.
2. Letters for type of service unless full rate (as NL).
3. Body with SS; message all WITHIN outlined border.
4. Clean, dark, neat type necessary.

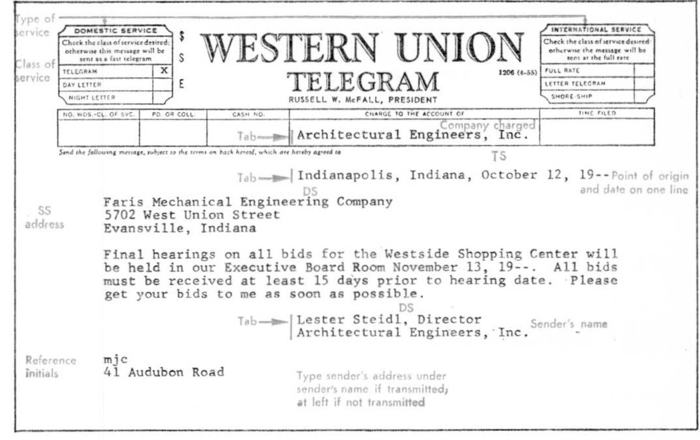

Architectural Engineers, Inc.

Indianapolis, Indiana, October 12, 19--

Faris Mechanical Engineering Company
5702 West Union Street
Evansville, Indiana

Final hearings on all bids for the Westside Shopping Center will be held in our Executive Board Room November 13, 19--. All bids must be received at least 15 days prior to hearing date. Please get your bids to me as soon as possible.

Lester Steidl, Director
Architectural Engineers, Inc.

mjc
41 Audubon Road

TELEGRAM

NOTE: Three cc's are often required: File, Customer, Accounting Office.

100B: Growth Index – Skill Transfer (25)

1. *Straight Copy.* Type a 5′ writing on 94B, page 152. Determine *gwam.* Circle errors.
2. *Rough Draft.* Type a 5′ writing on 79C, page 125. Determine *gwam*: Total Words ÷ 5. Circle errors. Compute % of transfer: rough-draft rate divided by straight-copy rate.
3. *Statistical Copy.* Type a 5′ writing on the statistical copy below. Determine *gwam.* Circle errors. Compute % of transfer: statistical-copy rate divided by straight-copy rate.

All numbers are used in each ¶.

	GWAM 1′	GWAM 5′	
 You requested me to send you some estimates of costs to produce a	13	3	48
letter. Studies show that some typists take as long as 10 minutes, or	27	5	51
even more, to type an average letter of say, 125, 167, or 190 words.	41	8	53
If the typist is paid from $1.80 to $2.40 an hour, this means that the	56	11	56
letter costs from 30 to 40 cents to produce in terms of the typist's	69	14	59
time alone. When other factors are considered, the ordinary business	83	17	62
letter may cost from $1.80 to $2.75 to produce. This is a rather shock-	98	20	65
ing statistic, isn't it?	102	20	66
 Filing costs, too, should be considered. On the average, it costs	13	23	68
6½ cents to retain a carbon copy of a letter in the files for one year.	28	26	71
Just to file the carbon copy costs a cent. It costs $7.50 annually to	42	29	74
maintain one cubic foot of records in the office, exclusive of employee	57	32	77
costs. It costs $196 a year to maintain a 4-drawer file, including	70	35	80
personnel. It has been estimated that it costs $6,200 just to create	84	37	83
and file the contents of a 4-drawer file. Add these cost factors to	98	40	85
the costs to produce a letter, and the ordinary business letter may	112	43	88
really cost as much as $1.93 to $2.88 to produce and retain.	124	45	90

1′ GWAM | 1 | 2 | 3 | 4 | 5 | 6 | 7 | 8 | 9 | 10 | 11 | 12 | 13 | 14 |
5′ GWAM | 1 | 2 | 3 |

100C: Letter Typing Evaluation (20)

60-space line
Modified block style
Current date on 14th line, followed by 3 blank lines
Mixed punctuation
Correct errors

Opening lines

Mr. James Krug | Grant Corporation | 8746 La Jolla Parkway | San Diego, Calif. 92135 | Dear Mr. Krug: |

Closing lines

Sincerely yours, | Mark Barshop | Your initials for reference.

1. Using the statistical copy of 100B above as the body of the letter, type a letter to the address given in Column 2.
2. Since a record is to be made of the time it takes you to produce a letter, you are to start typing the letter when your teacher tells you to start. When you have completed the letter, proofread it carefully to be sure the letter is mailable; then raise your hand and your teacher will give you the total time to that point.
3. Record this time on your letter; then determine your *words a minute rate* by dividing your time into 255 (total words).

LESSON 178

178A: Conditioning Practice (10) *each line three times; then 1′ speed writings on Lines 1 and 2*

Alphabet; shift	Jinx Bradley and Mose Gruzon packed excitedly for exquisite High View.	Quiet hands; quick snap stroke
Figure	One warehouse stored 205 tables, 183 chairs, 69 lamps, and 47 mirrors.	
Figure-symbol	Item #8293 was billed to West & Blair for $475.60 (less 10% for cash).	
Fluency	Some tabulations may have data arranged in groups for clearer reading.	
	| 1 | 2 | 3 | 4 | 5 | 6 | 7 | 8 | 9 | 10 | 11 | 12 | 13 | 14 |	

178B: Interoffice Correspondence (Memorandum or Memo) – Preview (5)

Features to Study in the Illustration Shown Below:

1. Special letterhead for within-company messages between offices or departments.
2. Heading data typed 2 spaces after appropriate guide word. (Use variable-line spacer to align.)
3. Personal titles (Mr., Mrs., Dr., etc.) usually omitted. No salutation or complimentary close.
4. TS after printed headings. SS ¶s; DS between ¶s.
5. Side margins usually 1″; may increase to 1½″ or 2″.
6. Reference initials included.

178C: Typing Interoffice Correspondence (35)

Type the following four interoffice memos for 25′ when directed to begin. If time permits, start over. Mark errors. Compute *g-pram*. **Goals:** Efficient procedure; good format.

Time Schedule	
Get ready to type	5′
Timed production	25′
Proofread; compute *g-pram* . .	5′

Problem 1

Words
To: Ward B. Schaap, Director Research 7
and Development Date: *(current)* File: 13
TI–501966 From: H. W. Adams, President 20
Subject: Cost Reduction (¶ 1) Our Board 25
of Directors periodically expresses anxiety 34
over increases in costs of operations. Typi- 43
cally, greater concern is voiced when profit 52
margins are modest than when they are 60
substantial. Yet there appears to me to be 68
little defense for only cyclical alarms over 77
an element having such a forceful impact 86
on the financial health of our company. 94
(¶ 2) Many of our competitors are now 100
either engaged in or actively planning for 109
a serious attack on operational costs, and 117
it is my plan to institute a zealous cost 126
reduction program in our company, too. 134
(¶ 3) I should like to review with you 140
a possible study of methods being em- 148
ployed in other cost reduction programs as 156
a means of gaining insights for designing 165
our economy program. (xx) + *Envelope* 169/182

NOTE: Special color envelopes are usually used for interoffice correspondence. In other cases, type COMPANY MAIL in the postage location. Include addressee's title. See illustration at top of page 269.

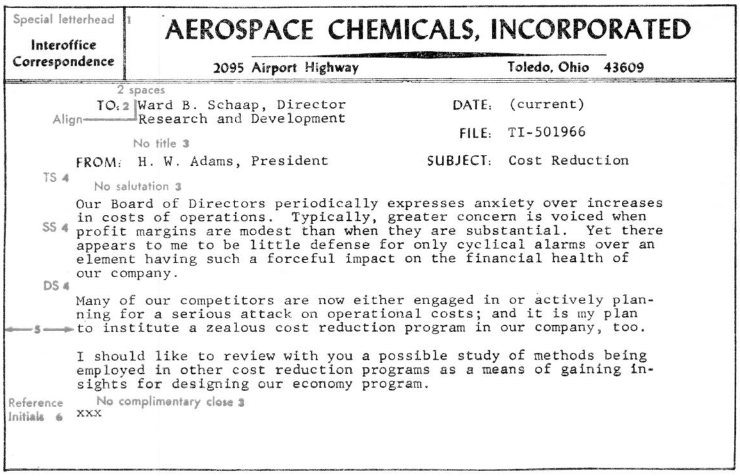

Special letterhead 1
Interoffice Correspondence

AEROSPACE CHEMICALS, INCORPORATED
2095 Airport Highway Toledo, Ohio 43609

2 spaces
TO: 2 Ward B. Schaap, Director DATE: (current)
Align Research and Development
FILE: TI-501966
No title 3
FROM: H. W. Adams, President SUBJECT: Cost Reduction
TS 4
No salutation 3
SS 4
Our Board of Directors periodically expresses anxiety over increases in costs of operations. Typically, greater concern is voiced when profit margins are modest than when they are substantial. Yet there appears to me to be little defense for only cyclical alarms over an element having such a forceful impact on the financial health of our company.
DS 4
5
Many of our competitors are now either engaged in or actively planning for a serious attack on operational costs; and it is my plan to institute a zealous cost reduction program in our company, too.

I should like to review with you a possible study of methods being employed in other cost reduction programs as a means of gaining insights for designing our economy program.

Reference Initials 6 No complimentary close 3
xxx

INTEROFFICE MEMORANDUM

Problem 2

Words
Retype Problem 1, but make these changes:
To: **Milton E. Shaw Director of Finance** *File:* 7
TI–502966 Substitute the following ¶ for ¶ 3 in
Problem 1: **Will you send me this week, for all** 137
departments, your cost analysis figures cover- 146
ing the last five-year period. I want to study 156
these data carefully prior to my meeting with our 166
R & D staff. (xx) + *Envelope* 169/178

Unit 17 | Lessons 101-110

Business Letters

Letter Stationery. Business letters are usually typed on 8½- by 11-inch letterhead stationery. The letterhead has the name and address of the company and sometimes other information printed at the top. The printed heading is *usually* no more than two inches deep.

If a letter is longer than one page, plain paper of the same size, color, and quality as the letterhead may be used for the additional pages. Special paper (onionskin or manifold-copy paper) is used for carbon copies.

Smaller letterheads (usually 8½ by 5½ or 5½ by 8½ inches) may be used for short letters.

Margins and Vertical Placement. Some offices use standard margins (a set line length) for all letters. Others vary the margins according to letter length.

A placement table, such as the one given below, will help you to place letters correctly. As you gain experience, you should be able to estimate letter length and place letters correctly without this "aid."

Notes About the Placement Table.

1. Vertical placement of the date varies according to letter length. The address, however, is always typed on the 4th line (3 blank line spaces) below the date.
2. Letters with special lines (attention, subject, etc.) or unusual features (tabulated material, extra lines in address or closing) may require adjustment in date-line placement. Also, when a deep letterhead makes it impossible to type the date on the designated line, type it a double space below the last letterhead line.
3. No change in margins is needed for letters in the 101–300 word classification: Use 1½-inch margins for all these letters.
4. For each 50-word increase in letter length in the "average" category, the date line is raised 2 lines.

LETTER PLACEMENT TABLE

Letter Classification		5-Stroke Words in Letter Body	Side Margins	Margin Description	Date Line Position (From Top Edge of Paper)
Short		Up to 100	2"	Wide	Line 20
Average	1	101 – 150	1½"	Standard	18
	2	151 – 200	1½"	"	16
	3	201 – 250	1½"	"	14
	4	251 – 300	1½"	"	12
Long		301 – 350	1"	Narrow	12
Two-page		More than 350	1"	Narrow	12

LESSON 101

101A: Conditioning Practice (5) *each line three times*

Eyes on copy

Alphabet	The view from the jungle peak was both exciting and amazing to Quincy.
Figure	The fishermen caught 84 albacore, 3,215 barracuda, and 7,690 mackerel.
Quiet hands	For many people their only exercise comes from jumping to conclusions.
Speed	They plan to see the ancient ornaments when they visit the old museum.

| 1 | 2 | 3 | 4 | 5 | 6 | 7 | 8 | 9 | 10 | 11 | 12 | 13 | 14 |

LESSON 177

177A: Conditioning Practice (10) *each line three times; then 1′ speed writings on Lines 1 and 4*

Alphabet; shift	Pearl Bizoc waxed novel discs with Gil Jackforth at unique Music City.	*Shift quickly*
Figure	The club had 170 plates, 93 cups, 62 saucers, and 548 knives in stock.	
Figure-symbol	Bill #8372 for 45 lbs. of meat @ $1.96 per lb. went to Jones & Millar.	
Fluency	Good typists are capable of handling business stationery of all sizes.	
	| 1 | 2 | 3 | 4 | 5 | 6 | 7 | 8 | 9 | 10 | 11 | 12 | 13 | 14 |	

177B: Technique Refinement – Space-Bar Control (8) *repeat 176B, page 266*

177C: Growth Index – Straight Copy (32)

1. Type one 5′ writing on both ¶s. Compute *nwam*.
2. Type two 3′ writings on ¶ 1:
   (a) Speed (exploration) level; (b) control level.
3. Repeat Step 2 procedure for ¶ 2.
4. Type one 5′ writing on both ¶s. Compute *nwam*. Record the better 5′ writing.

All letters are used.

	GWAM 3′		GWAM 5′	
Many people today are disquieted about their dreams for the future.	5	66	3	77
They think about the rapid and numerous changes that are taking place in	9	71	6	80
our society almost daily and ponder what the future may hold. There is	14	76	9	82
no doubt that the new discoveries of science, improved technology, and	19	81	12	85
amazing findings of research have led to changes in our way of life for	24	85	14	88
which we have felt quite unprepared; and there is good reason to assume	29	90	17	91
that we may anticipate even more unusual changes to which we shall have	33	95	20	94
to adjust in the immediate future. It is wise to keep in mind, though,	38	100	23	97
that the size of a problem in no way suggests its severity; thus, there	43	103	26	100
is sound premise for assuming that a future full of chance can be met	48	109	29	102
with minimum fear for ultimate success. There is hardly need, then, to	52	114	31	105
arouse anxiety about unknown crises which could be encountered at some	57	119	34	108
time in the future; instead, we should prepare for any eventuality.	62	123	37	111
To prepare well for the future, one should have a solid foundation	4	66	40	114
in all the subjects contributing to a basic, general education. History,	9	71	43	117
mathematics, social studies, and some science should form a part of all	14	76	46	119
educational experience; and well-chosen business courses should also be	19	80	48	122
a requisite. A person preparing for the future should be willing to	24	85	51	125
hazard the risk of having his ideas analyzed by critics and should al-	28	90	54	128
ways be sensible in his attitudes toward the merits of his own ability.	33	94	57	131
One should also reveal a rational respect for the work of others even	38	99	60	134
though one may hope to surpass what has been done previously. And in	42	104	63	136
this quest for success in the future, one must show a zest and vigor for	47	109	65	139
attempting jobs that have never been tried before. While most risks	52	113	68	142
and details of the future may seem vague at the present time, there is	57	118	71	144
no basis for fear if one prepares well and has a fine outlook on life.	61	123	74	148

3′ GWAM | 1 | 2 | 3 | 4 | 5 |
5′ GWAM | 1 | 2 | 3 |

101B: Manuscript Typing (15) *(Full sheets)*

1" side and bottom margins; 2" top margin
DS ¶ 1; SS the enumerated items

After typing the first paragraph, reset the margins to indent the enumerated items 5 spaces from the left and right margins.

Reset the left margin: (1) at the figure position with a tab stop for the lines of copy; OR (2) at the beginning of the lines of copy and use the margin release key and backspace to type the figures in their proper position.

Reset the right margin 5 spaces to the left.

SPECIAL LETTER PLACEMENT POINTS

TS

Certain points must be kept in mind when using a letter placement table. These points are listed below:

1. Paper-guide placement. Check the placement of the paper guide so that the horizontal centering of the letter will be accurate. The left and right margins of a letter should be approximately equal. *DS*
2. Date line. The horizontal placement of the date line varies according to the letter style used.
3. Address lines. When the letter is addressed to a person, his official title may be placed on the first or the second line of the address, whichever gives a better balance to the lines.
4. Attention line. Sometimes an attention line is used in business letters. When it is used, it is usually typed on the second line (a double space) below the letter address. (See illustration on page 202.)
5. Subject line. The subject line, when used, may be typed on the second line (a double space) below the salutation. It may be either centered or typed at the left margin. (See illustration on page 202.)
6. Company name. Sometimes the company name is typed in the closing lines. When this is done, it is typed in all capital letters two lines (a double space) below the complimentary close. The modern practice is to omit the company name in the closing lines; this is especially true when letterhead paper is used.
7. Typewritten name and official title. The name of the person who dictated the letter and his official title are typed four lines (3 blank lines) below the complimentary close, or four lines below the typed company name when it is used. When both the name and the official title are used, they may be typed on the same line or the official title may be typed on the next line below the typed name.
8. Two-page letters. If a letter is too long for a single page, at least two lines of a paragraph should be typed at the bottom of the first page and at least two lines should be carried to the second page. The second page of a letter, or any additional pages, requires a proper heading. Either of two forms may be used for typing the extra-page heading. (See illustrations on page 202.)

101C: Alertness Training (5)

Using the manuscript prepared in 101B, study and relate as many of the items as possible to Style Letter 2, page 164. Note the use of the word "Enclosures" to indicate the inclusion of separate items.

101D: Skill Applications (25) *(Plain sheets)*

Problem 1: Learning

Type Style Letter 2, page 164, in modified block style with 5-space ¶ indentions as shown.

In typing the letter in correct form, be guided by the placement and spacing notations in color.

Type on the *exploration (speed) level* and do not correct errors.

Problem 2: Proofreading

Proofread the letter you typed as Problem 1. Indicate by pencil corrections any changes that you need to make in the copy.

Use the standard proofreaders' marks you have learned (Reference: pages 90, 92, 100, and 125) to make the needed pencil corrections.

Problem 3: Skill Building

Using your corrected copy, retype the letter. As you type, make the corrections you have indicated in your copy.

Type on the *control level*; erase and correct neatly any errors you make as you retype the letter. Compare your letter with Style Letter 2.

LESSON 176

Special Business Communications

176A: Conditioning Practice (10) *each line three times; then 1′ speed writings on Lines 1 and 4*

Alphabet; shift	Reva Printz and Sally Jackwell exhibited quaint figurines on Art Mall.	*Finger-reach action*
Figure	We ordered 148 keys, 209 locks, 73 doors, and 65 files for a building.	
Figure-symbol	A late bill sent to Hall & Carr read: "$21\frac{1}{2}$ x $38\frac{1}{4}$ ft. @ $1.25 per ft."	
Fluency	Once a job is begun, it should not be left until it is done very well.	
	| 1 | 2 | 3 | 4 | 5 | 6 | 7 | 8 | 9 | 10 | 11 | 12 | 13 | 14 |	

176B: Technique Refinement – Space-Bar Control (8) *two 1′ speed writings on each line*

CUE | Strike the space bar rapidly, but firmly.

	Words
if he is to go or us by so do be am of it as up me an in we	12
for the and may but sir all men due box man six big own men	12
with they them make than when also work form both sign down	12

176C: Skill Comparison – Speed and Accuracy Emphasis (32)

1. Type two 3′ writings on ¶ 1 for speed. If you complete the ¶, start over. Compute *gwam.*
2. Type one 3′ writing on ¶ 1 for control (3-4 error limit).
3. Repeat Steps 1 and 2 for ¶ 2.
4. Type two 3′ speed writings, using both ¶s 1 and 2. Compute *gwam* and compare with Steps 1 and 2.

All letters are used.

	3′ GWAM Each ¶		3′ GWAM Both ¶s	
It is an odd, common thing for people to say that work in an office	5	31	5	58
is quite easy, since the day is spent typing letters. Yet the way in	9	36	9	63
which a letter must be typed suggests that this common point of view	14	41	14	67
is in error. If the job is completed attractively, with ideas stated	18	45	18	72
accurately and corrections made neatly, typing letters makes office	23	50	23	76
work a true challenge and requires unusual competencies.	27	53	27	80

	3′ GWAM Each ¶		3′ GWAM Both ¶s	
In a new buying surge, our retail sales rose to $8,127,000,000, a	4	31	31	85
sales annual cited. Durable goods hit $2,113,000,000, up 5% from a	9	36	36	89
year earlier; and nondurables hit $6,014,000,000, a climb of 19% from	14	40	40	94
the previous year. Department store sales came up 31% in a year; the	18	45	45	99
drug store and the furniture-appliance group each added 23%, and grocery	23	50	50	103
store and apparel sales added 16% over a year earlier.	27	54	54	107

3′ GWAM | 1 | 2 | 3 | 4 | 5 |

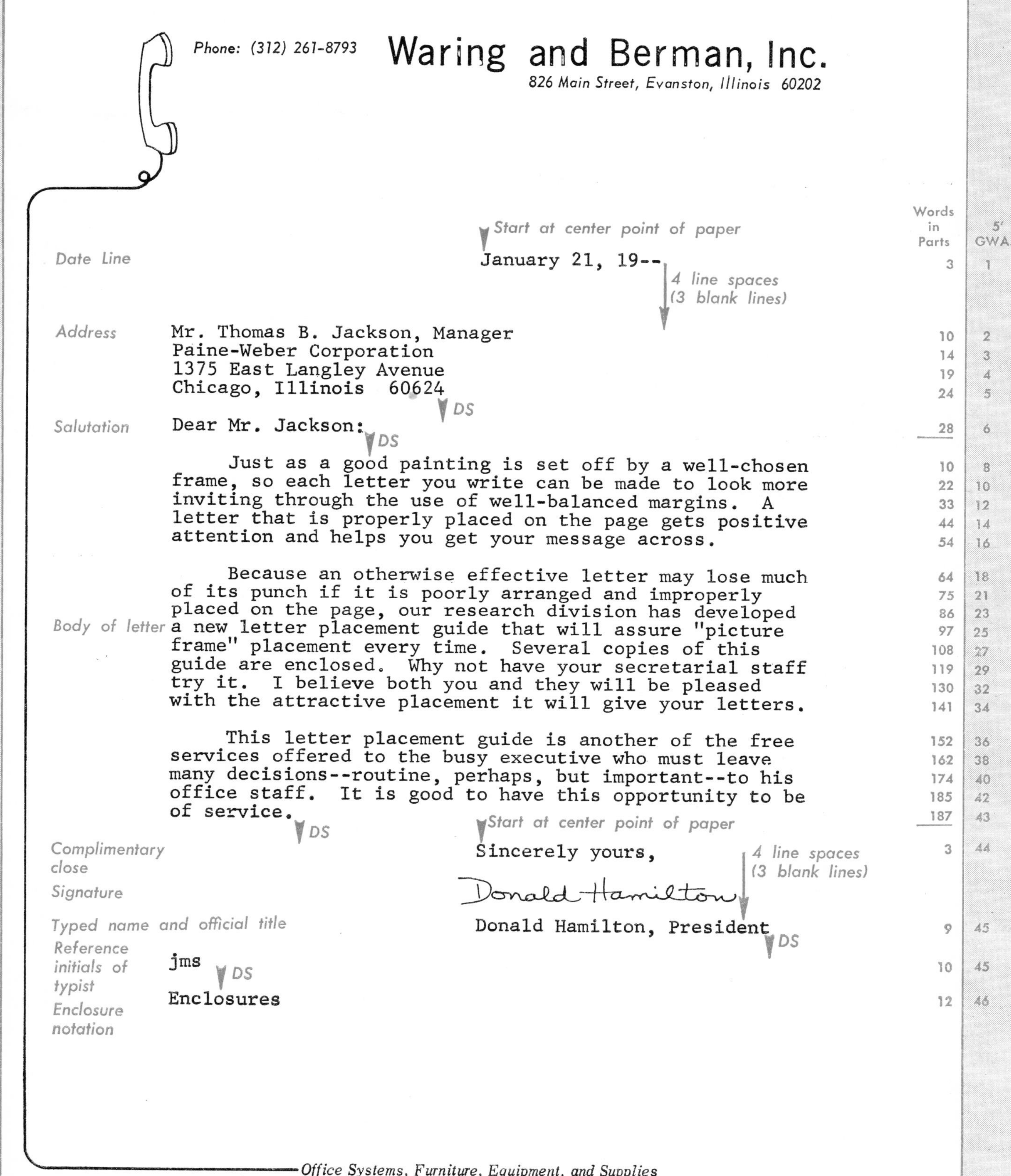

Phone: (312) 261-8793

Waring and Berman, Inc.

826 Main Street, Evanston, Illinois 60202

Words in Parts | 5' GWAM

Start at center point of paper

Date Line — January 21, 19-- 3 1

4 line spaces (3 blank lines)

Address — Mr. Thomas B. Jackson, Manager 10 2
Paine-Weber Corporation 14 3
1375 East Langley Avenue 19 4
Chicago, Illinois 60624 24 5

DS

Salutation — Dear Mr. Jackson: 28 6

DS

Just as a good painting is set off by a well-chosen 10 8
frame, so each letter you write can be made to look more 22 10
inviting through the use of well-balanced margins. A 33 12
letter that is properly placed on the page gets positive 44 14
attention and helps you get your message across. 54 16

Because an otherwise effective letter may lose much 64 18
of its punch if it is poorly arranged and improperly 75 21
placed on the page, our research division has developed 86 23
Body of letter — a new letter placement guide that will assure "picture 97 25
frame" placement every time. Several copies of this 108 27
guide are enclosed. Why not have your secretarial staff 119 29
try it. I believe both you and they will be pleased 130 32
with the attractive placement it will give your letters. 141 34

This letter placement guide is another of the free 152 36
services offered to the busy executive who must leave 162 38
many decisions--routine, perhaps, but important--to his 174 40
office staff. It is good to have this opportunity to be 185 42
of service. 187 43

DS — Start at center point of paper

Complimentary close — Sincerely yours, 3 44

4 line spaces (3 blank lines)

Signature — *Donald Hamilton*

Typed name and official title — Donald Hamilton, President 9 45

DS

Reference initials of typist — jms 10 45

DS

Enclosure notation — Enclosures 12 46

Office Systems, Furniture, Equipment, and Supplies

Style Letter 2: Modified Block with Indented Paragraphs and Mixed Punctuation

LESSON 175

175A: Conditioning Practice (5) *pretyping check; then each line three times*

Alphabet; shift	Dave Plietz saw John Quigley bowl six games for the Cedar Park trophy.	*Quick carriage return*
Figure	They replaced at cost 50 plates, 194 forks, 362 spoons, and 78 knives.	
Double letters	noon deed loose books accept assess immense running stopping opportune	
Fluency	The quantity of work that they may handle is quite well known to many.	
	| 1 | 2 | 3 | 4 | 5 | 6 | 7 | 8 | 9 | 10 | 11 | 12 | 13 | 14 |	

175B: Skill Building – Straight Copy (8) *repeat 174B, page 263*

175C: Tabulation Production Measurement (37)

Time Schedule	
Get ready to type	2′
Timed production	30′
Proofread; compute *n-pram* . .	5′

Arrange supplies. Type the following three tables for 30′ when directed to begin. Correct errors as you type. If time permits, start over. Mark uncorrected errors. Compute *n-pram*.

Problem 1 *Full sheet 1 cc DS body*
8 spaces between columns

Words

INSURANCE BENEFIT PAYMENTS
IN THE UNITED STATES * 10

Reported by Selected States 15
(000 Omitted) 18

State	Death Payments	Annuity Payments	Policy Dividends	Words
				23 / 36
Alabama	$ 67,700	$ 5,900	$17,700	44
Arizona	26,000	5,700	14,300	50
Florida	139,800	36,200	53,100	56
Georgia	94,500	6,600	29,000	62
Hawaii	10,500	6,100	9,600	67
Idaho	10,900	1,000	6,100	72
Iowa	52,200	10,300	38,000	78
Kansas	42,300	9,600	24,100	83
Maine	19,000	4,800	12,600	88
Nevada	6,500	800	3,400	94
				97

*Additional information available in source, for endowments and for disability 106 / 112

Source: Life Insurance Fact Book, 1966 125

Problem 2 *Half sheet 1 cc SS body*
6 spaces between columns
Type horizontal rulings

Words

INSURANCE BENEFIT PAYMENTS
IN THE UNITED STATES 10

Reported by Selected States 15
(000 Omitted) 18

State	Death Payments	Annuity Payments	Policy Dividends	Words
				29 / 40 / 45 / 51 / 62
Ohio	$258,000	$71,200	$151,400	69
Texas	196,800	50,500	58,500	75
Utah	18,600	2,000	10,300	80
Washington	53,900	11,600	31,100	87
Wisconsin	91,100	17,900	61,300	93
Wyoming	5,900	1,400	3,700	99
				110

Source: Life Insurance Fact Book, 1966 122

Problem 3 *Combine Problems 1 and 2 1 cc SS body*
Use typed horizontal and vertical rulings
8 spaces between columns; body in groups of 4
Word Count: 198
+ each vertical rule 9/225

LESSON 102

102A: Conditioning Practice (5) *each line three times*

Alphabet	New lake equipment may be purchased for the junior magazine executive.	*Uniform*
Figure-symbol	Order #2856 for 30 chairs and 47 desks will be shipped on November 19.	*stroking*
Double letters	Three letters will go to Bill and Betty Ott about the Tennessee deeds.	
Speed	The efficient way to gain speed is to type with continuity and rhythm.	
	| 1 | 2 | 3 | 4 | 5 | 6 | 7 | 8 | 9 | 10 | 11 | 12 | 13 | 14 |	

102B: Skill-Building Drills – Letter Parts (15) *1′ and 3′ writings (Plain paper; Margins: 1½″)*

1. Using Style Letter 2, page 164, type four 1′ writings on the opening parts (date through salutation). When you have typed through the salutation, DS, indent for the date, and repeat the drill. Type these lines as many times as you can during the 1′ timing. Determine *gwam.*

2. Using the same letter, type four 1′ writings on the closing parts (complimentary close through enclosure notation). When you have typed through the enclosure notation, DS, indent for the complimentary close, and repeat the drill. Type on the *speed level.* Determine *gwam.*

3. On another sheet of paper, type a 3′ writing on the body of the letter. Determine *gwam* by dividing the total words typed by 3.

On which of the timed writings did you make the greatest speed: opening lines? closing lines? body of the letter? Why?

102C: Application Skill Building – Letters (30) *(Plain paper)*

Style: Modified block, 5-space ¶ indentions, mixed punctuation; date and closing lines started at center.

Placement: Use the table, page 162. The number of words in the letter body is indicated by the number in parentheses at the end of the letter.

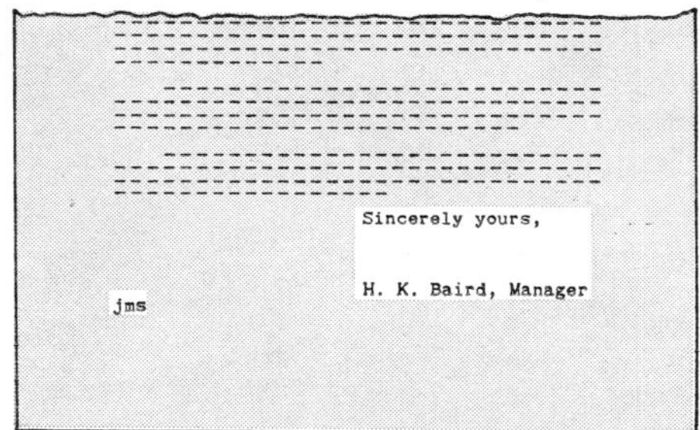

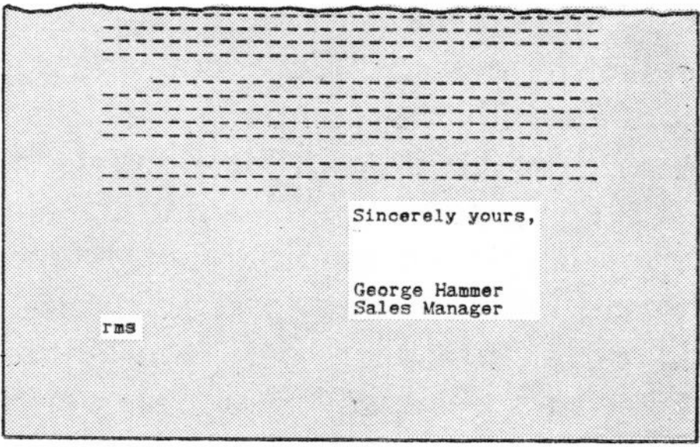

PLACEMENT OF OFFICIAL TITLE IN CLOSING LINES

Letter 1

Words
(Current date) | Mr. Jay O'Conner, General Manager | Western Industrial Products Company | 17
9574 South Indiana Avenue | Denver, Colorado 80201 | Dear Mr. O'Conner: | (¶ 1) Have you 33
stayed at the Bayshore Inn lately? We try to promote the Inn as a sensible hotel for the 51
busy executive who is stopping in Vancouver on business. But, frankly, it's been a losing 69
battle because the Bayshore Inn simply doesn't look like a sensible hotel. It looks like 87
a place you'd find in Rio or Acapulco. (¶ 2) The Bayshore Inn is built on the lee shore of 104
a yacht harbor, and the mountains are so near you can smell the evergreens on their slopes. 123
The Inn is only four blocks from the heart of Vancouver; but if you look out your window, 141
you'd think you were in a mountain retreat. A walk in the gardens of the hotel is an 158
adventure, and lunch at Trader Vic's is a reward. (¶ 3) The only sensible thing about the 175
Bayshore Inn is the price. Single rooms start at $12. Busy executives keep coming back 193
here again and again. They tell us it is the sensible place to stay. Perhaps you should 211
stop at the Inn the next time you're in Vancouver. We'd like the opportunity to pamper 228
you, too. | Sincerely yours, | H. K. Baird, Manager | jms | (199) 239

Letter 2 is on page 166.

Problem 1 *Executive Size (7¼" x 10½")*
Modified block, mixed

Words
(Current date) Mr. Keith L. Pierson 1907 W. 9
Kenton Avenue Columbus, Ohio 43205 Dear 17
Mr. Pierson: Subject: Executive Recognition 26
Plan (¶ 1) We are pleased to answer your 33
questions regarding our proposed "Executive 42
Recognition Plan." The Board of Directors has 51
given a great deal of thought to the problem 60
of attracting and retaining competent, insight- 70
ful, future-looking executives. Our company is 80
rapidly expanding. We believe that, to meet 89
successfully the challenge of competition and of 98
our increasing responsibilities, we must take 108
steps to gain and retain the services of men who 117
are able to achieve maximum earnings on the 126
investment of our stockholders. Therefore, we 136
are planning to adopt an incentive system called 145
the "Executive Recognition Plan." This plan is 155
designed to repay our top-level executives for 164
the contributions they make to the profit objec- 174
tives of the company. (¶ 2) Under this new 181
plan, incentive awards may be made in company 191
stock, thus increasing interest in the company's 200
business on the part of those executives who re- 210
ceive the awards. To encourage such executives 219
to stay with the company, the plan permits the 229
awards to be paid in installments over a number 238
of years, contingent, with certain exceptions, 248
upon continued employment. Hence, executives 257
would be motivated to remain with the company 266
in order to "earn out" the entire number of 275
award installments. (¶ 3) It is our hope that this 284
new plan will receive the enthusiastic approval 294
of our stockholders and that top executives in 303
the company will respond with many profitable 312
ideas and innovations. Very sincerely yours, 322
Donald E. Anderson Chairman of the Board 330
(xx) (301) *+ Envelope* **330/343**

Problem 2 *Standard Size (8½" x 11")*
Modified block, mixed

(Current date) Mr. Darwin Stevens, President 9
National Equipment Company 1205 Sunset Road 18
Waterloo, Iowa 50701 Dear Mr. Stevens: (¶ 1) 26
We welcome your inquiry regarding our special- 35
ized services in scientific industrial lighting. 45
Both our experience and our scientific research 55
support your viewpoint that the margin of dif- 64
ference between the most profitable business 73
firms and those that are somewhat less success- 82
ful can often be traced to the ability of some 91
companies to turn out better products at lower 101
costs than do their competitors. Therefore, we 110
attempt to help you to remain competitive 119
through attention to maximum production and 127
minimum cost factors. (¶ 2) Productivity is a 136
vital and continuing concern of management, 144
and studies which deal with critical elements 154
that influence production have revealed some 163
rather impressive data. Equipment, personnel 172
incentives, facilities, and company policy have 181
been recognized as factors which have a signifi- 191
cant impact on industrial output. But of all fac- 201
tors that influence production, illumination has 210
been identified as a factor of unusual importance. 221
(¶ 3) You are aware that we have long held the 229
lead in scientific research for improved industrial 239
lighting and that we are committed to helping 249
business firms increase their productivity through 259
the use of scientific systems of work-station illu- 269
mination. May one of our lighting engineer 278
representatives call on you soon to discuss 286
some of the services we offer? Yours very truly, 296
ILLUMINATING SYSTEMS, INC. James T. Thomp- 305
son Chief Engineer (xx) (270) 309
+ Envelope **328**

Problem 3 *Half-Size (5½" x 8½")*
Block, open

(Current date) Mr. John W. Snyder 4091 Circle 9
Hill Road Louisville, Kentucky 40207 Dear 18
Mr. Snyder (¶ 1) At its last meeting, the Advis- 26
ory Board recommended that steps be taken 34
soon to determine the feasibility of launching 44
a new concert series of light opera programmed 53
to appeal to young people interested in fine 62
theater. As a consequence, I am planning a 71
series of four to six concerts for Saturday mati- 81
nee performances. (¶ 2) Since you have ex- 88
pressed a personal interest in this new venture, 98
I should like to have you study the enclosed 107
tentative program and send me your reactions 116
to the listings shown. It would help greatly if 125
you could send your appraisal within a few 134
days. Very cordially yours Lawrence L. Davis 143
General Manager (xx) Enclosure (118) 149
+ Envelope **162**

Letter 2

	Words
(Current date) | Mr. John Seymour, Purchasing	9
Agent | Stone Mountain Products, Inc. | 1568	17
Peach Tree Avenue | Atlanta, Georgia 30309 |	26
Dear Mr. Seymour: | (¶ 1) Some people work	33
well at desks piled high with papers. Others	42
work equally well at neat, uncluttered desks.	52
Is someone right and someone wrong? (¶ 2)	59
With Gibralter desks, you're right either way.	69
Uncluttered, a Gibralter desk pays dividends in	78
good looks. It combines functional efficiency	88
with smart, contemporary styling. Cluttered with	98
a mountain of paper work, a Gibralter desk is a	107
bulwark of quality construction. It is made to	117
take rough use. (¶ 3) There is Gibralter furni-	125
ture for every office need. The next time you	135
need furniture, why not make it Gibralter.	143
You'll be right in your choice. | Sincerely yours, |	153
George Hammer | Sales Manager | rms (120)	160

LESSON 103

103A: Conditioning Practice (5) *each line three times*

Alphabet	This bright jacket has an amazing weave and is of exceptional quality.	*Finger-action reaches*
Figure-symbol	Order the #38, #56, and #79 dies and the #1204 (Diamond) machine tool.	
Concentration	He asked us to translate "Tenet insanable multos scribendi cacoathes."	
Speed	The auditor will send a statement to the firm by the end of the month.	
	| 1 | 2 | 3 | 4 | 5 | 6 | 7 | 8 | 9 | 10 | 11 | 12 | 13 | 14 |	

103B: Growth Index – Straight Copy (15) *two 5′ writings; circle errors; determine* gwam

All letters are used.

	GWAM 1′	5′	
The business letter is, in a sense, the personal envoy of the busi-	13	3	51
ness firm that writes it. All firms give much care to the content of	27	5	53
the letter so that it will be as effective as possible; however, if the	42	8	56
letter is carelessly typed or poorly placed on the page, much of its	55	11	59
effect may be lost. A letter tends to give a good or a poor image of	69	14	62
the firm that sends it, depending upon the first impression it makes.	84	17	65
All typists should recognize that good placement of the letter on the	98	20	67
page is, therefore, of primary importance.	106	21	69
A letter must be carefully proofread before it is removed from the	13	24	72
typewriter. Just be sure that you acquire this necessary habit. Here	28	27	75
is an idea of some of the steps to follow: First, check the placement	42	30	78
and the form of the letter. It should be well placed on the page, and	56	32	80
it should look much like a picture in a frame. Every key stroke should	70	35	83
be even or uniform. Second, be sure that all figures and amounts are	84	38	86
exact. Be sure to see that the address is correct. Lastly, verify the	99	41	89
content of the letter; also, the grammar and spelling. Be sure that	113	44	92
all typing errors have been neatly corrected, and that there are no	126	46	94
errors of word division, and the like.	134	48	96

1′ GWAM \| 1 \| 2 \| 3 \| 4 \| 5 \| 6 \| 7 \| 8 \| 9 \| 10 \| 11 \| 12 \| 13 \| 14 \|
5′ GWAM \| 1 \| 2 \| 3 \|

Unit 30 | Lessons 174-175

Measuring Basic and Production Skills

LESSON 174

174A: Conditioning Practice (5) *pretyping check; then each line three times*

Alphabet; shift	Wes Plascjak and Max Query gave a big jazz concert in Fort Penn Hotel.	*Quick, snap stroke*
Figure	They sold 85 rugs, 69 lamps, 402 shades, and 173 end tables this year.	
Double letters	aloof happy success million accords written accident approves approach	
Fluency	They wish to make a big profit for the firm in this part of the world.	
	| 1 | 2 | 3 | 4 | 5 | 6 | 7 | 8 | 9 | 10 | 11 | 12 | 13 | 14 |	

174B: Growth Index – Straight Copy (8) *5′ writing; circle errors; compute* nwam

All letters are used.

	GWAM 1′	5′	
One of the most vital of all sectors of our society is the one that	14	3	62
deals with education. Over a span of almost ten years, there has been	28	6	65
a growing interest in, and greater support for, all phases of our educa-	42	8	67
tional activity. Leaders from all walks of life have pointed to a	55	11	70
sizable need for more and richer education for all of us; and, to prove	70	14	73
the extent of their concern and interest, they have endorsed ambitious	84	17	76
programs of all descriptions for all types of people and their needs.	98	20	79
But just as there have been bold, strong efforts to improve both the	112	22	81
quality and the chances of getting an education in our society, so there	127	25	84
have been unusual challenges to those persons taking advantage of the	141	28	87
privilege of gaining more and finer education in our prized schools.	154	31	90
One of the big issues to be settled when you start to plan school	13	33	93
activities centers around the type and worth of subjects to be taken	27	36	95
while a student. So often a conflict arises over deciding the amount of	42	39	98
time that should be given to courses of a general, background nature and	56	42	101
the amount of time that should be devoted to work of a more practical	70	45	104
purpose. Sadly, such conflict produces wasteful confusion that should	84	48	107
not exist, for a wise student realizes the value of both kinds of study	99	51	110
and plans to maintain a balance between the two. Thus, when selecting	113	53	113
areas to be studied, try to include many courses that will enrich your	127	56	115
understandings and others that will equip you to earn an ample living.	141	59	118
1′ GWAM | 1 | 2 | 3 | 4 | 5 | 6 | 7 | 8 | 9 | 10 | 11 | 12 | 13 | 14 |			
5′ GWAM | 1 | 2 | 3 |			

174C: Business Letter Production Measurement (37)

Time Schedule	
Get ready to type	2′
Timed production	30′
Proofread; compute *n-pram* . .	5′

Arrange supplies. Type the following three letters on page 264 for 30′ when directed to begin. Make 1 cc and address an envelope for each letter. Use margins and date line as shown under TIPS on page 258. Correct errors. If time permits, start over. Mark uncorrected errors. Compute *n-pram*.

103C: Application Skill Building – Letters (30) *(Modified block style; 5-space ¶ indention; 2″ margins)*

1. Type a 3′ writing on the letter to establish a base rate. If you finish before time is called, start over.
2. Determine *gwam.* To this rate add 8 *gwam* to set a new goal. Divide the goal rate into four equal segments; note these quarter-minute check points for guided writings.
3. *Leave proper spacing between letter parts, but begin the letter (date line) near the top of the sheet.* Beginning with the date, type three 1′ guided writings on the opening parts of the letter and ¶ 1. *Begin the second and third writings a double space below the last line of the previous writing.*
4. Repeat Step 3, using ¶ 2 and the closing lines of the letter.
5. Type another 3′ writing on the complete letter. Try to maintain your new goal rate for this writing. Determine *gwam* and compare it with the rate you attained in Step 1.
6. Type the letter from your teacher's dictation.

	Words in Parts	3′ GWAM
September 21, 19-- | Mr. Scott Archer | 3011 Scottsdale	10	3
Drive | Phoenix, Arizona 85010 | Dear Mr. Archer: |	20	7
(¶ 1) We want to be sure to give you credit, but not the kind of credit which is	15	12
usually given by a credit manager. We mean the kind of credit which is defined	31	17
by Webster as "praise or approval to which a person is entitled."	44	21
(¶ 2) The way you have handled your account with us during the past year cer-	14	27
tainly merits our praise. We appreciate the promptness with which you pay your	30	31
account. So we want to say thank you, and "give credit where credit is due."	46	37
It is a pleasure to be of service to you.	54	39
Sincerely yours, | Dwight Nott, Credit Manager | lwe (98)	10	42

LESSON 104

104A: Conditioning Practice (5) *each line three times*

Alphabet	Jack Culep admired the vivid, waxy sheen of a Guatemalan quetzal bird.	*Space quickly; down-and-in motion*
Figure-symbol	He thought $24.36 too much for a 150# bag of sugar and offered $18.79.	
Quiet hands	This is my translation: The incurable itch of writing possesses many.	
Speed	Learn to space quickly between words in order to type with continuity.	
	| 1 | 2 | 3 | 4 | 5 | 6 | 7 | 8 | 9 | 10 | 11 | 12 | 13 | 14 |	

104B: Skill-Building Drills – Letter Parts (10) *1′ writings (Plain paper; 2″ margins)*

1. Using 103C, above, type three 1′ writings on the opening lines. Determine *gwam.*
2. Using the same letter, type three 1′ writings on the closing lines. Determine *gwam.*
3. Type a 1′ writing on each of the ¶s of the letter. Determine *gwam.* Compare your 1′ rates.

173B: Special-Size Stationery Production Measurement (45)

Arrange supplies. Type the following four letters for 30′ when directed to begin. Place date and margins as shown under TIPS, page 258. Make 1 cc and address an envelope for each letter. Correct errors. If time permits, start over. Mark uncorrected errors. Compute *n-pram.*

Time Schedule	
Get ready to type	7′
Timed production	30′
Proofread; compute *n-pram* . .	8′

Problem 1 *Half-Size (5½″ x 8½″)*
Modified block, mixed

Words

(Current date) Mr. John C. Gibson 3059 8
Mapleview Drive Frankfort, Kentucky 40601 16
Dear Mr. Gibson: (¶ 1) I am genuinely pleased to 25
be able to write to you that arrangements have 34
been made to offer Tchaikovsky's The Nut- 43
cracker Ballet during the coming Christmas Sea- 55
son. Three evening performances will be offered 65
during the week of December 26. (¶ 2) The pro- 73
duction has been completely redesigned; strik- 82
ing new sets and decor will add immeasurably 90
to the dazzling impression. All the young at 100
heart, from seven to seventy, will want to see 109
and hear The Nutcracker Ballet! (¶ 3) Next week, 122
I shall be mailing your complimentary tickets. 132
Very cordially yours, Lawrence L. Davis, General 141
Manager (xx) (111) + *Envelope* 143/157

Problem 2 *Executive-Size (7¼″ x 10½″)*
Modified block, open

Words

(Current date) AIRMAIL Mr. Ronald Seltzer 8
1209 Elm Lane Green Bay, Wisconsin 54303 17
Dear Mr. Seltzer SUBJECT: Announcement of 25
Meetings (¶ 1) The Annual Meeting and a Special 34
Meeting of Stockholders will be held concur- 42
rently on December 9, 19––, in Chicago, as 51
described in the enclosed notice. We invite you 61
to attend. (¶ 2) Our stockholders will vote on the 70
election of directors, a proposed two-for-one 79
split of common stock, the retirement of treasury 89
shares, stock option and incentive plans, and on 99
any other business that may properly come 107
before the assembly. (¶ 3) If you do not expect 116
to attend the meetings, please fill in, sign, and 126
return the enclosed proxy. A prompt return of 135
your proxy will save the expense of further mail- 145
ings. Proxies of stockholders who attend the 154
meetings and vote in person will not be voted by 164
the Proxy Committee. Very sincerely yours 173
Donald E. Anderson Chairman of the Board 181
(xx) Enclosures 2 (141) + *Envelope* 184/196

Problem 3 *Government-Size (8″ x 10½″)*
Modified block, mixed

Words

(Current date) AIRMAIL––CERTIFIED Mr. Gerald 9
L. Hershey Director, Research Planning State 18
Department of Education Harrisburg, Pennsyl- 27
vania 17101 Dear Mr. Hershey: (¶ 1) Your let- 35
ter inquiring about the availability of research 44
funds for projects involving other countries con- 54
tains some excellent proposals. As you are well 64
aware, among national leaders there is growing 73
interest in activities designed to strengthen rela- 83
tionships between the United States and other 92
nations of the world; and Congress has taken a 102
very positive attitude toward financing worth- 111
while undertakings. (¶ 2) The International Edu- 119
cation Act of 1966 represents a monumental 128
step forward in the development of overseas 137
programs. Section 3 (b) of the Act states in 146
part: "Grants under this section may be used to 156
cover part or all of the cost of establishing, 165
strengthening, equipping, and operating re- 173
search and training centers, including the cost 183
of teaching and research materials and re- 191
sources." Thus, there is specific provision for 201
financing the type of research endeavor you 210
suggest in your recent letter. (¶ 3) To enable the 219
proper authorities to evaluate your intended re- 228
search, I suggest that you formulate a detailed 238
description (including cost estimates) of the spe- 248
cific research study you have in mind. I am 257
enclosing a list of topics to be included and a 266
suggested format to be considered in framing 275
your proposal. You should definitely include a 285
fairly reasonable estimate of the amount of time 295
you feel will be necessary to complete the pro- 304
posed study. (¶ 4) If I may help you further, 312
please write me. Sincerely yours, Fairchild H. 322
Carter Vice Chairman Legislative Policy Com- 330
mittee *(Your reference initials on file copy only.)* 331
Enclosures 2 (282) + *Envelope* 334/356

Problem 4 *Retype Problem 2 to send to:* Words

Mr. Charles A. Fuller 4
4200 Broadway, N. E. 9
Portland, Oregon 97206 14

104C: Business Letter Production with Alertness Training (35) *(4 letterheads or plain sheets)*

Use the placement table, page 162, to place the following letters correctly.

Alertness Training. Supply needed punctuation, capitalization, or missing letter parts as you type. Be alert!

Problem 1 *(Modified block, indented ¶s)*

Words
Mr. Dale O'Brien, Office Manager | Metropolitan 12
Life Insurance Institute | 840 Madison Avenue | 21
New York, New York 10022 | *(Supply an appro-* 30
priate salutation) | (¶ 1) It has often been said 34
that "the spinal curve is directly related to the 44
efficiency curve." In other words, a seated 53
worker's "slump" leads to excessive fatigue and 63
a "slump" in production. It is a matter of record, 73
too, that correct posture increases speed, reduces 83
fatigue, and improves efficiency and morale. 93
(¶ 2) But don't take our word for these state- 101
ments. Just mail the enclosed card for two new 110
publications which are of interest to any forward- 120
looking person. One publication discusses the 130
value of correct sitting posture; the other de- 139
scribes the new Modern Posture Chairs. The 148
Modern Posture Chairs encourage sustained and 157
accurate work. The self-adjusting backs give the 167
utmost in correct body support. What's more, 176
there is a Modern Posture Chair for every execu- 186
tive and general office need. (¶ 3) Be sure to 194
mail the postpaid card today. The two new 203
publications will reach you promptly. | *(Supply* 210
closing) | Dan J. Belin | Sales Manager | (your 219
initials) | Enclosure (180) 221

Problem 2 *(Modified block, indented ¶s)*

mr. john h. norton | 320 harper street | pittsburgh, 13
pennsylvania 15206 | (¶ 1) Going places? 23
You'll go three times as far in the new Midas 98 33
Compact. Yes, one gallon of gasoline will take 43
you 36 or more miles even in city driving. 51
(¶ 2) Going places? You'll have more money to 60
spend if you invest in the best buy of all Com- 69
pacts––the Midas 98. The price is only $1,795. 79
You'll have more money to spend, too, because 88
the new Midas 98 is really a miser with gasoline 98
on the open road. (¶ 3) Going places? Then 106
go right to the nearest mailbox with the enclosed 116
postal card. Just indicate the most convenient 125
time for your free-trial demonstration. The sup- 135
ply of new Midas 98 Compacts is going fast, so 144
you better hurry. | joseph p. sansone | sales 156
manager | (127) 160

Problem 3 *(Modified block)*

Words
mrs. james w. robings | 6138 w. 75th place | los 12
angeles, california 90045 | (¶ 1) We dislike 23
using superlatives, but these are some of the 33
exclamations that were heard at our first public 42
showing of the new Electra typewriter: Sensa- 52
tional! Amazing! Fantastic! (¶ 2) This remark- 60
able all-electric compact typewriter for home 69
and office use has every basic feature of the 79
full-size electric typewriters––and many new 88
features which even they don't have. We are 97
proud of the new automatic-set margins. You 106
simply set a "guide number" for the approximate 115
number of words in a letter, and the margins 124
will automatically adjust for the typing of a letter 135
of that length. You decide on the margin you 144
want at the bottom of the paper, set an appro- 153
priate number, and when the paper reaches this 163
position, a light flashes––much as the turn signal 173
on your automobile––to warn you that you are 182
at the bottom of the paper. (¶ 3) There's much 190
more we could tell you about this typewriter, 199
but you'll just have to see it and try it to believe 210
it. Why not call us today for a demonstration 219
of the Electra in your home or office. You will 229
be under no obligation whatsoever to buy. | 238
kurt templeman | sales representative | (216) 249

Problem 4 *(Modified block)*

mr. michael g. verona | 23847 mountain avenue | 12
denver, colorado 80219 | (¶ 1) Your subscrip- 23
tion to the <u>Denver News</u> is being continued so 34
that you won't miss any of your favorite features 44
or the complete news coverage. This is being 53
done because I am sure that the only reason you 63
haven't renewed your subscription is that you 72
have been too busy. (¶ 2) The <u>Denver News</u> has 83
won national recognition for its complete and 92
objective news reporting. Its lively, picture- 101
packed sections devoted to sports, to modern 110
homemaking, to humor, to the theater, and to 119
other important facets of contemporary living 128
make it a great newspaper for the whole family. 138
(¶ 3) To insure getting the <u>Denver News</u> regu- 148
larly, just mail the enclosed card with your 157
renewal check in the postage-paid envelope. Be 167
sure to do it now. | (miss) tanya papach | mail 179
subscription department | (143) 186

Problem 2 →

Type enclosure for Problem 1 *1 cc*
8" x 10½" paper *Reading position*
4 spaces between columns (longest part)

				Words
FEDERAL PAYMENTS TO FIVE MIDWESTERN STATES UNDER				10
THE ELEMENTARY AND SECONDARY EDUCATION ACT OF 1965				20
(Payments for Fiscal Year 1966)				26
	Title II	Title III	Title V	32
State	Books; Materials	Services	State Depts.	49
Illinois	$5,361,699	$3,609,491	$547,040	58
Indiana	2,528,237	1,823,414	340,696	65
Michigan	4,671,827	2,976,979	519,753	72
Ohio	5,406,689	3,597,474	587,904	79
Wisconsin	2,278,827	1,583,119	281,896	87

Problem 3

Retype Problem 1 and Problem 2

		Words
Send to:	Dr. John Rich	3
	509 Cedar Lane	6
	Nashville, Tennessee 37212	11
Supply an appropriate salutation		15

LESSON 172

172A: Conditioning Practice (5) *pretyping check; then each line three times*

Alphabet; shift	Joe Zaretsky left Max Daquin above the new camp ledge on Piney Slopes.	*Finger action; quiet hands*
Figures; words	070892 pupils 434832 review 297712 slumps 564965 throng 687593 nimble	
Double letters	dresser possess platoon clogged putting toddles pollute success polling	
Fluency	Some executives like to use a standard style for all business letters.	
	| 1 | 2 | 3 | 4 | 5 | 6 | 7 | 8 | 9 | 10 | 11 | 12 | 13 | 14 |	

172B: Sustained Special-Size Stationery Letter Production (45)

Time Schedule

Get ready to type	7′
Timed production	30′
Proofread; compute *n-pram* . .	8′

Arrange supplies for rapid handling. Make a list of problems to be typed. Make 1 cc for each letter.

Type for 30′ when directed to begin, following the instructions given for each problem. Correct all errors neatly. Proofread each problem carefully before removing it from the typewriter. If you finish all problems before time is called, begin again.

Page 257, 169C, Problem 1
Page 259, 170C, Problem 1
Page 260, 171C, Problem 1

After computing *n-pram*, turn in all problems arranged in the order in which they are listed.

LESSON 173

173A: Conditioning Practice (5) *pretyping check; then each line three times*

Alphabet; shift	Zoe Marquet with Wendy Paxlin gave brief concerts in Jackson Seminary.	*Quiet hands*
Figures; words	5687593 thimble 0740923 purpose 2485865 writing 4320963 respond 201534	
Common words	against average benefit between capital changes courses receipt request	
Fluency	Try to have your work space well organized when typing office letters.	
	| 1 | 2 | 3 | 4 | 5 | 6 | 7 | 8 | 9 | 10 | 11 | 12 | 13 | 14 |	

LESSON 105

105A: Conditioning Practice (5) *each line three times*

Alphabet	H. Webb gives quick, extra quizzes as a means of judging top quality.	*Type with continuity*
Figure-symbol	Is the total charge on Order No. 2378, dated June 10, \$45.69 or \$4.56?	
Shift key	Jan C. McNeil and Paula O'Brien will speak at the Key West Convention.	
Speed	Keep your eyes on the copy and type with continuity to increase speed.	
	| 1 | 2 | 3 | 4 | 5 | 6 | 7 | 8 | 9 | 10 | 11 | 12 | 13 | 14 |	

105B: Skill Building – Straight Copy; Skill Transfer – Letter Copy (15)

1. Type a 5′ writing on 103B, page 166. Circle errors. Determine *gwam.*
2. Type a 5′ writing on Style Letter 2, page 164. Circle errors. Determine *gwam.*

105C: Production Skill Measurement – Letters (30) *(Modified block; indented ¶s; mixed punctuation)*

Time Schedule	
Planning and preparing	4′
Timed production writing . . .	20′
Proofreading; determining *g-pram*	6′

Type each letter on a separate letterhead or plain sheet. Use the word-count figures listed in parentheses at the ends of the letters and the placement table (page 162) for determining proper placement.

Type the official title below the typed name. Use your own initials for reference (xx).

If you complete both letters before time is called, start over. Type on the *control level*; do not correct errors as you type. When time is called, proofread each letter. Determine *g-pram* (gross production rate a minute): Total words divided by 20 (the typing time).

Problem 1

Words
(Current date) | Mr. Kenneth Beddow | 2495 8
Lakeview Street | Omaha, Nebraska 68103 | 16
Dear Mr. Beddow: | (¶ 1) Trouble free, econom- 23
ical operation of your car is vitally important to 34
you. To assure you of such performance for 42
your car, I would like to recommend Royal 51
Super gasoline––the finest premium gasoline on 60
the market today. (¶ 2) If you are not now 68
receiving the benefits of a Royal credit card, 77
may I personally invite you to complete and 86
return the application enclosed. The conven- 95
ience of a Royal credit card assures you the best 105
in products and services from thousands of 114
Royal stations throughout the United States and 123
Canada. (¶ 3) Even if you now have other oil 131
company credit cards, you owe it to yourself, to 141
your car, and to your budget to apply for a 150
Royal credit card. Take a moment now to fill in 160
and mail the application enclosed––we pay the 169
postage. Of course, there is no charge for the 178
card. | Sincerely yours, | Roger S. Kent | Con- 187
sumer Services | (xx) | Enclosure (160) 192

Problem 2

Words
(Current date) | Mr. Robert Leshin, Manager | 8
American Business Forms, Inc. | 3592 Lafayette 18
Avenue, South | Indianapolis, Indiana 46202 | 26
Dear Mr. Leshin: | (¶ 1) We have continued your 34
subscription beyond the date of its expiration. 44
We did this because of the importance of unin- 53
terrupted service to you. (¶ 2) Each issue of 62
THE WALL STREET JOURNAL forwarded to you 70
has contained valuable news, original informa- 79
tion, editorials, and interpretative articles that 89
you would not want to miss. The editors are 98
preparing some very important material for early 108
publication. This material will cover the many 118
changes now taking place in the business and 127
financial world. You can get such information 136
nowhere else at such nominal cost. (¶ 3) If your 145
check is not handy, your word as to payment is 154
as good as your bond with us. Just return the 164
enclosed card now. | Sincerely yours, | Jona- 172
than Kaufer | Circulation Manager | (xx) | 179
Enclosure (137) 181

LESSON 171

171A: Conditioning Practice (5) *pretyping check; then each line three times*

Alphabet; shift	Jack Hirtz sold Tony Marquis six new vests for playing at Brady Hills.	*Rhythmic stroking*
Figures; words	20863 spine 56492 throw 39875 climb 20945 sport 76314 under 04870 primp	
Left and right	recasts minimum sweater monopoly retreat minikin swerves mullion greater	
Fluency	You should develop skill in typing letters on all sizes of stationery.	
	| 1 | 2 | 3 | 4 | 5 | 6 | 7 | 8 | 9 | 10 | 11 | 12 | 13 | 14 |	

171B: Speed and Accuracy Emphasis (10) *compare rates on Steps 1 and 2; on Steps 3 and 4*

1. Type two 1′ writings, 169B, page 257; compute average *gwam* for performance on straight copy.
2. Type two 1′ writings, 170B, page 258; compute average *gwam* for skill on statistical copy.
3. Type one 1′ writing, 169B, page 257; circle errors. **Goal:** Not over 1 error per minute.
4. Type one 1′ writing, 170B, page 258; circle errors. **Goal:** Not over 1 error per minute.

171C: Typing Letters and Tables on Government-Size Stationery (8″ x 10½″) (35)

Type the following three problems for 25′ when directed to begin. If time permits, start over. Mark errors. Compute *g-pram*.

Time Schedule

Study problems; get ready . . .	5′
Timed production	25′
Proofread; compute *g-pram* . .	5′

Problem 1 *Modified block, mixed (TIPS, page 258) 1 cc*
Date on Line 10 — 3 blank lines after date
1½″ side margins — Envelope

Words

(Current date) AIRMAIL—SPECIAL DELIVERY Dr. Earl A. 11
Dvorak Director, Educational Programs State Depart- 21
ment of Education Springfield, Missouri 65801 My 31
dear Dr. Dvorak: (¶ 1) It is a pleasure for me to respond 41
to some of the points discussed in your recent letter con- 53
cerning provisions contained in the Elementary and Sec- 63
ondary Education Act of 1965. I appreciate your interest 75
in this legislation, and I hope it will be possible for you 87
to utilize some of the opportunities contained therein. 98
(¶ 2) As you can well imagine, this much-needed legisla- 108
tion has sparked unparalleled enthusiasm over the pos- 119
sibilities of developing and undertaking new programs 130
for which considerable financial assistance is needed. 141
To date, we have received scores of highly commendable 152
and reasonably plausible proposals for long-range proj- 163
ects dealing with special problems of children from low- 174
income families. We have not had, however, a 183
proportionate expression of interest in projects relating 194
to the utilization of instructional materials or to the 202
creation of supplementary educational services. (¶ 3) I am 216
enclosing, as you have requested, a summary report of 227
payments made to five midwestern states under three 238
titles of PL 89–10. This report will give you some idea 249
of the impact of the new Act on state educational pro- 260
grams. Sincerely yours, Fairchild H. Carter Vice Chair- 271
man Legislative Policy Committee *(Reference initials on* 279
file copy only.) Enclosure (227) *+ Envelope* 301

HEALTH, EDUCATION, AND WELFARE DEPARTMENT
OFFICE OF EDUCATIONAL SERVICES
WASHINGTON, D.C. 20202

Current date

Mailing notation → AIRMAIL--SPECIAL DELIVERY

Dr. Earl A. Dvorak
Director, Educational Programs
State Department of Education
Springfield, Missouri 65801

My dear Dr. Dvorak:

It is a pleasure for me to respond to some of the points discussed in your recent letter concerning provisions contained in the Elementary and Secondary Education Act of 1965. I appreciate your interest in this legislation, and I hope it will be possible for you to utilize some of the opportunities contained therein.

As you can well imagine, this much-needed legislation has sparked unparalleled enthusiasm over the possibilities of developing and undertaking new programs for which considerable financial assistance is needed. To date, we have received scores of highly commendable and reasonably plausible proposals for long-range projects dealing with special problems of children from low-income families. We have not had, however, a proportionate expression of interest in projects relating to the utilization of instructional materials or to the creation of supplementary educational services.

I am enclosing, as you have requested, a summary report of payments made to five midwestern states under three titles of PL 89-10. This report will give you some idea of the impact of the new Act on state educational programs.

Sincerely yours,

Fairchild H. Carter
Vice Chairman
Legislative Policy Committee

Reference initials are typed on file copy only → Enclosure

GOVERNMENT-SIZE STATIONERY

LESSON 106

106A: Conditioning Practice (5) *each line three times*

Alphabet	With the expert advice of Judge Jackson, I may be able to do the quiz.	*Fingers curved*
Figure-symbol	At a rate of $1.57 an hour, 10 men earned $43.96 for working 28 hours.	
Reach drill	qpa; wosl eidk rufj tygh *(Repeat this pattern for a full line; reach with the fingers.)*	
Speed	The chairman of the firm suggested that the statement be mailed to us.	
	| 1 | 2 | 3 | 4 | 5 | 6 | 7 | 8 | 9 | 10 | 11 | 12 | 13 | 14 |	

106B: Growth Index – Straight Copy (8) *5′ writing; circle errors; determine* gwam

All letters are used.

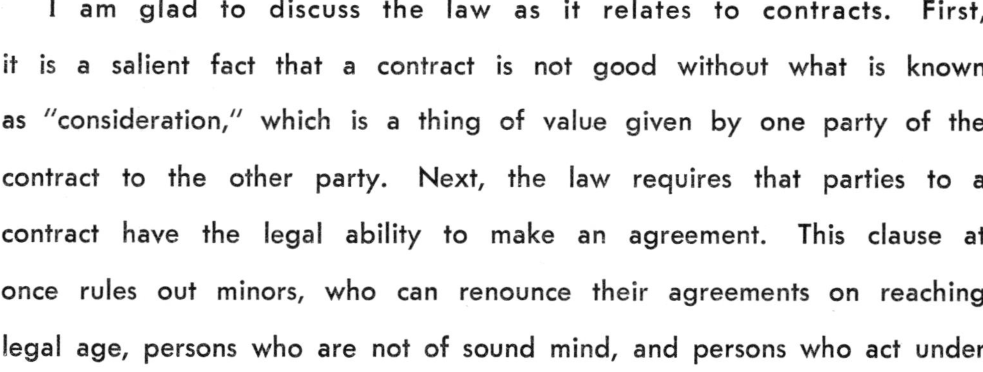

I am glad to discuss the law as it relates to contracts. First, it is a salient fact that a contract is not good without what is known as "consideration," which is a thing of value given by one party of the contract to the other party. Next, the law requires that parties to a contract have the legal ability to make an agreement. This clause at once rules out minors, who can renounce their agreements on reaching legal age, persons who are not of sound mind, and persons who act under duress or compulsion.

It is very important to have a full "meeting of the minds" in a contract, and to know the exact meaning of all the "fine print." A good practice to follow is to be sure to "read carefully before you sign." As business transactions become more complex, every person should realize that eternal vigilance is the price one must pay for peace of mind. The rule of law still is "caveat emptor," or "let the buyer beware."

In summary, it needs to be stressed that all of us must try to deal only with parties of integrity. We just must not make agreements on half understandings where the details of the contract have not been fully spelled out. *(231 words)*

GWAM 1′	5′	
13	3	49
27	5	52
42	8	55
56	11	57
70	14	60
84	17	63
98	20	66
102	20	67
13	23	69
28	26	72
42	29	75
57	32	78
71	35	81
84	37	84
13	40	86
27	43	89
41	46	92
45	46	92

1′ GWAM | 1 | 2 | 3 | 4 | 5 | 6 | 7 | 8 | 9 | 10 | 11 | 12 | 13 | 14 |
5′ GWAM | 1 | 2 | 3 |

170C: Typing Letters and Tables on Executive-Size Stationery (7¼" x 10½") (35)

Type the following three problems for 25′ when directed to begin. If time permits, start over. Mark errors. Compute *g-pram*. **Goals:** Efficient procedure and good format.

Time Schedule	
Study problems; get ready . . .	5′
Timed production	25′
Proofread; compute *g-pram* . .	5′

Problem 1

Modified block, open — *1 cc*
Date on line 12 — *3 blank lines after date*
1″ side margins (see TIPS, page 258) — *Envelope*

Words

(Current date) Mr. Lester Steidl 4214 Saratoga Drive 11
Minneapolis, Minnesota 55409 Dear Mr. Steidl Subject: 22
Income Tax Information (¶ 1) In compliance with the require- 32
ments of the United States Internal Revenue Code, we report 44
to the Internal Revenue Service all dividends paid to our 56
stockholders. A summary report of all dividends paid per 68
share in 1967 is enclosed for your assistance in completing 80
your income tax return. (¶ 2) Whenever a Hayeford Share- 90
holder purchases additional shares and the form of the Share- 102
holder's name or address, or the order of names in case of 113
joint ownership, varies even slightly from the form of the 125
earlier registration, a new account is automatically opened 137
and a duplicate registration is created. This procedure, of 149
course, results in considerable increased company expense 161
which could be eliminated by account consolidation. (¶ 3) If 172
you now have a duplicate registration and would like to con- 184
solidate your accounts into one holding, please advise our 196
Transfer Agent, the Main National Bank of Chicago, how you 208
would like all your shares listed. Please do not send your 220
stock certificates to our Transfer Agent unless you are 231
requested to do so. Very sincerely yours Donald E. Ander- 242
son Chairman of the Board (xx) Enc. (215) + *Envelope* 249/262

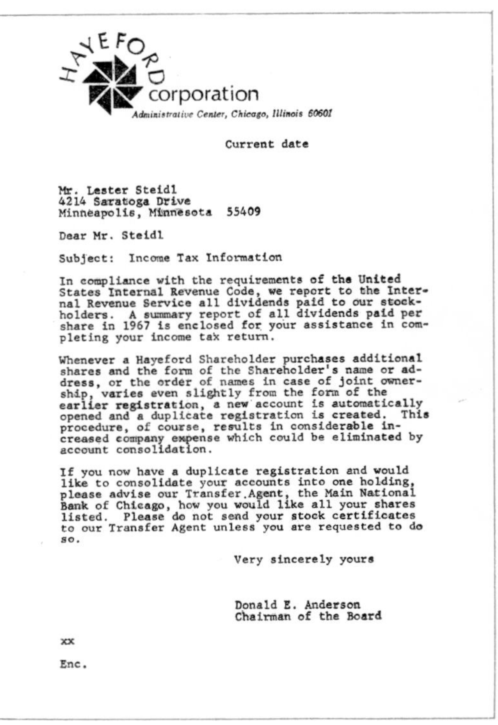
HAYEFORD corporation
Administrative Center, Chicago, Illinois 60601

Current date

Mr. Lester Steidl
4214 Saratoga Drive
Minneapolis, Minnesota 55409

Dear Mr. Steidl

Subject: Income Tax Information

In compliance with the requirements of the United States Internal Revenue Code, we report to the Internal Revenue Service all dividends paid to our stockholders. A summary report of all dividends paid per share in 1967 is enclosed for your assistance in completing your income tax return.

Whenever a Hayeford Shareholder purchases additional shares and the form of the Shareholder's name or address, or the order of names in case of joint ownership, varies even slightly from the form of the earlier registration, a new account is automatically opened and a duplicate registration is created. This procedure, of course, results in considerable increased company expense which could be eliminated by account consolidation.

If you now have a duplicate registration and would like to consolidate your accounts into one holding, please advise our Transfer Agent, the Main National Bank of Chicago, how you would like all your shares listed. Please do not send your stock certificates to our Transfer Agent unless you are requested to do so.

Very sincerely yours

Donald E. Anderson
Chairman of the Board

xx

Enc.

EXECUTIVE-SIZE STATIONERY

Problem 2 →

Type enclosure for Problem 1 — *7¼″ x 10½″ paper* — *1 cc*
Reading position — *DS body* — *6 spaces between columns*

Words

SUMMARY OF DIVIDENDS PAID ON HAYEFORD 8
CORPORATION COMMON STOCK—1967 14

Record Date	Payable	Per Share	Words
			16
			23
February 27, 1967	March 10, 1967	$ .40	32
May 8, 1967	June 10, 1967	.45	38
August 28, 1967	September 10, 1967	.50	45
December 7, 1967	December 31, 1967	.50	54
Total 1967 Dividends		$1.85	60

Problem 3

	Words
Retype Problem 1 and Problem 2	
Send to: Dr. Frank E. Liguori	4
2943 Blue Haven	7
Cincinnati, Ohio 45221	12
Supply an appropriate salutation	15

106C: Skill-Building Drills – Letter Parts (10) *1′ writings for speed (Plain paper; Margins: 1½″)*

Standard margins

Block style: All lines start at left margin.

Open punctuation: No marks of punctuation after any of the opening or closing lines, unless an abbreviation ends the line.

1. Type four 1′ writings on the *opening lines* in 106D, below (date line through salutation). Start date line near top edge. Leave proper spacing after each part. When you have typed through the salutation, DS, and repeat the drill. Determine *gwam.*
2. Type four 1′ writings on the *closing lines* in 106D (complimentary close through reference initials). Block style; open punctuation. When you have typed the reference initials, DS, and repeat the drill. Determine *gwam.* Compare rates with rates of Step 1.

106D: Skill Applications (27) *(Plain sheets)*

Problem 1: Learning

Type a letter with the *opening* and *closing* lines shown below, using the paragraphs of 106B, page 170, as the body of the letter. Type the letter in the BLOCK STYLE with open punctuation as illustrated. All lines start at the left margin when the *block style* is used. The body of the letter has 231 five-stroke words.

	Words
Opening lines:	
(Current date) | Mr. Jay Rademacher, Chair-	8
man | Business Education Department | Albu-	16
querque High School | Albuquerque, New	23
Mexico 87102 | Dear Mr. Rademacher	30
Closing lines:	
Sincerely | John Kingdon | Legal Consultant |	8
(xx)	8

Problem 2: Skill Building

Type the letter of Problem 1 to **Mr. Alan Fraser, Chairman | Business Education Department | Woodrow Wilson High School | Long Beach, California 90802** | *(Supply an appropriate salutation.)*

KAMBEL & KINGDON — PHONE: (505) 871-4009 — ATTORNEYS AT LAW
309 ELSMERE BUILDING, 1214 ANDERSON AVENUE, ALBUQUERQUE, NEW MEXICO 87106

April 25, 19--

Mr. Jay Rademacher, Chairman
Business Education Department
Albuquerque High School
Albuquerque, New Mexico 87102

Dear Mr. Rademacher

I am glad to discuss the law as it relates to contracts. First, it is a salient fact that a contract is not good without what is known as "consideration," which is a thing of value given by one party of the contract to the other party. Next, the law requires that parties to a contract have the legal ability to make an agreement. This clause at once rules out minors, who can renounce their agreements on reaching legal age, persons who are not of sound mind, and persons who act under duress or compulsion.

It is very important to have a full "meeting of the minds" in a contract, and to know the exact meaning of all the "fine print." A good practice to follow is to be sure to "read carefully before you sign." As business transactions become more complex, every person should realize that eternal vigilance is the price one must pay for peace of mind. The rule of law still is "caveat emptor," or "let the buyer beware."

In summary, it needs to be stressed that all of us must try to deal only with parties of integrity. We just must not make agreements on half understandings where the details of the contract have not been fully spelled out.

Sincerely

John Kingdon

John Kingdon
Legal Consultant

le

STYLE LETTER 3. BLOCK STYLE LETTER WITH OPEN PUNCTUATION

LESSON 107

107A: Conditioning Practice (5) *each line three times*

Alphabet	The brown fox jumped very quickly to grab those excited, fuzzy chicks.	*Fingers upright*
Figure-symbol	He sent $234.98 for the camera and $16.75 for the case (plus 20% tax).	
Reach drill	z/a; x.sl c,dk vmfj bngh *(Repeat this pattern for a full line; reach with fingers.)*	
Speed	It is a good plan to do your very best on each typing job that you do.	
	| 1 | 2 | 3 | 4 | 5 | 6 | 7 | 8 | 9 | 10 | 11 | 12 | 13 | 14 |	

Problem 2 *Enclosure for Problem 1* *5½" x 8½" paper; long side at left* *1 cc* *Reading position* *DS body* *4 spaces between columns*

			Words
	CELEBRITY CONCERT SERIES		5
	(Civic Auditorium)		9
		Front	10
Date	Production	Orch.	18
Oct. 10	Othello (Rossini)	$3.75	25
Nov. 4	Magic Flute (Mozart)	3.75	32
Dec. 28	Macbeth (Verdi)	4.50	37
Jan. 6	La Tosca (Puccini)	4.50	44
Feb. 5	Carmen (Bizet)	3.75	49
March 9	Parsifal (Wagner)	5.50	55

TIPS FOR SPECIAL-SIZE STATIONERY

For half-size stationery (5½ x 8½), side margins may be decreased from ¾" to ½" for longer letters.
(Date may vary from Line 8 to Line 10)

For executive stationery (7¼ x 10½), side margins may be decreased from 1" to ¾" for longer letter.
(Date may vary from Line 10 to Line 16)

For government stationery (8 x 10½), side margins may be decreased from 1½" to 1" for longer letters.

Government correspondence guides call for:

1. Date to begin DS below letterhead and 1½" from right margin.
2. Reference initials in lower case and on file copy only, DS from last notation.

Problem 3 *Retype Problem 1 and Problem 2*

	Words
Send to: Mr. Thomas Millea	3
4950 West Chester Avenue	8
Lexington, Kentucky 40501	14
Supply an appropriate salutation	18

LESSON 170

170A: Conditioning Practice (5) *pretyping check; then each line three times*

Alphabet; shift	Wade Hertz kept Jacquelyn Bexon from viewing our scenic Niagara Falls.	*Eyes on copy*
Figures; words	5637 they 2948 work 0975 pout 3480 drip 2186 spin 7986 join 4325 rest	
Left and right	decease opinion erasers million decades phonily readers pumpkin regrets	
Fluency	The best office workers are those capable of adjusting well to change.	
	| 1 | 2 | 3 | 4 | 5 | 6 | 7 | 8 | 9 | 10 | 11 | 12 | 13 | 14 |	

170B: Speed and Accuracy Emphasis – Statistical Copy (10)

1. Type two 1' writings for speed; compute *gwam* for better writing.
2. Add 4 words to *gwam* rate; divide into quarter-minute goals.
3. Type two 1' writings for new goal rate, the teacher calling each quarter minute.
4. Check speed; then mark errors to compare with accuracy writings.
5. Type two 1' writings for control.

During period from January 14, 1966, to February 15, 1967, stock options for the purchase of 76,320 shares of common stock were granted to the employees and officers of the Hayeford Corporation. All options expire on December 18, 1972, for 6,000 shares granted to company officers at $38.25 per share, the market value on date of grant. The options are exercisable until five years from the period of grant.

107B: Skill Transfer – Statistical Copy (8) *5′ writing; circle errors; determine* gwam

All figures are used.

	GWAM 1′	5′	
Here are the figures that I quoted at the last session of the	12	2	54
Council. In light of the census estimate, our population will grow to	27	5	57
more than 235 million by 1975. Of this total, nearly 64 million, or	40	8	60
27.2 percent, will be under 15 years of age. Nearly 50 million, or	54	11	62
21.4 percent, will be between the ages of 15 and 24. There will be	68	14	65
54 million souls, or nearly 23 percent, in the 25 to 44 age bracket.	82	16	68
In the 45 to 65 age group, there will be nearly 44 million persons,	95	19	71
or 18.8 percent of the grand total. Nearly 22 million folk, or	108	22	73
9.6 percent, will be in the over-65 age group.	117	23	75
Now for some of the employment statistics: In 1900, 2 of every 3	13	26	78
teen-age boys were already employed; today the proportion is less than	27	29	80
1 in 3. At the other end of the age scale--65 years and older--2 of	41	32	83
every 3 men were at work in 1900; today the figure is below 30 percent.	56	35	86
At the present time, nearly 44.8 percent of all girls enter the employ-	70	37	89
ment market in their early 20's. The ratio then falls again until age	84	40	92
35, after which it rises rapidly and reaches a peak between the ages of	98	43	95
45 to 54 when nearly half of all women (46.3 percent) are part of the	112	46	97
labor force. It is estimated that a girl in school today will likely	126	49	100
(257 words) spend approximately 25 to 27 years of her remaining life as a worker.	140	51	103

1′ GWAM | 1 | 2 | 3 | 4 | 5 | 6 | 7 | 8 | 9 | 10 | 11 | 12 | 13 | 14 |
5′ GWAM | 1 | 2 | 3 |

107C: Skill-Building Drills – Letter Parts (10) *(Follow directions of 106C, page 171, for 1–2 below)*

1. Type four 1′ writings on the *opening lines of* Problem 1, 107D, below. Determine *gwam.*
2. Type four 1′ writings on the *closing lines* of Problem 1, 107D, below. Determine *gwam.*

107D: Skill Applications (27) *(Plain sheets)*

Problem 1: Skill Building

Using the paragraphs of 107B as the body, type a letter in *block style*, open punctuation. Use the *opening* and *closing lines* at the right. Correct errors. (257)

Problem 2: Skill Building

Type the letter of Problem 1 to **Mr. Kevin McGlaze | 1835 Montana Avenue | Santa Monica, California 90402** | (*Supply an appropriate salutation*). Correct errors. (257)

	Words
Opening lines:	
(Current date) | Mr. Robert G. Neches |	7
Manager, Alton–King, Inc. | 815 Broadway	15
Avenue, So. | Los Angeles, California	22
90001 | Dear Mr. Neches |	27
(+ *Lines in Body*)	284
Closing lines:	
Sincerely yours | Robert Gibson | Executive	292
Secretary | (xx)	294

LESSON 169

169A: Conditioning Practice (5) *pretyping check; then each line three times*

Alphabet; shift	Mike Bozic fixed banquet dates for John Galvin at famous Wayside Park.	*Uniform stroking*
Figures; words	273 sue 035 pet 581 tip 495 rot 306 pen 284 sir 685 hit 277 sum 694 nor	
Near balanced	problem special provide quality profits display perhaps product payable	
Fluency	Some business firms require typists to use letterheads of mixed sizes.	
	| 1 | 2 | 3 | 4 | 5 | 6 | 7 | 8 | 9 | 10 | 11 | 12 | 13 | 14 |	

169B: Speed and Accuracy Emphasis – Straight Copy (10)

1. Type two 1′ writings for speed; compute *gwam* for better writing.
2. Add 4 words to *gwam* rate; divide into quarter-minute goals.
3. Type two 1′ writings for new goal rate, the teacher calling each quarter minute.
4. Check speed; then mark errors to compare with accuracy writings.
5. Type two 1′ writings for control.

Men and women who have succeeded in life reflect that it is important for ambitious people to gain attractive, appealing voices. They emphasize that the way we talk is almost as important as what we say. They remind us frequently that others usually remember us in relation to unique personal qualities rather than in terms of academic status. Try to speak consistently in amiable, vibrant tones.

169C: Typing Letters and Tables on Half-Size Stationery (5½″ x 8½″) (35)

Time Schedule	
Study problems; get ready . . .	5′
Timed production	25′
Proofread; compute *g-pram* . .	5′

Type the following three problems for 25′ when directed to begin. If time permits, start over. Mark errors. Compute *g-pram*.

Problem 1 *Modified block, mixed* — *1 cc* — *½″ side margins*
Date on Line 10 — *3 blank lines after date* — *Address envelope*

Words

(*Current date*) Mrs. Mary Ann Zabel 1905 Heddon Court New 11
Albany, Indiana 47150 Dear Mrs. Zabel: (¶ 1) As one of our most 23
interested and loyal patrons, you will be pleased to learn that plans 37
for our Celebrity Concert Series for the coming year have now been 51
made final. We have been fortunate in being able to schedule not 64
only unusually popular productions, but exceptionally talented artists 78
as well. From all indications, our new series should be one of our 92
most successful. (¶ 2) I am enclosing a summary of the performances 104
for which we have contracted, in the hope that this advance release 118
will interest you and that you will share my enthusiasm for the pros- 132
pects of our next concert season. Very cordially yours, Lawrence 145
L. Davis General Manager (xx) Enclosure (119) + *Envelope* 152/165

LOUISVILLE CIVIC ASSOCIATION — EXECUTIVE OFFICES 105 E. BROADWAY LOUISVILLE, KENTUCKY 40202

Current date

Mrs. Mary Ann Zabel
1905 Heddon Court
New Albany, Indiana 47150

Dear Mrs. Zabel:

As one of our most interested and loyal patrons, you will be pleased to learn that plans for our Celebrity Concert Series for the coming year have now been made final. We have been fortunate in being able to schedule not only unusually popular productions, but exceptionally talented artists as well. From all indications, our new series should be one of our most successful.

I am enclosing a summary of the performances for which we have contracted, in the hope that this advance release will interest you and that you will share my enthusiasm for the prospects of our next concert season.

Very cordially yours,

Lawrence L. Davis
General Manager

xx

Enclosure

HALF-SIZE STATIONERY

LESSON 108

108A: Conditioning Practice (5) *each line three times*

Alphabet	By his frequent adjustments, an amazing executive kept their goodwill.	Type with continuity
Figure-symbol	The 546 copies, priced at $3.78 each, may be shipped on June 19 or 20.	
Shift lock	A sample was printed in four colors on BEST Papers PKG #34110 BRISTOL.	
Speed	Send a draft of the statement to the union at the address on the card.	

| 1 | 2 | 3 | 4 | 5 | 6 | 7 | 8 | 9 | 10 | 11 | 12 | 13 | 14 |

108B: Accuracy Emphasis (10)

Type two 1′ writings on each of the ¶s of 108C on the *control level.* With the repetition try to increase your speed without losing control. Make the corrections written in the copy as you type.

108C: Skill Transfer – Rough Draft (8) *5′ writing; circle errors; determine* gwam

	Text	GWAM 1″	5″	
1.4 5.4 80	~~We are sending you~~ a sample of a cover which printed on	15	3	46
	Best Papers PKG. Pkg is a plastic coated paper with spe-	27	5	49
	cially treated surface. This produce is a new way by which	44	9	52
	the Best Paper Company is helping firms get much more value	59	12	55
	from their prined peices.	64	13	56
1.4 5.4 80	The catalog cover was made for the Life company of Saint	11	15	58
	Charles, a well known maker of prestige ~~goods~~. ~~Appearance~~	23	17	61
	and ~~durabiliey~~ were ~~important in~~ the dover since the cata-	34	20	63
	logue is used to acquaint ~~retail~~ dealers with the product	44	22	65
	line. The soil resistant surface is ideal for s uch use as	65	26	69
	it cleans easily. ~~Jan Blake planned~~ this cover forthe Life	79	29	72
	firm.	80	29	72
1.4 5.4 80	The catalog ~~utilizes~~ colored dividers which are alos of	10	31	74
	plastic-coated paper. These ~~dividers~~ give emphasis to the	23	33	77
	product displays ~~within~~ the catalog. ~~Complete production~~	33	35	79
	~~information~~ on these plastic-cotaed papers is given in the	43	37	81
	brochure. ~~Your local distributor~~ in your city can give you	55	40	83
	~~further information~~. Why not give him a call soon.	69	43	86
	(216 words)	72	43	86

LESSON 168

168A: Conditioning Practice (5) *pretyping check; then each line three times*

Alphabet; shift	John Coleman and Pat Gregory quizzed seven boys who work at Fort Knox.	*Keep carriage moving*
Figures: 4-4-4	1025 3946 7801 2435 6987 2015 6349 7810 2543 6789 5021 3946 8017 2354	
Common words	accept assist branch expect before credit except assure desire points	
Fluency	You should prepare all tabulated reports with much care and exactness.	
	| 1 | 2 | 3 | 4 | 5 | 6 | 7 | 8 | 9 | 10 | 11 | 12 | 13 | 14 |	

168B: Tabulation Production Measurement (45)

Time Schedule

Get ready to type . . . . 7′
Timed production . . . . 30′
Proofread; compute *n-pram* . . 8′

Arrange supplies for rapid handling. Type the following four problems for 30′ when directed to begin. Correct errors. If time permits, start over. Mark uncorrected errors. Compute *n-pram*. Arrange problems in order listed, to turn in.

Problem 1 ⟶

Full sheet 1 cc Reading position
DS body 4 spaces between columns

COUNTY REVENUE (1968)

	Cash Balance	Tax Levies	Other Revenues	Total	Words
COUNTY REVENUE (1968)					8
(headings)					12
(headings)					24
Current Expense . .	$16,303	$200,000	$ 86,000	$302,303	36
County Road . . .	5,200	232,000	190,000	427,200	46
Airport	1,000	4,000	–0–	5,000	55
State Highway . . .	30,500	45,000	–0–	75,500	64
Health Unit	3,500	19,556	–0–	23,056	73
Fair	–0–	21,200	–0–	21,200	82
Waterways Fund . .	–0–	–0–	10,000	10,000	90
Weed Program . . .	–0–	5,700	–0–	5,700	99
Junior College . . .	–0–	5,000	25,000	30,000	108

Problem 2 *Half sheet 1 cc Center vertically*
SS body 8 spaces between columns

ESTIMATED VALUES OF LIFE INSURANCE POLICIES * (Words 9)
OVER SHORT- AND LONG-TERM INTERVALS (16)

(Based on the January 1, 1967, Dividend Scale) (26)

Year	Cash Value	Accumulated Dividends	Total Cash Value	Words
				31
				44
3	$ 735.00	$ 135.00	$ 870.00	51
5	1,515.00	315.00	1,830.00	56
8	2,685.00	690.00	3,375.00	62
10	3,480.00	1,005.00	4,485.00	68
13	4,620.00	1,620.00	6,240.00	75
				78

*Adult policy having $15,000 face value (86)

Source: Company Report, 1966 (92)

Problem 3 *Retype Problem 2 with* addition *below 1 cc*
Full sheet DS body; show body in groups of 4
Omit underline; add rulings above and below column headings and table, as shown

Year	Cash Value	Accumulated Dividends	Total Cash Value	Words
				12
				12
				6
15	$5,325.00	$2,130.00	$ 7,455.00	6
18	6,345.00	3,015.00	9,360.00	6
20	6,990.00	3,720.00	10,710.00	6
				9

+ Problem 2 words **92/149**

Problem 4 *Retype Problem 3, but SS body 1 cc*
Type vertical lines for boxed table
Words: Each vertical rule 5
Total words 164

108D: Skill Applications (27) *(Plain sheets; 1 carbon sheet; copy sheets)*

Problem 1: Letter with Carbon Copy

Using the paragraphs of 108C, page 173, as the body, type a letter with one carbon copy in the *block style* with open punctuation. Use the *opening* and *closing lines* shown at the right. Correct errors. (216)

Problem 2: Skill Building *(Alertness Training)*

Type the letter of Problem 1 to **Mr. S. J. DeBrum, Purchasing Agent | ABC Manufacturing Company | 34890 Beauchamp Avenue | Dallas, Texas 75216 |**

Words

Opening lines:

(Current date) | Mr. Gerard Steinhardt, Man- 8
ager | Newman–Brown Manufacturing Com- 16
pany | 7495 Barnett Avenue, South | Kansas 23
City, Kansas 66123 | Dear Mr. Steinhardt | 31
(+ Words in body) 247

Closing lines:

Sincerely yours | Greg McGlaze, Sales Man- 255
ager | (xx) | Enclosures | 267

LESSON 109

109A: Conditioning Practice (5) *each line three times*

Alphabet	A jovial man in this plaza fixed Will's bicycle during a quick squall.	*Eyes on copy*
Figure-symbol	Number-symbol checkup: 2", 3#, 4$, 5%, 6, 7&, 8', 9(, 0), ¢, @, ½, ¼.	
Electric	@ ¢ * ' "	
Quiet hands	Purposeful repetition leads to rapid improvement of stroking patterns.	
Speed	Both of them will help the city auditor with the work that is pending.	
	| 1 | 2 | 3 | 4 | 5 | 6 | 7 | 8 | 9 | 10 | 11 | 12 | 13 | 14 |	

109B: Skill Transfer – Statistical Copy; Rough Draft (15)

1. *Statistical Copy.* Type a 5' writing on the ¶s of 107B, page 172. Circle errors; determine *gwam.*
2. *Rough Draft.* Type a 5' writing on the ¶s of 108C, page 173. Circle errors; determine *gwam.*

109C: Building Production Skill – Letters (30) *(Block style; open punctuation; type on control level)*

Time Schedule	
Planning and preparing	4'
Timed production writing . . .	20'
Proofreading; determining *g-pram*	6'

Type each letter on a separate letterhead or plain sheet. Determine proper placement: Use table, p. 162.

If you complete the letters before time is called, start over. Do not correct errors. When time is called, proofread each letter; determine *g-pram* (Reference: 105C, page 169).

Problem 1

Words

(Current date) | Mr. Michael C. Hewett, Jr. | 8
Space Technology Laboratories | 2746 Coronado 17
Avenue | Long Beach, California 90813 | Dear 26
Mr. Hewett | (¶ 1) Today many business firms 33
use the block style letter for their correspon- 42
dence. This letter is an example of that style. 52
You will note that all lines start at the left margin. 64
The advantage of this style is that the mechanical 74
process of indenting opening and closing lines, 83
or paragraphs, is eliminated. This practice saves 94
time and space. (¶ 2) Open punctuation is used 102
with this letter: Punctuation marks are omitted 112
after the date, address, salutation, and compli- 121
mentary close unless an abbreviation is used, in 131
which case the period is typed as a part of the 141
abbreviation. Elimination of these punctuation 150
marks helps to increase letter production rates. 160
Another recommended timesaving feature is to 169
type only the typist's initials for reference when 180
the dictator's name is typed in the closing lines. 190
(¶ 3) As you can see, the block style of letter 198
gives good placement appearance; and because 207
many extra typing strokes and motions are elimi- 227
nated, its use does help to increase letter produc- 217
tion rates. It is the letter style that I recommend 238
for use in the business office. | Sincerely yours | 248
J. Scott Miller | Communications Consultant | 256
(xx) (215) 256

(Please see page 175 for Problems 2 and 3.)

Problem 3 *Full sheet* *1 cc* *Reading position*
DS body *10 spaces between columns*
Type format as shown

			Words
EMPLOYEE AND DEPENDENT COVERAGE UNDER			8
GROUP LIFE INSURANCE IN THE UNITED STATES, 1965			17
(000,000 Omitted)			21
			33
			45
	Number of		47
Coverage	Policies	Amount	52
			64
Purchased During Year			68
Primary, Employee . .	43,640	$ 50,795	77
(Dependent)	2,530 *	590	86
Total	43,640	$ 51,385	98
In Force at End of Year			103
Primary, Employee . .	233,270	$301,298	112
(Dependent)	11,380 *	4,815	121
Total	233,270	$306,113	133
			145

*These policies covering dependents are included in primary coverage 157 159

Source: Life Insurance Fact Book, 1966 171

Problem 4 *Full sheet* *1 cc* *Reading position*
SS body *10 spaces between columns*
Correct the table as shown *Type all rules*

			Words
BUILDING PERMITS RELATED TO POPULATION			8
(Total City)			10
			19
			28
Year	Building Permits*		30
		Population**	36
			45
1930	793	18,900	48
1940	1,099	20,800	52
1950	8,682	35,900	56
1960	13,511	51,000	60
1963	23,660	67,100	64
1964	27,110	70,200	67
1965	23,658	72,600	71
1960	24,739	75,400	75
			84

* Residential permits only 89

**Rounded to the nearest hunderd 95

Source: Ch. of Commerce printing 103

+ each vertical rule 5/113

LESSON 167

167A: Conditioning Practice (5) *pretyping check; then each line three times*

Alphabet; shift	Max Quintz played five sets of tennis with Jack Moroney at Long Beach.	*Fingers curved and close to keys*
Figures: 4-3-2	1052 463 79 8021 354 96 7810 235 64 9708 125 43 6879 120 35 4697 801 2536	
Double letters	dazzle ribbon puzzle haggle jammed robber tarred ripple runner mapper	
Fluency	It is often helpful to assemble items so related data appear together.	
	| 1 | 2 | 3 | 4 | 5 | 6 | 7 | 8 | 9 | 10 | 11 | 12 | 13 | 14 |	

167B: Sustained Tabulation Production (45)

Arrange supplies for rapid handling. Make a list of problems to be typed. Include 1 cc for each. Review definition of acceptable words on page 249.

Type for 30′ when directed to begin, following the instructions given for each problem. Correct all errors neatly. Proofread each problem carefully before removing it from the typewriter. If you finish all problems before time is called, begin again.

Time Schedule		*N-PRAM
Get ready to type	7′	Total Acceptable Words
Timed production	30′	+
Proofread; compute *n-pram**	8′	½ Unacceptable Words ÷ by Time

Page 255, 166C, Problem 4 **Page 253, 165C, Problem 2**
Page 255, 166C, Problem 3 **Page 251, 164C, Problem 1**

After computing *n-pram*, turn in all problems arranged in the order in which they are listed.

Problem 2

Words
(Current date) | Mr. Shelby Popham | 9827 8
Hickory Hill Drive | Green Bay, Wisconsin 16
54301 | Dear Mr. Popham | (¶ 1) Do you know 23
how to get the most for your car at trade-in 32
time? Men who appraise trade-ins know that all 41
cars experience normal wear and tear. What 50
they do appraise, in effect, is how well you 59
cared for your car, and how competently repair 68
work was performed. The secret, then, is to 77
keep the value of your car high with planned 86
care. Periodic maintenance by our professional 96
staff will do just that; then when it's trade-in 105
time, your car will be worth more. (¶ 2) Remem- 114
ber that putting off scheduled maintenance may 123
allow minor troubles to grow into major ailments. 133
Why not let us help you keep your car good 142
looking and in top running order. Dents, wrin- 151
kles, dings, bumps, and blemishes disappear like 161
magic when we do the job. Our trained 169
mechanics have the "know-how" that it takes to 178
keep your car humming smoothly. (¶ 3) Just 186
give us a call and we'll arrange for a "loaner" 195
while your car is in the shop. Why not call us 205
right away. | Sincerely yours | James Robinson, 214
Head | Service Department | (xx) (187) 219

Problem 3

(Note special complimentary close)

Words
(Current date) | Mr. Steven Leish | 1135 San 8
Viciente Blvd. | Santa Monica, California 90402 | 18
Dear Mr. Leish | (¶ 1) Enclosed are four com- 25
plimentary theater tickets. These tickets will 35
admit you, and an entire carload of your guests, 45
to any West Coast Drive-In Theater. Each ticket 54
is good for one show of your choice during any 64
of the next three months. (¶ 2) We are making 72
this offer because our efforts for the past ten 82
years have been directed to upgrading the 90
drive-in theater concept. Today our screens are 100
the biggest being used for movie projection. 109
Our snack bars, and all other facilities, are 118
sparkling clean. You can understand, I think, 128
why we are eager for you to look us over. When 137
you come, remember there is no formality in 146
drive-in theater-going. (¶ 3) May we soon have 154
the pleasure of your company as one of our 163
honored guests. A first-run movie, leisure dress, 173
and no parking costs add up to a wonderful 182
evening of entertainment. | Yours for pleasant 191
relaxation | Robert E. Keislar | Public Relations 200
Department | (xx) Enclosures 4 (166) 205

LESSON 110

110A: Conditioning Practice (5) *each line three times*

Alphabet	Fay saw many zebra and quaint pink ducks in the exciting jungle movie.	*Wrists low; hands quiet*
Figure-symbol	The new prices are as follows: 12 @ $25.50; 24 @ $48.95; 36 @ $70.50.	
Shift key	The salesmen are from Dow & Co., J & B Products, Inc., and Lynn & Son.	
Speed	The right key stroke is made with your fingers held close to the keys.	
	| 1 | 2 | 3 | 4 | 5 | 6 | 7 | 8 | 9 | 10 | 11 | 12 | 13 | 14 |	

110B: Skill Building – Straight Copy (15)

1. Type a 5′ writing on the ¶s of 106B, page 170: *Control level* (5 or fewer errors).
2. Type another 5′ writing. If you made the goal of Step 1, increase your speed on this writing.

110C: Production Skill Measurement – Letters (30) *(Block style; open punctuation; correct errors)*

Time Schedule	
Planning and preparing	4′
Timed production writing . . .	20′
Proofreading; determining *n-pram*	6′

Repeat the letter problems of 109C, page 174 and above. In this timing, however, *all errors are to be erased and corrected.* When time is called, proofread each letter; determine *n-pram* (net production rate a minute—rate with all errors erased and corrected).

LESSON 166

166A: Conditioning Practice (5) *pretyping check; then each line three times*

Alphabet; shift	Jim Woznak sent Brad Huxley to equip five antique cars in Los Angeles.	*Wrists low and relaxed*
Figures: 3-4-2	102 5643 97 801 2453 96 780 1352 64 978 1205 43 697 8021 53 469 7801 25	
Near left and right	excess lining accede kindly stress liking reface unions reward nylons	
Fluency	Titles and headings in tabulated reports should be simple and concise.	
	| 1 | 2 | 3 | 4 | 5 | 6 | 7 | 8 | 9 | 10 | 11 | 12 | 13 | 14 |	

166B: Previewing Tables with Grouped Data and Notes (8)

Grouped Data: Items may be placed in groups to aid reading, provide emphasis, or make comparison easy. To group data, leave an extra line space between groups. (*See Problem 1 below.*)

Reference Note: Explains nature of data. Placed a DS after the last line, including ruling. Precedes "Source Note." (*See Problem 3, page 255.*)

Source Note: Explains origin of data. Placed a DS after the last line of a table (including ruling or reference note). Blocked at left margin or indented 3–5 spaces. (*See Problem 3, page 255.*)

Two-Line Main Heading: Usually single spaced. (*See Problem 1 below.*)

Leaders: Made by striking the period and space bar alternately. Align leaders by noting whether first leader is typed on odd or even number. (*See Problem 3, page 255.*)

DRILL: Type your full name, followed by 12 leader periods. Note whether first leader falls on even or on odd space. Now on line below your name, type the name of your city, followed by leaders, aligning the leaders with those on the line above. On the next line, follow the same procedure with name of your state.

166C: Typing Tables with Grouped Data and Notes (37)

Type the following four tables for 30′ when directed to begin. If time permits, start over. Mark errors. Compute *g-pram.*

Time Schedule

Get ready to type	2′
Timed production	30′
Proofread; compute *g-pram* . .	5′

Problem 1 *Half sheet 1 cc SS Reading position*
Data in groups of 3 6 spaces between columns
Type horizontal and vertical rules

	Words
LIFE INSURANCE IN FORCE IN THE UNITED STATES	9
INCLUDING ALASKA AND HAWAII	15
(000,000 Omitted)	18
	28
	38

Year	Ordinary	Group	Industrial	Words
				44
				54
1960	$340,268	$175,434	$39,563	61
1961	364,347	192,202	39,451	66
1962	389,150	209,178	39,638	72
1963	418,856	228,540	39,672	77
1964	455,860	252,182	39,833	83
1965	497,630	306,113	39,818	89
				98

+ each vertical rule 4/110

Problem 2

Retype Problem 1, but DS the body, leaving an extra line space between groupings. Use full sheet. Draw vertical rules.

Type an asterisk after the third column heading (*Group*) and add the following reference note and source note:

	Words
Problem 1	98
* Includes all group insurance sold by any form	107
of private business organization	114
Source: Life Insurance Fact Book, 1966	127

Unit 18 | Lessons 111-113

Speed and Accuracy Emphasis

LESSON 111

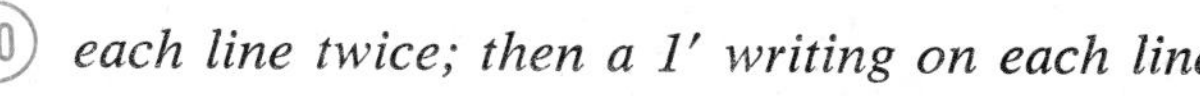

111A: Conditioning Practice (5) *each line three times*

Alphabet Liquid oxygen fuel was used to give this big jet rocket amazing speed.

Figure-symbol He bought 80 pencils @ 6¢ each; 23 erasers @ 9¢ each; 1 punch @ $4.75.

Long words These laboratories specialize in solid-state space propulsion systems.

Speed One of the heaviest loads to carry may be a bundle of bad work habits.

| 1 | 2 | 3 | 4 | 5 | 6 | 7 | 8 | 9 | 10 | 11 | 12 | 13 | 14 |

Quick, snap stroke

111B: Technique Improvement – Key Stroking (30) *each line twice; then a 1′ writing on each line*

Technique Goals

Fingers Curved

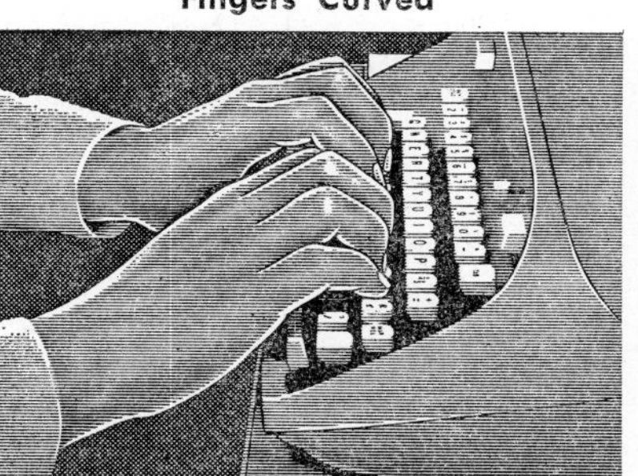

Fingers Upright

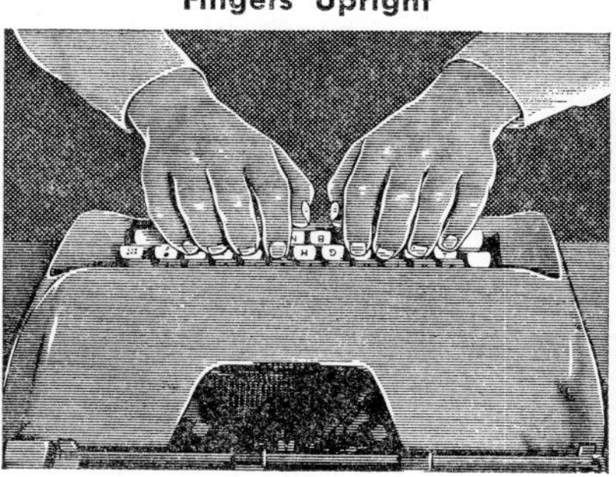

Finger-Reach Action

1 *Home row* J. J. Hall has had half a dish of hash. Ask the lads to wash glasses.

2 *3d row* Are you trying to type on the upper row by reaching with your fingers?

3 *1st row* Aza C. Bonham calmed an excited lynx as the men carried it to the van.

Fingers 3 and 4

4 Cool-as-a-breeze cottons, in the popular new azure color, are on sale.

5 Six zebra were seen eating wet, waxy poppy pods in the quaint old zoo.

6 Wally was appalled by the zealous opinion expressed by the quaint man.

Long, direct reaches

7 A number of union members may be at the unveiling of the unique mural.

8 An eccentric man bought bright, unique bronze statues at the ceremony.

9 A musical ceremony will have precedence over the unique presentations.

Double letters

10 A ragged puppy looked quizzically at the kitten sitting on the pillow.

11 Miss Booth will tell them to keep all supplies needed for class drill.

12 Betty will sell glass balls for a drill meet next week in Mississippi.

| 1 | 2 | 3 | 4 | 5 | 6 | 7 | 8 | 9 | 10 | 11 | 12 | 13 | 14 |

165C: Typing Tables with Rulings (37)

Time Schedule	
Get ready to type	2′
Timed production	30′
Proofread; compute *g-pram*	5′

Type the following four tables for 30′ when directed to begin. Use horizontal and vertical lines as indicated. Mark errors. Compute *g-pram*. **Goals:** Proper techniques; correct format.

Problem 1 *Full sheet* *Spread main heading (See Reference Guide, page x, if needed)* *Center vertically* *4 spaces between columns* *Type all lines*

FREEWAY CONSTRUCTION PROJECTS

Double-space / Double-space

Project	Freeway Miles	Construction Costs	Completion Date	Words
				12 / 24 / 37 / 44 / 49 / 61
Project A	17.0	$5,885,980	1972	68
Project B Overhead Viaduct	1.3	1,088,785	1972	74 / 78
Project C Rock Cut	3.1	3,900,500	1973	84 / 86
Project D	13.0	4,696,630	1973	93
Project E Land Acquisition	9.2	3,162,270	1973	99 / 103
Project F Four Overhead Sections	5.4	8,000,000 (Est.)	1974	109 / 114 / 117 / 130

Single-space / Double-space (after column headings)

DS between projects; SS (within project entry)

Single-space (before bottom rule) — 130

+ each vertical rule 8/154

Problem 2 *Half sheet* *Center vertically* *SS body* *6 spaces between columns* *Type horizontal lines; draw vertical lines with ruler*

MILLAR STEEL FABRICATORS, INC. — Words 6

Excerpts from Financial Statements — 13 / 24

Accounting Classification	1966 (000)	1967 (000)	Words
			28 / 34 / 44
Current Assets	$34,978	$51,269	51
Property and Equipment	57,291	64,143	58
Consumer Taxes Collected	750	896	66
Taxes Charged to Income	865	947	74
Shareholders' Equity	65,423	72,853	81
Salaries, Wages, Bonuses	12,346	18,745	89 / 99

Problem 3 *Retype Problem 2; add new Column 4* *1 cc* *Full sheet; DS body; 4 spaces between columns* *Center vertically* *Type horizontal lines* *Draw vertical lines before removing paper*

1970 (Est.) (000)	Words
	6 / 13 / 26 / 32 / 39 / 52
$75,372	60
86,205	69
1,342	78
2,065	87
91,460	95
46,987	105/117

Problem 4 *Retype Problem 3* *1 cc* *Type all lines; reinsert paper to type vertical lines*

Words: Each vertical rule 6
Total words 147

111C: Growth Index – Straight Copy (15) *two 5′ writings; circle errors; determine* gwam

All letters are used.

	GWAM 1′	5′	
Someone once said that it does not matter whether your ancestors	13	3	55
came to this country on the Mayflower; what does matter is what they did	28	6	58
after they got here. By the same token, it does not matter who your	41	8	61
parents are or what they do; what does matter is what you do with your	56	11	64
talents and abilities. Many persons sleepwalk through life; they have	70	14	66
no goal nor do they realize a just purpose in life. This blind effort is	84	17	69
quite unnecessary. If you formulate a goal while you are still young,	99	20	72
you will have a better chance of reaching that goal and succeeding in	113	23	75
life. Behavior habits that you form now carry over into adult life.	126	25	78
To improve your lot in life, you must first improve yourself. The	13	28	80
road to success is paved with many obstacles. To succeed, you must over-	28	31	83
come these problems and not be overcome by them, for problems are but	42	34	86
an opportunity to the person who is determined to win. Nothing worth-	55	36	89
while is easily won; extra effort will help you win your goal.	68	39	91
The key to success is still hard work. Don't accept the idea that "it	82	42	94
can't be done," because for every achievement made against unusual odds	97	45	97
it can be said, "It could not be done, but somehow it was done." Free-	111	47	100
dom to work, as well as a good education so that you can make the most of	126	50	103
your talents, has helped to make our country great.	136	52	105

1′ GWAM | 1 | 2 | 3 | 4 | 5 | 6 | 7 | 8 | 9 | 10 | 11 | 12 | 13 | 14 |
5′ GWAM | 1 | 2 | 3 |

LESSON 112

112A: Conditioning Practice (5) *each line three times*

Alphabet	Jack's brevity always complements his quietly expressed zeal for good.	Fingers curved, close to keys
Figure-symbol	The purchase price is $14,675.89 plus 3% sales tax and 20% excise tax.	
Long words	Systems engineers had complete responsibility in space communications.	
Speed	The successful typewriting student is one who has formed right habits.	

| 1 | 2 | 3 | 4 | 5 | 6 | 7 | 8 | 9 | 10 | 11 | 12 | 13 | 14 |

112B: Skill Building – Straight Copy (15) *(Repeat 111C above; Goal: Improved speed or accuracy)*

Problem 2

DO: Retype Problem 1, making these changes:

1. Change exact vertical placement to *reading position* by finding starting point for exact placement and then moving up two lines.
2. Leave 4 spaces between columns.
3. Change first three column headings:

	Words
Column 1: Company Name	2
Column 2: Common Stocks	2
Column 3: Municipal Bonds	3
+ *Problem 1 words*	88/95

Problem 3

Retype Problem 2. Substitute *Average Yield* column for *Total* column. Use 2 lines for column headings and 6 spaces between columns.

Average Yield	Problem 3 Words
	8
	14
	32
5%	40
3%	47
6%	55
5%	63
4%	70
7%	77
4%	84

Problem 4

Retype Problem 1, but omit *Total* column. Make 1 cc. Leave 6 spaces between columns.

LESSON 165

165A: Conditioning Practice (5) *pretyping check; then each line three times*

Alphabet; shift	Jack Voltz wrote Paul Bexley to request drama roles for Carnegie Hall.	*Quick, finger-action reaches*
Figures: 2-4-3	39 1056 482 72 5901 463 87 3206 159 48 7052 391 64 8520 137 94 2603 758	
Left and right	decade pinion reader limply grades poplin access Johnny regret uphill	
Fluency	Data set forth in tabulated reports should be grouped for clear study.	
	| 1 | 2 | 3 | 4 | 5 | 6 | 7 | 8 | 9 | 10 | 11 | 12 | 13 | 14 |	

165B: Previewing Typed and Nontyped Rulings for Tables (8)

RULED TABLES: When horizontal lines are placed above and below columnar headings and below the last line of a table, the table is said to be "ruled."

DRILL 1: Type a 3″ horizontal line on the left side of your paper. Space down twice and type your name. Space down once and type another 3″ horizontal line. Inspect to be sure that a blank line separates your name from the lines above and below it.

DRILL 2: Repeat the drill, *drawing* the horizontal lines by holding your pen or pencil firmly against the alignment scale (or card holder) and moving the carriage, using the carriage-release lever. See Reference Guide, page xi, for review, if necessary.

DRILL 3: Type your name and "rule" it as follows: Make light pencil marks at points where the lines should start and stop. Remove the paper and *draw* the lines with pen and ruler.

DRILL 4: Type a double rule as follows: Type a 3″ horizontal line. Before typing the second rule, use the variable line spacer to move the platen forward until the first line appears slightly above the alignment scale; then type the second underline.

DRILL 5: Type vertical side rulings for the drill of Step 1 by taking your paper from the typewriter, reinserting it sideways, aligning it carefully at the corners, and *typing* the rules.

BOXED TABLES: When a ruled table has vertical lines between columns, connecting the horizontal lines, the table is said to be "boxed." The sides may or may not be closed. Extend horizontal lines 1 space or more into margins for table with sides closed.

DRILL 1: Type the boxed table shown below, leaving 8 spaces between columns. Type horizontal lines. Then make light pencil marks at points for lines to be drawn for the boxed table; remove the paper from the typewriter and draw the lines, using a ruler.

Name	City	State
Your first name	Your city	State
A friend's name	Friend's city	State
A second friend's name	Friend's city	State

DRILL 2: Repeat Drill 1, but after you remove the paper from the typewriter to draw the lines, reinsert it sideways and type in the vertical lines.

DRILL 3: Repeat Drill 1, except draw the vertical lines while the paper is still in the typewriter. See Reference Guide, page xi, for review, if necessary.

TIP

When you single-space to the next line of typing and type an underline, the underline appears at the *bottom* of its line space, *leaving* the line space blank.

112C: Guided Writing – Progressive-Difficulty Paragraphs (15)

1. **Type** a 1′ writing on ¶ 1 for *speed*. Divide this *base* rate by 4 to get quarter-minute goals.
2. **Type** two 1′ guided writings at the base rate. *Goal: Control* with no loss of speed.
3. **Type** another 1′ writing at 4 to 8 *gwam* above the base rate. *Goal:* Improved speed with finger action and continuity of writing.
4. **Repeat** Steps 1–3 for ¶s 2 and 3 at ¶ 1 rate.

Response Patterns

¶ 1 — *51% Balanced-hand, 14% One-hand, 35% Combination*

Aim for a high goal and then work in the right way to reach such a goal. The right work habits and the right mind set are the format for achieving high goals. It is by working, not wishing, that you can and do reach goals. Start right now to work in the right way so that the right way of working will become a habit.

¶ 2 — *44% Balanced-hand, 18% One-hand, 38% Combination*

They will send the statement to the address shown on the card. The union requested that they do this and that the case be referred to the judge for further action. The judge has promised to consider all the facts and the other data of the case. He will probably be able to give us his decision by the end of the week.

¶ 3 — *25% Balanced-hand, 34% One-hand, 41% Combination*

It is no exaggeration to say that the decrease in rainfall has resulted in water reserves which are far below the average required for safety. We were told to refer this water problem to the committee for attention. New plans probably will be drafted after this committee has made a minimum study of the water problem.

112D: Technique Improvement – Control of Operative Parts (15) *each line four times: TE, TE, S*

		EMPHASIZE
Space-bar control	and and and, the the the, they they they, then then then, pay them for if it is, and the, they may pay, when they try, to help you, the drain They may pay them when they try to help you clean the old storm drain.	*Quick, down-and-in motion*
Shift-key control	Floyd Flynn, Paul McNeil, and Jack Burred attended the AMS Convention. R. J. Asham, T. O. Black, A. E. Byrd, and Jan Kane made A's in typing. H. V. McGil, President of McGil & Company, left for Chicago, Illinois.	*Little finger reach*

Center + 10 = ↓ TAB

Carriage return — *Quick, flick return*

A quick return
of the carriage ——— Tab ———→ with an immediate
start of the new line ——— Tab ———→ will result in an
increased speed rate. ——— Tab ———→ (*Repeat as many times as time permits.*)

Unit 28 | Lessons 164-168

Arranging and Typing Tables

(Backspace - from - Center Method)

LESSON 164

164A: Conditioning Practice
(5) *pretyping check; then each line three times*

Alphabet; shift	Steve Kaszycki had Jack Quero plan large craft exhibits at Bryn Mawr.	Type with continuity
Figures: 2-3-4	50 213 4697 80 512 3649 78 102 5643 79 801 5423 96 780 1253 64 798 1025	
Balanced-hand	profit handle bushel formal height panels burlap visual emblem airman	
Fluency	Try to type my tabulations in a style that is simple and easy to read.	

| 1 | 2 | 3 | 4 | 5 | 6 | 7 | 8 | 9 | 10 | 11 | 12 | 13 | 14 |

164B: Drill on Tabulating: Arranging Columnar Headings
(8) *eight spaces between longest items*

Review centering and tabulating in Reference Guide, pages x and xi. Then type the drills shown at the right as directed below:

Drill 1 – Center by columnar entries.

Drill 2 – Center by columnar headings.

Drill 3 – Center by the longest items, whether a heading or an entry. (This procedure should be used in future problems, unless otherwise directed.)

	Company	Assets	Funds
Drill 1.	International Fabrics	$42,375,980	$31,862,590

	No. of Shares	Market Value	Percent of Portfolio
Drill 2.	715	$28,640	3.7%

	Agency	Monthly New Car Quota	Sales
Drill 3.	Sakamoto Motors, Inc.	85	$345,000

164C: Typing Tables with Columnar Headings
(37)

Time Schedule

Get ready to type	2′
Timed production	30′
Proofread; compute *g-pram* . .	5′

Type the following four tables for 30′ when directed to begin. Mark errors. Compute *g-pram.*

Problem 1

Full sheet	*Center vertically*
DS body	*6 spaces between columns*

				Problem 1 Words	Problem 4 Words
SUMMARY OF CORPORATE FINANCIAL HOLDINGS				8	8
For Selected Companies in Area				14	14
Firm	Stocks	Bonds	Total	23	21
Allied Tire	$68,192,400	$87,635,500	$155,827,900	34	28
Atlas Drug	75,263,250	89,746,850	165,010,100	43	35
Custom Fiber	42,797,300	41,298,100	84,095,400	52	42
Forbes Paper	37,269,750	42,816,900	80,086,650	61	49
Pure Foods	29,346,900	38,921,350	68,268,250	70	56
Union Chair	24,167,050	36,287,050	60,454,100	79	62
U. S. Photo	31,246,750	47,919,650	79,166,400	88	69

LESSON 113

113A: Conditioning Practice (5) *each line three times*

Alphabet	The jovial kings welcomed six zealous queens by a formal garden party.	Rhythmic stroking
Figure-symbol	A 100% hardwood 3-shelf bookcase (38″ x 23″ x 7 3/4″) sells for $9.65.	
Long words	Electro-mechanical devices and servomechanisms solve systems problems.	
Speed	Keep the right thumb close to the space bar in order to space quickly.	

| 1 | 2 | 3 | 4 | 5 | 6 | 7 | 8 | 9 | 10 | 11 | 12 | 13 | 14 |

113B: Technique Improvement – Response Patterns (15) *each line three times: TE, TE, S*

High-frequency words emphasized.

		CHECK
Stroke response	are you was him best only dear upon date state opinion average minimum No, I was not able to get an opinion or to reserve a tax date for you. We can get him to give an opinion now on only a few extra trade cases.	✓ Finger action; upright fingers
Word response	their work, and the work, work with them, when they paid, sign the form He may work with their men when they sign the right form for the city. They wish to go to the city with the chairman to sign the right forms.	✓ Speedy, word-level typing response
Combination response	and the tax, only their, but they care, when they read, pay such rates state when they, in the reserve, were you paid, and their opinion then minimum profit, an average problem, reserve a quantity, for the estate	✓ Variable rhythm; uniform stroking
Variable rhythm	Quantities of problems are solved for the estate at a minimum profit. She will provide us with a statement of the case and added amendments. A million or more statements are mailed by the union staff each month.	✓ Continuity and rhythm

| 1 | 2 | 3 | 4 | 5 | 6 | 7 | 8 | 9 | 10 | 11 | 12 | 13 | 14 |

113C: Selected Goal Practice (15) (*Repeat 112C, page 178, as directed below*)

1. *Speed.* Type two 1′ speed writings on each paragraph. Force your speed to its highest level; type with continuity and rhythm, keep the action in the fingers with the hands and arms quiet; use quick, snap strokes.

2. *Control.* Type two 1′ guided writings on each paragraph on the *control level.* Select a rate that is about 4 to 8 words below your speed rate. *Goal:* Not over 1 error on each writing. Type without a sense of hurry to improve accuracy.

113D: Skill Building – Straight Copy (15) (*Repeat 111C, page 177*)

LESSON 163

163A: Conditioning Practice (5) *pretyping check; then each line three times*

Quiet hands and arms

Alphabet; shift	Jack Quigley sold Paul Zukov fixtures for a fine home in New Brighton.
4-2-3 grouping	5027 14 639; 8216 30 754; 9086 21 534; 7985 23 468; 7095 28 470; 963
Word endings	quire flect ingly tient spect ulate flict cient ology gency graph ville
Fluency	Your work future will improve as you learn to perform at higher rates.
	| 1 | 2 | 3 | 4 | 5 | 6 | 7 | 8 | 9 | 10 | 11 | 12 | 13 | 14 |

163B: Business Letter Production Measurement (45)

Time Schedule	
Get ready to type	7′
Timed production	30′
Proofread; compute *n-pram* . .	8′

TYPE: The following three letters for 30′ when directed to begin. Make 1 cc and address an envelope for each letter. Correct your errors as you type. If time permits, start over. Mark uncorrected errors. Compute *n-pram.*

Problem 1: Block, Open

Words
(*Current date*) Mr. Lloyd E. Lammey 213 East 9
14th Street Bloomington, Indiana 47401 17
Dear Mr. Lammey Subject: Lawn Development 25
(¶ 1) We are pleased that you wrote to us de- 33
scribing the problems which you encountered 42
while trying to plant a new lawn. This is a good 52
time of year to make plans by which future 60
efforts may be more productive. (¶ 2) The plant- 69
growing zone in which you live, as well as the 78
characteristics of your soil, places definite limi- 88
tations on the type of grass you may expect to 98
grow. We recommend that you arrange for a 106
soil analysis to learn as much as possible about 116
the ground you are trying to cultivate before 125
you attempt any further planting. (¶ 3) The 133
enclosed pamphlet discusses the growing zones 142
and some procedures for obtaining a reliable 151
soil analysis. Please accept it with our compli- 161
ments. Very sincerely yours Gary L. Fishel, 170
President (xx) Enclosure (137) + *Envelope* 174/188

Problem 2: Modified, Mixed

(*Current date*) American Builders' Supply Co. 9
1905 N. Madison Street Cape Girardeau, Mis- 17
souri 63701 Attention Mr. F. Kenneth Scott 26
Gentlemen: (¶ 1) That compact, under-counter 34
dishwasher for which you have waited has just 43
arrived! Using no more space than a 24-inch 52
base kitchen cabinet, our new appliance is a 61
performing miracle. (¶ 2) Available in either 70
built-in or portable models, the Leadon provides 79

Words
an effortless way to wash dishes after every meal. 90
It uses six automatic-cycle push-button controls 100
to handle all dishes from heavy pots and pans 109
to fine crystal. Powerful washing-rinsing water 119
jets do away with need for scraping and pre- 127
rinsing. Other features have been added to aid 137
the busy housewife. (¶ 3) Enclosed are descrip- 145
tive details and price lists. We shall be pleased 155
to handle your orders. Sincerely yours, L. 164
Eugene Jones Sales Manager (xx) Enclosures 172
(131) + *Envelope* 189

Problem 3: Modified, Indented ¶s; Mixed

(*Current date*) Mr. George Vanover 5926 West 9
Maple Avenue Ft. Dodge, Iowa 50501 Dear 17
Mr. Vanover: Subject: Office Illumination Re- 26
port (¶ 1) I am eager to report some findings 34
of our study for improving the quality of light 44
in your offices. (¶ 2) By correcting a few basic 53
weaknesses, you can, I believe, greatly improve 62
your office lighting. Our study revealed exces- 72
sive glare at many stations and a lack of uni- 81
formity of illumination at others. There were 90
undue shadows at the stenographic desks and 99
somewhat disturbing brightness ratios in the 108
accounting section. Your executive offices need 118
greater lighting flexibility. (¶ 3) A detailed re- 126
port of our analysis is enclosed. Shall we plan 136
to meet soon to discuss our recommendations? 145
Yours very truly, ILLUMINATING SYSTEMS, INC. 155
James T. Thompson Chief Engineer (xx) En- 162
closure (118) + *Envelope* 163/176

LESSON 114

Backspace-from-Center Tabulation

114A: Conditioning Practice (5) *each line three times*

Alphabet	The Aztec jewelry makes an exquisite gift of which everybody is proud.	*Finger action; quiet hands*
Figure-symbol	Order No. 8475 for 36 chairs ($9.75 ea.) will be shipped May 19 or 20.	
Shift key	Jack Flood, Mary E. Langs, and C. O. Quaile work for Black & Williams.	
Speed	The auditor will mail a new contract to them by the end of this month.	
	| 1 | 2 | 3 | 4 | 5 | 6 | 7 | 8 | 9 | 10 | 11 | 12 | 13 | 14 |	

114B: Technique Improvement – Figure Reaches (5) *four 1' writings*

Line: 70; Tab stops: 10-space intervals
Last two digits of each group give word count

									EMPHASIZE
Each figure used a minimum of 12 times.	3701	7302	4603	6404	5805	8506	9507	5908	*Finger-reach action*
	3409	7410	6311	8912	6713	9514	8315	7416	
	6517	7218	3819	4920	8921	5622	6823	7924	*Quick, tab spacing*
	4025	4926	5627	4728	5829	9430	8631	3732	

114C: Manuscript Typing (25) *(Margins: 1" side and bottom; 2" top; DS; ¶ indention: 5)*

TABULATING SUMMARY: BACKSPACE-FROM-CENTER

TS

Tabulating is the arrangement of material in columnar (table) form for ease of reading and reference. The steps to follow, as well as other information, are given below.

TS

Step 1: Vertical Placement of Material

Mathematical placement. To determine vertical placement, count the total lines to be used for the table (including the blank spaces between lines if the material is to be typed in double- or triple-spaced form); subtract this figure from the total lines available for use on the sheet; divide the remainder by 2. This new figure will indicate the number of blank lines to be left at the top of the sheet (ignore any "remainder" lines when dividing by 2). Use the formula: (Total Lines Available − Total Lines Used) ÷ 2 = Blank Lines to Be Left in the Top and in the Bottom Margin.

Spacing after heading lines. In counting lines to be used, allow a double space (1 blank line) between the main heading and the secondary heading. Allow a triple space (2 blank lines) after a main heading if a secondary heading is not used, or after the secondary heading when both a main heading and a secondary heading are used. Allow a double space after columnar headings (when used).

Reading position. A modern practice in centering material vertically on a full page (8½ x 11 inches) is to center the material in reading position (visual center), a point approximately 2 line spaces above actual vertical center. To center material in reading position, determine the top margin in the usual way, then subtract 2 from the number of lines to be left in the top margin. Actual vertical center is generally used in placing material on sheets smaller than 8½ x 11 inches.

TS

Step 2: Horizontal Placement of Columns

Backspace from center. First, move the margin stops to the ends of the scale and clear all tab stops. Then, to arrange the columns horizontally on the sheet, backspace from center 1 space for each 2 spaces in the longest line in each column and for each 2 spaces to be left between columns.* Set the left

Determining Acceptability of Production Problems

All problems should be marked as either *Acceptable* or *Unacceptable*, according to the following definitions:

Acceptable—any problem typed in complete agreement with directions given and containing no inaccuracy of any kind, on either the original or carbon copies, at the end of the measurement period.

Unacceptable—any problem having at the end of the measurement period, either on first copy or carbon copy, any inaccuracy of any kind including:

1. Deviations from directions.
2. Inaccuracy in problem format or arrangement.
3. Inaccurate use of materials.
4. Typographical errors, misspellings, incorrect word division, improper word usage, incorrect figures or totals, inaccurate punctuation, uncorrected errors.
5. Poor erasures or corrections on either original copy or on carbon copy.

162C: Sustained Business Letter Production (38)

Time Schedule		* N-PRAM =
Get ready to type . . .	5′	Total Acceptable Words
Timed production . . .	25′	+
Proofread; compute *n-pram**	8′	½ Unacceptable Words
		÷ by Time

USE: Letterhead; 2 sheets of carbon paper; envelopes, eraser and eraser shield.

Goals: Good work procedure and acceptability of copy.

DO:

1. Study instructions for *Acceptable* copy at the top of this page.
2. Arrange supplies neatly within easy reach. Plan placement of completed work. (See PRODUCTION TIP at the right.)→
3. Make a list of the letters given below; place the list close to your book so you can check off the letters as you complete them.

   Page 244, 159C, Problem 1
   Page 246, 160C, Problem 1
   Page 247, 161C, Problem 1

4. For each letter, prepare two cc's and an envelope.
5. Type each letter in the order listed, according to the directions included with that problem.
6. When directed to begin, type for 25′ from your prepared list, being sure that each letter meets the standards for *Acceptable* copy as explained at the top of the page. If you complete all letters in acceptable form, begin again.
7. Correct neatly any errors on first copy and carbons as soon as you detect the error.

PRODUCTION TIP

Here is a good way to assemble your work as it is completed:

Step 1 – Remove the letter from the typewriter, address an envelope, and place the letter under the envelope flap.

Step 2 – Place the letter and envelope face down on the desk.

Step 3 – When time is called, turn the stack face up, and your work will be in correct sequence to evaluate and turn in.

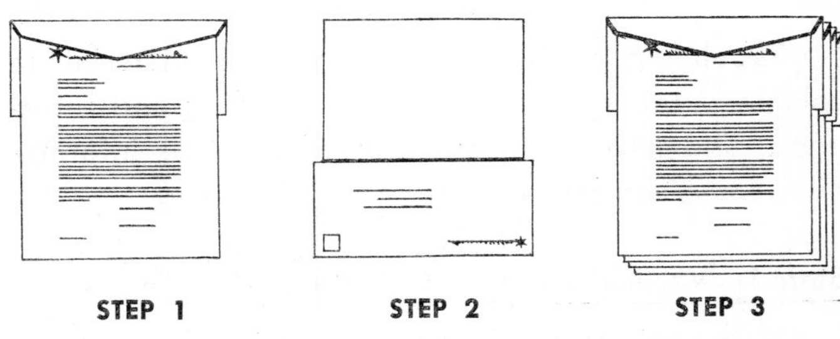

8. After typing the letter, proofread it again before removing it from the typewriter. Correct any errors not already corrected.
9. When the timed production is ended, indicate the nature of any error remaining on any problem and draw a diagonal line across that page to indicate that the problem is "Unacceptable" and will receive ½ credit.
10. On your computation sheet if you have one (or on your first page), compute your *n-pram* (net production rate a minute) for the timing (See box above, at left.).
11. Turn in all problems in the order in which they were listed.

> **Note.** *Footnotes may be shown at the end of a short report. Place a single explanatory footnote, indicated by the asterisk, in proper position after the last line at the end of the manuscript.*

margin stop at this point. From the left margin stop, space forward 1 space for each space in the longest line in the first column and for each space to be left between the first and second columns. Set a tab stop at this point for the second column. Follow a similar procedure for any additional columns.

Spacing between columns. An even number of spaces is usually left between columns (4, 6, 8, 10, or more). The number of spaces to be left between columns is governed by the space available, the number of columns used, and the requirement of ease of reading.

Columnar headings. Columnar headings (when used) are usually centered over the columns.

TS

Other Information

Spacing review. Most typewriters have 6 single line spaces to the vertical inch. Since there are 10 pica-type spaces or 12 elite-type spaces to the horizontal inch, paper 8½ x 11 inches has 66 writing lines of 85 pica or 102 elite spaces. The usual center point for pica-type machines is 42; for elite-type machines, 50 or 51.

Dollar sign. In a money column, place the dollar sign before the top figure in the column and the total (if shown). The dollar sign may be placed so that it will be one space to the left of the longest line in the column, or it may be placed next to the first digit of the top figure in the column, whether this be the longest line in the column or not.

______________ *SS*

DS

*When an extra space occurs at the end of a column, carry it forward to the next column. If the last column ends with an extra space, ignore the space.

114D: Backspace-from-Center Tabulating Drill (15) *center vertically and horizontally on half sheet*

Determine vertical and horizontal placement; check solutions with placement cues given at the bottom of this page

Learning cues: *Lines used for table indicated at right; longest line in each column underlined in color*

If time permits: Repeat drill, half sheet, short side up, 4 spaces between columns

WORDS FREQUENTLY MISSPELLED

TS

			Lines Used
WORDS FREQUENTLY MISSPELLED			1
			2
			3
advertisement	diagnosis	neither	4
			5
affidavit	dividend	nuisance	6
			7
agenda	efficiency	optimistic	8
			9
auxiliary	enable	oversight	10
			11
bankruptcy	erroneous	permission	12

HORIZONTAL PLACEMENT: 13 | 8 | 10 | 8 | 10

VERTICAL PLACEMENT

Formula: $\frac{\text{Lines Available} - \text{Lines Used}}{2} = \text{Top Margin}$

$\left(\frac{33 - 12}{2} = \right.$ 10 blank lines in top margin (extra line left at bottom))

Proof: Blank Lines Top Margin + Lines Used + Blank Lines Bottom Margin = Lines Available (10 + 12 + 11 = 33)

HORIZONTAL PLACEMENT

Backspace from center 1 space for each 2 spaces in longest columnar lines and for spaces between columns (*advertisement* — 8 — *efficiency* — 8 — *optimistic*):

ad|ve|rt|is|em|en|+4|te|ff|ic|ie|nc|+4|yo|pt|im|is|ti|

Learning recall: When backspacing, carry forward to the next column the extra space that may occur at the end of the longest line of a column. Ignore an extra space at the end of the last column. Remember to space forward to determine the tab stops.

Problem 3

Type second page of letter to Nicholas G. Angelucci
Block, open — *Current date*
See Reference Guide page vii for vertical form heading

Words

(*Second-Page Heading*) 10

are submitting bids for the complete installation, 20
with the understanding that we shall have an 29
opportunity to review our estimates at the time 39
of final contract negotiations. In the event that 49
major changes or revisions are proposed, we 58
understand that we shall be permitted to rework 67
our bids in terms of the changes suggested. (¶) 76
I am enclosing a projected time schedule for 85
work completion, to give you some idea of the 94
amount of time needed for our activities. Yours 104
very truly ILLUMINATING SYSTEMS, INC. James 113
T. Thompson Chief Engineer (xx) Enclosure 121

Problem 4

Retype second page of letter to Nicholas G. Angelucci
Modified block, mixed — *Horizontal form heading*

LESSON 162

162A: Conditioning Practice (5) *pretyping check; then each line three times*

Alphabet; shift	Jim Rosner placed Felix Lequey on a very tough job in West Kenzington.	*Start new line quickly*
4-3-4 grouping	3162 408 5791; 3804 295 7624; 3587 906 1320; 5147 689 2468; 1359 7045;	
Double letters	foggy tippy tinny tooth class lobby booth funny fuzzy messy jazzy peppy	
Fluency	Most business letters will look quite stylish if typed in simple form.	
	| 1 | 2 | 3 | 4 | 5 | 6 | 7 | 8 | 9 | 10 | 11 | 12 | 13 | 14 |	

162B: Learning Review Problem – Multiple Carbon Pack Assembly (7)

1. Turn to Reference Guide, page viii, to review carbon-pack assembly methods.
2. Assemble and insert a two-carbon pack, using the desk-top method. Observe the TIPS at the right. →
3. Position the pack to type at the left margin on line 7. Type your name.
4. Refer to Reference Guide, page viii, to review removal of the carbons. Remove carbon pack and try this removal-of-carbons step.
5. Again referring to Reference Guide, page viii, use the machine assembly method to assemble and insert the same pack.
6. Leave this pack in the typewriter for use in Step 7, erasing.
7. Turn to Reference Guide, page xii, and carry out each of the erasing steps indicated at the top of that page, erasing two letters of your name on each copy of the pack.

CARBON ASSEMBLY AND ERASING TIPS

Desk Method

1. Be sure dull side of the carbon is toward you as you assemble the carbon pack.
2. Insert the pack into the typewriter with the heading down and facing the back of the machine.
3. To straighten the pack in the typewriter, grasp the pack firmly, operate the paper-release lever, and move the pack until it is aligned properly; reset the paper-release lever.

Machine Method

4. Insert the letterhead and second sheets until they are barely gripped by the feed rolls.
5. Insert carbon paper between the gripped sheets, being sure the glossy side of the carbon is facing you.

Erasing

6. Insert a 5″ x 3″ card in front of first carbon before erasing on original sheet; move card to similar position in front of second carbon when erasing first carbon copy.

LESSON 115

115A: Conditioning Practice (5) *each line three times*

Alphabet	Six big juicy steaks sizzled in a pan as five workmen left the quarry.	*Fingers curved*
Figure-symbol	A special "J&B" rug (8′10″ x 12′) sells for $346.79 less 15% discount.	
Continuity	It will help to remember that anger is but one letter short of danger.	
Speed	The simple way to better our lot in life is to try to do a lot better.	
	| 1 | 2 | 3 | 4 | 5 | 6 | 7 | 8 | 9 | 10 | 11 | 12 | 13 | 14 |	

115B: Selected-Goal Practice – Progressive-Difficulty Sentences (15)

1. Select a speed goal and type each sentence three times on the call of the 20-, 15-, or 12-second return guide, as directed by your teacher. Pause briefly after each spurt writing to relax.

2. Type a 1′ writing on each sentence. Type on the *speed* level. Work for continuity and rhythm.

Note. The figures above the copy indicate the 1′ rates in terms of the guide call.

GWAM														
20″ Guide	3	6	9	12	15	18	21	24	27	30	33	36	39	42
15″ Guide	4	8	12	16	20	24	28	32	36	40	44	48	52	56
12″ Guide	5	10	15	20	25	30	35	40	45	50	55	60	65	70

1	*Balanced-hand*	They paid for the maps of the ancient land forms with their endowment.
2	*Combination*	Most of the statements are mailed by the staff at the end of each day.
3	*One-hand*	Only a few of your cases on monopoly were referred to the union staff.
4	*Figures*	He sold 126 bats, 573 balls, 48 gloves, and 90 Dopp-Kits to the teams.
5	*Long words*	Specialists are needed in magnetohydrodynamics and telecommunications.
6	*Shift key*	Jack A. MacDuff, President of MacDuff & O'Brien, lives in Walla Walla.
		| 1 | 2 | 3 | 4 | 5 | 6 | 7 | 8 | 9 | 10 | 11 | 12 | 13 | 14 |

115C: Tabulating Skill Applications (24)

Problem 1: Three-Column Table

Full sheet
Center vertically
DS data
10 spaces between columns

Problem 2: Skill Building

Retype table of Problem 1 with these changes: Reading position; 6 spaces between columns

WORDS FREQUENTLY MISSPELLED

			Words in Cols.	Total Words
				6
		TS		
advertisement	diagnosis	neither	6	12
affidavit	dividend	nuisance	12	18
agenda	efficiency	optimistic	18	23
auxiliary	enable	oversight	23	29
bankruptcy	erroneous	permission	30	35
brief	excusable	perpetuate	35	41
calendar	forfeit	privilege	40	46
capacity	genuine	prosecute	46	51
caution	illegible	receive	51	57
coincide	inferior	sacrifice	57	62
collusion	inhabit	schedule	62	68
concur	lease	statistics	67	72
curiosity	lenient	supersede	72	78
deceive	management	technique	78	84
depreciation	mileage	tragedy	84	89

115D: Tabulating Skill Building (6) *3′ writing on Problem 1, using columns only*

1. Determine quickly left margin stop and tab stops for columns. Do not center vertically.

2. Start writing about 1″ from top edge of sheet. If you complete problem, start over.

161B: Business-Letter Review – Modified Block, Indented ¶s (7)

Features to Review:

1. Opening, closing, and other *special* lines start as in modified block, page 245. Set tab stop at center point.
2. Paragraphs indented 5 spaces.
3. Company name, when used, typed in all capitals, DS below complimentary close.
4. Signer's name and title starting 4 lines below company name.
5. Reference initials and enclosure notation typed at left margin.

Adjusting Letter Length. In letters having special lines (attention, subject, company name, signer's title, enclosure notation, and the like), it is often necessary to type the date a line or two higher than the position suggested in the Reference Guide on page vii. Before typing the date, therefore, look over the letter to determine the number of special lines for which provision should be made. The date in the letters of this lesson should be typed two lines higher than recommended in the Reference Guide, because of the special lines.

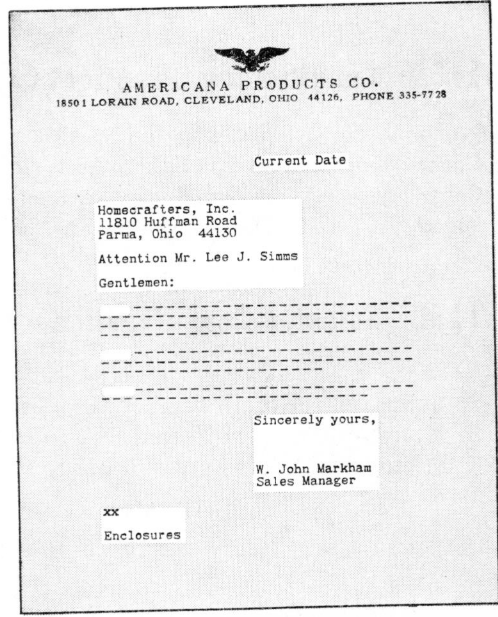

AMERICANA PRODUCTS CO.
18501 LORAIN ROAD, CLEVELAND, OHIO 44126, PHONE 335-7728

Current Date

Homecrafters, Inc.
11810 Huffman Road
Parma, Ohio 44130

Attention Mr. Lee J. Simms

Gentlemen:

Sincerely yours,

W. John Markham
Sales Manager

xx

Enclosures

MODIFIED BLOCK, INDENTED ¶s
MIXED PUNCTUATION

161C: Letters – Modified Block, Indented ¶s, Mixed Punctuation (38)

Time Schedule	
Get ready to type	5′
Timed production	25′
Proofread; compute *g-pram* . .	8′

TYPE: The following four letter problems for 25′ when directed to begin. Make 1 cc and address an envelope for each letter. If time permits, retype the letters. Mark errors. Compute *g-pram*.

Problem 1

Words

(Current date) Mr. Robert S. Crawford 4693 9
Frontier Street Ottumwa, Iowa 52501 Dear 17
Mr. Crawford: Subject: Installation of Flood- 26
lights (¶ 1) We have your request to study the 34
feasibility of installing decorative illumination 44
for the exterior of your Executive Office Build- 54
ing. The opportunity to investigate the possibili- 64
ties of this project should provide some interest- 73
ing and innovative challenges. (¶ 2) I am en- 81
closing a booklet, EXTERIOR ILLUMINATION, which 91
I should like to have you examine. At the time 100
we report the findings of our study to you, 109
perhaps you can take time to discuss some of the 119
ideas presented in our publication. (¶ 3) You 127
will hear from us soon on the progress we 136
are making on our study. Yours very truly, 145
ILLUMINATING SYSTEMS, INC. James T. Thompson 154
Chief Engineer (xx) Enclosure (114) 160
+ Envelope 172

Problem 2

Words

(Current date) Mr. Robert L. Hanson Modern 9
Products, Inc. 3500 Main Street Ottumwa, 17
Iowa 52501 Dear Mr. Hanson: Subject: Re- 25
ceipt of Contract (¶ 1) We are pleased to be 33
awarded the contract for indoor and outdoor 42
lighting of your new headquarters building. 51
Your plans for tying in your lighting with the 60
spacious grounds and the ultramodern architec- 69
ture of your new building make this contract an 79
exciting one to fulfill. (¶ 2) Our starting date, 88
as indicated in our project bid, will be exactly 98
one month from today. Therefore, we are eager 107
to discuss remaining details and to order the spe- 117
cial materials that this lighting system will re- 126
quire. May we meet with you on Friday after- 135
noon at your office to complete plans for this 145
project? Yours very truly, ILLUMINATING SYS- 153
TEMS, INC. James T. Thompson Chief Engineer 162
(xx) (117) *+ Envelope* 163/179

LESSON 116

116A: Conditioning Practice (5) *each line three times*

Alphabet	Jack will help move the boxes of zinc from the gondola cars at Quincy.	*Quiet hands*
Figure-symbol	The 5 reams of 8½" x 11" paper (No. 24) on Order #79 will cost $16.30.	
Adjacent key	Opportunity comes to a person as a result of dedication and hard work.	
Speed	The right techniques coupled with the right attitudes aid your typing.	
	| 1 | 2 | 3 | 4 | 5 | 6 | 7 | 8 | 9 | 10 | 11 | 12 | 13 | 14 |	

116B: Growth Index – Straight Copy (15) *two 5′ writings; circle errors; determine* gwam

All letters are used.

	GWAM 1′	5′	
There is an overwhelming amount of paper work in the modern office.	14	3	53
Because of this problem, many firms are using computers for the process-	28	6	55
ing of much of the data which make up the paper work of the firms.	42	8	58
Although the speed with which these data can be processed has been dazzling,	57	11	61
the use of computers for processing data is limited to work of a repetitive	72	14	64
nature. Contrary to the opinion of some people, a computer cannot think;	87	17	67
it can only react to the program that has been prepared for it. In this	102	20	70
process, the first step is for a person to study all the records of the	116	23	73
firm; then the next step is to prepare the program for the computer.	130	26	76

	GWAM 1′	5′	
More than ever, the modern office worker must get a good education	13	29	78
if he is to find and hold a job. His worth is increased if he knows how	28	32	81
to type. The basic tool of the computer is the punched card. This card	43	34	84
may be punched indirectly as new records are prepared, or it may be	56	37	87
punched directly by the use of a card punch machine. Did you know that	71	40	90
this card punch machine has the letter keyboard of a standard typewriter?	86	43	93
A good typist can, with a small amount of instruction, operate a card	100	46	96
punch machine. Learning to type, then, is another way to enter the	113	49	98
exciting field of automation.	119	50	99

1′ GWAM | 1 | 2 | 3 | 4 | 5 | 6 | 7 | 8 | 9 | 10 | 11 | 12 | 13 | 14 |
5′ GWAM | 1 | 2 | 3 |

160C: Letters in Modified Block, Mixed Punctuation (38)

Time Schedule

Get ready to type	5′
Timed production	25′
Proofread; compute *g-pram*	8′

TYPE: The following three letters for 25′ when directed to begin. Prepare a cc and address an envelope for each. If time permits, retype the letters. Mark errors. Compute *g-pram.*

Goals: Correct format; efficient work procedure.

Problem 1

Words
(*Current date*) The Home Appliance Company 8
5021 E. Poplar Avenue Rolla, Missouri 65401 17
Attention Mr. John F. Lee Gentlemen: (¶ 1) 25
Within a few days, we shall ship you the most 34
attractive household appliance you have seen in 44
many years! This beautifully styled refrigerator- 54
freezer with automatic ice maker is a real 63
dream––and a very pleasant one at that! (¶ 2) 71
Our fall sales promotion will feature the inclu- 80
sion of this unusual ice maker in all no-frost, 90
upright-model freezers. We are proud of this 99
new appliance. We know you will be pleased to 109
demonstrate it to your quality-conscious cus- 117
tomers. (¶ 3) I am enclosing some factory manu- 126
als together with some publicity items which I'm 135
sure will prove of genuine interest to you. Sin- 145
cerely yours, L. Eugene Jones Sales Manager 154
(xx) Enclosures (119) + *Envelope* 156/171

Problem 2

(*Current date*) Mid-States Supply Company 8
5170 W. Main Street Sikeston, Missouri 63801 17
Attention Mr. Gaza A. Katona Gentlemen: 26
(¶ 1) We are in the process of completing plans 34
for the annual exhibit to be held in Kiel Audi- 43
torium, February 16–21. Early reports suggest 52
a lively and well-attended convention. (¶ 2) 60
Since you at one time registered an interest in 70
exhibiting some of the appliances for which we 79
are distributor, we wonder whether you would 88
consider joining us in building one exhibit spon- 98
sored by both firms. We could furnish some of 107
the larger pieces of equipment, thus eliminating 117
for you the big problem of packing and trans- 126
porting appliances that are sometimes quite un- 135
wieldy. Our two firms could also share costs–– 145
an item of real consequence today. (¶ 3) I am 153
enclosing a copy of the floor plan on which is 162
designated the exhibit space allocated to us. If 172
you feel favorably inclined toward my sugges- 181
tion, I shall appreciate hearing from you soon. 191
We can discuss details later. Sincerely yours, 200
L. Eugene Jones Sales Manager (xx) Enclosure 209
(171) + *Envelope* **223**

Problem 3

(*Current date*) Modern Appliances 3740 Cen- 8
ter Street Sikeston, Missouri 63801 Attention 18
Mr. Sam Briggs Gentlemen: Subject: New 26
Model Appliances (¶ 1) Your enthusiasm about 34
our latest models of large kitchen appliances is 43
certainly gratifying. We have been able to build 53
more beauty and more practicality into both the 63
refrigerator and the range without having to 72
make a substantial price increase. (¶ 2) You will 81
be pleased to know that our test models have 90
brought an enthusiastic response regarding ease 100
of care and cleaning of these newest appliances. 110
We know you will be proud to demonstrate 118
these new value-packed refrigerators and ranges 127
to your customers. Sincerely yours, L. Eugene 137
Jones Sales Manager (xx) (102) 141
+ *Envelope* **154**

LESSON 161

161A: Conditioning Practice (5) *pretyping check; then each line three times*

Alphabet; shift	Jack Zabel with Rex Marquette made plans for visiting Yosemite Valley.	*Return carriage quickly*
3-2-3 grouping	703 46 285; 917 20 538; 716 49 258; 690 43 218; 509 67 413; 705 98 236;	
Left and right	trade pylon grade pupil taste hulky draft polyp grace onion extra lumpy	
Fluency	You will find it valuable to learn how to judge the length of letters.	
	| 1 | 2 | 3 | 4 | 5 | 6 | 7 | 8 | 9 | 10 | 11 | 12 | 13 | 14 |	

116C: Tabulating Skill Applications (24) *(4 half sheets)*

Problem 1: Five-Column Table

Half sheet
Center vertically
DS data
6 spaces between columns

					Words in Cols.	Total Words
VARIATIONS IN SPELLING OF LONG VOWEL SOUNDS						9
				TS		
a	name	grain	play	break	5	14
e	see	cream	shield	region	10	19
i	smile	light	died	style	15	24
o	float	doe	plateau	elbow	20	29
u	mule	few	continue	lieu	25	34
oo	stoop	chute	true	junior	30	39

Problem 2: Table with Columnar Headings

Half sheet
Center vertically
DS data
10 spaces between columns

Note. Centering columnar headings: 87D, page 140. Use margin release when centering heading for first column.

			Words in Cols.	Total Words
COMMON BUSINESS TERMS				4
	TS			
Insurance	Business Law	Accounting		17
		DS		
actuary	bailment	asset	5	22
annuity	decedent	balance	10	27
claim	executor	income	14	31
lapsed	intestate	invoice	19	36
policy	par value	journal	24	41
premium	probate	liability	29	47
term	repossess	voucher	34	51

Problem 3: Table with Columnar Headings

Half sheet
Center vertically
SS data
Spaces between columns: 10, 14, 10

				Words in Cols.	Total Words
AVERAGE HOURLY					3
WORK WEEK COMPARISON					7
	DS				
(1850 to 2000)					10
	TS				
Year	Work Week	Year	Work Week		21
1850 [10]	69.8 [14]	1930 [10]	45.9	4	25
1860	68.0	1940	44.0	8	29
1870	65.4	1950	40.0	12	33
1880	64.0	1960	37.5	16	37
1890	61.9	1970	30.0*	20	42
1900	60.2	1980	25.0*	24	46
1910	55.1	1990	20.0*	28	50
1920	49.7	2000	15.0*	32	54

SS ____________ *(Underline 1½" long)* 57

DS *Estimated. 60

Problem 4: Skill Building

Retype Problem 3 with these changes: Half sheet (short side up); center vertically; DS data; 16 spaces between columns—2 columns only, arranged in chronological order.

Footnotes or source notes may be typed at the left margin or indented 3 or 5 spaces.

116D: Tabulating Skill Building  *3′ writing on Problem 3, using columns only*

1. Determine quickly left margin stop and tab stops for columns. Do not center vertically.
2. Start writing about 1″ from top edge of sheet. If you complete problem, start over.

Words

Mrs. Oakland Subject: Tree Selection (¶ 1) 25
Thank you for asking us to help select and 34
arrange trees for your new property. (¶ 2) I am 43
enclosing three drawings of your building site 52
on which we have sketched alternative possibili- 61
ties for choosing and placing trees needed to 71
complete your landscaping. Please note that on 80
each drawing we have indicated possible loca- 89
tions for the tree plantings as well as the name 99
of each tree to be included in each group mak- 108
ing up a planting area. Throughout, we have 117
tried to achieve naturalistic balance while har- 126
monizing your preference for shade, bloom, and 136
evergreen trees. (¶ 3) Will you take time to 144
study these drawings carefully and let me have 153
your reactions to the recommendations. Perhaps 163
we can discuss these proposals soon. Very sin- 172
cerely yours Gary L. Fishel, President (xx) 180
Enclosures (144) + *Envelope* 182/196

Problem 3

Words

(Current date) Mrs. Clair Rowe 911 North Til- 9
lotson Muncie, Indiana 47304 Dear Mrs. 17
Rowe (¶ 1) We are pleased to have the oppor- 24
tunity to help you plan landscaping for your lake 34
cabin. This kind of planning has been one of 43
our specialties for many years. (¶ 2) The en- 51
closed brochure illustrates several basic land- 60
scaping plans to be selected largely according 70
to the nature of the particular setting. You will 80
note that special attention is given to landscap- 90
ing that requires little care by the vacationers 99
and plantings that can exist without attention 109
when the owners may be away from the site for 118
extended periods. (¶ 3) We shall be available 126
next Saturday to visit your cabin site with you 136
and Mr. Rowe, as you request. Very sincerely 145
yours Gary L. Fishel, President (xx) Enclosure 154
(124) + *Envelope* 165

LESSON 160

160A: Conditioning Practice (5) *pretyping check; then each line three times*

Alphabet; shift	Melvin Azrak and John Gower asked to buy antique lamps at Camp Oxford.	*Variable rhythm*
2-3-3 grouping	40 125 964; 38 561 734; 20 879 137; 80 256 920; 31 649 875; 39 506 782;	
Left and right	cedar union sweat nylon great polio erase pulpy crate nymph waste plump	
Fluency	One planning to work in a fine office should learn to read good books.	
	| 1 | 2 | 3 | 4 | 5 | 6 | 7 | 8 | 9 | 10 | 11 | 12 | 13 | 14 |	

160B: Business-Letter Review – Modified Block, Mixed Punctuation (7)

Features to Review:

1. Date and closing lines begin at horizontal center of paper. Set tab stop at the center point.
2. Letter address, attention line, salutation, and paragraphs typed at left margin. Subject line at left margin or centered.
3. Salutation "Gentlemen" used when letter is addressed to a company.
4. Mixed punctuation: colon after salutation, comma after complimentary close.
5. Reference initials and special notations typed at left margin.
6. Double space between all separate letter parts.

Adjusting Letter Length:

To avoid placing a letter too low on the page, you may condense the closing lines by (1) leaving only two blank lines for the signature, (2) raising the initials and special notations to appear opposite the last closing lines. For lower placement, leave more lines and lower the initials and notations.

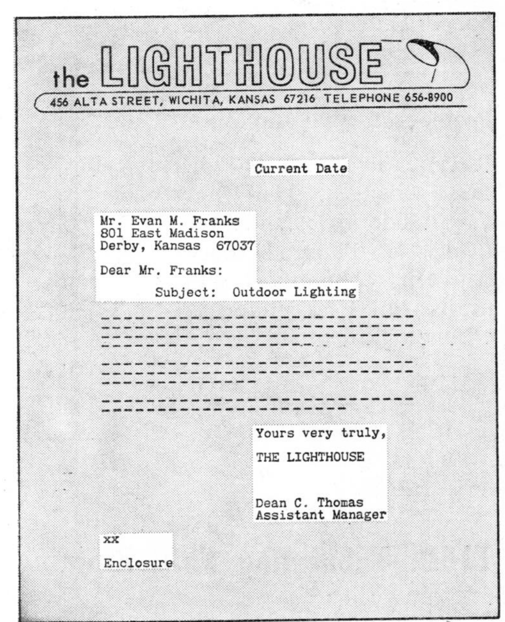

the LIGHTHOUSE
456 ALTA STREET, WICHITA, KANSAS 67216 TELEPHONE 656-8900

Current Date

Mr. Evan M. Franks
801 East Madison
Derby, Kansas 67037

Dear Mr. Franks:

Subject: Outdoor Lighting

Yours very truly,

THE LIGHTHOUSE

Dean C. Thomas
Assistant Manager

xx

Enclosure

MODIFIED BLOCK, MIXED

LESSON 117

117A: Conditioning Practice (5) *each line three times*

Alphabet	Maxine was puzzled by the lack of interest in the five good quay jobs.	Quick, snap stroke
Figure-symbol	We will ship your Order #35790 for 126 boxes and 48 cartons on Monday.	
Long words	Democracy is based upon the extraordinary possibilities in each of us.	
Speed	It is by our daily work that we make our future what we want it to be.	

| 1 | 2 | 3 | 4 | 5 | 6 | 7 | 8 | 9 | 10 | 11 | 12 | 13 | 14 |

117B: Skill Comparison – Straight Copy (15) *(Repeat 116B, page 183; compare rates)*

117C: Building Sustained Tabulating Skill (30)

Time Schedule	
Planning and preparing	3′
Timed tabulating production . .	20′
Proofreading; determining *g-pram*	7′

If you complete the following problem before 20 minutes are up, start over on a new sheet. Type on *control* level. Do not erase errors.

Note. Longest columnar item color underlined; also, note new two-letter state abbreviations (approved for use with ZIP Code only).

Full Sheet
Center vertically
DS data
2 spaces between longest items
Center ZIP Code number under col. heading

Each figure used a minimum of 16 times.

				Words in Cols.	Total Words
SELECTED BUSINESS FIRMS					5
IN MAJOR CITIES					8
TS					
Name	Street	City and State	ZIP Code		22
Air Reduction Sales Co.	150 East 42d Street	New York, NY	10017	13	34
American Can Company	4766 Sayre Avenue, N.	Chicago, IL	60635	25	46
Shell Oil Company	7253 Wilshire Blvd.	Los Angeles, CA	90002	37	58
Union Carbide Corp.	778 N. Wanamaker	Philadelphia, PA	19139	49	70
General Dynamics Corp.	6485 Chestnut Avenue	Detroit, MI	48218	61	83
Ethyl Corporation	639 Oakhill Road	Baltimore, MD	21228	72	94
Monsanto Chemical Co.	7378 Hutchins Avenue	Houston, TX	77004	84	106
Continental Can Co.	5698 Bayliss Avenue	Cleveland, OH	44103	96	118
Bankers Trust Company	6465 G Street, S.E.	Washington, DC	20019	109	131
American Cyanamid Co.	4399 California Ave.	St. Louis, MO	63111	122	142
Johns–Manville Corp.	7358 Clay Street	San Francisco, CA	94109	134	156
Lever Brothers Company	6486 Beloit Road, W.	Milwaukee, WI	53219	147	168
Dow Chemical Company	345 Kendall Avenue	Boston, MA	02118	158	180
Gulf Oil Corporation	8693 La Prada Street	Dallas, TX	75218	170	192
Celanese Corporation	599 LaSalle Avenue	New Orleans, LA	70112	182	204
Esso Standard Oil Co.	7890 Baldwin Street	Pittsburgh, PA	15234	195	217
Standard Brands, Inc.	4659 Nogales Street	San Antonio, TX	78237	208	229
Rand McNally & Company	345 Alvarado Road	San Diego, CA	92120	220	242
Occidental–Western Co.	465 North Canal	Seattle, WA	98103	231	253
Irving Trust Company	5783 Parkside Avenue	Buffalo, NY	14216	243	265

Unit 27 | Lessons 159-163

LESSON 159

Building Business-Letter Typing Power

159A: Conditioning Practice (5) *pretyping check; then each line three times*

Alphabet; shift Paul Zabik sent Gwen Joyce six novels compiled by author Fred Marquis.
2-2-3 grouping 39 57 204; 81 63 259; 78 40 612; 69 73 854; 10 38 206; 59 74 137; 80
Balanced-hand prowl handy proxy civic their visit right field world forms usual signs
Fluency This is the time to learn how to type business letters in proper form.
| 1 | 2 | 3 | 4 | 5 | 6 | 7 | 8 | 9 | 10 | 11 | 12 | 13 | 14 |

Space quickly; down-and-in motion

159B: Business-Letter Review – Block Style, Open Punctuation (7)

Features to Review:

1. All lines, including the date, typed at the LEFT MARGIN.
2. No punctuation after salutation or complimentary close.
3. Subject line at left margin; word *subject* in capitals or in upper and lower case, followed by colon and 2 spaces; DS before and after subject line. Note: Word *subject* sometimes omitted.
4. Name of signer typed on fourth line below complimentary close.
5. Title of signer either on line with name or on next line.
6. Reference initials a DS below signer's name and/or title.
7. Enclosure notation a DS below reference initials.

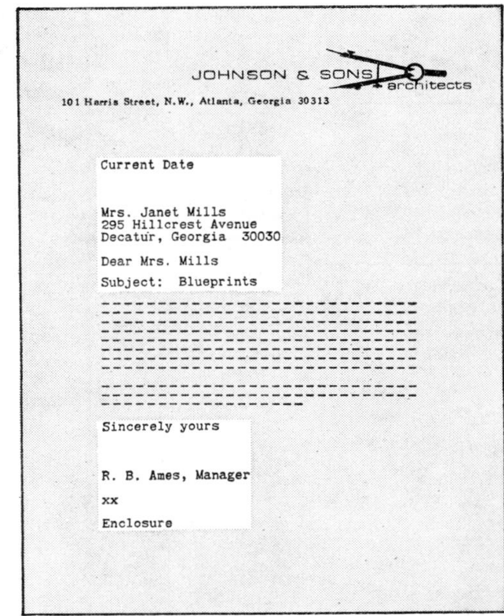
JOHNSON & SONS architects
101 Harris Street, N.W., Atlanta, Georgia 30313

Current Date

Mrs. Janet Mills
295 Hillcrest Avenue
Decatur, Georgia 30030

Dear Mrs. Mills

Subject: Blueprints

Sincerely yours

R. B. Ames, Manager

xx

Enclosure

BLOCK STYLE
OPEN PUNCTUATION

159C: Letters in Block Style, Open Punctuation (38)

Time Schedule		**G-PRAM =
Get ready to type	5′	Total Words Typed
Timed production	25′	÷ Time
Proofread; compute *g-pram* . **Gross Production Rate a Minute	8′	

USE: Margins and date placement as in Reference Guide, page vii; your initials for reference.

DO: Type the following three letters for 25′ when directed to begin. Address an envelope for each. If time permits, retype the letters. Mark typing and placement errors. Compute *g-pram*.

Problem 1

Words
(*Current date*) Mrs. Gladys Kermit 713 East 9
Cottage Grove Street Martinsville, Indiana 17
46151 Dear Mrs. Kermit Subject: Landscape 26
Planning (¶ 1) When choosing plants for your 34
landscape, try to make your selections in terms 43
of (a) their eventual size; (b) the purpose you 53
wish them to serve; and (c) their appearance at 63
eye level. To make choices without thinking 72
seriously about these factors can involve you in 81
undue expense as well as inferior results in the 91
appearance of your property. For example, 100
plants not reaching maturity for some years need 109
to be planted so they will be most appealing 118
when they reach full size. (¶ 2) The enclosed 127
brochure has been prepared especially for peo- 136
ple facing landscaping problems. I hope you 145
will find it helpful. Very sincerely yours Gary 154
L. Fishel, President (xx) Enclosure (121) 161
+ Envelope 176

Problem 2

(*Current date*) Mrs. Judy M. Oakland 315 East 9
Highland Avenue Muncie, Indiana 47303 Dear 18

LESSON 118

118A: Conditioning Practice (5) *each line three times*

Alphabet	Most companies emphasize extra valuable jobs for good quality workers.	*Quick carriage return*
Figure-symbol	These fishing boxes (9½" x 8¼" x 14½") with 6/0 reels sell for $23.75.	
Uniform stroking	Don't wonder about your ability—wonder if you are using your ability.	
Speed	To type rapidly, hold your arms quiet and let the fingers do the work.	
	| 1 | 2 | 3 | 4 | 5 | 6 | 7 | 8 | 9 | 10 | 11 | 12 | 13 | 14 |	

118B: Speed and Accuracy Emphasis – Statistical Script Copy (15)

1. Type four 1′ writings on the *speed* level.
2. Subtract 8 words from the best rate made in Step 1. Determine quarter-minute goals.
3. Type four 1′ guided writings at this new rate. *Goal:* Not over 1 error on each writing.
4. As time permits, type additional 1′ writings on either the *speed* or *control* levels, according to your needs.

All figures are used.

EMPHASIZE
Finger stroking action
Continuity
Fluent rhythm

The average man in his lifetime spends 20 years working. He spends another 20 years sleeping, 16 years playing, 5 years shaving and dressing, 5 years eating, and 3 years just waiting. In a lifetime an average man spends 8,764 hours telephoning, or the equivalent of 1 full year. In a lifetime of 70 years, his heart pumps about 77,179,000 gallons of blood—enough to lift a 10-ton weight 10 miles.

118C: Measuring Sustained Tabulating Skill (30)

Time Schedule	
Planning and preparing	3′
Timed tabulating production . .	20′
Proofreading; determining *n-pram*	7′

Repeat 117C, page 185, *but correct all errors.* When time is called, proofread carefully. Subtract 15 words from the total words typed for each uncorrected error. Determine *n-pram* (net production rate a minute)—rate with all errors corrected.

LESSON 119

119A: Conditioning Practice (5) *each line three times*

Alphabet	A fog-like haze developed quickly just as the workmen left the boxcar.	*Start new line quickly*
Figure-symbol	The new prices are as follows: 12 @ $25.50; 24 @ $48.95; 36 @ $70.50.	
Shift key	Order the Damp Proof Red Primer from Bartons & Delaney, New York, N.Y.	
Speed	They paid for the gowns with the money she received for her handiwork.	
	| 1 | 2 | 3 | 4 | 5 | 6 | 7 | 8 | 9 | 10 | 11 | 12 | 13 | 14 |	

158A: Conditioning Practice (8) *3′ for pretyping check; then each line three times*

Alphabet; shift	Valerie Klaus won six games bowling with Jacquelyn Ray and Fran Perez.	*Rhythmic continuity*
Credit Card Nos.	561 302 748; 926 410 385; 792 130 465; 879 024 163; 875 901 243; 56789	
Double letters	reef feet beet beef free loll reek hoop poll coop loom peep fuzz good	
Fluency	The eight firms own big maps of the key land shapes on the lake shelf.	
	| 1 | 2 | 3 | 4 | 5 | 6 | 7 | 8 | 9 | 10 | 11 | 12 | 13 | 14 |	

158B: Word Division Review (12) *half sheet; center vertically; 8 spaces between columns of words*

Type problem; correct results; discuss guides.

WORD DIVISION GUIDES

You may separate –

1. Two single-vowel syllables appearing together, between the vowels.
2. After a one-letter syllable in the middle of a word, but not in a word ending such as able, ible, ical, icle.

WORD DIVISION REVIEW

Word	Syllable Identification	May Be Divided
conciliation	con/cil/i/a/tion	
stereotype	ster/e/o/type	
megaphone	meg/a/phone	
gravitate	grav/i/tate	
habitable	hab/it/a/ble	
flexible	flex/i/ble	
historical	his/tor/i/cal	

158C: Inventorying Letters; Centering 

Problem 1: Business Letter

TYPE: The following letter in modified block style; mixed punctuation; 1½″ side margins; date, Line 18 followed by 3 blank lines; one cc; envelope. Enclose announcement typed as Problem 3.

September 24, 19–– | Mr. Leslie I. Combs, Jr. | District Manager | Recording Systems and Equipment | 1302 Fairthorne Avenue | Philadelphia, Pennsylvania 19128 | Dear Mr. Combs (¶ 1) We are now in the process of making plans for our next Sales and Promotion Conference. It is our hope that the meetings this year will be of special interest to the men in our organization and that great benefit will result from our discussions. (¶ 2) Will you please prepare copies of the enclosed announcement and distribute them to all men involved. It may be advisable, too, for you to make a larger copy in attractive style and display it prominently on a bulletin board. (¶ 3) If you have any specific questions or suggestions relating to our forthcoming meeting, please get in touch with me. Very sincerely yours | Robert R. Rankin | President | RRR:xx | Enclosure

Problem 2: Business Letter

TYPE: The same letter, but address it to **Mr. Angelo Fergerson** who is district manager of the same company, but with his office at **5657 Wilson Avenue, Richmond, Virginia 23228**. Again enclose announcement and type envelope.

Problem 3: Announcement

TYPE: 2 original copies on full sheets; DS; center the problem vertically; center each line horizontally.

ANNOUNCING | The Annual District Sales and Promotion Conference | To Be Held | in | The International House, Washington, D. C. | November 13–17, 19–– | All Meetings Held in the Industrial Seminar Wing | Suites A to J | Deadline for Reservations, October 20 | PLAN NOW FOR THIS IMPORTANT MEETING | Mail Registration Forms to | Mr. Stanley I. Gurnick, Personnel Relations | Home Office, Washington, D. C.

Problem 4: Composition

IF TIME PERMITS: See how rapidly you can plan and type a rough draft of an announcement relating to your school. Study it for completeness. You may wish to add a visual attention getter. Retype a final copy.

119B: Technique Improvement – Finger Facility (17) *each line twice; then 1′ writing on each line*

	REACHES		EMPHASIZE
1	*Adj. key*	Are you equipped to cover the action required to operate the abacuses?	*Fingers upright; close to keys*
2	*Long reaches*	Two men excelled in reporting the news received via the coaxial cable.	
3	*Finger 1*	Five hungry men helped James save a battered boat from further damage.	*Finger-reach action*
4	*Finger 2*	Dick decided to dedicate his new musical work to an educational group.	
5	*Finger 3*	An old wax sample was used by Wally Olds to wax those new wood floors.	*Quiet hands*
6	*Finger 4*	Aza Quinn quizzed a popular polo player about scaling the Alpine peak.	
		| 1 | 2 | 3 | 4 | 5 | 6 | 7 | 8 | 9 | 10 | 11 | 12 | 13 | 14 |	

119C: Tabulating Skill Applications (28)

Problem 1: Table with Rulings

Half sheet
Center vertically
SS data
4 spaces between columns

AVERAGE ANNUAL LIVING COST
IN SELECTED UNITED STATES CITIES* *DS*

(Family of Four) *TS*

Item	Amount	Percent	Words in Cols.	Total Words
AVERAGE ANNUAL LIVING COST				5
IN SELECTED UNITED STATES CITIES*				12
(Family of Four)				16
Item	Amount	Percent		23
Food and Beverages	$1,748	28.4	7	30
Housing	1,393	22.6	11	34
Clothing	563	9.1	15	38
Medical Care	332	5.4	19	42
Transportation	485	7.9	24	47
Other Goods and Services	699	11.3	31	54
Personal Taxes	669	10.9	35	58
Misc. (Life Insurance, etc.)	268	4.4	43	69
Indent 5 → Total	$6,157	100.0		77

SS

______________ 81

*Estimate of dollar amount required to maintain a "modest but adequate" level of living. 91 99

Problem 2: Skill Building

Retype table of Problem 1 with these changes: Full sheet, reading position; DS data; 6 spaces between columns.

Problem 3: Columnar Heading Placement

Half sheet
Center vertically
SS data
*6 spaces between columnar headings**

***Note.** Type the headings, then center the longest line of each column under the heading; set the stops, and type the data of the columns.

VALUE OF $1.00 INVESTED AT
4% AND 5% COMPOUNDED ANNUALLY

End of Year	Amount at 4%	Amount at 5%	Words in Cols.	Total Words
VALUE OF $1.00 INVESTED AT				5
4% AND 5% COMPOUNDED ANNUALLY				11
End of Year	Amount at 4%	Amount at 5%		26
1	$1.0400	$1.0500	4	30
2	1.0816	1.1025	7	33
3	1.1249	1.1576	10	36
4	1.1699	1.2155	13	39
5	1.2167	1.2763	16	42
6	1.2653	1.3401	20	46
7	1.3159	1.4071	23	49
8	1.3686	1.4775	26	52
9	1.4233	1.5513	29	55
10	1.4802	1.6289	32	58

LESSON 157

157A: Conditioning Practice (8) *3′ for pretyping check; then each line three times*

Alphabet; shift	Marvin Wesley sent Phil Boaz an exquisite jacket from Grandview Lodge.	*Curved, upright fingers*
Policy Nos.	328 75 93; 572 89 30; 496 32 76; 206 19 34; 801 54 86; 401 75 91; 4126	
Left and right	gave pomp bade polo serf yolk scab ploy fear jump feat hulk rare plop	
Fluency	They wish to name both panels for work in the field of civil problems.	
	| 1 | 2 | 3 | 4 | 5 | 6 | 7 | 8 | 9 | 10 | 11 | 12 | 13 | 14 |	

157B: Word Division Review (12) *half sheet; center vertically; 8 spaces between columns of words*

Type problem; correct results; discuss guides.

WORD DIVISION GUIDES

You may separate –

1. The suffix from a root word which ends in a double consonant.
2. Between double consonants, when a root word ends in a letter that is doubled in adding the suffix.
3. A compound word only at the hyphen.

WORD DIVISION REVIEW

Word	Syllable Identification	May Be Divided
dwelling	dwell/ing	
stressing	stress/ing	
planning	plan/ning	
programming	pro/gram/ming	
strapping	strap/ping	
self-control	self-/con/trol	
semi-invalid	sem/i-/in/va/lid	

157C: Inventorying a Report Outline (30) *full sheets; 6″ line; TS (triple space), DS, and SS as directed*

Problem 1: Outline

TYPE: The copy as an outline; omit leaders and page numbers. **Goals:** Efficient procedure and good format.

Problem 2: Table of Contents

TYPE: The copy as a TABLE OF CONTENTS with spaced leaders and page numbers. 2″ top margin, 1½″ left margin for leftbound manuscript.

Problem 3: Title Page

TYPE: A title page for a leftbound manuscript. Use title, your name, name of school, date.

IF TIME PERMITS: Retype problems for speed.

DEVELOPING A SOUND INVESTMENT PROGRAM

TS	I. Introduction.	1
DS	A. Economics in our daily living	5
	1. Status of national economy	5
	a. Gross national product (GNP)	7
	b. Employment index	9
	2. Projections for future economic growth .	12
	B. Need for sound individual program . .	13
	1. Personal financial responsibilities . . .	17
	a. Family	20
	(1) Current obligations	23
	(2) Anticipated commitments	25
	b. Federal government social programs . .	27
	2. Projected personal income and resources	30
DS	II. Basic principles of life insurance . . .	33
DS	A. Factors affecting risk	36
	1. Life expectancy	39
	2. Insurable risks	41
	B. Determination of premiums	43
	1. Reserve accumulation	45
	2. Cash and loan values	46
	C. Options for settlement	49
	1. Implications of lump-sum payment . . .	51
	2. Payments through periodic installments .	53
DS	III. Basic principles of annuities	56
DS	A. Definition and description of annuities .	59
	B. Different kinds of annuities	61
	1. Single premium versus annual premium .	65
	2. Straight-life and refund	69
DS	IV. Planning the investment program . . .	72
DS	A. Choosing the life insurance element . .	76
	1. Term insurance.	81
	2. Straight-life policies	87
	3. Limited-payment policies.	93
	B. Choosing the annuity contract	96

LESSON 120

120A: Conditioning Practice (5) *each line three times*

Alphabet	Six skaters jumped grotesquely in a veritable frenzy of wacky rhythms.	*Quiet hands*
Figure	His life insurance was under Group Policy Nos. OL 75423 and MCI 18960.	
Adjacent key	John asked Fred to cover the boxes for the six men before you came in.	
Speed	When typing the top-row figures, keep the reach action in the fingers.	

| 1 | 2 | 3 | 4 | 5 | 6 | 7 | 8 | 9 | 10 | 11 | 12 | 13 | 14 |

120B: Accuracy Emphasis (7) *1′ writing on each sentence of 120A; goal: not over 1 error each writing*

120C: Tabulating Skill Building (8) *3′ writing on Problem 1 below; data in columns only, plus leaders*

1. Determine quickly left margin stop and tab stops for columns. Do not center vertically.
2. Start writing about 1″ from top edge of sheet. If you complete problem, start over.

120D: Tabulating Skill Applications (30)

Problem 1: Table with Leaders*

Full sheet
Reading position
Space data as shown
20 spaces between columns
Leave 2 spaces after last leader period

EDUCATION AND LIFETIME EARNINGS — 6

DS

(Earnings from Age 18 to 64) — 12

TS

Grade Completed	Earnings	Words in Cols.	Total Words
			25
Elementary School:		4	29
Less than 8 years	$143,000	13	38
8 years	184,000	22	47
High School:		25	50
1 to 3 years	212,000	34	59
4 years	247,000	44	69
College:		46	71
1 to 3 years	293,000	55	80
4 years	385,000	64	89
5 years or more	455,000	73	98
All Education Groups	299,000	83	108

DS after headings; Indent 3 for subentries; *SS* before rule (112); *DS* after rule.

Source: Bureau of Census. — 116

Problem 2: Skill Building

Retype the table of Problem 1 with these changes: Half sheet (short side up); 10 spaces between columns; omit leaders.

*Leaders (made by alternating the period and the space) are sometimes used to connect typed material, as shown in the table of Problem 1. When typing leaders, check on the cylinder scale whether the first period is struck on an odd or an even number; then strike all additional lines of leaders on either the odd or the even number so as to align leaders vertically.

Unit 26 | Lessons 156-158

Basic Typing Operations Inventory

LESSON 156

156A: Conditioning Practice (8) *3′ for pretyping check; then each line three times*

Alphabet; shift	Jack Szabo and Vern Piquot sailed with six friends on new Lake Gramby.	*Wrists low; hands quiet*
Figure review	22 88 44 66 33 99 55 00 11 77 22 88 44 66 33 99 55 00 11 77 22 88 44	
Left and right	crab milk draw holy acts hymn deaf pink face puny gaze plum babe lily	
Fluency	This is a fine time for all of us to try to do the best work possible.	
	| 1 | 2 | 3 | 4 | 5 | 6 | 7 | 8 | 9 | 10 | 11 | 12 | 13 | 14 |	

156B: Word Division Review (12) *half sheet; center vertically; 8 spaces between columns of words*

1. Read word-division guides and problem directions.
2. Clear margins, set stops for 3 columns with 8 spaces between. (See Ref. Guide, pages x and xi, for review.)
3. SS (single space); use DS between two-word groups.
4. Center heading; center column headings over columns.
5. Type the 3 columns, tabbing across page. The diagonals show syllables. In the third column, type each word shown in the first two columns, using a hyphen at each acceptable division point.
6. Check results. Discuss questions with your teacher.

■ *Follow this same procedure for all word-division drills in this unit.*

WORD DIVISION GUIDES

Do not separate –

1. A one-letter syllable beginning a word.
2. A two-letter syllable at the end of a word.
3. A word written as a contraction.
4. A past tense that does not add another syllable (another enunciation).

WORD DIVISION REVIEW

Word	Syllable Identification	May Be Divided
abridged	a/bridged	
eclipsed	e/clipsed	
achiever	a/chiev/er	
strangely	strange/ly	
wouldn't	would/n't	
shouldn't	should/n't	
construed	con/strued	
programmed	pro/grammed	

156C: Inventorying Tabulation Skills 

TRY NEW LEARNING: To type lines over numerals ($\overline{V}$, $\overline{X}$): type the capital; backspace; roll platen toward you 1 line; type underline.

Problem 1

TYPE: The table on full sheet. ⟶

Center vertically; DS the body; decide spacing between columns. Review spacing for headings. **Goals:** Efficient procedure; good format.

Problem 2

RETYPE: The table at the right, as in Problem 1, but SS the body. Arrange the body in groups of 5 by a DS between lines 5 and 6.

IF TIME PERMITS: Retype the table in 4 columns.

ARABIC FIGURES WITH ROMAN NUMERAL EQUIVALENTS

1	I	11	XI	30	XXX	400	CCCC
2	II	12	XII	40	XL	500	D
3	III	13	XIII	50	L	600	DC
4	IV	14	XIV	60	LX	700	DCC
5	V	15	XV	70	LXX	800	DCCC
6	VI	16	XVI	80	LXXX	900	CM
7	VII	17	XVII	90	XC	1,000	M
8	VIII	18	XVIII	100	C	2,000	MM
9	IX	19	XIX	200	CC	5,000	$\overline{V}$ *
10	X	20	XX	300	CCC	10,000	$\overline{X}$ *

* A line over a numeral multiplies the value by 1,000.

Problem 3: Skill Building

Full sheet
Center vertically
DS data
Spaces between items in columns: 20, 6

			Words in Cols.	Total Words
HOW TEEN-AGERS SPEND THEIR MONEY				7
DS				
(Dollar Breakdown) *TS*				10
Item	Boys	Girls		16
		DS		
Cars, gas	.04	––	3	20
Clothing*	.07	.19	7	23
Dates	.10	––	9	26
Grooming	.02	.07	13	29
Hobbies	.03	.02	16	32
Movies, records	.09	.09	21	37
Savings	.07	.09	24	40
School supplies	.06	.08	29	45
School lunches	.23	.21	33	50
Snacks	.09	.05	36	53
Sports	.11	.06	39	56
Reading	.05	.06	43	59
Miscellaneous	.04	.08	47	63
________________		*SS*		67
*For girls, includes jewelry.				73

Problem 4: Skill Building

Retype the table of Problem 3 with these changes: Half sheet (short side up); DS data; spaces between items in columns: 10, 4

LESSON 121

121A: Conditioning Practice (5) *each line three times*

Alphabet	James saw a big gray fox move quickly along a building near the plaza.	*Uniform stroking*
Figure-symbol	The terms of discount on Order #47–2896 dated June 15 were 2/10, n/30.	
Fingers 3 and 4	A plump yellowtail swallowed the squid as I attempted to set the hook.	
Speed	They expect to make the audit of the offices at the end of this month.	

| 1 | 2 | 3 | 4 | 5 | 6 | 7 | 8 | 9 | 10 | 11 | 12 | 13 | 14 |

121B: Growth Index – Straight Copy (15) *two 5′ writings; circle errors; determine* gwam

All letters are used.

	GWAM 1′	5′	
Although not all systems are alike, most modern business units of	13	3	53
today realize that some degree of control over purchasing and requisi-	27	5	56
tioning of supplies is needed. One worker in an office or department	41	8	59
is usually given the job as supply clerk for that unit. If someone wants	56	11	62
a new supply of pencils, he will make out an order for pencils, give it	70	14	65
to the clerk, and the clerk will see that the order is filled. When the	85	17	68
supply clerk renews his stock of goods, he will send an order to a cen-	99	20	71
tral supply area where the order will be processed. At this time supplies	114	23	74
will be billed to the unit involved, and the articles will be sent. *(Continued)*	127	25	76

1′ GWAM | 1 | 2 | 3 | 4 | 5 | 6 | 7 | 8 | 9 | 10 | 11 | 12 | 13 | 14 |
5′ GWAM | 1 | 2 | 3 |

155B: Stroking Technique Refinement – Common Letter Combinations (7) *each line three times*

Avoid excessive hand-and arm motion as you type

stra	strays straws strain strait strand strange straight stranger strangled
impl	imply implant implore implied implicit implement implicate implication
stre	streaks streets streams stresses stretcher strength streamer strenuous
impo	impose import impolite impound imposter important impoverish impossible

| 1 | 2 | 3 | 4 | 5 | 6 | 7 | 8 | 9 | 10 | 11 | 12 | 13 | 14 |

155C: Growth Index – 5′ Straight-Copy Writings (30)

1. Type three 5′ writings; determine your *nwam* for each. Record the best of the three. This score will be used in grading your performance in this unit. Read the copy carefully!
2. Type one 5′ writing at your highest speed rate. Compare the *gwam* with the results of your best *nwam* writing. In future lessons, try to raise your net-rate score to your speed-rate level.

All letters are used.

	GWAM 1′	5′	
Men who have gained fame as astute leaders in the business world	13	3	61
remind us of crucial views which must be shared by all persons having	27	5	64
a vital concern about the continued welfare of our society. These men	41	8	67
emphasize with firmness that the chief reason for engaging in business	55	11	70
enterprise is to make a satisfactory profit. The idea that a company	69	14	73
should spend its time and funds on social goals is worth heeding, but	83	17	75
the success of a business venture must be gauged in terms of whether	97	19	78
or not a firm has been able to earn profits. The ability to do things	111	22	81
which society urges doing depends upon the fiscal resources of a firm	125	25	84
as well as upon the surplus of capital remaining after paying for the	139	28	87
added benefits requested by workers and the costs of normal operations.	154	31	89
One of the most important items influencing the profit made by a	13	33	92
corporation is the productive strength of its personnel. Though some	27	36	95
firms have been able to devise ways by which the output of machines may	41	39	98
be forecast and quoted with exactness, too few firms have been able to	56	42	101
find equally reliable methods for judging human traits having a great	70	45	103
impact on the productive behavior of young or old. Yet there are men	84	47	106
who like to prove close relationship between the output of workers and	98	50	109
the cost of operating an enterprise. For all who plan to find work in	112	53	112
a business area, there is real merit in helping a firm realize a just	126	56	115
profit by trying to work as skillfully as possible on all assignments.	140	59	117

1′ GWAM | 1 | 2 | 3 | 4 | 5 | 6 | 7 | 8 | 9 | 10 | 11 | 12 | 13 | 14 |
5′ GWAM | 1 | 2 | 3 |

155D: Related English Check (5) *correct as you type; check results; retype at increased speed*

excitedly she said, "john has published his article the big sound

GUIDES: Use double quotation marks to enclose quoted matter; single quotation marks to enclose a quotation within a quotation. Use quotation marks also to enclose titles of: (1) articles in magazines; (2) chapters in books; (3) essays and lectures; (4) headlines in newspaper stories.

	GWAM 1′	GWAM 5′	
If an office worker wants an item that is not in the inventory, a	13	28	79
purchase requisition will be sent by the supervisor to the purchasing	27	31	82
agent for the firm. This draft should contain a concise description of	42	34	85
the item. The buyer will then secure bids on the item to get the lowest	56	37	88
price. When the agent selects the supplier, he will have a purchase	70	39	90
order typed. The order is then forwarded to the supplier that gave the	84	42	93
lowest price on the item, often after a phone call has been made to	98	45	96
confirm the award. Extra copies of the order should be sent to account-	112	48	99
ing and receiving as well as to the department that wants to use the item.	127	51	102

1′ GWAM | 1 | 2 | 3 | 4 | 5 | 6 | 7 | 8 | 9 | 10 | 11 | 12 | 13 | 14 |
5′ GWAM | 1 | 2 | 3 |

121C: Tabulating Skill Applications (30)

Problem 1: Boxed Tabulation (*Full sheet; Reading position; Spaces between columns: 10–6–6–6*)

Type the table as shown below. After the table has been typed, type an underline one-half space above and below the columnar headings, and below the last line of the table.

The vertical lines may be ruled with a ball-point pen without removing the paper from the typewriter; use the ratchet release and roll the paper forward to rule the lines. *To type the vertical lines*, indicate with an apostrophe where each of these lines should be typed. Remove the paper; reinsert it with the long side up, and type the vertical lines with the underline key.

Note. Center the dates over the 2-digit items in each column.

OCCUPATIONAL DISTRIBUTION OF EMPLOYED PERSONS

(In Percent)

Classification	1910	1950	1960	1970*	Words in Cols.	Total Words
OCCUPATIONAL DISTRIBUTION OF EMPLOYED PERSONS						9
(In Percent)						12
Classification / 1910 / 1950 / 1960 / 1970*						19
White-collar	22	37	43	45	5	24
Professional, technical (Indent 3)	5	9	11	13	12	31
Proprietary, managerial	7	9	11	11	19	38
Clerical, sales	10	19	21	21	25	44
Blue-collar	37	41	36	36	30	49
Skilled	12	14	13	13	34	53
Semiskilled	14	21	18	18	39	58
Unskilled	11	6	5	5	43	62
Service	10	10	13	13	47	66
Farm	31	12	8	6	50	69
All workers	100	100	100	100	57	76

*Estimated projection. — 80

+ Rules 145

(*Please see page 191 for Problem 2*)

All letters are used.

	GWAM 1'	5'	
In a recent study made by top men who hire office workers, it was	13	3	62
found that the chief weakness among employees was a lack of ability in	27	5	65
analyzing and resolving problems. This was so for those who spent most	42	8	68
of their time typing letters as well as for those who were hired to do	56	11	71
only simple office tasks. There seemed to be quite a big fault among	70	14	74
all office people in doing problems, or jobs, which employers needed to	84	17	77
have done. Those zealous about improving performance in the offices of	99	20	80
the nation are quick to state the need for better skill in handling jobs	113	23	83
as the one vital need of this age. They urge the importance of building	128	26	85
correct work habits, of learning how to use equipment with ease, and of	142	28	88
gaining a usable skill to check all work for both neatness and accuracy.	157	31	91
This investigation, one of several completed by employers, points	13	34	94
to a glaring gap in the education of those planning to enter the busi-	27	37	97
ness world. It emphasizes the fact that one must know how to attack and	42	40	100
solve problems if one wants to succeed in industry. It is insufficient	56	43	102
for typists to be able to copy lessons or tasks from a textbook; there	70	45	105
must be in evidence the capacity to produce usable copy from any source	85	48	108
from which it may come and from any context in which it may appear. One	99	51	111
must possess insights into every facet of office work, must plan well,	114	54	114
and must survive unusual pressures. While potential to succeed depends	128	57	117
upon numerous qualities, ability to work efficiently forever ranks high.	142	60	120

1.6 HA 5.8 70

1' GWAM | 1 | 2 | 3 | 4 | 5 | 6 | 7 | 8 | 9 | 10 | 11 | 12 | 13 | 14 |

5' GWAM | 1 | 2 | 3 |

154D: Related English Check (5) *correct as you type; check results; retype at increased speed*

what kind of work may be expected from a person who "only half tries__

GUIDE: Place the question mark outside the quotation mark when the entire sentence is a question.

LESSON 155

Timed writings in this lesson will be scored in terms of NWAM—the best rate with fewest errors. You should pace yourself, then, to get your best NET rate. Stay mentally and physically relaxed.

155A: Conditioning Practice (8) *3' for pretyping check; then each line three times*

Alphabet; shift	Major Quinzy wrote Dick Laux to buy gifts for sale in South Plainview.	Uniform key stroke
Soc. Sec. Nos.	306-94-4586 279-26-4869 187-01-8959 310-42-3517 312-50-2455 307-10-8763	
Word endings	tion able tial ible sion ally cial ment tain port burg less cate ings	
Fluency	He may spend some time trying to find a plan for the local men to use.	

| 1 | 2 | 3 | 4 | 5 | 6 | 7 | 8 | 9 | 10 | 11 | 12 | 13 | 14 |

Problem 2: Boxed Tabulation

Full sheet
Reading position
DS data
4 spaces between columns

Center primary columnar headings (Male, Female) over the three columns to which each applies.

LABOR MARKET PARTICIPATION BY AGE AND SEX — Words Total: 8

(In Percent) — 11

Age	Male			Female			Words in Cols.	Total Words
								13
								14
	1900	1950	1960	1900	1950	1960		20
14 – 19	62.1	39.9	32.0	26.8	23.0	21.8	8	28
20 – 24	90.6	82.5	83.2	31.7	43.6	44.3	13	35
25 – 34	94.9	92.8	94.9	19.4	32.0	35.4	23	43
35 – 44	94.5	95.2	95.5	15.0	35.2	42.7	30	51
45 – 54	92.8	92.5	92.7	14.2	33.1	46.3	38	58
55 – 64	86.2	83.9	85.1	12.6	23.6	34.3	46	66
65 – up	63.1	41.5	29.7	8.3	7.9	10.1	53	73
All ages	85.7	79.4	77.4	20.0	29.3	34.5	61	81

+ Rules 162

LESSON 122

122A: Conditioning Practice (5) *each line three times*

Alphabet	Jay will make executive organizational plans for the old Quebec firms.	Finger-reach action
Figure-symbol	The #5346 item will cost Oakley & Company $921.78 (less 10% for cash).	
One-hand	Were you aware that the water polo player executed few exciting saves.	
Speed	It is easier to make the figure-key reaches if the fingers are curved.	

| 1 | 2 | 3 | 4 | 5 | 6 | 7 | 8 | 9 | 10 | 11 | 12 | 13 | 14 |

122B: Sentence Guided Writing (15)

TECHNIQUE CUE | Return carriage quickly and start the new line.

1. Type each sentence 3 times on the call of the 15″, 12″, or 10″ guide by your teacher.
2. Type each sentence at *gradually* increasing rates on the call of the 15″, 12″, or 10″ guides.

High-frequency balanced-hand words emphasized.

		Words in Line	GWAM 15″	12″	10″
1	She may work with them and also with us.	8	32	40	48
2	Did both of their men wish to go to the city?	9	36	45	54
3	They may do the work for the chairman of the firm.	10	40	50	60
4	The chairman may sign the form if they wish to be paid.	11	44	55	66
5	They may pay the men for the field work and sign both forms.	12	48	60	72

| 1 | 2 | 3 | 4 | 5 | 6 | 7 | 8 | 9 | 10 | 11 | 12 |

153C: Stroking Technique Refinement – Four-Letter Words (7) *each line three times*

GOAL: Try to type Lines 2, 3, and 4 as rapidly as you type Line 1.

Balanced-hand	down foam dial goal firm with city pair dock fork such wish both worn
Left and right	safe look read monk cave lion rate pool bead hill vase moon cede hull
Combination	such seat form noon then drew wish mill paid sear name hunk held fast
Double letters	been less cell hood door loop seep room peek root hook deed tool cook
	| 1 | 2 | 3 | 4 | 5 | 6 | 7 | 8 | 9 | 10 | 11 | 12 | 13 | 14 |

153D: Related English Check (5) *correct as you type; check results; retype at increased speed*

in a pleading voice she asked, _may I go to the pop concert with him_

GUIDE: Place the question mark inside the quotation mark when only the quoted matter is a question.

LESSON 154

154A: Conditioning Practice (8) *3′ for pretyping check; then each line three times*

Alphabet; shift	Paul Zahn spoke to Jan Axsom about five quick ways to see Dredge Lake.	*Quick, snap stroke*
Telephone Nos.	447-2885 738-7417 241-0290 638-9546 926-0275 357-9060 356-9081 332-1914	
Double Letters	seed pass meet book cool lass hall putt seek puff mass weed razz feed	
Fluency	There was good reason to believe that this work would be done on time.	
	| 1 | 2 | 3 | 4 | 5 | 6 | 7 | 8 | 9 | 10 | 11 | 12 | 13 | 14 |	

154B: Stroking Technique Refinement – Word Beginnings and Endings (7) *each line three times*

NOTE: If necessary see page 235 (152B) to review instructions.

Avoid excessive "bouncing" of the hands when making reaches	ban bar hab hal bro bur het hex cab can hon kin car cap lin lit cen cir
	mal man cli com mar mas con def mel men del des mis mod dif dis mon mys
	bute jury tend pose tric jure sult pute sive hood tive port ward city
	pire tual stic ical grim nity acle ship mity gram icle rity ture lity
	| 1 | 2 | 3 | 4 | 5 | 6 | 7 | 8 | 9 | 10 | 11 | 12 | 13 | 14 |

154C: Improving Sustained Speed and Accuracy (30)

1. Set your goal at the rate typed on your 5′ speed writing in Lesson 153B.
2. Type two 5′ writings on the ¶s on page 239, trying on each writing to reach or better your best speed rate.
3. Compute *gwam* for the higher speed writing.
4. Type two 5′ writings on the ¶s, trying to improve your accuracy. Relax, but concentrate.
5. Compute *nwam* for the more accurate writing.

■ *NWAM* means "net words a minute"; to figure, on a 5′ writing, deduct 2 for each error from your *gwam*.

122C: Building Sustained Tabulating Skill (30)

Time Schedule	
Planning and preparing	3′
Timed tabulating production . .	20′
Proofreading; determining *g-pram*	7′

Arrange the following problem in proper form as you type it. If you complete the problem before 20 minutes are up, start over on a new sheet. When time is called, proofread your copy and determine *g-pram*.

Full sheet
Reading position
DS data
4 spaces between columns

Each figure used a minimum of 25 times.

				Words in Cols.	Total Words
VERDUGO REALTY COMPANY					5
New Listings					7
Name	Address	Phone	Price		16
Lew Alcindor	8943 Valley Circle	678–9212	$56,750	10	26
Robert Anderson	6704 South Jackson	764–2378	69,500	20	36
Thomas Atkins	1410 Orange Grove	241–7609	19,975	30	46
Shirley Barber	1396 Laguna Place	246–7819	47,850	39	56
Lloyd Bush	1522 Allen Avenue	748–2364	39,950	48	65
Byron Callahan	9876 Devonshire Avenue	321–7812	39,500	59	76
James Craven	2460 Elk Drive	748–3062	59,950	68	84
Roger Day	1308 Victory Blvd.	240–1578	53,750	77	93
John Fallon	362 Briggs Terrace	746–1529	43,460	86	103
David Geren	5145 Collet Street	784–3612	62,795	96	112
Gail Goodrich	6331 Victory Blvd.	789–2314	42,500	106	122
Douglas Grant	1228 Irving Avenue	535–1869	17,845	115	132
Jeffrey Sellwood	16954 Strawberry Drive	783–8418	48,500	127	143
John Sutton	423 Valley View Road	563–7859	39,860	136	153
Peter Van Dyke	814 Winchester Avenue	361–2940	35,750	147	163
John Wynhoff	14830 Dickens Place	763–4048	45,900	157	173
Alex Xydias	2615 Delaware Road	257–9238	67,930	166	182

LESSON 123

123A: Conditioning Practice (5) *each line three times*

Quick, snap stroke

Alphabet	Six juicy steaks sizzled over a big wood fire as the quaint men slept.
Figure-symbol	He bought 80 pencils @ 6¢ each; 23 erasers @ 9¢ each; 1 punch @ $4.75.
Fingers 3 and 4	The zealous politician was appalled by the losses in the wool markets.
Speed	Some frustration in life may help us develop a better sense of values.
	| 1 | 2 | 3 | 4 | 5 | 6 | 7 | 8 | 9 | 10 | 11 | 12 | 13 | 14 |

123B: Skill Building – Straight Copy (15) *(Repeat 121B, pages 189–190)*

123C: Measuring Sustained Tabulating Skill (30)

Time Schedule	
Planning and preparing	3′
Timed tabulating production . .	20′
Proofreading; determining *n-pram*	7′

Repeat 122C, above, but erase and correct all errors. When time is called, proofread carefully. Subtract 15 words from the total words typed for each uncorrected error. Determine *n-pram* (net production rate a minute)—rate with all errors corrected.

LESSON 153

153A: Conditioning Practice (8) *3′ for pretyping check; then each line three times*

Alphabet; shift	Zelda Paxsom invited John Cagney for the banquet talk in Warren, Ohio.	*Finger-action reaches*
ZIP Codes	47403 15943 45227 65806 39803 98177 37904 39102 55811 58106 62406 96822	
Left and right	tear kiln were mink dart join bear pump care kink gear pull rare limp	
Fluency	The store selling radios will use much more space for the sales items.	
	| 1 | 2 | 3 | 4 | 5 | 6 | 7 | 8 | 9 | 10 | 11 | 12 | 13 | 14 |	

153B: Maintaining Speed and Accuracy Goals for Sustained Periods (30) *3′ and 5′ writings*

	Time
1. Type a 3′ speed writing on each ¶; determine *gwam*.*	8′
2. Practice difficult words and passages in the ¶ on which you had less *gwam*.	2′
3. Type a 3′ writing on this "slow" ¶.	4′
4. Using both ¶s, type a 5′ speed writing. Record *gwam* for use in Lesson 154.	7′
5. Practice difficult portions of the copy.	2′
6. Type a 5′ writing for accuracy.	7′

All letters are used.

	GWAM 1′	5′	
For one who may have big plans for spending his life in some fine	13	3	62
business firm, there is likely to come a time when that one will start	27	5	65
to think about the type of work being done to prepare for the new, and	42	8	68
probably quite novel, future work experience. And as interest turns to	56	11	71
a study of the entire area of work, some vital human facts are found.	71	14	73
There is a very close and most revealing relationship between the way	84	17	76
most people think and the way they act on the job. Those who like and	98	20	79
seem proud of their jobs tend to do more and better work than those who	113	23	82
have little interest in or who voice great concern about the many tasks	127	25	85
given them to do. There is much to be said for that valid point which	141	28	88
emphasizes the role of suitable attitudes in appraising fitness for work.	156	31	91
Since the way one thinks has much to do with the way one works, it	13	34	93
is essential that a person interested in becoming well prepared for the	28	37	96
rigors of business do many things that will result in truly realistic	42	40	99
attitudes. One of the best ways to develop a positive attitude toward	56	42	102
work is to acquire a sense of confidence; and it is usually true that	70	45	105
confidence is the result of learning how to do things well. Those who	84	48	107
are certain they have the ability to work with skill and with maximum	98	51	110
effectiveness should realize that, for most situations, they have both	112	54	113
the vital power and the potential necessary for job success. There is	127	57	116
much to be said for developing sureness through skill and mental poise.	141	59	119

1′ GWAM | 1 | 2 | 3 | 4 | 5 | 6 | 7 | 8 | 9 | 10 | 11 | 12 | 13 | 14 |
5′ GWAM | 1 | 2 | 3 |

*To convert 5′ *gwam* figures to use for a 3′ writing, multiply your 5′ *gwam* by 5/3.

Unit 20 | Lessons 124-125

Measurement and Evaluation

LESSON 124

124A: Conditioning Practice (5) *each line three times*

Alphabet	Jack Voguel expected to find a buzzing atmosphere in West Quincy, N.H.	*Wrists low and relaxed*
Figure	I sold Jet Record Nos. 47–2115–B, 86–2735–A, 92–0413–C, and 64–8015–Z.	
Long words	Propulsion system and applied aerodynamics specialists are needed now.	
Speed	Often, persons are lonely because they build walls instead of bridges.	
	1 | 2 | 3 | 4 | 5 | 6 | 7 | 8 | 9 | 10 | 11 | 12 | 13 | 14	

124B: Growth Index – Straight Copy  *two 5′ writings; circle errors; determine* gwam

All letters are used.

Education is available in a lot of different sizes and shapes, and it is all an important part of life. Remember when you suddenly realized, as a child, that your left shoe really didn't fit on your right foot? Remember when you learned to tie your shoes, to tell time, or to go to the store alone? These special times represented additions to your learning and to your progress. For some persons, getting an education is the result of just these kinds of day-to-day experiences. For example, a teen-ager who dents the fender on the family car is getting an education when he has to use part of his summer pay, or his allowance, to pay for the repair.

Think of what a loss it is for many millions of good minds to be bored nightly by television re-runs and old movies. The alert person puts an end to this waste of his time. He does this by getting more education––by going back to school. Our educational system is one of the unique things that make this country different from other countries. We must not sell it short and we must not neglect it. Your education does not come to an end when you are graduated from high school or from college––it is a lifelong process. Learning is an essential part of good living; the man who stops learning has, to a degree, stopped living.

1′ GWAM | 1 | 2 | 3 | 4 | 5 | 6 | 7 | 8 | 9 | 10 | 11 | 12 | 13 | 14 |
5′ GWAM | 1 | 2 | 3 |

GWAM 1′	5′	
13	3	54
28	6	57
43	9	60
57	11	63
70	14	66
85	17	68
100	20	71
114	23	74
127	25	77
131	26	78
13	29	80
27	32	83
41	35	86
56	37	89
70	40	92
84	43	94
98	46	97
113	49	100
126	52	103

124C: Letter Production Skill Building (30) *(20′ writing on letters, page 168, as directed below.)*

Time Schedule	
Planning and preparing	3′
Timed production writing . . .	20′
Proofreading; determining *n-pram*	7′

Type each letter, properly placed, on a separate letterhead or plain sheet. Correct all errors. When time is called, proofread each letter. Deduct 15 words from total words typed for each uncorrected error; divide remainder by 20 to determine *n-pram*.

152C: Increasing Stroking Rates (30)

PRACTICE PROCEDURE — Time

A. Type ¶ 1, then ¶ 2, as follows:
  1. Untimed to explore content. — 5′
  2. One 3′ timed writing on each ¶ for speed. — 8′

B. Add 4 *gwam* to your better rate on each ¶ and use this goal rate for an uninterrupted 3′ speed writing on each of the two ¶s as directed:

1. Type for 3 minutes on ¶ 1 for speed. At the end of 3 minutes, your teacher will call "Return." — 3′
2. At the call of "Return," start from the beginning of ¶ 1, again typing for speed. At the end of the second 3 minutes, your teacher will call "time." — 3′
3. At the call of "time," stop typing; determine *gwam* for the better 3′ writing; compare this rate with the 3′ rate recorded for 151B, page 234. — 2′
4. Repeat this procedure for ¶ 2. — 9′

All letters are used.

Text	1′ GWAM*	3′ GWAM*	
To those who may be faced with the need for making precise plans	13	4	104
for a good job in business, here are a few hints which, if kept in mind,	27	9	109
may be found to aid in wise planning. In the first place, it is a fact	42	14	114
well known that a person counting on making a big salary or on the slim	56	19	118
chance of having an income above that made by most workers must have	70	23	123
something of worth to offer a business. No company, in these times of	84	28	128
high and soaring costs, can expect to employ one who does not have top	99	33	132
skill, special traits, or broad experience which can work to the benefit	113	38	137
of the industry. There is no point in asking a firm to give a job to	127	42	142
one who offers little of worth to the company. Since business firms try	142	47	147
to make profit, those who work for firms must help to make that profit.	156	52	152
Although it may be a little difficult to believe, there are few, if	14	57	156
any, special powers or superior personal traits that are gained without	28	61	161
some extra effort on the part of the owner. Those famous men and women	42	66	166
who in the eyes of the world seem to have special gifts or even unique	57	71	170
qualities are people who have certainly paid a big price in the form of	71	76	175
long hours and zealous effort to produce the traits which impress. Not	85	80	180
too many folks strike it rich or make the big time without having some	100	85	185
quality that has been acquired rather than inherited. One of the most	114	90	190
important things all of us should do is pursue a sound program with the	128	95	194
objective of developing a quality that will be both useful and in demand.	143	100	199

1′ GWAM | 1 | 2 | 3 | 4 | 5 | 6 | 7 | 8 | 9 | 10 | 11 | 12 | 13 | 14 |
3′ GWAM | 1 | 2 | 3 | 4 | 5 |

*To convert the 3′ *gwam* figures to use for a 5′ writing, multiply your 3′ *gwam* by 3/5.

152D: Related English Check (5) *correct as you type; check results; retype for speed as time permits*

half voted "yes__ half, "no__ The bill then went "back to committee__

GUIDE: Commas and periods come before, but semicolons follow, quotation marks.

LESSON 125

125A: Conditioning Practice (5) *each line three times*

Alphabet	Fill the big jug quickly with five or six pints of Zimmer's Grape Ade.	Finger-reach action
Figure-symbol	McNeil, Jones & Sons refused to pay invoice #13405 dated May 28, 1967.	
Long reaches	Cecil will bring a number of bright lights to a civic center ceremony.	
Speed	Regrettably, nuances of techniques may be lost in the drive for speed.	
	| 1 | 2 | 3 | 4 | 5 | 6 | 7 | 8 | 9 | 10 | 11 | 12 | 13 | 14 |	

125B: Skill Transfer – Statistical Rough Draft (15) *two 5′ writings; circle errors; determine* gwam

All letters and figures are used.

	GWAM 1′	5′	
Jay Maroni, account ~~number~~ No. 503-30-6212, filed his federal	11	2	52
income tax form 1040 last year with the Internal Revenue serv-	23	5	55
vice. His gross income was $7320.56. After he had made allowances	37	7	57
for his dependents and his other deductions, his federal tax bill ~~amounted to~~ was $618.49.	53	11	60
W-2 forms ~~indicated~~ showed that $462.30 had been ~~deducted~~ withheld by his employer during the year. He had	71	14	64
~~already~~ paid the sum of $127.38 via his quarterly estimates.	82	16	66
Jay then ~~remitted~~ paid the ~~remaining~~ balance of his tax bill, which was $28.81.	94	19	69
No ¶ A state income tax return, as well as a check	103	21	71
for $17.20, was also filed by Jay when it was	112	22	72
due. Thus, his total income tax bill for the	122	24	74
year was $635.69.	125	25	75

	GWAM 1′	5′	
Jay has one son, Zolla, who graduated from college two	11	27	77
years ago. Zolla is single, and he has ~~on~~ no property. His total in-	24	30	80
come for last year was $7150.38. Zolla, account ~~number~~ No.	35	32	82
618-42-1574, filed his federal income tax form 1040-A last year on a	49	35	85
salary of $7150.38. ~~for last year~~ His tax bill amounted to	58	37	87
$1315.49. He also had to pay state taxes in the amount of	70	39	89
$102.64. Zolla and Jay then compared their tax bills. Even though their gross income was about the same,	92	43	93
Zolla paid $697.00 more in federal taxes and $85.44 more in state taxes than did his father.	111	47	97
Zolla's total taxes amounted to $782.44 more than	121	49	99
his father's taxes.	124	50	100

151C: Stroking Technique Refinement – Figures (7)

TYPE: The first line *once*; then each of the other lines at least four times, using good techniques.

IF TIME PERMITS: Select lines for speed emphasis. **Goal:** Increased speed on figure copy.

Avoid excessive hand and arm movement

3d 0; 5f 7j 2s 8k 4f 9l 6j 3d 0; 5f 7j 2s 8k 4f 9l 6j 3d 0; 5f 7j 2s 8k

333 000 555 777 222 888 444 999 111 666 333 000 555 777 222 888 444 999

33 00 55 77 22 88 44 99 11 66 33 00 55 77 22 88 44 99 33 00 55 77 22 88

3 0 5 7 2 8 4 9 1 6 3 0 5 7 2 8 4 9 3 0 5 7 2 8 3 0 5 7 2 8 4 9 1 6 3 0

| 1 | 2 | 3 | 4 | 5 | 6 | 7 | 8 | 9 | 10 | 11 | 12 | 13 | 14 |

151D: Related English Check (5) *correct it as you type*

1. Type the sentence, making needed corrections.
2. Check your corrected copy with your teacher.
3. Read the guide covering the corrections involved.
4. Retype corrected sentence for speed as time permits.

Goal: To learn to apply related English *as you type* for improved problem production

■ *Follow these procedures for all drills of this kind in Part 3.*

mr paul l ritchie has written a new book making your own good luck

GUIDES: Capitalize proper names; follow abbreviations with a period. Titles of books may be underlined or typed in all capital letters.

LESSON 152

152A: Conditioning Practice (8) *3′ for pretyping check; then each line three times*

Fingers curved

Alphabet; shift	Fritz Pomeroy asked Elvin Jacques to exchange news about North Dakota.
Figure review	777 333 999 555 000 444 666 222 888 111 333 000 222 666 444 888 555 50
Left and right	ease jump ward kill cart loin wear junk saws link ware pulp rest lump
Fluency	They mailed the checks to the group soon after the prices were listed.

| 1 | 2 | 3 | 4 | 5 | 6 | 7 | 8 | 9 | 10 | 11 | 12 | 13 | 14 |

152B: Stroking Technique Refinement – High-Frequency Two-Letter Combinations (7)

TYPE: Each line 3 times as follows:

1. At an easy pace to explore stroking patterns.
2. As rapidly as possible to increase speed.
3. At a slightly reduced rate for accuracy.
4. For extra practice, choose your own goal.

■ *Follow these procedures for all technique drills in this unit.*

Move the fingers without pulling the hand out of position

th	that earth bother theater health neither thought beneath weather their
he	hear tithe behead height breathe rehearse helmet seethe inherit reheat
in	incite strain prints infer within drinks insure violin originate begin
er	erupt neater inertia error greater energy errand former adversity verb

| 1 | 2 | 3 | 4 | 5 | 6 | 7 | 8 | 9 | 10 | 11 | 12 | 13 | 14 |

125C: Tabulating Production Measurement (30)

Time Schedule	
Planning and preparing	3′
Timed production writing . . .	20′
Proofreading; determining *n-pram*	7′

If you complete the following problem before 20 minutes are up, start over on a new sheet. Correct all errors. Proofread your work. Deduct 15 words from total words typed for each uncorrected error; divide remainder by 20 to determine *n-pram*.

Full sheet
Reading position
DS data
6 spaces between columns

Each figure is used a minimum of 20 times.

STUDENT SERVICE BUREAU				Words in Cols.	Total Words
					5
Name	Age	Telephone	Skills or Experience		20
Adamson, Judy Anne	15	472–9909	Baby-sitting	9	29
Blees, Jonathan	16	393–7784	Box boy––groceries	18	38
Brown, Steve	16	398–3920	Gardening	25	45
Cleave, James	14	262–8307	Gardening	32	52
Esensten, Mark	15	583–4890	Gardening	40	60
Geren, Jeff	15	304–8032	Typewriting	47	67
Holmes, Phyllis	17	202–0395	Stenographic	55	75
Jacobs, Trudy	16	208–4850	Housework––general	64	84
Jay, Robin	14	462–3489	Baby-sitting	71	91
King, Larry	17	585–0294	Carpenter's helper	80	100
Levitt, Kathy	17	260–3849	Typewriting	88	107
McGlaze, Greg	16	392–3570	Lifeguard	95	115
Nimmer, Becca	16	475–8293	Stenographic	103	122
Nott, Robert	15	478–9263	Gardening	110	129
Olson, Bjorn	15	474–7390	Office––general	118	138
Perry, Susan	16	582–4567	Secretarial	125	145
Prinzmetal, Carol	16	268–2098	Baby-sitting	134	154
Sellwood, Michael	17	580–0764	Painting––general	143	163
Steinberg, Bruce	15	469–9520	Typewriting	152	171
Tabbat, David	17	793–8745	Box boy––groceries	160	180
Wexler, Howard	16	583–5783	Selling––general	169	189
Wolfe, Ernie	16	302–9465	Selling––general	178	197
Wright, Lita	16	306–7802	Baby-sitting	185	205

Unit 25 | Lessons 151-155

Developing Speed with Accuracy

LESSON 151

151A: Conditioning Practice (8) *includes 3′ for pretyping check as directed on page 233*

RECALL: 70-space writing line; 5-space indention for paragraphs. Single-space (SS) sentence drills. Double-space (DS) ¶ writings.

TYPE: Each line three times:
1. Slowly, to refine techniques.
2. Rapidly, to push for speed.
3. Reduce rate slightly for accuracy.

AS TIME PERMITS: Retype selected lines, trying for errorless copy. Place a check mark at the end of each errorless line.

Alphabet; shift	Bromley Koufax was piqued at Gregory Pizor over jaunts to French Lick.	*Fingers curved*
Figure reaches	j7j j7j d3d d3d l9l l9l f4f f4f k8k k8k f5f f5f ;0; ;0; s2s s2s j6j j6j	
Balanced-hand	then work melt foam maid them mend sick pale lame soap they held pane	
Fluency	There is to be a new sales code passed for use in this city very soon.	
	| 1 | 2 | 3 | 4 | 5 | 6 | 7 | 8 | 9 | 10 | 11 | 12 | 13 | 14 |	

151B: Checking Your Present Status – Progressive Difficulty Paragraphs (30)

TYPE: 1′ writings; determine *gwam* on each.

	Time
A. For *each* of the three ¶s:	
1. Type once untimed to explore content.	5′
2. Type one 1′ timing for speed (push).	5′
B. For *each* of the two lower-rate ¶s:	
1. Practice difficult words and passages.	2′
2. Type one 1′ timing to increase speed.	3′

TYPE: 3′ writings; determine *gwam* on each.

	Time
C. Using all three ¶s:	
1. Type two 3′ timings for speed.	8′
2. Practice difficult phrases.	2′
3. Type one 3′ timing for accuracy.	5′

■ Record the better 3′ speed rate to compare with 3′ rates in Lesson 152.

All letters are used.

	GWAM 1′	3′	
The chief aim of all typing effort should be to try to build the	13	4	74
best skill possible. It does not make much difference whether you plan	27	9	79
to use this new skill for home, school, office, or other fine purpose;	42	14	84
the real object of all practice must be to try to gain top skill. The	56	19	89
best way you can get ready for the future is to build typing power now.	70	23	93
There is no magic method or simple system by which you can build	13	28	98
usable typing power. To be able to attain high levels, you must expend	27	32	102
extra energy, spend many hours in proper practice from copy that gives	42	37	107
ideas for growth, and try, as well, to make the best and most effective	56	42	112
work habits a focus in each action. Great skill is built, not bestowed.	70	47	117
Those who would head for the top of the skill ladder must be able	13	51	121
to adjust to various practice routines with great optimism. No single	27	56	126
activity can supply the variety of technique experiences so necessary	41	60	131
for sound growth and progress. Type awkward and fluent copy with equal	56	65	135
zest; and remember always that fine skill is a result of lively effort.	70	70	140

1′ GWAM | 1 | 2 | 3 | 4 | 5 | 6 | 7 | 8 | 9 | 10 | 11 | 12 | 13 | 14 |
3′ GWAM | 1 | 2 | 3 | 4 | 5 |

Unit 21 | Lessons 126-132

Office Typing Problems; Business Forms

LESSONS 126-132

126A: Conditioning Practice *(Lessons 126–132)* (5) *each line three times*

Type with continuity

Alphabet	Some Hi-Fi fans adopt with zeal or absorb quickly an extensive jargon.
Figure-symbol	Review of figures and symbols: "2," #3, $4, 5%, 6, 7&, 8', (9), (10).
	Electric: 2@, 6¢, 8*,
One-hand	Are you going to send an abstract of the monopoly case to him by noon?
Speed	The more that is left to chance, the less chance there is for success.
	| 1 | 2 | 3 | 4 | 5 | 6 | 7 | 8 | 9 | 10 | 11 | 12 | 13 | 14 |

126B: Selected Goal Practice – Progressive Difficulty Paragraphs *(Lessons 126, 129, 132)* (15)

1. *Speed.* Type two 1′ writings on each ¶ for speed. Do this by proper reading of the copy and by keeping the stroking action in your fingers. As you type ¶s 2 and 3, try to maintain the rate of ¶ 1. Your teacher will guide your writing by calling each quarter-minute interval.

2. *Control.* Type two 1′ writings on each ¶ for control (not over 1 error each minute). Select a rate that is 4 to 8 *gwam* below your speed rate. Try to type exactly at this rate as your teacher guides your writing by calling each quarter-minute interval. Type with continuity.

¶ 1
5.0 AWL

There are many kinds of energy. It takes energy to run or walk. It takes energy just to sit and think. To type the words on this page takes a great amount of energy. As you grow in typing skill, you will expend less energy and still type more words in the same amount of time.

¶ 2
6.0 AWL

An underlying concept in any skill is the ability to relax, but this does not imply the absence of mental and physical effort. Contrarily, a maximum amount of physical and mental effort must be maintained; yet the typist must remain calm, relaxed, and relatively free of tension.

¶ 3
7.0 AWL

As you become increasingly competent in typewriting, measurable returns in relation to practice may seemingly diminish. It is important not to reduce effort at this point. Accept this challenge to higher excellence, remembering that mankind has tremendous capabilities to excel.

Preparing for Business

In your prior study of typewriting you developed the ability to type with both speed and accuracy. In addition, you learned to type an impressive array of personal and business papers. You also built a solid foundation for further typing growth and development.

Now, in this first phase of advanced typewriting, you will build even greater speed and accuracy, and also acquire improved know-how and competence in performing office typing jobs.

You will learn to solve new problems, to handle variations in office procedure, and to follow a tested plan for developing real production typing proficiency. You will gain new skill and learn to transfer that skill from classroom to office typing situations.

DAILY PRETYPING CHECK

Three minutes are at first allowed as part of the conditioning practice for the "readiness" check. See how quickly you can learn to make a careful check. You may feel rushed, but only at first.

Make and Check Machine Adjustments: As an ace pilot checks important operating controls of his plane before takeoff, so you must check certain part of your typewriter to determine their readiness for work *before* you "take off" to type the materials of each lesson. So learn to check your machine both thoroughly and quickly. Your success in typewriting will be influenced by the operating readiness of your typewriter.

Daily, before typing, use the check list given at the right to determine the operating readiness of your machine.

1. Place PAPER GUIDE **8** at *zero* (0), or as otherwise directed.
2. Set PAPER-BAIL ROLLS **13** to divide the paper into thirds.
3. Set RIBBON CONTROL **22** on black.
4. Set MARGIN STOPS **7** and **15** for a 70-space line.
5. Clear TAB **31**; set TAB **23** for 5-space indention. Try TAB KEY or BAR **24**.
6. Try PLATEN (Cylinder) **14**; place RATCHET RELEASE **6** and PAPER RELEASE LEVER **16** in "set" position.
7. Move carriage from side to side using CARRIAGE-RELEASE **4** and **18**.
8. Set LINE-SPACE REGULATOR **5** and test RETURN LEVER or KEY **1** for accurate spacing.

Check Keyboard Action: To learn whether the keys are moving properly (not sticking or sluggish) and whether the shift keys and space bar have good action, type the alphabet, capitalizing alternate letters and spacing once between letters. Then, a double space below the alphabet, type a line of the figures 1 through 0. Your copy should look like that shown at the foot of this page.

Inspect Your Copy: If copy appears too light because of a worn ribbon or untidy because of dirty type, make plans with your teacher for you to change the ribbon or clean the type.

Shift for capitals and space between letters or figures with minimum waste motion.

A b C d E f G h I j K l M n O p Q r S t U v W x Y z

DS

1 2 3 4 5 6 7 8 9 0 1 2 3 4 5 6 7 8 9 0 1 2 3 4 5 6

126C: Growth Index – Straight Copy *(Lessons 128 and 131)* (15) *two 5′ writings*

All letters are used.

LA 1.4 54 80		GWAM 1′	5′	
	If you were to ask an employer what one quality he considers of most	14	3	54
	importance in an employee, chances are he would say dependability. To be	29	6	57
	able to depend on a worker is of great importance to an employer who has	43	9	60
	to plan the work so that it will be completed properly and on time. If	58	12	63
	the employer isn't sure that the worker will be on the job and that he	72	14	66
	can do the job, his problems increase. Another source of concern is the	86	17	69
	worker who arrives at work ten to fifteen minutes late. All workers	100	20	71
	should recognize that this practice does not make a good impression.	114	23	74
	Dependability starts with being at work every day and being there on time.	129	26	77
LA 1.4 54 80	Just being at work, however, is only the start on the road to depend-	14	29	80
	ability. The employer also considers how well you do your work and the	28	31	83
	way in which you do it. If he can assign an exacting task to you and	42	34	85
	depend on your doing the task in the right way and on time, you should	56	37	88
	quickly become a valued employee. If you are the type that can never	70	40	91
	quite finish the task without coming back for further instructions, or	84	43	94
	if the task sometimes must be corrected by someone else, watch out! Your	93	46	97
	type can be replaced--and probably soon will be. Make it a practice to	114	49	100
	be a dependable employee, and you can depend on continuous employment.	127	51	103

1′ GWAM | 1 | 2 | 3 | 4 | 5 | 6 | 7 | 8 | 9 | 10 | 11 | 12 | 13 | 14 |
5′ GWAM | 1 | 2 | 3 |

126D: Skill Transfer – Statistical Rough Draft *(Lessons 127 and 130)* (15) *two 5′ writings*

	GWAM 1′	5′	
A study of 225 regular-copy 5' writings of second-half	11	2	25
first-year typing students has shown a total of 1,673 errors,	23	5	27
and 315 were errors in another area			
of which 1,358 were keyboard errors. Of the 1,358 errors	42	8	31
of the first group, 56.1% were left-hand errors, and 43.9%	54	11	34
were right-hand errors. ~~Approximately~~ *about* 48.5% of the 1,358	64	13	36
keyboard errors were made on the third bank, 30.5% were made	76	15	38
on the home row, and 21.0% were made the on first bank. Of	88	18	40
the 315 other-area errors, 60.3% were space, 19.4% were shift-	101	20	43
key, and another 19.4% were ~~miscellaneous~~ *of one kind or another* reading errors.	114	23	46

(Continued on page 198)

3. Proofreading Skill Measurement—Alertness Check (15)

The "Correct-It-As-You-Type" letter shown below contains many proofreading errors: misspelled words; errors of word division, capitalization, punctuation, and number usage; errors of spacing and paragraphing; omitted words. Follow these steps:

1. Make all necessary proofreading corrections as you type the letter.
2. After you have completed the letter, circle any uncorrected proofreading errors you have as your teacher reads the corrections. Mark the necessary corrections on your copy.
3. Score your proofreading skill by deducting 2 points from 100 for each uncorrected proofreading error.

Modified block,
¶s indented
Current date on Line 12
Mixed punctuation
Correct all
typing errors

Words

Mr. Jeffrey Dasteel, Manager | Student Typewriting service | Ft. Wayne 17
High School | Ft. Wayne, Indiana 46807 28
Your letter about the need for proofreeding on the part of all 41
typist's is a reel concern to us, to. Listed hear are some of the st- 55
eps in profreading that we require our typist's to learn and to fo- 68
llow: 69
1. Check the placement and general form of the letter: 81
Is the letter well balanced on the page? Does it 91
look like a picture in a frame? Have all keys ben 101
struck with uniform force? Will the leter made a 111
good first impression. 116
2. Check the correctniss of all figures and amonts: Is the adress 130
correct? Are the street name and numbers correct? Has the typist been 145
consistent in typing figures, such as eight, 26, forty-two. 155
3. Check the exactness of the content, including the grammer and spel- 169
ling: does the letter make good cents and does it convay the intended 183
meaning? Are the words divided correctly at the ends of lines? Are their 198
any mispelled words in the letter? are there any errors of capitalization 213
or punctuation. 216
dont hesitate to rite to us for any other help we can give you. I 230
wish you continued success with your student typewriting service 244
sincerely yurs | christopher york | communications consultant | (215) 256

4. Spelling Skill Measurement (10) (*half sheet; SS data; 6 spaces between columns*)

Arrange the list of words given below in an attractive 3-column table as the words are dictated to you by your teacher. Do this:

1. Determine the vertical and horizontal placement of the table before dictation is started. There will be 12 words in each column. Assume the longest line in each column has 10 letters.
2. Center the main heading; then close your book and type and tabulate from column to column as the words are dictated to you.
3. After the list has been dictated, open your book and check the spelling of each word. Circle each word that you misspelled.

Main heading: WORDS FREQUENTLY MISSPELLED |

accommodate definition planned | argument desirable privilege | atten-

dance difference proceed | beginning enough profited | belief existence

quantity | believe government receive | brief losing recommend | busi-

ness mileage referring | calendar misspell separate | conferring occasion

studying | copying occurred supersede | definite permitted weird |

	GWAM 1'	5'	
The fact that *many* students do not type with good form *may have been* ~~was~~	14	3	26
~~probably~~ a reason for a sizeable percentage of the 1,358 key-	24	5	28
board errors. For example, 27.4% of these were adjacent-key	36	7	30
errors, of which 65.7~~$~~% were made with the left hand and 34.3%	49	10	33
were made with the right hand. ¶ Failure to use even stroking	89	18	41
pressure was a reason for 12.7% of the errors, and *inferior* ~~poor~~ typ-	102	20	43
ing response patterns *may have been* ~~probably were~~ the cause of another	113	23	46
20.9%. *Students may not know that such errors as these may be a result of hand-and-arm movement which forces the fingers out of proper position.*	114	23	46

126E: Skill Applications (*Lessons 126 to 132*) (30)

Problem 1: Interoffice Memorandum

Type the interoffice memorandum as illustrated below. Make a carbon copy. Use 1″ side margins; correct all errors that you make. Type on the control level.

INTEROFFICE CORRESPONDENCE **henderson and sons**

TO: Francene Nott, Steno. Dept. **DATE:** September 21, 19--

FROM: Jeffrey Sellwood, Manager **SUBJECT:** Letter Styles

Effective October 1, all our letters are to be typed in the block style (all lines beginning flush with the left margin). Will you please announce this policy change to all members of your department.

We are making this style letter change because research conducted in the sales department with this letter style during the past three months has indicated that its use enables typists to produce letters more quickly. The net result has been an amazing reduction in letter typing production costs.

Also, will you please assume responsibility for the retraining program that may be needed to familiarize our typists with the block letter style.

hj

LESSON 150

150A: Conditioning Practice (5) *each line three times*

Alphabet	Murky haze enveloped a city as jarring quakes broke forty-six windows.	*Type with continuity and rhythm*
Figure	Today Vi sold 34 dresses, 56 hats, 78 ties, 90 shirts, and 12 jackets.	
Adjacent key	Rewards received for services rendered are related to effort expended.	
Speed	In life, your position is not nearly so important as your disposition.	
	| 1 | 2 | 3 | 4 | 5 | 6 | 7 | 8 | 9 | 10 | 11 | 12 | 13 | 14 |	

150B: Skill Measurement – Employment Testing (45)

1. **Straight-Copy Skill Measurement** (8) *repeat 149B–1, page 229; goal: to improve your rate*

2. **Related Learning Measurement** (12) (*74-space line*)

Type the problem sentences given below, making appropriate corrections at the points of color underlines as the sentences are typed. Follow these steps:

1. Type the number of the sentence; then type the sentence in corrected form. Triple-space after each sentence.
2. Type the sentences from your teacher's dictation as they are dictated with the corrections indicated. Type the dictated sentence on the line below the sentence to which it applies.
3. Mark your sentences for related learning errors. Record number of errors with your name.

1. Colors of a spectrum are violet blue green yellow orange and red.
2. he will meet the governor at the century club on tuesday of next week.
3. As I was washing the sergeant a man no one liked suddenly appeared.
4. I shall be at my office at 10 30 am, and I shall leave at 11 30 am.
5. 8 visitors from the east are here; fifteen or 20 more will arrive soon.
6. Spectrum tables show to a ten-billionth of a millimeter color lines.
7. The letters exhibit 1 and the documents exhibit 13 will be needed.
8. He said, his exact words were I want to go there in a day or two.
9. The letter didnt arrive in fact it couldnt since it wasnt mailed.
10. A boys tricycle was found, but the girls bicycles are still missing.
11. It is difficult to tell your 5s from your 6s. Sell Chicago Fund 4's.
12. Before you leave today, please take the book to Sister Alexis office.
13. Johns class of 67 will meet today. cross your t s and dot your i s.

Study the telegram illustrated at the right below. Observe these items:

1. *Type of Service.* Domestic or International.
2. *Class of Service.* Telegram, Day Letter, etc. Class desired indicated by (X).
3. *Charge to.* Company to be billed for message. (Set tab 2 spaces inside box to start name.)
4. *Sender's Address; Date.* A triple space below the account name. (Use tab to start directly under the account charged.)
5. *Address.* A double space below the date and at the left margin; single-space.
6. *Body of Message.* 1″ margins; either single- or double-spaced.
7. *Sender's Name.* A double space below the message. (Use tab to start under sender's address and date that were typed under the printed heading.)
8. *Reference Initials.* If a company name is typed on the telegram, type the name or initials of the dictator and the typist at the left, a double space below the typed *sender's name.*
9. *Sender's Address and Telephone.* If not to be transmitted, type at left; if to be transmitted, type under sender's name.

Note. The number of carbon copies needed depends upon local needs as well as the type of telegraphic facilities available. Three carbon copies are often required: *File, Customer, Accounting Office.*

Problem 2: Telegram

Type the telegram as illustrated. Make two carbon copies on plain half sheets. Proofread and make all corrections needed.

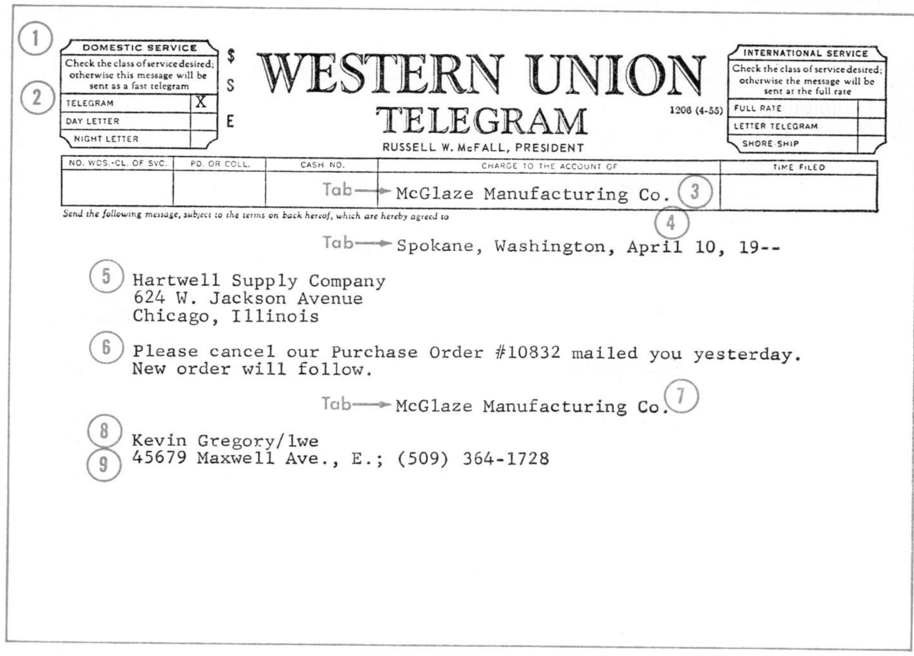

DOMESTIC SERVICE
Check the class of service desired; otherwise this message will be sent as a fast telegram

TELEGRAM	X
DAY LETTER	
NIGHT LETTER	

WESTERN UNION
TELEGRAM
1206 (4-55)
RUSSELL W. McFALL, PRESIDENT

INTERNATIONAL SERVICE
Check the class of service desired; otherwise the message will be sent at the full rate

FULL RATE	
LETTER TELEGRAM	
SHORE SHIP	

NO. WDS.-CL. OF SVC.	PD. OR COLL.	CASH NO.	CHARGE TO THE ACCOUNT OF	TIME FILED
		Tab→	McGlaze Manufacturing Co.	

Send the following message, subject to the terms on back hereof, which are hereby agreed to

Tab→ Spokane, Washington, April 10, 19--

Hartwell Supply Company
624 W. Jackson Avenue
Chicago, Illinois

Please cancel our Purchase Order #10832 mailed you yesterday.
New order will follow.

Tab→ McGlaze Manufacturing Co.

Kevin Gregory/lwe
45679 Maxwell Ave., E.; (509) 364-1728

Problem 3: Night Letter

Type the following as a night letter. Make 2 cc's on half sheets. Charge message to: **National Fiber Company**. Type your initials for reference.

Houston, Texas April 18, 19–– Continental Distributors, Inc. 5634 Middleground Road Savannah, Georgia On March 24 the Memphis plant shipped Invoice #163028 for American Weavers, Inc., New Orleans, Louisiana, in Crate #17, weighing 329#. A shortage of Item Z–29 has been reported. Investigate details of claim and report findings. Also report the reweight on the merchandise. Paul Smith *Address not to be transmitted:* 4250 Mayflower

Problem 4: Error Corrections (*Line: 60; DS; Center vertically on half sheet*)

Certain corrections may be made by squeezing letters into half spaces, or by squeezing or spreading the letters of an entire word into the available space. Such corrections are explained in 67D, p. 110.

Type the sentences (with numbers) as given below; then make the corrections shown in parentheses after each sentence. Use as a heading: PROBLEM 4: ERROR CORRECTIONS

1. This sentence has an omitte_letter at the end of a word. (Squeeze "d" into the half space.)
2. This sentence has an omitted letter at the_eginning of a word. (Squeeze "b" into the half space.)
3. This sentence has a leter omitted within a word. (Erase "leter" and type "letter.")
4. This sentence has a lettter added within a word. (Erase "lettter" and type "letter.")
5. This sentence has lettres of a word transposed. (Erase "re" and type "er.")

2. Tabulation-Copy Skill Measurement (*unarranged copy*) (28)

Time Schedule	
Planning and preparing	3′
Tabulation production timing . .	20′
Proofreading; determining *g-pram*	5′

Arrange the following problem in proper form as you type it. You will have about 3′ to determine the setup of the table; make pencil notations of the points at which heading lines are to be started. Stay ALERT as you type. Proofread; determine *g-pram*.

Full sheet
Reading position
DS columnar data
4 spaces between columns
Longest line in each column color underlined

Each figure is used a minimum of 15 times.

When a street has a number as its name, separate the house number from the street number by a hyphen preceded and followed by a space.

				Words in Cols.	Total Words
Main heading: NEW ACCOUNTS					3
Secondary heading: (Spring Quarter)					6
Columnar headings: Name	Street Address	City and State	ZIP Code		23
Colette Berman	7820 Thurston Circle	Los Angeles, Calif.	90049	12	35
Lyn Clark	848 Allen Street	Hackensack, N.J.	07601	22	45
Dorothy Ford	63 Sea Cliff Avenue	Sea Cliff, N.Y.	11579	33	56
Mary Garcia	8488 Fenton Street	Denver, Colo.	80227	44	66
John Iskra, Jr.	939 Riverview Drive	Columbus, Ohio	43202	55	78
Frank B. Johnston	483 Danbury Street	Wichita, Kansas	67220	67	89
William Lower	4659 Portola Drive	San Francisco, Calif.	94127	79	102
Keven McGlaze	5659 E. Upsal Street	Philadelphia, Pa.	19150	91	114
Warren Meyer, Jr.	8385 Sam Cooper Road	Knoxville, Tenn.	37918	103	126
Paul Mooradian	4668 Star Lane, N.E.	Minneapolis, Minn.	55421	115	138
David M. Phillips	3947 E. Broad Street	Tampa, Florida	33610	127	150
Jay W. Robertson	56 Gloucester Street	Boston, Mass.	02100	139	162
Richard Rogers	3948 W. Elm Street	Greensboro, N.C.	27406	151	174
Jasper Sawatzky	6789 Chicago Avenue	Evanston, Ill.	60201	162	185
Gary E. Thompson	1391 Fontaine Road	Lexington, Ky.	40502	174	196
Barton Wigge	4758 Indigo Street	Houston, Texas	77035	184	207
Barbara Wilson	629 – 19th St., N.W.	Oklahoma City, Okla.	73127	197	220
Kenneth Zimmer	3465 Clematis Blvd.	Pittsburgh, Pa.	15235	208	231

3. Envelope Skill Measurement (9)

a. Type as many small envelopes as you can (using the addresses above) as you are timed for 5′. Start with the first address. Use appropriate titles: *Miss* or *Mr.* with each name. DS a 3-line address.

b. Determine envelope *gwam* by dividing words typed (*Words in Columns* figures) by 5. Put addressed envelopes in order; record your name and rate on first envelope. Put a rubber band around envelopes.

AmegA Wholesale Supply Company

INVOICE

2742 Ferguson Street, Minneapolis, Minnesota 55403 (612) 247-9163

Sales Department

Sold To	Tridea Engineering, Inc. 22 North Grand Avenue Long Beach, California 90806	Date	November 19, 19--
		Our No.	GJ-5032
		Cust. Order No.	H-32068
Terms	2/10, n/30	Shipped Via	REA Express

Quantity	Description	Unit Price	Amount
2 ea.	J-2643 Cylinder Grinders	45.32 ea.	90.64
12 sets	FH 291 Bushing Driver Sets	5.98 set	71.76
24 ea.	KX 102 Oil Pan Gaskets	.75 ea.	18.00
1 ea.	W 2358 Torque Wrench	21.88 ea.	21.88
2 doz.	NX 4215 Weldor's Goggles	30.00 doz.	60.00
2 ea.	10-foot Engineer Rods	15.00 ea.	30.00
1 doz.	50-foot Steel Tapes	40.00 doz.	40.00
			332.28
Margin	Tab	Tab	Tab

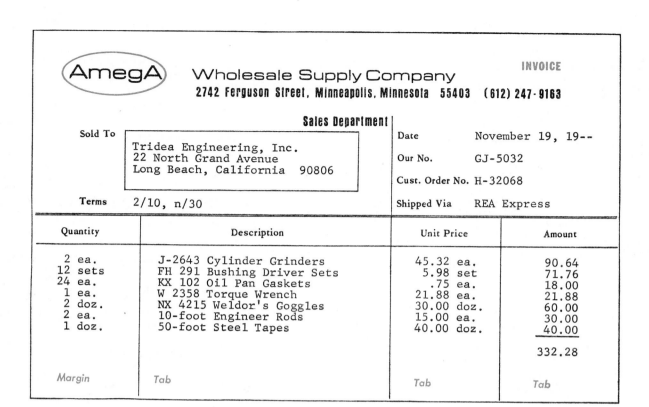

Problem 5: Invoice

Type an invoice from the illustration above. If the printed form is not available, do not type the material that would ordinarily be printed, but arrange the typewritten material in the same manner as that in which the insertions would be typed on the printed forms.

Set tab stops for the items to be typed. In typing invoice items, type across the line, using the tab key or bar to move from column to column. In the amount column underline the last amount, then double-space to type the total figure.

Proofread and correct the copy before removing it from the typewriter.

Fold the invoice for a window envelope (See Reference Guide, page vi).

Problem 6: Invoice

Type the following invoice on the appropriate form. Make 2 cc's on plain half sheets. Correct errors.

Sold To	Tridea Engineering, Inc. 22 North Grand Avenue Long Beach, California 90806	Date	November 20, 19––
		Our No.	GJ–5097
		Cust. Order No.	H–32086
		Shipped Via	Red Ball Express
Terms	2/10, n/30		

Quantity	Description	Unit Price	Amount
10 cases	10W–30 quart cans Modern Motor Oil	13.95 case	139.50
2 C	CX 4139 Plastic Funnels	20.00 C	40.00
1 M	1/2-inch, Galvanized Reducing Elbows	100.00 M	100.00
5 C	1 1/2-inch, 45° Elbows for Drainage	12.00 C	60.00
10 ea.	60-ft. coils 3/8-inch Copper Tubing	10.00 ea.	100.00
3 M	3/8-inch Coupling––Copper to Copper	20.00 M	60.00
50 rolls	KC 91, 1-inch Clear Repair Tape	.50 roll	25.00
			524.50

149B: Skill Measurement – Employment Testing (45)

1. Straight-Copy Skill Measurement (8) *5′ writing; circle errors; determine* gwam

	GWAM 1′	5′	

All letters are used.

Some of you may soon be moving from a somewhat structured school 13 3 69
situation to a relatively unstructured work situation. One of your ini- 27 5 72
tial problems may be the wise use of your work time. It is always easy 42 8 75
to waste time; this fact becomes even more obvious in a work situation. 56 11 78
For instance, most firms have a coffee or rest break in the morning and 71 14 80
again in the afternoon. An employee may take more than the allotted 84 17 83
time for the break. This practice is, in a very genuine sense, nearly 99 20 86
the same as stealing from the employer because the employee is being 112 22 89
paid for work time he is not spending on the job. Your employer has a 127 25 92
right to expect that you will use your work time in a conscientious and 141 28 94
responsible way. One way to do this is to plan and organize your work 155 31 97
so that it can be completed within a specified time period. 167 33 100

Still another distinct problem may be in the human relations domain. 14 36 102
In the world of work you will associate with many different kinds of 28 39 105
people. Some of these persons you may like and others you may dislike; 42 42 108
yet it is essential that you learn how to get along with those whom you 57 45 111
may not care for as well as with those whom you like. If you are to 70 47 114
improve your relations with others, you often will have to make an ear- 84 50 117
nest effort to do so. In trying situations, you will learn that good 98 53 119
manners are a positive asset. Also, you should realize that the irrita- 113 56 122
tions and issues of the work situation can easily be transmitted into 127 59 125
curt or impatient dealings with the clients of the firm by whom you are 141 62 128
employed. As you can see, your employer has a direct and distinct concern 156 65 131
in how well you can get along with others. 164 66 133

1′ GWAM | 1 | 2 | 3 | 4 | 5 | 6 | 7 | 8 | 9 | 10 | 11 | 12 | 13 | 14 |
5′ GWAM | 1 | 2 | 3 |

TRIDEA ENGINEERING, INC.
22 North Grand Avenue
Long Beach, California 90806

No. 217 November 24, 19 --

Pay to the Order of Amega Wholesale Supply Company $ 839.64

Eight hundred thirty-nine and 64/100------------------------------ Dollars

Long Beach National Bank
239 North Atlantic Blvd.
Long Beach, California 90825

⑆1214⑈007⑆ 1426938⑈

Treasurer, TRIDEA ENGINEERING, INC.

DETACH THIS STUB BEFORE CASHING ABOVE CHECK — VOUCHER CHECK

TO
Amega Wholesale Supply Company
2742 Ferguson Street
Minneapolis, Minnesota 55403

TRIDEA ENGINEERING, INC.
22 North Grand Avenue
Long Beach, California 90806

IN PAYMENT OF THE FOLLOWING INVOICES

DATE	INVOICE	AMOUNT
11/19	GJ-5032	332.28
11/20	GJ-5097	524.50
		856.78
	Less 2%	17.14
	Net	839.64

Note. One part of a voucher check is a standard check; the other lists or explains items covered by the check.

Problem 7: Voucher Check

Type a voucher check from the illustration. If the printed form is not available, type a specimen form; then type the appropriate information on the ruled lines and on the check stub. Correct errors as you type.

Problem 8: Voucher Check

Type a voucher check using the same firm names as shown in the illustration above: December 15, 19––; Check No. 982; $236.96. Invoices: 12/6, GJ–6894, $156.72; 12/8, GJ–7014, $85.08; total, $241.80; Less 2%, $4.84; Net, $236.96.

Problem 9: Index Card Mailing List

Mailing lists, as well as other reference items, are frequently typed on 5″ x 3″ index cards.

DO: 1. Type a 5″ x 3″ index card (or paper cut to that size) from the illustration. Type a similar index card for each of the firms given in 117C, page 185.
2. Arrange the typed cards in alphabetic order by firm name. Identify your index card mailing list by typing and centering vertically and horizontally the following information, double-spaced, on another index card: *MAILING LIST* | *your name* | *name of your school* | *city and state*. Put a rubber band around the completed cards and save them for later use.

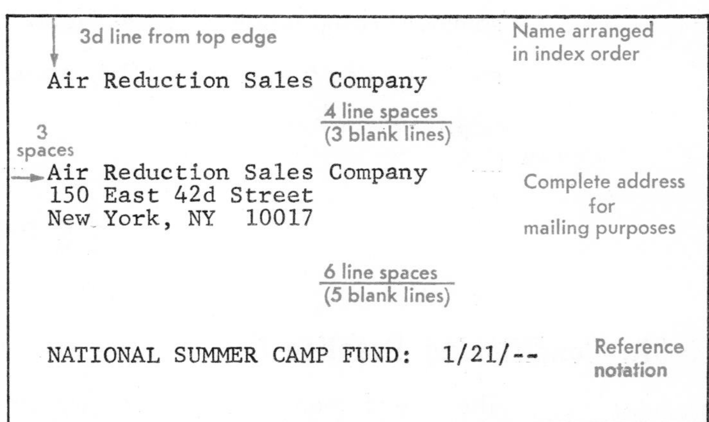

Problem 10: Addressing Large Envelopes

Drill: Type 12 large envelopes to the first 12 addresses of the *mailing list* you prepared in Problem 9. Mark the envelopes: **Attention Public Relations Director** (Reference Guide, page vi).

Note. Beginning office typists should be able to type about two envelope addresses a minute. Try to meet this standard. Do this by pre-positioning the envelopes for easy pickup: *Flaps down, face up.*

Note. Travel item refers to costs of operating a car or using public transportation.

All numbers are used.

	GWAM 1'	5'	
The findings of a recent poll show that 53 percent of the families	13	3	56
in our nation earn about $6,000 a year. The head of the house is near	28	6	59
40 years of age, he is married, and he has had from 10 to 12 years of	42	8	62
school. It takes $5,000 a year for the family to meet common costs.	56	11	65
The costs are as follows: food, 25%, shelter, 29%; clothing, 10%;	69	14	67
medical care, 6%; travel, 16%; personal care, 3%; recreation, 4%; educa-	83	17	70
tion, 1%; and other items, 6%.	89	18	71
In contrast, the findings show that 25 percent of the families earn	14	21	74
less than $3,000 a year. The head of the house is 59 years of age, and	28	23	77
he has had only 7 years of school. The assets of the families shrink	42	26	80
at a rate of $270 a year. A list of the common costs that must be met	56	29	83
is given here: food, 29%; shelter, 33%; clothing, 7%; medical care, 8%;	71	32	86
travel, 10%; personal care, 3%; recreation, 3%; education 0.4%; and	85	35	88
other expenses, 6.6%.	89	36	89
At the upper end of the scale, the findings reveal that 22 percent	13	38	92
of the families earn income of $13,000 a year. The head of the house	27	41	95
is just 46 years of age. He has had at least 12 years of school. The	42	44	98
family spends over $8,600 a year to pay for common costs. A list of the	56	47	100
common costs is given here: food, 23%; shelter, 28%; clothing, 12%;	70	50	103
medical care, 6%; travel, 16%; personal care, 3%; recreation, 5%; educa-	84	52	106
tion, 2%; and other items, 5%.	90	54	107

1' GWAM | 1 | 2 | 3 | 4 | 5 | 6 | 7 | 8 | 9 | 10 | 11 | 12 | 13 | 14 |
5' GWAM | 1 | 2 | 3 |

LESSON 149

149A: Conditioning Practice (15) *each line three times*

Alphabet	The proud man quickly won five prizes in the high jumping exhibitions.	Finger-reach action
Learning *	one, 1; forty, 40; one, twenty-seven, 127; twelve, seventy-three, 1273	
Figure	121 374 561 902 836 984 570 573 920 4682 3057 6481 9362 4857 1920 5647	
Speed	No job has a future—the future is with the person who holds that job.	

| 1 | 2 | 3 | 4 | 5 | 6 | 7 | 8 | 9 | 10 | 11 | 12 | 13 | 14 |

***** *Read, think, and type numbers in two-digit sequences, whenever possible.*

Problem 11: Addressing Small Envelopes—3′ writing

1. Type as many small envelopes as you can as you are timed for 3 minutes. Use the addresses shown on your mailing list. Arrange the envelopes for easy pickup. *Flaps down and away from you, face up; envelopes on left.*

2. Count the number of envelopes addressed. Record this information with your name in the upper left corner of the first envelope or on a separate slip of paper. Put the addressed envelopes in order, and put a rubber band around them.

Problem 12: Special Business Letter Variations

Step 1: Learning the Placement of Attention and Subject Lines

Preview. Study the illustration. Note that the *attention line* is typed a double space below the last line of the address. In the block and modified block letter styles, the attention line begins at the left margin. The *subject line* is typed a double space below the salutation. It may be centered, as illustrated or typed at the left margin. Also, the word SUBJECT (all capitals or first letter capitalized) may be used as a heading for the line.

```
SUBJECT:  National Summer Camp Fund
```

The trend in business offices is to omit the word *Subject.*

Special Drill. Type the opening parts of a business letter (given in unarranged form at the right) as follows: (1) Arrange the material in proper letter form; set stops for 1″ side margins; space four times (3 blank lines) between the date and the address; (2) after the first typing, DS, and repeat the lines two times.

```
                                        January 13, 19--



Air Reduction Sales Company
150 East 42d Street
New York, New York  10017

Attention Public Relations Director

Gentlemen:

                  NATIONAL SUMMER CAMP FUND

     Although the rest of the country may be battling knee-deep
snow drifts, here in our office "It's June in January" and we are
"knee deep in June."  It is in January that
```

MODIFIED BLOCK STYLE WITH AN ATTENTION LINE AND CENTERED SUBJECT LINE

January 13, 19–– Air Reduction Sales Company 150 East 42d Street New York, New York 10017 Attention Public Relations Director Gentlemen: NATIONAL SUMMER CAMP FUND (¶) Although the rest of the country may be battling knee-deep snow drifts, here in our office "It's June in January" and we are "knee deep in June." It is in January that

Step 2: Learning to Type the Heading for the Second Page of a Two-Page Letter

Preview. Two forms that may be used for the heading of the second page, as well as additional pages, of a letter are illustrated at the right. These headings are started about an inch from the top of the page. A triple space (two blank lines) is used between the heading and the first line of the body of the letter. The second page is typed on plain white paper of the same quality as that used for letterhead sheet.

Special Drill. Type three times each (using 1″ side margins) the heading and the opening lines of the second page (given in unarranged form at the right) in both forms illustrated. After the first typing, DS, and repeat twice.

```
Air Reduction Sales Company
Page 2
January 13, 19--


nation.  Your contribution will go 100 percent to the NATIONAL
SUMMER CAMP FUND because all fund raising, labor, and counseling
are supplied on a voluntary basis.  A return envelope is enclosed
for your convenience.
```

PAGE 2 HEADING, VERTICAL FORM

```
Air Reduction Sales Company        2        January 13, 19--


nation.  Your contribution will go 100 percent to the NATIONAL
SUMMER CAMP FUND because all fund raising, labor, and counseling
are supplied on a voluntary basis.  A return envelope is enclosed
for your convenience.
```

PAGE 2 HEADING, HORIZONTAL FORM

Note. With the *horizontal* form, the date line ends even with right margin; the page number is centered.

Heading: Air Reduction Sales Company | Page 2 | January 13, 19––

nation. Your contribution will go 100 percent to the NATIONAL SUMMER CAMP FUND because all fund raising, labor, and counseling are supplied on a voluntary basis. A return envelope is enclosed for your convenience.

3. Letter Production Skill Measurement (28) (*Letterhead or plain paper; 1 carbon copy; correct errors*)

Time Schedule	
Planning and preparing	3′
Letter production timing . . .	20′
Proofreading; determining *n-pram*	5′

Using the ¶s of the rough draft, page 226, as the body of the letter (332 words), type letters as directed below. If you complete the letters before time is up, start over. When time is called, proofread carefully. Subtract 15 words from the total words typed for each *uncorrected* error. Determine *n-pram*.

a. Block style letter (*open punctuation*)

	Words
Opening lines:	
(*Current date*) | Mr. Ben Blazina, Chairman |	8
Business Education Department | Grand Rapids	17
High School | Grand Rapids, Michigan 49512 |	25
Dear Mr. Blazina |	28
(+ *Body words*)	360
Closing lines:	
Sincerely yours | John Featherstone | Personnel	369
Director | (xx)	371

b. Modified block style with 5-space ¶ indentions (*mixed punctuation*)

	Words
Opening lines:	
(*Current date*) | Mr. Henry Nelson, Chairman |	8
Business Education Department | Des Moines	17
High School | Des Moines, Iowa 50317 | Dear	25
Mr. Nelson: |	27
(+ *Body words*)	359
Closing lines:	
Sincerely yours, | John Featherstone | Personnel	368
Director | (xx)	370

LESSON 148

148A: Conditioning Practice (5) *each line three times*

Thumb close to space bar

Alphabet	B. V. Mark recognized the quaint, jagged flowers with spurred calyxes.
Figure-symbol	The new pool (15′ wide x 60′ long x 7½′ deep) will cost but $3,248.90.
Shift key	He read the articles: "Fatigue," "How to Relax," and "Saving Energy."
Speed	Can we demonstrate to those who would be careless that life is a gift?

| 1 | 2 | 3 | 4 | 5 | 6 | 7 | 8 | 9 | 10 | 11 | 12 | 13 | 14 |

148B: Speed and Accuracy Emphasis (20) (*Repeat 146B, pages 222–223*)

148C: Skill Measurement – Employment Testing (25)

1. Straight-Copy Skill Measurement (8)
Type a 5′ writing using the paragraphs of 147B–1, page 225.

Goal: To improve your previous rate, or to reduce the number of errors made.

2. Rough-Draft Skill Measurement (8)
Type a 5′ writing using the paragraphs of 147B–2, page 226.

Goal: To exceed your previous rate and to maintain an accuracy goal of fewer than five errors.

3. Statistical-Copy Skill Measurement (9)
Type a 5′ writing on the paragraphs at the top of page 228.

Goal: To keep your eyes on the copy, to type with continuity and fewer than five errors.

Step 3: Learning to Type Closing Lines with Special Variations

Preview. The closing lines illustrated at the right introduce three business letter variations:

1. The typing of only the title below the complimentary close;
2. The typing of the name of the dictator and the typist's initials in the reference notation;
3. The typing of a postscript a double space below the last item of the closing lines.

Note. A postscript may be preceded by the letters P.S. (postscript), but the modern trend is to omit this abbreviation.

Special Drill. Starting with the last lines of the body of the letter, type three copies of the closing lines with special variations (given in unarranged form at the right). Arrange the material according to the illustration, and leave proper space between the various parts; after first typing, DS, and repeat. Use 1″ side margins.

```
We must not let them down.  We know that your Company will do all
it can to help.
                                    Sincerely yours,


                                    Executive Secretary

MJSellwood/hj

Enclosure

     We shall send you our summer camp brochure soon.  This bro-
chure shows, in concise, pictorial form, the highlights of these
summer camps.  You will enjoy thumbing through it.
```

CLOSING LINES WITH SPECIAL VARIATIONS

We must not let them down. We know that your Company will do all it can to help. Sincerely yours, Executive Secretary MJSellwood/hj Enclosure (¶) We shall send you our summer camp brochure soon. This brochure shows, in concise pictorial form, the highlights of these summer camps. You will enjoy thumbing through it.

Problem 13: Two-Page Form Letter

Type the letter with one carbon copy to the first addressee on your *mailing list* (prepared in Problem 9, page 201). As time permits in these lessons, type the letter (one *cc*) to as many additional addressees as possible. For each new letter, use your typed copy of the preceding letter as the copy from which you type; thus you can proofread the previous letter as the new letter is typed. Correct all errors. As you type each new letter, try to reduce your letter typing time.

Modified block style with 5-space ¶ indentions	*1″ side margins; approximately 1″ bottom margin*	*Mixed punctuation; vertical form second-page heading*	*Address large envelopes*

Words
January 13, 19—— Air Reduction Sales Company 9
150 East 42d Street New York, New York 17
10017 Attention Public Relations Director Gen- 26
tlemen: NATIONAL SUMMER CAMP FUND 33
(¶ 1) Although the rest of the country may be 41
battling knee-deep snow drifts, here in our office 51
"It's June in January" and we are "knee deep 60
in June." It is in January that those of us at the 71
National Summer Camp Center have to turn our 80
thoughts to June and make plans for summer 88
camps for children. It is a big job, and we need 98
your help. (¶ 2) Here in New York City alone, 107
we have the names of over 5,000 children on 115
our want-to-go-to-camp list this year. The same 125
situation is true for other major cities. These chil- 136
dren are between 9 and 14 years of age. They 145
are from underprivileged areas of the city. 154
Many of these youngsters have never been 162
away from the city, fished in a stream, been 171
swimming in a lake or pool, or slept under the 181
stars. Each one of the youngsters deserves coun- 191
try sun and fun. Winter in an urban center such 200
as New York doesn't give youngsters much 209
opportunity for outside play and fresh air. Their 219
mental and physical health is always improved 228
by a summer camp experience. (¶ 3) We must 236
not disappoint these youngsters in our cities—— 245
and we shall not, if you will put your love for 255
children into action by sending a contribution 264
to the NATIONAL SUMMER CAMP FUND. This 272
fund helps to support summer camps for needy 281
children throughout the country. The cost of 290
sending one child to summer camp is only $3 a 299
day. Why not "adopt" one or several children 309
for a two-week period this summer by spon- 317
soring their attendance at a summer camp. Your 327
contribution is tax deductible, of course. (¶ 4) 335
As soon as school is out next June, the first 345

(*Continued next page*)

2. Rough-Draft Skill Measurement (9) *5′ writing; circle errors; determine* gwam

Scan the copy quickly to be sure you understand the corrections; make indicated corrections as you type.

All letters are used.

	GWAM 1′	5′	
points / make			
Here are some of the things I would stress were I to	10	2	68
who are about to enter the world of work. / value			
talk to your students. First, I would stress the importance	30	6	72
of good personal traits. Our firm rapdily promotes workers	42	8	74
who can solve problems by themselves,			
who have a sense of duty, and who can promptly compl ete tasks	61	12	78
prescribed.			
assigned to them and the in manner in which we want them done.	71	14	80
well / e / who			
The employee who can wo rk effectively with othrs and is	82	16	82
tactful and kind			
courteous and considerate will always be in demand. The	90	18	84
Skill in communication			
ability to communicate effectively is also very important. I	100	20	86
suggest to a / person			
would like to caution young students that although the "cool"	112	22	88
jargon / suitable			
vocabulary of the teenager may be a satisfactory way to	122	24	90
talk / peer group / in			
communicate with his own fellow students while he is high	132	26	92
vocabulary			
school, it is a poor substitute for the words needed for	144	29	95
good / office			
adequate expression and communication in the business world.	155	31	97
¶ Next, I would have to say that attitude aboutthe job and toward	13	34	99
the work is exceedingly important. Our firm puts a premium on	25	36	102
employees who are willing to help others during a rush period.	48	41	106
d / a rush job			
We reware workers who have the ability to do work under pres-	61	43	109
sure and still retain the composure needed to get the job	73	46	111
as it should be done. / #			
done. Of equal value, too, is the employee whocan understand	90	49	115
straight			
and follow direc tions which may not be stated in a neat	102	51	117
spell numbers / be			
1, 2, 3 sequence; these may directions which requrie him to	114	54	120
i / (and then to work his plan if he is to get the task done.			
make some decisons, and to plan his work,	133	58	124
No ¶ A final job ingredient I would label simply as the applica-	145	60	126
tion of "common sense" to all work.	152	61	127
— even though this means working overtime now and then.			
¶ I am hopeful these suggestions will be of some	9	63	129
merit to you and your students in your	17	65	131
discussion of careers.	22	66	132

Words

excited group of youngsters will be loaded on 354
buses and will be off for a two-week summer 363
camp outing. In your own city, you will be 371
invited to be present on this special occasion, 381
your "adopted children" will meet you, and I 390
know you will say, "All of us feel better for 399
having helped to make this experience possible 409
for needy youngsters." (¶ 5) Won't you send us 417
your check today for as much as your Company 426
can contribute to this worthy cause. We are 435
asking that you help us to help a child experi- 444
ence and enjoy the benefits that a session of 454
summer fun, activity, and guidance will offer. 463
Consider your contribution as a good investment 473
in the future of our nation. Your contribution 482

Words

will go 100 percent to the NATIONAL SUMMER 491
CAMP FUND because all fund raising, labor, 500
and counseling are supplied on a voluntary basis. 510
A return envelope is enclosed for your conve- 519
nience. (¶ 6) Hundreds of children are counting 527
on us to give them this camping experience-- 536
it will be one that they will remember all their 546
lives. We must not let them down. We know 555
that your Company will do all it can to help. 564
Sincerely yours, Executive Secretary MJSell- 573
wood/hj Enclosure (¶) We shall send you our 581
summer camp brochure soon. This brochure 589
shows, in concise, pictorial form, the highlights 599
of these summer camps. You will enjoy thumb- 608
ing through it. 611/633

Problem 14: Letters on Half Sheets (Review of Letter Styles)

Short letters are often typed on half sheets (either 8½″ x 5½″ with the letterhead at the top of the long edge, or 5½″ x 8½″ with the letterhead at the top of the short edge). In this problem, you will use both types of stationery. The letters are to be addressed as directed in Steps 1 and 2 and are to be marked: **Attention Public Relations Director**. Use as the salutation: **Gentlemen**.

1. Type letters on 8½″ x 5½″ paper (long side up) to the first four addressees on your mailing list.

Modified block style	*Type date January 23, 19--*
Mixed punctuation	*on 5th line from top edge*
1″ side margins	*Space down 2 lines and*
Address small envelopes	*type the address*

2. Type letters on 5½″ x 8½″ paper (short side up) to the next two addressees on your list.

Block style	*Type date January 23, 19--*
Open punctuation	*on 10th line from top edge*
¾″ side margins	*Space down 4 lines and*
Address small envelopes	*type the address*

Words

(Date, address, attention line, salutation) 26

(¶ 1) Our summer camp brochure is in the mail. As you thumb through it, 39
notice the excited expressions on the faces of the youngsters as they 53
are shown arriving in camp, catching their first fish, splashing in the 68
lake, or eating "Western Style" around the campfire. (¶ 2) Your contri- 81
bution to our NATIONAL SUMMER CAMP FUND will make similar experiences a 95
reality for other underprivileged children. Won't you join the other 109
summer camp sponsors and "KICK IN FOR THE KIDS." Sincerely yours 123
Executive Secretary MJSellwood/hj (93) *(+ Envelope)* 129/152

Problem 15: Composing Thank-You Letters

The first two business firms on your mailing list have sent in contributions to the NATIONAL SUMMER CAMP FUND. Follow these steps:

1. Compose a brief thank-you letter that you can send to each firm. Invite the Public Relations Director to the Bus Loading Ceremony. Tell him that it will take place at 9 a.m. on June 20, and that he will be notified at a later date as to the exact location in his city. In this first draft, *x-out* any errors that you make. (See page 112, 69B.)
2. Make any needed corrections in the wording, spelling, or grammar with a pen or pencil and retype your rough draft of the letter. Use this form letter for the letters that you type with the date: January 26, 19--. Address a small envelope for each letter.

LESSON 147

147A: Conditioning Practice (5) *each line three times*

Alphabet	The maze box puzzle was quickly solved by the good students from Fiji.	*Eyes on copy*
Figure-symbol	Type these figures and symbols: "2," #3, $4, 5%, 6, 7&, 8', (9), (0). Electric 2@, 6¢, 8*,	
Related learning	"Will the campaign," the judge asked, "begin this week or next month?"	
Speed	True merit is like a river––the deeper it is, the less noise it makes. | 1 | 2 | 3 | 4 | 5 | 6 | 7 | 8 | 9 | 10 | 11 | 12 | 13 | 14 |	

147B: Skill Measurement – Employment Testing (45)

Many personnel departments of business firms require an applicant to come for a preliminary interview and to take certain basic skill tests as an initial screening device. If the applicant passes these tests, he is then considered for the position, and he may take other employment tests required by the company.

1. Straight-Copy Skill Measurement (8) *5' writing; circle errors; determine* gwam

All letters are used.

Text	GWAM 1'	5'	
To hunt for a job is a bit of an art. Before you begin, it helps	13	3	64
to review your education, work experiences, and skills. Be sure you	27	5	67
know your goal and what you want to do. Life is too short to go through	42	8	70
it doing work you do not like to do. When you are ready to hunt for a	56	11	73
job, plot your approach with care. First, collect needed personal data;	70	14	76
such as, your social security number, the names and addresses of persons	85	17	79
whom you can use for reference, and the dates of your education and work	100	20	82
experiences. Next, prepare a data sheet that lists or sums up your per-	114	23	84
sonal characteristics, education, and work experiences. If you possess	128	26	87
skills, such as typing or shorthand, be sure to list them. Finally,	142	28	90
give the names of two or three persons other than relatives who know	156	31	93
you well.	158	32	93

Text	GWAM 1'	5'	
Now you are ready to search for job leads. Inquire among friends,	13	34	96
relatives, and others who may be in a position to aid you. Your school	28	37	99
may have a placement office––be sure to use it. Check the "Help Wanted"	42	40	102
ads in your newspaper. When you locate a promising job lead, ask by	56	43	104
letter or telephone for an interview, unless you know that you are to go	71	46	107
at once for an interview. If you write a letter of application, realize	85	49	110
that it is a mirror of your work habits and your thinking. The letter	100	51	113
should be neatly and correctly typed. When you are called for an inter-	114	54	116
view, dress simply and in good taste; show an interest in the company	128	57	119
and the job; sell yourself, your skills, and your abilities; and you will	143	60	122
enhance your chances of getting the job.	151	62	123

1' GWAM | 1 | 2 | 3 | 4 | 5 | 6 | 7 | 8 | 9 | 10 | 11 | 12 | 13 | 14 |
5' GWAM | 1 | 2 | 3 |

Unit 22 | Lessons 133-142

Building Business Letter and Tabulation Production Skills

LESSON 133

133A: Conditioning Practice (5) *each line three times*

Alphabet	The travel expert frequently amazed us with talks about jungle dances.	*Shift quickly*
Figure-symbol	Send Order #1280–YL ($4,936.70 less 15%) for 4¼ C&B Pine via C&NW R.R.	
Shift key	Refer the papers to Miss Jan Q. O'Brien, secretary to McCrae & McGill.	
Speed	An efficient secretary paid the busy clerks for the eighty handy pens.	
	| 1 | 2 | 3 | 4 | 5 | 6 | 7 | 8 | 9 | 10 | 11 | 12 | 13 | 14 |	

133B: Related Learning – Punctuation Guides (15) *(Reference: 86C, page 138)*

Practice Plan:

1. Study explanatory guide or rule.
2. Type *Learn* sentence, noting rule application.
3. Type *Apply* sentence, making all needed corrections; then DS. Save sheet for 134B, page 207.

Machine Adjustments:

1. 70-space line; single spacing.
2. 1½″ top margin first page; 1″ margin on all other pages; bottom margin of about 1″ on all pages that are full.

1. **Comma**—Use the comma after (a) introductory words, phrases, or clauses; and, (b) words in a series.
2. **Comma**—Use the comma to set off short, direct quotations.
3. **Comma**—Use the comma to set off (a) words in apposition (words which come together and refer to the same person, thing, or idea); and, (b) words of direct address.
4. **Comma**—Use the comma to set off nonrestrictive clauses (not necessary to meaning of sentence); however, do not use commas to set off restrictive clauses (necessary to meaning).
5. **Comma**—Use the comma to separate the day from the year and the city from the state.

SERIES 3. PUNCTUATION GUIDE EXAMPLES

1 *Learn* After he leaves Atlanta, he will visit Richmond, New York, and Boston.
Apply If they leave early_they will have bacon and eggs_toast_and coffee.

2 *Learn* I asked, "When are you leaving?" She replied, "I plan to leave soon."
Apply H. D. Thoreau once said_"Be not simply good: Be good for something."

Note different meaning

3 *Learn* Mr. King, the owner, is out today. Yes, Dr. Felder, the owner is out.
Apply The manager_Mr. Jeffrey_said, "Ask my assistant_Mr. Lange_for it."

4 *Learn* His story, which no one believed, was told in detail to many visitors. *(nonrestrictive)*
Apply Chapters 7 and 8_which relate to this problem_are very well written.
Learn All students_who practice with a purpose_will be successful in typing. *(restrictive)*
Apply The building will have to be repaired, unless good care is taken of it.

5 *Learn* He was born September 20, 1873, and lived in Lexington, Massachusetts.
Apply They may plan to go to Stockholm_Sweden, on or about August 26_1980.

PERSONAL DATA SHEET

Center heading 1 inch from top of page
1-inch side margins
Use your judgment in arranging data

John L. Beck
1327 Valley Heart Drive
Burbank, California 91506
Telephone: 224–6539

Personal Information

Age:	18
Place of Birth:	Logan, Utah
Height and Weight:	6'1", 175 pounds
Health:	Excellent

Education

High School:	Burbank High School
Degree:	High school diploma, pending graduation
Major:	Business management––Academic
Grade Average:	B+ (Upper 15% of graduating class)

School Activities

Member of varsity baseball team for three years. Regular shortstop during junior and senior years.

President of Junior Achievement Club during junior year. Formed the Allied Products Company, which manufactured and sold tie racks.

Student body treasurer during senior year. Prepared purchase requisitions and kept records of receipts and disbursements of student body funds.

Work Experience

Newspaper route for one year. Delivered 120 papers a day. Made collections monthly.

Clerk-Typist in an insurance office for two summers. Typed insurance forms and letters, sorted company mail, and did other general clerical work.

References (by permission)

Mr. Charles Wheelock, Boys' Adviser; Burbank High School; 525 N. Glenoaks Boulevard; Burbank, California 91502

Mr. Lloyd Bartholome, Business Instructor; Burbank High School; 525 N. Glenoaks Boulevard; Burbank, California 91502

Mr. Edward Nelson, Office Manager; Western States Insurance Company; 2613 W. Olive Avenue; Burbank, California 91506

133C: Letter Skill Building (20) *(Block style, open; 2" margins; date on Line 20)*

1. Type a 3′ writing on the letter to establish a base rate. If you finish before time is called, start over.
2. Determine *gwam.* To this rate add 8 *gwam* to set a new goal. Divide the goal rate into four equal segments; note these quarter-minute check points for guided writings.
3. *Leave proper spacing between letter parts, but begin the letter (date line) near the top of the sheet.* Beginning with the date, type three 1′ guided writings on the opening parts of the letter and ¶ 1. *Begin the second and third writings a double space below the last line of the previous writing.*
4. Repeat Step 3, using ¶ 2 and the closing lines of the letter.
5. Type another 3′ writing on the complete letter. Try to maintain your new goal rate for this writing. Do this by using good techniques and by typing with continuity. Determine *gwam* and compare it with the rate you attained in Step 1.

RECALL: *Block style—all lines start flush with the left margin. Reference: p. 171.*

	Words	3′ GWAM	
May 10, 19-- / Mrs. Bernard Newman / 15867 Lakeview Drive	11	4	47
Washington, D.C. 20031 / Dear Mrs. Newman /	19	6	49
(¶1) The excellent way in which you have handled your	29	10	53
credit account with us is sincerely appreciated. We want	40	13	56
you to know that serving you has been a genuine	50	17	60
pleasure. Thank you for giving us this opportunity to	61	20	63
be of service.	64	21	64
(¶2) Although your account is paid in full, please do not	75	25	68
feel that it is closed. Your account is open in our files,	87	29	72
ready to serve you. We hope you will use it often.	97	32	75
Your credit record now entitles you to make purchases	108	36	79
with no down payment. We shall look forward to	118	39	82
seeing you.	120	40	83
Cordially yours / Robert Neches, Manager / jm	129	43	86

133D: Letter Production Typing – Skill Building (Short Letter) (10) *(Plain half sheets)*

Type the short letter of 133C to as many of the following addressees as time permits. Correct all errors neatly; make one carbon copy; address small envelopes.

Block style
Open punctuation
Supply appropriate salutations
Your initials as reference

(1) Mrs. Charles Zahl 1109 Chippewa Place Alexandria, Virginia 22312

(2) Mrs. Carole Bellucci 9 Stuyvesant Oval New York, New York 10009

(3) Mrs. Gayle C. Pickel 671 Glenwood Place Pittsburgh, Pa. 15209

(4) Mr. Fred Jarvis 4895 Fox Way, S.E. Washington, D.C. 20021

(5) Mr. Michael Armer 6789 Lincoln Dr. Charleston, W.Va. 25312

(6) Miss Claudia Koper 8349 Eastwood Ave. Huntington, W.Va. 25701

SET 3	*High-frequency two- and three-letter combinations emphasized*	Words	GWAM 15"	12"	10"
1	When are you and she going to the station for her?	10	40	50	60
2	During this testing session, you will be on your honor.	11	44	55	66
3	The youth will go to the area to seek the title to the tent.	12	48	60	72
4	When they leave at the end of this hour, are you going with them?	13	52	65	78
5	You and I were to go there to do the work before the end of this week.	14	56	70	84
	| 1 | 2 | 3 | 4 | 5 | 6 | 7 | 8 | 9 | 10 | 11 | 12 | 13 | 14 |				

146C: Applying for Employment (25)

AN OFFICE

AN INTERVIEW

TAKING A TYPING TEST

An applicant for employment in a business office may be required to write a letter of application and to complete a data sheet before he is considered for an interview. You will do so now.

Modified block style	*Start return address at*
Mixed punctuation	*center point on line 12*
1½" side margins	*Omit reference initials*

1. *Typing a Letter of Application.* The following letter was written in application for a position in a business office. Type the letter as directed; correct all errors.

Words

1327 Valley Heart Drive 5
Burbank, California 91506 10
(Current date) 13

Mr. Robert J. Thomas | Director of Personnel | 22
National Computers, Inc. | 4567 Washington 30
Boulevard | Los Angeles, California 90023 | 38
Dear Mr. Thomas: (¶ 1) Your announcement of 46
openings for the position of "Computer Pro- 55
grammer Trainee" was given to me by my school 64
adviser, Mr. Charles Wheelock. Programming is 73
an area of interest to me, and I should like to 83
apply for the position. (¶ 2) I shall be gradu- 91
ated from Burbank High School in June. My 100
field of study has been business management. 109
This program includes courses in general busi- 118
ness, business law, economics, typewriting, book- 128
keeping, office practice, and introduction to data 138
processing. In addition, I have completed the 148
regular required high school courses. I can type 158
60 words a minute on straight-copy materials, 167
and I have learned appropriate production skills. 177
I have been active in school organizations. Last 187
year I was president of the Junior Achievement 197
Club. This year I am student body treasurer. 206
(¶ 3) The enclosed personal data sheet will give 215
you additional information. I believe my high 224
school grade average, my work experience, and 233
my participation in school activities are an indi- 243
cation that I can succeed in the position for 252
which I am applying. May I come for an inter- 261
view at a time that is convenient for you? In 270
case you wish to call me, my telephone number 280
is 224-6539. Sincerely, | John L. Beck | Enclo- 288
sure (240) 289

2. *Typing a Personal Data Sheet.* Type the data sheet (page 224) to enclose with the letter of application. The illustration shows one style that may be used.

3. *Composition.* If time permits, assume you are applying for a job for which you have the requisite skills and education. Prepare a letter of application and data sheet appropriate for you.

LESSON 134

134A: Conditioning Practice (5) *each line three times*

Alphabet	Quiet Muscovy ducks from Brazil were judged by the experts as winners.	*Quiet hands; quick, snap stroke*
Figure-symbol	The 6.70 x 15, 2-ply tires (natural rubber) may cost more than $34.89.	
Adjacent key	As we drew near, a weaverbird wasted little time in vacating her nest.	
Speed	You can do the seemingly impossible if you have faith in your efforts.	
	| 1 | 2 | 3 | 4 | 5 | 6 | 7 | 8 | 9 | 10 | 11 | 12 | 13 | 14 |	

134B: Related Learning – Punctuation Guides (10) *(Reinsert sheet used for 133B, p. 205)*

6. Comma—Use the comma to separate two or more parallel adjectives.

7. Comma—Use the comma to separate (a) unrelated groups of figures which come together; and (b) whole numbers into groups of three digits each (however, policy, year, page, room, telephone, and most serial numbers are written without commas).

8. Exclamation Mark—Use an exclamation mark after emphatic interjections and after phrases or sentences that are clearly exclamatory.

9. Question Mark—Use a question mark at the end of a sentence that is a direct question; however, use a period after a question which is in the form of a request.

10. Dash—Use a dash for emphasis, to indicate a change of thought, to introduce the name of an author or a reference when it follows a direct quotation, and for other special purposes.

Note. The dash (made by typing two hyphens without space before or after) is an emphatic mark of punctuation.

6	*Learn*	That old-fashioned stove kept them warm on long, cold winter evenings.
	Apply	She traded her new_solid-gold watch for that big_friendly black dog.
7	*Learn*	During 1967, 1,249 cars, insured under Policy 80–643207, were damaged.
	Apply	In 1967_1250 new $100000 policies, series 1348–92,015, were written.
8	*Learn*	What a beautiful view! How lucky they are to be able to go to school!
	Apply	Oh, if I could only go_ I typed 80 w.a.m. today. Hurrah, you did it_
9	*Learn*	When are you leaving? May we have your check for $15.75 before May 8.
	Apply	How old is your uncle_ Will you please do this work before you leave_
10	*Learn*	The icy road--slippery as a silver-scaled fish--made driving a hazard.
	Learn	"To read good books is to enjoy life's greatest treasures."--Thompson.
	Apply	Excellence is not something that is thrust upon us_ it must be earned.

134C: Tabulation Timed Writing (20)

1. Type a 5′ writing on the *unarranged table* at the top of page 208. Arrange the material in proper form. Before time is started, you will have approximately 3′ to determine the left margin stop and the tab stops for the columns. Determine, also, the points at which the main heading and the columnar headings are to start. Make pencil notations of these points.
2. When time is called, proofread your copy and determine *gwam*.
3. Type another 5′ writing and try to improve your rate.

Unit 24 | Lessons 146-150

Determining Typewriting Competence

(Taking an Employment Test)

LESSON 146

146A: Conditioning Practice (5) *each line three times*

Alphabet	This quick quiz will cover exceedingly important factors of job skill.	*Fluent rhythm*
Figure-symbol	A 100% hardwood 3-shelf bookcase (38″ x 23″ x 7 3/4″) sells for $9.65.	
Long reaches	She executed many zany swan dives at the aquacade dedication ceremony.	
Speed	Is life so short that we no longer have time for courtesy and a smile?	

| 1 | 2 | 3 | 4 | 5 | 6 | 7 | 8 | 9 | 10 | 11 | 12 | 13 | 14 |

146B: Speed and Accuracy Emphasis (20)

1. **Speed Jump—Set 1.** Starting with Sentence 1, Set 1, gradually increase your speed as you type each new sentence on the call of the 15″, 12″, or 10″ guide by your teacher. Move from one sentence to the next when the "return" is called. Push your speed to its highest possible level.

2. **Accuracy Drive—Set 2.** Starting with Sentence 1, Set 2, gradually increase your speed on each new sentence as the 15″, 12″, or 10″ guide is called by your teacher. Your goal is errorless writing on each sentence; if you make an error, stay on that sentence until you type it without error.

3. **Speed and Accuracy—Set 3.** Type each sentence of Set 3, page 223, as a 1′ writing at a guided rate determined by the call of the 15″, 12″, or 10″ *return* guide. Start at a slow rate and gradually increase this rate on each new timing; try to type with not more than 1 error on each writing.

			Words	GWAM 15″	GWAM 12″	GWAM 10″
SET 1		*High-frequency balanced-hand words emphasized*				
	1	He may also make me go with them to do their work.	10	40	50	60
	2	They may sign the city amendment form for the chairman.	11	44	55	66
	3	The firm may make a profit if the men do a quantity of work.	12	48	60	72
	4	Their wish is to do the problem and then visit the city chairman.	13	52	65	78
	5	It is their wish to pay the firm for the work so it may make a profit.	14	56	70	84
		| 1 | 2 | 3 | 4 | 5 | 6 | 7 | 8 | 9 | 10 | 11 | 12 | 13 | 14 |				
SET 2		*High-frequency one-hand words emphasized*				
	1	After you rate him, read only a few reserve cases.	10	40	50	60
	2	John can get you only a minimum tax rate on the estate.	11	44	55	66
	3	We regret that you were referred to him for the tax opinion.	12	48	60	72
	4	The average reserve tax rate is greater than the minimum you set.	13	52	65	78
	5	Were you to refer all or only a few area tax cases to him for opinion?	14	56	70	84
		| 1 | 2 | 3 | 4 | 5 | 6 | 7 | 8 | 9 | 10 | 11 | 12 | 13 | 14 |				

(Please see page 223 for SET 3)

Full sheet
Reading position
4 spaces between columns
DS data of columns

Each figure is used a minimum of 12 times.

	Words
Main Heading: DELINQUENT ELECTRIC SERVICE ACCOUNTS	7

Name	Address	Bill Date	Amount	Words
Scott Archer	2819 W. 83d Street	March 20	$38.57	28
Mark Barshop	4664 Saticoy Street	March 10	57.90	38
Dan Beilin	4749 Woodcliff Road	March 1	73.50	47
David Eisner	3367 South Brockton	March 10	26.82	56
Anthony Grant	23751 Jackson Avenue	March 1	46.98	66
David Jadwin	10294 Hayvenhurst Avenue	March 1	56.73	77
Jon Kaufer	892 Lindo Street	March 10	41.95	85
Steven Leonard	74689 Thurston Circle	March 20	39.58	96
Thomas McDonald	3674 Adlon Road	March 10	28.95	105
Steven Philips	7460 Hinton Way	March 1	52.56	114
Ralph Simmonds	4569 Royal Oak Drive	March 20	18.78	124
Robert Spitzer	3948 Westwood Blvd.	March 20	56.72	134

(*Columnar Headings:* Name | Address | Bill Date | Amount — 19 words)

134D: Memorandum Typing (Review) (15) *(Full sheet)*

1″ side margins
All errors corrected
Carbon copy on plain sheet

Type the following material as an interoffice memorandum (Reference: Page 198). If a memorandum form is not available, type the problem on a full sheet with the heading lines starting about 1 inch from the top edge of the sheet. Save the carbon copy you make for use in 135C, page 209.

TO: Nicolas Nelken, Account Manager | *DATE:* May 25, 19-- | *FROM:* Carol Rogers, Accounting Dept. | *SUBJECT:* Delinquent Accounts |

(¶ 1) Electric service accounts that are now more than 30 days past due are shown below. These names are being sent to you so that the regular form letter on delinquent accounts can be sent to them.

(¶ 2) *(Triple-space and type the tabulation copy given in 134C, above; single-space the items. Center the table horizontally as directed. In the table, change the "Bill Date" to April, but use the same day as shown.)*

LESSON 135

135A: Conditioning Practice (5) *each line three times*

Alphabet	John V. Maze is able to type six words faster by using a quick stroke.	Fingers curved
Figure-symbol	He paid $1,830.45 in 1967 for an (8′ x 12′) oriental rug for his home.	
Long words	A habit may be an outgrowth of physiological or psychological motives.	
Speed	Keep the stroking action in the fingers to increase your typing skill.	

| 1 | 2 | 3 | 4 | 5 | 6 | 7 | 8 | 9 | 10 | 11 | 12 | 13 | 14 |

LESSON 144

144A: Conditioning Practice (5) *each line three times*

Alphabet	Six big flaming rocket ships zoomed over the picturesque wooden jetty.	*Finger stroking action*
Figure-symbol	Sell the #394 item (nylon) to J&B Company at list--120 gross @ $68.75.	
Fingers 3 and 4	Aza Q. Popoloux was asked to escort that popular but plump queen home.	
Speed	They had moved to a new address when the statement was mailed to them.	
	| 1 | 2 | 3 | 4 | 5 | 6 | 7 | 8 | 9 | 10 | 11 | 12 | 13 | 14 |	

144B: Skill Building – Statistical Copy (15) *two 5′ writings of 107B, page 172, as directed below*

1. In the first 5′ writing, try to type at your best rate. **Goal:** 5 or fewer errors.

2. In the second 5′ writing, increase your speed if you made the Step 1 goal; if not decrease it.

144C: Production Typing (Letter Style Review) (30) (*1 carbon; envelopes; correct errors*)

Type as many of the problems listed below as you can in the time allowed. Make pencil or typed notations of the problems, page numbers, and *general directions* so you need not refer to this page.

As each letter is typed, evaluate its acceptability:

An *acceptable letter* is attractively placed on the page; is typed with uniform (even) key stroking, and has all errors neatly erased and corrected. It has "eye appeal" and makes a good impression on all who see it.

1. Problem 1, *Style Letter 1*, page 86.
2. Problem 1, *Style Letter 2*, page 164.
3. Problem 1, *Style Letter 3*, page 171.
4. Problems 1 and 2, pages 165–166.

LESSON 145

145A: Conditioning Practice (5) *each line three times*

Alphabet	Invaluable new zoning rules were quickly expedited by the junior firm.	*Shift quickly*
Figure-shift lock	These 1,258 men have had FORTRAN, IBM 7094, and SYSTEM 360 experience.	
Shift key	Jack LeConte and Mary O'Brien accepted jobs with S. & J. Wooland, Inc.	
Speed	I will sign a contract by the end of the week so we can test the case.	
	| 1 | 2 | 3 | 4 | 5 | 6 | 7 | 8 | 9 | 10 | 11 | 12 | 13 | 14 |	

145B: Skill Building – Rough Draft (15) *two 5′ writings of 108C, page 173, as directed below*

1. In the first 5′ writing, try to type at your best rate. **Goal:** 5 or fewer errors.

2. In the second 5′ writing, increase your rate if you made the Step 1 goal; if not decrease it.

145C: Production Typing (30) (*Correct errors*)

Type as many of the problems listed below as you can in the time allowed. Make pencil or typed notations of the problems, page numbers, and *general directions* so you need not refer to this page.

As each problem is completed, evaluate it as to its acceptability: (1) placement on the page; (2) uniformity of key stroking; (3) neatness of error correction.

1. Problem 1, page 188 (*tabulation*).
2. Problem 1, page 190 (*tabulation*).
3. Problem 1, page 198 (*memorandum*).
4. Problem 5, page 200 (*invoice*).

135B: Growth Index – Straight Copy (15) *two 5′ writings* *Goal: Not over 1 error a minute*

All letters are used.

	GWAM 1′	5′	
 For most typing tasks, the typist must use paper, carbon sheets,	13	3	57
envelopes, and other items. Much time may be lost in using such supplies.	28	6	60
For example, supplies may be in utter disarray on or in the typist's desk.	43	9	63
The output of a typist can be increased by careful planning of the order	58	12	66
and layout of paper, carbon sheets, envelopes, and other supplies. In	72	14	69
this way, these items can be reached quickly and easily as they are	86	17	72
needed. The same rule or guide also applies to erasers, note pads, pen-	100	20	74
cils, pens, and other tools that may be used in the job to be done.	114	23	77
"A place for everything with each thing in its place," is a good rule	128	26	80
to follow.	130	26	80
 A second guide to effective work habits relates to the assembly,	13	29	83
pickup, and insertion of supplies into the typewriter. The typist may	27	31	86
use many waste motions in assembling and inserting a carbon pack into	41	34	89
the machine. He may not realize that much time may be lost with even	55	37	91
such a simple task as the insertion of a sheet of paper into the machine.	70	40	94
For example, the typist may fumble the paper, he may use both hands in the	85	43	97
pickup of the paper, he may turn the paper a few times, he may grind	99	46	100
rather than twirl the paper into the machine, and he may use many other	113	49	103
waste motions—each of which results in lost time. This is time that	122	51	106
can and should be turned into typing time and increased production rates.	142	54	109

1′ GWAM | 1 | 2 | 3 | 4 | 5 | 6 | 7 | 8 | 9 | 10 | 11 | 12 | 13 | 14 |
5′ GWAM | 1 | 2 | 3 |

135C: Letter Production Typing – Skill Building *(Average-Length Letter)* (30) *(Plain sheets)*

Type the form letter at the top of page 210 to as many of the names and addresses given on the carbon copy of the memo prepared for 134D, page 208, as possible. Use the name of your city and state in the address lines, and the *ZIP* code for your home address. Supply appropriate salutations. Make the necessary insertions in the first paragraph as it is typed.

With each repetition of the letter, try to reduce your typing time. Do this by typing without waste motions: Keep fingers close to keys, eyes on the copy, and the carriage moving.

Unit 23 | Lessons 143-145

Review of Basic Skills

The typist in the business office is frequently called upon to perform a variety of typing tasks—all of which must be completed with a minimum of confusion and waste motion.

This unit will review and help you improve the basic typing skills which may be measured in a typical employment test.

The unit has the following specific aims:

1. To help you improve your basic typing skills.
2. To help you learn to make notes of and to follow directions without asking unnecessary questions.
3. To help you learn to make critical judgments relating to the usability or mailability of your typed work.

LESSON 143

143A: Conditioning Practice (5) *each line three times*

Alphabet The queerly boxed package of zinc mixtures was delivered just in time.

Figure-symbol A $50 million 12-year 6 3/4% debenture was offered at $98 to yield 7%.

Long reaches Many economy-minded union men are numbered among Mr. Bright's friends.

Speed He will sign the contract and take title to the eight firms this week.

| 1 | 2 | 3 | 4 | 5 | 6 | 7 | 8 | 9 | 10 | 11 | 12 | 13 | 14 |

Finger-reach action

143B: Skill Building – Straight Copy (15) *two 5′ writings of 124B, page 193, as directed below*

1. In the first 5′ writing, try to type at your best rate. **Goal:** 5 or fewer errors. Do this by typing with rhythm and continuity.
2. In the second 5′ writing, increase your speed if you reached the Step 1 goal; if not, decrease your speed and try to type with greater *control.*

143C: Tabulation – Classifying Information on Index Cards (30)

1. Type a 5″ x 3″ index classification card (or use a slip of paper of the same size) from the illustration at the right. Using this card as a guide, type additional index cards for the names contained in 125C, page 195, classified according to the subject heading of *Skills or Experience.* Arrange the names of the students, their ages, and telephone numbers on the cards in tabulated columns, centered horizontally, with *4 spaces between columns.* In typing the cards, start the columnar headings a double space below the subject heading. Type the subject heading in the upper left corner, ½ inch from the left edge and on the third line from the top edge.

2. After you have completed the indexing and tabulating of the names according to the skills or experience classification, alphabetize the cards according to the subject classification. Then type an identification card containing the following information, centered vertically and horizontally, and double spaced:

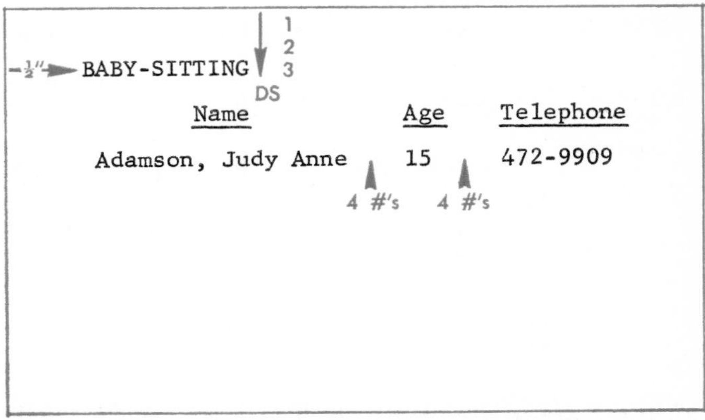

INDEX CARD WITH CLASSIFIED INFORMATION

STUDENT SERVICE BUREAU | *your name* | *name of your school* | *city and state* in which it is located. Put a rubber band around the cards, or a staple in the lower left corner if slips of paper were used, and submit them to your teacher for evaluation.

Modified block style	*Current date*	*Address envelopes*
Mixed punctuation	*Carbon copy*	*All errors corrected*

Words

20
(¶ 1) We are writing you, Mr. *(last name)*, to call 28
your attention to our *(date)* bill of *(amount)* for 39
electric service provided at *(street address)*, your 49
home address. This account now appears on our 59
delinquent or past-due list. This means that if we 69
do not hear from you within five days, we shall 79
be forced to discontinue electric service to your 89
home. (¶ 2) When a "prompt pay" account 96
appears on our delinquent list, we naturally 105
wonder why. Our previous reminders have not 114
brought the usual prompt reply from you. This 123
leads us to believe that some unusual circum- 132
stances have prevented payment. (¶ 3) It is 140
part of our policy to be of service to our cus- 148
tomers in every way we can. Your credit stand- 158
ing with us is now our prime concern. We 166
should like to help you take whatever steps may 176
be necessary to remove your name from our 184
delinquent list so that you can continue to enjoy 194
electric service. If you cannot make full payment 204
now, please contact this office. It is extremely 214
important that you do so at once. | Sincerely 223
yours, | Nicholas Nelken | Account Manager | 231/244

(For this letter and all remaining letters in Part 2, be sure to use your own reference initials.) (201)

LESSON 136

136A: Conditioning Practice (5) *each line three times*

Alphabet	Jolly housewives made inexpensive meals using quick-frozen vegetables.	*Fingers upright*
Figure-symbol	This rug (12′ x 13′6″) was $417.90, but it is now on sale for $381.50.	
Shift key	Joseph J. Tymczyszym won the London Conservatory of Music Scholarship.	
Speed	The good student is one who reads more, studies more, and thinks more.	
	| 1 | 2 | 3 | 4 | 5 | 6 | 7 | 8 | 9 | 10 | 11 | 12 | 13 | 14 |	

136B: Related Learning – Punctuation Guides *(Continued)* (15) *follow standard directions*

11. Colon—Use the colon to introduce an enumeration or a listing.

12. Colon—Use the colon to introduce a question, or a long, direct quotation.

13. Colon—Use the colon between hours and minutes expressed as figures. **Note.** Use figures with a.m. or p.m. (also, A.M. or P.M.).

14. Hyphen—Use the hyphen to join compound numerals from twenty-one to ninety-nine.

15. Hyphen—Use the hyphen to join compound adjectives preceding a noun which they modify.

16. Hyphen—Use the hyphen after each word in a series of words that modify the same noun.

11	*Learn*	Here are the reasons for his success: courage, industry, and honesty.
	Apply	She bought three items at the store_ a coat, a dress, and a suitcase.
12	*Learn*	The question is this: Are you using good technique at the typewriter?
	Apply	Ask James to answer the question_ Does inconsistency lead to failure?
13	*Learn*	When it is 4:30 p.m. in New York City, it is 1:30 p.m. in Los Angeles.
	Apply	Will the ceremony start at 1_30 p.m. on Friday, January 23, next year?
14	*Learn*	Spell these figures in this sentence: four, eighty-five, sixty-eight.
	Apply	At twenty_three, I never realized that I would live to be ninety_nine.
15	*Learn*	The good-natured teacher asked them to read only the best-known books.
	Apply	In the last five_year period, our business has increased tremendously.
16	*Learn*	First-, second-, and third-class mail is to be sorted before 9:30 a.m.
	Apply	All 6, 7, and 8_foot boards are to be used during the 10-day period.

(Problem 1—continued) Words

have the privilege of examining it free for two 242
weeks. Simply fill in the enclosed postpaid card 252
and drop it in the mail. We will do the rest. 262
Cordially yours, | LANE MAGAZINE & BOOK COM- 270
PANY | Lou Johnson, Sales Manager | Enclosure 279
(241)

Problem 2 *(2 carbon copies)*

Start date on 18th line. Center the subject line a double space below the salutation.

Mr. George Campbell 5934 Huntington Drive 11
Baton Rouge, Louisiana 70810 Dear Mr. Camp- 20
bell: DISABILITY INCOME INSURANCE CLAIM (¶ 1) 28
Enclosed is the form for your disability income 38
insurance claim. (¶ 2) Will you please complete 46
the Employee's Statement and have your doctor 56
complete the Physician's Statement on the other 65
side of the claim form. If you will then mail this 76
claim form to me, I shall see that the Employer's 86
Section is completed and that your claim is 94
processed. (¶ 3) Please call me if you have any 103
questions or if I can be of any service to you. 113
Sincerely yours, | John R. Keenan, C.L.U. | 121
Enclosure cc: Dr. Milton Tobias (82) 128

LESSON 142

142A: Conditioning Practice (5) *each line three times*

Alphabet	Jack Waxlof made amazing progress by using improved typing techniques.	*Release keys quickly*
Figure-symbol	Order #6890 for 2 gross of buttons totals \$3.72 (24 doz. @ 15½¢ each).	
Related learning	Osborne's is featuring men's shirts, women's dresses, and boys' shoes.	
Speed	Try to keep the fingers in typing position when shifting for capitals.	

| 1 | 2 | 3 | 4 | 5 | 6 | 7 | 8 | 9 | 10 | 11 | 12 | 13 | 14 |

142B: Tabulation Timed Writing (15) *(Full sheets)*

1. Type a 5′ writing on the table below. Determine quickly placement and needed stops. Use a full sheet, and start the centered heading about 1″ from the top edge. If you complete the table before time is up, DS, and start over. Proofread; determine *gwam*.
2. Type another 5′ writing and try to improve your Step 1 rate.

Full sheet
Proper spacing between parts
2 spaces between columns
DS data of columns

NEW SALES REPRESENTATIVES (Words: 5)

Name	Street	City and State	ZIP Code	Words
				19
Frank Baker	1639 Lake Forest Drive	Sacramento, Calif.	95826	31
George Campbell	5934 Huntington Drive	Baton Rouge, La.	70810	44
Andrew Chin	234 Kukaniloko Walk	Honolulu, Hawaii	96817	55
Steven Lasker	5078 Cervantes Blvd.	San Francisco, Calif.	94123	67
Bernard Newman	15867 Lakeview Drive	Washington, D. C.	20031	79
M. E. Olberding	5478 S. Indiana Avenue	Charleston, W. Va.	25304	92
Jack Roberts	29375 Barrett Avenue	Cleveland, Ohio	44108	103
Howard Towne	366 Azalea Lane	Billings, Mont.	59101	113
James Ziegler	7823 Boulder Ave., N.	Tulsa, Okla.	74126	124

142C: Letter Production Skill Measurement (30)

Time Schedule	
Planning and preparing	3′
Timed production measurement .	20′
Proofreading; determining *n-pram*	7′

Repeat 141D, pages 218–219, but *correct all errors.* When time is called, proofread carefully. Subtract 15 words from the total words typed for each uncorrected error. Determine *n-pram* (net production rate a minute—all errors corrected or penalties assessed).

136C: Building Letter Production Skill (30) *(Modified block; ¶ indention: 5; 1 cc; address envelope)*

Time Schedule	
Planning and preparing	3′
Timed production writing . . .	20′
Proofreading; determining *g-pram*	7′

Type each letter on a separate letterhead or plain sheet. Use *current date; mixed punctuation.*

If you complete the letters before time is up, start over; use plain paper for repeated problems. Do not correct errors. When time is called, proofread; determine *g-pram.*

Problem 1

(Because of the unusual number of enumerations, this letter should be treated as a long letter and placed accordingly. Indent the enumerated items 5 spaces from the left and right margins; leave a DS before and after each item.) (Reference: Page 147.)

Words

Mr. Thomas Harper | 930 Alta Vista Road | 11
Louisville, Kentucky 40205 | Dear Tom: (¶ 1) 19
This letter is being sent to you and to every other 29
representative of this Company. We are starting 39
a campaign to improve our customer relations, 48
and we need your help. In this letter to you, 57
I should like to list some of the things each of us 68
should keep in mind as we deal with our cus- 76
tomers. Perhaps a good beginning would be to 86
give some of the responses that might be made 95
to the question, "What is a customer?" 103

1. A customer is the most important per- 111
son with whom we can deal––in 117
person or by mail. 121
2. A customer is not dependent on 128
us––we are dependent on him. 134
3. A customer is not an interruption of 142
our work––he is the purpose of it. 149
4. A customer is not an outsider to our 157
business––he is the reason for it. 165
5. A customer is a person who brings 172
us his wants––it is our job to handle 180
them profitably to him and to our- 186
selves. 188

(¶ 2) These are some of the responses that might 197
be made to the question, "What is a customer?" 206
I hope we will remember these things when we 215
deal with our customers. They are our most 224
important asset. Without them, we could not 233
remain in business. Will you help us make each 243
of our customers a "King" by trying at all times 253
to give him the best possible service. We need 262
the goodwill and continued patronage of our 271
customers if we are to grow and prosper. Cor- 280
dially yours, | Scott Thorsen, Sales Manager | 289/302
(260)

Problem 2

Mr. Bryan Humphrey, Manager | Student Type- 11
writing Service | Huron High School | Huron, 19
South Dakota 57350 | Dear Mr. Humphrey: | 28
(¶ 1) Thanks for your inquiry about letter styles. 37
This letter is arranged in the modified block 46
style with 5-space paragraph indentions. Busi- 55
ness letters are usually typed on 8½- by 11-inch 65
letterhead stationery which has the name of the 75
company sending the letter, as well as other 84
identifying information, printed at the top of the 94
sheet. (¶ 2) The position of the date line is 102
varied according to the length of the letter. 111
More space is left before the date line of short 121
letters than of long letters. The address is typed 132
on the fourth line (3 blank lines) below the date. 142
Some business offices use standard margins (a 151
set line length) for all letters; others adjust the 162
margins according to the length of the letter. 171
(¶ 3) Other questions about letter placement are 178
answered in the letter style booklet which is 189
enclosed with this letter. Don't hesitate to write 199
to us if there is any other information you need. 210
Sincerely, | Steven Osborn | Communications 218
Consultant | Enc. (182) 221/241

LESSON 137

137A: Conditioning Practice (5) *each line three times*

Alphabet	Exquisite lace was found in the Topaz Village Market by the jolly man.	*Hands quiet*
Figure-symbol	The house located at 23968 Richmond Street sold for $14,750 last year.	
Shift key	Jack McNeil will meet Elvis C. O'Brien tomorrow in Idaho Falls, Idaho.	
Speed	The full value of happiness is gained through sharing it with someone.	
	| 1 | 2 | 3 | 4 | 5 | 6 | 7 | 8 | 9 | 10 | 11 | 12 | 13 | 14 |	

141C: Related Learning – Punctuation Guides *(End of Series)* (10) *follow standard directions*

32. Apostrophe—Use the apostrophe and s to form the plural of most figures, letters, and words (6's, A's, five's). In market quotations, the plural of figures is expressed by the addition of s only.

33. Apostrophe—To show possession, add the apostrophe and s to (a) a singular noun; and, (b) a plural noun which does not end in s.

34. Apostrophe—To show possession, add the apostrophe and s to a proper name of one syllable which ends in s.

35. Apostrophe—To show possession, add the apostrophe only after (a) plural nouns ending in s; and, (b) a proper name of more than one syllable which ends in s.

36. Apostrophe—To show possession, add the apostrophe after the last noun in a series to indicate joint or common possession of two or more persons. **Note.** Separate possession of two or more persons is indicated by adding the possessive to each of the nouns; as, the manager's and the treasurer's reports.

32	*Learn*	Be sure your f's don't look like 7's. Boston Fund 4s are due in 1972.
	Apply	Cross your ts and dot your i s. Be sure to sell United 6's this week.
33	*Learn*	A boy's bicycle has been found, but the men's shoes are still missing.
	Apply	Buy the girls dress today; childrens toys will be on sale Wednesday.
34	*Learn*	Do not pay Charles's bill for $230 today, but pay 75 cents at Jones's.
	Apply	Was it Bess' hat, Ross' shoes, or Chris' watch that was lost today?
35	*Learn*	Those lawyers' offices were about 15 miles from Anthony Roberts' home.
	Apply	The boys camp counselor said that he will visit the Adams home soon.
36	*Learn*	Men's hats and boys' shoes will be on sale at Levy and Stover's store.
	Apply	Jerrys and Philips bicycles were found at my aunt's and uncle's house.
		(separate possession) *(common possession)*

141D: Building Letter Production Skill (30) *(Modified block style; carbon copy)*

Time Schedule	
Planning and preparing	3'
Timed production writing . . .	20'
Proofreading; determining *g-pram*	7'

Type each letter on a separate letterhead or plain sheet. Use *current date*; *mixed punctuation.*

If you complete the letters before time is up, start over; use plain paper for repeated problems. Do not correct errors. When time is called, proofread; determine *g-pram*.

Problem 1

Because of the special lines, this letter of 241 words should be treated as a long letter and placed accordingly on the page. In the body of the letter, center the book title and the name of the author. Double-space these special lines.

Words

Mr. Steven Lasker 5078 Cervantes Blvd. San 12
Francisco, Calif. 94123 Dear Mr. Lasker: (¶ 1) 20
"Gold! This was the call, high and shrill, that 30
broke on the frosty California air early in 1848. 40
With the suddenness of a thunderclap, it killed 50
a way of life and brought forth another." It was 60
the event that "tore the American frontier loose 69
from its Missouri River moorings and sent it leap- 79
ing to the Pacific." (¶ 2) The whole exciting 87
story of the gold-rush days is now vividly and 97
authentically told in a distinguished new book 106
from the Ward Richie Press: 112
DS
GHOST TOWNS AND MINING CAMPS OF CALIFORNIA 121
DS
by Remi Nadeau 124
DS
This book brings you a panoramic portrayal of 132
the gold boom—covering all of California, sec- 142
tion by section and town by town. The book 150
contains 288 pages, 5 guide maps, and 55 his- 159
torical prints and photographs. It presents a 169
history of the gold rush that is fast-moving and 178
exciting. With its comprehensive index and 187
helpful bibliography, GHOST TOWNS AND MIN- 195
ING CAMPS OF CALIFORNIA will find a permanent 205
place on your library shelves for its unique ref- 214
erence value. (¶ 3) This is your opportunity to 223
reserve a first copy of this new book. You will 233

(Continued on page 219)

137B: Speed Emphasis (5) *1′ writing on each line of 138A, below; Goal: Speed with continuity*

137C: Related Learning – Punctuation Guides *(Continued)* (10) *follow standard directions*

17. Parentheses—Use parentheses to enclose parenthetical or explanatory matter and added information.

18. Parentheses—Use parentheses to enclose letters or figures used to identify enumerated items.

19. Parentheses—Use parentheses to enclose figures following amounts which are expressed in words (figures are used for added clarity or emphasis).

20. Underline—The underline, as is true for quotation marks, may be used to call attention to special words or phrases. **Note.** Use a continuous underline unless each word is to be considered separately from the rest; as, He misspelled steel, occur, and weird.

21. Underline—Use the underline to indicate titles of books and names of magazines and newspapers.

17 *Learn* The contracts (Exhibit A) and the mortgages (Exhibit B) were enclosed.
Apply This is the book_20TH CENTURY TYPEWRITING_that we use in this class.

18 *Learn* He stressed these factors: (1) speed, (2) accuracy, and (3) neatness.
Apply Check these techniques: _1_stroking,_2_rhythm, and_3_continuity.

19 *Learn* The undersigned agrees to pay the sum of three hundred dollars ($300).
Apply A balance of four hundred sixty-two dollars, $462, is due and payable.

20 *Learn* There is a difference between blazing a trail and burning up the road.
Apply They translated the Latin phrase, nemo non venit, as "everybody came."

21 *Learn* The book New Learning was reviewed in Harper's and the New York Times.
Apply Did you read the review of Learning to Learn in the Los Angeles Times?

(Make needed corrections—cues omitted in Apply sentences.)

137D: Letter Production Skill Measurement (30)

Time Schedule	
Planning and preparing	3′
Timed production measurement .	20′
Proofreading; determining *n-pram*	7′

Repeat 136C, page 211, but *correct all errors.* When time is called, proofread carefully. Subtract 15 words from the total words typed for each uncorrected error. Determine *n-pram* (net production rate a minute—all errors corrected).

LESSON 138

138A: Conditioning Practice (5) *each line three times*

Alphabet: Steven was intrigued by the quizzical expression on Judge Mark's face.

Figure-symbol: In 1967, 372 clerks worked for Jones & Martin. Quote Royal 4s at 58½.

Adjacent key: Were you going to trade a seesaw in the recreation area for the swing?

Speed: Actions speak louder than words––it is by our deeds that we are known.

| 1 | 2 | 3 | 4 | 5 | 6 | 7 | 8 | 9 | 10 | 11 | 12 | 13 | 14 |

Finger-stroking action

138B: Accuracy Emphasis (5) *1′ writing on each line of 138A; Goal: Not over 1 error each minute*

140B: Skill Building – Straight Copy (15) *(Repeat 135B, page 209)*

140C: Production Typing – Typing an Itinerary (30)

Type the itinerary given below in the form illustrated at the right. Use 1″ margins (approximate) on all sides; center heading lines; 1 carbon copy; correct errors. If time permits, retype for speed.

An itinerary (a travel schedule) usually includes a chronological listing of departure and arrival times; mode of travel and accommodations; and, often, a listing of scheduled activities.

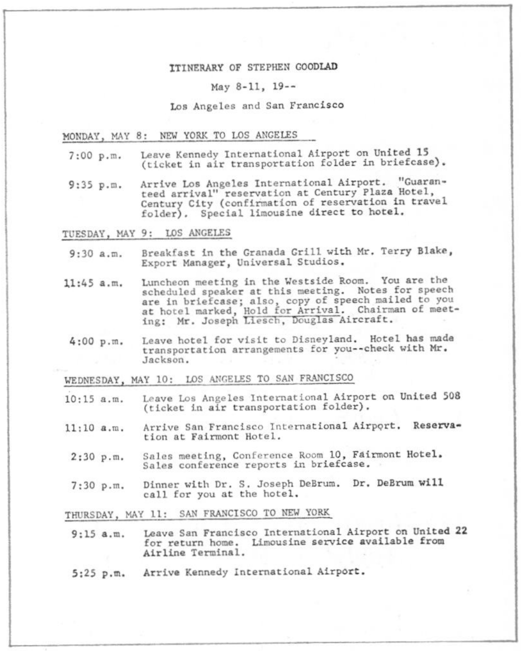

ITINERARY OF STEPHEN GOODLAD | May 8–11, 19–– | Los Angeles and San Francisco |

<u>MONDAY, MAY 8: NEW YORK TO LOS ANGELES</u>

7:00 p.m.	Leave Kennedy International Airport on United 15 (ticket in air transportation folder in briefcase).
9:35 p.m.	Arrive Los Angeles International Airport. "Guaranteed arrival" reservation at Century Plaza Hotel, Century City (confirmation of reservation in travel folder). Special limousine direct to hotel.

<u>TUESDAY, MAY 9: LOS ANGELES</u>

9:30 a.m.	Breakfast in the Granada Grill with Mr. Terry Blake, Export Manager, Universal Studios.
11:45 a.m.	Luncheon meeting in the Westside Room. You are the scheduled speaker at this meeting. Notes for speech are in briefcase; also, copy of speech mailed to you at hotel marked, <u>Hold for Arrival</u>. Chairman of meeting: Mr. Joseph Liesch, Douglas Aircraft.
4:00 p.m.	Leave hotel for visit to Disneyland. Hotel has made transportation arrangements for you––check with Mr. Jackson.

<u>WEDNESDAY, MAY 10: LOS ANGELES TO SAN FRANCISCO</u>

10:15 a.m.	Leave Los Angeles International Airport on United 508 (ticket in air transportation folder).
11:10 a.m.	Arrive San Francisco International Airport. Reservation at Fairmont Hotel.
2:30 p.m.	Sales meeting, Conference Room 10, Fairmont Hotel. Sales conference reports in briefcase.
7:30 p.m.	Dinner with Dr. S. Joseph DeBrum. Dr. DeBrum will call for you at the hotel.

<u>THURSDAY, MAY 11: SAN FRANCISCO TO NEW YORK</u>

9:15 a.m.	Leave San Francisco International Airport on United 22 for return home. Limousine service available from Airline Terminal.
5:25 p.m.	Arrive Kennedy International Airport.

ITINERARY OF STEPHEN GOODLAD

May 8-11, 19--

Los Angeles and San Francisco

<u>MONDAY, MAY 8: NEW YORK TO LOS ANGELES</u>

7:00 p.m. Leave Kennedy International Airport on United 15 (ticket in air transportation folder in briefcase).

9:35 p.m. Arrive Los Angeles International Airport. "Guaranteed arrival" reservation at Century Plaza Hotel, Century City (confirmation of reservation in travel folder). Special limousine direct to hotel.

<u>TUESDAY, MAY 9: LOS ANGELES</u>

9:30 a.m. Breakfast in the Granada Grill with Mr. Terry Blake, Export Manager, Universal Studios.

11:45 a.m. Luncheon meeting in the Westside Room. You are the scheduled speaker at this meeting. Notes for speech are in briefcase; also, copy of speech mailed to you at hotel marked, <u>Hold for Arrival</u>. Chairman of meeting: Mr. Joseph Liesch, Douglas Aircraft.

4:00 p.m. Leave hotel for visit to Disneyland. Hotel has made transportation arrangements for you--check with Mr. Jackson.

<u>WEDNESDAY, MAY 10: LOS ANGELES TO SAN FRANCISCO</u>

10:15 a.m. Leave Los Angeles International Airport on United 508 (ticket in air transportation folder).

11:10 a.m. Arrive San Francisco International Airport. Reservation at Fairmont Hotel.

2:30 p.m. Sales meeting, Conference Room 10, Fairmont Hotel. Sales conference reports in briefcase.

7:30 p.m. Dinner with Dr. S. Joseph DeBrum. Dr. DeBrum will call for you at the hotel.

<u>THURSDAY, MAY 11: SAN FRANCISCO TO NEW YORK</u>

9:15 a.m. Leave San Francisco International Airport on United 22 for return home. Limousine service available from Airline Terminal.

5:25 p.m. Arrive Kennedy International Airport.

LESSON 141

141A: Conditioning Practice (5) *each line three times*

Alphabet	Have you ever watched a quick jet zoom past as a bird in exact flight?
Figure-symbol	He bought the #39572 die for $84.60, taking an 11% discount of $10.46.
Related learning	Form possessives as follows: boy's hat, men's shirts, but boys' hats.
Speed	Faith carries the light of truth which eliminates the shadow of doubt.
	| 1 | 2 | 3 | 4 | 5 | 6 | 7 | 8 | 9 | 10 | 11 | 12 | 13 | 14 |

141B: Speed and Accuracy Emphasis (5) *1′ writing on each line of 141A; Goal: Speed with control.*

138C: Related Learning – Punctuation Guides (*Continued*) (10) *follow standard directions*

22. **Quotation Marks**—Use quotation marks to enclose direct quotations. **Note.** When the question mark applies to the entire sentence, it is typed outside the quotation marks.

23. **Quotation Marks**—Use quotation marks to enclose titles of articles, poems, plays, and the like.

24. **Quotation Marks**—Use quotation marks to enclose special words or phrases (for emphasis).

25. **Quotation Marks**—Use single quotation marks (the apostrophe) to indicate a quotation within a quotation.

26. **Semicolon**—Use a semicolon to separate two or more coordinate clauses (compound sentence) when the conjunction is not expressed.

22	*Learn*	Was it Emerson who said, "The only way to have a friend is to be one"?
	Apply	He quoted Samuel's statement, The electorate is the jury writ large.
23	*Learn*	Did any of you read Peter's latest article, "Frontier Thinking Today"?
	Apply	The musical Sound of Music won a top rating in the Atlantic Monthly.
24	*Learn*	The difficult "problem of space" is still that space between our ears!
	Apply	It is only by scratching for the facts that we arrive at real truth.
25	*Learn*	I think I wrote, "We must have, as Tillich said, 'the courage to be.' "
	Apply	I said, "We must be, as the poet said, One for all and all for one."
26	*Learn*	To be critical is easy; to be constructive and helpful is not so easy.
	Apply	We cannot live on past glory, we must strive to improve and go onward.

138D: Preview Practice – Special Letter Problem Applications (15)

Step 1: Typing a Table Within a Letter

a. Special Drill—Table I, page 214. Using 1″ side margins and drill paper, type the last two lines of the paragraph preceding Table I. Double-space; then type Table I according to the special directions given on page 214. Note that in Columns 2 and 3 the data are centered under the columnar headings; be sure to set tab stops for these points. After typing Table I, double-space and type the first two lines of the paragraph following Table I.

b. Special Drill—Table II, page 215. Using 1″ side margins and drill paper, type the last two lines of the paragraph preceding Table II. Double-space, then type Table II according to the special directions given on page 215. After typing Table II, double-space and type the first two lines of the paragraph following Table II.

Step 2: Typing a Company Name in the Closing Lines

Preview. When used in the closing lines, the company name is typed in all CAPITALS a double space below the complimentary close as shown in the illustration. The typed name of the dictator is then typed 4 spaces (3 blank lines) below the company name. **Note.** The *Copy to* notation may be abbreviated *cc:*.

Special Drill. Starting with the last two lines of the body of the letter, type the closing lines as shown in the illustration. Use 1″ side margins and drill paper; leave proper spacing between the various closing parts.

```
                                   Yours for safe driving,

                                   NATIONAL HIGHWAY SAFETY COUNCIL



                                   Frank Baker, Chief
                                   Traffic Safety

xx

Copy to Mr. Stephen Buffon
        A.A.A. Safety Engineer
```

COMPANY NAME IN THE CLOSING LINES; COPY TO NOTATION

LESSON 139

139A: Conditioning Practice (5) *each line three times*

Alphabet	A mad boxer shot a quick, gloved jab to the jaw of his dizzy opponent.	Fingers close to keys
Figure-symbol	Special sale items are identified by the *; as, 10 *, 631 *, 792 *, 845 *.	
Adjacent key	Robert tired quickly as he tried to remove the five turrethead rivets.	
Speed	This world is full of good intentions which are waiting to be applied.	
	| 1 | 2 | 3 | 4 | 5 | 6 | 7 | 8 | 9 | 10 | 11 | 12 | 13 | 14 |	

139B: Related Learning – Punctuation Guides (*Continued*) (10) *follow standard directions*

27. Semicolon—Use a semicolon to separate independent clauses when they are joined by a conjunctive adverb (however, consequently, nevertheless, etc.).

28. Semicolon—Use a semicolon to separate a series of phrases or clauses (especially if they contain commas) that are introduced by a colon.

29. Semicolon—Place the semicolon outside the final quotation mark; the period, inside.

30. Apostrophe—The apostrophe may be used as a symbol for feet in billings or tabulations, or for minutes.

31. Apostrophe—The apostrophe may be used as a symbol to indicate the omission of letters (as in contractions or figures).

27	*Learn*	He did not follow the rule; consequently, he made many serious errors.
	Apply	He had good typewriting techniques, consequently, he typed with speed.
28	*Learn*	Our sales were: 1965, $1,125,840; 1966, $1,531,450; 1967, $1,935,976.
	Apply	These are the new officers: John Van, President, Dee Ford, Secretary.
29	*Learn*	Mr. Carr spoke on "Building Speed"; Mr. Brown, on "Building Accuracy."
	Apply	You cannot use "therefore;" expenses will not increase "necessarily".
30	*Learn*	The billing was as follows: 15′ x 18′. Robert ran the mile in 3′54″.
	Apply	The apostrophe may be used to express feet in billings; as, 20 ft. x 24 ft.
31	*Learn*	Shouldn't we pay tribute to the "Spirit of '76" in celebrating July 4?
	Apply	Cant the class of 67 meet today? We shouldnt upset our scheduling.

139C: Letter Production Typing (35) (*Complete the problem of 138E, pages 214–215.*)

LESSON 140

140A: Conditioning Practice (5) *each line three times*

Alphabet	The quick, ambiguous quiz on job pay vexed all who had studied for it.	Eyes on copy
Figure-symbol	Did he order the 16–, 20–, and 24–foot beams (5 7/8″ x 9 3/4″) for us?	
Script	Competence as a part of success must be earned and re-earned each day.	
Speed	Some people never escape from the confinement of their own prejudices.	
	| 1 | 2 | 3 | 4 | 5 | 6 | 7 | 8 | 9 | 10 | 11 | 12 | 13 | 14 |	

138E: Letter Production Typing (15) *(Additional time is provided in Lesson 139 for completion of letter)*

Three-Page Letter with Title Line, Tabulations, Enumerated Items, Company Name in Closing Lines, and Copy Notation

Modified block style with 5-space ¶ indentions
Current date; mixed punctuation
1" side and bottom margins (approximate)
Horizontal form heading (page 202) for pages 2 and 3

Center title line in all capitals with a DS before and after the line
Indent enumerated items (page 215) 5 spaces from left and right margins; DS before and after each item

Words

(Current date) | Dr. M. E. Oliverio, President | Fairmont Glass, Incorporated | 15
5599 South Indiana Avenue | Charleston, West Virginia 25304 | Dear Dr. Oliverio: | 31

This letter is being sent to all business firms in the United States. Your 46
cooperation and help are needed. Won't you see that the following portion of this 62
letter is duplicated and distributed to all your employees. This is one step your 79
National Council is taking in its efforts to reduce the highway accident rate. 95

SAFETY ON THE HIGHWAYS 100

With most epidemics, our highly developed society is very harsh. Offending 115
microorganisms are hit and destroyed with arsenals of wonder drugs and batteries 131
of hypodermic needles. Yet there is one epidemic we permit, almost as if we were 147
unaware of its existence. This is the auto accident plague. Every driver should 164
ask himself if the minutes saved by excessive speed are worth the consequences of 180
highway accidents—broken bones, disfigured bodies, or even sudden death. Every 196
driver should remember that a car driven at any speed is, in reality, a guided 212
missile, but without built-in and programmed controls. It can be only as safe as 229
the degree of control and caution exercised by the driver. 241

"Murder by Motor," as the dread havoc of the roads has been called by the 255
American Trial Lawyers Association, is this nation's most serious accident prob- 272
lem. During a recent year, auto accidents took 53,500 lives. The minute you 287
start your car, you have an "accident potential" that varies with your age group. 304
Although all age groups are involved, young people are particularly susceptible 320
as is indicated by the following table: 328

4 spaces between longest line of Col. 1 and columnar heading for Col. 2;
4 spaces between Col. 2 heading and Col. 3 heading
In Cols. 2 and 3, center data under headings
DS data

TABLE I. AGE OF DRIVERS IN ACCIDENTS 336

Age Group	Fatal Accidents	Nonfatal Accidents	Words
Under 24 years	30.3%	28.3%	358
25–64 years	62.3	67.2	363
65 and over	7.4	4.5	367

(Heading line: 353)

Since most boys and girls start driving a car at about age 16, this table 382
indicates, in terms of the 8-year age span, that the greatest number of fatal 397
and nonfatal accidents occur in the "Under 24 years" age group. The hazard of 413
driving for a young person is indicated by the fact that motor vehicle accidents 429
constitute two thirds of all accident fatalities among males 15 to 19 years of age. 446

Because more and more young people will be driving in the years ahead, every 462
effort must be made to make everyone safety conscious so that the trend toward 477

Words

increased "slaughter on the highways" can be reversed or at least halted. SAFETY 494
ON THE HIGHWAYS must begin at home and in our schools if we are to reduce the 509
auto accident rate. Listed here are some of the things that you as an individual 526
can do: 528

1. Learn thoroughly how to operate an automobile with safety. Always 542
   follow the best driving practices and allow no exceptions to occur. 556
2. Always keep your car in a safe mechanical condition. Be aware of 570
   the road conditions as you drive. 577
3. Set a good example for others by observing all traffic laws and by 591
   practicing courtesy on the highways. 598
4. Keep well within the speed limits at all times. 609

Accidents are basically the result of a failure to recognize risk. One of 624
the real keys to safe driving is to anticipate danger and to get ready for it 640
while you still have plenty of time to stop. In this way, you can avoid the need 656
for most quick stops. It is well to know, too, the total stopping distance needed 673
when it is necessary to make sudden or quick stops. The following table gives 688
this information: 692

4 spaces between longest lines of columnar headings
SS data and center under columnar headings

TABLE II. STOPPING DISTANCE CHART 699

Miles per Hour	Feet Traveled per Second	Driver Reaction Distance*	Vehicle Braking Distance	Total Stopping Distance	Words
					706 / 713 / 730
20	29	22	23	45	733
30	44	33	45	78	735
40	59	44	81	125	739
50	73	55	133	188	742
60	88	66	206	272	745
70	103	77	304	381	749

752

*Based on 3/4-second reaction time 759

In normal driving, an extra factor known as Perception Distance must be added 775
to the Total Stopping Distance. Perception Distance is the distance traveled from 791
the point where you could and should recognize a hazard to the point where you do 808
actually recognize it. This distance varies widely among individuals according 824
to their alertness. 828

A rather grim picture has been presented here; but if it saves the life of 843
even one person who reads it, then it will have served its purpose. It is too 859
late to be sorry after an accident occurs. The scars of accidents, like rubbish, 875
litter our highways. Why take a chance when with the exercise of due care and 891
caution you can greatly reduce your chances of having an automobile accident. 907
Always, when you press your foot on the accelerator, ask yourself this question: 923
Is the time I save by the extra speed worth the chance I may be taking? If you 939
prefer living to "sudden death," then Drive with Care! Remember: The life you 962
save may be your own. 971
Yours for safe driving, | NATIONAL HIGHWAY SAFETY COUNCIL | Frank Baker, Chief | 986
Traffic Safety | (xx) | Copy to Mr. Stephen Buffon | A.A.A. Safety Engineer | 999

Reference Guide

TYPEWRITER OPERATIVE PARTS

Typewriters have similar operative parts, the names of which vary somewhat from typewriter to typewriter even when the function is the same. These similar operative parts are identified in the four segments of a typewriter given below and on page ii. Each segment is a composite and not an exact segment of any one typewriter. For this reason, the exact location of a part identified in the segment may be slightly different from that on your typewriter; but the differences are, for the most part, few and slight.

Extra parts that are peculiar to the typewriter you operate and not common to most typewriters can be identified by reference to the instructional booklet distributed by the manufacturer of the typewriter. This booklet can be very helpful to you because all its content is directed to the operation of one specific make of machine.

In using the illustrations, follow the line from the number to the part location. Know the function of each part, as explained in the textbook, and learn to operate it with maximum efficiency.

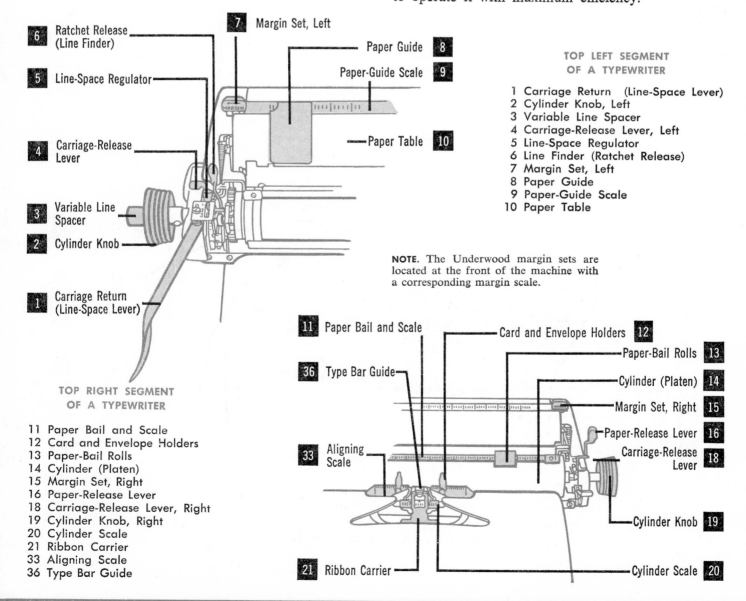

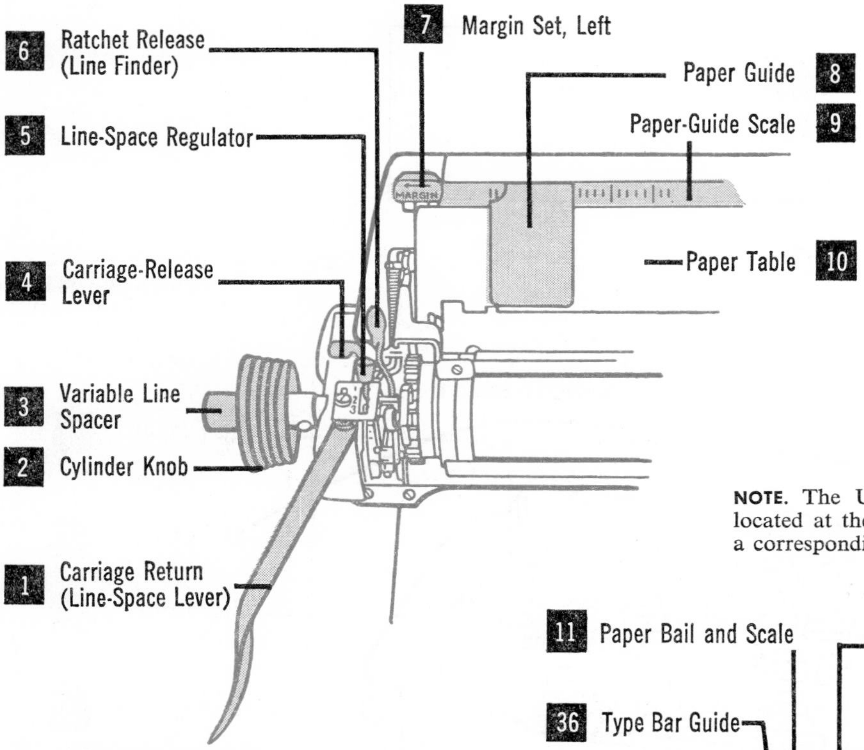

TOP LEFT SEGMENT OF A TYPEWRITER

1 Carriage Return (Line-Space Lever)
2 Cylinder Knob, Left
3 Variable Line Spacer
4 Carriage-Release Lever, Left
5 Line-Space Regulator
6 Line Finder (Ratchet Release)
7 Margin Set, Left
8 Paper Guide
9 Paper-Guide Scale
10 Paper Table

NOTE. The Underwood margin sets are located at the front of the machine with a corresponding margin scale.

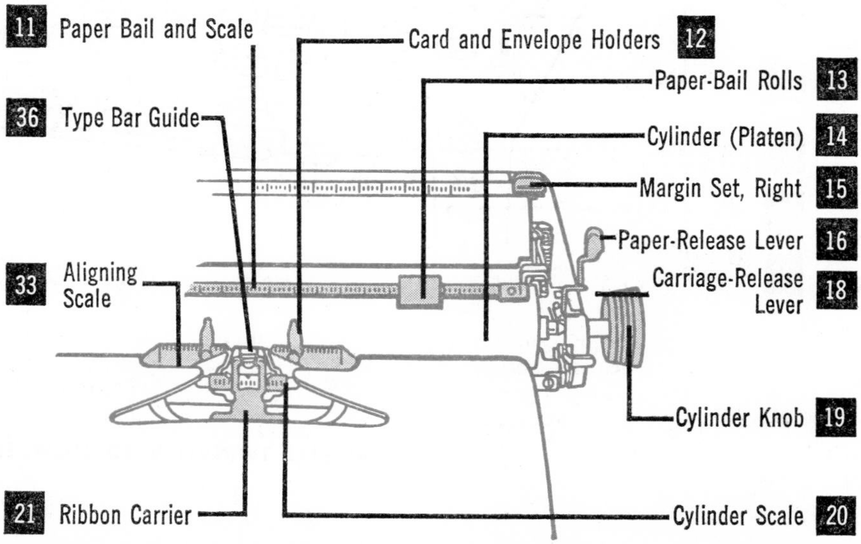

TOP RIGHT SEGMENT OF A TYPEWRITER

11 Paper Bail and Scale
12 Card and Envelope Holders
13 Paper-Bail Rolls
14 Cylinder (Platen)
15 Margin Set, Right
16 Paper-Release Lever
18 Carriage-Release Lever, Right
19 Cylinder Knob, Right
20 Cylinder Scale
21 Ribbon Carrier
33 Aligning Scale
36 Type Bar Guide

LOWER SEGMENT OF A MANUAL TYPEWRITER

22 Ribbon Control and Stencil Lock
23 Tab Set Key
24 Tabulator Bar or Key
25 Margin-Release Key
26 Shift Key, Right
27 Space Bar
28 Shift Key, Left
29 Shift Lock, Left and Right
30 Backspace Key
31 Tab Clear Key
32 Ribbon Reverse
34 Touch Regulator

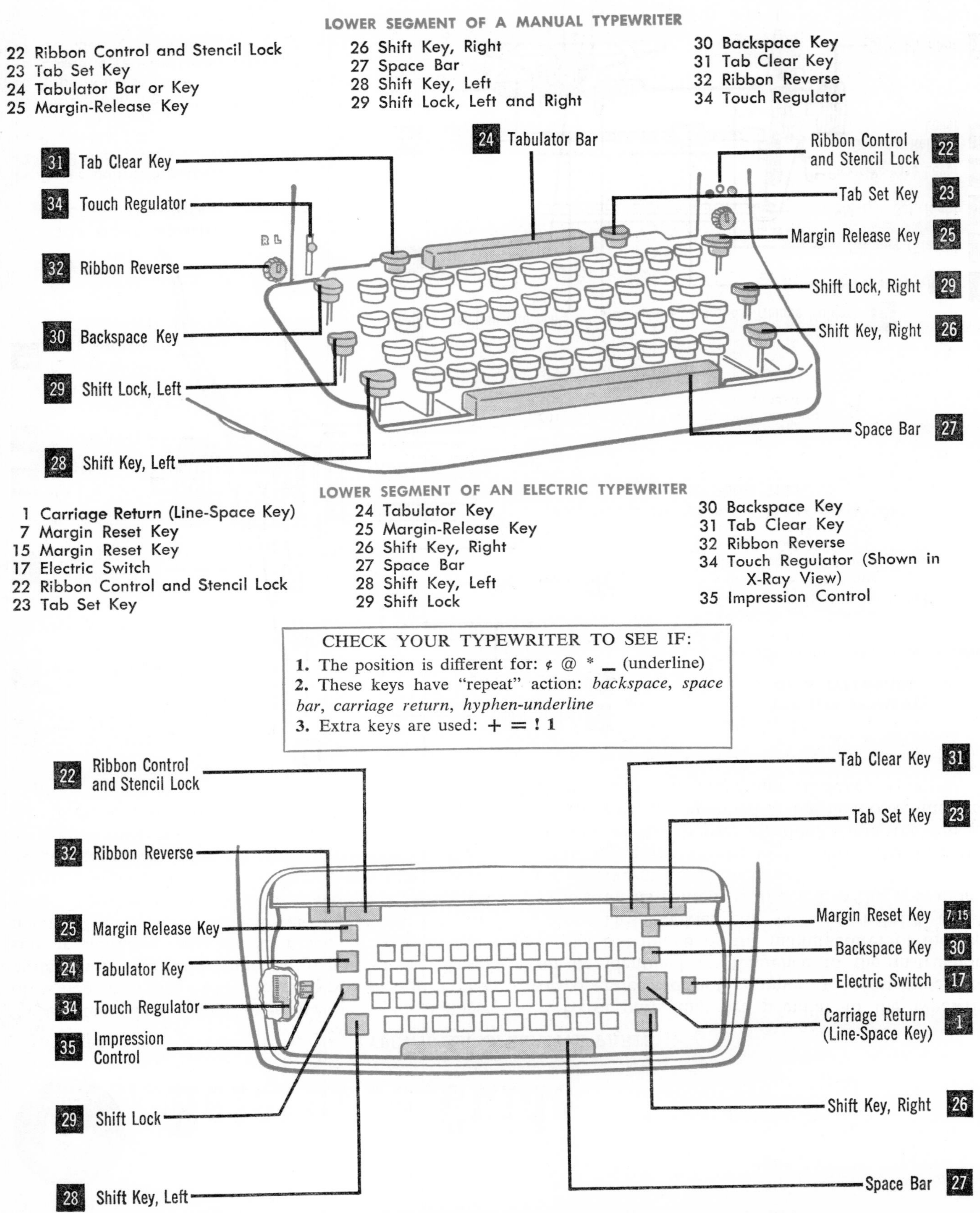

LOWER SEGMENT OF AN ELECTRIC TYPEWRITER

1 Carriage Return (Line-Space Key)
7 Margin Reset Key
15 Margin Reset Key
17 Electric Switch
22 Ribbon Control and Stencil Lock
23 Tab Set Key
24 Tabulator Key
25 Margin-Release Key
26 Shift Key, Right
27 Space Bar
28 Shift Key, Left
29 Shift Lock
30 Backspace Key
31 Tab Clear Key
32 Ribbon Reverse
34 Touch Regulator (Shown in X-Ray View)
35 Impression Control

CHECK YOUR TYPEWRITER TO SEE IF:

1. The position is different for: ¢ @ * _ (underline)
2. These keys have "repeat" action: *backspace, space bar, carriage return, hyphen-underline*
3. Extra keys are used: + = ! 1

SETTING THE PAPER GUIDE; CENTERING THE PAPER

IBM, Olympia, R. C. Allen, Royal, Smith-Corona. Set the paper guide **8** so the indicator at the left will point to *0* on the paper-guide scale **9**, which is on the paper table **10**. When paper of standard size (8½″ by 11″) is inserted with the guide at *0*, the centering point will be:

42 for machines with pica type

50 or 51 for machines with elite type

(Note the difference between pica and elite type illustrated in the two lines above. Compare this type with the type on the machine you are using.)

Note. The Smith-Corona provides for "Automatic Centering" of 8½″ by 11″ paper. Two pointers on the paper table scale indicate the position for setting the paper guide when paper of this size is used. For paper 8½″ wide, set the guide at the inside pointer. The center of the sheet is indicated by the pointer on the paper bail.

Remington. The fixed centering point is *0* for both pica- and elite-type machines. Before inserting the paper, line up the left edge of the paper guide with the paper edge mark. This will give the same readings on the scale at both edges of the paper.

Underwood. Scale numbers on the paper table correspond to the width of the paper used. To center 8½″-width paper, move the outer edge of the paper guide until it corresponds with the 8½″ mark on the left paper centering scale. After you have placed the paper inside the guide and moved it into typing position, the right edge will also be at 8½ inches on the right scale.

PLANNING THE MARGIN STOPS

To have the typed material centered horizontally, set stops for the left and right margins. Typewriters differ in their mechanical adjustments and the bell rings at different points on different typewriters, but the carriage locks at the point where the right margin stop is set. After the bell rings, there will be from 8 to 11 or more spaces before the carriage locks, some machines allowing more but none fewer than 8 spaces.

Test out your typewriter and determine the number of spaces the bell rings before the carriage locks. Take this into consideration when setting the right margin stop. Since the ringing of the bell is a cue to return the carriage, set the right stop 5 to 8 spaces beyond the desired line ending so the bell will ring approximately 3 spaces before the point at which you want the line to end.

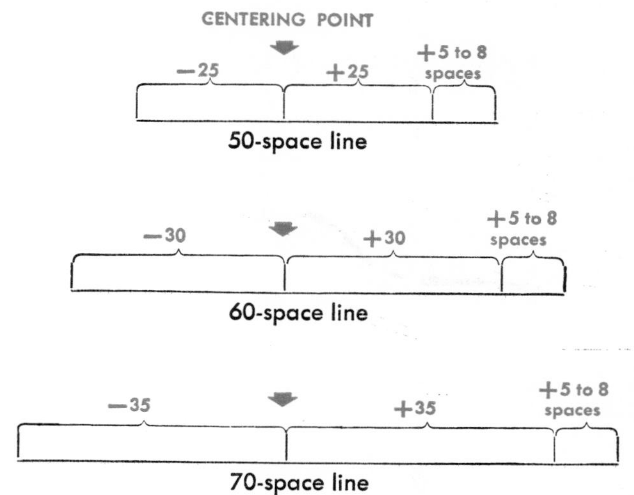

MECHANICS OF SETTING THE MARGIN STOPS

Royal Standard and Electric. *To set the left margin stop,* place your left index finger behind the left "Magic" margin control and move it forward; move the carriage to the desired position; then return the margin control to its original position. *To set the right margin stop,* move the right "Magic" margin control forward; move the carriage to the desired position; then return the margin control to its original position.

IBM Electric. *To set the left margin stop,* move the carriage until it is against the left margin stop; depress and hold down the margin set key as you move the carriage to the desired new position; then release the set key. *To set the right margin stop,* move the carriage until it is against the right margin stop; depress and hold down the margin set key as you move the carriage to the desired new position; then release the set key.

IBM Selectric. Move stops to desired position. This is easy to do by relating their location to the keyboard. As there is no movable carriage as on other typewriters, stops can be moved left or right as the line length requires.

R. C. Allen and Olympia. *To set the left margin stop,* depress the left margin stop, move the carriage to the desired position, and set and then release the stop. Use the same procedure for setting the stop for the right margin.

Remington Standard and Electric. *To set the left margin stop,* move the left margin stop to the desired position to begin the line of writing. Move the stop for the right margin to the desired position to set the stop for the right margin.

Smith-Corona Standard. *To set the left margin stop,* press the left margin set button to the left in the direction of the arrow as you move the carriage to the desired position; then release the margin set button. *To set the right margin stop,* press the right margin set button to the right in the direction of the arrow as you move the carriage to the desired position; then release the margin set button.

Smith-Corona Electric. *To reset the left margin,* depress the left carriage release button and the left margin button, move the carriage to the right to the desired location and release the two buttons simultaneously. The same operation is used to reset the right margin.

Underwood. Set both right and left margins simultaneously. You do not have to move the carriage. The margin indicators (shaded geometric shapes) on the front scale indicate balanced margin set positions.

KNOW YOUR TYPEWRITER. Your machine may have timesaving features not included in this discussion of operating parts. Learn these features from a study of the manufacturer's pamphlet which describes and illustrates the operating parts of the typewriter you are using. You can get this pamphlet without cost from the manufacturer of your typewriter. The pamphlet will have many ideas for your operative improvement.

CHANGING TYPEWRITER RIBBONS

The technique for changing ribbons is not the same for all machines, but in no case is it particularly difficult. The basic steps for changing the ribbon are listed:

1—*Wind the ribbon on one spool, usually the right.*

2—*Raise and lock the ribbon carrier 21.* Do this by pressing down the shift lock **29**, moving the ribbon control **22** for typing on the lower portion of the ribbon, and by depressing and locking any two central keys, such as *y* and *u*.

3—*Remove the ribbon from the carrier 21 and remove both spools.*

4—*Hook the new ribbon to the empty spool and wind several inches of the new ribbon on it.* Be sure that the ribbon winds and unwinds in the proper direction.

5—*Place both spools on their holders and thread the ribbon through the ribbon carrier.*

6—*Release the shift lock, and return the ribbon indicator to the position for typing on the upper portion of the ribbon.* Unlock the two type bars, and the typewriter will be ready for use.

7—*Clean the keys, if necessary.* When a new ribbon is first used, it may be necessary to clean the keys so that all typed letters will be clear and bright.

Nonelectric (Underwood)

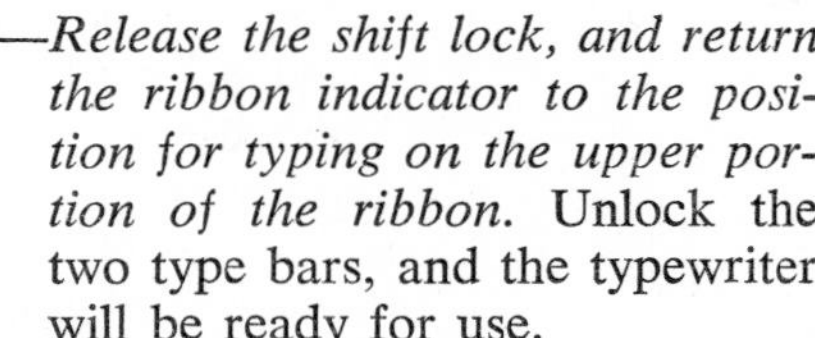

PATH OF THE RIBBON AS IT WINDS AND UNWINDS ON THE TWO SPOOLS

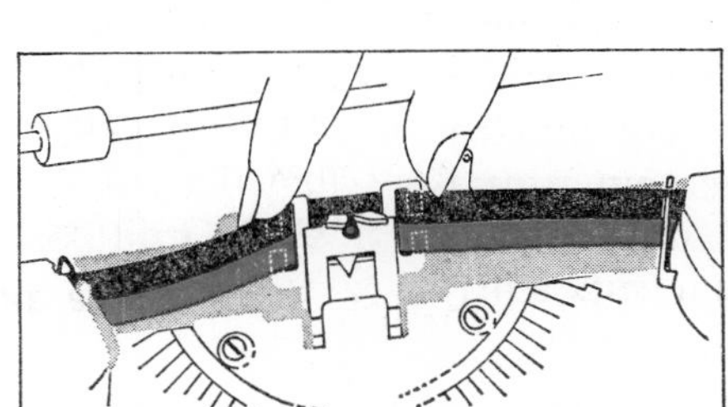

RIBBON THREADED THROUGH THE RIBBON-CARRIER MECHANISM

Electric

IBM RIBBON

LETTER STYLES

August 24, 19--

Mr. Michael C. Hewett, Jr.
Space Technology Laboratories
2746 Coronado Avenue
Long Beach, California 90813

Dear Mr. Hewett

Today many business firms use the block style letter for their correspondence. This letter is an example of that style. You will note that all lines start at the left margin. The advantage of this style is that the mechanical process of indenting opening and closing lines, or paragraphs, is eliminated. This practice saves time and space.

Open punctuation is used with this letter: Punctuation marks are omitted after the date, address, salutation, and complimentary close unless an abbreviation is used, in which case the period is typed as a part of the abbreviation. Elimination of these punctuation marks helps to increase letter production rates. Another recommended timesaving feature is to type only the typist's initials for reference when the dictator's name is typed in the closing lines.

As you can see, the block style letter gives good placement appearance; and, because many extra typing strokes and motions are eliminated, its use does help to increase letter production rates. It is the letter style that I recommend for use in the business office.

Sincerely yours

J. Scott Miller

J. Scott Miller
Communications Consultant

hj

BLOCK, OPEN

January 15, 19--

Dr. James E. Seitz, President
Seitz Business College
San Francisco, California 94126

Dear Dr. Seitz:

This letter is an example of the modified block style. It is one of the most popular business letter styles in use today. As you will observe, it differs from the block style in that the date line and the closing lines (the complimentary close and the typed name and title) are indented and blocked. Mixed punctuation is frequently used with this letter style: a colon after the salutation and a comma after the complimentary close.

When the modified block style is used, letter production efficiency dictates that the date line, the complimentary close, and the typed name and title be started at the same point. Actual practice in the business office, however, varies widely. For instance, the date line may be centered, it may be typed so that it ends at the right margin, or it may be given special placement in relation to the letterhead. Similarly, the closing lines may be started five spaces to the left of center or may be typed so that they end approximately at the right margin.

Although the modified block style gives good placement appearance, it is difficult to account for its popular appeal since, as compared with the block style, additional typing motions are involved in the placement of the various parts. The problem may be that no one has really given serious consideration to the effect of the letter style used on letter production efficiency.

Cordially yours,

John E. Homan

John E. Homan, Director

DR

MODIFIED BLOCK, MIXED

September 13, 19--

Mr. Bryan Humphrey, Manager
Student Typewriting Service
Huron High School
Huron, South Dakota 57350

Dear Mr. Humphrey:

Thanks for your inquiry about letter styles. This letter is arranged in the modified block style with 5-space paragraph indentions. Business letters are usually typed on 8½- by 11-inch letterhead stationery which has the name of the company sending the letter, as well as other identifying information, printed at the top of the sheet.

The position of the date line is varied according to the length of the letter. More space is left before the date line for short letters than for long letters. The address is typed on the fourth line (3 blank lines) below the date. Some business offices use standard margins (a set line length) for all letters; others adjust the margins according to the length of the letter.

Other questions about letter placement are answered in the letter style booklet which is enclosed with this letter. Don't hesitate to write to us if there is any other information you need. Good luck to you and the other students at your school with your typing service.

Sincerely,

Steven Osborn

Steven Osborn
Communications Consultant

hj

Enclosure

MODIFIED BLOCK, INDENTED ¶s, MIXED

December 3, 19--

Dr. Donald Howell, Chairman
Business Education Department
Central State University
Muncie, Indiana 47301

AMS SIMPLIFIED LETTER STYLE

The unique Simplified letter style for business correspondence is sensible, streamlined, and effective. It is a simplified "block style" with all lines beginning at the left margin. Other features are listed below:

1. The address is typed 3 or more blank lines below the date.
2. The salutation and complimentary close are omitted.
3. A subject heading in all capitals is typed a triple space below the address.
4. Unnumbered listed items are indented 5 spaces, but numbered items are typed flush with the left margin.
5. The dictator's name and title are typed in capitals 5 line spaces (4 blank lines) below the body of the letter.
6. Reference initials consist of the typist's initials only.
7. Copy notations are typed a double space below the reference lines.

Because of the timesaving features of this AMS Simplified style letter, its use will reduce your letter-writing costs and give your letters a distinctive "eye appeal." Try it. You will like it.

Lee Clarke

LEE CLARK - SECRETARY

rc

AMS SIMPLIFIED

ADDRESSING ENVELOPES

1. **Typing the Address.** Set a tab stop (or margin stop, if a number of envelopes are to be addressed) 5 spaces to the left of the horizontal center of the envelope. Start the envelope address at this point at or slightly below vertical center of the envelope.

   Observe the amount of space to be left above the address. Learn to judge by *eye measurement* the proper point for starting the first line of the address.

2. **Style.** Most envelopes are typed in *block style* without punctuation at the ends of lines, except when an abbreviation ends a line. The ZIP Code is typed 2 spaces after the state name.

   Note. As a rule, double-space a three-line address; single-space a four-line address.

3. **Placement of Special Notations**

   Airmail. Use an airmail envelope; or in the space between the stamp and the address, place an airmail sticker or type AIRMAIL.

   Special Delivery or *Registered.* Type these notations in all CAPITALS in the space between the stamp and the address.

   Attention Line, Hold for Arrival, or *Personal.* Type these notations in the lower left corner of the envelope. Capitalize the first letter of each principal word.

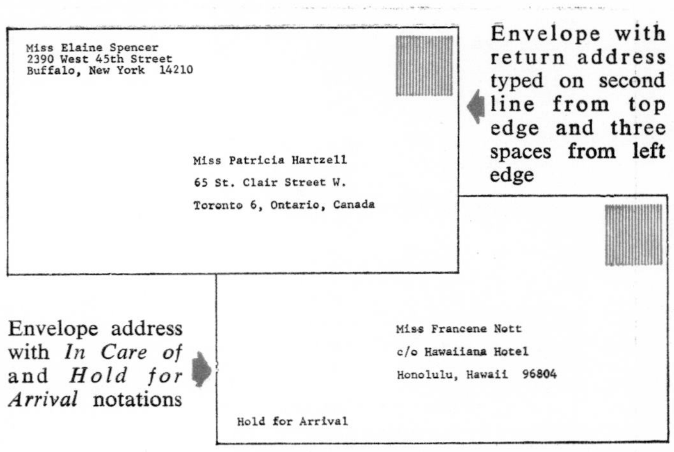

Miss Elaine Spencer
2390 West 45th Street
Buffalo, New York 14210
Miss Patricia Hartzell
65 St. Clair Street W.
Toronto 6, Ontario, Canada
Miss Francene Nott
c/o Hawaiiana Hotel
Honolulu, Hawaii 96804
Hold for Arrival

Envelope with return address typed on second line from top edge and three spaces from left edge

Envelope address with *In Care of* and *Hold for Arrival* notations

SMALL ENVELOPES

Envelope address with AIRMAIL notation and attention line

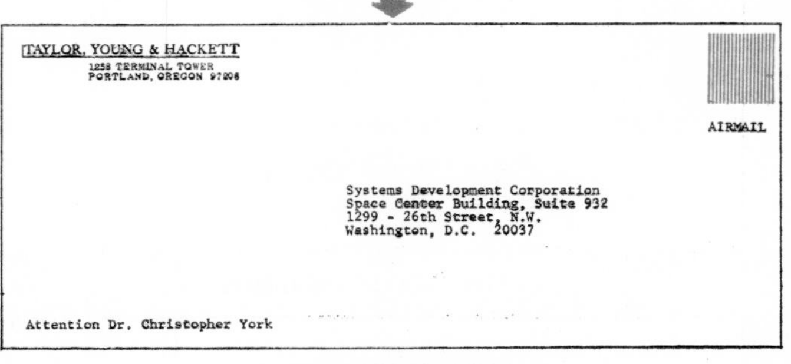

TAYLOR, YOUNG & HACKETT
1258 TERMINAL TOWER
PORTLAND, OREGON 97208
AIRMAIL
Systems Development Corporation
Space Center Building, Suite 932
1299 - 26th Street, N.W.
Washington, D.C. 20037
Attention Dr. Christopher York

LARGE ENVELOPES

FOLDING-AND-INSERTING PROCEDURE FOR ENVELOPES

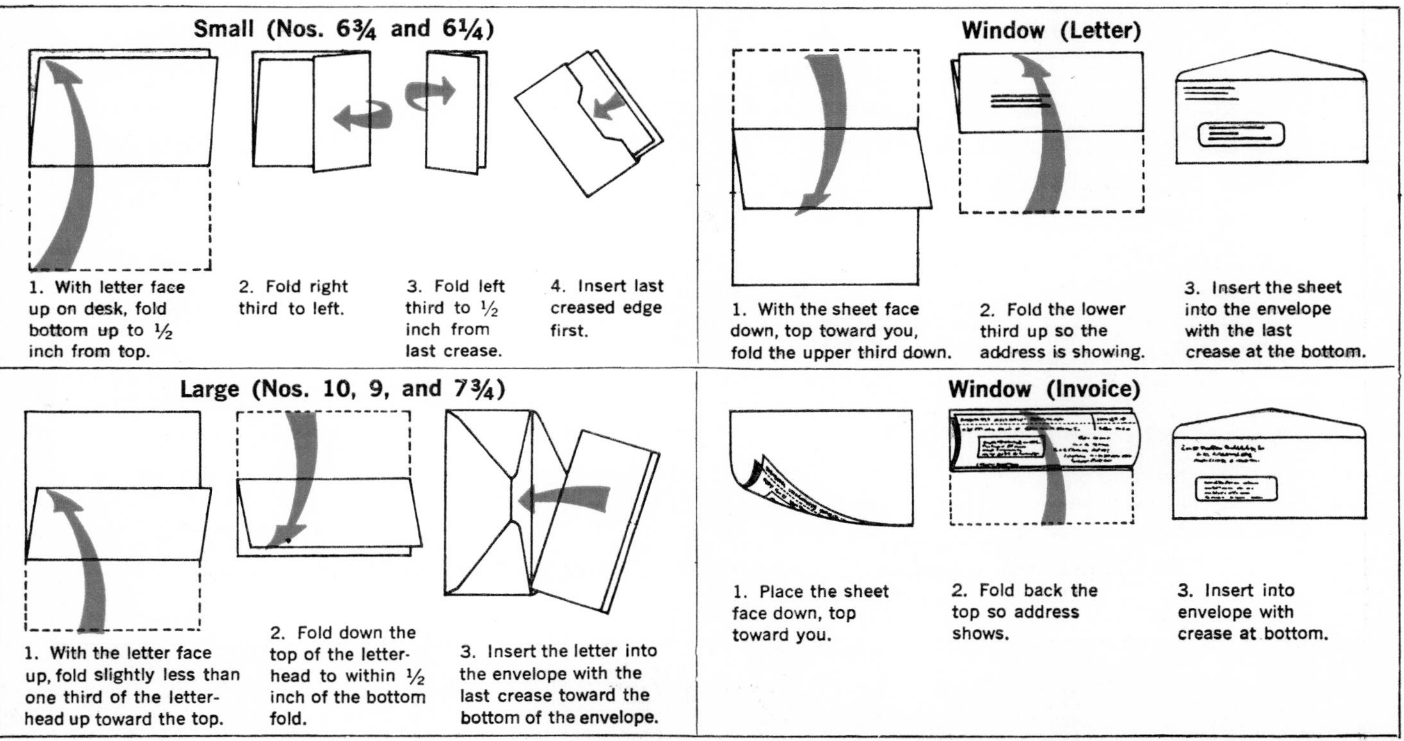

Small (Nos. 6¾ and 6¼)
1. With letter face up on desk, fold bottom up to ½ inch from top.
2. Fold right third to left.
3. Fold left third to ½ inch from last crease.
4. Insert last creased edge first.
Window (Letter)
1. With the sheet face down, top toward you, fold the upper third down.
2. Fold the lower third up so the address is showing.
3. Insert the sheet into the envelope with the last crease at the bottom.
Large (Nos. 10, 9, and 7¾)
1. With the letter face up, fold slightly less than one third of the letterhead up toward the top.
2. Fold down the top of the letterhead to within ½ inch of the bottom fold.
3. Insert the letter into the envelope with the last crease toward the bottom of the envelope.
Window (Invoice)
1. Place the sheet face down, top toward you.
2. Fold back the top so address shows.
3. Insert into envelope with crease at bottom.

SPECIAL LETTER-PLACEMENT POINTS

Paper-Guide Placement. Check the placement of the paper guide so that the horizontal centering of the letter will be accurate.

Margins and Date Placement. Use the following guide:

5-Stroke Words in Letter Body	*Side Margins*	*Date Line*
Up to 100	2″	20
101 – 300	1½″	18–12*
Over 300	1″	12

*Date line is moved up 2 line spaces for each additional 50 words.

Horizontal placement of date varies according to the letter style.

Address. The address is typed on the 4th line (3 blank line spaces) below the date. An official title, when used, may be typed on the first or the second line of the address, whichever gives better balance.

Attention Line. An attention line, when used, is typed on the second line (a double space) below the letter address.

Subject Line. A subject line is typed on the second line (a double space) below the salutation. It may be either centered or typed at the left margin.

Company Name. Sometimes the company name is typed in the closing lines. When this is done, it is typed in *all capital letters* two lines (a double space) below the complimentary close. The modern practice is to omit the company name in the closing lines, particularly if a letterhead is used.

Typewritten Name and Official Title. The name of the person who dictated the letter and his official title are typed 4 lines (3 blank lines) below the complimentary close, or 4 lines below the typed company name when it is used. When both the name and official title are used, they may be typed on the same line or the official title may be typed on the next line below the typed name.

Unusual Features. Letters having unusual features, such as tabulated material, long quotations, or an unusual number of lines in the address or the closing lines, may require changes in the adjustments normally used for letters of that length.

Two-Page Letters. If a letter is too long for one page, at least 2 lines of the body of the letter should be carried to the second page. The second page of a letter, or any additional pages, requires a proper heading. Either the vertical or the horizontal form may be used for the heading; each is followed by a triple space.

Second-Page Headings

```
Dr. J. W. Orr
Page 2
May 14, 19--
```

Vertical Form

Horizontal Form

```
Dr. J. W. Orr        2        May 15, 19--
```

GUIDES FOR WORD DIVISION

1. Divide a word between syllables only. Type a hyphen at the end of the line to indicate the division. Type the rest of the word on the succeeding line.
2. Do not divide a word of five or fewer letters.
3. Do not divide from the remainder of the word:
   a. A one-letter syllable at the beginning or end of a word; as, *around, steady*
   b. A syllable without a vowel; as, *wouldn't*
   c. A two-letter syllable at the end of a word; as, *greatly*
4. Avoid dividing after a two-letter syllable at the beginning of a word. Try to divide elsewhere in the word; as, *express-ing.*
5. Avoid dividing initials, abbreviations, numbers, and proper names; but a surname may be separated from the initials or given name, when necessary.
6. Divide after a one-letter syllable within a word, as *sepa-rate*, unless the word ends with *able*, *ible*, or *ical* (the two-syllable endings you must keep as a unit); as, *depend-able.* If two one-letter syllables come together, divide between the vowels; as, *gradu-ation.*
7. When dividing words, type *cial, tial, cion, sion*, or *tion* as a unit; as, *impar-tial, impres-sion.*
8. If the final consonant in a word is doubled when adding a suffix, divide between the double letters; as, *control-ling*; but when a syllable is added to a word that ends in double letters, divide after the double letters; as, *express-ing, unwill-ing.*
9. Divide hyphened or compound words only at the hyphen that connects the two words; as, *self-explanatory.*
10. If separating the parts of the date is unavoidable, separate between the day of the month and the year.
11. Avoid dividing words at the ends of more than two successive lines, or the final word on a page.

CARBON-PACK ASSEMBLY METHODS

DESK-TOP ASSEMBLY METHOD

1. Assemble letterhead, carbon sheets (*dull side up*), and second sheets as illustrated below. *Use one carbon and one second sheet for each copy desired.*

2. Grasp the carbon pack at the sides, turn it so that the *letterhead faces away from you*, the *glossy side of the carbon faces you*, and the *top edge of the pack face down*. Tap the sheets gently on the desk to straighten.

3. Hold the sheets firmly to prevent slipping; insert pack into typewriter. Hold pack with one hand; turn platen with the other.

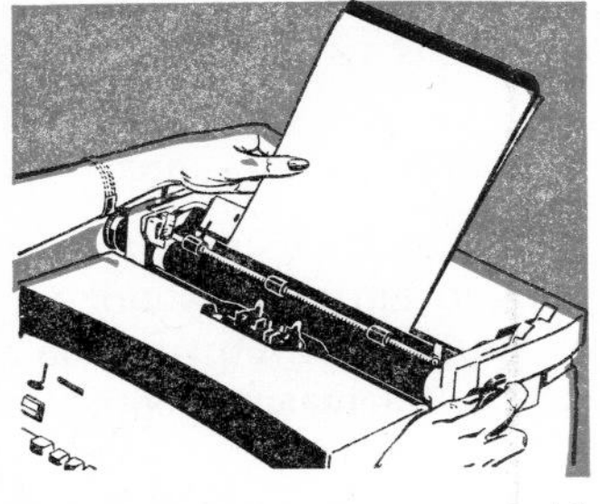

Tip for Wrinkle-Free Assembly

Start pack into typewriter with paper-release lever forward; then reset the paper-release lever and turn pack into the machine.

Inserting the Pack with a Trough

To keep the carbon pack straight when feeding it into the typewriter, place the pack in the fold of a plain sheet of paper (paper trough) or under the flap of an envelope. Remove the trough or envelope when the pack is in place.

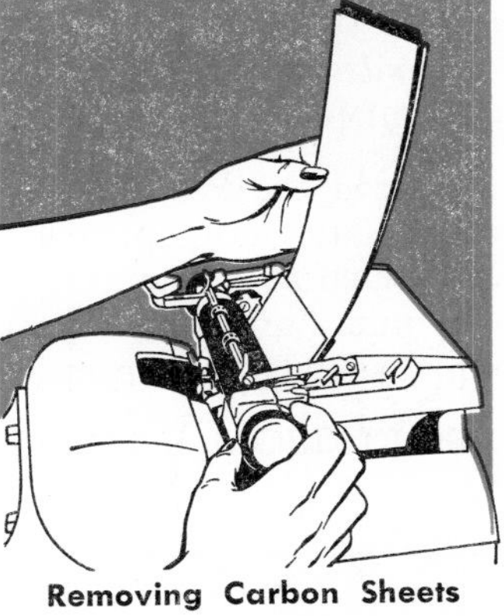

Removing Carbon Sheets

Hold the left edge of the letterhead and second sheets; remove all carbons at one time with the right hand.

MACHINE ASSEMBLY METHOD

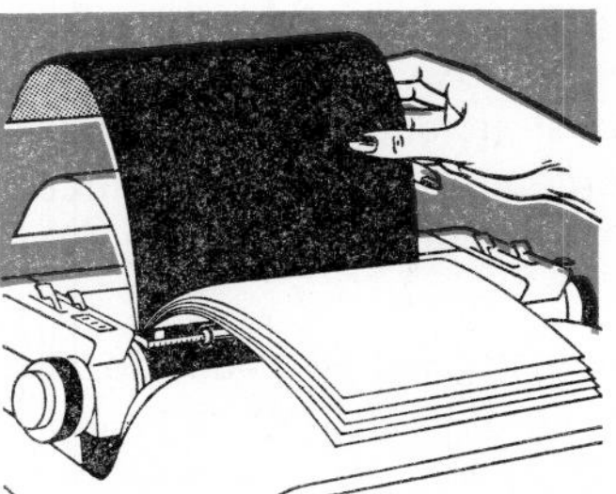

1. Assemble paper for insertion (original on top; second sheets beneath). Turn the "pack" so *original faces away from you* and the *top edge faces down.*
2. Insert sheets until the tops are gripped by the feed rolls; then pull the bottom of all sheets except the last over the top (front) of the typewriter.
3. Place carbon paper between sheets, *glossy side toward you.* Flip each sheet back (away from you) as you add each carbon sheet.
4. Roll pack into typing position.

SLOTTED DRAWER ASSEMBLY METHOD

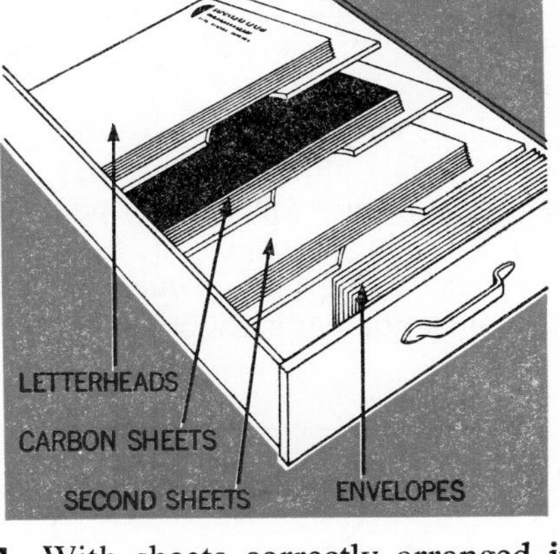

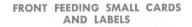

1. With sheets correctly arranged in slotted drawer, pick up a letterhead with left hand and a sheet of carbon paper with right hand; pull sheets slightly forward; grasp both sheets with left hand as right hand reaches and pulls second sheet into position.
2. Pull sheets from slots. Straighten pack by tapping gently on desk as the sides of the sheets are held loosely by both hands.
3. Add extra sets (a second sheet and a carbon) for any additional copies that may be needed.
4. Insert into typewriter as with desk-top assembly method.

FRONT FEEDING SMALL CARDS AND LABELS

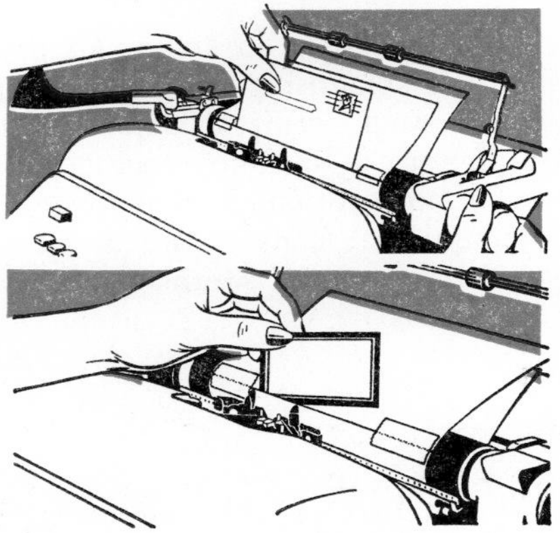
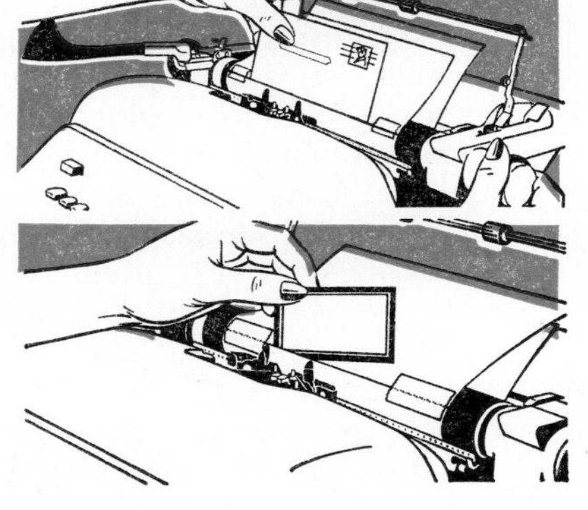

SUMMARY OF MANUSCRIPT FORM

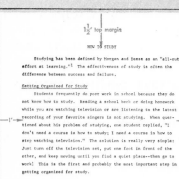

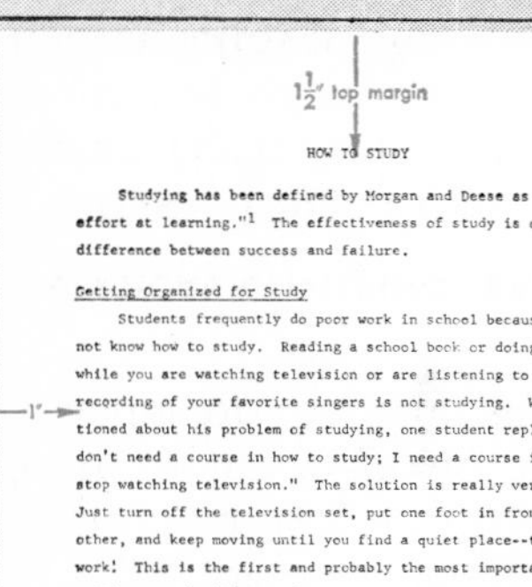

HOW TO STUDY

Studying has been defined by Morgan and Deese as an "all-out effort at learning."[1] The effectiveness of study is often the difference between success and failure.

Getting Organized for Study

Students frequently do poor work in school because they do not know how to study. Reading a school book or doing homework while you are watching television or are listening to the latest recording of your favorite singers is not studying. When questioned about his problem of studying, one student replied, "I don't need a course in how to study; I need a course in how to stop watching television." The solution is really very simple: Just turn off the television set, put one foot in front of the other, and keep moving until you find a quiet place--then go to work! This is the first and probably the most important step in getting organized for study.

Basic Aspects of Study

Only a few study techniques can be given in this brief report. The first technique is to get organized. Good organization includes three important aspects of study: (1) a place to study, (2) a time for study, and (3) a desire to learn.[2]

[1]Clifford T. Morgan and James Deese, How to Study (New York: McGraw-Hill Book Co., Inc., 1957), p. 2.

[2]Loren Reid, "The Lost Art of Studying," School and Community, XLVI (March, 1960), 16-17.

1

FIRST PAGE, UNBOUND

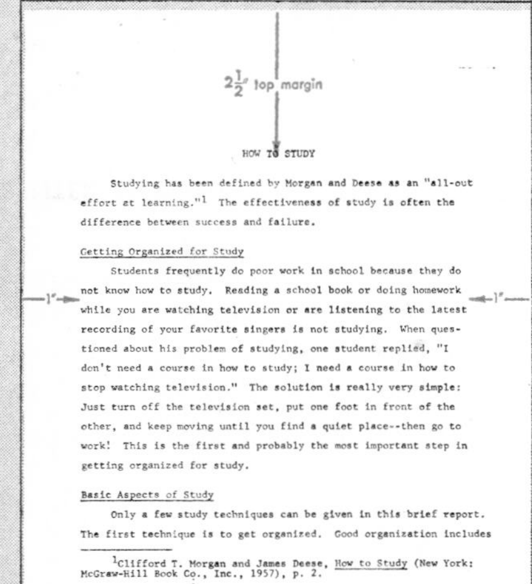

HOW TO STUDY

Studying has been defined by Morgan and Deese as an "all-out effort at learning."[1] The effectiveness of study is often the difference between success and failure.

Getting Organized for Study

Students frequently do poor work in school because they do not know how to study. Reading a school book or doing homework while you are watching television or are listening to the latest recording of your favorite singers is not studying. When questioned about his problem of studying, one student replied, "I don't need a course in how to study; I need a course in how to stop watching television." The solution is really very simple: Just turn off the television set, put one foot in front of the other, and keep moving until you find a quiet place--then go to work! This is the first and probably the most important step in getting organized for study.

Basic Aspects of Study

Only a few study techniques can be given in this brief report. The first technique is to get organized. Good organization includes

[1]Clifford T. Morgan and James Deese, How to Study (New York: McGraw-Hill Book Co., Inc., 1957), p. 2.

1

FIRST PAGE, TOPBOUND

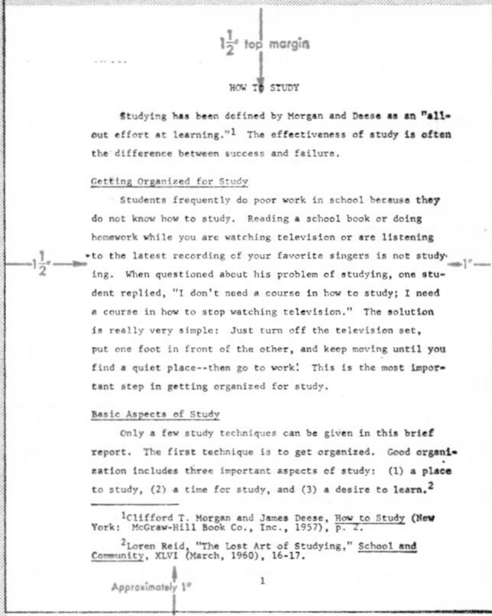

HOW TO STUDY

Studying has been defined by Morgan and Deese as an "all-out effort at learning."[1] The effectiveness of study is often the difference between success and failure.

Getting Organized for Study

Students frequently do poor work in school because they do not know how to study. Reading a school book or doing homework while you are watching television or are listening to the latest recording of your favorite singers is not studying. When questioned about his problem of studying, one student replied, "I don't need a course in how to study; I need a course in how to stop watching television." The solution is really very simple: Just turn off the television set, put one foot in front of the other, and keep moving until you find a quiet place--then go to work! This is the first and probably the most important step in getting organized for study.

Basic Aspects of Study

Only a few study techniques can be given in this brief report. The first technique is to get organized. Good organization includes three important aspects of study: (1) a place to study, (2) a time for study, and (3) a desire to learn.[2]

[1]Clifford T. Morgan and James Deese, How to Study (New York: McGraw-Hill Book Co., Inc., 1957), p. 2.

[2]Loren Reid, "The Lost Art of Studying," School and Community, XLVI (March, 1960), 16-17.

1

FIRST PAGE, LEFTBOUND

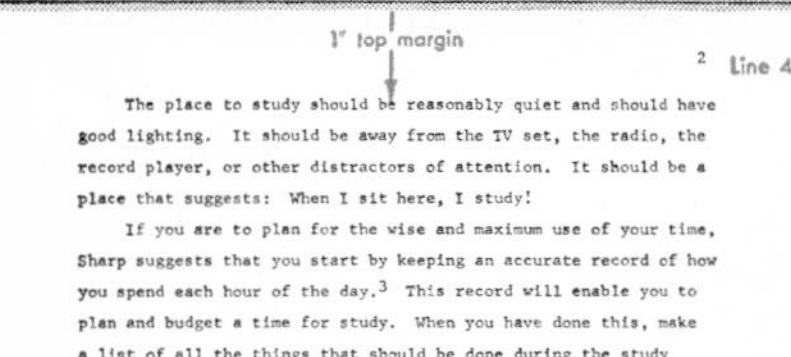

2

The place to study should be reasonably quiet and should have good lighting. It should be away from the TV set, the radio, the record player, or other distractors of attention. It should be a place that suggests: When I sit here, I study!

If you are to plan for the wise and maximum use of your time, Sharp suggests that you start by keeping an accurate record of how you spend each hour of the day.[3] This record will enable you to plan and budget a time for study. When you have done this, make a list of all the things that should be done during the study period. Next, make a decision as to the approximate time needed for each study task, the best procedure to follow, the equipment and materials needed--then go to work and stick to your schedule.

The final aspect of getting organized for study is to have a desire to learn. This is something that you must do for yourself; no one can do it for you. You--not your dad or mom or a friend--are getting the education. Nason, commenting on this phase of learning, has said:

> There is nothing wrong with asking for advice and examples. But the basic work should be your own--not that of another person. After getting help from someone, you should test whether you can do the problem for yourself.[4]

The practice of self-reliance will help you learn to solve problems on your own. It will help you discover practical applications of what you learn; it may add interest and excitement to your school work.

[3]S. L. Sharp, "Effective Study Methods," Journal of Higher Education, XIV (May, 1943), 271.

[4]Leslie J. Nason, "10 Good Rules for Improving Study," San Francisco Chronicle (January 31, 1961), p. 2.

SECOND PAGE, UNBOUND

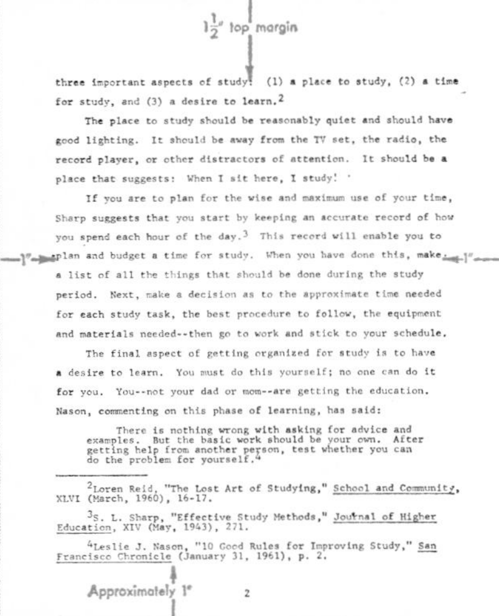

three important aspects of study: (1) a place to study, (2) a time for study, and (3) a desire to learn.[2]

The place to study should be reasonably quiet and should have good lighting. It should be away from the TV set, the radio, the record player, or other distractors of attention. It should be a place that suggests: When I sit here, I study!

If you are to plan for the wise and maximum use of your time, Sharp suggests that you start by keeping an accurate record of how you spend each hour of the day.[3] This record will enable you to plan and budget a time for study. When you have done this, make a list of all the things that should be done during the study period. Next, make a decision as to the approximate time needed for each study task, the best procedure to follow, the equipment and materials needed--then go to work and stick to your schedule.

The final aspect of getting organized for study is to have a desire to learn. You must do this yourself; no one can do it for you. You--not your dad or mom--are getting the education. Nason, commenting on this phase of learning, has said:

> There is nothing wrong with asking for advice and examples. But the basic work should be your own. After getting help from another person, test whether you can do the problem for yourself.[4]

[2]Loren Reid, "The Lost Art of Studying," School and Community, XLVI (March, 1960), 16-17.

[3]S. L. Sharp, "Effective Study Methods," Journal of Higher Education, XIV (May, 1943), 271.

[4]Leslie J. Nason, "10 Good Rules for Improving Study," San Francisco Chronicle (January 31, 1961), p. 2.

2

SECOND PAGE, TOPBOUND

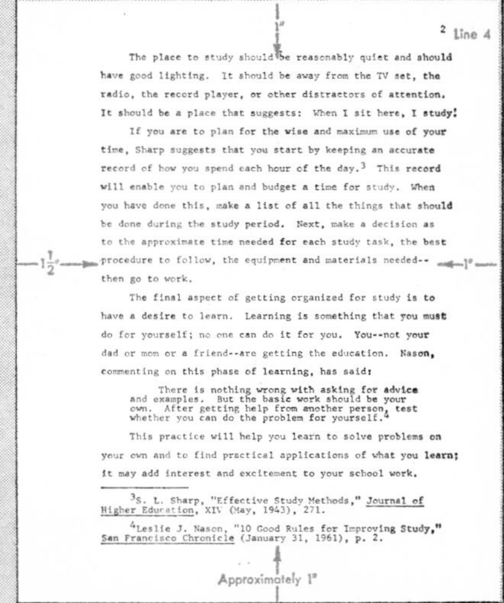

2

The place to study should be reasonably quiet and should have good lighting. It should be away from the TV set, the radio, the record player, or other distractors of attention. It should be a place that suggests: When I sit here, I study!

If you are to plan for the wise and maximum use of your time, Sharp suggests that you start by keeping an accurate record of how you spend each hour of the day.[3] This record will enable you to plan and budget a time for study. When you have done this, make a list of all the things that should be done during the study period. Next, make a decision as to the approximate time needed for each study task, the best procedure to follow, the equipment and materials needed--then go to work.

The final aspect of getting organized for study is to have a desire to learn. Learning is something that you must do for yourself; no one can do it for you. You--not your dad or mom or a friend--are getting the education. Nason, commenting on this phase of learning, has said:

> There is nothing wrong with asking for advice and examples. But the basic work should be your own. After getting help from another person, test whether you can do the problem for yourself.[4]

This practice will help you learn to solve problems on your own and to find practical applications of what you learn; it may add interest and excitement to your school work.

[3]S. L. Sharp, "Effective Study Methods," Journal of Higher Education, XIV (May, 1943), 271.

[4]Leslie J. Nason, "10 Good Rules for Improving Study," San Francisco Chronicle (January 31, 1961), p. 2.

SECOND PAGE, LEFTBOUND

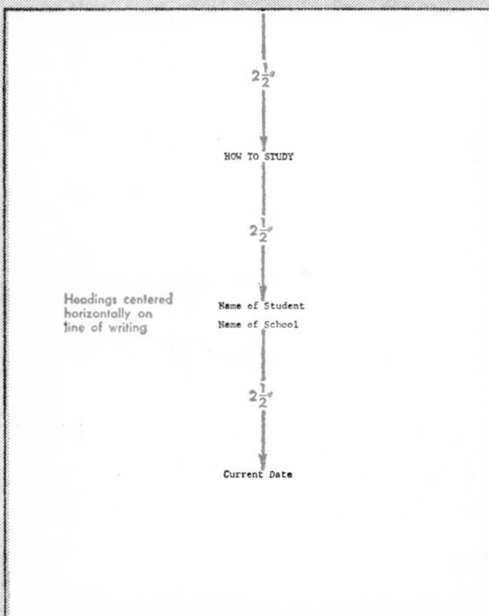

HOW TO STUDY

Name of Student

Name of School

Current Date

TITLE PAGE

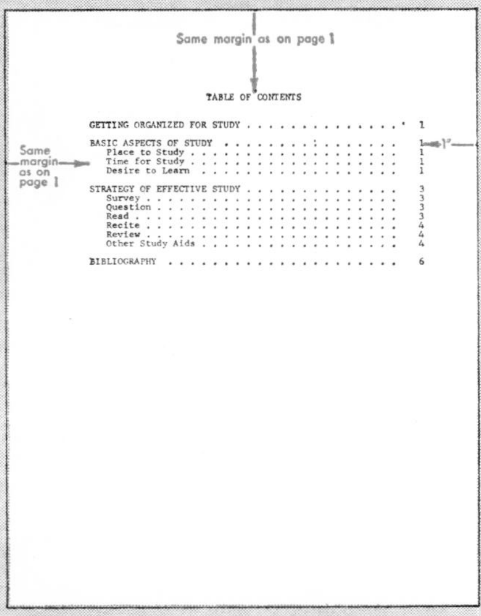

TABLE OF CONTENTS

TABLE OF CONTENTS

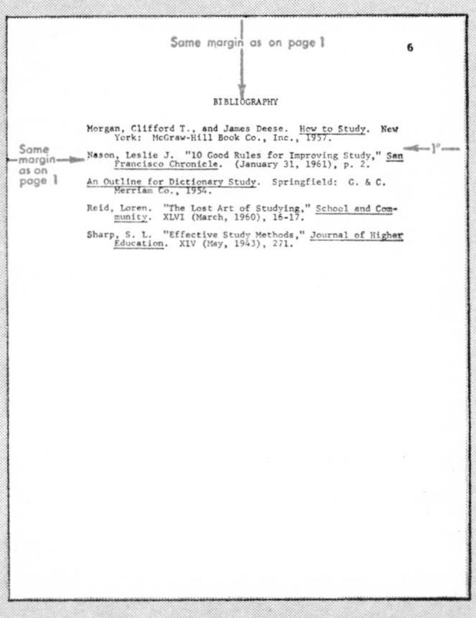

6

BIBLIOGRAPHY

Morgan, Clifford T., and James Deese. How to Study. New York: McGraw-Hill Book Co., Inc., 1957.

Nason, Leslie J. "10 Good Rules for Improving Study," San Francisco Chronicle. (January 31, 1961), p. 2.

An Outline for Dictionary Study. Springfield: G. & C. Merriam Co., 1954.

Reid, Loren. "The Lost Art of Studying," School and Community. XLVI (March, 1960), 16-17.

Sharp, S. L. "Effective Study Methods," Journal of Higher Education. XIV (May, 1943), 271.

BIBLIOGRAPHY

CORRECTION SYMBOLS (PROOFREADERS' MARKS)

Sometimes typed or printed copy may be corrected with proofreaders' marks. The typist must be able to interpret correctly these marks in retyping the corrected copy or *rough draft* as it may be called. The most commonly used proofreaders' marks are shown below.

Mark	Meaning	Mark	Meaning	Mark	Meaning
‖	Align type; set flush	∨ʼ	Insert apostrophe	¶	Paragraph
Cap or ≡	Capitalize	∨“ ∨”	Insert quotation marks	No new ¶	No new paragraph
⁐	Close up		Move right	#	Space
℘	Delete		Move left	◯ sp	Spell out
∧	Insert		Move down; lower	stet	Let it stand (ignore correction)
∧,	Insert comma		Move up; raise	∽ or tr	Transpose
∧# or #/	Insert space	lc or /	Set in lower case	___	Underline or Ital.

CENTERING SUMMARY

HORIZONTAL CENTERING

1. Move marginal stops to extreme ends of scale.
2. Clear tab stops; then set a tab stop at center of paper.*
3. Tabulate to center of paper; backspace *once* for each *two* letters, figures, spaces, or punctuation marks in the line to be centered. Start typing where the backspacing ends. (In backspacing, disregard odd or leftover stroke.)

***FORMULA FOR FINDING HORIZONTAL CENTER OF PAPER**

	Example
Scale reading at left edge of paper	0
+ Scale reading at right edge of paper	102
Total ÷ 2 = Center Point	102 ÷ 2 = 51

Spreading Headings

1. To center a spread heading, from center backspace once for each letter, character, and space in the heading. Begin to type where the backspacing ends.
2. In typing a spread heading, space once after each letter or character and three times between words.

VERTICAL CENTERING—BACKSPACE-FROM-CENTER METHOD

Basic Rule. From vertical center of paper, roll platen (cylinder) back once for each two lines, two blank line spaces, or line and blank line space. Ignore odd or leftover line.

Steps to follow:

1. To move paper to vertical center, start spacing down from top edge of paper—
   - **a.** Half sheet: Down 6 TS (triple spaces) — 1 SS
   - **b.** Full sheet: Down 11 TS + 1 SS
2. From vertical center—
   - **a.** Half sheet, SS or DS: Follow Basic Rule (back 1 for 2).
   - **b.** Full sheet, SS or DS: Follow Basic Rule (back 1 for 2); then back 2 SS for *reading position.*

VERTICAL CENTERING—MATHEMATICAL METHOD

1. Count lines and blank line spaces needed to type problem.
2. Subtract *lines used* from *lines available* (66 for full sheet and 33 for half sheet).
3. Divide by 2 to get top and bottom margins. If fraction results, disregard it. Space down from top edge of paper *1 more than number of lines to be left in top margin.*

For reading position, which is above exact vertical center, subtract 2 from exact top margin.

FORMULA FOR VERTICAL MATHEMATICAL PLACEMENT

$$\frac{\text{Lines available} - \text{Lines used}}{2} = \text{Top Margin}$$

TABULATION SUMMARY

VERTICAL PLACEMENT

1. *Vertical centering.* Follow either of vertical centering methods explained on page x.
2. *Spacing after heading lines.* Double-space (1 blank line space) between *main* and *secondary* headings, if both are used; triple-space (2 blank line spaces) between last line of heading (whether main or secondary) and first line of columns (or columnar headings). Double-space (1 blank line space) between columnar headings (when used) and first line of columns.

HORIZONTAL PLACEMENT—BACKSPACE-FROM-CENTER METHOD

1. *Preparatory Steps*
   - a. Clear margin stops by moving them to the extreme ends of the scale.
   - b. Clear all tab stops.
   - c. Move carriage to center of paper.
   - d. Decide spacing between columns—preferably an even number of spaces (4, 6, 8, 10, etc.).
2. *Center Heading Lines*
3. *Determine and Set Left Margin Stop*

   Backspace from center of paper 1 space for each 2 letters, figures, symbols, and spaces in *longest line* of each column and for each 2 spaces between columns. Set left margin stop at this point. (If an extra space occurs at the end of the longest line when backspacing, carry it forward to the next column. Ignore an extra space at end of last column.)

Note. If a columnar heading is longer than the longest line in the columns, it may be treated as the longest line in determining placement. The longest columnar line must then be centered under the heading, and tab stops set accordingly.

Example:

advertisement		efficiency		optimistic
13	8	10	8	10
ad|ve|rt|is|em|en	+4	te|ff|ic|ie|nc	+4	yo|pt|im|is|ti

4. *Set Tab Stops*

   From the left margin stop, space forward 1 space for each letter, figure, symbol, and space in the longest line in the first column and for each space to be left between the first and second columns. *Set a tab stop at this point for the second column.* Follow similar procedure when additional columns are to be typed.

CENTERING COLUMNAR HEADINGS

1. *Forward-Space, Backspace Method*

   From point at which column begins, space forward once (→) for each 2 letters, figures, or spaces in the longest line (the line that requires the most strokes to type). From center of column, backspace (←) once for each 2 spaces in heading. Begin to type where backspacing ends. (In both steps ignore an extra space.) The typed heading will be centered over the column.

2. *Mathematical Method*

   To the number of the cylinder (platen) or line-of-writing scale immediately under the first letter, figure, or symbol of the longest line of the column, add the number shown under the space following the last stroke of the line. Divide this sum by 2; the result will be the center point. From this point on the scale, backspace to center the columnar heading.

DRAWING RULED LINES

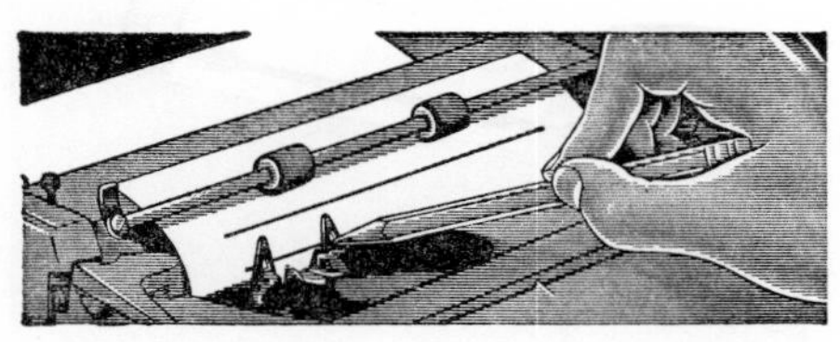

To Draw Horizontal Lines: Place the pencil point through the cardholder (or on the type bar guide above the ribbon); depress the carriage-release lever to draw the carriage across the line.

To Draw Vertical Lines: Operate the line finder. Place the pencil point or pen through the cardholder (or on the type bar guide above the ribbon). Roll the platen up the page until you have a line of the desired length. Remove the pen or pencil and reset the line finder.

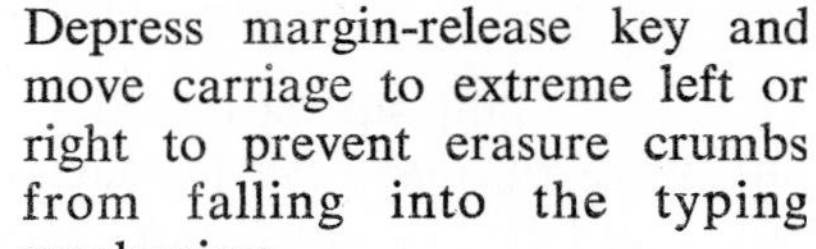

HOW TO ERASE AND CORRECT ERRORS

USING AN ERASER SHIELD

1. Depress margin-release key and move carriage to extreme left or right to prevent erasure crumbs from falling into the typing mechanism.
2. To avoid disturbing the paper alignment of the type, turn the cylinder forward if the erasure is to be made on the upper two thirds of the paper; backward, on the lower third of the paper.
3. To erase on the original sheet, lift the paper bail out of the way, and place a 5″ x 3″ card *in front of* the first carbon sheet. Use an eraser shield to protect the writing that is not to be erased. Brush the eraser crumbs away from the typewriter.
4. Move the protective card in front of the second carbon, if more than one copy is being made. Erase the errors on the carbon copy with a soft (or pencil) eraser first, then with the hard typewriter eraser used in erasing on the original copy.
5. When the error has been erased on all copies, remove the protective card, position the carriage to the proper point, and type the necessary correction.

SQUEEZING AND SPREADING OF LETTERS

In correcting errors, it is often possible to "squeeze" omitted letters into half spaces or to "spread" letters to fill out spaces.

1. *An omitted letter at the beginning or end of a word:*

Error: `an omitte letter`
Correction: `an omittedletter`

Corrective steps:

1. Move carriage to the letter *e*.
2. Depress and hold down the space bar; strike the letter *d*.

Note. On an electric typewriter, it may be necessary to hold the carriage by hand at the half-space point.

2. *An omitted letter within a word:*

Error: `a leter within`
Correction: `a letter within`

Corrective steps:

1. Erase the incorrect word.
2. Position the carriage at the space after the letter *a*.
3. Press down and hold the space bar; strike the letter *l*.
4. Release the space bar, then press it down again and hold it; strike the next letter.
5. Repeat the process for any additional letters.

3. *Addition of a letter within a word:*

Error: `a lettter within`
Correction: `a letter within`

Corrective steps:

1. Erase the incorrect word.
2. Position the carriage as if you were going to type the letter *l* in its regular position following the space.
3. Press down and hold the space bar; strike the letter *l*.
4. Release the space bar; then repeat the process for each remaining letter.

QUARTER-MINUTE CHECK POINTS

Use this scale to identify the quarter-minute goals for guided writing. First, decide the goal rate at which you want to type for the minute; then get from the scale the quarter-, half-, three-quarter-, and one-minute goals and check the copy at these points.

The paragraphs in the guided writings are marked with the 4-word count shown in figures and with an in-between count shown by a • (dot). To check the goals, place a small mark above each quarter-minute goal. If your goal is not shown in the copy by a figure or a dot, spot the approximate midpoint between the dot and the figure and check this point. Do not take time to count the exact strokes; rather, estimate the correct placement of the goal check when there is no figure or dot to show the exact count.

Goal	Quarter	Half	Three-Quarters	One
16	4	8	12	16
20	5	10	15	20
24	6	12	18	24
28	7	14	21	28
32	8	16	24	32
36	9	18	27	36
40	10	20	30	40
44	11	22	33	44
48	12	24	36	48
52	13	26	39	52
56	14	28	42	56
60	15	30	45	60
64	16	32	48	64
68	17	34	51	68
72	18	36	54	72
76	19	38	57	76
80	20	40	60	80
84	21	42	63	84
88	22	44	66	88
92	23	46	69	92
96	24	48	72	96
100	25	50	75	100

SPECIAL INDEX

Alphabetic Sentences[1]

Figure Sentences[2]

Figure-Symbol Sentences[3]

Fluency (Speed) Sentences[4]

Alphabetic Paragraph Writings

Concentration Drills

Technique Drills

Pre-Application Manipulative Drills

Related Learning Drills

Skill Transfer Writings

Guided Writing Copy

Straight-Copy Timed Writings

[1] An alphabetic sentence appears in every Conditioning Practice beginning on page 25.
[2] A figure sentence appears in most of the Conditioning Practices beginning on page 55.
[3] A figure-symbol sentence appears in many of the Conditioning Practices beginning on page 42.
[4] Beginning on page 27, an easy sentence, designed for speed building or fluency practice, appears in every Conditioning Practice throughout the book.

INDEX

A, control of, 3

B, control of, 23

C, control of, 11

D, control of, 3

E, control of, 5

F, control of, 3

R, control of, 13

S, control of, 3

T, control of, 8

U, control of, 11

V, control of, 19

W, control of, 15

X, control of, 21

Y, control of, 23

Z, control of, 13